WealthWarn

I0333474

WealthWarn

A Study of Socioeconomic Conflict in Hebrew Prophecy

Michael S. Moore

PICKWICK *Publications* • Eugene, Oregon

WEALTHWARN
A Study of Socioeconomic Conflict in Hebrew Prophecy

Copyright © 2019 Michael S. Moore. All rights reserved. Except for brief quotations in critical publications or reviews, no part of this book may be reproduced in any manner without prior written permission from the publisher. Write: Permissions, Wipf and Stock Publishers, 199 W. 8th Ave., Suite 3, Eugene, OR 97401.

Pickwick Publications
An Imprint of Wipf and Stock Publishers
199 W. 8th Ave., Suite 3
Eugene, OR 97401

www.wipfandstock.com

PAPERBACK ISBN: 978-1-5326-3812-1
HARDCOVER ISBN: 978-1-5326-3813-8
EBOOK ISBN: 978-1-5326-3814-5

Cataloguing-in-Publication data:

Names: Moore, Michael S., author.

Title: WealthWarn : a study of socioeconomic conflict in Hebrew prophecy / by Michael S. Moore.

Description: Eugene, OR: Pickwick Publications, 2019. | Includes bibliographical references and index.

Identifiers: ISBN 978-1-5326-3812-1 (paperback). | ISBN 978-1-5326-3813-8 (hardcover). | ISBN 978-1-5326-3814-5 (ebook).

Subjects: LCSH: Bible. OT. Prophets—Criticism, interpretation, etc. | Social justice—Religious aspects. | Prophets.

Classification: BR1700.3 M66 2019 (print). | BR1700.3 (ebook).

Manufactured in the U.S.A. 08/08/19

Contents

Abbreviations | vii

1. Introduction | 1

2. Prophetic Socioeconomic Motifs in Ancient Near Eastern Texts | 4
   Mesopotamia 4
      Inanna's Descent 4
      The Babylonian Creation Epic 17
      Prophetic Texts from Tell Koujunjik (Nineveh) and Tell Ḥarīrī (Mari) 25
   Anatolia 31
   Syria-Palestine 36
   Summary 54

3. Socioeconomic Conflict Motifs in Hebrew Prophetic Texts | 56
   Elijah vs. the Prophets of Ba`al 57
   Isaiah 65
   Jeremiah 73
   Ezekiel 84
   Book of the Twelve 88
      Hosea 89
      Joel 97
      Amos 103
      Micah 107
      Habakkuk 111
      Haggai 113
      Zechariah 117
      Malachi 119
   Summary 121

4. Prophetic Socioeconomic Motifs in Early Jewish Texts | 122
Ezra-Nehemiah 122
Letter of Reḥum and Shimshi to King Artaxerxes 123
Response of King Artaxerxes 126
Letter of Tattenai and Shethar-bozenai to King Darius 128
Response from King Darius 130
Letter of Artaxerxes to Ezra 133
Epistle of Jeremiah 140
Tobit 142
Summary 155

5. Prophetic Socioeconomic Motifs in the Greek New Testament | 157
Gospel of Matthew 158
Galilean Encounters 159
Judean Encounters 172
Acts of the Apostles 180
Summary 195

6. Summary and Conclusion | 196
Fertility/Procreation 196
Inheritance/Possession 197
"House"/Temple 198
Tithing/Taxation 199
Land 200
Conclusion 201

Bibliography | 203
Subject Index | 265
Author Index | 283

Abbreviations

1QapGen	*The Genesis Apocryphon* from Qumran Cave 1
1QH	*The Hodayot Scroll* from Qumran Cave 1
1QM	*The War Scroll* from Qumran Cave 1
1QS	*The Scroll of the Rule* from Qumran Cave 1
2mp	second-person masculine plural
4QMMT	*The Halaka Letter* from Qumran Cave 4
A	Codex Alexandrinus
AASF	Annales Academiae scientarium fennicae
AAWG.PH	Abhandlungen der Akademie der Wissenschaften in Gottingen, Philologische-Historische Klasse
AB	Anchor Bible
ABD	*Anchor Bible Dictionary*, edited by David Noel Freedman, 6 vols. (New York: Doubleday, 1992)
ABS	Archaeology and Biblical Studies
AcBib	Academia Biblica
act.	active
ad loc.	"to the (appropriate) place"
AE	Anthropology and Ethnography
AEL	*Ancient Egyptian Literature*, by Miriam Lichtheim, 3 vols. (Berkeley: University of California Press, 1973)
AfO	*Archiv für Orientforschung*
AG	Analecta Gorgiana
AGH	*Die akkadische Gebetsserie "Handerhebung,"* by Erich Ebeling (Berlin: Akademie, 1953)
AHw	*Akkadisches Handwörterbuch*, by Wolfram von Soden, 3 vols. (Wiesbaden: Harrassowitz, 1965–81)
AIL	Ancient Israel and Its Literature

A.J.	*Antiquities of the Jews*, by Flavius Josephus, translated by William Whiston (London: Bell, 1889)
AJEC	Ancient Judaism and Early Christianity
AJES	*American Journal of Economics and Sociology*
AJSL	*American Journal of Semitic Languages*
AJT	*Anglican Journal of Theology*
AKG	Arbeiten zur Kirchengeschichte
ALASP	Abhandlungen zur Literatur Alt-Syren-Palästinas und Mesopotamiens
ALGHJ	Arbeiten zur Literatur und Geschichte des hellenistischen Judentums
AnBib	Analecta biblica
ANE	Ancient Near Eastern
ANEM	Ancient Near East Monographs
ANESSup	Ancient Near Eastern Supplement Series
ANET	*Ancient Near Eastern Texts Relating to the Old Testament*, edited by James B. Pritchard, 3rd ed. (Princeton: Princeton University Press, 1969)
AOAT	Alter Orient und Altes Testament
AOTC	Abingdon Old Testament Commentaries
APR	annual percentage rate
AR	Assyrian Recension
ARM	Archives royales de Mari
ARTU	*An Anthology of Religious Texts from Ugarit*, by Johannes C. de Moor (Leiden: Brill, 1987)
AS	*Aramaic Studies*
ASNU	Acta seminarii neotestamentici upsaliensis
ASOR	American Schools of Oriental Research
ASV	American Standard Version
ATD	Das Alte Testament Deutsch
Atr	Atraḫasis Epic
AYB	Anchor Yale Bible
AYBRL	Anchor Yale Bible Reference Library
B	Codex Vaticanus
BASOR	*Bulletin of the American Schools of Oriental Research*
BBB	Bonner biblische Beiträge
BBR	*Bulletin for Biblical Research*
BCE	before the Common Era
BCH	*Bulletin de correspondance hellénique*

BDB	Brown, Francis, S. R. Driver, and Charles A. Briggs, *A Hebrew and English Lexicon of the Old Testament* (Oxford, 1907)
BETL	Bibliotheca ephemeridum theologicarum lovaniensium
BHS	*Biblia Hebraica Stuttgartensia*, edited by K. Elliger and W. Rudolph (Stuttgart, 1983)
BI	*Biblical Interpretation*
Bib	*Biblica*
BibEnc	Biblical Encyclopedia
BibIntSer	Biblical Interpretation Series
BibOr	Biblica et orientalia
BibSem	Biblical Seminar
B.J.	*Bellum judaicum*, by Flavius Josephus, translated by William Whiston (London: Bell, 1889)
BJS	Brown Judaic Studies
BLS	Bible and Literature Series
BRLA	Brill Reference Library of Ancient Judaism
BSOAS	*Bulletin of the School of Oriental and African Studies*
BVB	Beiträge zum Verstehen der Bibel
BWAT	Beiträge zur Wissenschaft vom Alten Testament
BWL	*Babylonian Wisdom Literature*, by Wilfrid G. Lambert (Oxford: Clarendon, 1960)
BZ	*Biblische Zeitschrift*
BZAW	Beihefte zur Zeitschrift für die alttestamentliche Wissenschaft
BZNW	Beihefte zur Zeitschrift für die neutestamentliche Wissenschaft
CAD	*Chicago Assyrian Dictionary*
CAH	*Cambridge Ancient History*
CANE	*Civilizations of the Ancient Near East*, edited by Jack M Sasson, 4 vols. (1995; reprinted in 2 vols., Peabody, MA: Hendrickson, 2006)
CAP	*Aramaic Papyri of the Fifth Century B.C.*, by Arthur E. Cowley (Oxford: Clarendon, 1923)
CAT	*The Cuneiform Alphabetic Texts from Ugarit, Ras Ibn Hani and Other Places*, edited by Manfried Dietrich, Oswald Loretz, and Joaquín Sanmartín (Münster: Ugarit-Verlag, 1995)
C. Ap.	*Contra Apionem*, by Flavius Josephus, translated by William Whiston (London: Bell, 1889)
CBET	Contributions to Biblical Exegesis and Theology
CBQ	*Catholic Biblical Quarterly*

CBQMS	Catholic Biblical Quarterly Monograph Series
CBS	Classic Bible Series
CC	Continental Commentaries
CCT	*Cuneiform Texts from Cappadocian Tablets in the British Museum*, edited by Paul Garelli and Dominique Collon (1921; reprint, London: Trustees of the British Museum, 1975)
CD	*Damascus Document*
CDA	*A Concise Dictionary of Akkadian*, edited by Jeremy Black et al. (Wiesbaden: Harrasowitz, 2000)
CDOG	Colloquien der Deutschen Orient-Gesellschaft
CE	Common Era
CEJL	Commentaries on Early Jewish Literature
Cf.	compare/see
CH	Codex Hammurabi
CHANE	Culture and History of the Ancient Near East
CHD	*Chicago Hittite Dictionary*, edited by Hans G. Güterbock et al. (Chicago: Oriental Institute of the University of Chicago, 1980–)
CM	Cuneiform Monographs
CMHE	*Canaanite Myth and Hebrew Epic*, by Frank Moore Cross (Cambridge: Harvard University Press, 1973)
CML	*Canaanite Myths and Legends*, edited by J. C. L. Gibson (Edinburgh: T. & T. Clark, 1978)
ConBOT	Coniectanea biblica, Old Testament Series
COS	*Context of Scripture*, edited by William W. Hallo and K. Lawson Younger (Leiden: Brill, 2003)
CovQ	*Covenant Quarterly*
CPNIV	College Press NIV Commentary
CRINT	Compendia rerum iudaicarum ad Novum Testamentum
CSICL	Cambridge Studies in International and Comparative Law
CSAWC	Contributions to the Study of Ancient World Cultures
CT	*Christianity Today*
CTH	*Catalogue des textes hittites*, by Emmanuel Laroche (Paris: Editions Klincksieck, 1971)
D	the intensive form
DA	*Deir ʿAllā* Texts
DANE	*Dictionary of the Ancient Near East*, edited by Piotr Bienkowski and Alan Millard (Philadelphia: University of Pennsylvania Press, 2000)

DBGGKL	Dresdner Beiträge Geschlechterforschung in Geschichte, Kultur, und Literatur
DCLS	Deuterocanonical and Cognate Literature Studies
DDD	*Dictionary of Deities and Demons in the Bible*, edited by Karel van der Toorn et al. (Leiden: Brill, 1999)
DH	The Deuteronomistic History
DI	Descent of Ishtar
DJG	*Dictionary of Jesus and the Gospels*, edited by Joel B. Green (Downers Grove, IL: InterVarsity, 1992)
DMWA	*A Dictionary of Modern Written Arabic*, edited by Hans Wehr and J. Milton Cowan (Ithaca, NY: Cornell University Press, 1966)
DN	divine name
DOTHB	*Dictionary of the Old Testament Historical Books*, edited by Bill Arnold and Hugh G. M. Williamson (Downers Grove, IL: InterVarsity, 2005)
DOTPr	*Dictionary of the Old Testament Prophets*, edited by Mark Boda and J. Gordon McConville (Downers Grove, IL: InterVarsity, 2012)
DR	*Dictionnaire des religions*, edited by Mircea Eliade and Ioan Peter Couliano (Paris: Presses Universitaires, 1983)
DSB	Daily Study Bible
DSSSE	*The Dead Sea Scrolls Study Edition*, edited by Florentino García Martínez and Eigbert J. C. Tigchelaar, 2 vols. (Leiden: Brill, 1997–98)
DT	Disappearance of Telipinu
DTTM	*Dictionary of Targumim, Talmud and Midrashic Literature*, by Marcus Jastrow (London: Luzac, 1903)
DULAT	*Dictionary of the Ugaritic Language in the Alphabetic Tradition*, edited by Gregorio del Olmo Lete and Joaquín Sanmartín (Leiden: Brill, 2003)
EA	*Die el-Amarna Tafeln*, edited by Johannes A. Knudtzon, 2 vols. (1915; reprint, Aalen: Zeller, 1964)
EBC	Expositor's Bible Commentary
EBD	*The Egyptian Book of the Dead*, edited by Peter Le Page Renouf and Edouard Naville (London: Society of Biblical Archaeology, 1904)
ECC	Eerdmans Critical Commentary
EDSS	*Encyclopedia of the Dead Sea Scrolls*, edited by Lawrence H. Schiffman and James VanderKam, 2 vols. (New York: Oxford University Press, 2000)
Ee	*Enūma eliš*
Eg	Egyptian

EHJ	*Encyclopedia of the Historical Jesus*, edited by Craig A. Evans (London: Routledge, 2008)
EIC	*Encyclopedia of Intelligence and Counterintelligence*, edited by Rodney P. Carlisle (London: Routledge, 2015)
EJ	*Encyclopedia Judaica*
Eng	English
EpJer	Epistle of Jeremiah
ER	*Encyclopedia of Religion*, edited by Lindsay Jones, 2nd ed., 15 vols. (Detroit: MacMillan Reference, 2005)
ErIsr	*Eretz-Israel*
ESV	English Standard Version
esp.	especially
ET	English translation
et al.	"and others"
Eth	Ethiopic
ETSMS	Evangelical Theological Society Monograph Series
f.	feminine
FAT	Forschungen zum Alten Testament
FB	Forschung zur Bibel
FBBS	Facet Books Biblical Series
FCB	Feminist Companion to the Bible
FH	Folio Histoire
FoSub	Fontes et Subsidia ad Bibliam pertinentes
FOTL	Forms of the Old Testament Literature
fr.	from
FRC	Family, Religion and Culture
FRLANT	Forschungen zur Religion und Literatur des Alten und Neuen Testaments
FS	Festschrift
fut.	future
G	the simple form
GAG	*Grundriss der akkadischen Grammatik*, by Wolfram von Soden, 2nd ed. (Rome: Pontifical Biblical Institure, 1969)
GAP	Guides to Apocrypha and Pseudepigrapha
GBH	*A Grammar of Biblical Hebrew*, by Paul Joüon, translated and revised by T. Muraoka, 2 vols. (Rome: Pontifical Biblical Institute, 1991)
GE	Gilgamesh Epic

Gk	Greek
GKC	*Gesenius' Hebrew Grammar*, edited by Emil Kautzsch, translated by Arthur E. Cowley, 2nd ed. (Oxford: Clarendon, 1910)
GLH	*Glossaire de la langue hourrite*, by Emmanuel Laroche (Paris: Editions Kliencksieck, 1980)
GMTR	Guides to the Mesopotamian Textual Record
GN	geographical name
GNT	Greek New Testament
GRBS	*Greek, Roman, and Byzantine Studies*
GTR	Gender, Theory and Religion
HAL	*Hebräisches und aramäisches Lexikon zum Alten Testament*, by Ludwig Koehler et al., translated and edited by Mervyn E. J. Richardson, 4 vols. (Leiden: Brill, 1994–99)
hapax legomenon	"used only once"
HAR	*Hebrew Annual Review*
HAT	Handbuch zum Alten Testament
HBM	Hebrew Bible Monographs
HCSB	Holman Christian Standard Bible
HA	Handbuch der Archäologie
HO	Handbuch der Orientalistik
HE	*Historia Ecclesiae*
HED	*Hittite Etymological Dictionary*, by Jaan Puhvel (Berlin: Mouton de Gruyter, 1984–)
Heb	Hebrew
HPQ	*History of Philosophy Quarterly*
HRel	Historia Religionum
HS	*Hebrew Studies*
HSK	Handbücher zur Sprach- und Kommunikationswissenschaft
HSM	Harvard Semitic Monographs
HSS	Harvard Semitic Studies
HTKAT	Herders theologischer Kommentar zum Alten Testament
HUCA	*Hebrew Union College Annual*
Hur	Hurrian
HW	*Hethitische Wörterbuch*, edited by Johannes Friedrich and Annelies Kammenhuber (Heidelberg: Carl Winter, 1975)
ICC	International Critical Commentary
ID	Inanna's Descent

IEJ	*Israel Exploration Journal*
inf.	infinitive
in se	"in itself"
Int	*Interpretation*
ipf.	imperfect
IPT	*Iscrizione puniche della Tripolitania*, by Giorgo Levi della Vida Giorgio and Maria Giula Amadasi Guzzo (Rome: "L'Erma" di Bretschneider, 1987)
ipv.	imperative
ITC	International Theological Commentary
JAAPOS	*Journal of the American Association of Pediatric Ophthalmology and Strabismus*
JANER	*Journal of Ancient Near Eastern Religions*
JAOS	*Journal of the American Oriental Society*
JB	Jerusalem Bible
JBL	*Journal of Biblical Literature*
JBLMS	Journal of Biblical Literature Monograph Series
JCS	*Journal of Cuneiform Studies*
JEA	*Journal of Egyptian Archaeology*
JESHO	*Journal of the Economic and Social History of the Orient*
JFSR	*Journal of Feminist Studies in Religion*
JL	Jeremiah's Laments
JNES	*Journal of Near Eastern Studies*
JNSL	*Journal of Northwest Semitic Languages*
JNTS	*Journal of New Testament Studies*
JÖAI	*Jahreshefte des Österreichischen archäologischen Instituts*
JP	*Journal of Politics*
JRE	*Journal of Religious Ethics*
JSJ	*Journal for the Study of Judaism in the Persian, Hellenistic, and Roman Periods*
JSJSup	Supplements to the Journal for the Study of Judaism
JSNT	*Journal for the Study of the New Testament*
JSNTSup	Journal for the Study of the New Testament Supplement Series
JSOT	*Journal for the Study of the Old Testament*
JSOTSup	Journal for the Study of the Old Testament Supplement Series
JSSI	*Journal of Sport and Social Issues*
JTS	*Journal of Theological Studies*

KAI	*Kanaanäische und aramäische Inschriften*, edited by Herbert Donner and Wolfgang Röllig (Wiesbaden: Harrassowitz, 1969)
KAT	Kommentar zum Alten Testament
KBANT	Kommentare und Beiträge zum Alte und Neuen Testament
KBo	*Keilschrifttexte aus Boghazköi*
ketib	"that which is written"
KHC	Kurzer Hand-Commentar zum Alten Testament
KJV	King James Version
KUB	*Keilschrifturkunden aus Boghazköi*
L	Lucianic recension of OG (Old Greek)
LAI	Library of Ancient Israel
Lane	Lane, Edward William, editor, *An Arabic-English Lexicon*, 8 vols. (London: Williams & Norgate, 1863)
LAS	Leipziger Altorientalische Studien
LCBI	Literary Currents in Biblical Interpretation
LD	Lectio divina
LEC	Library of Early Christianity
LHBOTS	Library of Hebrew Bible/Old Testament Studies
lit.	literally
LNTS	Library of New Testament Studies
LSJ	Liddell, Henry George, Robert Scott, and Henry Stuart Jones, eds., *A Greek-English Lexicon*, 9th ed. with revised supplement (Oxford: Clarendon, 1996)
LSTS	Library of Second Temple Studies
LXX	Septuagint
m.	masculine
MARI	*Mari: Annales de recherches interdisciplinaires*
MBCBSup	Mnemosyne: Bibliotheca Classica Batava Supplements
MIO	*Mitteilungen des Instituts für Orientforschung*
MSK	Tell Meskene
MT	Masoretic Text
n.	neuter
N	simple passive form
NA	Neo-Assyrian
NAB	New American Bible
NAC	New American Commentary
NASB	New American Standard Bible

N.B.	*nota bene*, "note carefully"
NEA	*Near Eastern Archaeology*
NDA	New Directions in Archaeology
NEB	New English Bible
NEchtB	Neue Echter Bibel
Neot	*Neotestamentica*
NET	New English Translation
Nevi'im	The Prophets
NICOT	New International Commentary on the Old Testament
NIGTC	New International Greek Testament Commentary
NIV	New International Version
NIVAC	New International Version Application Commentary
NKJV	New King James Version
NLH	*New Literary History*
NLT	New Living Translation
NovTSup	Supplements to Novum Testamentum
NRSV	New Revised Standard Version
NSKAT	Neuer Stuttgarter Kommentar Altes Testament
NTL	New Testament Library
NTOA	Novum Testamentum et Orbis Antiquus
NTS	*New Testament Studies*
NW	Northwest
OA	Old Assyrian
OAN	Oracles Against the Nations
OB	Old Babylonian
OBO	Orbis biblicus et orientalis
OBT	Overtures to Biblical Theology
OED	*Oxford English Dictionary*
OG	Old Greek (LXX)
OL	Old Latin
OLA	Orientalia lovaniensia analecta
OTL	Old Testament Library
ORA	Orientalische Religionen in der Antike
OrAnt	*Oriens antiquus*
OTM	Old Testament Message
OTP	*Old Testament Pseudepigrapha*, edited by James H. Charlesworth, 2 vols (Garden City, NY: Doubleday, 1983–85)

OtSt	*Oudtestamentische Studiën* (journal)
OtSt	Oudtestamentische Studiën (series)
pace	"with all due respect"
Pal	*Paléorient*
pass.	passive
passim	"throughout/frequently"
PEQ	*Palestine Exploration Quarterly*
pf.	perfect
PJT	*Pacific Journal of Theology*
pl.	plural
PN	proper name
POS	Pretoria Oriental Series
PRU	*Le palais royale d'Ugarit*
PSB	*Princeton Seminary Bulletin*
PSD	*A Compendious Syriac Dictionary*, by Robert Payne Smith (Oxford: Clarendon, 1903)
Ps.-J.	*Pseudo-Jonathan*
ptc.	participle
Q	Qur'an
qere	"that which is read"
RA	*Revue d'assyriologie et d'archéologie orientale*
RB	*Revue biblique*
RBL	*Review of Biblical Literature*
refl.	reflexive form
ResQ	*Restoration Quarterly*
RevExp	*Review and Expositor*
RevQ	*Revue de Qumran*
RGRW	Religions in the Graeco-Roman World
RHR	*Revue de l'histoire de religions*
RIDA	*Revue internationale de droits de l'antiquité*
RN	royal name
RS	Ras Shamra
RST	Regensburger Studien zur Theologie
RSV	Revised Standard Version
RT	*Rural Theology*
RTU	*Religious Texts from Ugarit*, by Nicolas Wyatt (Sheffield: Sheffield Academic, 2002)

S	Codex Sinaiticus
Š	the causative form
SAA	State Archives of Assyria
SAACT	State Archives of Assyria Cuneiform Texts
SAALT	State Archives of Assyria Literary Texts
SAAS	State Archives of Assyria Studies
Sam	Samaritan Pentateuch
SB	Standard Babylonian
SBL	Society of Biblical Literature
SBLAB	Society of Biblical Literature Academia Biblica
SBLDS	Society of Biblical Literature Dissertation Series
SBLMS	Society of Biblical Literature Monograph Series
SBLSP	*Society of Biblical Literature Seminar Papers*
SBLSymS	Society of Biblical Literature Symposium Studies
SBLStBL	Society of Biblical Literature Studies in Biblical Literature
SBLWAW	Society of Biblical Literature Writings from the Ancient World
SBS	Stuttgarter Bibelstudien
StBT	Studien zu den Boğazköy-Texte
SCL	Sather Classical Lectures
SCM	Student Christian Movement
SCS	Septuagint and Cognate Studies
SDIOAP	Studia et Documenta ad Iura Orientis Antiqui Pertinentia
SDSS	Studies in the Dead Sea Scrolls and Related Literature
SEÅ	*Svensk exegetisk årsbok*
SEAJT	*Southeast Asia Journal of Theology*
SEL	*Studi epigrafici e linguistici*
SemeiaSt	Semeia Studies
sg.	singular
SHANE	Studies in the History and Culture of the Ancient Near East
SHCT	Studies in the History of Christian Traditions
SHR	Studies in the History of Religions
SJLA	Studies in Judaism in Late Antiquity
SJOT	*Scandinavian Journal of the Old Testament*
SJud	Studies in Judaism
SMS	*Syro-Mesopotamian Studies*
SNTSMS	Society for New Testament Studies Monograph Series

SOTSMS	Society for Old Testament Studies Monograph Series
SPOT	Studies on Personalities of the Old Testament
SSI	*Textbook of Syrian Semitic Inscriptions*, by J. C. L. Gibson, 3 vols. (Oxford: Clarendon, 1971–82)
SSN	Studia semitica neerlandica
ST	*Studia theologica*
STDJ	Studies on the Texts of the Desert of Judah
StPohl	Studia Pohl
STW	Suhrkamp Taschenbuch Wissenschaft
subj.	subjunctive
SUNT	Studien zur Umwelt des Neuen Testaments
s.v.	*sub verbo* ("under the word")
SVC	Supplements to Vigiliae Christianae
SWBA	Social World of Biblical Antiquity
Sym	Symmachus' Greek translation
SymS	Symposium Series
Syr	Syriac (Peshitta)
TADE	*Textbook of Aramaic Documents from Ancient Egypt*, edited by Bezalel Porten and Ada Yardeni, 5 vols. (Winona Lake: Eisenbrauns, 1986–99)
Tanak	Hebrew Bible/Old Testament
TBSAW	Topoi. Berlin Studies of the Ancient World
TCL	Textes cunéiformes, Musée du Louvre
TDNT	*Theological Dictionary of the New Testament*, edited by Gerhard Kittel and Gerhard Friedrich, translated by G. W. Bromiley, 10 vols. (Grand Rapids: Eerdmans, 1964–76)
TDOT	*Theological Dictionary of the Old Testament*, edited by G. Johannes Botterwick and Helmer Ringgren, translated by J. T. Willis, G. W. Bromiley, and D. E. Green (Grand Rapids: Eerdmans, 1974–2016)
Tg.	*Targum*
Tg. Ps.-J.	*Targum Pseudo-Jonathan*
Tg. Onq.	*Targum Onqelos*
Theo	Theodotian's Greek translation
ThF	Theologie und Frieden
ThT	*Theologisch tijdschrift*
T. Job	*Testament of Job*

TLOT	*Theological Lexicon of the Old Testament*, edited by Ernst Jenni and Claus Westermann, translated by Mark Biddle, 2 vols. (Peabody, MA: Hendrickson, 1997)
TNTC	Tyndale New Testament Commentaries
TO	*Textes ougaritiques: Mythes et légendes*, edited by André Caquot et al. (Paris: Cerf, 1974)
Torah	The Pentateuch
TOTC	Tyndale Old Testament Commentaries
Transeu	*Transeuphratène*
TRu	*Theologische Rundschau*
TSAJ	Texte und Studien zum antiken Judentum
ThTo	*Theology Today*
TUGAL	Texte und Untersuchungen zur Geschichte der altchristlichen Literatur
TynBul	*Tyndale Bulletin*
UBCS	Understanding the Bible Commentary Series
UF	*Ugarit-Forschungen*
Ug	Ugaritic
UNP	*Ugaritic Narrative Poetry*, edited by Simon B. Parker, SBLWAW 9 (Atlanta: Society of Biblical Literature, 1997)
USQR	*Union Seminary Quarterly Review*
UT	*Ugaritic Textbook*, by Cyrus H. Gordon, 3 vols., AnOr 38 (Rome: Pontificium Institutum Biblicum, 1965)
UTB	Uni-Taschenbücher
Vg	Latin Vulgate
VSKMB	*Vorderasiatische Schriftdenkmäler der Königlichen Museen zu Berlin*
VT	*Vetus Testamentum*
VTE	*Vassal Treaties of Esarhaddon*, by Donald J. Wiseman (London: British School of Archaeology in Iraq, 1958)
VTSup	Supplements to Vetus Testamentum
WBC	Word Biblical Commentary
WF	*Western Folklore*
WGW	Wissenschaftliche und Gesellschaftlicher Wandel
WI	Worlds of Islam
WMANT	Wissenschaftliche Monographien zum Alten und Neuen Testament
WO	*Die Welt des Orients*
WUNT	Wissenschaftliche Untersuchungen zum Neuen Testament
WW	*Word and World*

ZA	*Zeitschrift für Assyrologie*
ZAW	*Zeitschrift für die alttestamentliche Wissenschaft*
ZBK	Zürcher Bibelkommentare
ZNW	*Zeitschrift für die neutestamentliche Wissenschaft und die Kunde der älteren Kirche*
ZTK	*Zeitschrift für Theologie und Kirche*

1

Introduction

Socioeconomic concerns cast long shadows over the collection of ancient texts commonly called "the Bible."[1] Students of Torah (תורה)[2] investigate the contours of these shadows via sociohistorical,[3] socioliterary,[4] and other methods,[5] while students of the Writings (כתובים)[6] gravitate to mythopoeic,[7] anthropological,[8] sociological,[9] rhetorical,[10] and sociohistorical approaches.[11] Similar variety characterizes contemporary analyses of the rabbinic,[12] puritan,[13] and apocalyptic texts.[14] Continuing the approach of the previous book in this series,[15] the following pages will examine some of the major socioeconomic motifs embedded in the largest single section of the Bible, the Prophets (נביאים, "Nevi'im"),[16] prefacing this with a survey of cognate motifs sculpting literary texts in Mesopotamia (Inanna's Descent, *Enūma eliš*), Anatolia (the Disappearance of Telipinu), and Syria-Palestine (the Ba'al Cycle, Kirta, Aqhat, the Betrothal of Nikkal-Ib).[17] After this attention focuses on relevant Jewish

1. Gk τὰ βίβλια, "the scrolls."

2. Genesis, Exodus, Leviticus, Numbers, Deuteronomy.

3. Pleins, *Visions*, 41–92.

4. Moore, *WealthWatch*, 100–167.

5. Cf. Chelst, *Exodus*.

6. Psalms, Proverbs, Job, Ecclesiastes, Esther, Lamentations, Song of Songs, Ruth, Ezra-Nehemiah, 1–2 Chronicles.

7. Girard, *Psalms*.

8. Meyers, "Neighborhood," 110–28.

9. Whybray, *Wealth*.

10. Sandoval, *Wealth*.

11. Washington, *Wealth*.

12. Neusner, *Economics*; Ohrenstein and Gordon, *Talmud*.

13. Murphy, *Wealth*.

14. Gordon, "Scepticism," 33–42.

15. Moore, *WealthWatch*, 22–25.

16. Joshua, Judges, 1–2 Samuel, 1–2 Kings, Isaiah, Jeremiah, Ezekiel, Book of the Twelve.

17. Though the present study distinguishes between "literary texts" and "non-literary texts," the boundaries between the two can often be blurry. Reiner ("Literatur," 15–210) delimits "literary texts" to

(Ezra-Nehemiah, Epistle of Jeremiah, Tobit) and Nazarene texts (Gospel of Matthew, Acts of the Apostles).

Previous passes through this "great literature" tend to read it through lenses ground by at least four theoretical models: (a) the "rent capitalism" model;[18] (b) the "ancient class society" model;[19] (c) the "tributary state" model;[20] and (d) the "patronage" model.[21] Each has its strengths and weaknesses,[22] yet all are helpful not least because of a persistent problem; viz., the fact that so many readers simplistically portray the poverty-wealth polarity as "the result of random idiosyncratic personal differences of ability or industry, on the one hand, or the inordinate greed and moral corruption of particular individuals, on the other."[23] This situation is unacceptably problematic for several reasons, but not least because "the struggle for justice is too important . . . to benefit from the repetition of slogans."[24]

---

myths, epics, autobiographies, propaganda literature, poetry (including hymns and prayers), love lyrics, laments, elegies, wisdom literature (both philosophical and didactic), humorous literature, and elevated prose. Foster (*Muses*, 13–18) basically agrees with this taxonomy (cf. Moore, *WealthWatch*, 3–4).

18. Lang ("Peasant," 85), e.g., argues that no peasant society is self-subsistent, but depends on "a propertied, educated, and merchant élite often resident in towns and always monopolizing control of public affairs."

19. Kippenberg ("Typik," 41) sees in eighth-century Israel a "transformation of the archaic tribal society," a situation which, like the socioeconomic landscape of Greece and Italy, has much to do with the problem of "indebtedness."

20. Gottwald ("Class," 5) contends that "the productive processes generating wealth and power in the biblical world center on land and are precapitalist. The vast majority of people produce food and other life necessities from the earth, working in household or village teams. Since technology and transport are not sufficiently developed to create a large consumer market for manufactured goods, the route to concentrating wealth and power in such circumstances is to gain control over agrarian and pastoral products, which the appropriators can themselves consume or assign to retainers at their discretion or convert into other valuables through trade and the acquisition of land. This is achieved in the ancient Near East by the so-called dawn of civilization, distinguished by the emergence of strong centralized states which siphon off agrarian and pastoral surpluses through taxation, spawn landholding and merchant groups who profit from peasant indebtedness and high-level international trade, and engage in warfare and the conquest of neighboring lands."

21. Simkins ("Patronage," 128) argues that "in spite of the social and economic hierarchy, the exchange between patrons and clients is based on reciprocity, and the relationship between them is idealized as friendship and expressed in terms of kinship. The patron is a 'father' to his clients, who honor him as 'sons' and faithful 'servants.' Patron-client relations are foremost personal bonds to which one's identity and honor are committed. The bonds are held together by mutual commitments of loyalty, though rarely ever formalized. The patron commits himself to protect and support his clients, and the client commits himself to serve his patron. By means of these interpersonal obligations, exercised through a generalized exchange, patron-client relations function to regulate and mitigate the effects of economic inequalities."

22. Cf. Houston, *Contending*, 26–48.

23. Gottwald, "Class," 3. Cf. Kessler, *Introduction*, 113–14; Gerstenberger, *Theologies*, 174; Albertz, *History*, 322; and Nolan and Lenski, *Macrosociology*, 174–75.

24. Guillaume, *Finance*, 107.

That being said, very few (if any) studies attempt to read these motifs through intertextual lenses ground by the bleak realities of ANE economics.[25] Granted, comprehensive analysis will try to take into account as much recoverable evidence as possible, whether artifactual,[26] epigraphical,[27] textual,[28] literary,[29] historical,[30] numismatic,[31] iconographic,[32] or even ecological.[33] But the present study, like its predecessor, does not pretend to be comprehensive. Instead it seeks to evaluate the "big problems"[34] afflicting ANE economies *only* as they are signified, epitomized, and symbolized via literary motifs structuring the contours of *actual texts*,[35] particularly the prophetic texts of the Bible.[36]

25. Like the previous book, the present study does not focus on theoretical modeling because, as Morley (*Theories*, 1) points out, "the place of 'theory' in ancient history remains controversial. Its advocates (normally advocates of one particular theoretical approach rather than of theory in general) insist that un- or under-theorised historical accounts are inadequate because they depend on a set of implicit and problematic assumptions masquerading as 'common sense.' Its opponents maintain that any account of antiquity using modern concepts and theories is illegitimate and misleading, as the evidence has been corrupted and distorted with anachronism (and, more often than not, a political agenda)." Further, Nolan and Lenski (*Macrosociology*, 156) rather pragmatically point out that postmodern readers tend to approach "Mother Goose rhymes and stories as charming survivals from a simpler, happier world of the past. Yet if we look at them closely, and at other older folktales, a very different picture emerges. It is a picture of widespread poverty and despair, except for the fortunate few who live in palaces."

26. Faust, *Archaeology*, 243–54; Dever, *Archaeology*, 74–89.

27. Hutton and Rubin, *Epigraphy*, 1–9; Rollston, *Writing*, 1–10.

28. Tov, *Textual*, 1–20; Elliott, *Textual*, 13–52.

29. Wilder, *Literary*, 37–50; Alter, *Narrative*, 1–24.

30. Halpern, *Historians*, 1–36; Levenson, *Historical*, 1–32.

31. Howgego, *Coins*, 1–23.

32. Schroer and Keel, *Ikonographie*, 11–36; De Hulster et al., *Iconographic*, 135–242.

33. Habel, *Earth*, 25–37; Moore, *Eco-Wisdom*.

34. Cf. Polanyi, *Livelihood*, xli.

35. Ro (*Poverty*, 3) justifiably criticizes approaches which ignore or minimalize "the analysis and treatment of . . . texts"; and Hallo ("Cuneiform," 12–13) contends that "in the area of literary techniques the evidence from the literate neighbors of ancient Israel is not only relevant . . . but enjoys a scholarly consensus based on a maximum of facts and a minimum of theories." Cf. Reiner, "Akkadische," 151–210; Groneberg, "Definition," 59–84.

36. For a more detailed introduction, cf. Moore, *WealthWatch*, 1–25.

2

Prophetic Socioeconomic Motifs in Ancient Near Eastern Texts

SOCIOECONOMIC MOTIFS COMPARABLE TO those utilized in Nevi'im animate several "great texts" from Mesopotamia, Anatolia, and Canaan.

Mesopotamia

Whereas the previous volume spotlights the mythopoeic epics of Gilgamesh, Atraḫasis, and Erra as motif repositories comparable to those in Torah,[1] the following pages will examine the socioeconomic motifs structuring two other "great texts"—Inanna's Descent[2] and the Creation Epic[3]—plus a representative sample of "prophetic texts"[4] preserved in governmental correspondence from the libraries of Zimri-Lim (at Tell Ḥarīrī/Mari) and Assurbanipal (at Tell Koujunjik/Nineveh).[5]

Inanna's Descent

Mythopoeic epics about mother/fertility goddesses fiercely committed to protecting devotees from the pain of *infertility* deeply impact the "great literature" of the ancient

1. Moore, *WealthWatch*, 26–99. Mugerauer ("Literature," 407–15) discusses the indispensable role of "great literature" in criticizing value-systems (whether they be tribal, confederate, or imperial), and Davenport ("Twist," 1–23) shows how such critical thinking permeates GE.

2. Cf. Kramer, "Inanna," 52–57.

3. Cf. Lambert, *Creation*, 50–133.

4. Nissinen (*Perspectives*, 52) defines "prophecy" as "a process of divine-human communication in which the prophet is the mediator between the divine and human worlds, transmitting divine messages to human recipients"; and further, that "the literarization of prophecy presupposes a community that adopts, repeats, interprets, and reinterprets prophetic messages for its own purposes."

5. See, conveniently, Nissinen, *Prophets*, 13–199; Roberts, "Mari," 166–253; Parpola, *Prophecies*, 4–43; Gordon, "Prophecy," 37–58; Weippert, *Götterwort*, 207–26; Stökl, *Prophecy*, 1–28; Radine, *Amos*, 80–109.

world.[6] Procreation in these texts is no genteel, "optional" concern,[7] at least not like it is depicted in much postmodern Western fiction.[8] This is true for several reasons, but not least because procreation for the ancients has more to do with tribal *survival* than individual *choice*.[9] Incessant debate over the moral, ideological, and societal complexities of abortion, for example, belabored *ad nauseum* in postmodern Western literature,[10] does not seriously concern (much less preoccupy) the ancients.[11] Instead the overwhelming tendency is to celebrate *fertility* and *procreation* as divine blessings bestowed on the "black-headed people"[12] to promote the success and prosperity of family, clan, tribe, and nation.[13] Devotees of "the goddess" appeal to her regularly

6. "Fertility" is a buzzword in many circles. Cf. the astute critical analyses of Hackett ("Sexist," 65–76), Moss and Baden (*Infertility*, 229–38), Keefe (*Hosea*, 66–103), and Stol (*Women*, 651–52). Use of the term here is limited predominantly to economic categories; i.e., Keefe's ("Politic," 81–83) critique is well taken.

7. Keefe's (*Hosea*, 158) perspective is judicious: "Ancient Israelite women are largely defined by their procreative potential and constrained within a male-dominated social system. A modern, liberated person may respond to this . . . with horror and conclude that ancient Israel is a misogynistic society . . . But in a social context where the individual is not the primary locus of human meaning and value, sex and gender will carry meanings which are quite distinct from our own and the equations most central to feminist analysis will not necessarily hold . . . In such social situations personal autonomy is not definitive to the structures of human meaning and therefore should not be taken as the normative criteria upon which to evaluate woman's status and ascribed worth within ancient Israelite society."

8. See Barth, *Road*; Drabble, *Bird-Cage*; Wilt, *Fiction*, 37–66; and the essays in Evans, *Child*. Distinguishing between "economic" and "sentimental," Zelizer (*Child*, 171) documents how contemporary attitudes toward adoption have changed over the past few decades. Involuntary childlessness, of course, is an entirely different matter (cf. May, *Barren*, 1–20).

9. Inhorn (*Infertility*, 3–38) documents cultural attitudes toward infertility in ancient Egypt, and Koepf-Taylor (*Survival*, 33–64) emphasizes the great value of children and how infertility spawns not just emotional, but socioeconomic distress. Goodchild ("Market," 230) focuses on "the direct contradiction between the mechanics of market forces and individual freedom."

10. Cf., e.g., Irving, *Rules*; Jordan, *Woke*; Cody, *Juno*; and Rabe, *Hurlyburly*. Girgus (*Law*) outlines the evolution of the impact of individualism on Poe, Emerson, Brownson, Whitman, Howells, Henry James, Ives, Fitzgerald, and William James.

11. Granted, ANE legal texts do mention abortion (cf. Frymer-Kensky, "Virginity," 83–84; Bergman, *Childbirth*, 9–59), and the practice does find attention in late Hellenized sources (cf. Gorman, *Abortion*, 13–18), but it's difficult to think of a single second-millennium text in which abortion functions *as a literary motif*. Contrast this with how its prevalence in postmodern culture shares, in Levine's (*Economics*, 3) opinion, "some of the features of a standard economic treatment of insurance" in that "it provides protection from downside risk in the form of giving birth to a child that is unintended." Because "this insurance is available at very low cost," moreover, it often "leads to changes in behavior which increase the likelihood of its being needed."

12. Akk *niši*^{meš} *ṣal-mat qaqqadi* is a common idiom for "the Babylonians" (*Ee* 6.107; *Erra* 1.120).

13. Tanak is no exception. Cf. the divine command פרו ורבו ("be fruitful and multiply") in Genesis (Gen 1:22, 28; 8:17, 9:1, 7) in what Schmutzer (*Fruitful*, 226) calls the "creation mandate" (cf. Moss and Baden, *Infertility*, 70–102), and N.B. that these motifs feature heavily in childbirth incantations designed to secure the fortunes of both mother and child (Farber, *Lamaštu*, 1–6; Beckman, *Birth*, 170–71; Blackman, "Egyptian," 199–206).

in this regard,[14] and the mythographers responsible for articulating their petitions employ covert literary strategies like those later retreaded in Nevi'im.[15] The Hebrew prophet Jeremiah, for example, castigates his fellow Egyptian exiles for burning incense to the מלכת השמים ("Queen of Heaven"),[16] using an epithet most likely shaped by Mesopotamian[17] or Canaanite sources.[18] Indeed, practically every ANE pantheon boasts a "heavenly queen" of one sort or another whose primary *raison d'être* is to champion fertility and prosperity in the face of war, famine, disease, and death.[19] In Egypt she goes by several names: Nut,[20] Hathor,[21] Mut,[22] Isis,[23] even the cerebral Ma`at.[24] Canaanites call her Astarte,[25] Athirat,[26] and/or Anat,[27] and Anatolians call her Kubaba, Šauška, and/or Cybele.[28]

14. Cf. Black, "Mother," 202; Gadotti, "Feminine," 28–58; Bachvarova, "Pregnancy," 272–306; Urbin-Chofray, "Déesse-mère," 380–81.

15. Frymer-Kensky, *Goddesses*, 99. Van der Toorn (*Scribal*, 48) asks, "Were there authors in antiquity? Yes, there were. How about individual talent, literary genius, and outstanding artistic skill? All of that existed."

16. Jer 44:17 (cf. 7:18). Cogan (*Imperialism*, 85–86) views her as the outgrowth of a local astral cult, but Ackerman ("Queen," 110) believes her to be an amalgamation of several Canaanite goddesses (Anat, Qudšu, Astarte, Hathor, even Šapšu).

17. Parpola (*Prophecies*, xv) imagines Ištar to be a "mother goddess" presiding over an Assyrian mystery cult promising "transcendental salvation and eternal life."

18. The Canaanite goddess Anat is called *b`lt šmm rmm* ("Lady of the High Heavens") in *CAT* 1.108.7. That Jeremiah's home village is named ענתות ("Anathoth") doubtless represents some indication of her (vestigial) presence, perhaps sensitizing the prophet early on to her pervasive influence (cf. Patai, *Goddess*, 62–66; Van der Toorn, "Anat-Yahu," 97).

19. The ancients regularly personify disease and catastrophe as demonic beings (cf. *Erra* 1.23–44; Geller, *Medicine*, 146–49; Scurlock, *Medicine*, 361–645; Fohrer, "Krankheit," 172–87; Moore, *Babbler*, 212–25; cf. the (re)symbolization of these demons in GNT, Rev 6:1–8). Some see in early Israel an original Hebrew goddess eventually subsumed into monotheistic Yahwism (e.g., Lang, *Goddess*, 5–7)—a polytheistic predilection later carried over into the cults of Mary and Sophia (cf. Spretnak, *Mary*; Kinsley, *Goddesses*; Moore, *Goddesses*, 178–81; Moore, "Trajectory," 87–103).

20. Nut is the primeval sky-goddess responsible for birthing the Egyptian pantheon (Lesko, *Goddesses*, 22).

21. Hathor takes over Nut's fertility mandate (Lesko, *Goddesses*, 85–87).

22. Mut is an Egyptian word for "mother" (Lesko, *Goddesses*, 130).

23. Associated with the annual inundation of the Nile, Isis is the great *reviver* of parched land mythopoeically represented by a dead husband, Osiris (Lesko, *Goddesses*, 156).

24. Cf. Karenga, *Ma`at*, 148–51; Allen, *Egyptian*, 147–48.

25. Ug *`ṯtrt* (*CAT* 1.2.1.40; cf. Heb עשתרת, 1 Kgs 11:5; Wyatt, "Astarte," 109–14; Olyan, "Queen," 163). N.B. the title *`štrt šmm 'drm* ("Aštarte of the Lofty Heavens") on the Ešmunazar sarcophagus from Sidon (*KAI* 14.16).

26. Ug *aṯrt* (*CAT* 1.4.6.46; cf. Wyatt, "Asherah," 99–105).

27. Ug *`nt* (*CAT* 1.3.2.4; cf. Day, "Anat," 36–43).

28. *GLH* 150; Goetze, *Kleinasien*, 131–35; Roller, *Cybele*, 44–53; Hutter, "Shaushka," 758–59. Cf. Frymer-Kensky, *Goddesses*, 9–82; Ackerman, *Heroes*, 87; Buchan, *Frozen*, 124; Jacobsen, *Harps*, 168; Townsend, "Revitalization," 179–203; and Moore, *WealthWatch*, 34, 52–53, 59, 62–64. The degree to which "fertility" colors her résumé can be difficult to discern, but contemporary "analyses" based on little more than a desire to redefine the notions of "gender" and "sexuality" tend to be

In Sumer—home of the world's oldest literature—several goddesses "sponsor the cultural arts and learned occupations,"[29] but the most powerful by far is Inanna, a complex character embodying "an amalgam of several different Sumerian, or southern Mesopotamian goddesses,"[30] thus making her one of the "most intriguing"[31] and "most fascinating of the goddesses, both to the ancients and to modern writers."[32] Championing fertility and prosperity in the face of infertility, famine, disease and death, *this* heavenly queen comes to a point where she earnestly "desires" (AL BI_2-IN-DUG_4)[33] (at least, in the minds of her mythographers)[34] to exit "the great above" (AN GAL) and enter "the great below" (KI GAL).[35] So strong is this "desire," in fact, it compels her to invade the Netherworld realm of her sister Ereškigal[36] to neutralize, if not vanquish altogether the tentacled power of Death.[37] Some imagine this "desire" as little more than a thinly disguised "covetousness" much like that prompting her to target the hero Gilgamesh.[38] Others dismiss it as the swagger of a brassy celebrity starring in an ANE version of her own tawdry "reality show."[39] Yet like Gilgamesh, the hero

embarrassingly uninformed.

29. Levenson, *Goddesses*, 50. Jacobsen (*Treasures*, 23–73) situates the origins of the "dying gods of fertility" in the fourth millennium BCE. Frymer-Kensky (*Goddesses*, 213–20) argues that the Hebrews demythologize and reassign these functions, not eliminate them.

30. Abusch ("Ishtar," 453). For Frymer-Kensky (*Goddesses*, 27), "Inanna has enormous power, and in some sense has control over heaven, earth, and lordship," even though "her great power and role are ill-defined."

31. Jacobsen, *Treasures*, 135.

32. Frymer-Kensky, *Goddesses*, 222.

33. Lit. "speak a desire" (ID 191).

34. Hobson (*Mammon*, 44) recognizes that "belief in the power of the religious experts to control the productive forces of nature, and to avert the injurious forces, is early realized as a means of easy living by a priestly caste, the members of which soon learn how to apply to their own material advantage the sacrifices, gifts, or blackmail which experience enables them to appropriate." The priesthood controlling Eanna (Inanna's temple) has its headquarters in the city of Uruk.

35. ID 191. Carter ("Inanna," 9) presumes that "if we understand the primary quality of the heart to be compassion," then "Inanna has compassion enough to risk her descent."

36. ^{d}EREŠ.KI.GAL (lit. "Lady of the Great Below," ID 93) rules ^{d}Irkalla, a common designation for the Netherworld (DI 4; cf. Sum KUR, ID 4; Flückiger-Hawker, *Urnammu*, 332) alongside her male consort Nergal (Hutter, *Unterwelt*, 98; Penglase, *Myths*, 246–47; Launderville, *Celibacy*, 185–89). The conflict between these sisters is fierce, but not necessarily because one is the "dark side" of the other (*contra* Schneider, *Religion*, 49).

37. Cf. Gadotti, *Netherworld*; Haas, "Death," 2021; and Moore, *Babbler*, 166–79. Katz (*Netherworld*, 182) observes that the status of dead Sumerians "corresponds to terrestrial social standards"; i.e., that "the netherworld is conceived as paralleling the world of the living."

38. GE 6.6–21; cf. Sladek, "Inanna," 20, 205; Moore, *WealthWatch*, 51–67. Other opinions appear in the essays edited by Maier (*Gilgamesh*).

39. Cf. Jacobsen, *Harps*, 205.

who breaches the *itu*-fence surrounding the Cedar Forest,[40] Inanna, too, breaches a "sacred boundary"—the one separating *life* from the invasive power of *death*.[41]

The socioeconomic dynamics personified by this character are not easily cartooned.[42] "Jealousy" is not *the* reason for her "ill-considered attempt at a *coup d'état*,"[43] nor is it appropriate to depict her as a postmodern professional woman determined "to reject societally approved ways."[44] Simplistic anachronistic analyses tend to ignore the socioeconomic "elephant in the middle of the room"; viz., How does ID/DI engage the "big problems" afflicting the Mesopotamian economy?[45]

As with Gilgamesh or any other "literary text," the clearer one's understanding of its literary structure, the more likely it is to be fully understood:[46]

Inanna leaves the Upperworld

Inanna descends into the Netherworld

Inanna dies

The gods (Enki and Ninšubur) intervene

Inanna revives

Inanna ascends from the Netherworld

Inanna reenters the Upperworld

40. GE 3.55. Cf. Moore, *WealthWatch*, 43–46.

41. Eliade, *Sacred*, 25, 181; Moore, *Babbler*, 212–14. Franco and Zimbardo ("Heroism," 505) insightfully observe that "it is easy to consider heroism as invariably motivated by positive intentions and engaged in only by 'good' people. However, there are many examples in which the impulsivity that plays into deviant behavior also prepares individuals with checkered pasts to act in heroic ways."

42. Harris, "Images," 219–30.

43. *Pace* Jacobsen, *Harps*, 205. Parpola (*Prophecies*, xxxi–xxxvi) drifts to another extreme when he argues, in his effort to characterize Ishtar religion as an "ecstatic mystery cult," that "to understand ID correctly it is essential to realize that it has nothing to do with 'fertility.'" Porter (*Trees*, 18–19) is justifiably critical of such extremism.

44. *Pace* Frymer-Kensky, *Goddesses*, 25. Green (*Enki*, 284) counters that "in both *Inanna and Enki* and *Enki and the World Order* Inanna appeals to Enki for a share in the powers of the world," while "in a third myth, *Inanna's Descent*, she tries to extend her sphere of power into the Netherworld. Her character is thus depicted as greedy and her acts as thefts or illegitimate usurpations. Analogies may be seen in the Akkadian *Myth of Anzu* and the Sumerian *Ninurta and the Turtle*, where Anzu and Ninurta each try to wrest powers from the Abzu. On the other hand, Inanna claims in *Enki and the World Order* that she is requesting merely her own deserved share, which has been denied her; and the goal sought in *Inanna and Enki*—self-beautification—is not outside the proper character of Inanna. The possibility that Inanna is legitimating her powers by honest claims, at least in *Inanna and Enki* and *Enki and the World Order*, must also be considered."

45. Polanyi (*Livelihood*, xli) distinguishes minor concerns from "big problems" (cf. Aubet, "Polanyi," 17–39). Olson ("Gate," 19) argues that the Sumerians "first join knowledge to culture, and, with this weapon, shape dignities of economics and value."

46. Cf. Moore, *WealthWatch*, 30, on the literary structure of GE. Whether or how much ID operates (like *Ee*) within a ritual context is important, but immaterial here (cf. Groneberg, "Ištar," 291–303; Böck, "Inanna," 21–23).

Inanna Leaves the Upperworld

Conspicuously missing from DI,[47] the first seventy-two lines of ID describe not only Inanna's frustration with *infertility* and *death*, but her amorphous scheme to (a) marshal the resources necessary for mounting a successful invasion of KUR-RA (the Netherworld),[48] including (b) the formulation of an escape plan should things turn ugly.[49] Since nothing can accompany her on her chthonic journey,[50] she cannot proceed without first "forsaking" (MU-UN-ŠUB)[51] the primary fixtures of her cult—the male priesthood,[52] the female priesthood,[53] and the temple-complexes where they work. This isolates her not only from her most fervent devotees, but indeed, from *all* sources of Upperworld help. It also affects her clandestine decision to smuggle the "sacred blueprints" (Sum ME) of the cosmos through "customs";[54] i.e., hide in her

47. DI (138 lines) is much shorter than ID (412 lines).

48. ID 5 (lit. "the mountains"). Sladek ("Inanna," 61–62) observes that "many texts make it clear that the Mesopotamians think that the netherworld is directly under the ground. Yet not only does the word KUR suggest mountains, but . . . some passages seem to indicate that they think it is located in the mountains to the northeast. One of the most prominent of these is the description of the route taken by Inanna to the netherworld in ID . . . Inanna leaves her city Uruk and travels north on the Iturungal canal, finally arriving at Agade. She then heads east overland towards the mountains, as is shown by her answer to the doorman's questions, 'I am Inanna (and I am going) eastward' (ID 81). This is supposed to be a plausible reason for her being at the entrance to the Netherworld. Moreover, in the cultic reenactment of Dumuzi's journey to the netherworld (so his sister Geštinanna can come out after her half-year stay), the statue of Dumuzi is taken to the mountains in the east. In addition one may point to the fact that *arallu*, an Akkadian poetic name for the Netherworld, is considered in some texts to be an actual mountain that is a source of gold."

49. Penglase (*Myths*, 246) thinks "the view that Inanna seeks to acquire Ereškigal's throne . . . conflicts with certain other elements in ID. If Inanna intends to usurp Ereškigal's throne, then it appears that she does not intend to retain it permanently, for which she would have to remain in the Netherworld." This, however, contradicts "her instructions to Ninšubur," which specify "that she intends to make her way back to the Upperworld."

50. Inanna/Ishtar is not the only deity who descends into the Netherworld. Nergal, too, has to pass through seven gates to return to his wife Ereškigal (*Nergal and Ereškigal*, trans. in Foster, *Muses*, 517), and several Canaanite texts allude to things chthonic; e.g., El says, "[After Baʿal] I shall descend into the Earth" (*ʾard bʾarṣ*, *CAT* 1.5.6.24–25). In Anatolian myth the LÚNI.DUḪ ("gatekeeper") of the Netherworld opens the 7 ^{GIŠ}IG ("seven doors") to seize Telipinu's "anger, wrath, sin, and anxiety" (Hoffner, *Hittite Myths*, 2.26–27).

51. ID 6–13 (lit. "cause to fall down," Flückiger-Hawker, *Urnamma*, 353).

52. NAM-LAGAR (cf. van Dijk, "Marduk," 68; Alster, "NAM-EN," 117; Sladek, "Inanna," 183).

53. NAM-EN (cf. van Dijk, "Marduk," 68; Alster, "NAM-EN," 117).

54. ID 130–63. Sassoon (*Sumer*, 65) contends that the ME (pl.) "are a collection of abstract qualities related to or underlying all aspects of life . . . an uncannily modern sounding statement of the behavior and concepts out of which human life on earth is in fact built." Sum ME denotes "tangible object" (Kramer, "Inanna," 53) as well as intangible "divine power" (Sladek, "Inanna," 17). Enki gives several ME to Inanna in the myth commonly known as *Enki and Inanna*, including heroism, power, wickedness, righteousness, plunder, lamentation, rejoicing, deceit, rebellion, kindness, movement, settlement, carpentry, copper-making, writing, blacksmithing, leatherworking, construction, wisdom, discernment, holy purification rites, the shepherd's hut, piled-up glowing charcoals, the sheepfold, respect, awe, reverent silence, the kindling of fire, the extinguishing of fire, hard work, the family,

clothing the "cultural traits and complexes"[55] she soon has to abandon, one by one, at each of Ganzir's (seven) gates.[56]

Particularly important is the escape-plan entrusted to Ninšubur, her loyal SUKKAL ("vizier/prime minister").[57] The plan is simple. Should Inanna for some reason become stranded "down there," Ninšubur is to don the dress of a mourner and make the rounds of the Enlil, Nanna, and Enki temples, chanting the following lament:

A-[A] ᴰMU-UL-LÍL DU_5-MU-ZU	Father Enlil,[58] let no one in the
MU-LU KUR-RA	Netherworld
NAM-BA-DA-AN-GAM-E	kill your child
KÙ-$ŠA_6$-GA-ZU SAḪAR-KUR-RA-KA	Let no one mix your fine silver with
NAM-BA-DA-AB-ŠÁ-RE	crude ore
ZA-GÌN-$ŠA_6$-GA-ZU ZA-ZADIM-MA-KA	Let no one replace your fine lapis lazuli
NAM-BA-DA-AN-SI-IL-LE	with fine-cut stone
ᴳᴵŠTAŠ KARIN-ZU ᴳᴵŠNAGAR-RA-KA	Let no one engrave your fine mahogany
NAM-BA-DA-AN-DAR-DAR-RE	like it is everyday lumber
ᴷᴵSIKIL ᴰGA-[ŠA]-AN-NA KUR-RA	Let no one in the Netherworld kill
NAM-BA-DA-AN-GAM-E	the young lady Inanna.[59]

Structurally this lament consists of three equations framed by a "prophetic" warning, each contrasting something precious with something mundane; i.e., fine silver ≠ crude ore, lapis lazuli ≠ lapidary stone, and mahogany ≠ everyday lumber. These polarities fuse into focus when intertextually read alongside other Sumerian laments.

descendants, strife, triumph, counselling, comforting, judging, and decision-making. In *Enki and Ninmaḫ* the gods say, A-A TUD-DA-GIN_7 ME NAM TAR-TAR-RA ME ZA-E AL-ME-EN-NA, "You (Enki) are our non-impotent father, the one who holds the ME to decide destinies; in fact, you are the ME" (text posted at http://etcsl.orinst.ox.ac.uk/cgi-in/etcsl.cgi?text=c.1.1.2&display=Crit&charenc=&lineid=c112.44#c112.44; cf. Farber-Flügge, *Inanna*, 97–115; Ceccarelli, *Enki*, 108–9; and Lambert, *Creation*, 336–37.

55. Kramer, *Sumer*, 99. Cf. the transliteration of Sum ME in OB *mê ᵈNanâ* (CH 1.63).

56. ID 14–24, 73. Ganzir is another name for the Netherworld, specifically its entrance (*CAD* G.43; Katz, *Netherworld*, 88–89). Sladek ("Inanna," 74–75) points out that the Sumerian tradition varies the number of clothing items, eventually settling on *seven* as the ideal number.

57. ID 34–64. Ninšubur is Inanna's SUKKAL ZID (lit. "good vizier," DI 29). Cf. Akk *sukkallu* (*CAD* S.354–60); Sallaberger, "Ur," 188–90.

58. Alongside the deity Enlil here cf. ᵈNANNA (the moon-god Nanna) in line 52 and ᵈAM-ANKI (Enki) in line 60.

59. ID 43–47 (reconstructed according to George, "*Inanna*," 109–11). The words of this lament appear no less than six times in ID.

One of the ERŠEMA hymns,[60] for example, contains the following request: "When will she (Ereškigal) release her (Inanna), the silver she has accumulated? When will she release her? When will she release her, the lapis she has accumulated? When will she release her? The silver I had, my silver has been used up! The lapis lazuli I had, my lapis has been used up!"[61]

Ninšubur's lament, in other words, praises Inanna by comparing her to several things considered "precious."[62] Whether it also references the physical elements used to construct her humanoid image is not clear,[63] even though few doubt the existence of a correlation between her *mythical* journey and her *geographical* "journey";[64] i.e., the journey her cult-image sometimes makes when, for whatever reason,[65] it leaves her "house."[66]

60. Cf. Cohen, *Eršemma*, 63–64; Gabbay, *Eršema*. The root of ERŠEMA is ŠEM$_3$ ("drum," ID 35) and according to Dalglish (*Patternism*, 20) refers to a rhythmic hymn "filled with epithetic and laudatory invocations, often with a repetitious formula to induce the deities to repent."

61. ME-NA KÙ MU-UN-TU$_9^{TU}$ MU-UN-DUḪ-E ME-NA MU-UN-DUḪ-E / ME-NA ZA MU-UN-TU$_9^{TU}$ MU-UN-DUḪ-E ME-NA MU-UN-DUḪ-E / KÙ Ì-TU-KA KU-MU BA-TÌL / ZA-GÌN Ì-TU-KA ZA-GÌN Ì-TU-KA ZA-MU BA-TÌL (cited from Cohen, *Eršemma*, 63–64).

62. George, "*Inanna*," 111–13. Something similar occurs with the "precious throne" built by Nergal to appease Ereškigal in *their* chthonic encounter (text cited in Foster, *Muses*, 515).

63. Jacobsen, *Treasures*, 57; Buccelatti, "Inanna," 5; Walker and Dick, *Cult-Image*, 4–31.

64. Hurowitz ("Image," 155) recognizes that "the juxtaposition of the death of the goddess with damage to what can only be her cult statue indicates that the two are one and the same," and Buccellati ("Inanna," 7) understands that the story of Inanna's descent "may have been (central to) an annual renewal ceremony, which may have been a part of the regular, recurrent caring of the goddess, and might have originated in response to the breaking of a given statue, whether accidental or through enemy intervention."

65. In George's ("*Inanna*," 112–13) opinion, "evidence for divine statues in the third millennium BCE, when Inanna's Descent probably finds its canonical form, is scant," but DI appears to "describe Inanna's unhappy fate in terms of the desecration of her statue and its dismantling for the reuse of its component parts. This is understandable if we consider the function of the divine statue in ancient Mesopotamia. It is clear from historical episodes, such as Marduk's sojourn in Elam, that whatever befalls a god's statue is thought automatically also to befall the god . . . The god and its statue are identified in a very real way and are accordingly, for all practical purposes, one and the same. It should come as no surprise, then, if a myth describes the loss of Inanna in the Netherworld as if it is her statue that has been captured and in danger of being despoiled by 'he of the Netherworld.'" Hurowitz (*Temple*, 196–204) prefers to view temple-building more as the result of barter and acquisition than conquest and plunder.

66. N.B. that on one occasion Ishtar's image *atmanša ēzibu ūšibu ašar lā simātīša*, "abandons her temple and dwells where it is not her destiny" (Nissinen, *Prophets and Prophecy*, 99.10–11). Paralleling the stories of the "blind seer" in Torah (Num 22–24) and "Ark capture" in Nevi'im (1 Sam 5–7), DI/ID is a major contributor to the "captured deity" genre (cf. Miller and Roberts, *Hand*, 10–11; Sharp, *Irony*, 139–40; and Mann, *Prophets*, 116).

Inanna Descends into the Netherworld

Once Inanna starts making her way through the seven gates of "the palace Ganzir,"[67] the language of the poem turns formulaic and repetitive, much like that of a Greek χορός:[68]

- Inanna and Neti meet at a gate;[69]
- Inanna removes an item of clothing and asks, "What is going on?" (TA-AM$_3$ NE-E);[70] and
- Neti replies, "Be silent, Inanna—a ME of the Netherworld is perfectly sufficient. Do not presume to 'negotiate'[71] with a Netherworld GARZA."[72]

Interpretation of this χορός, of course, hinges on the meaning of these two Sumerian terms. Samuel Noah Kramer translates ME as "ordinances" and GARZA as "rites."[73] Jeremy Black translates ME as "divine power" and GARZA as "rites."[74] Esther Flückiger-Hawker translates ME as "cultic norms"[75] and William Sladek, refraining from translating ME at all, translates GARZA as "sacred customs."[76] Casting about for language more familiar to Westerners, Thorkild Jacobsen translates ME as "office of Hades" and GARZA as "Hades' sacred functions."[77] Regardless of the options, it's important to recognize something else here; viz., the fact that DI takes two Sumerian terms in ID and fuses them into one—*parṣū*—an Akkadian word frequently associated in administrative texts with "compensatory expenses."[78] *Question:* What drives this fusion, if not the

67. ID 73. "GANZIR is the 'entrance to the netherworld' in ID and appears only in the phrase É-GAL GANZIR, 'palace at the entrance to the netherworld'" (Sladek, *Inanna*, 59).

68. LSJ 1999 (cf. Peponi, "Chorus," 15–34). N.B. the similar repetitiveness in the phrase ויהי ערב ויהי בקר יום in Gen 1:3–31—"and there was evening and there was morning, day __." Ferrara (*Inanna*, 351) calls for more study on the "techniques of repetition" (to borrow a phrase from Alter, *Narrative*, 111) to clarify the aesthetics of Mesopotamian myth.

69. ID 77. Neti (^{d}NE-TI) is the name of the deity responsible for guarding the gate into the Netherworld. Humbaba plays the same "guardian-protector" role in Gilgamesh (GE 2.221–29).

70. ID 156 (lit. "What is this?").

71. ID 133 (Sum KA-ZU NA-AN-BA-E, lit. "position the mouth").

72. SI-A ^{d}INANA ME KUR-RA-KE$_4$ ŠU AL-DU$_7$-DU$_7$ ^{d}INANA ĜARZA KUR-RA-KE$_4$ KA-ZU NA-AN-BA-E. This line repeats itself seven times in ID 127–63.

73. Kramer, "Inanna," 55.

74. Black, http://etcsl.orinst.ox.ac.uk/cgi-bin/etcsl.cgi?text=t.1.4.1#.

75. Flückiger-Hawker, *Urnamma*, 116.

76. Sladek, "Inanna," 164–65, 254–55. Falkenstein ("Unterwelt," 115) translates Sum ME with Akk *parṣū*, as in DI 44.

77. Jacobsen, *Harps*, 213–15. "Hades," of course, is a Greek deity (ᾅδης). Taking this Western predisposition to the extreme, Boulay (*Serpents*, 253) imagines the ME as "mechanized robots." Snell (*Flight*, 2–3) details the types of problems which arise when ANE literature is misread through a Hellenized lens.

78. See DI 44, 47, 50, 53, 56, 59, 62, and texts cited at *CAD* P.199–200. Cf. Pun פרצם ("coins," *IPT* 134); فريضة ("distributive shares in estate," *DMWA* 706); "inroads" (*DTTM* 1238); "rules" (Foster,

Akkadian translator's preoccupation, like that of later targumists working on texts in Nevi'im, with overtly socioeconomic questions and concerns?[79]

Inanna's Death

Once Inanna passes through all seven gates a violent clash erupts between the two sisters.[80] In ID Ereškigal vacates her throne, Inanna seats herself upon it, the Annunaki mount a "lawsuit,"[81] and "the afflicted woman becomes a corpse."[82] In DI, however, Ereškigal "trembles" at Ishtar's invasive "presence,"[83] Ishtar "impulsively assaults her,"[84] and Ereškigal unleashes a squadron of sixty demons/diseases.[85] Conspicuously missing in the Akkadian tradition is any mention of a "corpse."[86] Instead, DI laments the result of this conflict with the dreary mantra, "the bull does not mount the cow; the ass does not impregnate the jenny; the lad does not impregnate the lass."[87] Having lost its greatest champion, in other words, the Upperworld collapses into a barren, empty place where nothing "(pro)creates" or "(re)produces" or "succeeds" or "prospers."[88]

Muses, 500–501); "ancient rules" (Speiser, "Ishtar," 107–8); "ancient rites" (Dalley, *Myths*, 156–57). N.B. that Marduk establishes his *parṣū* before receiving the *ṭuppi šīmāti* ("Tablet of Destinies," *Ee* 5.67–69).

79. Cf. below. In DI 38 Ereškigal modifies *parṣū* via the adj. *labīru* ("ancient"), but this hardly eliminates the likelihood of socioeconomic influence. Moreover, if "rites" is the only semantic possibility for *parṣū*, why does Lambert translate "offices" in *BWL* 36.103?

80. ID 165–72. Perera (*Descent*, 13) sees in ID "the necessity for sacrifice and descent in order to gain wholeness" as well as an "openness to being acted upon"—in short, something she calls "the essence of the experience of the human soul faced with the transpersonal"—but this quintessentially postmodern interpretation is but one of several options.

81. ID 167 (Sum DI MU-UN-DA-KU$_5$-RU-NE, lit. "cut a lawsuit"). Jacobsen ("Democracy," 159–72) rather famously writes about the pervasiveness of politics in mythopoeic Mesopotamian literature. Cf. the use of ריב ("to sue") in Nevi'im (Judg 6:32; Jer 25:31; Hos 2:4; cf. discussion below).

82. Sum MUNUS TUR$_5$-RA UZU NIĜ$_2$ SAG$_3$-GA-ŠE$_3$ BA-AN-KUR$_9$ (ID 171). Exactly *how* Inanna becomes a corpse is not indicated.

83. DI 64, *ina paniša ir'ub*. Whether Ereškigal's "trembling" (*ra'ābum*) is driven by fear or anger is left to the reader's imagination.

84. DI 65, *^{d}Ištar ul immalik elēnušša ušbī*. Ambiguous terminology and syntax trigger a variety of translations: "Ishtar did not deliberate (?), but leant (?) over her" (Dalley, *Myths*, 157); "Ishtar, without thinking, sat (?) (in the place of honor)" (Foster, *Muses*, 501); "Ishtar, without reflection, rushed at her" (Sladek, "Inanna," 256, reading *šubê'u* with von Soden, *AHw* 1257//*GAG* 109j, instead of *wašābu* with Oppenheim, "Mythology," 141).

85. DI 69. Whereas the Anunnaki punish her in ID, Ereškigal punishes her in DI, though the demons/diseases are launched by Namtar (cf. Abusch, *Maqlû*, 1–40; Scurlock, *Medicine*, 1–4).

86. ID 171 (Sum UZU-NÌ-SÌG-GA).

87. DI 77–78, 87–88. Similar mantras portray the invasion of infertility/death when Telipinu's disappearance leads to the *wešuriya* ("stifling") of livestock: UDU-*uš-za* SILA$_4$-*ŠU mi-im-ma-aš* GU$_4$-ma AMAR-*ŠU mi-im-ma-aš*, "the mother sheep rejects her lamb; the cow rejects her calf" (Hoffner, *Hittite Myths*, 2.2).

88. Loucas ("Prospérité," 227) calls Inanna and Ishtar "prosperity goddesses."

WEALTHWARN

The Gods (Enki and Ninšubur) Intervene

Three days pass without a word, generating a silence so loud it convinces Ninšubur to trigger the aforementioned escape-plan. Altering her appearance to look like a mourner, the vizier starts making the rounds of the temples, endorsing her mistress's value to her colleagues via the aforementioned lament-song. This elicits from Enlil and Nanna a conservative reaction,[89] each dismissing her with the proverb, "Those who desire the ME of the Netherworld must remain in the Netherworld."[90] Enki, however, takes a different tack.[91] As in Atraḫasis and other "great texts," Enki is the deity most willing to deal with conflict, often quite "creatively."[92] In Atraḫasis, for example, he advises the "black-headed people" to save themselves from Enlil's wrath by bribing their way into the good graces of his vizier Namtar.[93] Something similar happens here when he dispatches two messengers to persuade Ereškigal into extending her royal hospitality.[94] To the first messenger (the KUR-GAR-RA) he entrusts a "life-giving plant."[95] To the second (the GALA-TUR-RA) he furnishes "life-giving water."[96] Thus, even as Enki's "bribery option" in Atraḫasis circumvents Enlil's "thin-the-herd" scheme,[97] so his "Inanna procurement policy" in ID circumvents Ereškigal's "Inanna entrapment ploy"

89. Nanna is the Sumerian moon-god (cf. Sjöberg, *Mondgott*; Hall, "Nanna-Suen").

90. ID 193, 207, ME KUR-RA ME AL NU-DI-DA SA_2 BI_2-IN-DUG_4-[GA-BI KUR]-/RE\ ḪE_2-EB-US2. Black translates "The divine powers of the underworld are divine powers which should not be craved, for whoever gets them must remain in the underworld" (http://etcsl.orinst.ox.ac.uk/cgi-bin/etcsl.cgi?text=t.1.4.1#). Sladek translates "The ME of the Netherworld are ME which are not to be coveted, for [whoever gets them] must remain [in the netherworld]" ("Inanna," 168, 169). Green (*Inanna*, 285) recognizes that "the proper distribution of power is a theme of great importance" because "the distribution of power is depicted as part of the process of the organization of the universe."

91. A dedication to Enki during the reign of Rim-Sin (d. 1699 BCE) describes him as ḪÉ-ĜÁ ŠÁR-RE, "wealth-multiplier" (cited from Espak, *Enki*, 110). Cf. Sollberger, *Ur*, 141–39; Jacques, *Vocabulaire*, 123–24; Selz, "Babilismus," 663–71; Galter, "Ea/Enki," 3–7; and Ceccarelli, *Enki*, 3–4. Espak (*Enki*, 210) posits that "contrary to widely shared opinion, the religious thinking of ancient Mesopotamia reflects continuous change"; i.e., that "there is no constant and static divine figure Enki" (cf. Kitz, "Ea," 191–214).

92. Abigail plays this mediatorial role in the David-Nabal conflict (1 Sam 25), Solomon in the "two-prostitutes" conflict (1 Kgs 3:16–28), and Yeshu`a in the "render unto Caesar" incident (Mark 12:14–17; cf. below). Standing in the shadow of Lévi-Strauss (*Anthropology*, 206–31), Fontaine ("Inanna," 85) recognizes that myth "attempts to resolve basic perceived conflicts through substitution of a series of mediating terms which eventually render the initial oppositions 'livable.'"

93. *Atr* 1.383 (cf. Moore, *WealthWatch*, 81–83).

94. ID 222–56. Draffkorn-Kilmer ("Ereshkigal," 304) contends that Enki's messengers "bait her (Ereškigal) by vocalizing the guest's part of the oath, whereupon she, unthinking and off guard, responds with the host's part of the oath, thus *automatically* committing herself to (a) providing them with food and drink, and (b) placing them under the aegis of the host-guest bond."

95. ID 224 (U_2 NAM-TIL_3-LA BA-AN-ŠUM_2; cf. *CAD* K.557–59, and the יניקה-"shoot" in the "Parable of the Two Eagles," Ezek 17:4; cf. below).

96. ID 225 (A NAM-TIL_3-LA BA-AN-ŠUM_2; cf. *CAD* K.107–8 and 1 Kgs 18:33–34 below).

97. *Atr* 4.11' AR (*mur-ṣu di-'u šu-ur-pu-u a-sa-ku*, "disease, sickness, plague, pestilence").

by (a) sneaking his messengers past Neti,[98] (b) homeopathically aligning *her* "pain" with *their* "pain,"[99] and (c) forecasting through this realignment enough sympathy to lower her guard long enough to take the "hospitality oath."[100] The strategy succeeds. She says to the two messengers, "If you are gods, I will promise you something, (but) if you are mortal, I will decree for you a pleasing fate."[101] Implementing this oath she offers them a river to drink and a grainfield to eat, but in lieu of these gifts they ask for Inanna's corpse, knowing full well that she is now obligated to hand it over to them.

Inanna Revives

Once Inanna's corpse leaves Ereškigal's control, the KUR-GAR-RA and GALA-TUR-RA[102] sprinkle it with the "water of life" and "plant of life," and thanks to the power of Enki's "word,"[103] it "revives."[104] Examination of this "resurrection" against the larger belief-complex associated with "dying-rising" deities,[105] an important task in its own right, is immaterial here because it takes attention away from the following two questions: (a) how does ID/DI symbolically portray the character and scope of

98. Some define these messengers in sexual categories under the presumption that procreative sexuality is Ereshkigal's greatest nemesis. Sladek ("Inanna," 93–97), e.g., imagines their "abnormal" sexuality to be what enables them to slip past Neti (i.e., their lack of "procreative male potency"). Jacobsen (*Harps*, 220), however, prefers to define their behavior in liturgical categories, translating KUR-GAR-RA as "myrmidon" and GALA-TUR-RA as "elegist"; and Zsolnay ("*Assinnu*," 91) imagines them as "professional mourners." Intratextually speaking, it is far more likely that the role enacted by these messengers has more to do with *shrewdness* than *sexuality* ("abnormal" or otherwise).

99. DI 240 (ŠAG$_4$-ĜU$_{10}$-[TA] ŠAG$_4$-ZU-ŠE$_3$ BAR-ĜU$_{10}$-TA BAR-<ZU>-ŠU$_3$ DUG$_4$-GA-NA-AB -ZE$_2$-EN). Black translates "speaking to you from my heart to your heart, from my body to your body" (http://etcsl.orinst.ox.ac.uk/cgi-bin/etcsl.cgi?text=c.1.4.1&display=Crit&charenc=gcirc#). Jacobsen (*Harps*, 221) translates "I have spoken from my heart to your heart, from my liver to your liver." Sladek ("Inanna," 171) more idiomatically translates "(Who) is echoing my cry of pain?" Foster (*Muses*, 506) sees her pain in *Nergal and Ereškigal* as sexual frustration/isolation, but whatever its cause in ID she suffers the despair of never being able to produce a child.

100. Hospitality is a serious socioeconomic commitment in Middle Eastern culture (cf., e.g., Luke 10:25–37; Moore, *WealthWatch*, 204–9). Lucian (*Dea Syria* 12) alleges that, according to *Deucalioneia* (the Greek flood myth), the first generation of humanity perishes because οὔτε γὰρ ὅρκια ἐφύλασσον οὔτε ξείνους ἐδέκοντο οὔτε ἱκετέων ἠνείχοντο, "they neither keep oaths nor practice hospitality (lit. 'accept guests') nor address the needs of supplicants." Commitment to hospitality is what saves Lot from the destruction of Sodom (Gen 19:3) and defines one of the essential qualities expected of Christian leaders (φιλόξενος, lit. "love of strangers," 1 Tim 3:2).

101. ID 242–43, 269–70. Albright ("Patriarchs," 24–25) traces a linguistic connection between Enki, Atra-*Ḫasis* (Akk *ḫasāsu*, *CAD* Ḫ.122–25) *Koṯar-wa-Ḫasis* (Ug *kṯr wḫss*, "wise architect," *CAT* 1.6.6.59–60), and the Heb term כשר ("*kosher*," Esth 8:5; *HAL* 479).

102. DI 92 condenses these two messengers into one, Aṣušunamir, whom Dalley (*Myths*, 158) translates as "good looking playboy."

103. ID 284 (INIM ^{d}EN-KI-[KA3-TA]).

104. Sum ^{d}INANA BA-GUB (ID 281; lit. "Inanna stands up").

105. See Mettinger, *Riddle*, 60–64; Smith, "Gods," 521–27; Moore, *Riddle*.

Mesopotamia's "big problems?";[106] and (b) how does the Inanna/Ishtar cult in the ID/DI ritual tradition imagine their resolution?[107]

Inanna Ascends from the Netherworld

One transaction remains before Inanna can return to the Upperworld. Someone must be found to take her place.[108] Simply to have "living" food and "living" water resuscitate her corpse is not enough. A life must be exchanged for hers. As the Annunaki put it,[109] "If Inanna wants to rise from the Netherworld, she must furnish for herself a substitute."[110] Dumuzi and his sister Geštinanna fulfill this requirement in the Sumerian tradition, each spending six months of the year in Irkalla.[111] In the Akkadian tradition, however, Tammuz alone is the substitute—the diffident shepherd[112] specially acquired for this task via a hefty "ransom payment" (*ipṭiru*).[113]

DI (a) fuses together several key ideas separately expressed in ID, and (b) compresses their semantic bandwidth. That is, just as DI utilizes the administrative term *parṣū* to compress the semantic possibilities in ME and GARZA,[114] the term Aṣušunamir (DI 103) compresses the two terms in ID indicating Enki's messengers

106. Polanyi (*Livelihood*, xli) distinguishes minor economic concerns from "big problems."

107. Not to be forgotten is the fact that this section of ID is the chiastic pivot around which everything else structurally revolves.

108. ID 289. Why this is so is never explained, simply presumed. Reading ID through a lens hypersensitive to postmodern gender polarities, Gardner ("Mother," 456) speculates that "at one level, this story is a metaphor for the agricultural cycle—half the year for growing and farming, the other half for regeneration. At another, it tells of the takeover by men of what had previously been female responsibilities." Should this be the case, however, then why do Dumuzi *and his sister Geštinanna* each do time in the Sumerian Netherworld?

109. The Annunaki serve a literary function in ANE epics much like that of the Greek χορός (cf. Bertman, *Mesopotamia*, 116).

110. ID 288–89 (UD-DA ^{d}INANA KUR-TA BA-ED$_3$-DE$_3$ SAĜ-DILI SAĜ-ĜA2-NA ḪA-BA-AB-ŠUM$_2$-MU; lit. "exchange a single head").

111. At first the demons accompanying Inanna choose Ninšubur (ID 307–27), then Šara (ID 328–39), then Lulal (ID 340–46). Inanna rejects each of these choices for various reasons, but when the shepherd Dumuzi comes into view she passionately condemns him via the same three verdicts trained earlier on her by the Annunaki (i.e., "the look of death," "the speech of anger," and "the cry of guilt," ID 354–56; cf. 168–70). ID does not mention Geštinanna by name, but the Sumerian myth *Dumuzi and Geštinanna* makes it clear that this brother-sister *combination* is the only way to fulfill this substitutionary requirement (http://etcsl.orinst.ox.ac.uk/cgi-bin/etcsl.cgi?text=c.1.4.1.1&display=Crit&charenc=gcirc#).

112. Cf. Alster, "Tammuz," 828–34. "In cult rites of sacred marriage and death" devotion to Tammuz consists of "irresistible attraction" and "possessive love" (Jacobsen, "Tammuz," 101)—what contemporary psychologists call "addiction." Ezekiel condemns this addiction when it takes over the Hebrew women weeping for Tammuz at the north gate of the Jerusalem temple (Ezek 8:14).

113. DI 126–27 (*napṭīrša*, "her ransom"), reading *napṭīru* as a variant of (*CAD* I.173) or error (*CDA* 240) for *ipṭirū*.

114. See above.

(KUR-GAR-RA and GALA-TUR-RA).[115] The single figure Tammuz compresses together the brother-sister team of Dumuzi and Geštinanna, and the term *ipṭirū* compresses together the semantic options laid out in the terms SAĜ-ĜA$_2$-NA and SAĜ-BI-ŠE$_3$.[116] This semantic compression is difficult to explain apart from some understanding of and appreciation for the socioeconomic motifs infusing this mythopoeic tradition.

Inanna Reenters the Upperworld

Whereas the foregoing analysis seeks to identify the socioeconomic motifs structuring a famous literary text, in no way does it seek to imply that all other analyses are somehow "inadequate." With anthropologist Joseph Campbell one might well ask whether one of ID/DI's goals is to disclose how time spent in the "dark places of the soul" helps Inanna-like "travelers" develop the inner resources needed to survive and prosper.[117] And with Joseph Mark one might wonder whether ID/DI simply focuses on "one of the gods behaving badly and the other gods . . . suffering" for it.[118] Like all great literature, this tradition speaks to different readers on different planes.[119] From the perspective of the present study, however, it's important to recognize three things: (a) the shape and significance of ID's chiastic literary structure, (b) the shape and significance of DI's semantic compression strategy, and (c) the ways and means by which these literary features help shape ID/DI's depiction of the Mesopotamian economy.

The Babylonian Creation Epic

Of all the creation epics,[120] the "exceptionally long Babylonian poem"[121] commonly known by its opening line, *Enūma eliš* ("When on high . . ."),[122] conflates several priestly traditions about Marduk,[123] the vanguard deity worshiped at the annual *akītu*

115. Cf. Dalley, *Myths*, 158.

116. ID 289. Semantic compression is not uncommon in Akkadian translations of Sumerian texts, but its significance is often downplayed (cf. Vanstiphout, "Ambiguity," 155–66; Westenholz, "Language," 183–206; and Veldhuis, *Cuneiform*, 1–4).

117. Campbell, *Hero*, 88–90.

118. Mark, "Inanna," http://www.ancient.eu/article/215/.

119. Mugerauer, "Literature," 407–15. As Lewis ("Myth," 45) puts it, "the same story may be a myth to one . . . and not to another."

120. Other Mesopotamian creation epics include *Enmešarra's Defeat*, *Enki and Ninmaḫ*, *The Slaying of Labbu*, *The Murder of Anšar*, *The Theogony of Dunnu*, and *Atraḫasis* (cf. Lambert, *Creation*, 281–401; Lambert and Millard, *Atra-ḫasīs*).

121. Gabriel, *Weltordnung*, 7. The self-designation in *Ee* 7.161 is *zamāru* ("song").

122. *Ee* 1.1. See King, *Creation*; Lambert, *Creation*, 50–133; Dalley, *Myths*, 228–77; Buccellati, "*Quando*"; Foster, *Muses*, 439–85; Talon, *Enūma*, 3–108; Speiser, "Creation," 60–72; and Heidel, *Creation*, 1–60.

123. Seri, "Creation," 4. Arguably the most important deity in Babylonian history, "Marduk" (Sum

festival,[124] including (a) his displacement of Anšar as "king of the gods";[125] (b) his defeat of the leviathan Tiamat;[126] (c) his victory over Tiamat's puppet-consort Qingu;[127] (d) his monster-slaying adventures in general;[128] and most importantly, (e) his displacement of the "great god" Enlil.[129] Sensitive to this multidimensionality, W. G. Lambert finds in *Ee* a "compositely written masterpiece" depicting Marduk as the "victor and hero" via several "mythological themes."[130] One theme in particular, however, carries significant *socioeconomic* weight. As Walter Sommerfeld shows, the displacement of a major deity (Enlil) by one much less so (Marduk) is not only literarily, but socioeconomically significant.[131] *Ee* is many things, but not least a mythopoeic testimony to the *socioeconomic* success of the Marduk priesthood headquartered at Esagila.[132] In many ways Ba'al's displacement of El reflects this same dynamic,[133] as does Tešub's victory

---

^{d}AMAR.UTU; Akk ^{d}*marūtuk*) means "bull-calf of Utu" (Lambert, *Creation*, 252) or, more generically, "son of the sun" (*Ee* 101–02; cf. Hurowitz, "Name," 89–90).

124. Cf. Sum A-KI-TA ("source"). Pallis (*Akītu*, 306) identifies this new-year ritual as the annual moment in which the king "leads Marduk's statue by the hand to *bît akītu* and there, as Marduk, defeats all evil in order to create the means of existence for the new year, spiritually as well as materially." Bidmead ("Akitu," 1) emphasizes that the *akītu* eventually comes to exercise greater and greater "political prominence, especially in the Neo-Assyrian and Neo-Babylonian periods" when the Marduk priesthood turns it into "a propagandistic tool wielded to promote state ideology." Pongratz-Leisten (*Akītu*, 42–47) attends to the laborious task of reconstructing the ritual's spatiotemporal and liturgical details. Bell (*Ritual*, 18–19) rehearses the celebrated dispute between Eliade (*Sacred*, 88–89) and Smith (*Religion*, 91–94) over whether *Ee* is intentionally (Eliade) or incidentally (Smith) connected to the *akītu* ritual/festival.

125. *Ee* 1.12; 2.8–9; 119–52. Anšar is the commander of the forces arrayed against Tiamat and her armies, the deity who recruits Marduk to fight against chaos and uncertainty. As *Ee* 4.28 puts it, ^{d}*marūtuk-ma šarru*, "Marduk is king." Cf. Gunkel, *Creation*, 16.

126. *Ee* 4.97–104 (Alster, "Tiamat," 867–69).

127. *Ee* 4.119–20. Reckoning the "ng" (ĝ) phoneme to be Sumerian in origin, Lambert (*Creation*, 221) cites a parallel between Early Dynastic ^{d}KIN and Akk ^{d}*qingu*. Additionally, a *kingu* is a "sealed tag-receipt" (cf. *kanāku*, "to seal") exchanged by managers to document the work done by laborers under their direction (cf. *CAD* K.387).

128. *Ee* 3.27–34. Lambert, *Creation*, 448, 457; Wiggermann, *Spirits*, xi-xiii.

129. *Ee* 4.145–46. Sommerfeld, *Aufstieg*, 185–212. As Maul ("Hauptstadt," 113) sees it, *Ee* documents "what must have been, for the tradition-conscious Mesopotamian, an incredible break: Marduk appears in place of Enlil as king of the gods, and Babylon in place of Nippur as the center of the world."

130. Lambert, *Creation*, 458.

131. Sommerfeld, *Aufstieg*, 185–212. Batto (*Dragon*, 168) suggests that *Ee* "rewrites the common Semitic Combat Myth as a story of the inadequacy of the traditional high gods of Mesopotamia to meet newer challenges."

132. *Ee* 6.62. Esagila (Sum É-SAĜ-IL; lit. "house of the upraised head") is Marduk's temple-complex in Babylon. Oshima (*Marduk*, 81) situates the genesis of Enlil's displacement "not in the theo-propaganda of the Babylonian palace" but in the "framework of temple scholarship." Crouch ("Ištar," 129–42) contends that Ištar's role increases at Marduk's expense in Neo-Assyrian retellings of *Ee* because the Ištar cult houses the only powerbrokers strong enough to legitimate the Assyrian priest-king.

133. Pope, *El*, 83. One of Ba'al's dreams is to commandeer, like Ra, "a boat in the clouds" (*ṯkt bglṯ*, *CAT* 1.4.5.69; cf. *EBD* 181).

over Kumarbi,[134] and the triumph of Zeus over the Titans,[135] not to mention modern-day *coups d'état* like Lenin's assassination of the Romanovs[136] and Castro's ouster of Batista.[137] Each of these takeovers illustrates to some extent the phenomenon of *cosmogony*—that clash of generations often necessary before younger, stronger rulers can come to power.[138] Granted, *Ee* avoids the mention of Enlil until the last line of tablet 4, and then only to explain (a) his removal from the throne (*Ee* 4.145–46); (b) his reassignment to a subordinate place in the heavens (5.8); and (c) his payment of "tribute" to his new boss (5.80).[139] But this hardly lessens the impact of its significance. *Question:* What socioeconomic realities does *Ee* convey via this cosmogonic tradition?[140]

Analyses of this *zamāru*-song's literary structure are several,[141] but careful attention to the text itself reveals significant activity underneath the surface.[142] In Tablet 1, for example, the poet launches several ideas into orbit over the "increase-decrease" polarity. The primeval divine pair Laḫmu-Laḫamu "grows and matures,"[143] but only until Anšar-Kišar "surpasses" them.[144] Yet when the "divine brothers convene,"[145] the

134. Güterbock, "Hurrian," 123–34.

135. Ζεὺς δὲ θεῶν βαςιλεύς ("Now Zeus, king of the gods," Hesiod, *Theog.* 885–86). Olympian displacement of the divided Titans occurs in lines 627–819 (cf. Hadas, *History*, 38–39).

136. Massie, *Romanovs*, 283–92; Rappaport, *Romanovs*, 203–7.

137. Coltman, *Castro*, 137–38.

138. Cross, *Canon*, 73. Gabriel (*Weltordnung*, 412) thinks *Ee*'s primary objective is to argue that the only way to establish world peace is via the "*pax Mardukiana*."

139. Akk *qištū* (cf. *CAD* Q.275–80 and below). Lambert ("Marduk," 1) thinks that "the rise of Marduk, city god of Babylon, is one of the most striking phenomena known from ancient Mesopotamia. From being an utterly insignificant god in third-millennium Sumer, he rises to become head of the Babylonian pantheon by the first millennium."

140. Lambert (*Creation*, 449–51) argues that *Ee*'s story of Tiamat's defeat closely parallels the Anzû myth because each features a challenger threatening the established order, as well as a hero strong enough to meet this challenge. "In each case the gods are in danger from an evil-intending being. In each case, two well-esteemed gods are invited to deal with the threat but decline. Then a deity suggests his own son, who, with promises of reward, agrees to go. At his first meeting with the foe he fails, but on the second time, succeeds. It is impossible to suppose that these two accounts are entirely independent, and certainly the Anzû myth is the earlier of the two. The evidence for conscious dependence consists of a number of points, some of which alone would be inadequate, but in combination their force is great." The most significant of these is the Tablet of Destinies. "When the gods gather around to congratulate Marduk after his arrangement of the universe, he promptly hands over the Tablet of Destinies to Anu, who is most commonly considered the god to hold it. Marduk is certainly not parting with any of his supreme power in this disposition of the Tablet, and one is left with the feeling that the author does not take it too seriously. Why then does he bring it in at all? If the story of Anzû is the model on which he is forming his own account of Marduk's heroic deed, then everything is understandable."

141. Gabriel lists several in his dissertation (*Weltordnung*, 112–16).

142. Cf. the similar approach to Lamentations in Moore, *Babbler*, 226–44.

143. *Ee* 1.11 (*ir-bu-ú i-ši-ḫu*). Cf. פרו ורבו ("Be fruitful and multiply," Gen 1:22).

144. *Ee* 1.12 (*at-ru*). Akk *atāru* often appears in economic texts to denote "excessive wealth" (*CAD* A/2.489–91).

145. *Ee* 1.21 (*in-nen-du-ma at-ḫu-ú ilāni*$^{meš-ni}$); i.e., the pantheon.

resulting "clamor"[146] is so loud, it elicits great "distress"[147] and "disorder,"[148] dividing those who "compromise"[149] with the partygoers and "endure"[150] their shenanigans from those who "scatter and destroy" them, along with their entire "way of life."[151]

The song's climax comes on Tablet 4 with Marduk's "reception of the kingship":[152]

^{d}*marūtuk kab-ta-ta*[153] *i-na ilāni rabûti*	You, O Marduk, are honored by the great gods
ši-mat-ka[154] *la ša-na-an sè-kàr-ka* ^{d}*a-nu-um*	Your destiny unequalled, your command (like) Anu's

146. *Ee* 1.22 (*na-ṣir-šu-nu*) // 1.25 (Akk *ri-gim-šu-un*). Akk *ragāmu*, in addition to meaning "to call" and/or "to prophesy," can also mean "to lodge a claim," *CAD* R.63–64). On the use of *rigmu* in Atraḫasis and Gilgamesh, cf. Moore, *WealthWatch*, 33, 36, 76, 82).

147. In addition to the meanings "to be ill" and "to be troubled," Akk *marāṣu* (*Ee* 1.27, 37, 46) can also mean "to be distressed." In the Amarna correspondence, e.g., the king of Mitanni (Tušratta) writes to his son-in-law (Pharaoh Nimmureya) hoping that *ḫurāṣu ša ērišu ina libbi aḫija lu la im-mar-ra-aṣ*,"the gold I ask does not cause distress in the heart of my brother."

148. Akk *sapā-ḫu* (*Ee* 1.39). Cf. *mā-rū bīt abišunu i-sa-pa-[ḫu]*, "the sons may squander the father's house/estate" (text cited from *CAD* S.153). The cosmological question, of course, hides behind the classic "chicken-vs.-the-egg" dilemma: is this distress/confusion/squandering *caused* by the divine brothers' misconduct, or merely *amplified* by it?

149. Akk *gamālu* (*Ee* 1.28). Cf. *ina mitgurtišunu eqlam mala eqlim awīlum mala awīlum išk[u] nma eqlam uš-ta-ag-mi-lu*, "in their agreement they give evidence, person to person, concerning each field (until) they reach a compromise with regard to the (disputed) field" (text cited from *CAD* G.23).

150. Akk *šadādu* (*Ee* 1.46). In addition to its literal meaning ("to pull taut"), Akk *šadādu* can mean "to bear a yoke, to measure out"; e.g., *šumma kaspam watram ša-ad-da-ti anāku libbaka uṭab*, "If you will indeed measure out additional silver, I will personally repay you" (text cited from *CAD* Š/1.24).

151. *Ee* 1.39 (Akk *lu-uš-ḫa-liq-ma al-kàt-su-nu lu-sa-ap-pi-iḫ*). Akk *alaktu* ("course of behavior/way of life"; cf. הלך; Syr ܗܠܟ; Ug *hlk kbkbm*, "walk of the stars," *CAT* 1.19.2.3) appears several times in this opening section (*Ee* 1.28, 37, 46) to describe adolescent behavior often appearing (in the eyes of "olden gods") to be "wildly lawless" (*al-ka-ta e-ši-ta*, *Ee* 1.49). For a discussion of *rigmu u ḫubūru* ("noise and tumult") in *Atraḫasis*, see Moore, *WealthWatch*, 33–36, 76–79.

152. *Ee* 4.2 (Akk *a-na ma-li-ku ir-me*).

153. Cf. the nominal derivative *kubuttu* ("wealth") in *Ee* 7.21.

154. Bottero (*Mésopotamie*, 189) singles out in *Ee* the Akkadian term *šīmtu* ("destiny") as "le terme le plus fort et le plus riche et significatif." Sometimes it occurs in *status constructus*, as in the phrase *šīmat* ^{d}*Marūtuk* ("destiny of Marduk," *Ee* 6.96). Sometimes it appears in refrains like "unrivaled is 'your destiny'" (*šī-mat-ka*, *Ee* 4.4, 6). Sometimes it marks dramatic turning points in the plot line, as when the gods "decree a destiny . . . for Marduk" (*a-na* ^{d}*marūtuk . . . i-ši-mu šim-ta*, *Ee* 3.138); i.e., when the great gods finally accept his demand for the authority to "decree destinies" (*ši-ma-ta lu-šim-ma*, *Ee* 2.160) before committing himself to battle on their behalf (N.B. how each of these passages utilizes the noun *šīmtu* in combination with its verbal root, *šiāmu* via the cognate accusative, *GKC* 117p). Distinguishing between *Festsprechung* ("conferred word of destiny"), *Festsprechungsakt* ("conferred act of destiny"), and *Festsprechungsmacht* ("conferred power of destiny"), Gabriel (*Weltordnung*, 260) defines *šīmtu* as "the power to confer destiny denoting the capability and authority to establish permanence for a third party through a particular word." Marduk, in other words, is no banana republic dictator. Everything he does is "by the book." He never conquers or creates or dictates policy unless authorized to do so by "the words of destiny" issued from an authoritative source to which he is voluntarily submissive. Only after the gods fully authorize him does he take responsibility for the *ṭuppi šīmāti*^{meš} ("Tablet of Destinies," *Ee* 4.121).

iš-tu u$_4$*-mi-im-ma la in-nen-na-a qí-bit-ka*[155]	Today your promise remains "intact."[156]
za-na-nu-tum[157] *er-šat pa-rak ilāni-ma*	The shrines of the gods require provisioning
a-šar sa-gi-šu-nu lu-ú ku-un[158] *aš-ruk-ka*	So that you may be certified in their chapels
^{d}*marūtuk a-ta-ma mu-tir-ru gi-mil-li-ni*	O Marduk, since you "pay our bills,"[159]
ni-id-din-ka šar-ru-tu$_4$ *kiš-šat kal gim-re-e-ti*	We authorize you to handle "all our expenses."[160]

Later, when Marduk slaughters Tiamat and imprisons her consort Qingu, the gods follow through on their promise:

ab-bu-šu iḫ-du-ú i-ri-šu	His fathers rejoiced and celebrated
igisê šul-ma-ni[161] *ú-ša-bi-lu*[162] *šu-nu ana šá-a-šu*	Bringing him tribute and gifts.[163]

155. Akk *qibītu* here denotes "divine pronouncement creating and maintaining the proper functioning of the world" (*CAD* Q.247). Cf. Sum ME (Sladek, "Inanna," 85).

156. *Ee* 4.5–7 (i.e., "un-nullified"). Akk *enû* ("to renege/annul") often applies to the forging of a contract (cf. texts cited in *CAD* E.175–76).

157. The verbal root of this term (*zanānu*) often denotes the socioeconomic provisioning of corporations (temples, cities) as well as individuals (*CAD* Z.43–45).

158. Akk *kunnu* (*CAD* K.540). Talon (*Enūma*, 91) translates "curateur."

159. Although *mu-tir-ru gi-mil-li-ni* (*Ee* 4.13; cf. 3.116 and 3.138) is often translated "avenger" (Lambert, *Creation*, 87; Talon, *Enūma*, 91; lit. "returner of the favor") or "champion" (Foster, *Muses*, 457; Dalley, *Myths*, 250), the *gimlu/gimru* word pair contains too many socioeconomic connotations to ignore (cf. texts cited in *CAD* G.73–75, 77–78; and N.B. *gamālu* in *Ee* 1.28).

160. *Ee* 4.11–14. Tanak readers will doubtless note a parallel between these words and those demanding from Samuel a human מלך ("king"), a sociopolitical shift which throws Israel into a pyramidical economic system much like that attested in the Amarna correspondence (cf. 1 Sam 8:6–20; 12:1–6; Moran, *Amarna*, xxvi–xxxix).

161. As is well known, the line between "gift" and "bribe" is sometimes blurry (cf. Moore, *WealthWatch*, 45–47). Of the thirty or so Akk terms for "gift," however, some connote "bribery" more than others—e.g., *ṭātu*, *katrû* (Sum KADRU), *qīštu*, *ṭā'tu*, and the word found here—*šulmānu*. The king of Cyprus, e.g., says to Pharaoh, *mi-nu-um-me-e šul-ma-nu ša ú-še-bi-lu a-na ia-ši a-na-ku 2-šu a-na muḫḫi-ka ú-te-ir-ru*, "Whatever 'gift' he [Pharaoh] delivers to me, I will send it back to you doubled" (*EA* 35.51–53; other pertinent texts cited at *CAD* Š/3.245–47).

162. The first meaning cited in *CAD* Z.1 for *š/zabālu* is "to carry, transport (a load), to deliver (goods to fulfill a tax obligation)."

163. *Ee* 4.133–34.

Just as Baʿal goes to great lengths to build *his* "house,"[164] so Marduk (after destroying *his* "leviathan")[165] goes to great lengths to build *his* "house,"[166] relocating the "great gods" to *their* new "shrines."[167]

ú-ba-áš-šim man-za-za[168] *an ilāni rabûti*	He designated galaxies for the great gods
kakkabāni^meš^ *tam-šil-šu-nu lu-ma-ši uš-zi-iz*[169]	Allocating the stars (to) their constellations.[170]

Utilizing Tiamat's corpse to invent *time* (twelve months, three stars per month) and *space* (Tigris and Euphrates flow from her eye-sockets), Marduk

iš-tu pi-lu-di-šu uṣ-ṣi-ru ú-ba-ši-mu par-ṣi[i-šu]	Draws up his procedures and determines his compensation.[171]
[ṣer-r]r-e-ti it-ta-da-a ^d^*é-a uš-ta-aṣ-bit*[172]	Taking over the controls, he entrusts them to Enki.
[tuppi š]īmāti^meš^ *ša* ^d^*[q]ingu i-ki-mu ú-bil-lam-ma*	The Tablet of Destinies[173] (which) Qingu confiscates and impounds

164. *CAT* 1.3–4 (see below). Cf. also the closing lines of *Inanna and Ebiḫ*: "I have built a palace and done much more. I have put a throne in place and made its foundation firm. I have given the *kurĝara* cult performers a dagger and prod. I have given the *gala* cult performers *ub* and *lilis* drums. I have transformed the *pilipili* cult performers" (http://etcsl.orinst.ox.ac.uk/cgi-bin/etcsl.cgi?text=t.1.3.2&display=Crit&charenc=&lineid=t132.p33#t132.p33).

165. Akk Tiamat // Ug Yam (cf. below).

166. *Ee* 4.144–45.

167. Akk *māḫāzū* (*Ee* 4.146). Cf. *CAD* M.85–89.

168. Akk *bašāmu* (*Ee* 5.1) usually means "to design(ate), build," but an OB letter from Tell Harmal reads *šīm-šu . . . bi-iš-ma-am-ma*, "Propose its price" (cited from *CAD* B.139). N.B. that Akk *manzāzu* derives from the verb *zāzu* (occurring in the next line).

169. The socioeconomic roots of *zāzu* (// *bašāmu* in the previous line) are firmly established. See, e.g., *šittam . . . ammala šīmat abišunu i-zu-zu*, "they will allocate the rest (of the inheritance) according to their father's 'disposition'"; *ina ālim ammala šīmātišunu i-zu-zu*, "they will allocate (the silver) in the city according to their 'arrangements'" (texts cited from *CAD* Z.78; N.B. the socioeconomic use of *šīmtu* in these examples).

170. *Ee* 5.1–2. Dalley (*Myths*, 255): "He fashioned stands for the great gods. As for the stars, he set up constellations corresponding to them." Lambert (*Creation*, 99): "He fashioned heavenly stations for the great gods and set up constellations, the patterns of the stars." Talon (*Enūma*, 95): "Il créa une station pour les grands dieux, fit surgir des étoiles, des astres à leur image." Foster (Muses, 463): "He made the position(s) for the great gods; he established (in) constellations the stars, their likenesses."

171. N.B. Akk *parṣū* in DI 44, 47, 50, 53, 56, 59, and 62 (where it translates Sum ME // GARZA; cf. above).

172. Akk *ṣabātu* ("to seize, take possession," *Ee* 5.68) often occurs to describe (re)possession of real estate and other commodities; e.g., *aššum eqlētim ša aḫ Purattim zâz[i]m u ina eqlētim ša ṣābim ṣa-ba-[t]im*, "as to the distribution of the fields along the Euphrates and the (re)possession of people's fields . . ." (ARM 1.6.24).

173. The Tablet of Destinies is the cosmological equivalent of the Sum ME collection given by Enki

re-eš ta-mar-ti it-ba-la ana ^{d}anim iq-ti-šá	He reappropriates, handing it over to Anu as a trophy.[174]

Then, in another grand remunerative gesture,

[^{d}a]-num ^{d}en-líl u ^{d}é-a u-qa-i-šu-uš qí-šá-a-ti	Anu, Enlil, and Enki shower him with gifts[175]
ka-innim-ma-ak dum-qí ù taš-me-e šu-a-šú iz-zak-ru	invoking over him a wish for prosperity and success, (saying),[176]
ul-tu u_4-me at-ta lu za-ni-nu pa-rak-ki-ni	"Henceforth are you the provider for our temples."[177]

Eventually he reveals the blueprints for his new "house":

lu-pu-uš-ma bi-ta lu-u šu-bat la-le-e-a	"I will build a house for myself, a 'wealth depository.'[178]
qir-bu-uš-šu ma-ḫa-za-šu lu-šar-šid-ma	Within whose (walls) I will construct a 'toll-booth'[179]
ku-um-mi lu-ud-da-a lu-kín šar-ru-ti	I will set up my 'sanctuary'[180] and establish my kingship."[181]

to Inanna (and later reclaimed) in the Sumerian myth *Inanna and Enki* (http://etcsl.orinst.ox.ac.uk/cgi-bin/etcsl.cgi?text=c.1.3.1&display=Crit&charenc=gcirc#).

174. *Ee* 5.67–70. Of the seventy or so Akk terms for "giving," some occur in contexts more intentionally economic than others; e.g., *kânu, kašāru, kezēru, nadānu, naḫāsu, raṣûm, tadānu*, and this term, *qâšu*. Cf., e.g., *kūm iski atûtu* PN NÍG.BA *ana* PN2 *iq-ti-iš*, "PN deeded (x silver) as payment to PN2 for the doorkeeper's fee" (text cited from *CAD* Q.157). Cf. *u-qa-i-šu-uš qí-šá-a-ti*, "they deeded gifts" (*Ee* 5.80).

175. *Ee* 5.80.

176. Cf. the similar word pair *dumqu//nuḫšu* in the treaty blessing *du-um-ka u nuḫša lu nimur*, "May we see fortune and plenty" (*KBo* 1.3.40; cf. also *nuḫšim u ṭuḫdim*, "wealth and abundance," CH 1.55–56). Foster misses the socioeconomic intentionality of this word pair (*Muses*, 467), as does Dalley (*Myths*, 259, "blessing and obedience") and Talon (*Enūma*, 80, "de bien et de concorde").

177. *Ee* 5.114–15. See above on *za-na-nu-tum* (*Ee* 4.11).

178. The first term describing Marduk's temple is the generic *bītu* ("house," Ug *bt*; בית, بيت, ܒܝܬܐ), but the second occurs in the epithet *šu-bat la-le-e* (lit. "seat of wealth"), a significant parallel because *lalû* is an economic, not a religious term. See, e.g., *ibaššu ālam šâti ana 1 awēlim ša la-la-am šaknuma kullašu ile'u luddinšumma*, "Maybe I will give this town to some wealthy man who is able to take care of it" (ARM 4.11.16).

179. Akk *māḫāzu*, esp. when used in sequence with terms like *parakku* and *kummu*, usually denotes a religious structure, but given the context, it is not insignificant that *māḫāzu* also refers to the cities occupied by such religious structures; e.g., *ina qereb ma-ḫa-zi šatu qaqqarāti mādāte*, "I grabbed much territory inside that *māḫāzu*" (text cited from *CAD* M/1.87).

180. Akk *kummu* can denote any private room; e.g., *ittil eṭlu ina kummīšu*, "the young man sleeps in his room" (DI 89). Whereas *māḫāzu* is public, *kummu* is private.

181. *Ee* 5.122–24.

The final section of the epic, often called "Marduk's Fifty Names,"[182] proves especially revealing.[183] The first name celebrates the accomplishments of Babylon's new "shepherd" as *ša-kin mi-re-ti ù maš-qí-ti*, "the one who supplies rich pasture and clean water."[184] Another praises him as *ša-rik*[185] *mi-riš-ti*[186] *ša is-ra-ta*[187] *ú-kin-nu*, "the donor of arable fields who cultivates (even) the alleyways in between."[188] In another he is *šu-u-ma za-nin-šu-nu*[189] *mu-ad-du-ú is-qí-[šu]-un*[190] *šá šu-ku-us-su*[191] *ḫegalla*[192] *uṣ-ṣa-pu a-na ma-a-ti*, "the provisioner who assigns their inheritances, utilizing his share to generate a land surplus."[193] Another addresses him as *mu-šab-ši ṣi-im-ri u ku-bu-ut-te-e*[194] *mukin ḫegalli ša mim-ma-ni i-ṣi a-na ma-'-de-e*[195] *ú-tir-ru*, "the creator of

182. See Litke, *God-Lists*; Lambert, *Creation*, 147–68. Since name lists are a popular literary device (Olmo Lete, "Lists," 305–52), Seri ("God-Lists," 508) views Marduk's Fifty Names not as "the result of the composer's creative genius" but as something copied "from already existing god-list(s)."

183. Still the template for onomastic analysis is Gelb, *Names*; and Huffmon, *Names*; followed by Noth, *Personnamen*, 1–15; Grøndahl, *Personnamen*; and Hess, *Names*.

184. *Ee* 6.124. Cf. בנאות דשא // מי מנוחות, "grassy meadows // still waters" (Ps 23:2). *Ee* 7.72 depicts Marduk as a *rē'û kīnu*, "reliable shepherd." Like other texts praising the attributes of ANE leaders, many of *Ee*'s socioeconomic motifs focus on the agrarian task of "shepherding" (cf., e.g., *RN rē'ûm nibīt Enlil anāku mukammer nuḫšim u ṭuḫdim*, "I am Ḫammurapi, Enlil's chosen shepherd, the one who heaps up plenty and prosperity," CH 1.51–56; cf. יהוה רעי, "Yahweh is my shepherd," Ps 23:1; Vancil, "Symbolism," 39–43).

185. Akk *šarāku* (*Ee* 7.1) is another one of the seventy or so Akk terms for "give" (see above), a word which, while occasionally used to describe the "giving" of votive offerings (*CAD* Š/2.41–42), draws its most basic meaning from the world of practical economics; e.g., *i-šar-ra-ak terdennu ana katî ti'ûta*, "the younger son gives food to the destitute" (*BWL* 84.250).

186. Akk *mēreštu* (*Ee* 7.1). Cf. *mukinnu apšenni šá mi-reš-ta elleta úkinnu ina ṣe-e-ri*, "who plows furrows, who clears arable fields, even in the outlying countryside" (*Ee* 7.62).

187. Lambert (Creation, 482) points out that according to a fragment of the *Ee* commentary, *i-ra-tum* = *ta-mir-tu*, and according to von Soden (AHw 1341), *tamertu* = *tawwertu*, as in the expression *ana ta-mer-ti ali*, "in the land contiguous to the city(-walls)."

188. *Ee* 7.1.

189. Akk *zanānu* occurs in *Ee* 4.11, "the shrines of the gods require *provisioning*," and cf. *mu-ša-az-nin nuḫša eli erṣetim rapaštim*, "he provides wealth over the entire earth" (7.69).

190. Following Foster (*Muses*, 476). Lambert (*Creation*, 125) reads "income," but Akk *isqu* fundamentally denotes not "wages," but "a share of inheritance (or booty)" (*CAD* I.199; cf., e.g., *zi-it-ti is-qa-am*, ARM 2.13.13). Cf. Heb נחלה in 1 Kgs 21:3 and *niḫlātu* in Nissinen, *Prophets*, 1.4 (below).

191. Akk *šukūsu* can refer to an ornamental headdress like a turban (Lambert, *Creation*, 125) or tiara (Foster, *Muses*, 476), but Dalley (*Myths*, 267) stays close to the socioeconomic context, translating "farmland." *CAD* translates "the field which he allotted" (Š/3.236).

192. Akk *ḫegallu* occurs five times on Tablet 7 in lines 8, 21, 65, and twice in line 68, where it is deified (*dḫé-gál*) just as it is in Hittite and Hurrian texts (some cited in *CAD* Ḫ.168). N.B. that *bīt ḫegalli* (lit. "house of plenty") denotes a "treasury."

193. *Ee* 7.7–8. Elsewhere Enlil is the one who *ša-i-im ši-ma-at mâtim a-na ilu Marduk*, "decrees the fate of the land for Marduk" (CH 1.6–8).

194. Akk *kubuttu* derives from the verb *kabātu* (*Ee* 4.5), a word which, like Heb כבד, radiates multiple connotations of "wealth" over the base meaning "to be heavy" (cf. Gen 13:2; Num 22:17; and the texts cited in *CAD* K.14–15).

195. Echoing the "increase ≠ decrease" polarity on Tablet 1, Akk *iṣu* ≠ *mādu* occurs on a Mari

riches and wealth, the architect of abundance who turns that which is immaterial into valuable treasure."[196] Elsewhere he is *be-lum mu-deš-šú-u-šú-nu*[197] *šu-ú-ma dan-nu na-bu-šu-nu . . . ša ri-i-ta maš-qi-ta*[198] *uš-te-eš-še-ru*, "the lord who endows them abundantly, the great champion . . . who ensures the accessibility of the pastures and ponds";[199] and *be-el ḫé-gál-li ṭuḫ-di*[200] *iš-pi-ki rabûti*[meš], "lord of plenty, prosperity, and great storehouses."[201]

Each of these epithets stands atop a long-revered history of tradition as it accentuates a vital aspect of Marduk's socioeconomic power.[202] To identify them as indicators of the socioeconomic concerns of ancient Mesopotamians would seem fortuitous were it not for the fact that so many feature overtly agrarian metaphors tightly packed into dense titular displays. What this implies, of course, is that the priests responsible for regularly reciting this *zamāru*-song seem more than a little aware of what it takes to make the "black-headed people" in their care achieve some semblance of success and prosperity.[203]

Prophetic Texts from Tell Koujunjik (Nineveh) and Tell Ḥarīrī (Mari)

In addition to the great *literary* texts, socioeconomic motifs often appear in government correspondence written by fretful officials[204] charged with the difficult task of

tablet: *ṣābum i-ṣú-um u[l i]ṣṣabbat ṣābum mādumma iṣṣabbat*, "not a small troop, but a large one should be taken prisoner" (ARM 3.18.8).

196. *Ee* 7.20–22.

197. With only two exceptions (*Ee* 7.26, 102) each of the "Fifty Names" segment praising Marduk as *bēl* ("lord") alludes to his *socioeconomic* authority (*Ee* 7.20, 57, 61, 65).

198. This word pair on Tablet 7 (*ri-i-ta maš-qí-ta*, *Ee* 7.59) practically repeats verbatim the word pair on Tablet 6 (*mi-re-ti ù maš-qí-ti*, *Ee* 6.124).

199. *Ee* 7.57–59.

200. In one of the *šu-ila* prayers Anu's devotee promises that if the deity comes to his aid, *lu-da-ḫi-id bita[-ka]*, "I will abundantly furnish (your) house" (*AGH* 36.21).

201. *Ee* 7.65 (cf. Gen 41:48). After this his colleagues lay out for him several *katrū* -gifts (*Ee* 7.110; Akk *katrû* // Sum KADRU denotes the kind of "gift" little different from a "bribe") and *erbū* -gifts (*Ee* 7.111). Akk *erbu* often refers to "revenue" or "income"; e.g., a listing of temple funds, *guqqû šagikarê ir-bi tēlīt u mimma šūrubti ekurri mala bašû*, "monthly offerings, votive offerings, *irbu*-funds, *tēlītu*-tax, and any other type of temple income" (cf. *CAD* I.174).

202. Cf. Lambert, *Creation*, 147–68.

203. Polanyi, *Livelihood*, xli. Sommerfeld (*Aufstieg*, 174–81) locates *Ee* in the Kassite Period (1531–1155 BCE), while Lambert (*Creation*, 273–74) situates it in the reign of Nebuchadnezzar I (1125–04 BCE). Katz ("Babylon," 123–24) and Abusch ("Marduk," 548) date it to the first millennium as a response to Assyrian pretensions.

204. Often these texts are called "prophetic" because within them occur "predictions, or apparent predictions, eschatology or apocalyptic, social or religious criticism, and commissioned messages from deities" (Huffmon, "Prophecy," 477). Other government texts, like the Amarna correspondence, readily manipulate a number of socioeconomic motifs, but lacking the aforementioned criteria are not usually called "prophetic" (see, e.g., *EA* 1.61; 3.15; 4.36–50; 7.69–72; 10.19–20; 19. 68–69; 20.46–59; 29.70–75; 35.50–53; cf. Liverani, "Powers," 23–26; Moore, *Babbler*, 140–55).

protecting the welfare of the king's "house."[205] Situating themselves within overlapping categories, they tend to focus on the notions of *inheritance/possession*, *socioeconomic identity*, and *socioeconomic conflict resolution*.[206]

Inheritance/Possession

In an Assyrian oracle to King Esarhaddon,[207] Ishtar of Arbela[208] identifies herself as "great midwife,"[209] "wet-nurse," and "pregnant treasure,"[210] all epithets rooted in the socioeconomic notions of *fertility* and *procreation*. In Ištar's eyes (that is, in the eyes of the Ištar *priesthood*)[211] Esarhaddon is the legitimate king not so much because he is Sennacherib's biological son, but because he is *her* "son" and "legitimate heir."[212] Whether or not this renders him an incarnate "Son" in some sort of Assyrian "trinity" (*pace* Simo Parpola),[213] is less significant a question than this oracle's determination to redefine the king's persona in terms of "sonship" and "inheritance." Disputes over "inheritance"

205. These include (a) texts of oracles "received" from this or that deity, as well as (b) texts about the socioeconomic concerns of individuals involved in the communication of such oracles (cf. Nissinen, *Prophets*, 5).

206. Unless otherwise indicated, the citations below refer to the transliterated texts published by Martti Nissinen in *Prophets and Prophecy* (SBLWAW 12).

207. Westermann, *Oracles*, 42; cf. Grayson, "Esarhaddon," 574; and Leichty, "Esarhaddon," 949–58.

208. Grayson ("Nineveh," 1118) observes that "Nineveh is one of the four great cities of Assyria, the others being Asshur, Calah, and Arbela. The patron deity of Nineveh is Ishtar, goddess of love and war, who is also the patron deity of Arbela."

209. Akk *sa-ab-su-ub-ta-k[a]*, identified by Parpola (*Prophecies*, 7) as a variant of *šabsūtu* (*CAD* Š/1.16). Elsewhere Ishtar is *abūka ummaka*, "your father and mother" (Nissinen, *Prophets*, 82.26′) and Esarhaddon is *mūrī ša anāku urabbûni*, "my calf, whom I rear" (Nissinen, *Prophets*, 92.11).

210. Nissinen, *Prophets*, 73.15′–16′, 19. Parpola (*Prophecies*, 8) and Nissinen (*Prophets*, 107) translate *arītka de'iqtu* as "good shield," but *arītu* can also mean "pregnant" (*CAD* E.301) and *damqu* usually refers to "good fortune." Cf. *anākû ina bītika dam-qa-am ul ušabšīma*, "Have I not brought good fortune to your house?" (cf. *CAD* D.74).

211. Cf. Parpola (*Prophecies*, xlvii-xlviii). Commenting on the connection between myth and reality in the *Adapa* myth, Liverani (*Politics*, 21) argues that "the priesthood cannot ruin the economy of the country" because Adapa "cannot exaggerate his function at the expense of others."

212. Akk *aplu kēnu mār Mullissi*, "legitimate heir, son of Mullissu" (repeated twice for emphasis, Nissinen, *Prophets*, 73.5, 20). "Mullissu," the consort of the national deity Aššur, is one of Ishtar's most popular nicknames (Parpola, *Prophecies*, 54), and probably means "she who raises up" (causative ptc. of Akk *elû*).

213. Parpola, *Prophecies*, xxvi–xxxi. Cf. Weippert, "Prophetien," 71–113; Cooper, "Prophecies," 440; Moore, *Prophecies*, 551–52; and Hunt, *Value*, 22.

(Marduk's vs. Enlil's,[214] Yam's vs. Ba'al's,[215] Anat's vs. Yam's)[216] constantly pervade the mythopoeic epics of the ancient Near East, so it is no surprise to find this motif occurring in otherwise routine government correspondence.[217] Nor is it surprising, given Esarhaddon's rocky family history,[218] to find his supporters using it to to carve out a "reputable" religious way of legitimizing his (and their) "inheritance."[219]

Socioeconomic Identity

In other correspondence an official named Urad-gula complains to King Assurbanipal about his misfortunes in a brief letter Karel van der Toorn dubs "the case of the forlorn scholar."[220] Under Esarhaddon's administration Urad-gula laments the usual woes of being a "poor man,"[221] that is, until the moment arrives when

issu libbi kiqilliti intatḫanni	He (Esarhaddon) lifted me up from the trash heap
[nāmu]rātēšu amaḫḫaršu issi ṣābi	(and) I received audience-gifts[222] from him.

214. Cf. above and the description of Marduk as *aplu ku-nu-ú ša* ^{d}*en.lil*, "Enlil's legitimate heir" (*BWL* 212). Elsewhere Esarhaddon is *māru rēdūtīya*, "the son of my (Sennacherib's) succession" (Nissinen translates "my heir") and *tēnûka*, "your (Sennacherib's) replacement" (Nissinen, *Prophets*, 96.12, 14), and N.B. that Esarhaddon takes the throne after proceeding through the *bīt rēdûti*, "House of Succession" (Nissinen, *Prophets*, 96.21).

215. *CAT* 1.2.1.35 (cf. below).

216. *CAT* 1.3.44 (cf. below).

217. Dandamaev, "Economy," 252–75.

218. According to Assyrian sources, Sennacherib picks his youngest son Esarhaddon to be his heir, renaming him *Aššur-eṭil-mukin-apli* ("Assur establishes the young man as heir"; cf. texts cited in Leichty, "Esarhaddon," 951), but according to Tanak, Sennacherib's sons Adrammeleḫ and Šarezer assassinate their father, a crime which forces them to flee the country, thereby ensuring that the throne falls to Esarhaddon (Isa 37:38 // 2 Kgs 19:37).

219. At one point Esarhaddon gives thanks for the *šipir maḫḫe kayyān suddurā ša išid kussī šangûtīya šuršudi*, "prophetic oracles legitimating the foundation of my priestly throne" (Nissinen, *Prophets*, 98.12–16; cf. Lohfink, "ירש," 368–96). Milgram ("Gifting," 39) insists that the three fundamental features of tannaitic inheritance law (asset disposal, property transferral, and partibility) originate not from Hebraic sources, but from "the adoption and adaptation of well-known ancient legal traditions."

220. Nissinen, *Prophets*, 108 (cf. van der Toorn, "Lions," 629–33).

221. Akk *amēlu lapnu* (Nissinen, *Prophets*, 108.14). The adjective *lapnu* derives from the verb *lapānu* ("to impoverish, make destitute"), and appears alongside *aplu* ("heir") in an OB literary text—*tami DN u DN2 epqam imalla i-la-pi-in u aplam ula erašši*, "he who swears (falsely) by DN and DN2 will be covered with leprosy, become poor, and leave no heir" (cf. *CAD* L.81).

222. Nissinen, *Prophets*, 108.16. According to Postgate (*Bureaucracy*, 182) "a *nāmurtu* (pl. *nāmurātu*) is a gift given to someone, usually a superior, on the occasion of an audience with him: this no doubt varies with the social standing of both giver and recipient, and with the gravity of the issue leading to the need for an audience" (cf. *CAD* N/1.255).

damqāti šumī izzakkar	My name was whispered among the fortunate few;[223]
[rē]ḫāti ma'dāti akkal	I ate from the surplus of his provisions;[224]
ina birit ibašši kūdunu alpu ittanna u	Occasionally he gave me a mule or an ox, and
šattīya ṣarpu issēn manû šina mane akaššad	Each year I earned[225] an allotment or two of silver.
[ūmē] ša mār šarri bēlīya	(When) my lord (Assurbanipal) was crown prince
issi āšipīšu[226] *rēḫāti*[227] *amaḫḫar*	I skimmed the bounty along with his exorcists.[228]

After Assurbanipal succeeds Esarhaddon, however, Urad-gula falls back into poverty,[229] begging his employer for help:

šumm[u] illaka ummânī[230] *dannūti*	If it's appropriate for both tenured and adjunct[231]
u šaniūti kūdini inaššiū	faculty to be given mules,
yâši issēn mūru liddi[n]ūni	Then why can I not be granted just one donkey?[232]
atâ ina libbi Ekallāti[233] *rēš āšipi*[234] *šarru*	Why does the king summon an exorcist from Ekallatu

223. Cf. the description above of Ištar as *arītka de'iqtu* ("your pregnant good fortune," Nissinen, *Prophets*, 73.19).

224. Nissinen, *Prophets*, 108.17; lit. "remainder of the compensation," a phrase occurring in the line, *kî rabûti issi panēšu ētiqūni ittalka ina panīya rīḫte issi ma-da-te naṣṣa*, "after the ambassador left he came to me, bringing the 'remainder of the compensation'" (text cited from *CAD* M/1.14).

225. Nissinen, *Prophets*, 108.18. Akk *kašādu* usually means "to amount to, be sufficient in value"; e.g., *šumma luqūssu ana kaspim . . . la i-kà-ša-ad*, "if his merchandise does not equal the silver in value . . ." (text cited from *CAD* K.275).

226. Akk *āšipu* denotes the magico-religious specialist responsible for exorcism/ritual purification (cf. אשף, Dan 2:27; cf. Moore, *Balaam*, 34–41).

227. Akk *rēḫtu* occurs above in line 17.

228. Nissinen, *Prophets*, 108.15–19.

229. Urad-gula may be struck by the same type of political windshear as that unsettling the Egyptian official Sinuhe (cf. Lichtheim, *Literature*, 1.222–35; Moore, *WealthWatch*, 121–24).

230. Nissinen, *Prophets*, 108.31. Akk *ummânu* usually denotes an "expert" of some kind (e.g., *umma-ni ki-nu*, "legitimate creditor," *BWL* 32.118).

231. Akk *dannūti u šaniūti* fundamentally means "primary and secondary"; Nissinen (*Prophecies*, 160) translates "most prominent and even lesser."

232. Nissinen, *Prophets*, 108.31–32.

233. Nissinen, *Prophets*, 108.16. Ekallatu is a city on the Tigris twenty-five kilometers north of Aššur (Hallo, "Emar," 72).

234. Nissinen, *Prophets*, 108.16. Akk *rēš āšipī* likely refers to the "chief exorcist" of Ekallutu. Assurbanipal's "chief exorcist" is Adad-šumu-uṣur (*rab āšipī*; cf. Parpola, *Scholars*, 2.xv).

iššī u anāku ḫ[ūlu] ša mudabbiri aṣṣabat	While I am forced to take the desert road
issu pan ša nišē iša' 'ulūninni	to avoid those who jibe,
mā atâ ina šēpēka ta[llak]a	"Still traveling on foot, eh?"
nišē bēti ettiqū dannūti[235] *ina kussî šaniūti*[236]	People pass by my house—the upper class on litters,
ina saparrāti ṣeḫrūti[237] *ina libbi kūdinī*	the middle class on carts, the lower class on mules—
anaku ina šēpēya i-SAK-KUL[238]	While I am forced to travel on foot![239]

Finally he throws himself on the mercy of the crown:

kunnūni šummu ammar maš'enni	I cannot afford a pair of sandals
ammar igrī[240] *ša gallābi maṣṣākūni*[241]	I cannot pay the tailor
tēnû ša guzippīya ibaššûni[242]	I cannot afford a change of clothes
u šiqlē maṭṭi ana šeššet mana ṣarpu	I have run up a debt of approximately
kaqqudu lā ḫabbulākūni[243]	*six minas of silver.*[244]
[libbu . . . ša šar]ri lēṭib[245]	O, that the heart of the king might soften
lišpuranni ammar šinā umāmē	enough to send me two [draught] animals
[. . .] -kē u tēnê ša guzippi	and a spare change of clothes.[246]

235. Nissinen, *Prophets*, 108.18; lit. "primary, strong, great" (cf. the translation "tenured" above in Nissinen, *Prophets*, 108.31).

236. Lit. "secondary" (cf. the translation "adjunct" above in Nissinen, *Prophets*, 108.31).

237. Nissinen, *Prophets*, 108.19 (lit. "lowly").

238. Nissinen, *Prophets*, 108.20. Curiously, Akk *sakālu* ("to get stuck") can homonymously mean "to acquire fraudulently" (*CAD* S.68–69)

239. Nissinen, *Prophets*, 108.16–20.

240. Nissinen, *Prophets*, 108.27. Akk *igru* means "rent, wage" (*CAD* I.44–45).

241. Nissinen, *Prophets*, 108.28. Akk *maṣû* in the D form means "to make sufficient, available, to provide," but this is likely the homonym derived from *wiāṣum*, "to be insufficient" (*CAD* M/1.350).

242. Nissinen, *Prophets*, 108.28. Akk *bašû* fundamentally means "to exist, be available," but takes on more specific connotations in socioeconomic contexts; e.g., *kasap aḫika i-li-bi*$_4$*-ka la i-ba-ší-ú*, "your brother's silver is not charged to your account" (lit. "does not exist," *CAD* B.146).

243. Nissinen, *Prophets*, 108.29. Akk *ḫabālu* means "to borrow/owe"; cf. *kasapka ša úḫ-ta-bi-la-ku-ni šabbu'āti*, "Are you satisfied with your silver I borrowed from you?" (*CAD* Ḫ.6).

244. Nissinen, *Prophets*, 108.27–29. Galil (*Families*, 92) calls this "a relatively large sum."

245. Nissinen, *Prophets*, 108.34 (lit. "become good"); cf. ויאכל בעז וישת וייטב לבו, "Boaz ate and drank and his heart 'became good'" (Ruth 3:7).

246. Nissinen, *Prophets*, 108.34–35.

WealthWarn

Socioeconomic Conflict Resolution

Much like the Egyptian correspondence from Tell Amarna,[247] the correspondence recovered from Tell Ḥarīrī in Syria (ancient Mari)[248] recounts numerous conflicts threatening the health and wealth of Zimri-Lim, a northern rival of the southern Babylonian monarch Hammurabi.[249] Loyalty is a major concern for Zimri-Lim because, as Stuart Lasine points out, tense political environments tend to set apart "who is loyal to whom and who 'loves' whom by who shares information with whom."[250] Surrounded by constant intrigue, Zimri-Lim finds himself forced to commission servants ("spies") to gather intelligence on his enemies.[251] In a message from one of these servants an official named Nur-Sîn notifies the king that an *āpilu* ("answerer")[252] of Adad warns him to beware a plot designed to seize his *niḫlatum* ("inheritance").[253] In another brief another *āpilu* demands from Zimri-Lim that he send a valuable batch of items downstream to Ebabbara,[254] the solar deity's temple-complex at Sippar,[255] including (a) Zimri-Lim's daughter (probably Erišti-Aya);[256] (b) an *asakku*-trophy for Adad at his temple in Aleppo;[257] (c) a *qištu* ("gift") for Dagan to redeem the "vitality" of Zimri-Lim's "soul";[258] (d) a "hefty bronze sword" (probably to secure the support of a neighboring warlord;.[259] and (e) a "great throne" for *his* "wealth depository" (*šu-*

247. Rainey and Schniedewind, *Amarna*; Izre'el, "Amarna," 2411–19.

248. Heimpel, *Mari*, 3–6.

249. Huffmon, "Prophecy," 478–81; Margueron, "Mari," 885–99; Gordon, "Prophecy," 37–58.

250. Lasine, *Kings*, 48.

251. Sheldon ("Intelligence," 30) observes that "the Mari and Tell Leilan tablets disclose how rulers of the second millennium BCE deploy spies, scouts, and 'eyes' to check up on each other's activities" (cf. Weiss, "Leilan," 39–52; Ronczkowski, *Terrorism*, 1–16).

252. Huffmon ("Prophecy," 478–81) attempts to explain all the terms denoting the various magico-religious specialists attested in the Mari correspondence (cf. also Stökl, "Prophets," 51–54).

253. Nissinen, *Prophets*, 1.4, 20, 32. Cf. Ug *nḥlt* in *CAT* 1.4.8.14; Heb נחלת in 1 Kgs 21:3 (*contra* Guillaume, *Finance*, 20). Dossin ("Mari," 78) reads *niḫlatu* as a GN, but Malamat ("Patterns," 148–49) reads "estate, inherited property" (cf. Roberts, "Mari," 173). Cf. Fleming, *Time*, 98–126; *Priestess*, 71; and Lafont, "Adad," 7–18.

254. Nissinen, *Prophets*, 4. In a lament before his friend Gilgamesh, Enkidu curses the magnificent "door" (*gišdaltu*, GE 7.32) earlier given to Enlil (GE 5.295), musing that he might chop it up and send the pieces down the river to Ebabbara (GE 7.50–52).

255. Akk *bît Ebabbarra ša ki šu-ba-at ša-ma-i*, "the temple of Ebabbara, which is like the dwelling-place of heaven" (CH 2.30–31).

256. Nissinen, *Prophets*, 4.5. Though not mentioned by name, Erišti-Aya seems the most obvious *mārtu* ("daughter") referenced here since she already lives in Sippar as a *nadītum* ("priestess"; cf. Durand, *Mari*, 390–91).

257. Akk *asakku* denotes the name of a demon, the disease it causes, or a consecrated item attached to a temple or shrine. Cf. *aššat šagîm a-sa-kám ištanarriq*, "the temple manager's wife is constantly stealing that which is taboo" (cf. *CAD* A/1.327; another *asakku* appears in Nissinen, *Prophets*, 16.20).

258. The text of Nissinen, *Prophets*, 4.22 is corrupt, but Nissinen (*Prophets*, 24) supports the reconstruction *[balāṭk]a u napi[štaka]*.

259. Nissinen, *Prophets*, 4.24–31. Additionally the *āpilu* demands that Zimri-Lim pay Nergal of

ba-at la-l[îya]).[260] Evidently aware that Hammurabi occasionally marches his armies north to test his rival's defenses,[261] this *āpilu* further urges Zimri-Lim to "release" those Babylonian subjects suffering from the problem of "debt-slavery."[262]

Anatolia

Turning now to one of the "great texts" of Anatolia[263]—the Old Hittite myth commonly known as The Disappearance of Telipinu (DT)[264]—it is important to note at the outset that few contemporary studies (if any) survey or catalogue DT's socioeconomic motifs in a systematic way.[265] Previous portrayals of Anatolian economics, in fact, tend to be rather monochromatically restricted to little more than "land and livestock."[266] Careful intertextual analysis of DT alongside other *deus absconditus* myths, however, reveals much more.[267]

The first legible lines of DT depict an economy on its last breath, a crisis conveyed via repeated use of the Hittite term *wešuriyaš* ("stifled").[268] Like the "altars of the

Ḫubšalum "whatever you have vowed" (*mal takrubu*; cf. *CAD* K.192–98).

260. Nissinen, *Prophets*, 4.4 (lit. "seat of my wealth"). Marduk uses the same epithet to describe *his* "house" (*Ee* 5.122; cf. above).

261. Akk *[s]arrātim ittīka i[dbub] u qāssu ašar šanê[m*, lit. "he speaks lies to you while his hand operates elsewhere" (Nissinen, *Prophets*, 4.34–35). This is the same Hammurabi whose lawcode, etched onto a basalt stele and dedicated to Šamaš, now stands in the Louvre.

262. Occurring twice in this letter (Nissinen, *Prophets*, 4.38, 42) Akk *andurārum* denotes "release" from long-term indebtedness, a release often enabled by the *mīšarum* ("release-decree," *CAD* M/2:116–17; cf. שמטה, Deut 15:1). Cf. Postgate, *Mesopotamia*, 196; Kraus, *Verfügungen*, 80; Charpin, "Mari," 253–70; Lemche, "Edicts," 11–22; and Snell, *Flight*, 23–29.

263. Haas (*Literatur*, 16) complains that too many definitions of Hittite "literature" tend to be arbitrary, particularly with regard to what is or is not "great" literature.

264. *CTH* 324. "Telipinu" is Old Hattic for "strong lad" (Haas, *Literatur*, 104). See Rieken, "CTH 324.1"; and Hoffner, *Myths*, 14–20. Telipinu is the son of the storm-god (Gurney, *Hittites*, 184). Beckman ("Wrath," 151) prefers to call this text *The Wrath of Telipinu*.

265. Cf. Goetze, *Kleinasien*, 118–22; Bryce, *Hittites*, 84–87, 374–76; Sandars, *Peoples*, 23–45; Beckman, "Anatolia," 538–43; and Liverani, *Politics*, 27–52. Klengel ("Wirtschaftsgeschichte," 426) tries to sketch a picture of Hittite economics from administrative reports (tax receipts, land grants, product inventories, etc.), but basically ignores the literary texts. Van den Hout ("Literature," 857–78), on the other hand, wrestles with the problem of identifying what the Hittites themselves consider to be "great literature."

266. Goetze, *Kleinasien*, 118. Haas (*Literatur*, 103), e.g., calls Telipinu a "Vegetationsgott" predominantly concerned with "Landwirtschaft." Nolan and Lenski (*Macrosociology*, 154) emphasize that "in these societies land and control of those who work it is the most important economic resource."

267. Other, more fragmentary Hittite texts relevant to this study include the Disappearance of the Storm God (Hoffner, *Hittite Myths*, 3) and the Disappearance of the Sun God (Hoffner, *Hittite Myths*, 7; cf. Nutkowicz and Mazoyer, *Disparition*, 40–42).

268. Melchert ("Telipinu," 218) elaborates: "When neatly stacked logs burn they inevitably collapse on each other and become twisted and pressed together . . . When herds of domestic animal are disturbed, they typically crowd together and even attempt to climb onto each other. Finally, the altars of the gods are neatly ordered and (the images of) the gods on them, (so) their being crowded together

gods," the country's sheep and cattle are "stifled" (*wešuriyaš*).[269] Ewes and cows "reject" (*mimma*) their offspring,[270] while *ḫalki* ("barley"), *ᵈim-mar-ni-in* ("fertility"),[271] *ša-al-ḫi-an-ti-en* ("increase"),[272] *ma-an-ni-it-ti-en* ("success"),[273] and *iš-pí-ya-tar-ra* ("satisfaction")[274] all teeter on the edge of exhaustion. Signs of depletion are everywhere:

- the grain fields *Ú-UL ma-a-i* ("fail to ripen")[275]
- the animals (including humans) no longer *ar-ma-aḫ-ḫa-an-zi* ("conceive")[276]
- the mountains, trees and pastures *ḫa-a-te-er* ("wither up");[277]
- the fresh water *ḫa-a-az-ta* ("dries up");[278] and to make matters worse,
- a terrifying *ka-a-aš-za* ("famine") blankets the land,[279] causing everything to *ki-iš-ta-an-ti-it ḫar-ki-ya-an-zi* ("perish from hunger").[280]

Just as the Mesopotamian economy collapses with Inanna's chthonic defeat,[281] and the Canaanite economy with Ba'al's defeat[282] so Anatolia collapses with Telipinu's

---

and made crooked with the disappearance of Telipinu is a serious sign of a world gone awry."

269. Hoffner, *Hittite Myths*, 2a.2–3. Spanning the earthly and heavenly realms, these same three entities become "stifled" in another myth about a disappearing deity (*wešuriyas*, lit. "twisted, squeezed," Hoffner, *Hittite Myths*, 5a.2) in a situation ᵈKamrušepaš describes as the "stifling" of Telipinu's "soul" (ZI.*ŠÚ*; Hoffner, *Hittite Myths*, 2a.19; cf. Steiner, *Souls*, 21).

270. Hit *wešuriyaš* is intransitive; *mimma* is transitive (Rieken, "Translatio").

271. Whatever the exact meaning of this term—Hoffner (*Myths*, 15) reads "animal fecundity"; Müller (*Quaestio Thesauri*) reads "Fruchtbarkeit"—the DINGIR determinative identifies it here as a deity.

272. Hoffner (*Myths*, 15) reads "luxuriance"; Kimball and Slocum (https://lrc.la.utexas.edu/eieol/hitol/20) read "growth"; Müller (*Thesauri*) reads "Wachstum"; Friedrich (*Elementarbuch* 2.97) reads "Subst. unbestimmter Bedeutung."

273. Hoffner (*Literatur*, 15) reads "growth"; Kimball and Slocum (https://lrc.la.utexas.edu/eieol/hitol/20) read "luxuriance"; Friedrich (*Elementarbuch* 2.93) reads "Subst. unbestimmter Bedeutung." Müller (*Quaestio*) reads "Gedeihen."

274. Hoffner (*Myths*, 15) reads "abundance," followed by Kimball and Slocum (https://lrc.la.utexas.edu/eieol/hitol/20); Friedrich (*Elementarbuch*, 2.89) reads "Sättigung," followed by Müller (http://www.hethport.uni-wuerzburg.de/txhet_myth/q2.php). These six aspects of a healthy economy correspond in many ways to the seven ME in ID.

275. Hit *māi*, "to grow, blossom; to prosper" (Hoffner, *Hittite Myths*, 2.3).

276. Hit *armaḫ* ("to conceive/get pregnant"). Moreover, those already pregnant cannot *ḫa-aš-ša-an-zi* ("give birth," Hoffner, *Hittite Myths*, 2.3).

277. Hit *ḫād* (pl., "to dry up, wither," Hoffner, *Hittite Myths*, 2.4). Cf. יבשׁ ("to wither, dry up," Ezek 17:9).

278. Hit *ḫād* (sg.). Cf. 1 Kgs 18:33–38 (below).

279. Hit *kašt*, "famine" (Hoffner, *Hittite Myths*, 2.4). Cf. the wordplay on רעב ("famine") in Amos 8:11.

280. Hit *kištanu* ("to vanish, delete," Hoffner, *Hittite Myths*, 2.4).

281. See above.

282. *CAT* 1.5–6 (see below).

decision to "abandon" (*ar-ḫa i-ya-an-ni-iš*)[283] his post and "hide" (*ú-li-iš-ta*) in a "swamp" (*marmarra*).[284]

The first respondent to this predicament is ^{d}UTU-*uš* (the solar deity),[285] who throws a feast for his famished colleagues, the *LÍ-IM* DINGIR^{meš} ("thousand gods").[286] This backfires when it becomes painfully clear that there is not enough food—not even for the gods (!).[287] The next respondent is Telipinu's father ^{d}IM-*uš* (the storm-god),[288] a peevish bully prone to rationalizing his son's behavior simplistically as the product of his *ša-a-i-et-wa-ra-aš-za* ("intense anger").[289] Deflecting this assessment, the solar deity releases the *ḫa-a-ra-na-ri*^{MUŠEN} *le-e-li-wa-an-da-an* ("swift eagle")[290] to search for Telipinu in all the usual hiding places: (a) "the high mountains" (*pár-ga-mu-uš* ḪUR.SAG$^{DIDLI.ḪI.A}$);[291] (b) "the deep valleys" (*[ḫa]-a-ri-i-uš-kán ḫal-lu-[w]a-mu-uš*);[292] and (c) "the deep/quiet waters" (*ḫu-wa-an-ḫu-eš-šar-kán ku-wa-a-li-ú*).[293]

283. Lit. "walk far away" (cf. Sum MU-UN-ŠUB, repeated eight times in ID 6–13).

284. Hoffner, *Hittite Myths*, 2.2–4 (Hit *ule*, "to hide, conceal"). Smith (*Monotheism*, 121–22) and Mettinger (*Riddle*, 78–79) read DT intertextually alongside the Ba'al-Mot cycle, but Mettinger's claim that "the Hittite myth contains no reference to the motif of the descent to the Netherworld" is misleading (see below). Telipinu's behavior resembles that of Anat in Canaanite myth and Achilles in Greek myth, two other willful adolescents.

285. "The sun deity has a variety of manifestations: a male sun-god; the sun-goddess of Arinna; and a sun-goddess of the earth (that is, the sun traveling underground at night)" (McMahon, "Theology," 1985).

286. Van Gessel (*Onomasticon*) attempts to identify as many of these deities as possible, and Cimok (*Hittites*, 117–40) points out that one of the best places to see representational images of these deities is the Yazilikaya chapel next to the Ḫattuša palace complex.

287. Cf. Ahab's foraging for food during the drought sent by Yhwh (1 Kgs 18:5; Kilmer, "Tricked," 299–309; Liverani, *Politics*, 3–26). It's one thing for hunger to cripple the inhabitants of earth; it's quite another for it to affect the inhabitants of heaven.

288. Sometimes called Tarḫunta, the Ḫurrian name for ^{d}IM-*uš* is Tešub.

289. *Why* Telipinu is angry, of course, is "not stated" (Gurney, *Hittites*, 184), though this is hardly the only adolescent to behave selfishly, nor is it the only time anger drives otherwise heroic characters to deplorable extremes. In Canaanite myth the goddess Anat goes berserk in the name of "protecting" Ba'al (Walls, *Anat*, 217–24). In Greek myth Achilles pouts like a diva to "spite" Agamemnon (Muellner, *Achilles*, 5–31). In Tanak, Samson on occasion runs detrimentally amok (Judg 14:18–19). Telipinu is very much the classic "rebel without a clue."

290. Another eagle goes on a similar mission in Canaanite myth when the goddess Anat turns her assistant Yaṭpan into an eagle—but this one not only finds its target; it devours it (*CAT* 1.18.4.16–42).

291. Hit *park-* ("to be high, elevated," CHD P.155).

292. Hit *ḫallu-* ("deep," Friedrich, *Elementarbuch*, 2.85).

293. Puhvel (*HED* 4.303) suggests "dunkel, blau"; Hoffner (*Myths*, 15) reads "Blue Deep"; Beckman ("Telipinu," 152) reads "blue sea"; Haas (*Literatur*, 106) reads "blaugrünen Meereswogen"; Pecchioli-Daddi and Polvani (*Ittita*, 79) read "limpide acque"; Rieken (*Translatio*) reads "rühigen Fluten."

When all this fails the "mother-deity" (^{d}NIN.TU-*ni*)[294] takes charge, bluntly admonishing the storm-god to stop criticizing his colleagues.[295] Like Athtar at Ugarit, however,[296] the storm-god does not respond well to constructive criticism.[297] Not only is he passive-aggressively unwilling to get involved himself, he sees it as his mission to sabotage the efforts of those who do,[298] even though (as the text carefully states) he cannot even figure out how to secure the gate to his own village.[299] In short, just as Athtar fails to restore prosperity to Canaan,[300] so ^{d}IM-*uš* fails to restore prosperity to KUR ^{URU}Ḫatti ("Ḫatti-land").[301]

Undeterred, ^{d}NIN.TU-*ni* (the "mother-deity") recruits one of the tiniest of all creatures to help with the search, the "honeybee" (NIM.LÀL).[302] From other Hittite texts we know that these two characters—the mother-deity and the honeybee—often team up to solve intractable problems no one else wants to face.[303] Sometimes she sends out the NIM.LÀL to relay messages to this or that ^{d}LAMMA ("local protector-deity").[304] Sometimes she commissions it to retrieve items for ritual use, like the

294. Sum DINGIR.MAḪ (Hoffner, *Hittite Myths*, 9a.3); Hit *Ḫannaḫanna*. Interestingly enough, Hit *ḫanna* ("grandmother") can homonymously mean "to direct, decide" (Friedrich, *Elementarbuch* 2.85). Ceccarelli (*Enki*, 5) contends that "the most frequent names for the mother-deity are Ninhursanĝa, Nintur and Ninmaḫ in Sumerian texts as well as Mami/Mama and Bēlet-ilī in Akkadian texts." Cf. Laroche ("Koubaba," 113–28).

295. The Anatolian ^{MUNUS}ŠU.GI ("wise woman") plays a similarly "decisive" role in Hurro-Hittite ritual (Moore, *Balaam*, 21–29), as does Abigail in her mediation of the David-Nabal conflict (1 Sam 25; cf. Rodin, *Mother*, 297; Moore, *Reconciliation*, 23–34).

296. *CAT* 1.2.3.18–25 (see below).

297. In a parallel myth the storm-god himself is the one who carries away "everything good" (Hoffner, *Hittite Myths*, 3). Following Craigie ("Athtar," 224), Day (*Yahweh*, 173) views Athtar as the Canaanite equivalent of the Hurrian war-god Aštabi.

298. He says, *nu-wa-ra-an* DINGIR^{meš} GAL.GAL DINGIR^{meš} TUR *ša-an-ḫi-iš-ke-er . . . nu-wa-ra-an pa-iz-zi ka-a-aš [pa]r-ta-u-wa-aš-še-et-wa a-mi-ya-an-ta a-pa-aš-ša-u-wa a-mi-ya-an-za . . . nam-ma-wa-ra-aš ḫa-an-ti túḫ-ša-an-zi*, "If the great and small gods are searching but cannot find him, (how) will this (bee) find him? His wings are too small, and he himself is too small" (Hoffner, *Hittite Myths*, 2a.8).

299. Hoffner, *Hittite Myths*, 2.7. The storm-god goes *I-NA* URU-*ŠU* KÁ.GAL, "to his city (at) the great gate" (lit. "great mouth"), but *nu Ú-UL tar-ḫu-uz-zi ḫa-a-ši* (Hoffner, *Hittite*, 15: "he cannot manage to open it"; Haas, *Literatur*, 107: "he breaks its bolt with his hammer").

300. *CAT* 1.6.1.54–65 (see below).

301. This is one of the more common designations in the Hittite texts for describing the contiguous lands and peoples of second millennium Anatolia. Much like the Hebrew prophet Elijah (1 Kgs 19:13), the Hittite storm-god becomes so depressed he "hides" himself away (Hoffner, *Hittite Myths*, 2a.7, Hit *karuššiya*; *HED* K.83).

302. This PN does not appear on *CTH* 324.1, but it does appear on other tablets preserving various aspects of the "disappearing deity" tradition (e.g.,Hoffner, *Hittite Myths*, 3.12; 9a.3; 9b.4; 9c.2; 13b.3).

303. In this she very much much resembles the Mesopotamian god Enki.

304. Hoffner, *Hittite Myths*, 9. One manifestation of ^{d}LAMMA is the Hittite goddess Inara.

KUŠ*kurša* ("ephod").[305] Sometimes other deities (like the storm-god) enlist the NIM.LÀL to do jobs for *them* (like find *other* "lost deities"),[306] but the bottom line is that the NIM.LÀL succeeds where others do not, locating Telipinu "asleep in a meadow in the town of Liḫzina."[307]

Disabling him with its stinger, the NIM.LÀL applies medicinal wax to the resulting welps, and with the help of the aforementioned eagle flies him home.[308] Upon his arrival another female deity, the exorcist-deity dKamrušepaš,[309] takes charge of purifying Telipinu of all defilement, ritually "removing" (*da-a-aḫ-ḫu-un*) his "sin,"[310] "fury,"[311] "anger,"[312] "irritation"[313] and "anxiety"[314] via a typical MUNUSŠU.GI exorcism.[315] This results not only in Telipinu's "purification,"[316] but in a much-longed-for revival of economic prosperity.[317] Further, mirroring the ritual sequence in ID/DI, dKamrušepaš (a) transfers the "sin-fury-anger-irritation-anxiety" just "removed" from Telipinu to bronze *palḫi*-pots, (b) secures these pots with lead lids and iron locks, and (c) buries them deep within the "dark earth" (*da-an-ku-i da-ga-an-zi-pí*) where "nothing ever rises again."[318]

305. Hoffner, *Hittite Myths*, 9b.4 (i.e., "leather bag"). Güterbock reads "hunting bag" ("Hunting," 113), followed by Hoffner (*Hittite*, 17). Rieken (*Translatio*) reads "fleece," but N.B. the functions of the אפד ("ephod") in Nevi'im (e.g., Judg 17:5; Hos 3:4).

306. Hoffner, *Hittite Myths*, 9c.2. Gurney (*Hittites*, 180) points out that Hittitologists tend to separate the Anatolian myths into (a) tales about "finding disappearing deities," and (b) tales about "slaying the (cosmic) dragon."

307. Haas (*Literatur*, 104) argues that north-central Anatolia is the most likely center of the Telipinu cult, esp. the cities of Ḫanḫana, Turmita and Liḫzina.

308. Hoffner, *Hittite Myths*, 2c.2.

309. N.B. the DINGIR determinative (in *KUB* 56.17 she is called by her Hurrian name, Kataḫzipuri). Cf. Melchert ("Telipinu," 212–13).

310. Hit *uš-du-ul-še-et* (reading *du* instead of *túl* with Mazoyer, *Télipinu*, 48; and Rieken, *Translatio*).

311. Hit *kar-pí-iš-ša-an.*

312. Hit *kar-di-mi-ya-at-ta-aš-ša-an.*

313. Hit *wa-ar-ku-uš-ša-an*. Hoffner (*Myths*, 16) reads "picque?"; Beckman ("Telipinu," 152) reads "irritation."

314. Hit *ša-a-u-wa-ar*. Hoffner (*Myths*, 16) reads "sullenness."

315. Hoffner, *Hittite Myths*, 2a.22. On the magico-religious roles enacted by the MUNUSŠU.GI ("old/wise woman"), see Haas, *Orakel*, 17–66; Kammenhuber, *Orakelpraxis*, 9–13, 27–28; and Moore, *Balaam*, 21–29; *Babbler*, 9.

316. Hit *pár-ku-nu-nu-[un]* (Hoffner, *Hittite Myths*, 2a.22; cf. the numerous ritual texts cited in *CHD* P.165).

317. Hit *[šal-ḫa-a]n-t[i-i]š m[a-an-ni-it-ti-iš . . .]* (Hoffner, *Hittite Myths*, 2a.30; reconstructed from the sequence of terms in 2.2a.3).

318. Hit *na-aš-ta nam-ma ša-ra-a Ú-UL ú-ez-zi* (Hoffner, *Hittite Myths*, 2a.27). Like Irkalla/Ganzir in ID, the "dark earth" is protected by seven gates locked by seven bolts whose keys are held by a "gatekeeper" (LÚNI.DUḪ; cf. dNE.TI in ID 77). The major difference between the two traditions is that where Inanna herself descends into the Netherworld in ID/DI, only Telipinu's

With Telipinu returned the economy revives as he replenishes not only the "land and livestock," but whatever else is requested by the "royal couple."[319] To commemorate this revival they symbolically commission the construction of a new cult object—a ^{KUŠ}*kurša* ("ephod/leather bag")[320]—and hang it in the atrium of Telipinu's temple, stocking it with several ingredients depicting various aspects of the new prosperity: UDU-*aš* Ì-*an* ("choice mutton");[321] *ḫalki* ("barley");[322] ^{d}GÌR; GEŠTIN ("grapes"),[323] GU$_4$ ("beef"), UDU ("mutton"), MU^{KAM} GÍD.DA ("longevity"),[324] and DUMU^{meš} ("posterity").[325]

Syria-Palestine

Should the Hebrew GN כנען ("Canaan") derive from a root for "merchant/trader,"[326] then this furnishes insight, if only etymologically, into why so many of the Hebrew prophets so strongly criticize the socioeconomic behavior of their friends and neighbors.[327] Greater specificity comes from isolating several socioeconomic motifs animat-

"sin-fury-anger-irritation-anxiety" descends in DT.

319. Specifically he helps the royal couple experience *ḫu-iš-wa-an-ni in-na-ra-u-wa-ni* EGIR.UD-*MI*, "life, health, longevity" (Hoffner, *Hittite Myths*, 2a.28). Hutter (*Behexung*, 113–20) documents how Hittite magico-religious specialists (like the ^{MUNUS}ŠU.GI) go out of their way to protect the "royal couple" from spiritual, economic, and political harm.

320. ^{KUŠ}*kurša* ("ephod"); Güterbock ("Hunting," 113) translates "hunting bag" here and in Hoffner, *Hittite Myths*, 9b.4. In some temples the sacrality of the *kurša* is indicated by the determinative for deity (i.e., ^{dKUŠ}*kurša*; cf. texts cited in Güterbock, 117).

321. Lit. "oil of sheep" (likely idiomatic). Hoffner (*Myths*, 17) reads "Sheep Fat"; Beckman ("Telipinu," 153) reads "mutton fat"; Gonnet ("Rhyton," 321) reads "graisse de mouton."

322. This term sometimes appears in ritual texts as ^{d}*ḫalkiš*, i.e., "Grain." The grain goddess to whom prayer is directed in Mesopotamia is ^{d}Nisaba (Frechette, "Nisaba," 70–93).

323. Friedrich and Kammenhuber (*HW* Ḫ.54) identify ^{d}GÌR with the cattle-deity ^{d}Sumuqan/Šakkan (GE 1.109); Pecchioli Daddi and Polvani (*Ittita*, 84) read "e dentro c'è il dio GÌR del grano e del vino"; Hoffner (*Myths*, 18) reads "in it lie (symbols of) Animal Fecundity and Wine"; Beckman ("Telipinu," 153) reads "in it are grain, the fertility of the herds, and the grape"; Haas (*Literatur*, 114) reads "dann sind (die Gaben) des Getreides, des Viehs (und) des Weines hineingelegt."

324. Lit. "long years."

325. Lit. "children." Fontenrose (*Python*, 129) contends that in lieu of the "combat" theme, DT focuses on "appeasement." Bryce (*Society*, 215) argues that the "disappearing god" myths, in spite of their parallels to the "Netherworld journey" myths, are "of a different order" because "there is no sense here of a recurrent pattern; rather the emphasis is on the god's whimsical behavior." But if there is no recurrent pattern, why so many socioeconomic parallels?

326. Ug *kn`n* (*UT* 19.1272; *DULAT* 449; cf. كنخ); Heb כנען (Isa 23:8 [//סחר]; Zech 14:21 [≠ קדש]; Prov 31:24 [//מכר]; cf. Zobel, "כנען," 213–17).

327. See, for now, Isa 23:11–12; Hos 12:7–8; Ezek 27:1–36; Zech 9:3–4; Moore, *Babbler*, 122–39; Jemielity, *Satire*, 11–18. Lemos (*Gifts*, 1–19) justifiably censures the excesses of parallelomania, but Gnuse (*Property*, 63) still recognizes that "during the period of the judges Israel resists the economic state system. The Israelites remain in the highlands in unwalled villages, where there is economic equality, communal ownership, self-sufficiency in the production of goods, and social structures built upon kinship models." Yet "the influence of Canaanite economics penetrates Israelite communities"

ing the "great texts" of Canaan,[328] particularly those preserved in the mythopoeic epics inscribed on the clay tablets recovered from Ras Shamra (ancient Ugarit).[329] This is not the only lens through which to read this literature, of course,[330] yet it hardly seems coincidental that the motif-trajectories flowing through *these* "great texts" readily fall into categories similar to those within the Mesopotamian texts: *inheritance/possession*, *socioeconomic identity*, and *conflict resolution*.

Inheritance/Possession

Irritated by construction delays on his palace, and persuaded by his chief engineer that Baʿal is responsible,[331] the sea-deity Yam[332] dispatches messengers[333] to a divine council presided over by their "father" El[334] to demand that his brother Baʿal be remanded over into his custody, along with his entire "inheritance":[335]

---

because "the compromise with Canaanite values begins at an early stage."

328. Iser ("Staging," 887) recognizes in "great literature . . . its mimetic reflection of social conditions and its regenerative force in constituting reality," and Wyatt (*RTU* 35) observes that the "mythological material" at Ugarit "has important affinities with Hittite, Greek, Mesopotamian, and Israelite-Judahite material," being only "one recension of a widespread and important tradition."

329. Yon, *Ugarit*, 9–47.

330. Nor is this the only way to examine the form and/or function of Canaanite economics. Heltzer ("Ugarit," 423–54) submits a thorough ground-level summary, and McGeough (*Exchange*, 359) analyzes the forms and functions of various types of economic exchange. Monroe (*Scales*, 241–74) posits a paradigm for understanding reciprocal gift-giving, and Feldman (*Diplomacy*, 15–16) casts a net wide enough to engage the question of international gift-giving.

331. Ug *bʿl* (*DULAT* 205–09; *UT* 19.493); Heb בעל (*HAL* 137–38). Fleming (*Religion*, 71) suggests that the constant mixture of Hittite, NW Semitic, and Mesopotamian peoples at Emar (Tell Meskene, a seaport village on the Euphrates) makes it highly likely that the Sumerogram ^{d}IM at Emar refers to the storm-gods Teššup, Baʿal and/or Hadad (cf. Herrmann, "Baʿal," 132–39).

332. Ug *ym* (*DULAT* 965–66; *UT* 19.1106); ים (*HAL* 395–96); ܝܡܐ (*PSD* 193); يم (*DMWA* 1109; cf. Stolz, "Sea," 737–42). Wyatt (*Mind*, 113) reasonably contends that there is "every reason to regard the Greek and Ugaritic myths of the *Chaoskampf* as cognate," which would mean that "an equivalence between Typhoeus and Typhon on the one hand, and Yam on the other, is beyond reasonable doubt."

333. Correspondence between Hittite officials reveals a strong expectation of immunity for messengers from mistreatment and abuse: "Why are you not sending my messengers back to me? Are your servants too tired (to do so)? Do these messengers not belong to our lord?" (cited from Hoffner, *Letters*, 201).

334. Ug *il* (*UT* 19.163); אל (*HAL* 47–49); ܐܠܗܐ (*PSD* 17); الله (*DMWA* 24). Cf. Pope, *El*, 25–35; Herrmann, "El," 274–80.

335. See Mullen, *Council*, 57; Handy, *Pantheon*, 119; and Kloos, *Combat*, 22. Personalization of "the sea" can and does occur in Hebrew poetry; cf. כי תנוס מה לך הים, "Why is it, O Sea, that you flee?" (Ps 114:5).

tn ilm dtqh[336]	Give up, O gods, the one whom you protect
dtqynh hmlt[337]	The one whom you protect, O multitude.
tn b'l w'nnh[338]	Give up Ba'al and his retinue,
bn dgn[339] *artm*[340] *pdh*[341]	The son of Dagan, that I may inherit his gold.[342]

Like Enki at another divine council,[343] El responds immediately to this demand:

'bdk b'l yymm	Ba'al is your slave, O Yam,
'bdk b'l ynhrm[344]	Ba'al is your slave, O Nahar,
bn dgn asrkm[345]	The son of Dagan your prisoner.
hw ybl argmnk[346] *kilm*	Let him bring you tribute like the gods,
[hw] ybl wbn qdš mnḥyk[347]	Let him bring you gifts like the holy ones.[348]

336. Reading Ug *dtqh* from the verbal root *yqy* with Gordon (*UT* 19.1143), Kaiser (*Israel*, 60) and Gibson (*CML* 41) *contra* Wyatt (*RTU* 61) and Smith ("Ba'al," 99). Cf. وقى, "to guard, protect" (*DMWA* 1094).

337. Cf. המלה (// מחנה, "camp," Ezek 1:24).

338. Ug *'nn* (*DULAT* 170; *UT* 19.1885). It hardly seems coincidental that one homonym of *'nn* means "cloud"; N.B. *b'l diph* ("Ba'al of the mist") // *hd d'nn* ("Hadad of the clouds") in *CAT* 1.10.2.32–33 (Wyatt, *RTU* 158), and note also that in Ps 68:4 Hebrew scribes apply to Yhwh one of Ba'al's most characteristic epithets, *rkb 'rpt* ("rider on the clouds," *CAT* 1.2.4.8, 29; Wyatt, *Whisper*, 32–36).

339. Tanak readers recognize this grain-deity from the story of the Philistine capture of the Ark (1 Sam 5:2–7; see Healey, "Dagon," 216–19). Cf. ^{d}*ḫalkiš* ("grain-deity") in Hittite ritual texts (see above).

340. Ug *yrṯ* (*DULAT* 982–83; *UT* 19.1161); cf. Heb ירש (Judg 14:15; Isa 54:3; *HAL* 421). This mythopoeic conflict hardly reflects an atypical situation. In two Akk texts from Ugarit (*RS* 17.352.4–11 and 17.035), for example, royal siblings ferociously fight over their inheritance (texts cited from *PRU* 4.121–24; cf. Singer, "History," 678–80).

341. Cf. פז (// זהב, Ps 19:11).

342. *CAT* 1.2.1.18–19, 34–35. That gold and silver are abundant commodities in Ugaritic commerce hardly deflates the socioeconomic realities behind this mythopoeic text (Healey, *Ugarit*, 589).

343. *Atr* 1.208–17. See Mullen, *Council*, 260; Handy, *Pantheon*, 134–35; Jindo, "Courtroom," 81; Moore, *WealthWatch*, 80–81. Cf. Kramer and Maier, *Enki*, 1–13; Bertman, *Mesopotamia*, 118. Citing another parallel, Gordon (*Sumer*, 249) suggests that "the tipsy Enki" is to "be compared with the drunken El."

344. Ug *nhr* ("river/flood," *DULAT* 626; *UT* 19.1623). Cf. נהר ("river, flood" 2 Sam 8:3); ܢܗܪܐ (*PSD* 330); نهر (*DMWA* 1003); and the "roaring" (דכים) of the "rivers" (נהרות) associated with Yhwh's "voice" (קול, Ps 93:3).

345. Ug *asr* (*UT* 19.284); Heb אסר ("to bind," *HAL* 73); Akk *esēru* (*CAD* E.332–34); ܐܣܪ (*PSD* 25); اسر (*DMWA* 16). The PN ישׂראל ("Israel") derives from this verb (i.e., "the one who 'wrestles with/is bound to' God").

346. Ug *argmn* (*UT* 19.340); cf. ארגמן, lit. "purple cloth" (Ezek 27:16; Esth 1:6; *HAL* 81–82).

347. Ug *mnḥ* (*DULAT* 562–63; *UT* 19.1500); cf. מנחה, "gift" (Judg 3:17; 2 Sam 8:2; *HAL* 568–69). Smith (*History*, 37) observes that "the language describing the Ugaritic divine court includes . . . many elements derived from royal *realia* of the second millennium," including "royal treaty terminology for tribute (*argmn*) and royal gifts from an inferior king to a superior king (*mnḥ*)."

348. *CAT* 1.2.1.36–38. Smith (*Ba'al*, 62) recognizes *bn qdš* to be "a common epithet of the gods," but Rahmouni (*Epithets*, 209) only occasionally applies it directly to El.

All this falls on deaf ears, however, because the gods want nothing to do with this old rivalry.[349] Frustrated by their recalcitrance, Ba'al decides to take matters into his own hands, assaulting Yam's messengers[350] in what turns out to be the first of several successful attacks against the Canaanite "leviathan."[351] Destroying Yam completely, he then butchers the corpse in a mutilation ritual similar to that executed by Marduk against Tiamat[352] and Anat against Mot (and Aqhat).[353]

Watching from the sidelines, Anat—Ba'al's "sister/consort"—reframes all this from *her* perspective, boldly seizing credit for Yam's demise:[354]

lmḫšt mdd il ym	Look here! *I* struck down El's darling Yam
lklt nhr il rbm	Yes! *I* destroyed the great god Nahar[355]
lištbm tnn ištm[]h	Indeed![356] *I* bound and cuffed Tunnan[357]

349. "The gods tremble before Yam's messengers" (Fontenrose, *Python*, 130).

350. Indicating that a "sacred boundary" is being crossed, the Ugaritic mythographer shows Athtart and a female colleague (probably Anat) each taking one of Ba'al's arms to hold him back, apparently chiding him for failing to treat Yam's messengers as neutral non-combatants (*CAT* 1.2.1.38–44; cf. Greene, *Messenger*, 232–66; Bederman, *Law*, 88–136). Ober ("Ideology," 102–26) lists several more unlawful assaults perpetrated against neutral non-combatants during the Peloponnesian War.

351. Ug *ltn* (*DULAT* 507; cf. לויתן, "leviathan," Job 41:1) appears at the beginning of the Ba'al-Mot cycle (*CAT* 1.5.1.1) in a poetic celebration of Ba'al's victory over Yam. Some read this as a "creation text" (Mowinckel, *Psalms* 1.134; Fisher, "Creation," 314–15; Cross, *Canon*, 80), but others see it as an idealistic priestly attempt "to settle the problem of kingship over the gods and sovereignty over the cosmos" (Green, *Storm-God*, 182; cf. Smith, *Ba'al*, 77–78; Wyatt, *Mind*, 197).

352. *Ee* 4.106–40 (see Lambert, *Creation*, 232–40). Whether this Ugaritic text references an "act of creation" is vigorously disputed because "one scholar will claim that the old Canaanite myths do not speak of 'creation' (while) another will characterize the entire complex cycle as an elaborated cosmogonic myth, and hence properly called a 'creation story'" (Cross, *CMHE* 120). Korpel and Moor (*Adam*, 235–45) attempt to circumvent this by trying to reconstruct a Canaanite "creation myth" from ritual texts like *CAT* 1.100 and 1.107, even though this defies their earlier insistence that "Ba'al may be the champion among the gods to subdue the forces of evil, but he does not create anything new" (Korpel and Moor, "Poetry," 244).

353. *CAT* 1.6.2.30–37 (Mot); 1.19.1.10–11 (Aqhat). Cf. Walls, *Anat*; Day, "Anat," 36–43; Day, "Mistress," 181–90; Maier, "Anath," 225–27; and Cornelius, *Goddess*, 80, 85, 92–93. Segal (*Corpse*, 2) recognizes that "the theme of the mutilation of the corpse" is "well embedded in the epic tradition."

354. Anat is nothing if not opportunistic, as the Ugaritic texts repeatedly make clear. Pitard ("Monsters," 86) contends that the enemies of Anat fall "into two groupings—water-based and land-based deities. The former, with five names and epithets, appears to represent most likely one, but no more than two creatures (Yamm/Nahar, Tunnan/snake/Powerful One)," concluding that "the evidence suggests that this is only one deity." Whether Yam and Lotan are identical or not, the Ugaritic texts clearly state that "Anat, together with Ba'al, defeats Yam, Leviathan, and the other monsters" (Day, *Dragon*, 15).

355. Although Ug *nhr* technically means "river/canal" (cf. Heb נהר, Syr ܢܗܪܐ, Arab نهر), Wyatt (*Mind*, 197) suggests that "the various personages listed in these passages," though possessing "a kind of independence, are ultimately all aspects of the sea."

356. The translation here attempts to capture the intent of the thrice-repeated vocative *lamed* without surrendering "wiliness" (one of Anat's characteristic traits) for "woodenness" (cf. Miller, "Vocative," 617–38; Sivan, *Grammar*, 186–87).

357. Ug *tnn* (*DULAT* 873–74; *UT* 19.2575; cf. תנין (Isa 27:1; 51:9; Ps 74:13). See Diewert, "Tannin,"

mḫšt bṯn ʿqltn	*I* struck down the coiled Serpent[358]
šlyṭ d šbʿt rašm	The seven-headed Sulṭan[359]
mḫšt mdd ilm ar[š]	*I* struck down Aršu, the beloved of the gods
ṣmt ʿgl il ʿtk[360]	*I* silenced Atik, El's pet bull
mḫšt klbt ilm išt[361]	*I* put down Sparky, El's guard-dog
klt bt il ḏbb	*I* snuffed out Blaze, El's daughter
imtḫṣ[362] *ksp itrṯ ḫrṣ*	*I* seized the silver; *I* inherited the gold.[363]

Since ANE inheritance law privileges the rights of firstborn males,[364] it's more than a little puzzling to see Anat try to muscle in on Yam's "inheritance."[365] Further, it seems odd that elsewhere El assures a mortal king (Kirta)[366] that the "firstborn blessing" sometimes extends "even to the youngest" (Ug *ṣġrthn abkrn*).[367] Translators quibble over phraseology,[368] but the socioeconomic implications are not unclear. Not only is "the appointment of an heir . . . an important matter,"[369] but divinely bestowed wealth cannot be routinely subjected to "proportional division."[370] *Inheritance/possession*,

203–15; and Heider, "Tannin," 835–36.

358. Ug *ʿqltn* (*DULAT* 177; *UT* 19.1908; cf. עקלתון "twisty," Isa 27:1); عقال ("woven headband").

359. Gordon (*UT* 19.2423) reads *šlyṭ* as a Š-form of *lyṭ* (cf. Sivan, *Grammar*, 170; לט, "stealthy," Ruth 3:7), proposing a morphological parallel with the PN *šʿtqt* (*CAT* 1.16.6.1; see *UT* 19.1938). Others, on the basis of Heb שׁלט, ("to dominate," *HAL* 1408–10) read "tyrant" (Gibson, *CML* 50) or "potentate" (Smith, "Baʿal," 111); cf. سلطان, "sultan."

360. Defining the relationship between Aršu and Atik is difficult. Some associate Atik with the "Bull of Heaven" in Gilgamesh (GE 6.94; see Pope, *Job*, 321–22), while others find this comparison problematic (e.g., Day, *Dragon*, 81–82). Batto ("Behemoth," 168) discusses whether and/or how much resonance there may be between Atik (at Ugarit) and Behemoth (in Job).

361. Ug *išt* lit. means "fire, spark" (*DULAT* 119; *UT* 19.391); cf. אשׁ (Job 28:5; *HAL* 89).

362. Ug *mḫṣ* in G means "to wound, beat, crush, kill," but in Gt it means "to seize, fight" (*DULAT* 540). N.B. the // here with *yrṯ*.

363. *CAT* 1.3.3.35–44.

364. See, conveniently, the legal texts gathered by Greenspahn (*Brothers*, 36–59). Mowat ("Shakespeare," 31) documents the bard's attraction to biblical stories where "the younger brother usurps the dignity of the firstborn by displacing his elder and seizing his inheritance."

365. Cf., however, the exceptional inheritance claim filed by בנות צלפחד, "the daughters of Zelophehad" (Num 27:1–4; Sakenfeld, "Daughters," 179–96; Claassens, "Daughters," 319–37).

366. *CAT* 1.15.2.16–3.16. Korpel ("Exegesis," 106–11) wonders whether the underlying historical context to Kirta might be the absence of *any* male heir, a claim Marsman (*Ugarit*, 360) finds "speculative."

367. *CAT* 1.15.3.16 (i.e., to the new sons and daughters of the Kirta-Ḥuray union).

368. Greenstein ("Kirta," 26) reads "the youngest of them I name firstborn"; Gray (*Krt*, 19) reads "to the youngest of them I shall give the birthright"; Wyatt (*RTU* 212) reads "their last one I shall treat as the firstborn." The translation here is most indebted to Gibson (*CML* 92).

369. Marsman, *Ugarit*, 359.

370. Wyatt, *RTU* 212. Some wonder whether the "firstborn blessing" in Kirta covertly alludes to a succession crisis in the Ugaritic royal dynasty (van Selms, *Marriage*, 141; Gray, *Krt*, 60; Marsman, *Ugarit*, 360); i.e., like that affecting the Davidic dynasty (cf. Moore, *Reconciliation*, 49–60; *Faith*,

in other words, is no minor concern in the "great literature" of second millennium Canaan,[371] but instead walks arm in arm with the palace-construction motifs structuring the titanic conflicts between Yam, Athtar, and Ba'al.[372] Whenever these characters lament their plights, the words in their mouths help vent the *angst* of the priestly scribes writing them down, especially when they use literary tropes designed to engage important *socioeconomic* issues.[373] In short, the "great texts" of Canaan serve to (a) validate the religio-political power of the priesthoods controlling each deity's cultic machinery,[374] and (b) justify the "inheritance/seizure/possession" of the primary subsidy needed to maintain this machinery: *socioeconomic wealth*.[375]

Taking another look at Yam, it is instructive to note in this initial encounter that El makes his aspirations quite clear:

bn bht[376] *zbl ym*	Build a house for Prince Yam
[rm]m hkl ṯpṭ nhr	Raise a palace for Judge Nahar.[377]

59–64; *WealthWatch*, 125–27).

371. Ba'al identifies his "holy mountain" (Mt. Zaphon) as his *nḥlt* ("inheritance," *CAT* 1.3.3.30; cf. *niḫlatum* in Nissinen, *Prophets*, 1.4; and נחלת in 1 Kgs 21:3). Mauss (*Gift*) points out that gift-giving involves *giving*, *receiving* and *reciprocation*, but Godelier (*Enigma*, 29–55) adds a fourth dimension; viz., that some objects, too sacred to be exchanged, can only be *inherited*. Perhaps this influences the Canaanite mythographer's decision to use *yrṯ* in his depiction of Yam's demands.

372. Wyatt (*Mind*, 26) calls these three deities "the potential cosmic kings." Green (*Storm-God*, 210) defines Ug *'ṯtr* (*DULAT* 193–94; *UT* 19.1941) via the cognate عثر, translating "soil artificially irrigated," but Caquot ("'Athtar," 59) and Moor (*Pattern*, 205) find the sources marshalled to substantiate this position porously problematic. Following Craigie ("Athtar," 224), Day (*Yahweh*, 173) thinks of Athtar as a Canaanite parallel to the Hurrian war-god Aštabi, but others posit (in light of south semitic cognates) an astral context (Caquot, "'Athtar," 47–49; Leslau, *Ge'ez*, 73). Scanning for middle ground, Smith (*Ba'al*, 247–48) defines 'Athtar as "an important astral god who is considered a strong protector and at least occasionally a provider of water through natural irrigation."

373. Spencer ("Priests," 269) illustrates this by pointing to "turmoil at the highest levels of the Karnak priesthood" as something utterly "unsurprising, given the amount of influence and wealth at stake."

374. Weber (*Sociology*, 119) contends that "the intellectual influence upon religion of the priesthood, even where it is the chief carrier of literature, is of quite varied scope, depending on which non-priestly classes oppose the priesthood and on the power position of the priesthood itself."

375. According to Fletcher (*Egypt*, 84), the court of Thutmosis III sees the Amun priesthood in Thebes accumulate enough "wealth and power to rival that of the monarchy itself." And according to Black (*Sumer*, 100) Enlil's anger (*Atr* 1.87–96) reflects the anger of the Nippur priesthood over its displacement at the hands of the Babylonian priesthood of Marduk (cf. Sommerfeld, *Aufstieg*, 87, 104; Foster, *Muses*, 881; Cross, *CMHE* 195–216). Lenski (*Power*, 260) argues that in addition to religious duties, priests focus on two goals: (a) legitimizing the power of the governing elite, and (b) collecting enough taxes to enable such legitimation (goals repeated by the silversmith Demetrius in Acts 19:24–27; cf. below).

376. Ug *bht* ("house," *DULAT* 245–50) in this context doubtless connotes "temple" (N.B. // *hkl*) because to work in an opulent temple is the desire of every priesthood. David's desire to build a "house" for Yahweh well reflects this desideratum (2 Sam 7:1–16). Feinman ("Temples," 76–78) traces the contours of the relationship between economics and priesthoods in Mesoamerican culture.

377. *CAT* 1.2.3.7.

Seeking to explain these aspirations, it's instructive to note that the solar deity Šapšu[378] instructs Athtar[379] on why Yam needs his own "house":

[yṯ]ir[380] *ṯr il abk*	The bull El, your father, must avenge
l pn[381] *zbl ym*	The dignity of Prince Yam
l pn [ṯ]pṭ nhr	The dignity of Judge Nahar.[382]

Thus, when Athtar does the math and realizes that he will never have *his* own "house," this throws him into deep depression:

ank in bt [l]y [km i]lm	As for me, I have no house like the gods
[w]ḥẓr [kbn] [qd]š	No courtyard like the holy ones
lbdm ard bnpšny[383]	Alone, I will descend with my soul
trḥṣn kṯrm[384]	As the orderlies wash me (for burial)
bb[ht] zbl ym	In the house of Prince Yam
bhkl ṯpṭ nh[r]	In the palace of Judge Nahar.[385]

From a macroliterary perspective these stanzas not only explain why Yam and Athtar do not receive "houses."[386] They also serve as negative foils to "Baʿal the Great Hero."[387] Not only do they help explain the rationale for Baʿal's victory over Chaos (Yam) and

378. Cf. Handy (*Pantheon*, 107–08) and Lewis ("Dead," 227–28).

379. Wyatt's (*Myths*, 307–22, 341–45) attempt to interpret Athtar not as a tragic character in a "deposition myth," but as "the apotheosis of the human institution of kingship" has not found many takers. Athtar looks more like King Lear than King Arthur; more like King Saul than King David.

380. Ug *ṯar* (*DULAT* 891–92). Gordon (*UT* 19.2632) proposes emending *ṯar* to *ṯ`r* ("to arrange"), but also suggests the possibility of there being an Ug homonym cognate to Arab ثار ("to avenge," *UT* 19.2631). Gibson (*CML* 38) follows the first option; Smith ("Baʿal," 97) and Pardee ("Canonical," 247) the second. Watson ("Comments," 79–80) translates "be victorious" (cf. Akk *šaʾāru*), while Moor (*ARTU* 37) reads "grant his favor," followed by Wyatt (*RTU* 54).

381. Ug *pn* (lit. "face") here suggests "presence" and/or "dignity" (*HAL* 887; Moore, "Presence," 166).

382. *CAT* 1.2.3.16.

383. Challenging earlier opinion, Steiner (*Souls*, 21) contends that "belief in the existence—and afterlife—of disembodied 'souls' (*nb/pš*) is extremely widespread in the ancient Near East."

384. Cf. Eth *ktr*, "to cordon off, enclose" (Leslau, *Ge`ez*, 298); and N.B. the *kṯrt* ("Kotharat"), a quasi-divine group of female attendants (*CAT* 1.24.6, 11, 15; Wright, *Aqhat*, 81–86). Fitzenreiter ("Grabdekoration," 67–140) lists several types of cleansing rituals associated with Egyptian funerary praxis.

385. *CAT* 1.2.3.19–20. Cf. the "corpse-washing" motif in the Egyptian *Tale of Sinuhe* (Lichtheim, *Literature* 1:222–35).

386. Like the eclipse of Enlil's cult in Babylon, the removal of Athtar from power in these texts doubtless reflects the eclipse of Athtar's *cult* (Caquot, "`Athtar," 55; Smith, *Monotheism*, 65).

387. Walton (*Thought*, 61) recognizes that "the deity who may be considered the hero of a narrative may be portrayed in more positive ways than other deities who may serve as opponents, foils, or supporting characters."

Death (Mot),[388] they legitimize his leadership by predicating its validity on the success of his palace-building project.[389] Sociohistorically, of course, they concretize the fears of those priesthoods ever anxious, in Max Weber's words, to "infuse their views into the religion of the laity (and) secure their own position."[390] Thus, Yam dies at Ba'al's hands before receiving a palace, Athtar fails to acquire anything even resembling a palace, and Ba'al displaces both rivals by building *his* palace (with Anat's help) after extracting permission from a dithering "father" who gives in to his demands:[391]

ybn bt lb'l km ilm	Let a house be built for Ba'al like the gods
wḥẓr kbn aṯrt	A dwelling like (that for) Astarte's sons . . .[392]

Echoing her husband, Lady Athirat-Yam[393] reiterates El's decree:

bt arzm[394] *ykllnh*	Let a cedar house be completed for him
hm bt lbnt y'msnh	Let a house of bricks be mortared for him
ltrgm laliyn[395] *b'l*	Yes! Let it be said to Mightiest Ba'al,
ṣḥ ḫrn[396] *bbhtk*	"Summon (produce from) Ḫauran into your house

388. Ug *mt* (*DULAT* 597–98; *UT* 19.1443); cf. מות (*HAL* 532–34); ܡܘܬܐ (*PSD* 260); موت (*DMWA* 930); Watson, "Mot," 136–71; Hays, *Death*, 122–24.

389. Baines and Yoffee, "Legitimacy," 13–17.

390. Weber, *Sociology*, 67. The classic analysis of Mesopotamian priesthood is Renger's study ("Priestertum"); the classic study of Hittite priests is Sturtevant's ("Hittite"); and Cody ("Priesthood") outlines the peculiarities of the Hebrew priesthood (cf. Moore, *Babbler*, 25–41; Cross, *CMHE* 195–215; and the essays published in Anderson and Olyan, *Priesthood*).

391. Eissfeldt, *El*, 59–60; Pope, *El*, 25–54; Herrmann, "El," 274–80; Rose, "Names," 1004; Cross, *CMHE* 13–15. Pope (*El*, 102) and Oldenburg (*Conflict*, 142–46) attempt to ascertain the *degree* of conflict between El and Ba'al.

392. *CAT* 1.4.4.62–5.1. Generational tension is the primary conflict driving Kirta (Smith, *Monotheism*, 135–37) as well as *Ee* (Harris, *Mesopotamia*, 67–79), not to mention the Tanak book of Genesis (Steinmetz, *Conflict*, 147–53).

393. Ug *rbt aṯrt ym* ("the great lady who tramples Yam," or "the great lady who traverses the sea"). Cf. אשרה ("A/asherah," 1 Kgs 15:13; 18:19; 2 Kgs 21:7); Day, "Asherah," 385–408; Hadley, *Asherah*, 42–53.

394. The "house of cedar" (בית ארזים) most familiar to Tanak readers is the one David promises to build for Yhwh (2 Sam 7:7). Cf. also Akk *erēnu* ("cedarwood") in Ištar's speech to Gilgamesh (GE 6.12).

395. Ug *ilyn* (*DULAT* 68), from Ug *l'y*, *DULAT* 486 (?); cf. Akk *le'û* (*AHw* 547) and ܠܐܝܐ ("lion," *PSD* 233), but also لأى ("slow, tedious," *DMWA* 853) and לאה ("weak"; PN "Leah," Gen 29:16). Cf. Pardee, "Nouns," 483, and the honorific title of the Hurrian storm-god: *ᵈU-up ḫu-te-tù-a* ("Mightiest Teššup," MSK 74.192a.49 and *passim* (cf. Salvini, *Hourrites*, 2.65).

396. Gibson (*CML* 61), Wyatt (*RTU* 102), and Smith ("Ba'al," 130) read "caravan," but the philological evidence is hardly convincing (Gordon refrains from suggesting a translation, *UT* 19.1010). The translation here identifies Ug *ḫrn* with Arab حوران ("Ḥauran"), an early reference to the highlands of Syria-Lebanon known for their prize orchards and other "supplies." As Raczka (*Land*, 23) observes, "ubiquitous apple orchards have made the apple a symbol of the Golani Druze."

'dbt[397] *bqrb*[398] *hklk*	Supplies into the storerooms of your palace
tblk ġrm[399] *mid ksp*	Let the caves produce much silver for you
gb'm mḥmd[400] *ḫrṣ*	The hills precious gold
yblk udr[401] *ilqṣm*	Let the quarries produce the finest gems for you
wbn bht ksp ḫrṣ	To build a house of silver and gold
bht ṭhrm iqnim	A house of finest lapis-lazuli."[402]

Evidently unwilling to treat palace occupancy as a "divine right,"[403] the Canaanites expend a great deal of energy contemplating who receives what and when and for what reason,[404] even when assessing the claims of "great gods" like "Mightiest Baʿal."[405] Still, no Canaanite scribe[406] ever elevates another deity *over* Baʿal.[407] Such is the persistent power of "the Landlord" (Ug *b'l arṣ*) in Canaanite culture.[408] Like an NFL or NBA

397. Cf. עזבון ("supplies," Ezek 27:12, 14, 16, 19, 22, 24, 33). Coogan (*Canaan*, 101) reads "wagon train" (as a parallel to *ḫrn*, "caravan"), but then later reads *'dbt* as "supplies" (Coogan and Smith, *Canaan*, 132), doubtless to correlate with Smith's "wares" ("Baʿal," 130). Wyatt (*RTU* 102) reads "merchandise."

398. Technically Ug *bqrb*, like בקרב, means "in the midst of," but in the spirit of maintaining the quartermaster imagery, "storerooms" seems appropriate (cf. the צלעות in 1 Kgs 6:5–8; Ezek 41:6–11).

399. *Contra* Gordon's attempt to derive *ġrm* from **ġwr* ("mountain," *UT* 19.1953), N.B. that غار means "cave" (*DMWA* 687), a geological formation for which the Ḫauran plateau is well known.

400. Ug *mḥmd* (*DULAT* 362, 537); cf. מחמד (Isa 64:10; Lam 1:10), the parallel triad in Joel 4:5, מחמד/זהב/כסף ("silver, gold, precious things"), and the PN محمد ("Muḥammad").

401. *UT* 19.94. Wyatt (*RTU* 102) adopts Gordon's definition in order to preserve the "rocks/hills/quarries" triad.

402. *CAT* 1.4.5.1, 10–19. Anat repeats this chorus in lines 29–35, and the narrator follows suit in lines 35–40.

403. Relying heavily on Homeric and Eblaite parallels, Stieglitz ("Ideology," 225–34) posits the existence of a "divine kingship" ideology in second millenium Ugarit, but this ideology does not fully coalesce in the West until the programmatic essay of King James I (*Basilikon Doron*, "Royal Gift"; cf. Fischlin and Fortier, *Basilikon*, 83–176).

404. In Mesopotamia Naram-Sin, king of Agade, lavishes time and money on the (re)building of temples in the cities of Agade and Nippur, while Gudea, king of Lagash, builds no less than 15 "houses" for various deities (Roaf, "Built," 338).

405. David's drawn-out conflict with Saul comes to mind as a parallel (1 Sam 17–25), as does the plight of the long-absent Odysseus attempting to reclaim *his* inheritance (*Od.* 21–22; cf. Barnouw, *Odyssey*, 259–346).

406. Van der Toorn (*Scribal*, 104–05) recognizes that it matters whether scribes "see themselves as guardians of a secret or teachers of the ignorant; whether the writings they study are accessible to all or the preserve of the fortunate few; and whether their authority is based on their knowledge or on their affiliation with those in positions of political power."

407. Ug *'aliyn b'l* (*CAT* 1.3.3.13–14). Based on his reading of Beowulf, Gilgamesh, and the *Odyssey*, Rouland ("Sociological," 90–99) defines "heroism" as a sociological phenomenon. Thamm ("Emotions," 28) lists the major power- and status-identity types on a "hero-antihero" spectrum, and Schein (*Hero*, 69–70) suggests that what makes *mortal* heroes "heroic" is that unlike the gods, they risk something which can be permanently lost—their lives.

408. *CAT* 1.3.1.3–4.

all-star,[409] the "Landlord" receives constant, fawning attention from priestly "fans" and other stakeholders (the ancient equivalents of "referees," "owners," "competitors," and "the media").[410] None of this is extraordinary. The god Marduk displaces his challengers,[411] the hero Gilgamesh triumphs over the "wild man" Enkidu,[412] and the god Osiris constantly clashes with the "wild man" Seth.[413] This polarity applies to Canaanites as well because the principal socioeconomic question—"Who controls the land?"—is too important to leave to chance.[414] From a socioliterary perspective it therefore seems obvious why Canaanite scribes work so hard to make doubly sure that the gods authorize a "house" for the "Landlord" (Ug *b'l arṣ*).[415] Making him obtain a building permit (like Marduk)[416] through "proper channels" (i.e., El's approval; Yam's defeat; survival against Mot) reflects layers of priestly debate, to be sure. Yet even great gods like El recognize that there is no room in the cosmos for two "Landlords."[417]

Less dramatic, yet no less significant are the questions behind the question; viz., What is the value of the land? How is it to be measured? How is value to be assigned to the socioeconomic commodity in which so many invest their entire lives? Conceptualizing these questions within socioreligious polarities, What renders the land "blessed" vs. "cursed?"[418] Several Canaanite myths engage these questions. The Aqhat myth, for example, depicts an Inanna-like figure (Anat) attacking a privileged prince (Aqhat) in much the same way (and for many of the same reasons) that Ba'al attacks

409. NFL=National Football League; NBA=National Basketball Association. Cf. Simmons (*Basketball*, 3–29) and Crepeau (*Football*, 155–70).

410. Smith, *Warriors*, 326–32. One of the most interesting attempts to blur the realms of sports and myth is the 1989 film *Field of Dreams*, based on W. P. Kinsella's 1982 novel, *Shoeless Joe*.

411. *Ee* 4.95–5.64 (cf. above).

412. Wolff, "Heroic," 392–98.

413. Griffiths, *Osiris*, 185–215. Day (*Conflict*, 61) argues that "the divine conflict with the dragon and the sea undergoes a process of demythologization" in Tanak . . . "especially in Genesis 1, but also in other passages." Moreover, he believes that "contrary to a widespread view, Genesis 1 is neither dependent upon, nor polemicizing against the Babylonian *Enūma Elish*. Rather, as elsewhere, the traditions are ultimately Canaanite" (cf. Korpel and Moor, *Adam*, 57–59, 94–101).

414. Guillaume's (*Land*, 109) insistence that all possessions are privatizable *except* land provokes Kletter ("Land," 113) into retorting that such unsupportable claims betray "the crucial place of land tenure in our own ideologies."

415. Douglas, *Purity*, 67–68.

416. *Ee* 5.122–24 (cf. above).

417. *CAT* 1.3.1.3–4 (cf. Toombs, "Ba'al," 618; Gabriel, *Weltordnung*, 382–92). In essence this is the primary *raison d'être* for the production of cosmogonic myth itself (Cross, *Canon*, 80–81). On the motif of "frailty-leading-to-succession" cf. Moore, *Babbler*, 251; *Faith*, 155–59; *Reconciliation*, 139–50.

418. Finley's (*Economy*, 95–122) analysis is socioeconomically seminal, but literarily vacant. Brueggemann's (*Land*, 173–96) is rhetorically brilliant, but mythopoeically vacuous. Dietrich ("Altisrael," 219–36), Kossmann ("Diaspora," 237–58), and Isaac (*Land*, 5–7, 364–72) address some of the thorny problems affecting contemporary attempts to develop a "theology of the land."

Yam.[419] Subduing him through a trusted lieutenant (Yaṭpan),[420] she even follows Ba'al's example and mutilates the corpse:

tšṯḫrṣ[421] *klb ilnm*	She chops as at the heart of a mighty oak
wṯn gprm mn gprh	She cuts the carcass in two . . .[422]

Again, as barbaric as this all seems to postmoderns, it's important to recognize what the ancients feel to be at stake. Should Anat's efforts fail, then the only option left for the land is devastation—what the Hebrew prophets designate as its "mourning":[423]

pr' qẓ yb[l]	The shoots of summer shrivel up
šblt bġlph	The ear of corn in its husk . . .[424]
[ ] bgrn yḫrb	[ ] on the threshing floor dries up . . .[425]
'l bt abh nšrm trḫpn	The vultures encircle her[426] father's house
ybṣr ḥbl diym	A flock of hawks hovering overhead.[427]

The same applies to Mot *vis-à-vis* his conflict with Ba'al:

kḥrr zt	He (Mot) scorches the olive
ybl arṣ wpr 'ṣm	The produce of the earth and the fruit of the trees
yraun aliyn b'l	Mightiest Ba'al fears him.[428]

Even after Mot sucks Ba'al down into his cavernous gullet,[429] however, El refuses to stop believing that some spark of the "Landlord" survives, especially after seeing

419. See Parker, "Aqhat," 49–80; Moor, *ARTU* 224–65; Gibson, *CML* 103–22; and Wright, *Ritual*, 13–17.

420. Ug *tqḥ ytpn mhr št*, "she took Yaṭpan, warrior of the lady" (*CAT* 1.18.4.27). Smith (*Warriors*, 118) suggests that "if Yaṭpan is a 'Sutean warrior' . . . then this portrayal comports with the reputation of Suteans for killings and ambushes."

421. Most (e.g., Wright, *Ritual*, 142) read two terms *tšt* (from *št*, "to set, put") + *ḥrṣ* ("to "cut, slash," *DULAT* 369; *UT* 19.900; cf. חרץ, Exod 11:7; Josh 10:21), but Caquot ("Nouvelle," 100) and Wyatt (*RTU* 291) read *tšṯḫrṣ* as a single word (i.e., as a fem. Št form of *ḥrṣ*).

422. *CAT* 1.19.1.10–11. With Dijkstra and Moor ("Aqhatu," 197) and Wyatt (*RTU* 291), this translation seems to pose the fewest problems (cf. Segal, *Mutilation*, 72–73).

423. Hos 4:3; Isa 33:9. Hayes (*Mourns*, 235) argues that this metaphorical use of אבל ("to mourn") "reflects a state of disaster which has befallen, or is about to befall, the human community and at the same time introduces a contrasting perspective, as the state of the earth itself is held up as a silent witness against the state of its inhabitants" (cf. below).

424. *CAT* 1.19.1.18–19.

425. Waters, *Threshing*, 151–64.

426. The "her" in this poem is Paġit, Dan'el's daughter and Aqhat's sister.

427. *CAT* 1.19.1.30–33.

428. *CAT* 1.5.2.5–6. Pardee (*Ritual*) and Wright (*Ritual*) thoroughly explore the myth-ritual connections in this "great text."

429. "Like a kid sliding down my throat" (*klli bṯbrn qny*, *CAT* 1.6.2.23).

šmm šmn tmṭrn	The heavens rain oil;
nẖlm tlk nbtm	The ravines run with honey.[430]

Socioeconomic Identity

Three motifs find long-term parking in this "literary garage": *gift-giving/bribery*,[431] *bridewealth*,[432] and *slavery*.[433] The first helps shape the Ba'al cycle after Anat's encounter with El; i.e., when the "tomboy goddess"[434] threatens to make El's "grey hairs run with blood" should he refuse to approve the construction of Ba'al's "house."[435] Failing to intimidate him via the "direct approach,"[436] she deftly changes course, praising El for his (a) "eternal wisdom"[437] and (b) willingness to bestow "a life of good fortune."[438] Yet in spite of El's glowing *résumé*, she doggedly insists that

mlkn aliyn b`l	Mightiest Ba'al is our king,
ṯpṭn in d`lnh	Our judge, with none above him.
klnyy qšh[439] *nbln*	All of us must bring a gift to him;
klnyy nbl ksh	All of us must carry his cup.[440]

430. *CAT* 1.6.3.6–7, 12–13; cf. Stern, "Flowing," 554–57; Day, *Yahweh*, 116–18. Mettinger (*Riddle*, 217–22) champions the position most famously argued by Frazer (*Bough*, 183–542); viz., that the ancients believe in and worship deities which "die-and-revive." Despite critiques from Vaux ("Adonis," 33–56), J. Z. Smith ("Gods," 521–27), and M. Smith (*Monotheism*, 104–31), Mettinger still finds the primary evidence persuasive (regardless of how uncritically Frazer argues the case).

431. Cf. Moore, *WealthWatch*, 51–57, 66–70, 82–87, 120–27, 131–35, 144–46, 155–56, 184–88.

432. Termed "bride-price" in an earlier age, this category includes "bridewealth" (payment from groom's family to bride's family) as well as "dowry" (payment from bride's family to bride). Cf. Goody and Tambiah, *Bridewealth*, 14; Westbrook, *Marriage*, 24–25; and Lemos, *Marriage*, 1–19.

433. Moore, *WealthWatch*, 75–89, 132, 140–43, 148–53, 157–59, 175–79, 212–14, 228–30.

434. Walls, *Anat*, 75.

435. *CAT* 1.3.5.1–3.

436. "Overt-vs.-covert" approaches to conflict resolution define the Enlil-Enki, Saul-Jonathan, and Mordecai-Esther polarities (cf. Moore, *Reconciliation*, 87–98).

437. Ug *tḥmk il ḥkm / ḥkmk `m `lm*, "Your decree, O El, is wise; your wisdom everlasting" (*CAT* 1.3.5.38–39; repeated by Lady Athirat to El in 1.4.4.41–42).

438. Ug *ḥyt ḥẓt tḥmk*, "A life of good fortune is your legacy" (*CAT* 1.3.5.39; repeated by Lady Athirat to El in 1.4.4.42–43). Cf. حظ (Lane 1.595; *DMWA* 187; cf. بشر, "good luck," Q 12.19) and Akk *ẖadû balaṭa* ("good life," GE 1.226–33). Torah offers a very different take on "what is good for you" (לטוב לך, Deut 10:13).

439. An OB cognate of this Ug term appears in *Ee* 5.80, where "Anu, Enlil and Ea give him (Marduk) 'gifts' (*qištū*)," a line paralleled in 7.110, "Let the gods bring their 'gifts' (*katrū*, "bribe-gifts") before him (Marduk)."

440. *CAT* 1.3.5.33–34 (cf. Gen 44:2). Lady Athirat later sings the same song to her husband El (*CAT* 1.4.4.43–46).

Having clearly established her loyalties, Anat then retreats with Baʿal to draw up the blueprints for his new "house," financially buttonholing El's wife for support.[441] To prepare this "bribe/gift," Baʿal briefs his chief engineer to

šskn m ʿ mgn[442]	Prepare a gift (for)
rbt aṯrt ym	Lady Athirat-Yam
mǵẓ[443] *qnyt ilm*	An entreaty for the mother of the gods.[444]

Having been entrusted with this brief, the scribe Ilimilku[445] coats it with a thick layer of shellac:

yṣq ksp yšlh ḫrṣ	He casts silver, he pours gold
yṣq ksp lalpm	He melts thousands of silver (ingots)
ḫrṣ yṣqm lrbbt	Ten thousand (ingots) of gold
yṣq ḫym[446] *wtbṯh*	To make a canopy and a bed
kt il dt rbtm	A grand dais of twenty thousand (ingots)
kt il nbt bksp	A great dais adorned with silver
šmrgt bdm ḫrṣ	Overlaid with gold veneer.[447]

Whereas gift-giving-as-political-strategy ("bribery") well characterizes the routines of first millenium Persians[448] and Greeks,[449] second millennium Canaanites are hardly immune to its actuarial potential.[450] Anat's decision to bribe Athirat-Yam, in fact, reflects a well-worn socioeconomic strategy not unlike that reflected in other texts. In Atraḫasis,

441. Whether or not this "gifting" is "bribery" (Wyatt, *RTU* 92; Pardee, "Canonical," 256), Anat's strategy involves much more than just "following protocol" (*contra* Liverani, *Interest*, 211–23; Smith and Pitard, *Baʿal*, 38—yet cf. p. 103!). Anat's behavior toward El rather precisely parallels that of the black-headed people toward Enlil in *Atraḫasis*, a behavior there explicitly called *katrû* ("bribe," *Atr* 1.383; see *CAD* K.32–33; Moore, *WealthWatch*, 46, 82–83). Sowada (*Egypt*, 31) documents the "gift-vs.-bribe" debate among Egyptologists.

442. Ug *mgn* ("gift," *DULAT* 531; *UT* 19.1419); מגן ("gift," Hos 4:18; *HAL* 518); ܡܓܗܢܐ ("that which sets free," from ܓܗܐ, "to be set free, escape," *PSD* 249); مجانى ("free of charge," *DMWA* 894).

443. Gordon (*UT* 19.1958) wonders whether this might be a D participle of *ǵẓy*, "to entreat" (with gifts).

444. *CAT* 1.4.1.21–23. Following Wyatt (*RTU* 91) "mother" seems preferable to "progenitress" (Ginsberg, "Baʿal," 131), "mistress" (Gibson, *CML* 55, n. 6), or "creatress" (*UT* 19.2249; Smith, "Baʿal," 121). Cf. Rahmouni, *Epithets*, 275–77; Day, *Babel*, 79.

445. Ilimilku is the scribe responsible for preserving the Baʿal cycle found in the ruins of Ras Shamra (Ug *ilmlk*, *CAT* 1.6.6.53; cf. Korpel, "Ilimilku," 86–111).

446. Ug *ḫym* (*DULAT* 416; *UT* 19.956); cf. خيمه ("tent, pavilion" *DMWA* 269).

447. *CAT* 1.4.1.26–33. To reaffirm the Judean-Roman alliance, Simon the Hasmonean sends a similarly ostentatious gift to his Roman counterpart (1 Macc 14:18).

448. Cf. Sancisi-Weerdenberg, "Gifts," 129–45; Knoppers, "Economic," 55–56.

449. Cf. MacDowell, "Bribery," 57–78.

450. As Tandy (*Traders*, 141) puts it, "gift-giving networks . . . establish a special collective that can exchange goods . . . unencumbered by community demands."

for example,[451] Enki advises the "black-headed people" to avoid confronting the great god Enlil,[452] encouraging them instead to take the offerings earmarked for their personal gods[453] and reroute them to the door of Enlil's vizier Namtar.[454] When Namtar receives this *katrû* ("bribe/gift")[455] Enki hopes it will motivate him to plead their case to his boss. Whether or not such efforts ultimately succeed, the strategy itself changes little: "If the front door is locked, try the side door." *Translation:* "If the 'manager' is unavailable (Enlil/El), try the 'assistant manager' (Namtar/Athirat-Yam)."

The *bridewealth* motif appears in the Kirta Epic[456] as well as a short text called The Betrothal of Nikkal-Ib.[457] Like the Book of Ruth and the Abraham cycle in Genesis,[458] the Kirta Epic focuses on the socioeconomic challenges associated with "the near extinction of a house."[459] Responding to these challenges, Kirta pursues the hand of the daughter of a neighboring warlord, retreating to a sanctuary near Tyre to petition the "Queen of Heaven" about it:

aṯrt ṣrm	O Athirat of Tyre
wilt ṣdynm	O Goddess of Sidon
hm ḥry bty iqḥ	If I take Ḥuraya into my house
aš ʿrb ġlmt ḥẓry	If I bring the maiden into my dwelling
ṯnh kspm atn	I will donate twice (her weight) in silver[460]

451. *Atr* 1.372–410 (Lambert and Millard, *Atra-Ḫasīs*, 69–71).

452. Enlil is the netherworld lord who attempts to "thin out the human herd" via drought, famine, plague and flood (cf. Black, *Sumer*, 100–125).

453. Di Vito, *Names*, 272–76.

454. Namtar tends to be associated in Akkadian myth with plague and pestilence (Foster, *Muses*, 506–24; Lewis, "First-Born," 333), but the fact that SB *Atrahasis* consistently replaces him with Adad (e.g., SB *Atr* 5:11 // OB *Atr* 2:2:11) probably implies a later adaptation to the expectations of a NW Semitic audience (Lipiński, "Adad," 27–29).

455. *Atr* 1.383 (*CAD* K.33).

456. *CAT* 1.14–16. Cf. Greenstein, "Kirta," 9–48; Gibson, *CML* 82–102; Wyatt, *RTU* 176–243; Moor, *ARTU* 191–223.

457. *CAT* 1.24. Cf. Marcus, "Betrothal," 215–18; Gibson, *CML* 128–29; Wyatt, *RTU* 336–41. Students of this text debate whether it (a) is adapted from a Hurrian original, or (b) is alluded to in *CAT* 1.111.20–22 (cf. Moor, *ARTU* 141).

458. Ruth 1:1–5; Gen 12–22. Cf. Hendel, *Patriarch*, 48–59; Blenkinsopp, *Abraham*, 1–26; Van Seters, *Abraham*, 309–12; Moore, "Ruth," 309–14.

459. Greenstein, "Kirta," 9. Like the Baʿal Cycle, Kirta is also preserved by the scribe Ilimilku (*CAT* 1.16.6.58).

460. Matching a person's weight in precious metals is not uncommon in antiquity. Kim (*Incubation*, 245) cites a Hittite ritual which symbolically assesses the "weight" of a dead king in gold and other precious elements. Achilles refuses to return Hector's body *σ' αὐτὸν χρυσῷ ἐρύσασθαι ἀνώγοι*, "even if a command is issued to you in gold" (Homer, *Il.* 22.351), and a Hebrew poet laments that חר ש לנבלי נחשבו איכה בני ציון היקרים המסלאים בפז, "Zion's precious sons, weighed out in fine gold . . . are now reckoned as earthen jars" (Lam 4:2).

w ṯlṯh ḫrṣm	And three times (her weight) in gold.[461]

Cloaking this petition with economic images, he adds,

tn ly mṯt ḥry	Give me the maiden Ḥuraya
n`mt šbḥ bkrk	The "Naomi"[462] of the family, your firstborn[463]
dkn`m `nt n`mh	Whose charm is like that of Anat
km tsm `ṯtrt tsmh	Whose beauty is like that of Athirat
d`qh ib iqni	Whose pupils are lapis lazuli gemstones
`p`ph sp trml	Set into eyes gleaming like alabaster bowls.[464]

In The Betrothal of Nikkal-Ib the moon-deity Yariḫ asks the "matchmaker" Ḫirḫib[465] to arrange an introduction to the goddess Nikkal (a Canaanite deity cognate to the Sumerian goddess Ningal).[466] But Ḫirḫib balks, suggesting that Yariḫ consider Ba'al's daughter Pidray instead, or should this "make Athtar jealous,"[467] an otherwise unknown goddess named Yabrudemay.[468] Rejecting both options, Yariḫ decides to "freeze his desire"[469] for Nikkal by dispatching to her family a hefty *mhr* ("betrothal-gift"):[470]

461. *CAT* 1.14.4.36–43. "Silver, gold, land, slaves"—this sequence appears three times in Kirta (*CAT* 1.14.1.51–2.3; 3.33–34, and 6.17–18), but Wyatt (*RTU* 201) doubts whether Kirta ever literally fulfills the economic requirements of this vow because "quite apart from Kirta's stupidity in not taking care to fulfill so important a vow, there is the question of the implicit impiety of its making in the first place."

462. Ug *n`m* ("sweetness, charm," *DULAT* 613–15; *UT* 19.1665) has for many readers its most recognizable cognate in the PN נעמי ("Naomi").

463. Greenspahn (*Brothers*, 30) emphasizes that the socioeconomic significance of *primogeniture* cannot be overstated (cf. Moore, *WealthWatch*, 127–35).

464. *CAT* 1.14.6.24–30. The irony, of course, is that this economic imagery comes from a king hitherto suspicious of all economic bids (*CAT* 1.14.1.53–58).

465. Ug *mlk qẓ* (*CAT* 1.24.17; *DULAT* 722). Marsman (*Women*, 98) translates "counsellor for exchange-marriages," but admits this is disputable. Moor (*ARTU* 141) suggests that lines 34–39 are recited at marriage ceremonies during the distribution of *mhr*-gifts.

466. In Sumerian myth Ningal is the consort of the moon-god Nanna (cf. Sjöberg, *Mondgott*; Hall, "Nanna-Suen," 518–34; Bertman, *Mesopotamia*, 122; Dalley, "Legends," 59; Herrmann, *Nikkal*, 14; Marsman, *Women*, 98–99).

467. Ug *yġtr*, here taken (with Caquot, *TO* 394, and Gibson, *CML* 129) as the Gt form of *ġr*; cf. غر (*DMWA* 667).

468. Pidray appears frequently in the Ugaritic texts (Wyatt, *RTU* 71–72), but this is the only known mention of Yabrudemay. Should Ug *pdry* be cognate to بدرى (*bdry*, "cold rain," Lane 166) and Ug *ybrd* cognate to برد (*brd*, "cold, chilly," Lane 184), and should "Pidray's name be meteorological" (Smith and Pitard, *Ba'al*, 120), then it's not unlikely that the PN "Yabrudemay" symbolizes a meteorological phenomenon (cf. ברד, "hail-stones," Isa 32:19).

469. Buchan (*Frozen*, 14) uses this metaphor to describe the moment money changes hands in a business transaction.

470. Ug *mhr* ("brideprice," *DULAT* 536–37); cf. מהר ("Brautgeld," *HAL* 525); ܡܗܪ ("marriage portion or gift from the bridegroom to the bride," *PSD* 256); مهر ("nuptial gift, dowry," Lane 2740).

watn mhrh labh	I will give her betrothal-gift to her father
alp ksp wrbt ḫrṣ	A thousand (pieces) of silver, ten thousand of gold
išlḥ ẓhrm iqnim	I will send jewels of fine lapis-lazuli
atn šdh krmm	I will make her field like a vineyard
šd ddh ḥrnqm	The field of her love like an orchard."[471]

Working on these texts from an anthropological perspective, Tracy Lemos makes a strong case (a) that *bridewealth* payments tend to occur more in tribal/kinship societies than in urban/stratified societies, and (b) that the latter tend to gravitate to the custom of *dowry*, suggesting that "these two sets of changes, rather than being separate phenomena, are intricately related."[472] Applying Lemos' thesis to the story of Dinah in Genesis,[473] Sam Adams finds it exegetically fruitful,[474] and Naomi Steinberg appreciates the way it helps "situate Israelite marriage gifts within the larger social context of ancient Israel" without ignoring "the variation in marriage gifts within a cross-cultural setting."[475]

Given the paucity of textual, historical, and artifactual data, the task of measuring the dynamics of socieconomic institutions like betrothal and marriage can be tricky.[476] Karel van der Toorn thinks that this is (a) because evidential detail from "the West Semitic world (with the exception of Israel and Judah) remains poorly documented," and (b) because "the main source of information is the fourteenth- to twelfth-century texts from Ugarit (Ras Shamra), texts which have little to say about . . . ordinary families."[477]

471. *CAT* 1.24.19–23. Opinion is divided over whether these last two lines are metaphorical.

472. Lemos, *Marriage*, 19 (cf. Braaten, "Land," 135–219; Goody and Tambieh, *Bridewealth*, 1–58). The key verb here in Kirta (*CAT* 1.14.1.14) and Betrothal of Nikkal-Ib (*CAT* 1.24.18) is Ug *trḫ* ("to give bridewealth," *DULAT* 878; *UT* 19.2603; cf. Akk *terḫatu*, "Brautpreis," *AHw* 1348). Fafchamps and Quisumbing ("Marriage," 3224) observe that "one of the main ideas in the economic literature on dowry and bride-price is that these represent prices paid for future services." Lipiński ("מהר," 142–49), however, contends that the relationship between *trḫ* and *mhr* is a blurry one.

473. Gen 34:1–31.

474. Adams, *Economic*, 30–33.

475. Steinberg, *Marriage*, 527.

476. Recognizing this paucity, Lemos cautiously limits herself to the philological and anthropological possibilities (*Marriage*, 38–39), a caution well justified by two OA letters (cited in Kienast, *Eherecht*, 217, 220) where, in an exchange between an Assyrian bride and her parents, the father writes, "When I gave PN (an Assyrian man) to you as your bridegroom I paid out five minas of silver. After PN died you married a 'local man' (*nu-a-um*, 'Anatolian/ barbarian'), and I paid out five minas of silver for the wedding. Yet in your eyes my sons and I are worth nothing, for if my sons and I were worth something to you, I would be held in the same esteem as that bestowed by other daughters." To this complaint the daughter replies, "Write me a positive letter (lit. a "good words tablet," *ṭup-pá-am a-wa-tim dam-qá-tim lá-pí-ta-m*) . . . Extend your love to me! Concern yourselves not with the requests of your employees, but with my request. Send me a letter as soon as possible. Give me your love! If your letter does not come to me soon, I will die!"

477. Van der Toorn, *Family*, 153.

Slavery, of course, is a socioeconomic institution for which there is a surfeit of evidence accompanied by a surfeit of ways to interpret it.[478] For example, when El attempts to pacify Yam with the words, "Ba'al is your 'slave' (*'bd*), O Yam / Ba'al is your 'slave' (*'bd*), O Nahar / The son of Dagan your 'prisoner' (*asr*),"[479] this *'bd/asr* word pair refers to an institution still cloaked in layers of sociohistorical ambiguity.[480] Following the lead of Ignaz Gelb,[481] therefore, Daniel Snell counsels readers engaging this material to be cautious and circumspect.[482]

Socioeconomic Conflict Resolution

When Mot defeats Ba'al this throws the cosmos into a crisis so deep, its impact rivals that depicted in ID/DI and DT.[483] To be sure, one of the reasons Mot succeeds is (a) because El is too old to wear the mantle of "Landlord" (*b'l arṣ*), and (b) his first choice to replace him (Yam) is long dead and gone. But from a socioeconomic perspective, Ba'al's defeat signals the defeat of the economy's Provider,[484] a crisis to which El quickly reacts:[485]

gm[486] *yṣḥ il lrbt aṯrt ym*	Doggedly El cries out to Lady Athirat-Yam,

478. Patterson (*Slavery*, 337) defines "slavery" as a socioeconomic institution in which "slaveholders" use "slaves" to gain "the very direct satisfaction of power over another." Thus, a "slave" is a person who is intentionally and systematically "degraded and reduced to a state of liminality." Snell ("Slavery," 5) recognizes that "the appearance of slaves in literary texts is more limited" than in occasional letters and idealistic lawcodes, but that this hardly diminishes the fact that "the slave is a social type that sometimes has to be dealt with in texts copied for scribal education." Starr ("Slavery," 21) dismisses the existence of "solid evidence for the common view that industry and commerce . . . rest on the backs of slaves," but Chirichigno (*Debt-Slavery*, 344–57), following Gelb ("Serfdom," 195–207) and Dandamaev (*Slavery*, 107) divides Mesopotamian society into three categories: (a) free citizens, (b) semi-free citizens, and (c) chattel slaves.

479. *CAT* 1.2.1.36–37 (discussed above). Olmo Lete and Sanmartín (*DULAT* 139–41) distinguish between *'bd* I ("slave"), and *'bd* II ("servant"), but few find this distinction defensible. Smith (*History*, 137), e.g., argues that "the language of *'bd*, lit. 'slave,'" indicates only "the context of an inferior to a superior" (cf. Ballentine, *Conflict*, 54).

480. Not just contemporary, but ancient writers wrestle with how, exactly, to define slavery. *Atraḫasis*, e.g., identifies several factors associated with the "big problem" of slavery, but never proposes a strategic way to "resolve" it (cf. Snell, "Slavery," 4–21; Perdue, *Wisdom*, 132; Moore, *WealthWatch*, 84).

481. Gelb, "Serfdom," 195–207; "Freedom," 81–92.

482. Snell (*Flight*, 99–120). N. B. that even Torah uses extreme caution when describing the "slavery-redemption" polarity (Exod 3–20; cf. Moore, *WealthWatch*, 148–58).

483. *CAT* 1.4–6. Cf. Hays, *Death*, 122–24 (*pace* Bryce, *Society*, 215).

484. Watson, "Mot," 172–221.

485. Judah experiences a similar crisis when an aged David passive-aggressively resists the choosing of a successor (1 Kgs 1:1–2:10; Moore, *Faith*, 155–59).

486. Gordon (*UT* 11.5) and Sivan (*Grammar*, 179) read *gm* as an example of "adverbial *mem*."

tn aḥd[487] *bbnk amlkn*	"Choose one of your sons, and I will crown him,"
wtʿn rbt atrt ym	To which Lady Athirat-Yam replies,
bl[488] *nmlk ydʿ ylhn*	"Right. Let's crown a wise, educated king."[489]

Sensing something off-kilter in his wife's response (maternal bias? satirical disdain? political fatigue?), El launches a corrective negatively describing the attributes of an "ideal king":

dq anm lyrẓ ʿm[490] *bʿl*	"One feeble in strength cannot run like Baʿal
lyʿdb mrḥ[491] *ʿm bn dgn*	Nor throw the lance like the son of Dagan
ktmsm[492]	While floundering on his knees."[493]

Nevertheless Athirat refuses to change her mind:

blt nmlk ʿṯtr ʿrẓ	"Right. Let's crown Athtar the Prosperous.[494]
ymlk ʿṯtr ʿrẓ	Let Athtar the Prosperous be king!"[495]

Similar tensions arise when Prince Yaṣṣib, Kirta's son by his wife Ḥuray, criticizes his father for what he brashly characterizes as a lack of commitment to social justice,[496]

487. Wyatt (*RTU* 131) reads Ug *aḥd* as an ordinal number ("first"), but to posit Athtar as El's firstborn instead of Yam or Baʿal is problematic, to say the least.

488. The Ug particle *bl* can have both negative and positive connotations (Sivan, *Grammar*, 184–85).

489. *CAT* 1.6.1.43–48. Following Margalit (*Baʿal-Mot*, 143, 145), Marsman (*Ugarit*, 358) reads "someone who knows how to moisten," and Smith ("Baʿal," 153) transliterates as a PN, neither of which make much sense.

490. Ug *ʿm* (lit. "with"; cf. עם). Emerton ("Ugaritic," 441–43) reads a noun ("people") followed by Day ("Inheritance," 81) and Wyatt (*RTU* 132), but Tropper (*Grammatik*, 764) reads "against," and Moor (*Baʿalu*, 203) reads "like, as."

491. Doubtless "lance" is a metaphor for "lightning bolt." Miller and Hayes (*History*, 110) publish a photograph of the famous Louvre frieze depicting Baʿal with a club in one hand ("thunder") and a lance in the other ("lightning").

492. Reading *ktmsm* as an Ug cognate of Akk *kitmusu*, itself a reflexive iteration of *kamāsu* ("to kneel down," *CAD* K.117, 466; cf. Smith, "Baʿal," 154, and Marsman, *Ugarit*, 358).

493. *CAT* 1.6.1.50–52. Cf. Watson, "Poetry," 188.

494. Athirat's choice to replace Baʿal is *ʿṯtr ʿrẓ*, often translated "Athtar the Terrible" (Gibson, *CML* 75), "Athtar the Strong" (Smith, "Baʿal," 154), "Athtar the Luminous" (Craigie, "Athtar," 223), or "Athtar the Brilliant" (Wyatt, *RTU* 132), depending on which derivation of this root seems most appropriate. Moor (*ARTU* 85), however, translates "Athtar the Rich" because (a) he sees a play on the Ugaritic verb *rẓ* ("to compete," *DULAT* 750) a few lines earlier, and (b) observes similar wordplay in Prov 11:16, עריץ // עריש ("awe-inspiring"//"rich").

495. *CAT* 1.6.1.53–55. Trading on the structural parallels between the Canaanite and Vedic traditions, Wyatt (*Mind*, 32) suggests that Athtar represents "both *alter ego* of Yam and Mot *and* substitute for Baʿal."

496. The prophet Malachi voices a similar critique (Mal 3:5), and one of the closest Nevi'im parallels to the Kirta-Yaṣṣib cycle is the David-Absalom cycle (2 Sam 13–15).

even to the point of "prophetically" demanding that his father abdicate the throne. At first glance this critique looks like something straight out of *Amos*:

kġz ġzm tdbr	When bandits pillage, you (Kirta) govern
wġrm ṯṯwy[497]	And rule from [outposts in] the mountains.
šqlt bġlt ydk[498]	You let your hand touch any base thing;
ltdn dn almnt	You do not pursue the widow's case;
lṯpṭ ṯpṭ[499] *qṣr npš*[500]	You do not judge the cause of the wretched,
ltdy ṯšm[501] *ʿl dl*	You do not expel the oppressor of the poor;
lpnk ltšlḥm ytm	You feed neither the orphan in front of you
bʿd kslk almnt	Nor the widow behind you.[502]

Yet careful examination of this "prophecy" shows it to look more like something uttered by the angry prince Absalom than the prophet Amos.[503] The point is moot, however, because as soon as Kirta recovers his health he quickly reestablishes his grip on the throne.[504]

Summary

This brief survey spotlights several truths. *First*, socioeconomic motifs regularly, strategically, and creatively appear in prophetically minded literature recovered from ancient Mesopotamia, Anatolia, and Canaan.[505] Doubtless the same holds true for other,

497. Ug *dbr* may be translated "turn your back" (Gibson, *CML* 102; cf. *DULAT* 263), but D forms of دبر can mean "to govern" (*DMWA* 270), which is a strong parallel to *ṯwy* ("to rule," *DULAT* 938–39).

498. Greenstein ("Kirta," 41) reads "You've let your hand fall to vice." Cf. "I will not set before my eyes any 'base thing'" (Ps 101:3, דבר בליעל; lit. "thing of Belial").

499. N.B. that Absalom repeatedly uses the cognate term שפט ("to judge," 2 Sam 15:4) when making accusations against *his* royal father.

500. Lit. "short of soul"; cf. קצר רוח ("short of spirit," Exod 6:9).

501. Cf. שׂסה/ס (*HAL* 1485); Lambdin, *Loanwords*, 155; Schniedewind, *Hebrew*, 36.

502. *CAT* 1.16.6.43–50. According to Yaṣṣib's *ggn* ("genie," 1.16.6.26; cf. جن, "jinn/daemon," *DMWA* 138), Kirta falls short of the ideal exemplified by Aqhat's father Dan'el, the patriarch who *ydn dn almnt yṯpṭ ṯpṭ ytm*, "judges the widow's cause and tries the orphan's case" (1.17.5.7–8).

503. 2 Sam 15:1–6. As Daube ("Absalom," 317) notes, the ancients are conflicted over what to do with Absalom. Witnessing David do nothing in response to Amnon's violation of Tamar, Absalom ויחר לו מאד, "becomes very angry" (2 Sam 13:21 MT), but OG posits a reason for this anger: viz., because David shows favoritism toward Amnon as the πρωτότοκος ("firstborn"), a socioeconomic rationale Josephus (*A.J.* 7.173) later commends to Hellenistic readers.

504. This parallels David's behavior after the death of Absalom (2 Sam 20:3). Kim (*Kirta*, 211) contends that Yaṣṣib criticizes his father because "Kirta's absence from the throne due to illness coincides with a period of extended drought" (cf. Knoppers, "Kirta," 579).

505. This conclusion parallels that put forward in the previous volume of this series (cf. Moore, *WealthWatch*, 99, 223–24).

neighboring cultures (Egyptian, Hurrian, Persian),[506] but irregardless there seems no reason to presume that the texts surveyed here are in any way "extraordinary" or "exceptional." *Second,* these motifs readily fall into several overlapping categories, including *inheritance/possession, socioeconomic identity,* and *conflict resolution.* Doubtless these are not the only categories to consider, but again, there seems no reason to presume that the categories themselves are "contrived" or "artificial."[507] *Third,* ANE scribes animate their "great texts" with socioeconomic motifs because they feel a "prophetic" need to address—even if only covertly—the "big problems" impacting their lives and the lives of their constituents.[508] Not to recognize this point-of-contact is to segregate this literature from its historical context, and thereby exclude from consideration one of the most important resources for understanding this context.[509] *Fourth,* these socioeconomic motifs reflect issues and concerns profoundly central to the lives of the priesthoods responsible for ritually performing them at regular festivals.[510]

Question: How do the scrolls in Nevi'im address the "big problems" impacting *their* constituents?

506. Cf. Muhs, *Egyptian,* 1–12; Wilhelm, *Hurrians,* 42–51; Waters, *Persia,* 92–113.

507. Freedman ("Motif," 123) contends that "although most critics concentrate primarily on the metaphoric members of language families, it seems obvious that the literal components, in conjunction with the figurative, form a larger unit that may prove more revealing still. And when we combine the literal and the figurative into a single family unit, we emerge with perhaps what is most accurately called the literary 'motif.'"

508. Gruenwald (*Ritual,* 64) observes that "the priesthood is never the poor sector of the population." Thus "the image of a priesthood that is wealthy, greedy, and corrupt runs through the criticism of the prophets."

509. Cline (*Archaeology,* 4) states it simply and clearly: "Leaving aside for the moment the religious significance and the questions of the historical accuracy of the text, there is no question that the Bible is an historical document of seminal importance. . . The use of ancient sources by biblical archaeologists finds its parallel in the practices of Classical archaeologists who study the texts of the people who live in ancient Greece and Italy." For example, "those specializing in the Bronze Age will cautiously use the Homeric texts."

510. Cf. Pongratz-Leisten (*Akītu,* 42–47), and Hopkins (*Highlands,* 195–202). Ro (*Poverty,* 28) suggests that the motivation of lower-ranking priests to take the side of the materially poor" may (a) "derive from the theological rivalry with higher-ranking priests and lower-ranking priests," and/or (b) the "extreme misery of the materially poor offending the conscience of the lower-ranking priests and resonating with the priests' sense of disenfranchisement."

3

Socioeconomic Conflict Motifs in Hebrew Prophetic Texts

INFERTILITY, FAMINE, DISEASE, DEATH—THESE realities generate high levels of anxiety within every culture, ancient or modern.[1] First millenium Hebrews are no exception, but what makes Hebrew literature distinctive is its straightforward, irrepressible, against-the-grain alterity.[2] That is, where the ANE texts surveyed above feature linguistic,[3] literary,[4] anthropological,[5] and mythemical[6] landscapes similar to those in Nevi'im,[7] the ideologies behind them develop within conceptual worlds geared not so much to their *explanation* as their *deification*,[8] each deity a projection of this or that vital concern.[9] The prospect of a transcendent deity personally dealing with these

1. Ps 89:48 reads מי גבר יחיה ולא יראה מות ימלט נפשו מיד שאול, "What man can live and never see death? Whose soul can escape the power of Sheol?" and N.B. that Enlil's weapons against *a-me-lu-te* ("humanity") are *mur-ṣu di-'u šu-ur-pu-u a-sa-ku*, "disease, sickness, plague, pestilence" (*Atr* 4.11′AR).

2. I.e., "otherness" (cf. Hazell, *Alterity*, 38–46; Roberts, *Alterity*, 41–68). Tillich (*Culture*, 38) thinks "the Jewish nation is the nation of time in a sense which cannot be said of any other," even though Assmann's (*Moses*, 2) question is prescient: "Does not every construction of identity by the very same process generate alterity?" Cuffari (*Judenfeindschaft*, 188) thinks the Egyptians in Exodus and the Babylonians in Jeremiah engage in "brutal military measures against the Israelites," but that it is not until Judith, Esther, Daniel, and Maccabees that Hebrew literature begins to engage the problem of anti-semitism.

3. Craigie, "Ugarit," 104–06.

4. Talmon, "Comparative," 320–56.

5. Lemos, *Marriage*, 1–19.

6. Lévi-Strauss, *Anthropology*, 65.

7. Roberts, "Environment," 75–96.

8. Feuerbach (*Essence*, 11) contends that ancient religionists "fancy their . . . ideas to be superhuman," and Jong and Halberstadt (*Death*, 37) characterize this as an example of "projection theory." Snell (*Religions*, 17) thinks that "because the contrast with our own (scientifically informed) views is frequently extreme and surprising, we may find ourselves generalizing about the ancients' experiences, but this is not actually such a good idea because the ancients are mostly not interested in generalizing. They are concerned about the particular god and his or her particular power."

9. Machinist, "Distinctiveness," 420–42; *pace* Saggs, *Divine*, 1–29. According to Hamilton (*Sociology*, 26), Auguste Comte (*Philosophy*, 1–34) views "religion . . . as an attempt to understand and explain reality," but Rav Joseph (*b. Shab.* 83b) argues that the usual Gentile habit is to עשה דמות יראתו

harsh realities via a divine-human alliance based on "covenant loyalty"[10] is evidently too bizarre to imagine,[11] much less embrace.[12] Keenly aware of this polarity, Arthur Ferch cautions readers on one end of the spectrum not to dismiss those on the other, whether (a) those determined to "conceive Israel's religion as radically and wholly discontinuous with its environment," or (b) those determined to "neglect the differences evidenced by the data."[13]

Elijah vs. the Prophets of Ba'al

Conflict between these worldviews, at any rate, reaches a tipping point in ninth-century Israel when the Yahwistic prophet Elijah challenges the נביאי הבעל ("prophets of Ba'al") to a public contest.[14] The prophetic narrator of Kings[15] sets the stage for this

ומניחה בתוך כיסו, "make a likeness of his fear and put it in his bag" (cf. the *kurša*-bag hung in the palace courtyard after Telipinu's "return," Hoffner, *Hittite Myths*, 9b.4).

10. Yhwh עשׂה חסד . . . לאהבי ("expresses steadfast loyalty . . . to those who love me," Deut 5:10). Mendenhall and Herion ("Covenant," 1180) recognize that most ANE treaties/covenants include a "description of norms for future behavior, but whether Heb ברית ("covenant") parallels Ug *brt* ("omen," *DULAT* 238; cf. Akk *bārûtu*) or *brr* ("to be pure/clean," *DULAT* 237) remains uncertain, even in light of the theophoric epithets בעל ברית ("Ba'al of the Covenant," Judg 8:33; 9:4) and אל ברית ("El of the Covenant," Judg 9:46; cf. Mulder, "Berith," 141–44)."

11. *Pace* Frymer-Kensky's (*Goddesses*, 218) depiction of "the partnership (as) so uneven, the human position so precarious, and the human task so enormous," it creates "an almost irresistable attraction to posit intermediary figures, beings lesser than God, but other than human."

12. Oshima (*Poems*, 61) is doubtless correct to argue (*pace* Abusch, "Ghost," 378) that "the (personal) god guides a person's religious conduct with respect to the higher gods," but this hardly rivals the distinctively Hebrew notion of divine-human *covenant*. As the prophet Micah puts it, כל העמים ילכו אישׁ בשׁם אלהיו, "every people walks in the name of its gods" (Mic 4:5). Stanley (*Bible*, 532) observes that "all of the religious systems of the ancient Near East, apart from the more absolutist forms of Yahwism, are polytheistic," yet Beck (*Elia*, 28–29) sees little reason to disagree with those who see "Yhwh-only" faith as a pre-exilic phenomenon. The question for Beck is simply whether it is *henotheistic* (one deity to the exclusion of all others) or *monotheistic* (only one deity in existence). Even the Ethical Decalogue, for example, presumes the existence of אלהים אחרים ("other gods," Exod 20:3). Smith ("Excursus," 344) thus finds it problematic to presume that "the theological intelligibility of a single deity (must) depend on Judean social structure at the end of the seventh century and afterwards."

13. Ferch, "Ugarit," 86. Nolan and Lenski (*Macrosociology*, 172) argue that "regardless of its dominant religion, every advanced agrarian society is much like the rest with respect to its fundamental characteristics. Class, structure, social inequality, the division of labor, the distinctive role of urban populations in the larger society, the cleavage between urban and rural subcultures, the disdain of the governing class for both work and workers, the widespread belief in magic and fatalism, (and) the use of the economic surplus for the benefit of the governing class."

14. 1 Kgs 18:19. Cf. Ben Zvi, "Backgrounds," 125–35; Melugin, "Reconstruction," 63–78; Rusak, "Cults," 29–46; Peckham, *Anecdotes*, 88–169; Wyatt, "Asherah," 99–105; and Moore, *Faith*, 97–102. Whether Elijah is from a village called "Tishbi" (תשׁבי, 1 Kgs 17:1, so OG, Vg, and *A.J.* 8.13.2) or is simply "the inhabitant from the settlers in Gilead" (התשׁבי מתשׁבי גלעד, 1 Kgs 17:1; *Tg. Ps.-J.* reads מתותבי גלעד, "among the settlers of Gilead," a clause in which the *nomen constructus* is not a PN), the Ugaritic texts confirm that his knowledge of Ba'alism is fundamentally accurate.

15. Peterson (*History*, 257–92) speaks of an "Anathothian tradition" of authorship. Reacting to attempts to date Nevi'im late, Floyd ("Historicity," 20) states the obvious; i.e., "the mere fact that the

contest by taking the first words out of the prophet's mouth, molding them into a sharp dagger, and pressing it up to Baʿal's exposed jugular:[16]

חי יהוה	As Yhwh lives,[17]
אלהי ישׂראל	The God of Israel
אשר עמדתי לפניו	Before whom I stand,
אם יהוה השנים האלה	There shall cease for two years[18]
טל ומטר	All "dew and rain,"[19]
כי אם לפי דברי	Except by my word.[20]

Innocuous as this vow now seems, it's difficult to imagine a more powerful assault on the Baʿalist lobby because of the simple fact that Elijah and the prophetic narrator of Kings, like all Mosaic Yahwists,[21] believe "Baʿal" (widely known as "Rainmaker")[22] to be nothing more than a figment of the Canaanite imagination.[23] Baʿal may "triumph" over Yam ("Sea") and Mot ("Death") in festival after religious festival on the Canaanite calendar,[24] but these Yahwists find the claims of the Baʿalist lobby preposterous.[25] On

biblical prophets are literary characters in prophetic books does not necessarily imply that they are fictional figures."

16. Debate is lively, but the present consensus about Kings is that its basic ideology (esp. when compared with Ezra-Chronicles), is "prophetic." Cf. Noth, *Israel*, 13–17, 33–35; von Rad, *Theology*, 1.334–47; Gottwald, *Bible*, 193–94; Kratz, *Komposition*, 14–98; Richter, *History*, 1–7; O'Brien, *History*, 129–73; Walsh, "Elijah," 463–66; Mead, "Elijah," 249–54; and Moore, *Faith*, 97–102.

17. Hosea tells his audience to stop reciting the oath-formula חי יהוה, "As Yhwh lives" (Hos 4:15) because few any longer understand its sacral significance. Oath-taking is very serious business in preliterate cultures (cf. *GKC* 149; Barré, "Treaty," 81–83; Weidner, "Hochverrat," 1–9; Weeks, *Admonition*, 49–50).

18. As Noegel ("Unearthing, 227) puts it, "implicit in a drought is the fear that Baʿal has died." Talmud (*b. Taʿan.* 8b) cites 1 Kgs 17:1 to suggest that rain is not always a blessing, but can also indicate סימון קללה (the "sign of a curse").

19. Canaanite scribes deify these meteorological phenomena (טל ומטר) as Baʿal's "daughters" (*CAT* 1.4.1.17–18; cf. Smith, *Baʿal*, 49, 119; Wyatt, *RTU* 71–72).

20. 1 Kgs 17:1.

21. Hauser and Gregory (*Elijah*, 145) understand that "Elijah and the significance of his struggle against Baʿalism . . . stands in the tradition of Moses" (cf. Bluedorn, *Baʿalism*, 281–82).

22. Following Margalit's (*Aqht*, 259) suggestion, Ug *hrnmy* (*CAT* 1.17.1.19) is likely a neologistic epithet for "rainmaker." Elijah's critique, however, hardly implies that he holds the Baʿal *prophets* responsible for the two-year drought (*contra* Holt, "Jezebel," 96).

23 כי שקר נסכו ולא רוח בם הבל המה מעשה תעתעים בעת פקדתם יאבדו הביש כל צורף מפסל, "Every smith is ashamed of his molten images because they are fakes, devoid of breath, worthless, ridiculous entities which perish at the moment of their visitation" (Jer 10:14–15). Millgram (*Elijah*, 278) sees Kings insisting that Baʿal "is not vanquished by a change of heart on the part of the people," but by "his own weapon: brute force."

24. *CAT* 1.1–6. Connections to the lunar (cultic) calendar sometimes occur in non-mythical Ugaritic texts (cf., e.g., *CAT* 1.87.54; 127.1), yet Gorman (*Ritual*, 13–38) is doubtless correct to posit that the boundary in priestly thinking between ritual reenactment and historical reality is porous.

25. Cf. *CAT* 1.6.1.21, 23, 25, 27, 41–42; Handy, *Pantheon*, 99–102; Herrmann, "Baʿal," 132–39;

the other hand, no self-respecting Ba'alist would ever affirm a tradition so strange as the one in which a Hebrew-Egyptian expatriate from the royal house of Pharaoh treks into the Midianite wilderness to receive marching orders from a desert shrub.[26] Most would rather believe that "Ba'al" is what his name claims him to be—the "husband/lord"[27] responsible for protecting the economy from "invasion," not some shadowy wilderness deity demanding compliance to a "covenant/treaty"[28] requiring obedience to a copious inventory of priestly "commandments."[29]

Yet just as Elijah promises, drought *does* strike the land, and this forces the Israelite king to sit up and take notice.[30] At first glance Kings' presentation of this looks straightforward and direct, yet careful examination of the language here shows it to be surprisingly playful. It is significant, for example, that the narrator structures his memory of this conflict around a single verb, כרת ("to cut"). Where the first mention of Jezebel depicts her as a pampered princess determined to "cut off" (כרת) Yhwh's prophets,[31] the king does everything he can to make sure that none of the palace livestock is "cut off" (כרת).[32] Thus with a single word Kings introduces not only Elijah's detractors, but a twisted value-system in which barnyard animals have more value than human beings.[33]

Anderson, *Monotheism*, 47–62. Bronner (*Elijah*, 8) believes that "it is to Elijah an intuitive truth that Yhwh can brook no rival."

26. Exod 3:4. Morgenstern ("Elohist," 249) argues that a nascent form of Yahwism already exists in the cult presided over by "Jethro, priest of Midian" (Exod 18:1; N.B. the priestly blessing in 18:10–11), but few any longer support this "Midianite hypothesis" (Wyatt, *Mind*, 87–88). So many Israelites abandon Yahwism, however, it takes an actual theophanic encounter for Elijah to trust that he is not the only one left (1 Kgs 19:18; cf. Peckham, "Phoenicia," 79–99). Niebuhr (*Culture*, 60–61) classically explores the larger question of "religion-based-on-historical-revelation" vs. "religion-based-on-numismatic-experience."

27. Ug בעל (*DULAT* 206–09; cf. *HAL* 137–39). Hosea forbids his listeners to call Yhwh בעלי ("my lord/husband," Hos 2:16), and rabbinic teachers covertly preserve this prohibition via the shorthand phrase בית בעל (lit. "house of *Ba'al*") when designating land which, though fertile, is nevertheless off-limits (*b. Mo'ed Qaṭ* 2a-b).

28. Identifying two types of ברית ("covenant")—one of "salt" (Lev 2:13) and one of "sufferings" (Deut 28:69)—Talmud posits that salt gives taste to meat, and יסורין ממקרין כל עונותיו של אדם ("sufferings scour away all of a man's sins," *b. Ber.* 5a).

29. Elijah tells Ahab that עזבכם את מצות יהוה ותלך אחרי הבעלים, "you have abandoned the 'commandments' of Yhwh and gone after the Ba'als" (1 Kgs 18:18).

30. 1 Kgs 18:5. Cf. Thiel, "Ahab," 100–104; Oded, "Ahab," 522–25; and Walsh, *Ahab*, 24–32.

31. Jezebel, daughter of Ethba'al, king of Tyre (1 Kgs 16:31) occupies her days בהרג איזבל את נביאי יהוה/בהכרית ("with the cutting off/killing of Yhwh's prophets," 18:4, 13). Sadly, some readers fail to understand that balanced interpretation ≠ caricature. Just as Inanna is a complex character, e.g., Jezebel cannot simply be "a beautiful and malicious adder coiled upon the throne of a nation" (*pace* Lee, *Payday*, 16; cf. Yee, "Jezebel," 848–49). On the other hand, to portray her only as a courageous heroine fighting against "injustice" is just as simplistically extremist (*pace* Trible, "Strangers," 3–19).

32. 1 Kgs 18:5. Ironically, this is the same verb found in the common construction כרת ברית, "make (lit. 'cut') a covenant" (cf. Day, "Covenants," 91–110).

33. The same contrast of values occurs in Ahab's abusive treatment of Naboth, where securing land for a vegetable garden is treated as something more important than human life (1 Kgs 21:1–16;

Two years later Elijah informs Ahab of Yhwh's decision to end the drought,[34] and this leads to a turn of events eventually contextualizing the Mt. Carmel contest, the goal being to force Israel into facing a single question, "Who is the Rainmaker?"[35] Densely structured, the episode as a whole hangs together like a multi-layered tapestry—*layer one* the conflict between Elijah and Ahab; *layer two* the conflict between Elijah and Israel; *layer three* the conflict between Elijah and the Baʿal prophets; and *layer four* the conflict between Yhwh and Baʿal.[36] Underneath it all rests a prefatory layer about Gideon,[37] the שופט ("judge") renamed "Jerubbaʿal" (ירבעל)[38] for "filing suit" (ריב)[39] against Baʿal.[40] Pushing away a mob trying to lynch his son for tearing down a Baʿalist altar and its accompanying *ašerah*,[41] Gideon's father asks, "Are you here to 'file suit' (ריב) for Baʿal?[42] If Baʿal is God, let him file his own suit" (ריב).[43] Here the prophet Elijah throws down a similar gauntlet: "If Baʿal is God, follow him . . . but if Yhwh is God, follow him."[44]

cf. also 2 Kgs 6:24–7:20 and Moore, *Faith*, 148–52). Hobson (*Technology*, 3–72) eloquently criticizes the thinking responsible for such dehumanization, and Suter ("Christians," 649) makes international application: "The question is whether the labor and resources of the Third World nations should contribute more to the opulence of America's cats and dogs than to the elementary good health of Third World humans." Chaney ("Micah," 158–60) thinks that many, if not most examples of prophetic paronomasia are socioeconomically oriented.

34. אתנה מטר על פני האדמה, "I will give rain upon the face of the land" (1 Kgs 18:1).

35. Cf. Stienstra, *Husband*, 96–100.

36. Other famous Tanak showdowns include the Moses-vs.-Pharaoh (Exod 7–14) and David-vs.-Saul conflicts (1 Sam 17–28). Post-biblical examples are addressed in the essays edited by Mayer and Neil (*Conflict*) and Gort (*Conflict*). Roberts' ("Prophet," 632–44) attention to the implications of "food and drink" in 1 Kgs 18:41 is well taken, but discounts the episode's multilayeredness.

37. גדעון ("Scattergun"; cf. Heb גדע, "to scatter," Zech 11:10, 14).

38. Lit. "Let Baʿal sue." To the question "Why is גדעון renamed ירבעל?" Talmud responds, שעשה מריבה עם הבעל, "because he made a lawsuit against Baʿal," *b. Roš. Haš.* 25a). Levin's ("Baʿal," 206) translation of ירבעל as "Baʿal-Fearer" or "Founded by Baʿal" ignores the prophetic intertextual context (see below), and Bluedorn's (*Baʿalism*, 179) translation ("the Baʿal-fighter") ignores its legal (not to mention satirical) connotations.

39. ריבו באמכם ריבו כי היא לא אשתי ואנכי לא אישה, "File suit against your mother, file suit—for she is not my wife and I am not her husband" (Hos 2:4a).

40. Judg 6–9. Cf. Bluedorn (*Baʿalism*, 182–265) and Kelle (*Hosea*, 289–98). Fishbane (*Interpretation*, 19–22) discusses the multilayeredness of Tanak tradition generally.

41. Judg 6:32. Deut 16:21 reads לא תטע לך אשרה כל עץ, "You shall not plant for yourself any tree as an *ašerah*," so אשרה probably denotes both a cult object as well as a deity. Jezebel is a premier sponsor of the Ašerah cult (1 Kgs 18:19). Ackerman ("Queen," 183) carefully examines the nature of Jezebel's relationship to Ašerah.

42. Heb ריב, "to contend, sue for, dispute, defend" (*HAL* 1141–44).

43. האתם תריבון לבעל אם אתם הושיעון אותו . . . אם אלהים הוא ירב לו (Judg 6:31; repetition of the 2mp pronoun אתם conveys emphasis). Ringgren ("ריב," 474–78) documents the semantic range of ריב, and Trotter ("Lawsuit," 63–74) compares older studies like Ringgren's with newer studies determined to read the term through a redactoral lens.

44. אם יהוה האלהים לכו אחריו ואם הבעל לכו אחריו (1 Kgs 18:21; cf. Beyerlin, "Richterbuch," 27–29). Qur'an poses a similar contrast when Elijah asks, اتدعرن بعلارتذزرناحسنا لخالقين, "Will you invoke Baʿal, yet abandon the best of creators?" (Q 37.125).

Layer One: Elijah vs. Ahab

Layer one begins with a character slur. Ahab brands Elijah a "troubler" (עוכר),[45] a pejorative label used by Jonathan to denigrate his father Saul: "My father is a 'troubler' (עוכר) of the land."[46] The king uses this term to impugn Elijah for doing what prophets are called to do—hold the powerful accountable[47]—but Elijah turns the tables: "I have not made 'trouble' (עכר) for Israel; you and your father's house have!"[48] Tongue-in-cheek, Hermann Gunkel describes this exchange as a "depiction in forceful language of how each party hates the other."[49] Talmud comments that "if it is not good to be partial toward the wicked,[50] then it is certainly not good to show partiality to Ahab."[51]

The prophetic narrator of Kings is similarly frank. No one decides to "walk after the Ba'als," he argues, until or unless one decides to "forsake (עזב) the commandments (מצות)."[52] Behind this contention, of course, stands one of the clearest distinctions between Yahwism and Ba'alism; viz., the simple fact that no known Canaanite text even *alludes* to the central component of Mosaic Yahwism—*covenant*.[53] No archaeologist has ever uncovered a clay tablet preserving Ba'al's מצות ("commandments") or Ašerah's חקות ("statutes"), and of the thousands of Canaanite texts

45. This term appears about a dozen times in Tanak and is primarily associated with (a) the rebellious individual who touches the חרם ("taboo things") and is punished for it in the עמק עכור ("Valley of Trouble," Judg 6:18; 7:24–25; 1 Chr 2:7); (b) King Saul (1 Sam 14:29); and (c) the proverbial saying עכר ביתו בוצע בצע ושׂונא מתנת יחיה, "The one looking to make a 'profit' (lit. 'his cut') 'troubles' his house, but the one who hates bribes will live" (Prov 15:27).

46. 1 Sam 14:29. Edelman (*Saul*, 89) coyly observes that "Achan brings trouble by stealing booty," while "Jonathan claims that Saul has brought trouble by preventing the legitimate taking of booty." One rabbi suggests that the perpetrator in Josh 7 is called עכן ("Achan") because שעיכן עונותיהן של ישראל, "he causes Israel's sins to 'coil up' like a snake" (*b. Sanh* 44b, deriving from Heb עכן, "to coil").

47. Cf. Boadt, *Prophets*, 40; Carlson, *Prophets*, 68; Stiebert, *Shame*, 95. Ahab and Naboth disagree over how to define מחיר ("value/worth," 1 Kgs 21:2). To Naboth, מחיר is a sacred idea rooted in historical tradition about the נחלה אבות ("ancestral inheritance," 21:3). To Ahab it is an expendable commodity generated by the ups and downs of the marketplace. Israelites like Naboth recoil from the argument that נחלה can be bought or sold like ארץ or אדמה ("land, ground"). Where Naboth believes נחלה to be priceless, Ahab believes that anything can be bought.

48. 1 Kgs 18:18. Ahab's father, Omri, founds the dynasty eventually purged by Jehu (2 Kgs 9–10). One of the kings bowing down before Assyrian king Shalmeneser III on the Black Obelisk is *Ia-ú-a mār Ḫumri* ("Jehu, son of Omri"; cf. *ANET* 281).

49. Gunkel, *Elijah*, 18. Ahab treats the prophet Micaiah ben Imlah with the same contempt, telling Jehoshaphat that he "hates" him (שׂנא, 1 Kgs 22:8).

50. שאת פני רשע לא טוב (lit. "to lift up the face of the wicked is not good," *b. Yom.* 87a, citing Prov 18:5).

51. לא טוב לו לאחאב שנשאו לו פנים בעולם הזה (lit. "it was not good for him, for Ahab, when his face was lifted up in this world," b. Yom. 87a).

52. 1 Kgs 18:18. Q 37.125 (cited above) captures the essence of Heb עזב ("abandon, forsake") via the Arab term ذرى ("to scatter, disperse, throw down, winnow").

53. Cf. Cook, Yahwism, 15–45; Moberly, *Yahwism*, 93; Eichrodt, *Theology*, 1.36–69; Koch, "Monotheismus," 9; *contra* Dijkstra, "Moses," 93.

published so far (Ugaritic, Phoenician, Punic),[54] not one of them preserves anything even remotely approximating an "ethical decalogue."[55] Instead, the allusions to "self-mutilation" (התגדד) in this episode rather tellingly reveal what the Ba'al prophets themselves deem vitally important.[56]

Layer Two: Elijah vs. Israel

In *layer two* Elijah changes his tone of voice. He "draws near" (נגשׁ), gathering his "flock" around him like so many lost sheep[57] before voicing another Gideon-esque polarity, "How long will you go on poking around between two opinions?"[58] No one responds to this question, of course,[59] yet this does not stop him from laying down the parameters of the forthcoming contest. Later, after the Ba'alist prayer marathon winds down, he again invites Israel to "draw near" (same word, נגשׁ),[60] and again he receives a vacuous response. The Israelites in attendance simply stare at him as he "repairs" Yhwh's altar.[61]

54. Peckham's (*Phoenicia*, 16) attempt to catalogue Ugaritic as non-Canaanite is not convincing.

55. Exod 20:2–17//Deut 5:6–21. Cf. Philips, *Criminal*, 2–4; Hoffman, "Decalogue," 32–49.

56. 1 Kgs 18:28 (*HAL* 616; cf. Favazza, *Bodies*, 20–42). Schniedewind (*Book*, 116) observes that Gentiles "do not understand his (Yhwh's) legal customs" (משפטים בל ידעום, Ps 147:20) because some habitually "gash themselves" (התגדד) on behalf of the dead (Deut 14:1; cf. Jer 41:5; 47:5). Mendenhall ("Conquest," 76) argues that Hebrew Yahwism is a "radical rejection of Canaanite religious and political ideology (esp. the divine authority underlying the political institutions) and that the Canaanite concept of religion is essentially a phenological cultic celebration of . . . economic concerns."

57. Ackerman (*Elijah*, 265) contends that even though "the Middle Ages do not bequeath a connection between Elijah and pastoral work," the Kings narrator thinks that he "is sent to recapture the heart of his entire nation."

58. עד מתי אתם פסחים על שתי הסעפים, 1 Kgs 18:21 (lit. "for how long will you poke around the two branches"; cf. OG ἰγνύαις, "hamstrings"; Syr ܦܠܓܘܬܐ, "divisions"). *Tg. Ps.-J.* reads עד אמתי אתון פליגין לתרתין פלגון, "How long will you argue (and) promote divisions?" Debate over פסח tends to be animated (cf. OG χωλαίνω, "to be lame, defective"; Syr ܗܓܐ, "to meditate, muse upon"), esp. since the term reappears in 18:26 to describe the activity of the Ba'alists around their altar. Yet the more relevant question here is, "Why does Elijah voice this question *during a time of socioeconomic crisis*?" Not only does it resonate with previous questions put to the prophet about sin and death (from the Sidonian widow and Obadiah), it (a) overtly challenges his listeners to face the twin demons of ambivalence and fatalism crippling the economy as a whole, while (b) trying to pull them away from the *papier-mâché* "solutions" promoted by the Ba'alist lobby (cf. Peterson, "Yahwism," 138–43).

59. For Sweeney (*Kings*, 227) Elijah's question "is clearly rhetorical (because) it points to the futility of attempting to accommodate both sets of gods and demands." Cf. the same conspicuous silence in response to Nehemiah's questions (Neh 5:8; see below).

60. 1 Kgs 18:30.

61. 1 Kgs 18:30. Heb רפא (lit. "heals"); Syr ܬܪܣ ("to nourish, restore"); OG ἰάομαι, (to heal, cure, repair"); Vg *curavit* ("to cure"). Nevi'im often uses הרס to describe "damaged" altars (1 Kgs 19:10, 14; Ezek 13:14; 16:39). Yhwh even commands Gideon to "damage" (הרס) Ba'al's altar (Judg 6:25). N.B. that "Raphael" (רפאל, "God heals") plays a major role in restoring the household economy of Tobit (Tob 3:17; cf. below). Eventually the response on Carmel becomes an obligatory "Okay" (טוב הדבר, lit. "good is the thing," 1 Kgs 18:24).

Layer Three: Elijah vs. the Ba'al Prophets

In *layer three* Elijah turns to the Ba'al prophets, his tone shifting back to that governing his exchange with the king. To fellow Israelites he "draws near" (נגשׁ), but to the prophets of Ba'al he barks out commands like a drill sergeant, his earlier pleas now hardening into sharp invectives: *Choose! Prepare! Call! Don't ignite!* Doubtless it's possible to misconstrue his intentions,[62] but regardless of what they might be the response of these colleagues is to "poke around" (פסח) the altar of their deity.[63] As with all magical ritual, their intention is not to *worship* the "Cloudrider," only *engineer* a response to their liking.[64] Kings is silent about the contents of their incantations, but the Ugaritic ritual texts are quite revealing. In one ritual text, for example, Ba'al's devotees chant:

y b`lm [a]l tdy `z l ṯġrn	Repel the strong one from our gate, O Ba'al
y qrd [l]ḥmytny	The warrior from our walls
ibr y b`l nšqdš	A bull,[65] O Ba'al, we sanctify
mḏr b`l nmlu	A vow, O Ba'al, we fulfull
dkr b`l nšqdš	A ram,[66] O Ba'al, we sanctify
ḥtp b`l nmlu	A ritually slaughtered offering,[67] O Ba'al, we fulfill
`šrt b`l n`šr	A banquet-offering, O Ba'al, we prepare
qdš b`l n`l	To Ba'al's sanctuary we ascend
ntbt bt b`l ntlk	To Ba'al's "house" we trek
w šm` b`l l ṣlt	Please listen, O Ba'al, to (our) plea![68]

62. For Jeremiah there is no possibility of misconstrual when it comes to things Ba'alistic: בנביאי שמרון ראיתי תפלה הנבאו בבעל ויתעו את עמי את ישראל, "In the prophets of Samaria I saw a disgusting thing: they prophesied by Ba'al and led my people Israel astray" (Jer 23:13). In Talmud (*b. Sanh.* 103b) the failure to share one's wealth with the needy "alienates those who are near and draws near those who are distant, causing God's eyes to be averted from the wicked and even cause the Shekinah to rest on the נביאי הבעל" ("prophets of Ba'al").

63. 1 Kgs 18:26 (Gerleman, "פסח," 411–12). N.B. the similar magico-religious behavior in 1 Kgs 22:10–13 (Merkur, "Terrorism," 64–66).

64. Cf. Ug *rkb `rpt* ("cloud rider," *CAT* 1.3.2.40 and *passim*, echoed in Yhwh's title: רכב על עב קל, "rider on a swift cloud" (Isa 19:1). Like many other anthropologists, Goode ("Magic," 172–82) highlights the coercive manipulation associated with homeopathic magic.

65. Earlier the ritual references *alp l mgdl b`l*, "a bull for the tower of Ba'al" (*CAT* 1.119.12), which Miller (*Religion*, 96–97) parallels with Kirta's sacrifice on another *mgdl*-"tower" (*CAT* 1.14.2.20–21). Wagenaar (*Judgement*, 295) associates the *mgdl*-"tower" with the siege-defense mentality (cf. Mic 5:4–5).

66. Ug *dkr* (lit. "male animal," *DULAT* 269); cf. זכר ("male," Gen 1:27; *HAL* 259–60).

67. Ug *ḥtp* (*DULAT* 376). Akk *ḫātapu* "seems to denote a special method for slaughtering animals for ritual purposes" (*CAD* Ḫ.149)

68. *CAT* 1.119.28–34 (Ug *ṣlt* from *ṣly*, "to implore," *DULAT* 783–84); cf. Levine, "Ritual," 467–75; Pardee, *Ritual*, 50–53.

Whatever the wording, the heavenly reaction to this prayer marathon is profound silence—no "sound" (קוֹל), no "answer" (עֹנֶה), no "response" (קֶשֶׁב) of any kind.[69] Charging into this silence, Elijah starts "taunting" (חתל)[70] his colleagues, even to the point of following a discernible sequence; i.e., the more he taunts, the more they "rave" (נבא),[71] and the more they rave, the more they "mutilate themselves" (יתגדד).[72] Elijah also "wonders" about the nature of this silence—is it due to their deity's "meditating" (שׂיח), or "sleeping" (יָשֵׁן),[73] or change in "travel plans" (שִׂיג)?[74]

Layer Four: Yhwh vs. Ba'al

Like the stories of Inanna-vs.-Ereškigal,[75] Marduk-vs.Tiamat,[76] and Ba'al-vs.-Yam,[77] this ANE text engages the problem of *divine conflict*.[78] Should Elijah's prayer go

---

69. 1 Kgs 18:29. The first and last of these terms occur when Gehazai lays Elisha's staff on a dead boy's face and senses neither קוֹל nor קֶשֶׁב (2 Kgs 4:31). Note also the contrast between these three types of "silence" and the three "silences" following Yhwh's overtures to Elijah on Horeb (1 Kgs 19:11–12).

70. Taking into account that the root of חתל is a lexical first-cousin to התל (causative of תלל, "to deceive"), Elijah's strategy looks more than a little intentional. Satire and parody are not uncommon in Nevi'im (Jemielity, *Satire*, 22, 84), nor is the loss of final reduplicated radicals on prefixed stems in Classical Hebrew (*GBH* 82).

71. 1 Kgs 18:29. Heb נבא in the G-passive form (*nipal*) tends to describe the "prophesying" of prophets (1 Sam 10:11), but in the reflexive form (*hitpael*) it denotes uncontrollable "raving" (18:10). Moreover, the Akk cognate appears to denote the "invoking" of the dead in adoption rites at Emar, perhaps referring, in Stökl's opinion, to "some form of ancestor worship" (*Prophecy*, 164).

72. 1 Kgs 18:28 (cf. Favazza, *Bodies*, 20–42). In Talmud גדד occurs in the G form, as in the phrase גוּד אוֹ אֲגוּד, "Cut or I will cut," meaning "Affix a price, or I will" (*b. Bath.* 33a), but in the reflexive form it usually refers to self-mutilation, a practice strictly forbidden by Torah (Deut 14:1). Of interest is the fact that self-flaggelation is still practiced in some quarters (cf. Nakash, "Rituals," 122; Carroll, *Penitente*, 77–88).

73. 1 Kgs 18:27. Jacobson ("Sleeping," 413) suggests that Elijah's reference to Ba'al's sleeping reflects Enlil's desire for sleep (*Atr* 1.72–73), but Jagersma ("יָשֵׁן," 674–76) wonders whether Elijah might be mocking the Canaanite "sleep of death" associated with rituals for the first rainfall (*CAT* 1.3.2.38–40). More likely, Elijah here satirizes the belief of his detractors in the "death-sleep" of Ba'al (*CAT* 1.5.5.5–17), Telipinu (Hoffner, *Hittite Myths*, 2/3.3), or the storm-gods in general (cf. Smith, *Monotheism*, 128).

74. Attempts to link שִׂיג with "defecation" are rare today (cf. *HAL* 1229–30; Rendsburg, "Mock," 414–17). Kings is satirical (Moore, *Babbler*, 122–39), but under the surface lie several questions: What happens to Ba'al after Mot swallows him (*CAT* 1.5.5.1–6.25)? Does he die? Does a hastily created substitute take his place? Does the substitute also die or does Ba'al disappear (like Telipinu)? Lacunae in the recovered Ugaritic tablets presently preclude immediate answers to these questions (cf. Mettinger, *Riddle*, 55–81; Hays, *Death*, 122–23).

75. ID 164–72 (see above).

76. *Ee* 4.101–04 (see above).

77. *CAT* 1.2-1-2 (see above).

78. Peckham (*Phoenicia*, 95) sees here a Yhwh-vs.-Melqart conflict (cf. Gunkel, *Creation*, 3–4; Day, *Conflict*, 1–16; Batto, *Dragon*, 176–84). Ballentine (*Conflict*, 71) contends that divine conflict myths are "produced by authors, redactors and copyists utilizing the conflict *topos* to accomplish ideological work," and further, that "the legitimating ideology developed within combat traditions is employed to promote specific kings." Ideological analyses which ignore the socioeconomic component, however,

unanswered—like those of his colleagues—it becomes very difficult to explain (a) why the story climaxes with a descent of heavenly fire,[79] and (b) why the Mt. Carmel episode headlines that segment of Nevi'im known as הנביאים הראשנים ("Former Prophets").[80] Further, Elijah's decision to douse Yhwh's altar with the precious commodity of *potable water* rather persistently points attention back to the "Rainmaker" question.[81] When the heavenly fire "licks up"[82] not only the flesh and blood of the sacrifice, but the wood, the stones, the soil, and yes, even the *potable water*, it becomes very difficult to deny the likelihood that this text comes from the hand of a writer determined to challenge the populist rhetoric of his day about "rainmaking" and "cloudriding."[83]

Isaiah

Socioeconomic conflict motifs infuse the Isaianic tradition on many levels, but nowhere more cogently than the fourth Servant Song,[84] a signature Isaianic poem unmistakably framed by the socioeconomic motif of "prosperity":[85]

הנה ישׂכיל עבדי	Behold, my servant shall prosper,[86]

are patently deficient.

79. Rofé (*Prophets*, 87) defines Israelite history as "a series of prophetic realizations."

80. Zech 7:12 (cf. Mann, *Prophets*, 295–300). This is not the only time Kings shows Elijah calling down heavenly fire (cf. 2 Kgs 1:10–14), so any decision to excise this climax in the name of "relevancy" seems purely arbitrary (cf. Hobson, *Technology*, 3–71).

81. Cf. ID 225. Baukal ("Hydrotechnics," 63–79) notes that Yhwh uses water to silence Ba'al in three ways: (a) *withdrawal* (three years of drought); (b) *evaporation* (elimination of a large quantity of water on and around the altar; and (c) *precipitation* (eventual descent of rain).

82. לחך (1 Kgs 18:38 // אכל, "to devour").

83. Mann, *Prophets*, 288–92. Miller (*Religion*, 388) contends that this text is "clearly a polemic against Ba'al, the Canaanite storm-god." Qur'an remembers Elijah's vindication on Carmel as initiated by لاموسلين ("the agents," Q 37.123, from وسيلة, "medium, instrument, agent, messenger," *DMWA* 1069), but in Ap-Thomas's opinion ("Elijah," 155), the Mt. Carmel story pursues "a single motive from beginning to end: the bringing of rain, that Yahweh's supremacy might be established in Israel"—a theme to which Saul of Tarsus appeals in his Lycaonian speech (Acts 14:15–17; see below).

84. Isa 52:13–53:12. Cf. Hägglund, *Isaiah*, 35–45; Walton, "Imagery," 734–43; Baltzer, *Isaiah*, 394; Goldingay and Payne, *Isaiah*, 273–335; Hermisson, "Abschied," 209–22; Laato, *Servant*, 16–21; and Whybray, *Prophet*, 2–61. N.B. that the Isaianic "vineyard" allegory (Isa 5:1–7) parallels the Ezekielian "two eagles" parable (Ezek 17:1–10; see below).

85. Cf. שׂכל in Isa 52:13 // צלח in 53:10 and the identical word pair in Josh 1:8 (noted by Paul, *Isaiah*, 399; cf. Watters, *Poetry*, 39–59; Stuart, "Exegesis," 684). Paul (397) sees here (a) a divine declaration; (b) the term עבדי ("my servant"); and (c) the verb נשׂא ("to lift up"), but Oswalt (*Isaiah*, 378) marginalizes the socioeconomic connotations of שׂכל. *Tg. Isa.* repeats צלח in 52.13 *and* 53.10.

86. MT ישׂכיל; OG (συνήσει) and Vg (*intelleget*) connote שׂכל in a way similar to its usage in Daniel (cf. Moore, *Babbler*, 178). Syr ܢܬܡܨܐ ("all-sufficient," *PSD* 287), however, reads it through a lens more sensitive to socioeconomic concerns (cf. 1 Sam 18:15; Jer 10:21; 20:11; Prov 17:8; Ps 41:1). Citing Luther, Westermann (*Isaiah*, 258) marginalizes the socioeconomic connotations of שׂכל, but as Hägglund observes (*Isaiah*, 36), the term "occurs rather frequently in the wisdom tradition with the understanding that the one who has the insight will also be prosperous."

Exalted, high, and lifted up . . .[87]	ירום ונשא וגבה מאד
It is Yhwh's will that he be bruised and injured	ויהוה חפץ דכאו החלי
When you make his soul a guilt offering.[88]	אם תשים אשם נפשו
He will see (his) offspring "prolong (their) days,"[89]	יראה זרע יאריך ימים
And by his hand Yhwh's agenda prospers.[90]	וחפץ יהוה בידו יצלח

Cursory examination of this song shows it to utilize a number of agrarian metaphors sensitive to both *flora* and *fauna*:

He grew up before him like a young shoot,[91]	ויעל כיונק לפניו
Like a root out of dry ground . . .[92]	וכשרש מארץ ציה
All of us stray like sheep	כלנו כצון תעינו
Each choosing our own path . . .[93]	איש לדרכו פנינו
Like a sheep led to slaughter	כשה לטבח יובל
And like a lamb before its shearers is silent	וכרחל לפני גזיה נאלמה
So he opens not his mouth . . .[94]	ולא יפתח פיו

Ultimately, though, "wealth" has the last word:

Driven out from the land of the living,[95]	נגזר מארץ חיים
Punished for the transgression of my people,	מפשע עמי נגע למו
He makes his grave with the wicked,	ויתן את רשעים קברו

87. Isa 52:13. Doubtless these three terms (ירום ונשא וגבה) modify the verb שכל in the previous line to indicate the *scope* of the Servant's "success/prosperity."

88. Cf. the root אשם ("guilt offering") in Jer 2:3 (discussed below); Levine, *Presence*, 9–19; Milgrom, *Cult*, 25–43. On נפש as "soul," cf. Steiner, *Souls*, 68–80.

89. The stock phrase ארך ימים occurs in Deut 11:9; 17:20; 22:7; 32:47; Josh 24:31; Judg 2:7; Job 12:12; Ps 93:5; 143:5; Prov 3:2, 16; 28:16; Lam 5:20; and *passim*.

90. Isa 53:10. Early interpreters read this text from a priestly messianic perspective; e.g., *Tg. Isa.* 53.10 reads "It is the Lord's will to purify and cleanse the remnant of his people that by cleansing their souls of sins they might 'gaze upon the kingdom of their Messiah' (יחזון במלכות משיחהון), procreate sons and daughters, prolong their days, observe the teaching of Yhwh, and 'prosper' (צלח)," using participial phrases much like those found in "Marduk's Fifty Names" (*Ee* 6.124–7.136).

91. MT יונק (lit. "suckling"). OG (παιδίον, "child") and Syr (ܝܠܘܕܐ, "babe") ignore the agrarian image in the parallel line (שרש, "root"), but not Vg (*virgultum*, "sapling"). Cf. the use of יניקה ("shoot") in Ezekiel's "Parable of the Two Eagles" (Ezek 17:4, 22, see below).

92. Isa 53:2a. The stock phrase ארץ ציה occurs in Isa 41:18; Jer 2:6; 51:43; Ezek 19:13; Jos 2:5; Joel 2:20; Ps 63:2; 107:35; and *passim*.

93. Isa 53:6a. Cf. תעיני כשה אבד, "I have strayed like a lost sheep" (Ps 119:176).

94. Isa 53:7. Cf. נאלמתי לא אפתח פי, "I am become dumb; I open not my mouth" (Ps 39:10).

95. The stock epithet ארץ החיים ("land of the living") occurs in Isa 38:11; Jer 11:19; Job 28:13; Ps 27:13; 52:5; 116:9; 142:5. The ID/DI tradition and its successors irrigate the archetypal "lake" buoying up several "boats" leading to what Walton ("Imagery," 734–43) identifies as the "substitute king ritual."

את עשיר במתיו	And his death with the wealthy.[96]

Often downplayed, ignored or dismissed, the socioeconomic significance of this song emerges from the literary interface between the "prosperity" motif and the revolutionary notion of vicarious suffering.[97] This sets it apart from the rest of Nevi'im, to be sure, but Bernd Janowski sees more, arguing that "the Servant's 'success' prophesied by the two framing Yhwh statements" insightfully reflects how "an innocent one bears the guilt of others, perishes by it, but nonetheless achieves success."[98]

Moreover, the *redemption* brought by the Servant to those deservedly suffering for *their* sins occurs only because of the עמל נפשו ("labor of *his* soul"),[99] a development which in turn leads to (a) the Servant's חלק/שלל ("portion/spoil") for this "labor" growing into something רבים ("great"),[100] plus (b) the prospect of every recipient of this "labor" receiving an opportunity to become צדיק ("righteous"):[101]

אחלק לו ברבים	I will allot him a "portion"[102] among the great
ואת עצומים יחלק שלל	As he doles out the spoil of the powerful.[103]

96. Isa 53:8b-9a. MT עשיר, "wealthy" (sg.); 1QIsa[a] עשירים, "wealthy" (pl.); OG πλουσίους, "rich" (pl.); Vg *divitem*, "rich" (sg.); Syr ܥܬܝܪܐ, "rich" (sg.); *Tg. Isa*. 53.9, עתירי, "rich" (pl.). Stock usage of the מות/קבר ("death/grave") word pair occurs elsewhere in Tanak (Gen 23:4, 6, 11, 15; 2 Sam 19:38; cf. Hays, *Covenant*, 48–55). Some readers, struggling to link "the wicked with the rich in a burial site" (Childs, *Isaiah*, 417), emend עשר ("wealthy") to רשע ("wicked"), but Barrick's ("Palestine," 580–88) argument against this emendation remains persuasive, not only for textual/linguistic reasons, but because many contemporary discussions about wealth tend to come housed within structures affected (if not dominated) by simplistic polarities (i.e., "rich" vs. "poor"), even though prophetic, sapiential and even priestly attitudes in Tanak tend not to be simplistic (cf., e.g., the actuarial tables laid out in Torah assessing the relative values of individuals and their possessions according to "tax bracket," ערך נפש, Lev 27:1–34; cf. 2 Kgs 12:5; 23:35; Moore, *Faith*, 248–54).

97. Spieckermann, "Suffering," 1–15.

98. Janowski, "Sins," 70–71.

99. Isa 53:12. To Fitzmyer (*One*, 41), none of this occurs without "the suffering and triumphant עבד יהוה ('Servant of Yhwh')."

100. Similar "compensation" motifs appear in Isa 58:10–11; Joel 2:25; 4:4, 8. Soulen (*Israel*, 110–11) contends that "by restricting the concept of divine economy to God's work as Redeemer, Christians tend to imply that God's work as Consummator is in itself devoid of economy, that is, of God's care and providential management of the households of creation." Against this reductionist approach he challenges readers to "consider the possible Christian significance of an *economy of consummation*."

101. יצדיק צדיק עבדי לרבים, "My servant will make many righteous" (Isa 53:11). Aware of this interface, Tobit employs צדקות ("righteous deeds") as a synonym for ἐλεημοσύναι ("almsgiving," 4Q200.2.6–9; i.e., Tob 4:7–8; cf. below).

102. One of Tanak's most persistent motifs, MT חלק repeats twice in this couplet (cf. the חלק יעקב, "Portion of Jacob," in Jer 10:16; see below). Zechariah predicts a time when ונחל יהוה את יהודה חלקו ("Yhwh will inherit Judah, his 'portion,'" Zech 2:16).

103. Isa 53:12a. Syr reads the twice-repeated verb חלק each time with ܦܠܓ ("to divide in two"), but OG reads αὐτὸς κληρονομήσει πολλοὺς καὶ τῶν ἰσχυρῶν μεριεῖ σκῦλα ("this one will inherit many things and divide the spoil of the mighty") in what appears an obvious attempt to move חלק under the semantic umbrella of "inheritance." Thus the Maccabean question: ποῖον ἔθνος οὐκ ἐκληρονόμησεν βασίλεια καὶ οὐκ ἐκράτησεν τῶν σκύλων αὐτῆς, "What nation has not inherited the kingdom and seized its spoils?" (1 Macc 2:10; cf. Moore, *WealthWatch*, 177).

Isaiah utilizes the "inheritance" and "success/prosperity" motifs to contrast the character of the Creator with his flawed creation, using imaginative wordplay to rework many of the same metaphors utilized in earlier scrolls like Hosea, even though, as Sharon Moughtin-Mumby points out, this in no way implies the existence of a "sustained theme underpinning Isaiah 1–39's sexual and marital metaphorical language":[104]

ואתם קרבו הנה בני ענננה	Come here, you sons of a "cloud-reader,"[105]
זרע מנעף ותזנה	You seed of an adulterer and a prostitute.[106]
על מי תתענגו	Against whom do you so defiantly rebel?[107]
על מי תרחיבו פה	Against whom do you open (your) mouth
תאריכו לשון	And stick out (your) tongue?[108]
הלוא אתם ילדי פשע	Are you not children of transgression,
זרע שקר	A deceitful seed
הנחמים באלים	Taking comfort in gods[109]
תחת כל עץ רענן	Under every green tree,[110]
שחטי ילדים בנחלים	Butchering children in the valleys[111]
תחת סעפי הסלעים	Under the clefts of the rocks?
בחלקי נחל חלקך	Your "portion" lies in areas of the wadi;[112]

104. Moughtin-Mumby, *Isaiah*, 117.

105. Isa 57:3. Heb ענן means "to divine" (Lev 19:26), but the nominal form (ענן) also means "cloud" (*HAL* 811–12), and Jastrow (*DTTM* 1095) identifies ענן-divination as something rooted in cloud observation. The versions offer little help, but Vg *filii auguratricis* ("sons of a diviner") is at least more anthropologically specific than OG υἱοὶ ἄνομοι ("lawless sons"). *Tg. Isa.* 57.3 reads ואתון דמנצבתא אתקרבו הלכא עם דרא דעובדיהון בישין, "Draw near, you who walk with the generation of those who 'support' (lit. 'take their stand with') the business of the wealthy."

106. Ackerman (*Green*, 152) argues that "the predominant image of Isa 57:3–13 is sexual," but Hays (*Covenant*, 360) disagrees.

107. MT ענג. OG ἐντρυφάω ("make sport of"); Vg *ludo* ("to mock"); Syr ܠܚܒ ("to be greedy, indulgent"). In the next chapter Isaiah commends those who forsake their own "pleasure" (ענג, Isa 58:13) to "take pleasure" in Yhwh (ענג, 58:14).

108. Hays (*Covenant*, 360) observes in Isa 5:14 a parallel use of רחב and פה to describe Sheol.

109. Cf. OG οἱ παρακαλοῦντες ἐπὶ τὰ εἴδωλα, "take comfort in idols"; Vg *consolamini in diis*, "take comfort in gods"; Syr ܡܬܒܝܐܝܢ ܒܦܬܟܪܐ, "console yourselves with the idol" (sg.). The versions apparently read נחם ("to comfort"), not חמם ("to become warm"), and אלים as "god(s), not "oaks." Note also that MT prefixes no copula to תחת ("under").

110. Ackerman (*Green*, 165–212).

111. Cf. גיא בן הנם, "valley of the son of Hinnom" in Jer 7:31. Whether this refers to a separate "cult of Moloch," or merely the "chthonic side of Ba'alism" (Spronk, *Afterlife*, 233), Wyatt ("Hell," 176–77) argues persuasively that the practice of child sacrifice in Jerusalem, Moab, and Carthage helps shape later Western notions of hell.

112. Isa 57:6. Translators take many directions with this text, but N.B. the polysemantic wordplay on חלק ("smooth, slippery"/"portion") and נחל ("wadi"/"inheritance") here and in succeeding lines of

הם הם גורלך	They, *they* shall be your lot.[113]
גם להם שפכת נסך	Even though you pour out libations (and)
העלית מנחה	Dedicate food-offerings to them,[114]
העל אלה אנחם	Am I to be appeased by such things . . . ?[115]

Lest there be any question as to who has the power to defeat the forces of infertility, famine, disease, and death, Isaiah poses another Gideon-esque choice:

בזעקך יצילך קבוציך	Let your "pantheon" deliver you when you cry out;[116]
ואת כלם ישא רוח יכח הבל	Let a wind lift them all away (and) a vapor smother them.
והחוסר בי ינחל ארץ	But let those who take refuge in me inherit land[117]
ויירש הר קדשי	And take possession of my holy mountain.[118]

Isaiah responds to a variety of problems habitually recurring whenever bogus barricades and fabricated facades segregate ideology from praxis.[119] Like the young

MT. Cf. OG ἐκείνη σου ἡ μερίς οὗτός σου ὁ κλῆρος, "that is your portion; this is your lot"; Vg *in partibus torrentis pars tua haec est sors tua*, "in parts of the brook is part of your lot"; Syr ܡܢܬܟܝ ܘܝܪܬܘܬܟܝ ܥܡ ܡܢܬܐ ܗܝ، ܕܙܢܝܘܬܐ ܘܪܘܓܙܐ ܥܠܝܗܘܢ, "your portion and your inheritance—it is with the portion of prostitution and anger against them." Lewis (*Cults*, 157) reads בחלקי נחל as "among the dead of the wadi" (reading חלק III, *HAL* 310), but N.B. that Jeremiah uses this term in the epithet חלק יעקב ("Portion of Jacob," Jer 10:16//51:19; see below).

113. Daniel (Dan 12;3, 13) encourages the משׂכלים ("wise," cf. Moore, *Babbler*, 178–79) to wait לגרלך לקץ הימין ("for your lot at the end of days").

114. Some see "cult of the dead" language here (Lewis, *Cults*, 143–58; Kennedy, "Tombs," 47–52; Hays, *Death*, 360) or, more specifically, the מרזח–ritual (McLaughlin, *Marzēaḥ*, 180–83). Hays (*Death*, 360) contends that "cults of the dead continue to be a major preoccupation in the postexilic period," but this hardly precludes the socioeconomic perspective.

115. Isa 57:3–6. MT נחם ("to console, comfort") is supported by Syr (ܒܝܐ in *ethpael*), but OG ὀργίζομαι ("to be angry") and Vg *indignabor* ("to be scornful") allude to the "vengeful" aspect of נחם (cf. Ezek 24:14; Jon 3:9).

116. MT קבוציך, lit. "your assemblage" (NRSV reads "idols"); cf. OG ἐξελέσθωσάν σε ἐν τῇ θλίψει σου τούτους, "let these (things) deliver you in your ordeal"; Vg *liberent te congregati tui*, "let your congregation liberate you"; Syr ܢܦܨܘܢܟܝ ܐܠܗܐ, "let the gods deliver you." Cf. Ug *bpḫr qbṣ*, "in the gathering of the (divine) assembly" (*CAT* 1.15.3.15).

117. Cf. וענוים יירשו ארץ, "the poor will inherit/possess/seize land" (Ps 37:11, no definite article). OG γῆν ("land") becomes τὴν γῆν ("*the* land") in Matt 5:5.

118. Isa 57:13 (Baʿal claims Mt. Zaphon as *bġr nḥlty*, "the rock of my inheritance," *CAT* 1.3.3.27). Childs (*Isaiah*, 471) contends that Yhwh here welcomes all faithful refugees to his holy mountain (Zion), including foreigners and eunuchs (Isa 56:4–7), but use of the נחל/ירש word pair clearly tips the semantic scales in a socioeconomic direction (cf. Watters, *Formula*, 1–38).

119. Barr (*Ideology*, 102) observes that "ideology" can be "a worldview or set of ideas that is so intensely held that factual realities and practical considerations have no power to alter or affect it." Addressing Christians, Moberly ("Prophets," 32) posits that for "a Christian account of 'moral causality' is to be meaningful, it will need explicitly to be inclusive of, and not alternative to, political, economic, and social categories; that is, it is primarily the injustices that characterize public life and social interactions, more than those that characterize private life, which need to be in the forefront of a Christian

man asking, "Who is my neighbor?"[120] Isaiah's readers balk at the holistic criteria necessary for achieving "success":[121]

למה צמנו ולא ראית	Why do we fast and you do not see?
עניגו נפשנו ולא תדע	Why do we humble our souls and you do not know?[122]

Against such hesitation Isaiah challenges readers to reimagine the world from a perspective invested in the likelihood of renewal:

הן ביום צמכם תמצאו חפץ	Look, when you fast, you pursue your own business[123]
וכל עצביכם תנגשׂו	And tyrannize all your debtors . . .[124]
הלא זה צום אבחרהו	Is not *this* the fast I choose—
פתח חרצבות רשע	To loosen the bonds of evil,[125]
התר אגדות מוטה	And undo the thongs of the yoke,
ושלח רצוצים חפשים	To free the mistreated,[126]
וכל מוטה תנתקו	And break apart every yoke?[127]

concern standing in continuity with the prophets."

120. Luke 10:29.

121. Isa 58:1–14 (Schottroff, "Ökonomie," 263–78). N.B. the recurrence of נחל (נחלת יעקב, "inheritance of Jacob") in 58:14 (cf. Deut 32:9), a critical *Leitwort* Smith-Christopher (*Micah*, 83) links "not to property of any kind, but to ancestral property that, according to the Mosaic lawcodes, is an inherent right of possession for families, to be divided among descendants, but always maintained in the family and the tribe."

122. Isa 58:3. Oswalt (*Isaiah*, 498) sees "the prophet engaging in heavy irony here. The people believe they are fasting for one purpose, but in fact, whether they know it or not, they are fasting for an opposing reason."

123. Westermann (*Isaiah*, 335) takes חפץ (lit. "desire") to mean "business" because, to cite Oswalt (*Isaiah*, 498) "the point may be simply to say that their religious exercises are primarily for themselves, primarily to serve those covetous instincts that motivate all our lives far more than we care to admit."

124. Isa 58:3. Cf. Syr ܘܡܨܥܪܝܢ ܐܢܬܘܢ ܦܠܚܘܪܝܟܘܢ ܕܠܘܬܟܘܢ ("you disparage the foreigners right next to you"); OG πάντας τοὺς ὑποχειρίους ("everyone under your control"); Vg *omnes debitores vestros repetitis* ("all your habitual debtors"). Fohrer (*Jesaja* 3.206) explains Vg by emending עצב to עבט. The Aramaic tradition (again) reads the prophetic text through an overtly economic lens: ביום תעניתכון אתון תבעין צורכיכון וכל תקלתכון אתון מקרבין, "On the day you 'humble' yourselves, you list your own needs and all the shekels you invest" (*Tg. Isa.* 58.3).

125. Abernethy (*Isaiah*, 7) agrees with Hoffman ("Zechariah," 169–218) that "the memorial fasts alluded to in Zech 7–8 are the by-product of the fall of Jerusalem," i.e., the "catastrophe in the national memory" which many try to memorialize "through commemorative fasting." If Podella (*Fasten*, 271–72) is right, however (i.e., that these memorial fasts have their origin in the cult of the dead), then Isaiah's discussion of them here, right after Isa 57:3–13, seems more than a little intentional. Cf. Boda ("Fasts," 390–407).

126. The Akk cognate to חפשׁ, *ḫupšu*, denotes marginalized folk considered to be of lower status (*EA* 117:90; 118:23; 125:27; *CAD* P.37–49; cf. Moore, *WealthWatch*, 122–24).

127. Isa 58:6 (cf. אשבר מטהו, "I will break his yoke," Nah 1:13). Linking the socioeconomic oppression here with that condemned in Neh 5:1–4, Schottroff ("Ökonomie," 271) argues that as "large

Pondering this question, the prophet insists that no authentic response can afford to exclude the socioeconomic element:

הלוא פרס לרעב לחמך	Is it not to share your food with the hungry?
ועניים מרודים תביא בית	And bring the homeless poor into your house?[128]

Like the Servant's חלק ("portion"),[129] the "compensation" set aside for those who *appropriately* fast will be ample:

ותפק לרעב נפשך	If you offer your soul to the hungry
ונפש נענה תשׂביע	And gratify the soul of the needy . . . ,
ונחך יהוה תמיד	Yhwh will guide you continually,
והשׂביע בצחצחות נפשך	Gratifying your soul in parched places,
ועצמתיך יחליץ	And strengthening your bones.
והיית כגן רוה	You shall be like an irrigated garden
אשר לא יכזבו מימיו וכמוצא מים	Like a fountain (flowing) with never-ending water.[130]
והרכבתיך על במותי ארץ	I shall let you climb the peaks of the land
והאכלתיך נחלת יעקב	And dine on Jacob's inheritance.[131]

Agrarian motifs help shape the subsection of Isaiah commonly known as the "Isaiah Apocalypse,[132] i.e., that segment where prophetic and sapiential components meld together to form composite configurations often labeled "proto-apocalyptic."[133] This confluence produces a uniquely transformative effect. Previous allusions to

portions of the Jewish underclass slide into debt to their prosperous countrymen," this forces them "to take out loans" which only lead them deeper and deeper into "debt-slavery." The Aramaic tradition clearly recognizes this: הלא דא היא תעניתא דרעינא בהפרדו כנשת רשעא שׂרי קטרי כתבי דין מסטי ופטרו דהון אניסין בני חורין וכל דין מסטי תסלקון, "Is it not the humbling of our wills and the breaking up of the evil accumulated by the officials enslaved by the decrees of the Chief Quibbler and the dismissal of those who force the sons of light to give him everything?" (*Tg. Isa.* 58.6). Jastrow (*DTTM* 806) reads דין מסטי as the derogatory moniker of a specific official, like the הכוהן הרשע ("Wicked Priest") in 1QpHab 1.13.

128. Isa 58:7a. The word pair מרוד//עני appears again in Lam 1:7; 3:19. Gray (*Isaiah*, 84) concludes that the "thrust of this verse is that those rendered homeless by the trauma of exile should now not tolerate homelessness in their midst, even if it means opening their doors to the homeless poor."

129. Isa 53:12.

130. Isa 58:10–11. "Eternal fountain" imagery comes to a head in Ezek 47:1–23 (another passage ending with the *Leitwort* נחל), but cf. also 1QH 16.4–7.

131. Isa 58:14. Cf. חלק יעקב, "Jacob's Portion" (Jer 10:16 // 51:19), and N.B. that the search for Telipinu extends to the "high peaks" (*pár-ga-mu-uš* ḪUR.SAG$^{DIDLI.ḪI.A}$; Beckman, "Telipinu," 152).

132. Isa 24–27. Cf. Coggins, "Isaiah," 328–33; Millar, *Isaiah*, 1–21; Polaski, *Isaiah*, 49–70; Johnson, *Isaiah*, 1–18; Doyle, *Isaiah*, 24–27; Hibbard, *Isaiah*, 19–20.

133. Taylor (*Apocalyptic*, 36) defines "proto-apocalyptic" as "an incipient form of apocalyptic ideas that anticipate what is found in the later apocalypses." On the confluence of prophetic and sapiential "streams" into apocalyptic "lakes," cf. Moore, *Babbler*, 166–79.

"covenant values," for example, break away from historical categories to evolve into something very new, yet very tethered to a creation ideology rooted in ברית עולם ("eternal covenant").[134] Unlike earlier incarnations of ברית, *this* "covenant" transcends the taxonomies of time and space to forecast a prophetic dream only fully realizable on יום יהוה ("Yhwh's Day").[135]

הנה יהוה בוקק הארץ ובולקה	Behold, Yhwh destroys the land[136] and demolishes it,[137]
ועוה פניה והפיץ ישביה	Grinding up its surface and scraping off its inhabitants.
הבוק תבוק הארץ והבוז תבוז	The land is utterly devastated, totally ruined.
אבלה נבלה הארץ אמללה נבלה תבל	It dries up and withers, decimating the economy.[138]
אמללו מרום עם הארץ	The heavens wilt with the land,
והארץ חנפה תחת ישביה	And the land decomposes under its inhabitants.[139]
כי עברו תרות חלפו חק	For they transgress Torah, violate statute,
הפרו ברית עולם	And debase the eternal covenant.[140]
על כן אלה אכלה ארץ	Therefore a curse devours the land,
ויאשמו ישבי בה	And its inhabitants pay for their crimes.[141]

134. Isa 24:5 (cf. Gen 17:7). Smith ("Crux," 242) argues that the first Servant Song (Isa 42:1–7) "hearkens back to the old dynastic promise in order to present the new picture of Israel's place before the nations." For Smith, "the obvious phonetic resemblance between ברית עולם and ברית עם" suggests a socioliterary strategy designed to "play on the memory of the Davidic covenant theology."

135. Isa 13:9. For Petersen ("Twelve," 3–10), "Yhwh's Day" is the only motif consistently found throughout the Book of the Twelve. Cf. Schwesig, *Tag-JHWHs*, 20–44; Beck, *Tag-JHWHs*, 70–139; and Moore, *Babbler*, 56.

136. For Smend ("Anmerkungen," 166), Oort ("Jezaja," 175), and Watts (*Isaiah*, 316–17), ארץ likely refers to "land," not "earth," but for socioeconomic, not ethnocentric reasons (*pace* Polaski, *Isaiah*, 96).

137. This no-holds-barred description obviously looks less like the "mourning of the land" metaphor (אבל, Joel 1:10), and more like the desolate descriptions in texts like ID/DI and DT (cf. above).

138. OG οἰκουμένη, translating MT תבל.

139. Presuming a complex macroliterary understanding of "metaphor," Doyle (*Apocalypse*, 154) perceives this opening section of the Isaiah Apocalypse to be comprised of "three rather distinct isotopes: the divine, the enemy/hostility, and the earthly/human reaction."

140. Responding to attempts to identify ברית עולם with the Noachic (e.g., Mason, "Covenant," 177–98), Abrahamic, and Mosaic covenants, Polaski (*Isaiah*, 116–17) concludes that ברית עולם most likely denotes "a Deuteronomic covenant made cosmic and perpetually valid." In light of Knoppers' ("Economic," 70) argument that Chronicles transforms ברית in 1 Kgs 5:12 (cast as a kinship relationship between brothers) into a patron-client relationship resembling "an asymmetrical system of transnational economic exchange," it seems more than appropriate to note that ברית עולם is part of a trajectory which includes the ברית ראשנים ("ancestral covenant," CD 1.4; 6.2; 4Q266.2.1.9) and ברית (ל)אבות ("patriarchal covenant," CD 8.18; 19.31; 1Q28b 2.1; 1QM 14.8), which in turn encourages Qumran covenanters to imagine participation in an "eternal covenant" (ברית לעולם, CD 3.4).

141. Isa 24:1, 3–6 (excerpted). Kaiser (*Isaiah 13–39*, 182) and Polaski (*Isaiah*, 106) attribute the

Like Hosea and Jeremiah, Isaiah is careful to preserve the link between literary imagination and socioeconomic reality:

והיה כעם ככהן	As with layman,[142] so with priest[143]
כעבד כאדניו	As with slave, so with master
כשפחה כגברתה	As with maid, so with mistress
כקונה כמוכר	As with buyer, so with seller
כמלוה כלוה	As with lender, so with borrower
כנושה כאשר נושה בו	As with creditor, so with debtor.[144]

Summary: Even as Torah imagines socioeconomic relief for land and people through regularly scheduled שנות היבל ("Jubilee Years"),[145] Isaiah envisions a great and glorious יום ("day") when "all ranks and classes fare alike."[146]

Jeremiah

Like DI with ID, the Jeremiah scroll methodically adjusts the semantic bandwidths of the socioeconomic metaphors inherited from older scrolls in Nevi'im, resituating them under rubrics like *profitability*, *prosperity*, *slavery*, *relational alliance*, and *inheritance*.[147] Like Hosea, for example, Jeremiah fearlessly uses graphic sexual imagery to describe the love of the divine "husband" for his human "bride,"[148] drawing its deepest understanding of this "love" from the memory banks of Torah:

loss of viticulture to divine wrath and human confusion, but do not attend to the deeper (i.e., mythopoeic) dimension of this loss (cf. Milgrom, *Cult*, 1–12).

142. Lit. "people." *Tg. Isa.* 24.2 reads חילונאה, "outsider, layman" (Aram חול III, "that which stands outside the sanctuary," *DTTM* 433).

143. Working with Lenski's (*Power*, 86–88) notion of "status inconsistency," Ro (*Poverty*, 27) cautions that the "merits and demerits of priestly contributions . . . need to be examined more precisely" because "the priests are often unsuccessful in realizing the ideals they profess and contribute to the status quo of inequality by legitimizing and supporting the ruling class."

144. Isa 24:2. Morse (*Isaiah*, 148) interprets this to mean that "God's calamitous judgment will not discriminate. Accountability will put us all in the same boat. Not even the most powerful will escape."

145. Lev 25:11. North (*Jubilee*, 198, 45) sees "no internal textual reason why the Jubilee may not be of very great antiquity," even though "the Bible contains no evidence of the historical observance of the Jubilee year. Lemche ("Jubilee," 38–59), however, limits everything associated with יובל to the minds of disenfranchised Jews anxious to resettle Palestine.

146. Alexander, *Isaiah*, 405 (cf. Lev 25:40). Herms (*Apocalypse*, 249) underlines the fact that early respondents to Isaiah (e.g., *Tg. Isaiah*) tend to "nuance the text so as to highlight the issues of repatriation of the land and restoration of wealth and prosperity."

147. Cf. Weider, *Ehemetaphorik*, 205; and Lalleman-de Winkel, *Jeremiah*, 231–32. Kessler (*Statt*, 22) sees metaphorical language as a problem whenever it obscures socioeconomic reality; so also do some of the earliest rabbinic readers—e.g. פרח ("blossom") becomes ממון ("mammon/wealth," *Tg. Isa.* 5.24), and צו ("vanity") becomes ממון דשקר ("deceptive mammon/wealth," *Tg. Hos.* 5.11).

148. Moughtin-Mumby, *Jeremiah*, 80–116. As Thompson (*Jeremiah*, 81–85) makes clear, this is not the only parallel between Hosea and Jeremiah. In fact, Lundbom (*Prophets*, 125) calls Hosea

I remember the loyalty[149] of your youth,	זכרתי לך חסד נעוריך
Your love as a veiled bride,[150]	אהבת כלולתיך
How you followed me through the desert[151]	לכתך אחרי במדבר
Through an unseminated land . . .[152]	בארץ לא זרועה
No one asks, "Where is Yhwh,	ולא אמרו איה יהוה
Who brings us up from the land of Egypt,	המעלה אתנו מארץ מצרים
Who leads us through the wilderness[153]	המוליך אתנו במדבר
Through a desolate,[154] pockmarked land,[155]	בארץ ערבה ושוחה
Through a drought-stricken, deadly land,[156]	בארץ ציה וצלמות
Through a land none can *cross*,	בארץ לא עבר בה איש
Much less *inhabit*?"[157]	ולא ישב אדם שם

Into this metaphorical stew he injects a few drops of agrarian seasoning:

Israel is holy to Yhwh	קדש ישׂראל ליהוה

"Jeremiah's predecessor."

149. Jer 2:2. MT חסד. OG (ἔλεος), Vg (*miseror*), and Syr (ܚܣܕܐ) all emphasize the "merciful" dimension of חסד (*HAL* 323b), even though the root notion has to do with "joint obligation between relatives, friends, host and guest, master and servant; closeness, solidarity, loyalty" (*HAL* 323a). Glueck (*Hesed*, 3), Sakenfeld (*Hesed*, 45–82), and Clark (*Hesed*, 256–68) each address a different aspect of this "joint obligation." N.B. that for Jeremiah the polar opposite of חסד ("loyalty") is טמא ("defilement," Jer 2:2, 7).

150. MT כלולות likely derives from כלל, "to veil" (cf. Akk *kulūlu*; e.g., *bēlet-ilī la tašmûni tuk-tal-li-la panīša*, "The divine lady did not listen (for) she veiled her face," *CAD* K.518). Jauss (*Liebe*) publishes an encyclopedic study of ANE/Hebraic "love."

151. Gravitating to agrarian language like that found in DT (Hoffner, *Hittite Myths*, 2a.2–3), Jeremiah poetically describes "wilderness life": על ההרים אשׂה בכי ונהי ועל נאות מדבר קינה כי נצתו מבלי איש עבר ולא שׁמעו קול מקנה מעוף השמים . . . נדדו, "Take up weeping and wailing for the mountains and a dirge for the pastures of the wilderness, for they are so laid waste that no one can pass through, for the lowing of cattle is no longer heard and the birds of the sky . . . have flown away" (Jer 9:9).

152. Jer 2:2. MT זרוע (G pass. ptc.); Syr ܡܙܕܪܥ ("seminated," reflexive ptc. of ܙܪܥ, "to seminate"); Vg *in terra quae non seminatur* ("in a land which is not seminated"). Braaten ("Twelve," 111) sees זרוע as a major motif in the *Twelve*: "What does God sow? On the one hand God sows judgment on a people who violate their neighbor and God's land through bloodshed and whoredom. On the other hand, God promises to act for the sake of the created order and reverse this judgment and sow salvation for God's people, land, and even the animals."

153. Where other cultures revere entities deifying land and possessions, the Hebrews (from עבר, "to wander") worship a deity more interested in loyalty than land: והארץ לא תמכר לצמתת כי לי הארץ כי גרים ותושבים עמדי, "The land is not subject to 'final sale' for the land is mine; you are resident aliens settling 'alongside me'" (עמדי, Lev 25:23).

154. Heb ערבה ("desert, steppe"); Syr ܚܪܒܐ ("desolate"); غزب ("to be absent, separated, banished," *DMWA* 668; cf. PN "Arabia").

155. Lit. "land of desert and pit."

156. Lit. "land of drought and shadow of Mot (death)"; cf. צלמות ("shadow of death") in Ps 23:4.

157. Jer 2:6. On the sequence עבר → ישב ("wander" → "inhabit") cf. Moore, *Babbler*, 205–08.

ראשית תבואתה	The finest of his produce.[158]
כל אכליו יאשמו	All who devour it are guilty[159]
רעה תבא אליהם	(as) evil enters into them . . .[160]
ואביא אתכם אל ארץ הכרמל	I brought you into a land of orchards[161]
לאכל פריה וטובה	To devour[162] its fruit[163] and resources.
ותבאו ותטמאו את ארצי	But you wastefully defiled[164] my land
ונחלתי שׂמתם לתועבה	Twisting my inheritance into an abomination.[165]
עזבתי את ביתי	I have forsaken my house,
נטשתי את נחלתי	I have laid fallow my inheritance.[166]

158. Jer 2:3; lit. "the first of his '(forth)coming'" (תבואה, from בוא, "to go/come," 2:3d). Syr ܪܫ ܚܠܠܬܗ ("first of his seedlings"); OG ἀρχὴ γενημάτων αὐτοῦ ("beginning of his harvest"); Vg *primitiae frugum eius* ("beginning of his crops"). Cf. ארץ עבור // ארץ תבואה in Judg 5:12, Akk *ebūru*, "harvest/crop" (*CAD* E.16–20), and the repeated Torah epithet מעשׂר תבואתך, "tithe of your produce" (Deut 14:28, 26:12). Sensitive to socioeconomic concerns, *Tg. Jer.* 2.3 reads קדשא אנון בית ישׂראל קדם יוי על בזיהון כדימע ארמות עללא, "Holy is the house of Israel's annual payroll before Yhwh with regard to the proportioning of the wave-offering revenue."

159. Contra Milgrom (*Cult*, 25–43), Levine (*Presence*, 9–19) argues that אשם probably originates as an economic offering of silver or its equivalent.

160. Jer 2:3. N.B. that evil does not come "upon" (על, *pace* OG ἐπ' αὐτούς), but "into" (אל).

161. MT כרמל = (a) "orchard"; and (b) the PN "Carmel."

162. In Jer 2:7 Israel "eats" what Yhwh gives, but in 2:3 Yhwh condemns those guilty of "devouring" (אכל) Israel. Of all the prophets, Joel assigns the greatest strategic importance to this verb (Joel 1:4, 19–20; 2:3, 5, 25–26).

163. Embracing the agrarian presumptions of Métral ("Risk," 123–44) Guillaume ("Strategies," 141–42) postulates that the ברוך-"blessing" Yhwh "commands" (צוה) over the land in the sixth year of the sabbatical cycle (Lev 25:21–22) is a "theological device indicating that no taxes are raised on the produce of the sixth year in order not to deplete the reserves that have to last two years and to ensure that all surpluses are stored locally," and further, that the whole procedure is designed to ensure that "the local population that misses a harvest can survive and feed the new immigrants (incl. all the Persian soldiers on perennial bivouac) during the five to six months between the sowing time and the harvest of the ninth year."

164. MT טמא ("to defile"); OG μιαίνω ("to stain, defile"); Syr ܛܡܐ ("to defile"); Vg *contaminastis* ("contaminate"). Douglas (*Purity*, 1–41) elucidates the "purity-defilement" polarity from an anthropological perspective.

165. Jer 2:7 (MT תועבה). The Temple Sermon (7:9–10) lists the following תועבות ("abominations") as inherently responsible for damaging the economy: גנב ("theft"), רצח ("murder"), נאף ("adultery"), השבע לשקר ("swearing falsely"), and קטר לבעל ("sacrificing to Ba'al"). Later Yhwh explains why his judgment of Jerusalem cannot reasonably be labeled "unexpected": אשלח אליכם את כל עבדי הנביאים השכם ושלח לאמר אל נא תעשׂו את דבר התעבה הזות אשר שׂנאתי, "I persistently sent to you my servants the prophets, saying, 'Please do not do this תעבה ("abominable thing") which I hate,'" 44:4). MT נחלה finds a cognate echo in Nur-Sin's warning to Zimri-Lim about a priesthood plotting to seize his *niḫlatum* ("inheritance," Nissinen, *Prophets*, 1.4, see above), and N.B. that the "three traps of Belial" in early Judaism are זנות ("prostitution"), הון ("wealth"), and טמא ("defilement"; CD 4.17–18).

166. Jer 12:7. MT נטשׁ often appears in parallel with עזב to convey "waste" or "abandonment," but in this context the better choice is "fallowness" (cf. Exod 23:11).

Concerned about the way Judah so blithely ignores its covenant promises, Jeremiah marshals these images to alert readers to the simple fact that religious decisions have socioeconomic consequences. Yhwh does not abandon *his* covenant promises, but he *will* allow his delinquent partners to abandon theirs . . . and let them correspondingly "reap what they sow."[167]

Of all the scrolls in Nevi'im, Jeremiah is most prone to conveying this "bottom line" mentality via "ledger language"; i.e., that pragmatic, "profit-loss" shorthand accountants use to warn their clients about the dangers of debt.[168] For example,

הכהנים לא אמרו איה יהוה	The priests do not say, "Where is Yhwh?"
תפשׂי התורה לא ידעוני	The "torah-handlers" know nothing of me,[169]
והרעים פשׁעו בי	The shepherds rebel against me,
והנביאים נבאו בבעל	And the prophets prophesy by Ba'al,[170]
ואחרי לא יועלו הלכו	Pursuing things which yield no profit.[171]
לכן עד אריב אתכם	Therefore I file suit[172] against you . . .
ואת בני בניכם אריב	And I file suit against your grandchildren . . .[173]
ההמיר גוי אלהים	Does a nation exchange[174] (its) gods
והמה לא אלהים	For counterfeits?[175]

167. Job 4:8; Deut 27–28 (cf. Linafelt, *Bible*, 83; Flusser, *Judaism*, 11–14).

168. Chirichigno (*Debt-Slavery*, 140) observes that "the existence of debt-slaves and landless people may be attributed on the one hand to the burden of taxation, and on the other to the growing monopoly the rich landholding elite hold over resources." Cf. Chaney ("Micah," 148–49).

169. In v. 3 Yhwh's alliance with Israel is so close, it's unnecessary for Jeremiah to ask his whereabouts, but in v. 8 his priestly colleagues are put on notice (Num 27:21; 2 Kgs 22:13; cf. Ps 27:4).

170. Hosea mentions Ba'al(ism) 3 times, but Jeremiah triples that number.

171. Jer 2:8. Isaiah uses יעל to explain a sober theological tenet: אני אגיד צדקתך ואת מעשׂיך ולא יועילוך, "I will tell of your righteousness and your works—how they yield you no profit" (Isa 57:12). For Ben Zvi ("Successful," 27–50), economic power is the strongest incentive for pursuing profit, something impossible to achieve apart from חכמה ("wisdom").

172. Like Hosea and Dtr (who includes the story of ירבעל, "Jerubba`al," in Judg 6:32), Jeremiah gravitates to the legal term ריב/ירב ("to sue"/"lawsuit"). Whereas Dtr focuses on the ריב ("lawsuit") between Yhwh and Ba'al, Jeremiah broadens its parameters to "sue the nations" not only for their sin (Jer 25:31), but to release Judah from slavery (50:34). Even when Jeremiah struggles with his call he sardonically calls himself the "lawsuit man" (15:10, MT איש ריב; cf. Syr ܓܒܪܐ ܕܝܢܐ, "judgement man"; OG *ἄνδρα δικαζόμενον*, "contentious man"; Vg *virum rixae*, "man of strife").

173. Jer 2:9. Noting the repeated use of ריב in Hosea and Jeremiah, Braaten ("Twelve," 108) parallels Jeremiah's "call to participate in a legal action" with "Isaiah's appeal to the people to render judgment against the 'vineyard' (Isa 5:1–7)."

174. MT מור; OG *ἀλλάσσω* ("to give in exchange, barter"); Syr ܡܚܠܦ ("to exchange, barter"; cf. the epithet ܡܥܘܬܐ ܡܚܠܦ, "money-changers," *PSD* 144).

175. Should anyone ask, Jeremiah later adds, they will hear the nations lament, אך שׁקר נחלו אבותינו הבל ואין בם מועיל, "Our fathers have surely passed down to us worthless, unprofitable lies as our 'inheritance'" (Jer 16:19). *Tg. Jer.* 2.11 applies this directly to the economy: הא עממיא לא שׁבקו פלחן טעותא ואנון טעון דלית בהון צרוך, "Do Gentiles ever forsake the service of idols and the annual income

ועמי המיר כבודו	Why, then, do my people exchange their wealth[176]
בלוא יועיל	For things which yield no profit?[177]

When *everything* is for sale it can be tempting to believe that "newer" and "bigger" are automatically "better"—never mind "profitable," "beneficial," or "equitable."[178] Watching this ideology infect the thinking of his friends and family makes Jeremiah weep, to be sure,[179] but it hardly surprises him, not after years of watching them bow down to pillars of stone and stakes of wood.[180]

Alongside "profitability" Jeremiah parodies Judah's perceptions about "prosperity":[181]

ואיה אלהיך אשר עשית לך	Where are your gods which you make for yourself?
יקומו אם יושיעוך בעת רעתך	Let *them* rise up and save you in your time of distress.
כי מספר עריך היו אלהיך יהודה	O Judah! You have as many gods as you do villages![182]

Then he *really* "takes off the gloves":

they garner from grapevine production?"

176. Heb כבוד can, when context warrants, mean "wealth" (cf. Gen 31:1; Isa 10:3; 61:6).

177. Jer 2:11. Mentioning Jerubba`al (Gideon) by name, Samuel chides Israel for demanding a king, validating his message by calling down a rainstorm at קציר חטים ("wheat harvest") and warning his audience to stop pursuing התהו אשר לא יועילו ("useless things which yield no profit," 1 Sam 12:11–21).

178. Duhigg (*Productivity*, 6) insists that "productivity isn't about working more or sweating harder . . . Rather the difference between being merely busy and genuinely productive is about taking control of how we think and making better choices—instead of simply reacting to life's constant demands."

179. Jer 8:23; 48:32. Cf. 2:5, מה מצאו אבותיכם בי עבל כי רחקו מעלי וילכו אחרי ההבל, "What evil did your fathers find in me that they would distance themselves from me and pursue worthlessness?"

180. Jer 2:27; 3:9. Lundbom (*Jeremiah*, 285) suggests that Jeremiah's decision to connect "tree" with "father" and "stone" with "mother" intentionally reverses the usual association (tree = Ašerah; stone = Ba'al), probably to make the Hebrew worshipers of these objects look *especially* "stupid."

181. Philo (*Vita Mosis* 1.30–31) posits that "men in general, even if the slightest breeze of prosperity only blows their way for a moment, become puffed up and give themselves great airs, becoming insolent to all those in a lower condition than themselves, and calling them dregs of the earth, and annoyances, and sources of trouble, and burdens of the earth, and all sorts of names of that kind, as if they had been thoroughly able to establish the undeviating character of their prosperity on a solid foundation, though very likely they will not remain in the same condition even till tomorrow, for there is nothing more inconstant than fortune, which tosses human affairs up and down like dice."

182. Jer 2:28. Mastnjak (*Deuteronomy*, 225) links the question in Jer 2:28 with those in 2:6, 2:8, and Deut 32:37–38, presuming the standard Wellhausenian view that the prophetic texts in Jeremiah influence Torah (not *vice versa*).

You shall be treated as contemptuously[183] in Egypt[184]	גם ממצרים תבושי
As you were in Assyria.	כאשר בושת מאשור
For from there you shall be marched out	גם מאת זה תצאי
With your hands on your head.	וידיך על ראשך
For Yhwh rejects those in whom you trust	כי מאס יהוה במבטחיך
And you will not share in their "prosperity."[185]	ולא תצליחי להם

This critical spirit sets the tone for much of the material in JL:[186]

You are vindicated, O Yhwh, when I file suit against you;[187]	צדיק אתה יהוה כי אריב אליך
Only let me argue before you my case:[188]	אך משפטים אדבר אותך
Why does the way of the wicked prosper?[189]	מדוע דרך רשעים צלחה
Why do the most contemptuous[190] thrive?	שלו כל בגדי בגד
You plant them; they take root; they even bear fruit.[191]	נטעתם גם שרשו ילכו גם עשו פרי
You are near to their mouths, but far from their hearts.[192]	קרוב אתה בפיהם ורחוק מכליותהם

183. MT בוש ("to reproach, treat with contempt," *HAL* 112). Cf. Akk *šiṭutum* (*Erra* 1:20), and Gk καταφρονήσις ("contempt, disdain," 2 Macc 3:18). Frankena ("Irra-Epos," 5) views "contempt" as "the *Leitmotif* of the *Erra* epic" and Sommerfeld (*Aufstieg*, 27) shows that the historical referent for "contempt" in *Erra* is Marduk's takeover of Enlil's throne, a mythopoeic reflection of the Chaldean conquest of Babylon (cf. Bodi, *Erra*, 69–81).

184. Jeremiah himself goes into exile in Egypt (Jer 44:1).

185. Jer 2:36b-37. One of the earliest uses of צלח ("to succeed, prosper") in Nevi'im occurs when the Danites ask Micah to שאל נא באלהים ונדעה התצליח דרכנו, "inquire of the gods so that we might know whether our path will 'prosper'" (Judg 18:5).

186. Cf. Sneed, "Theodicy," 180–83; Moore, *Babbler*, 58–121.

187. On ריב, cf. Judg 6:31–32; Hos 2:2; Jer 2:9; 15:10; 25:31 (Huffmon, "Lawsuit," 291). Boda (*Praying*, 56–57) successfully dismantles Crenshaw's (*Amos*, 142–43) attempt to relegate all use of ריב to a post-exilic editor.

188. Cf. similar legal usage of משפט in 1 Kgs 18:28 (*HAL* 616).

189. Sharply segregating ריב ("to sue") from צלח ("to prosper"), Lundbom (*Moses*, 101) reads this question as a "legal challenge."

190. N.B. the repetition of בגד for emphasis (cf. Jer 2:28; *Erra* 1.19–20; Frankena, "Irra-Epos," 5).

191. Even when describing the behavior of the רשעים ("wicked") the prophet uses agrarian economic metaphors, a practice enthusiastically adopted by John the Baptist (see below). Elsewhere the prophet laments that the "wicked" לא דנו דין יתום ויצליחו, "do not judge the orphan's case" in a way that "enables him to prosper" (Jer 5:28).

192. Jer 12:1–2. KJV translates כליות as "reins" (i.e., "kidneys"; *HAL* 456). Isaiah cites a similar proverb, "near with their mouths . . . while hearts are far," using לב in lieu of כליות (Isa 29:13).

Whether this prophet genuinely struggles with Yhwh's decision-making process or simply enacts the *role* of "faithful struggler" to make a point,[193] his parody of Judahite "prosperity" closely follows the prophetic pattern laid down by Elijah at Mt. Carmel.[194]

The Chaldean siege of Jerusalem results in socioeconomic disaster, but in the midst of Judah's collapse Jeremiah's cousin Ḥanamel pitches an "investment opportunity":[195]

קנה נא את שׂדי	Please buy my field
אשר בענתות אשר בארץ בנימין	Which is in Anathoth in the land of Benjamin;
כי לך משפט הירשה	For the right of inheritance[196]
ולך הגאלה	And redemption[197] are yours.[198]
קנה לך	Buy it for yourself, so that
ואדע כי דבר יהוה הוא	I may know that this is Yhwh's word.[199]

Affirming his "right" (משפט) to this "inheritance" (ירשׁה), Jeremiah purchases Ḥanamel's field:

ואכתב בספר ואחתם	I signed and sealed the deed,[200]
ואעד עדים	And gathered witnesses.

193. Reventlow (*Jeremia*, 205) accepts JL as the authentic words of Jeremiah, but argues that the first-person "I" is representatively spoken on Judah's behalf. Clines and Gunn ("Persuade," 20–27) try to soften פתה in the last of JL to mean "persuade" (Jer 20:7), *contra* Balentine (*Prayer*, 165) and Moore (*Babbler*, 61).

194. 1 Kgs 18:27 (cf. Carroll, "Humour," 177).

195. Davidson (*Jeremiah*, 76) recognizes that "attention to both the kinship ties and the ancestral linkages sets the foundation in the narrative for the assertion of tribal and family loyalties."

196. MT ירשׁ ("to inherit," possess") occurs often in Nevi'im. Cf. יורשׁ עצר, "possessing prosperity" (Judg 18:7; cf. جَذر, Lane 395). Raphael uses the same epithet when he informs Tobias that σοὶ δικαιοῦται κληρονομῆσαι, "you have the right to inherit" (Tob 6:12; see below).

197. Ḥanamel evidently views Jeremiah as his גאל-"redeemer" (Lev 25:25–32; cf. Moore, "הגאל," 27–35). *Tg. Jer.* 32.8 reads ארי לך חזיא ירותא ולך אחסנתא, "for you are the inheritance decision-maker, and I would have you take possession."

198. Leota ("Possession," 60) recognizes that these are not identical assertions: משפט גאלה ("right of redemption") presumes the work of a financial rescuer, while משפט הירשה ("right of inheritance") presumes the possibility of prior (family) ownership. At any rate, the law in Lev 25:25 is designed to "restrain social and economic forces with the potential to threaten a family's enjoyment of property, particularly vulnerable families" (Davidson, *Empire*, 77).

199. Jer 32:8. MT reads "Buy it" (Ḥanamel's last statement), followed by "And I knew it was Yhwh's word" (i.e., an editorial comment from Jeremiah). Syr basically follows this syntax, but OG and Vg do not. OG reads ὅτι σοὶ κρίμα κτήσασθαι καὶ σὺ πρεσβύτερος καὶ ἔγνων ὅτι λόγος κυρίου ἐστίν ("because to you belongs the right of purchase, for you are an elder and know that it is the Lord's matter"). Vg reads *quia tibi competit hereditas et tu propinquus ut possideas intellexi autem quod verbum Domini esset* ("for the inheritance is appropriate for you; you are the relative in line to possess, but I know it because it is the Lord's word"). In other words, OG and Vg attribute the entire statement to Ḥanamel.

200. Lit. "I wrote in the scroll."

ואשקל הכסף במאזנים	I weighed out the silver on the scales.[201]
ואתן את הספר המקנה	I submitted the deed of purchase[202]
אל ברוך בנ נריה בן מחסיה	To Baruch, son of Neriah,[203] son of Maḥseiah
לעיני חנמאל דדי	Before the eyes of Ḥanamel my cousin
ולעיני העדים	And the eyes of the witnesses
הכתבים בספר המקנה	Ratifying the deed of purchase.[204]

Why does Jeremiah enter into this real estate transaction? Readers are divided,[205] but whatever the reason(s), the transaction itself goes a long way toward encouraging his audience to reimagine a future in which

עוד יקנו בתים ושדות	Houses and fields and vineyards
וכרמים בארץ הזות	Will again be purchased in this land.[206]

One of Jeremiah's most sordid episodes focuses on King Zedekiah's decision to "cut a covenant" to "declare the release" (קרא דרור)[207] of Jerusalem's slave population:[208]

201. Jer 32:10. Both Amos (8:5) and Hosea (12:8) accuse Hebrew merchants of using falsely weighted מאזנים ("scales").

202. MT ספר מקנה (lit. "scroll of property"; cf. שׂדה מקנתו, "field of his acquisition," Lev 27:22); OG reads κτῆσις ("acquisition/property"), contrasted by Aristotle (*Rhet.* 1410a.6) with ἀπόλαυσις ("enjoyment"). Talmud uses phrases like שׁטר זבינא ("writ of purchase," *b. Qidd.* 9a) and שׂדה מקח ("acquired field," *b. Git.* 67a).

203. The PN ברוך בנ נריה surfaced in 1975 on a clay bulla in a private collection (Avigad, "Baruch," 52–56), but has since been proven a forgery (Goren and Arie, "Bullae" 147–58).

204. Jer 32:12. King (*Jeremiah*, 85–91) and Dearman (*Jeremiah*, 296–97) detail the ins and outs of ANE property transfer.

205. Jer 32:15. Wang ("Jeremiah," 15) sees in this episode a strong message of hope, but Wanke ("Jeremia," 265–76) does not, even though this episode stands in the "Book of Consolation" (Jer 30–33), over which some posit a pre-exilic (Rudolph, *Jeremia*, 172–88), others a post-exilic date (Carroll, *Jeremiah*, 568–70). Dinter (*Priesthood*, 86) thinks that "the point of this public ceremony is to impress on the witnesses what the Lord is saying by this bizarre transaction"; i.e., "'houses and fields shall again be bought.'" Clements ("Jeremiah," 363), however, views it as a "great turning-point" because "in the hour of greatest crisis, when the human supports for hope appear to have been swept away by the calamity that engulfs Judah in the years 588–87, Jeremiah becomes aware that the true ground for hope lies with God himself."

206. *Contra* Carroll ("Strategies," 111), Rudolph (*Jeremiah*, 209) argues that Jeremiah purchases this land before the Babylonian takeover.

207. Jer 34:8. This is not the only example of wartime manumission. In the eighteenth century BCE, e.g., Hammurapi uses conscripts of "released slaves" (OB *wardim wuššurim*) to lay siege to a town on his northern border (ARM 23.363; Anbar, "Libération," 255), and in second-century CE Sicily, the slave-general Salvius (according to Diodorus Siculus, Hist. 36.4.4) "by proclamation, offers the slaves in the city (of Morgantina) their freedom. Then, when their masters counter with a like offer . . . they join them to repel the siege. Later, however, the praetor rescinds their emancipation, forcing the majority of them to desert to the rebels." The difference here, of course, is that Jeremiah anchors its critique in the "Law of Jubilee" with its clear prohibition against re-enslavement (Deut 15:1–18).

208. Jer 34:8–11. While many read this text as Dtr redaction (Duhm, *Jeremia*, 279–80; Rudolph, *Jeremia*, 203; Nicholson, *Jeremiah*, 63; McKane, *Jeremiah*, 882), Anbar ("Libération," 253) presumes

הדבר אשר היה אל ירמיהו מאת יהוה	The word came to Jeremiah from Yhwh
אחרי כרת המלך צדקיהו ברית	After King Zedekiah "cut a covenant"[209]
את כול העם אשר בירושלם	With all the people of Jerusalem
לקרא להם דרור	To "declare them released,"[210]
לשלח איש את עבדו ואיש את שפחתו	For each to send out his male and female slaves
העברי והעבריה [211]חפשים	As free Hebrew men and women (so that)
לבלתי עבד בם ביהודה אחיהו איש	No one's kin might again be a slave in Judah.[212]
וישובו אחרי כן וישבו את העבדים	But afterwards they turned round and took back
ואת השפחות אשר שלחו חפשים	The male and female slaves they had just set free,
ויכבשום לעבדים ולשפחות	And subjugated them again into slavery.[213]

Dwelling on the phrase קרא דרור ("declare the release"),[214] Jeremiah depicts the socioeconomic institution of slavery via paronomasiacal language much like that found in

---

it to be "an historical event." The Babylonian epic most preoccupied with the problem of slavery is *Atraḫasis* (cf. Moore, *WealthWatch*, 73–89). Chavel ("Emancipation," 73) argues that "the willingness of the Judeans to overturn (the Mosaic) covenant highlights the fact that they do not regard the general emancipation as an opportunity to purge an evil institution from their midst. Rather, accepting the enslavement of their fellow Hebrews as a legitimate institution, even if an unfortunate one from the viewpoint of the enslaved, the citizens of Jerusalem view historical circumstances as forcing their somewhat reluctant hand." Hiebert ("*Agrarian*," 438–39) similarly observes that while Hebrew writers "bequeath us admirable values about creation, land, and community," they "also hold many untenable principles, including the acceptance of slavery *per se* (regardless of their restraints on the economic forces leading to slavery)."

209. Jer 34:8, כרת ברית (cf. Day, "Covenants," 91–110).

210. Jer 34:8, קרא דרור. Isaiah uses this phrase to describe the eschatological "release of the captives" (לקרא לשבוים דרור, Isa 61:1).

211. Akk cognate *ḫupšū* in the Amarna correspondence refers to "undesirables" of low socioeconomic status (*EA* 117:90; 118:23; 125:27; *CAD* Ḫ.241–42) and is semantically equivalent to Eg *retenu* (cf. Moore, *WealthWatch*, 122–24).

212. Jer 34:8–9. Manumission of slaves can occur for military (David, "Manumission," 63–79), religious (Kessler, "Manumission," 107), economic (Lemche, *History*, 37–39), or some combination of reasons (Hyatt, *Jeremiah*, 55; Thompson, *Jeremiah*, 610). Chavel ("Emancipation," 72) suggests that "the fact that the people later reclaim their slaves may testify only to their . . . greed rather than to premeditated treachery."

213. Jer 34:11. Slavery comes to the fore again in the Nehemiah scroll when the realities of socioeconomic distress derail the celebration of Jubilee: כבשר אחינו בשרנו כבניהם בנינו והנה אנחנו כבשים את בנינו ואת בנתינו לעבדים, "Our flesh is the same as that of our brothers, our children are the same as their children, yet here we are subjugating our sons and daughters into slavery" (Neh 5:5; see below). Blenkinsopp (*Nehemiah*, 257) explains that "the only way in which the Judean farmer, who practices a subsistence economy, can possibly meet his tax obligation is by producing and marketing a surplus. His situation drives him inevitably, therefore, into the hands of the middleman or wealthy landowner, and the frequent cases of default and expropriation contribute to the great estates and absentee landlords of the Hellenistic and Persian periods."

214. *HAL* 221; cf. Akk *andurāru* (*CAD* A/2.115–17). In the seventeenth century BCE the

Kings, with its play on the word עוכר ("troubler"). As noted above, when Ahab calls Elijah a "troubler" (עוכר), the prophet responds by calling the *king* a "troubler" (עוכר).[215] Here Jeremiah upbraids a king for "declaring the release" of Hebrew slaves only to go back on his word, warning him that such duplicity will soon trigger the "declaration" of another "release" to "pestilence, famine and the sword."[216] Moreover, since Zedekiah has "wandered away" (עבר) from the covenant "cut" (כרת) with Jerusalem's slaves, the Chaldeans will cut up (כרת) the land of Judah into bloody pieces, then force Zedekiah to "wander" (עבר) among them.[217]

Repetition and doubling are common literary devices,[218] yet to replicate an entire poem in two different places within the same scroll is extraordinary,[219] indicating if nothing else the writer's desire to widen the contours of the socioeconomic motif-trajectory in Nevi'im:

עשׂה ארץ בכחו	He creates the land with his power,
מכין תבל בחכמתו	He maintains the economy[220] with his wisdom,
ובתבונתו נטה השמים	He stretches out the heavens with his understanding,[221]

Babylonian king Ammiṣaduqa issues a *mīšarum*-decree (*ANET* 526–28) designed to release his subjects from tax-induced debt (*CAD* M/2:116–17; *TDOT* 6:1–7). Hallo ("Sharecropping," 205–16) details the socioeconomic context of this decree, and Kraus (*Verfügungen*, 1–126) documents over one hundred examples of royal manumission decrees from Babylonia, Mari, Assyria, Hana, Elam, Kanesh, and Ešnunna. Otto ("Vertragsrecht," 125–60) analyzes the problem of debt-slavery from an ideological perspective, but Lemche ("Edicts," 11–22) rejects all parallels between Akk *andurārum* (*Atr* 1:243) and Heb דרור (Lev 25:10).

215. 1 Kgs 18:17 (cf. above and Chaney, "Micah," 158–60).

216. Jer 34:17 (cf. the similar play on רעב in Amos 8:11). Allen (*Jeremiah*, 241) interprets this to mean that "while the Babylonians (Chaldeans) conduct the siege from the outside, Yhwh will be at work inside, bringing about death-dealing pestilence in the besieged city."

217. Jer 34:18. Cf. also the paronomasiacal usage of כרת in 1 Kgs 18 (discussed above). Horsley (*Covenant*, 73) contends that "toward the end of the monarchy in Judah a number of signs appear that some officers of the monarchy believe that it should take covenantal principles seriously." Of course, by then it is "too little too late"—Nebuchadnezzar tortures and kills Zedekiah's family, gouges out his eyes, and hauls him into captivity (2 Kgs 25:7). Cf. Kline, *Soundplay*, 1–17; Noegel, *Puns*, xvi.

218. Alter, *Narrative*, 111–42. For Lundbom (*Rhetoric*, xxxvi), "it is difficult to overestimate the importance of repetition, which Muilenberg ("Rhetoric," 97–111) considers the very basis of Hebrew rhetoric."

219. Jer 10:12–16 // 51:15–19. Allen ("Jeremiah," 436) thinks the reason for this replication is to champion "Yhwh's superiority to Babylon's images." Repetitive poetic sequences also occur—albeit not so far apart—in the Ugaritic texts (e.g., *CAT* 1.2.4.11–26; cf. Sasson, "Ugaritic," 94).

220. Heb תבל doubtless derives from the root אבל (cf. Akk *abālu*, "to dry up," and *tābalu*, "dry land," *EA* 10.133), but OG οἰκουμένη is too frequent a translation of תבל to ignore (cf. OG 2 Sam 22:16; Isa 14:17; 24:4; Ps 9:9; 18:16; Lam 4:12; Hayes, *Mourns*, 12–18).

221. Sandoval (*Wealth*, 86–87) examines the prevalence of חכמה//תבונה and other, similar word pairs in Hebrew wisdom literature.

לקול תתו המון מים השמים	His voice stirs up the abundant[222] waters of heaven,
ויעלה נשאים	He makes the mists rise up
מקצה ארץ	From the alleyways of the land,[223]
ברקים למטר עשה	He creates the thunders attending the rain,[224]
ויוצא רוח מאצרתיו	He hurls the wind from its storehouses.[225]
נבער כל אדם מדעת	Everyone is reckless, foolish,[226] and ignorant,
הביש כל צורף מפסל	Every smith ashamed of his molten images[227]
כי שקר נסכו ולא רוח בם	Because they are fakes, devoid of breath,
הבל המה מעשה תעתעים	Worthless,[228] ridiculous entities which
בעת פקדתם יאבדו	Perish at their “moment of visitation.”[229]
לא כאלה חלק יעקב	The Portion of Jacob[230] is not like these,
כי יוצר הכל הוא	For he is the Sculptor of all things,
וישראל שבט נחלתו	And Israel is the “tribe of his inheritance.”[231]

222. MT המון often connotes “wealth/abundance”; e.g., when Nebuchadnezzar conquers Egypt ונשא המנה ושלל שללה ובזז בזה והיתה שכר לחילו, “he will carry off her wealth, capture her spoil, seize her plunder, and convert it into wages for his army” (Ezek 29:19).

223. Jer 10:13//51:16. On קץ (“edge/fringe/end”) as “alleyway,” N.B. that one of Marduk’s “Fifty Names” is *ša-rik mi-riš-ti ša is-ra-ta ú-kin-nu*, “the donor of arable fields who cultivates the alleyways in between” (*Ee* 7.1). *Ketib* ארץ is preferable to *qere* הארץ in 10:13 because (a) הארץ does not appear as *qere* in 51:16, (b) previous use of ארץ in this poem eschews the definite article, and (c) it generally fits better with the hymn’s pattern of non-articulated nouns.

224. Several readers (e.g., Patai, “Rain,” 225; Mulder, *Ba'al*, 37) imagine the heavenly fire striking the Yhwh altar on Carmel as a bolt of lightning (1 Kgs 18:38).

225. The term describing the place from which רוח (“wind”) emanates often describes the place from which tithes and offerings are distributed (i.e., the אוצר, “treasury,” Neh 13:12; cf. בית אוצר, “storehouse,” Mal 3:8).

226. The reflexive Syr cognate of בער (ܐܬܒܥܪ) can mean “to grow wild” (*PSD* 51).

227. MT בוש (to shame”) is a much-used word in Jeremiah: the “thief” is ashamed (Jer 2:26); the “wise men” are ashamed (8:8); the “daughter of Egypt” is ashamed (46:24); “Bēl” (Marduk) is ashamed (50:2).

228. MT הבל (“vanity”) is a *Leitwort* in Qohelet, often contrasted with יתרון (“profit”; cf. Kugel, “Money,” 374–99; Sneed, “Worthless,” 879–94).

229. On the negative eschatological connotations of פקד cf. Watts (“Socio-Economic,” 117, 120–21) and Moore (*Babbler*, 45–57).

230. MT חלק often appears in the phrase חלק ונחלה, (“portion and possession,” Gen 31:14; Deut 10:9; 12:12; 14:27, 29; 18:1), but a key verse in Torah (Deut 32:9) replicates the socioeconomic elements embedded here: כי חלק יהוה עמו יעקב חבל נחלתו, “For the portion of Yhwh is his people, Jacob the share of his inheritance.”

231. Jer 10:12–16//51:15–19. N.B. the same word pair (חלק/נחל) in 1 Kgs 12:16: מה לנו חלק בדוד ולא נחלה בבן ישי, “What ‘portion’ do we have with David? What ‘inheritance’ with the son of Jesse?” Cf. also Ps 135:12: נתן ארצם נחלה נחלה לישראל עמו, “He gave their land (i.e., the land of “the kingdoms of Canaan,” v. 11) as an inheritance, an inheritance for his people Israel.”

Depicting the consequences of idolatry via a socioeconomic epithet, Jeremiah's use of נחלה resonates with "inheritance" motifs occurring in several prophetic texts.[232] The Song of Moses,[233] for example, preserves an imaginative retelling of the creation story in which `Elyon ("Most High")[234] subdivides the גוים ("nations") into two companies: (a) בני אדם ("sons of Adam"), and (b) בני ישראל ("sons of Israel").[235] From the latter group Yhwh extracts a חלק ("portion") of עמו ("his people") while "Jacob retains the חבל ('territory') of his נחלה ('inheritance')."[236] *Summary:* Many "reject" (מסא) it, but Torah is unquestionably the primary source of Jeremiah's understanding about the dangers threatening the economy of late pre-exilic Judah.[237]

Ezekiel

Of all the prophets, Ezekiel may well be the fiercest critic of profligate wealth.[238] Addressing the merchants of Tyre,[239] for example, he notes that among their many clients

תרשיש סחרתך מרב כל הון	Tarshish trades with you, flush with exorbitant wealth,[240]

232. Polaski, *Isaiah*, 35–36. Cf. the socioeconomic epithets anchoring many of Marduk's "Fifty Names" (*Ee* 6.123–7.144; cf. above), the frequent use of *niḫlatum* in the Mari correspondence (Nissinen, *Prophets*, 1.4; cf. above), and Naboth's refusal to surrender the נחלת אבתי ("inheritance of my fathers," 1 Kgs 21:3).

233. Deut 32:8–9. Mastnjak (*Deuteronomy*, 212) wrestles with whether or not the Song of Moses is older than Jeremiah, and Van Ruiten ("Controversies," 224) sees this section of the Song portraying "Yhwh's mercy . . . in connection with Israel's apostasy."

234. Elnes and Miller, "Elyon," 293–99; Rose, "Names," 1004.

235. MT, Sam, *Tg. Onq.*, Syr, and Vg read בני ישראל ("sons of Israel"); OG reads ἀγγέλων θεοῦ ("angels of God"), which some see reflecting an older Hebrew *Vorlage* utilizing the phrase בני אלהים ("sons of God"). The readings in 4QDt[q] (. . .] בני אל; Skehan, "Fragment," 12) and 4QDt[j] (בני אלוהים; Tov, *Textual*, 269) appear to buttress this possibility, yet it remains to be proven whether OG (a) represents an older, more "original" *Vorlage*, or (b) revises this reading so as not to offend the sensitivities of monotheistic Hebrews (*pace* Sanders, *Deuteronomy*, 156–58).

236. Deut 32:9b. Doubtless this חלק ("portion") refers to the faithful שאר ("remnant") to which Isaiah refers (e.g., Isa 10:19–22; cf. Leuchter, *Identity*, 136–42).

237. Jer 6:19. *Contra* Mastnjak (*Deuteronomy*, 212), Sanders (*Deuteronomy*, 431–32) convincingly argues that the Song of Moses is pre-exilic.

238. ברב הוניך ומערביך העשרת מלכי ארץ . . . ויגבה לבבך בחילך, "With your great wealth and provision you (Tyre) enrich the kings of the earth . . . but your heart is full of pride in your wealth" (Ezek 27:33b, 28:5b). Joyce (*Ezekiel*, 178) suggests that for Ezekiel, Tyre's "commercial wealth" is her "temple."

239. Zechariah posits that even though Tyre "heaps up silver like dust and gold like the mud in the streets" (תצבר כסף כעפר וחרוץ כטיט חוצות), it will be "dispossessed" (ירש) and its "wealth" (חיל) tossed "into the sea" (Zech 9:3–4). Peckham (*Phoenicia*, 203) observes that "Tyre, after Tiglath-Pileser III, begins to redefine itself as the creative center of its world . . . able to monopolize overland and overseas trade, to invent money, and to revolutionize how business is done. Its products and distinctive pottery begin to show up everywhere" as "the Tyrian people produce works of art, collect and sell heirlooms and luxuries, and set the standards for refinement and good taste." Sedlmeier (*Ezechiel*, 34) recognizes that Ezekiel "devotes considerably more attention" to Tyre than any other city-state.

240. Sennacherib brags that all the islands of the great sea from Cyprus to Tarshish ([kur]*tar-si-si*) lay

בכסף ברזל בדיל בעופרת נתנו עזבוניך	Trading for your wares with silver, iron, tin and lead.[241]

Doubtless Tyre is singled out not because it is any more corrupt than Joppa or Sidon, but because it is such an obvious target, seeing as it houses one of the Mediterranean's most conspicuously wealthy economies,[242] an affluent bazaar[243] filled with merchants willing to buy and sell practically anything—*animals* (horses, mules, rams, goats), *precious metals* (gold, silver), *precious stones* (incl. ebony and ivory),[244] *carpets, clothing, foods, wines, spices*, and the like.[245] One item on this invoice, however, innocuously hides behind the simple epithet נפש אדם (lit. "soul of a man").[246] English Bibles translate the phrase as "human beings" (NRSV, ESV), "persons of men" (KJV, ASV), "human lives" (NKJV), and "lives of men" (NASB), but given the context,[247] it probably refers to the ugly business of human trafficking.[248]

Several socioeconomic motifs animate the "Parable of the Two Eagles":[249]

הנשר הגדול גדול הכנפים	A great eagle with huge wings
ארך האבר למלה הנוצה אשר לו הרקמה	And long pinions, rich with colored plumes,

under his dominion (*ANET* 290), suggesting a locale for Tarshish somewhere on the western shores of the Mediterranean (cf. Lipiński, "תרשיש," 790–93).

241. Ezek 27:12. *Tg. Ezek.* 27.12 locates Tyre's wealth in its בית גנז, "treasury house." Cf. Joyce, *Ezekiel*, 176–77; Pohlmann, *Ezechiel*, 381–91; and Saur, *Tyroszyklus*, 197–237. Schütte (*Schriftprophetie*, 4) insists that Ezekiel addresses "both Israelite as well as Judahite constituents of the two communities living in Judah."

242. Cf. Peckham, *Anecdotes*, 67–69.

243. MT עזבון (Ezek 27:12, 14; OG ἀγορά, "marketplace"); מערב (27:13; OG ἐμπορία, "shops").

244. Harrell et al. ("Gemstones," 6–7) painstakingly describe the gemstones adorning the Prince of Tyre's מסכה ("canopy," Ezek 28:13).

245. Doubtless the inventory in Ezek 27:1–27 is not intended to be exhaustive. This list of trading partners closely reflects the "Table of Nations" in Torah (Gen 10:2–4), and may well reflect Tyre's primary trading network (Liverani, "Tyre," 79; Saur, *Tyroszyklus*, 197). Rüger ("Tyrusorakel," 111–15), however, sees it referring to caravan routes in southern Arabia (cf. Zimmerli, *Ezekiel* 2.70–71; Allen, *Ezekiel*, 84; Block, *Ezekiel* 52).

246. Ezek 27:13. Cf. the same epithet in Num 19:11, 13; 31:46.

247. Cf. Block, *Ezekiel*, 46–59.

248. Cf. NET, NLT, and HCSB. Exactly what *type* of trafficking is not specified (Dandamaev, "Slavery," 56–85, lists several possibilities), but Ezekiel is not the only scroll to condemn this highly profitable business (cf. Joel 4:3 below). Bechard (*Unspeakable*, 2) reports that even today "children are trafficked mostly into the international sex trade for prostitution, sex tourism, and pornography. Outside of sexual exploitation children are used for organ harvesting, forced labor, soldiers in rebel armies, domestic servitude, street beggars and camel jockeys. Whatever their purpose, whatever act they are forced to perform, the victims of child trafficking become, by any definition, slaves."

249. Ezek 17:2–10. Eichrodt (*Ezekiel*, 223) recognizes that this משל (17:2; OG παραβολή) "treats plants and animals like persons, making them behave like human beings even when such behavior is not in consonance with their own natural characteristics." Renz (*Ezekiel*, 249) argues persuasively that "the book of Ezekiel hangs together" as a "rhetorical unit" specifically designed to address the needs of a "community in crisis."

בא אל הלבנון	Flies into the Lebanon,[250]
ויקח את צמרת האזר	Seizes the top of the cedar,
את רוש יניקותיו קטף	Breaks off its highest branch,[251]
ויביאהו אל ארץ כנען	And carries it into a land of merchants,[252]
בעיר רכלים שמו	Depositing it in a city of peddlers.[253]

According to the *political* interpretation of this parable,[254] the יניקה ("shoot") signifies the Davidic heir (זרע המלוכה, "royal seed," i.e., Zedekiah) who "cuts" a ברית ("covenant") with the Chaldeans.[255] Then afterwards,

ויקח מזרע הארץ	The eagle takes (the shoot) from a seminated land
ויתנהו בשדה זרע	And deposits it[256] in a seminated field,
קח על מים רבים	A healing plant[257] beside mighty waters,[258]

250. Houston Smith ("Lebanon," 269–70) tries to describe in a few paragraphs the magnificence of the Lebanese forest which George (*Gilgamesh*, 456) takes to be the geo-historical referent to the "sacred cedar forest" in Gilgamesh (GE 3.52–62).

251. N.B. that Ezekiel retains this term when Yhwh "breaks off" his own ינקה ("branch," Ezek 17:22), and that it also denotes the "branch (יונק) out of dry ground" in the fourth Servant Song (Isa 53:2). The common synonym נצר appears in Isa 11:1; 60:21; 1QHa 14.15; 15.19; 16.10 (נצר קדש, "holy shoot"); and DA 2.5 (*nqr*).

252. OG γῆν Χαναaν ("land of Canaan"); Vg *terram Chanaan* ("land of Canaan"); Syr ܐܪܥܐ ܟܢܥܢ ("land of Canaan"); *Tg. Ezek.* 17.4 reads בית ישראל ("house of Israel"). In spite of all the attempts to read כנען as a GN, "merchants" still seems the most appropriate translation here, esp. in light of the poetic parallel with רכלים ("peddlers").

253. Ezek 17:3–4. Nahum mocks the security forces of Nineveh for "increasing 'your peddlers' (רכליך) like the stars of heaven" (Nah 3:16), symbolizing them as locust grubs who, once matured, spread their wings and fly (cf. Roberts, *Nahum*, 75–76). Altmann ("Economy," 117), argues that Nehemiah's critique of "external traders in Jerusalem who provide elite consumption (Neh 13:15–18) points to an interregional trade profitable enough to be worth the risks involved in undertaking it."

254. Simian-Yofre ("Enigma," 17–43) views Ezek 17:11–21 as *political* interpretation and 17:22–24 as *theological* interpretation of the משל in 17:1–10. Further, he views this משל to be amenable to multiple interpretations besides the political and the theological.

255. Ezek 17:13. Zedekiah violates two covenants, one external and one internal: (a) one to "guarantee" Judah's political/economic loyalty to Nebuchadnezzar (Ezek 17:13); (b) the other to "guarantee" the freedom of former slaves (Jer 34:8). Zechariah predicts a time when Judah והיו שלל לעבדיהם ("will become plunder for their own slaves," Zech 2:13).

256. MT נתן (lit. "gives"). The 3ms suffix refers to the cut-off יניקה ("branch").

257. Ezek 17:5. *HAL* (1020) reads MT קח as a *hapax*, translating "pasture/meadow." OG reads πεδίον φυτὸν ("healing fruit?"), but Syr reads ܚܒܫܬܐ ("healing plant," from ܚܒܫ, "to heal, bind up," *PSD* 423).

258. MT מים רבים retains its mythopoeic connotations in several ANE texts. Cf. 2 Sam 22:17; Isa 17:13; Ezek 1:24; 31:15; 43:2; Hab 3:15; Cant 8:7; Ps 18:16; 29:3; and Hit *ḫu-un-ḫu-wa-na-aš-ša* ("watery abyss," *CTH* 321.63). May ("Waters," 10) argues that the phrase refers to "the chaotic, disorderly, insurgent elements" of the cosmos.

צפצפה שׂמו	Planting it as a river willow.[259]
ויקח מזרע הארץ	Having thus been taken from a seminated land,[260]
ויצמח ויהי לגפן סרחת שׁפלת קומה	It sprouts and grows into a low-hanging climber,
לפות דליותיו אליו ושׁרשׁיו תחתיו ויהי	Its tendrils spreading, its roots curling underneath,
ותהי לגפן ותעשׂ בדים	A potentially productive vine
ותשלח פארות	Unfolding its branches.[261]

In true Ezekielian style another eagle repeats the entire sequence as a "failsafe" measure in which a second "shoot" is transplanted to yet another illicit "water-source."[262] Taken together, these parables thus hammer home two truths: (a) periods of "prosperity" are always temporary, never permanent; and (b) the price for cozying up to foreigners to sustain such "prosperity" can be distressingly high, enough to make the Divine Investor ask some rather tough "business questions":

תצלח הלוא את שׁרשׁיה ינתק	Will it prosper?[263] Will he uproot it?
ואת פריה יקוסס ויבשׁ	Will he allow its fruit to dessicate and decay?
כל טרפי צמחה תיבשׁ	Will all the leaves on its branches wither up . . . ?[264]
והנה שׁתולה התצלח	Will it prosper after transplantation?[265]

In the political interpretation of this parable Ezekiel focuses on the motif of *prosperity*. By condemning the "royal seed" for siding with the Egyptians to fend off the Babylonians—even after promising not to do so—Ezekiel processes this "prosperity" motif through a prophetic motherboard programmed by even tougher "business questions":[266]

259. Cf. صغصاف ("a variety of willow," *DMWA* 518).

260. Pikor (*Ezekiel*, 20–22) observes how Ezekiel repeatedly gravitates to the "metaphor of land."

261. Ezek 17:5–6. Cf. the "vine" parable in Isa 5:1–7. Manning ("Ezekiel," 36–40) thinks this parable is christologically retreaded in GNT (John 15:1–10), and Tuckett ("Ezekiel," 101–02) sees a parallel between the leafy tree in this parable and the one featured in the parable of the mustard seed (Matt 13:31–33//Mark 4:30–32//Luke 13:18–19).

262. Ezek 17:15 (i.e., Egypt).

263. Ezek 17:9. As noted above, this term (צלח) combines with שׂכל to form an *inclusio* framing the fourth Servant Song in Isaiah (Isa 52:13 and 53:10).

264. Ezek 17:9.

265. Ezek 17:10. As Joyce (*Ezekiel*, 136) notes, MT שׁטל does not require the nuance "transplant" (NRSV), esp. since it appears so many times in Ezekiel (17:8, 10, 22; 19:10, 13), but given the context here "transplant" seems most appropriate (BDB 1060).

266. Craigie (*Ezekiel*, 126) summarizes: "For those in exile who think they can discern a glimmer of hope in the news they hear of Zedekiah's pro-Egyptian policy, Ezekiel draws a picture: the homeland they love so dearly is little more than a scrap of carrion plucked and pulled at between two

הימלט העשה אלה	Shall someone who does such things escape?[267]
והפר ברית ונמלט	Shall someone who violates the covenant escape?[268]
היצלח	Shall someone like this "prosper?"[269]

Summary: Ezekiel has a good deal to say about wealth and prosperity.[270] Ian Duguid recognizes that the prophet condemns Judah for replacing the "allure of Egypt" with the "allure of wealth," where "money seems to offer the same things that Egypt offers: independence, freedom from outside controls and limits, the power to choose, and comfortable affluence."[271] Peter Craigie, however, argues that the prophet's "point is not to criticize wealth as such; rather it is a matter of perspective. If there is no food to buy, silver will not satisfy hunger; if a sword is penetrating one's abdomen, gold quickly loses its offer of security. It is *dependence* on wealth that Ezekiel condemns, and the delusion of money's 'security.'"[272]

Book of the Twelve

Contemporary students of the Twelve argue over whether it is a singular entity, a diverse anthology, or some mixture of the two.[273] The fact that OG, Vg, apocryphal, pseudepigraphal,[274] rabbinic,[275] and late sectarian texts[276] all treat the Twelve as a singular entity suggests to Jakob Wöhrle that it is the "product of a conscious

---

scrapping eagles."

267. Hasel ("פלט," 552–55) traces the intricate philological connections between Akk *balāṭu*, Ug *plṭ*, Arab فلط, Syr ܦܠܛ, Heb פלט (Mic 6:14) and Heb מלט (Ezek 17:15), concluding that all denote varying degrees of "escape."

268. Otto (*Deuteronomium*, 15–32) has long argued that Hebraic notions of "covenant" derive from the "loyalty oaths" of ANE emperors. Koller ("Ezekiel," 419) basically ignores this משל-parable in his attempt to redefine "loyalty," *not* as an "ongoing reciprocal relationship," but as "an all-encompassing debt owed by Jerusalem from her childhood."

269. Ezek 17:15b (listing the first question last). To Allen's (*Ezekiel*, 75) suggestion that Tyre stands to prosper at Jerusalem's fall in political instead of economic terms, Duguid (*Ezekiel*, 334) pushes back, noting that "the oracles themselves focus entirely on Tyre as a leader in international commerce."

270. Even as Solon (cf. Adkins, *Greece*, 53) tries to distinguish between "god-given wealth" (θεόδοτα) and "illicit gain" (ὕβρις), so Ezekiel similarly discriminates.

271. Duguid, *Ezekiel*, 377.

272. Craigie, *Ezekiel*, 55 (emphasis in original).

273. *Unitary scroll*: Schneider, "Twelve"; Lee, "Unity"; Coggins, "Twelve," 64. *Diverse anthology*: Ben Zvi, "Twelve," 131–38; Floyd, "Prophetic," 409; Sweeney, *Twelve*, i–xxxix; Petersen, "Twelve," 3–10 ("thematized anthology"). Contemporary scholarship, as House ("Twelve," 314) observes, "reflects the unsettled state of Old Testament scholarship."

274. Sir 49:10; 4 Ezra 1:39–40; Mart. Isa. 4:22.

275. E.g., *b. B. Bat.* 13b-14b. Josephus (*Ag. Ap.* 1.40) lists only 13 prophets, which implies counting the Twelve as one scroll.

276. 4Q12^{a} (Qumran); 8Ḥev12gr (Naḥal Ḥever); Mur12 (Muraba`at).

book-building process."[277] Ehud ben Zvi staunchly disagrees,[278] but following the lead of James Nogalski,[279] many students view the Twelve as a singular entity incorporating several motifs binding it altogether, including "Yhwh's Day,"[280] "Jerusalem/Zion,"[281] "love,"[282] "marriage,"[283] and "Gentile judgment/salvation."[284] Of greatest interest here, however, is Laurie Braaten's thorough investigation of the "land" motif, particularly how the Twelve manipulates it through "the frequent use of vegetational imagery,"[285] an observation which, while anthropologically relevant,[286] does little to explain the contribution the land *motif* makes to the prophetic socioeconomic trajectory coursing through Nevi'im.[287]

Hosea

Contemporary readers of Hosea view its graphic sexual metaphors from widely differing perspectives.[288] Some read them as little more than pornographic sledgehammers designed to shame Israel into ceasing its "prostitutions" (זנונים)[289] with all her "lovers" (מאהבים).[290] Exactly who these "lovers" are, however, is far from clear.[291] Some imag-

277. "Das Produkt einer bewußten buchübergreifenden Gestalt" (Wöhrle, *Zwölfprophetenbuch*, 2).

278. Ben Zvi, "Books," 131–38.

279. Nogalski, "Intertextuality," 102–24.

280. Rendtorff, "Twelve," 420–32; Nogalski, "Yhwh," 192–213; Wolff, *Joel*, 33–34.

281. Sweeney, "Twelve," 153.

282. Watts, "Twelve," 209–17.

283. Baumann, "Ehemetaphorik," 214–31.

284. Wöhrle, *Zwölfprophetenbuch*, 1; Timmer, *Nations*, 221–42.

285. Braaten,"Twelve," 105 (cf. "Hosea," 1–26). Cf. Collins, *Elijah*, 67–68.

286. Cf. Stovell, "Agricultural," 37–61.

287. One of the reasons for this is because Braaten ("Twelve," 104, 108) reads Hosea via a "thematic approach based primarily on a synchronic reading of the MT," identifying Yhwh's "bride" as the land itself instead of the Israelite people, an approach which apparently reflects Habel's (*Nature*, 28) quasi-deification of ארץ ("land"; cf. Braaten, "Earth," 190–95; Moore, *Nature*).

288. Cf. Moughtin-Mumby, *Metaphors*; Baumann, *Metaphor*; Törnqvist, *Imagery*.

289. Hos 2:4. Jeremiah uses the root זנה repeatedly (a) to identify Israel's infidelity, and (b) link it to the collapse of the Judahite economy; e.g., ואת זנית רעים רבים, "You prostitute yourself with many 'neighbors'" (Jer 3:1); ותחניפי ארץ בזנותיך, "You pollute the land with your prostitutions" (3:2); והיה מקל זנותה ותחנף את הארץ, "She trivializes her prostitution and pollutes the land" (3:9).

290. Hos 2:7. Cf. Setel, "Pornography," 86–94; Brenner-Idan,"Pornoprophetics," 63–86; Exum,"Pornography," 101–28. One cannot read Nevi'im and not recognize the use of crude language. Besides Hosea, e.g., Jeremiah portrays Israel as a wild donkey so driven by sexual lust that multiple partners have their way with her without becoming the least bit "tired" (יעף, Jer 2:24), after which she shamelessly says, לא נטמאתי אחרי הבעלים לא הלכתי, "I am not defiled; I have not pursued the Ba'als" (Jer 2:23). Koller ("Ezekiel," 402–21) finds similar indignation in the Ezekiel scroll.

291. Great literature uses ambiguity to pull in readers and challenge them to think through difficult questions. In Starr's ("English," 78) opinion, "great literature, if it entertains well, will also educate without falling into the trap of being merely educational."

ine them to be agrarian deities staffed by powerful priesthoods in and around the capital city of Samaria.[292] Others suggest that מאהבים ("lovers"), a masculine plural participle repeated five times in chapter 2,[293] refers to Israel's *political* allies.[294] Brad Kelle, for example, argues that "the legal texts dealing with marriage and divorce . . . constitute" Hosea's "primary database," and that the scroll's oracles do not symbolize actual "physical punishments like stripping and exposure," but "financial and property stipulations" linked to "inheritance and possessions."[295] Attractive as this hypothesis looks, however, it problematically presumes (like other academic hypotheses about the Bible) an unwarranted degree of mutual exclusivity. That is, Kelle seems to presume that Hosea's metaphors cannot symbolize *both* sociopolitical *and* socioeconomic concerns at the same time.[296]

Scanning for middle ground, Alice Keefe suggests that at the center of Hosea stands "an image of something familiar to Hosea's ancient audience—the structure of Israelite marriage—to evoke a renewed understanding of something less familiar or perhaps forgotten; i.e., the requirements of the covenant relationship between Yhwh and the nation."[297] This attempt at a "golden mean," however, while attentive to Hosea's understanding of "covenant," (again) avoids the task of identifying the realities *symbolized* by these graphic metaphors.[298] Granted, many interpreters stumble when,

292. N.B. in Nevi'im the overt mention in Samaria of a בית הבעל ("house of Ba'al," 2 Kgs 10:21). Cf. Mays, *Hosea*, 39; Bons, *Hosea*, 44; MacIntosh, *Hosea*, 48; Wolff, *Hosea*, 35.

293. MT מאהבים (Hos 2:7, 9, 12, 14, and 15). *Tg. Hos.* 2.7, 9, 12, 14 reads עממיא רחמי, "Gentile lovers."

294. In *EA* 53 Akizzi of Qatna complains to Pharaoh that the Hittite emperor has empowered one of his vassals, Aitukama, to harrass and pull him away from his alliance with Egypt. Thus he writes to Amenhotep III to assure him that he has no intention whatsoever of abandoning his "love" (Akk *ra'âmu*, *EA* 53.41). Cf. Moran, "Love," 80; Olyan, "Honor," 202; Westbrook, "Law," 38; Moore, *Babbler*, 145, 147–48. In addition to the Amarna sources, N.B. that Hosea mentions Assyria by name (Hos 5:13), causing Kelle (*Hosea*, 291–92) to suggest that "the civil war in Israel between Hoshea and Pekah at the close of the Syro-Ephraimite conflict in 731–730 BCE most closely matches all the elements presupposed by and reflected in Hos 2."

295. Kelle, *Hosea*, 290. As will soon become clear, however, it is not necessary to restrict analysis to "official sources" to arrive at this conclusion.

296. Schwartz (*Taxes*) argues that "it's possible to suggest a political economic framework for all of this without denying the religious," yet reductionism is not new. Talmud, e.g., records a dispute over the meaning of Gomer's name in which one rabbi suggests that her name (גמר, "to finish, conclude") reflects her "profession" (i.e., שהכל גומרים בה, "that everyone 'finishes' inside her," *b. Pes.* 87a), while another suggests that her name merely alludes to a troubled time when hostile forces בקשו לגמר ממונן של ישראל, "seek to 'finish' Israel's wealth" (*b. Pes.* 87b). Philo (*Mosis* 1.24) roundly condemns all who would "contend violently for only one side of a question."

297. Keefe, "Hosea," 824. Dearman (*Hosea*, 11) observes that "in Hosea's poetic descriptions of Israel, Ephraim, and Judah's failures, one often cannot easily distinguish between indications of political actions (e.g., a coronation, a coup, international diplomacy) and those related to the cult (e.g., sacrifice, polytheism, veneration of images) . . . Most interpreters (rightly) see the imagery primarily in covenantal terms, where Israel's polytheism is rejected, but there may be political overtones as well to Gomer's lovers." Cf. Wyatt, *Whisper*, 47–84.

298. Frick ("Hosea," 202) affirms Keefe's rejection of all attempts to depict Israel as the adulterous

after recognizing an echo of Ba'alism in Hosea,[299] anachronistically imagine it to refer to a full-blown "orgiastic cult."[300] But just as problematic are the presently fashionable attempts to drain Hosea of all religious meaning whatsoever, even its core prophetic warning against covenant disloyalty.[301]

Reading Hosea through an intertextual socioeconomic lens makes extremist sandtraps easier to avoid because this approach recognizes (a) that the "great texts" of the ancient Near East *routinely* use sexual metaphors,[302] but (b) that more often than not their *raison d'être* is mythopoeically symbolic—not "pornographic"—in that they routinely contrast "fertility" with "barrenness,"[303] "civilization" with "wilderness,"[304] and "(pro)creation" with "chaos."[305] In other words, the intertextual web[306] where Hosea sits plays an important role in the shaping of its literary character.[307] Hosea is no postmodern self-help manual on how to deal with sexual abuse[308]

---

wife of God because many of those who champion this view tend to emphasize individual over tribal/familial concerns. Yet Frick illuminates the opposite extreme when he argues that "the social body of the nation is like the sexual body of an adulterous wife—transgressive and threatening to the order of society."

299. Kelle's (*Hosea*, 163–64) attempt to remove all possibility of בעל referring to Ba'alism (even in Hos 2:8 and 13:1) is patently unpersuasive.

300. Sherwood's (*Prostitute*, 215–16) critique of Albright (*Monotheism*, 281) is justifiable. Orgiastic behavior occurs in the ancient world (Hos 4:18), but evidence for it comes overwhelmingly from Graeco-Roman sources (e.g. the cult of Cybele and Attis; cf. Augustine, *Civitas Dei* 6.7; Turcan, *Cultes*, 35–75). Fuchs (*Metaphors*, 378) contends that "the shockingly offensive language used by the prophets is meant to convey a message of much-needed reform in the face of imminent destruction," and further, that this "message depends on the literary effectiveness of the imagery, not on the actual historical correlation to the social practices of prostitution, adultery, and fornication."

301. Students of a previous generation used to call such disloyalty "idolatry" (גלולים, Ezek 23:49), but this is a much-avoided term in contemporary biblical studies. Attempts to eliminate even the descriptor συγκρητίσμος ("syncretism," Plutarch, *Mor.* 490a) are also problematic because such strategies, like recent attempts to eliminate all distinctions between "magic" and "religion," glaringly expose the tender underbelly of postmodern relativism (cf. Grenz, *Primer*, 14–15; Provan, "Israel," 585–606).

302. Cf. the highly sexualized roles enacted by Shamḫat and Ištar in Gilgamesh (GE 1.162–94; 6.6–21; Moore, *WealthWatch*, 51–71). A contemporary example for North American culture is *hokum*, a musical genre characterized by "a humorous lyric with sexual overtones" (Campbell, *Popular*, 101).

303. Shamḫat, e.g., uses sex to *domesticate*; i.e., lead Enkidu to the threshold of "human reason" (Akk *ṭēmu*, GE 1.202), while Ištar uses sex to *enslave*: "Come to me, Gilgamesh, and be my "lover" (*ḫa'iru*, GE 6.6). Give me the gift of your "fruit/treasure" (*inbu*, GE 6.7). These texts have to do with socioeconomic success, not pornographic lust.

304. Hendel, *Patriarch*, 118; Gardner and Maier, *Gilgamesh*, 69.

305. Weigle, *Creation*, 1–14; Anderson, *Creation*, 144–54. Cf. discussion above on ID/DI.

306. Polaski's (*Intertextuality*, 32–49) explanation of this "web" is thorough and detailed.

307. Haddox ("Hosea," 140) thinks that Hosea "criticizes the improper political and economic relations of the male elites by attacking from multiple angles their masculinity, a part of their identity that they usually use to justify their power and prestige."

308. Baumann (*Violence*, 52–55), e.g., never even *alludes* to the DI/ID tradition in her comments about "nakedness." Diamond and O'Connor ("Coding," 123) contend that metaphors should be understood as "context dependent, intention relative, and polyvalent," but contemporary attempts to label Hosea's metaphors as "pornoprophetic"—however understandable, given the global pandemic

or ecological neglect,[309] but a passionate plea to Yhwh's "bride" to "come home." This is clear from the outset:

ריבו באמכם ריבו	File suit[310] against your mother.[311] File suit—
כי היא לא אשתי ואנכי לא אישה	(for she is not my wife and I am not her husband)—
ותסר זנוניה מפניה	That she turn her prostitutions[312] away from her face
ונאפופיה מבין שדיה	And her adulteries[313] away from her breasts,
פן אפשיטנה ערמה	Lest I uncover her nakedness[314]
והצגתיה כיום והלדה	And expose her, as on the day of her birth.[315]

Careful not to overexpose these images, Hosea quickly herds them into an agrarian economic "corral":

ושׂמתיה כמדבר	I will make her like a wilderness,
ושתיה כארץ ציה	I will make her like a dry land,[316]

of sexual abuse—only expose the desperation driving one of contemporary America's "revitalization movements" (Townsend, "Revitalization," 180–203; *pace* Brenner-Idan, "Pornoprophetics," 63–86).

309. *Pace* Braaten, "Earth," 194–95.

310. Hos 2:4. MT ריב ("to sue"); cf. Syr ܕܘܢܘ ("sue, judge"); OG κρίνω ("judge, decide"); Vg *iudicate* ("judge, adjudicate"). *Tg. Hos.* 2.4 reads אוכחו לכנשתא דישׂראל ("Let me gather evidence against Israel"). Competent translation (a) takes the versions seriously because it (b) takes the ancient context seriously (e.g., refuse to divorce the use of ריב from its use in the Gideon tradition—ירבבעל, "Let Ba'al Sue," Judg 6:25). Braaten ("Land," 108) recognizes that "Yhwh summons his children to join him in a lawsuit against their mother."

311. Since the children of adulterous mothers tend to be mistreated, N.B. that the negative names given to Gomer's children—לא רחמה ("Not pitied"), לא עמי ("Not my people," Hos 1:6, 9)—coupled with their "foreignness/ strangeness" (זר) provokes in Hosea the "devouring" (אכל) of their "portions" (חלק, Hos 5:7 // נחלה, "inheritance," Num 18:20).

312. OG consistently translates this pl. Heb noun (זנונים) with a singular one, πορνεία, a nominal form of the verb πέρνημι, "to sell" (as in the phrase τοῖς ξένοις τὰ χρήματα περνάντα σ' εἶδον, "I saw you selling goods to these foreigners" (Euripides, *Cycl.* 270–71). Munn (*Sovereignty*, 173) explains the connection: "The essence of prostitution (πορνεία) is the taking of payment (πορνεία being cognate with πέρνημι, 'to sell')." The primary dynamic, in other words, is more economic than sexual.

313. Heb נאפופים (from the root נאף, "to commit adultery") is an abstract pl. noun with a reduplicated third radical indicating "either the *conditions* or *qualities* inherent in the idea of the stem, or else the various single *acts* of which an action is composed" (*GKC* 124d). MacIntosh (*Hosea*, 39) translates as a jussive: "Let her give up her brazen promiscuity and her adulterous embraces."

314. Israel's "stripping" here parallels Inanna's "stripping" (ID 94–122) in that both connote vulnerability, not titillation.

315. Hos 2:4–5a. Ezekiel uses this imagery to remind fellow exiles of their procreative potential: "You were abhorred on the day you were born . . . (but) as you lay in your blood, I said to you, 'Live! Grow strong like prairie grass!'" (Ezek 16:5–7).

316. The word pair ארץ ציה // מדבר appears in Isa 41:18; Jer 2:6; Ezek 19:13; Ps 63:1; 107:35. Cf. a second-century BCE hymn from Qumran: "I pr[aise you, my Lord] because you make me a source of streams in a 'wilderness' (יבשה) and a spring of water in a 'dry land'" (ארץ ציה, 1QH 16.4).

והמתיה בצמא	I will make her die with thirst.[317]

And there is no hesitation about identifying the socioeconomic realities standing behind them:

אלכה אחרי מאהבי	I will go after my lovers,
נתני לחמי ומימי	Those who give me my bread and my water,
צמרי ופשתי	My wool and my flax
שמני ושקויי	My oil and my drink.[318]

Simply put, Hosea posits a twofold strategy for corralling Israel's "prostitutional spirit":[319] (a) plow under her cultivated fields into what Jeremiah calls "unseminated land,"[320] and (b) block off all attempts to rejuvenate them:

לכן הנני שׂך את דרכך בסירים	Therefore I will fence in[321] her[322] way with thorns
וגדרתי את גדרה	And enclose her behind a wall[323]
ונתיבותיה לא תמצא	So she will not be able to find her furrows . . .[324]

Question: How does Yhwh's "bride" respond to being "corralled?" *Answer:* She attaches herself to "better lovers," even while pretending to herself that her first husband remains a failsafe option:

ורדפה את מאהביה	She will pursue her lovers,
ולא תשׂיג אתם	But will not (re)produce with them.[325]

317. Hos 2:5b.

318. Hos 2:7b (six agrarian gifts). *Tg. Hos.* 2.7 is even more economically specific: אהך בתר עממיא רחמי מספכי מיכלי ומשתי כסות מילא ובוץ משח וכל פרנוסי, "I will go after the Gentiles I love—the suppliers, sustainers, those who drink from oaken flagons, who supply me with oil and fine linen and all my provisions."

319. Hos 5:4 (רוח זנונים).

320. ארץ לא זרועה (Jer 2:2). Classical Torah thinking focuses on the "creation-uncreation-recreation" sequence (Clines, *Theme*, 80–82; Blenkinsopp, *Creation*, 5), echoed in Braaten's ("Twelve," 109) observation that "the agricultural bounty of the land is a gift of God" which "God can take back as an act of judgment." Less convincing, however, is his attempt to hold the land itself responsible for "committing whoredom" (calling it "the bride land"). Davis (*Agriculture*, 2) more accurately suggests that "in contrast to ourselves biblical writers belong to a culture that recognizes land care as the life-and-death matter it unquestionably is."

321. "The prosecutor" (השׂטן) uses this term (שׂוך, "to fence in") to accuse Yhwh of artificially protecting Job's wealth.

322. OG maintains the 3fs suffix.

323. Cf. ארחי גדר ולא אעבור, "He has walled up my way and I cannot pass" (Job 19:8). One of Marduk's "Fifty Titles" is *ša-rik mi-riš-ti ša is-ra-ta ú-kin-nu*, "the donor of arable fields who cultivates (even) the alleyways in between" (*Ee* 7.1, see above), an epithet promoting his ability to make crops grow even in the beaten-down walkways separating furrowed fields.

324. Hos 2:8. Given the influence of the דרך//נתיב word pair (Isa 42:16; Jer 6:16; Job 24:13; Lam 3:9), many translate נתיבה as "path," but given the agrarian context, "furrow" seems more appropriate.

325. MT נשׂג, "to (re)produce" (Ezek 46:7; *HAL* 686). OG καταλαμβάνω ("to overtake, apprehend")

She will seek, but not find them,[326]	ובקשתם ולא תמצא
Then say, "I will return to my first husband;	ואמרה אלכה ואשובה אל אישי הראשון
For it was better for me then than it is now."[327]	כי טוב לי אז מעתה

Question: Why does the "bride's" covenant commitments so wildly vacillate?[328] *Answer*: Not because she is desperate to escape "spousal abuse,"[329] but because she no longer *understands* (ידע)[330] who her "husband" is or what he does to protect her:

She does not understand that	והיא לא ידעה כי
I am the one who gives her	אנכי נתתי לה
The grain, the new wine, and the new oil,	הדגן והתירוש והיצהר
That *I* am the one who lavishes the silver upon her	וכסף הרביתי לה
And the gold she transfers[331] to Ba'al.[332]	וזהב עשו לבעל

Wounded by her petulance, the "husband" starts the painful process of reclaiming his "dowry-gifts":

is followed by Vg *adprehender* ("to apprehend, seize"), but Syr ܕܪܟ usually means "to obtain/attain" (*PSD* 97). Cf. Num 6:21; Ezek 46:7.

326. Cf. *Tg. Hos.* 2.9: ותרדוף שלם עם עממיא רחמחא ולא תדביק ותבעי סעיד, "She shall pursue peace with her Gentile lovers but not unite with them and produce food." MT Hosea elsewhere resonates with this agrarian economic sentiment: בצאנם ובבקרם ילכו לבקש את יהוה ולא ימצאו חלץ בהם, "With their flocks and herds they come to seek, but do not find Yhwh, (for) he has 'withdrawn' from them" (Hos 5:6; cf. the socioeconomic implications of חלץ in the "sandal-removal" ceremony in Deut 25:10; Ruth 4:7–8).

327. Hos 2:9. The problem with this strategy, of course, is that Torah expressly forbids it (Deut 24:2), in part because of its "well-defined economic consequences" (Collins, "Divorce," 116).

328. For many interpreters this is an irrelevant question because contemporary interpreters tend to fixate on a very different one; viz., "Why does this 'husband' treat this 'bride' so 'harshly?'" Mandolfo (*Zion*, 124), e.g., sees "Yhwh sidestepping issues of divine culpability" without "admitting that he fails in his duty as a husband." Responding to this, Kim ("Husband," 139) observes that "jealousy is an appropriate response to Israel's idolatry and may be justified on the basis of mutually held legitimate expectations," and McLaren (*Faith*, 138) argues that "if some overmasculinize their image of God, we aren't helping ourselves and our children . . . by overfeminizing God." Cf. Haddox, "Hosea," 49–83.

329. It will always be fashionable in agnostic circles to place *all* of the blame for Israel's problems on the shoulders of Yhwh.

330. As is well known, Hosea's focus on ידע ("to know") is one of its most dominant themes (cf. Huffmon, "Treaty," 31–37; McKenzie, "Hosea," 22–27; Holt, "Hosea," 87–103; Haymes, *Knowledge*, 61–95). Mowinckel's (*Erkenntnis*, 6, 33) clarification of ידע remains definitive: "Knowing God means (for those Israelites who stand with him in an interactive relational community) the recognition of his name, his being, his will and his feelings, so that one might obtain the direction, the quality, the content, and the directive for their own lives."

331. Lit. "makes, does." Vg (*fecerunt*) and Syr (ܥܒܕܘ) read 3pl. with MT, but OG (ἐποίησεν) reads 3msg.

332. Hos 2:10. Cf. the much longer list in *EA* 14, an inventory of marriage-gifts designed to solidify the shaky relationship between Egypt and Mitanni (Kühne, *Chronologie*, 70–72).

אשוב ולכחתי דגני בעתו	I will return and take back my grain in its time[333]
ותירושי במועדו	And my new wine in its season,
והצלתי עמרי ופשתי	I will seize my wool and my flax
לכסות את ערות	Which cover up her nakedness.[334]
והשמתי גפנה ותאנתה	I will lay waste her vines and her fig trees
אשר אמרה	(of which she says,
אתנה המה לי אשר נתנו לי מאהבי	"These are the wages[335] my lovers give me"),[336]
ושמתים ליער	And I will transplant[337] them into a wild thicket
ואכלתם חית השדה	For consumption by the beasts of the field.[338]

In spite of everything, however, the "husband" never *completely* abandons the "bride":

זרעו לכם לצדקה	Sow justice among yourselves
קצרו לפי חסד	Reap the "benefits"[339] of covenant loyalty
נירו לכם ניר	Re-plow for yourselves the fallow ground.[340]
ועת לדרוש את יהוה	For it is time to search for Yhwh so that
עד יבוא וירה צדק לכם	He may again rain justice down upon you.[341]

In fact, he even revisits the question of marriage, suggesting to his estranged "bride" the prospect of "renewing their vows":

333. דגן ("grain") is divinized in Anatolian (*^{d}ḫalkiš*; cf. Hoffner, *Myths*, 18; see above), Philistine (Judg 16:23; 1 Sam 5:1–7), Canaanite (*CAT* 1.5.6.24), and other sources (cf. Healey, "Dagon," 216–19; Handy, "Dagon," 1–3).

334. Hos 2:11. Cf. the nakedness of Inanna (ID 94–122), *pace* Magdalene ("Terror," 326–52) and Lanner (*Lament*, 129–31).

335. Syr ܐܢܘܢ ܝܗܒܘ ܠܝ ܪ̈ܚܡܝ ("my lovers give these to me") holds on to the "giving" nuance embedded in MT אתנה (a rare nominal form of נתן, "to give"; *Tg. Hos.* 2.14 reads יקר, "prize"), but OG *μισθώματά μου* ("my wages") and Vg *mercedes* ("wages") do not. The irony, of course, is that Israel chooses to exchange "gifts" for "wages."

336. Ignoring contextual questions entirely, Baumann ("Prophetie," 221) eisegetes this text by reading into it "a scene of sexual power" designed to "punish Israel."

337. Heb שׂים normally means "to put/place," but Syr ܢܨܒ can mean "to bear" fruit (*PSD* 395), so in light of the agrarian context, "transplant" seems an appropriate reading.

338. Hos 2:14.

339. Lit. "a mouthful" (*HAL* 865).

340. Hos 10:12a. MT ניר; cf. Ug *nrt* ("tilled field," *DULAT* 643). Jeremias (*Hosea*, 136) contends that Hosea "employs the notion of newly broken ground (i.e., of the creation of new agricultural land by cultivation)" that he might "adroitly combine the imagery of land acquisition and the urgent call to his contemporary listeners concerning the matter at hand. The point is to bring about a completely new orientation" (cf. Vg *innovate vobis novale*, "innovate a change for yourselves").

341. Hos 10:12b (NRSV; lit. "throw justice to you"). Cf. 6:3: ויבוא כגשם לנו כמלכוש יורה ארץ, "he will come to us like rain, like showers soaking the land."

וכרתי להם ברית ביום ההוא	I will cut a covenant with them on that day
עם חית השׂדה ועם עוף השׁמים	With the wild beasts, the birds of the air, and
ורמשׂ האדמה	The creeping things of the earth.
וקשׁת וחרב ומלחמה	But the bow, the sword, and war
אשׁבור מן הארץ	I will abolish from the land,[342]
והשׁכבתים לבטח	So that I may lay her down in a safe place.[343]

He even "betroths" (ארשׂ)[344] her to himself again, sealing this betrothal with a new round of dowry-gifts:

וארשׂתיך לי לעולם	I will betroth you to myself forever.
וארשׂתיך לי בצדק ובמשׁפט	I will betroth you with righteousness and justice,
ובחסד וברחמים	With loyalty and compassion.
וארשׂתיך לי באמונה	I will betroth you to myself with truth,[345]
וידעת את יהוה	And you shall know Yhwh.[346]

Utilizing agrarian images rooted in sturdy tradition-histories, Hosea even tries to convert these metaphorical abstractions into concrete provisions via a testimonial "conversation with the cosmos":

אענה את השׁמים	I will answer the heavens
והם יענו את הארץ	And they will answer the land.
והארץ תענה את הדגן ואת התירושׁ ואת היצהר	The land will answer the grain, wine, and oil;

342. Whether this is intended to be temporary or permanent is not stated; cf. the war imagery in other prophetic texts (e.g., "The Parable of the Two Eagles," Ezek 17:2–10).

343. Hos 2:20. This internal-external sequence (covenant protection alongside weapons removal) later apocalypticizes into the "sealing" of believers alongside the "marking" of unbelievers (Ezek 9:1–11; 1 QM 6.1–7; Rev 7:3, *σφραγίζω*; 14:9, *χάραγμα*). Jassen ("Imaginaries," 175–76) sees behind it a literary world in which "depictions of violence . . . fulfill a rhetorical role in empowering the disempowered."

344. That ארשׂ is an explicitly economic term is clear from מהר // ארשׂ in the Covenant Code: כי יפתה איש בתולה אשר לא ארשׂה ושכב עמה מהר ימהרנה לו לאשׁה, "if a man seduces a virgin who is not betrothed and sleeps with her, he shall endow her and make her his wife" (Exod 22:15). Talmud teaches that fathers should clothe and cover their daughters and "give them something" (ניתיב לה מידי, usually taken as a reference to "dowry") so that a young man might be motivated "to leap (!) upon her and marry her" (דקפצי עלה ואתו נסבי לה, *b. Ketub.* 52b). Launderville (*Celibacy*, 88) recognizes that the מהר ("dowry") is "the wife's form of social security in case the marriage fails."

345. *These* "gifts," of course, are of infinitely greater value than "grain, wine and oil."

346. Hos 2:21–22. At Ugarit Yariḫ gives a *mhr* to Nikkal consisting of silver, gold, lapis-lazuli, orchards, and vineyards (*CAT* 1.24.19–23; see above), but Yhwh gives gifts to *his* betrothed unabashedly celebrating the character traits developed by what Peterson (*Obedience*, 201–06) calls "a long obedience in the same direction."

והם יענו את יזרעאל	And *they* will answer Jezreel,[347]
וזרעתיה לי בארץ	But *I* will inseminate her in the land.[348]

Summary: Yhwh's desire to (re)establish covenant intimacy with *his* "bride" on *his* land seems genuine,[349] but the prophet harbors lingering doubts that Israel's addictions prohibit her from understanding the seriousness of Torah's warnings to wayward wives.[350]

Joel

Where the metaphors in Hosea focus on the "fertility-infertility" and "marriage-divorce" polarities, Joel's metaphors cluster around the "destruction-restoration" polarity.[351] Where the imagery in Hosea focuses on the pain ravaging the heart of a broken-hearted husband, the horror of locust plague generates a different type of pain-imagery.[352] Many ANE texts explain such plagues as the absence or death of the "deity-in-charge,"[353] but not Joel. Here it is interpreted as a signal call for שׁובה

347. On יזרעאל ("God inseminates"), Dearman (*Hosea*, 92) argues that whatever its use elsewhere (e.g., Hos 1:3), here "Jezreel" denotes "fruitfulness and prosperity."

348. Hos 2:23b-25a. Sexual procreation is not the *only* way to be "creative," but in Hosea it appears to be the image to which his audience most readily relates. Moughtin-Mumby (*Metaphors*, 71–72) spins this positively by suggesting that Hosea "may be tempted away from its 'prostitution' motif only rarely, but when it is attracted by wider sexual or marital metaphorical language, even these passing metaphors reflect and engage in the innovative and distinctive persuasive strategies of this playful and creative prophetic poetry."

349. Cf. Stienstra, *Husband*, 96–126; Sohn, *Husband*, 67–83. Daniels (*Hosea*, 114) contends that "Yhwh is here the bestower of the produce of the land rather than the land itself, but that Hosea should dissociate the two is highly unlikely. Only the Lord of the land can cause it to bring forth its fruit, and only the Lord of the land can give it to Israel."

350. Explicitly economic is the rationale for this Torah prohibition: כי תועבה הוא לפני יהוה ולא תחטיא את הארץ אשר יהוה אלהיך נתן לך נחלה, "For that would be an abomination in the presence of Yhwh, and you shall not cause the land to sin which Yhwh your God is giving you as an inheritance" (Deut. 24:4; cf. Jer 3:1). Vg comes closest to preserving the causative dimension of MT תחטיא (*ne peccare facias terram tuam*, "you shall not cause your land to sin"), *contra* Syr (ܠܐ ܬܚܛܐ ܒܐܪܥܐ, "you shall not sin in the land") and OG (οὐμιανεῖτε τὴν γῆν, "you shall not defile the land"). This line of interpretation hardens in Sirach: "A woman who leaves her husband and presents him with an heir by another man has, first of all, disobeyed the law of the Most High; second, she has committed an offense against her husband; and third, through her fornication she has committed adultery and brought forth children by another man" (Sir 23:22–23).

351. Barton (*Joel*, 63) bluntly contends that "Yhwh has an interest in bringing about a restoration of material prosperity."

352. ANE treaties commonly mention locust plague in their curse-lists (*VTE* 442–43; *ANET* 538; Deut 28:38; cf. Wiseman, "Vassal," 78). Duhm (*Propheten*, 398–99) marginalizes the significance of the locust plague in Joel, but Crenshaw (*Joel*, 15) thinks that the land to which Joel refers suffers "from a widespread infestation of locusts and a dry summer during which all streams have failed." Seitz (*Joel*, 125–26) cites a recent report on the utter devastation caused by a contemporary locust swarm.

353. Cf. DT (discussed above) and Ahlström (*Joel*, 62–63). Assis (*Joel*, 41) argues the majority opinion that "in chapter 1 of Joel the exclusive meaning of locusts is literal, a plague of actual locusts,"

(“repentance”),[354] which upon implementation carries the potential of producing divine שׁלם (“compensation”):[355]

גוי עלה על ארצי	A nation[356] rises up against my land,[357]
עצום ואין מספר	Strong and innumerable . . .[358]
שׂם גפני לשׁמה ותאנתי לקצפה	Uprooting my vines and exposing my fig trees
חשׂף חשׂפה והשׁליך	Stripping off the bark and shredding it,
הלבינו שׂריגיה	Turning white its tendrils . . .[359]
הכרת מנחה ונסך	Cutting off the grain and drink offerings
מבית יהוה	From Yhwh’s house.[360]
אבלו הכהנים משׁרתי יהוה	The priests—Yhwh’s ministers—mourn,
שׁדד שׂדה אבלה אדמה	The fields are devastated, the ground mourns.[361]
כי שׁדד דגן	For the grain languishes,[362]
הוביש תירושׁ אמלל יצהר	The wine dries up, the oil runs out.[363]

but “when readers progress to chapter 2 they enter a metaphorical realm” where “the disaster described is compared to a human enemy.”

354. Joel 2:12. Crenshaw (“Joel,” 188–89) suggests that שׁובה does not always imply pre-existent transgression.

355. Joel 2:25; 4:4. Given the semantic flexibility of the Ug and Akk cognates, Eisenbeis (*Wurzel*, 353) argues that the root idea of שׁלם is “totality, wholeness,” but Gerleman (*Wurzel*, 1–2) argues that the root idea (brought out most clearly in the D form) is “compensation” (*HAL* 1418–23 excludes neither option). Levine (*Presence*, 28) defines the שׁלם-sacrifice in Leviticus (Lev 7:18, 20–21) as an “efficacious gift of greeting offered in the presence of the Lord.”

356. Barton (*Joel*, 43) cites Canaanite (*CAT* 1.14.2.51–3.7) and Sumerian texts to show that Joel is not the first ancient text to depict locust plague in sociopolitical terms (cf. Thompson, “Locusts,” 52–55).

357. Use of first person is a major characteristic of chapter 1: ארצי (“my land”); גפני (“my vines”); תאנתי (“my fig trees”); עמי (“my people”); נחלתי (“my inheritance”).

358. Joel 1:6a. OG *ἰσχυρὸν καὶ ἀναρίθμητον* (“strong and without number”); Vg *fortis et innumerabilis* (“strong and innumerable”; Syr ܚܣܝܢ ܘܠܝܬ ܠܗ ܡܢܝܢ (“strong and without number”). Crenshaw (*Joel*, 15) suggests that “the ensuing graphic description of Yhwh’s army appears to combine elements of an invasion of locusts, human soldiers, and perhaps celestial beings.”

359. Joel 1:7. Noting גופני עמי (“vines of my people”) in *Tg. Joel* 1.7, Finley (*Joel*, 29) suggests that “even though the plague and its effects are literal, the sequence ‘my land . . . my vine . . . my fig tree’ is surely intended to evoke the thought of Judah and the people who inhabit it.”

360. Hurowitz (“Joel,” 597–603) points out that an early Akkadian hymn to Nanāya (daughter of Anu) depicts two species of locusts who *pārisu sattukkī ša ilī u ištarā[ti]*, “cut off the regular offerings to the gods and goddesses” (cited from Streck and Wasserman, “Nanāya,” 183–201). *Tg. Joel* 1.9 reads קורבנין ונסכין, “*qorban*-gifts and libations” (on קרבן, see below).

361. Hayes (*Mourns*, 12–18) posits an organic connection between the “mourning” (אבל) of the priests and the “mourning” (אבל) of the land.

362. MT שׁדד. Cf. Hit *wešuriyaš* (“stifled”) in DT (Hoffner, *Hittite Myths*, 2a.2–3). Should the cereal-deity Dagan be in the back of the prophet’s mind (cf. *CAT* 1.2.1.19; 5.6.24), Syr (ܐܬܒܙܙ ܥܒܘܪܐ, “the produce is pillaged”) later tries to erase it.

363. Joel 1:9–10.

Having depicted this crisis with such grim images, Joel's attention quickly moves away from the "what" question to the "how" question—"How can the economy survive?"—then engages it with a step-by-step sequence of actions:[364]

Step One—"Ask Yhwh for help"

בין האולם ומזבח	Between the porch and the altar[365]
יבכו הכהנים משרתי יהוה	Let the priests—Yhwh's ministers[366]—weep,
ויאמרו חוסה יהוה על עמך	And say, "Spare[367] your people, O Yhwh!
ואל תתן נחלתך לחרפה	Let not your inheritance[368] suffer disgrace,
למשל בם גוים	Or be taunted by the nations!"[369]

Step Two—"Bear witness to Yhwh's answer"

ויקנא יהוה לארצו	Yhwh becomes jealous for his land
ויחמל על עמו	And shows renewed interest in his people . . .[370]
ויען יהוה ויאמר לעמו	Yhwh replies to his people, saying,
הנני שלח לכם	"Look, I am sending to you
את הדגן והתירוש והיצהר	The grain, the new wine, and the fresh oil.
ושׂבעתם אתו	You will be sated by it, and
ולא אתן אתכם עוד חרפה בגוים	I will let the nations reproach you no longer."[371]

364. Cf. Prinsloo (*Joel*, 123), *contra* Wolff's (*Joel*, 7) vision of Joel as a "nearly complete symmetry" (cf. Richter, *Richterbuch*, 319–43).

365. The אולם-"porch" is the boundary beyond which no one enters the temple except ordained priests. So for priests to exit the temple and congregate "between the אולם and the מזבח" signals heightened empathy for a suffering populace (Joel 2:17 // Ezek 8:16).

366. Allen (*Joel*, 53–54) contends that "the twice-mentioned priests are "particularly concerned because of the disastrous effect on the cultic routine," seeing that "all three products (grain, wine, oil) are the principle crops of Palestinian farmers."

367. MT חוס ("to feel sorry for, spare"); Syr ܚܣ ("to sympathize with, spare; cf. حس, "to feel compassion/ sympathy," *DMWA* 174). Vg reads *dicent parce* ("they speak sparingly").

368. MT repeats the now-familiar ANE *Leitwort* נחלה ("inheritance/possession").

369. Joel 2:17a–b. Assis (*Joel*, 37–38) finds Simkins's (*Joel*, 272–73) attempt to draw a parallel between the "locusts" in the first half of Joel and the "nations" in the second half "refreshing," but "inaccurate."

370. Joel 2:18. MT חמל, Vg *parco*, and Syr ܚܣ all carry socioeconomic connotations; moreover, the nominal form of OG φείδομαι (φειδός) can mean "thrifty" (Homer, *Od*. 14.92; Hesiod, *Works* 369).

371. Joel 2:19. Isaiah ridicules those who look to Pharaoh for "help" (עזר) and "profit" (יעל), but find only "shame" (בשת) and "reproach" (חרפה, Isa 30:5).

Step Three—"Rejoice at the prospect of economic revival"

אל תיראי אדמה גילי ושמחי	Fear not, O land! Rejoice and be glad!
כי הגדיל יהוה לעשות	For Yhwh will do great things.
אל תיראי בהמות שדי	Fear not, O beasts of my fields!
כי דשאו נאות מדבר	For the pastures of the wilderness will sprout,[372]
כי עץ נשא פריו	The tree bearing its fruit,
תאינה וגפן נתנו חילם	The fig and the vine producing their full yield.[373]
ובני ציון	O children of Zion,
גילו ושמחו ביהוה אלהיכם	Rejoice and exult in Yhwh your God!
כי נתן לכם את המורה לצדקה	For he sends the early rain for your vindication,
ויורד לכם גשם	And pours down for you the heavy rain,[374]
מורה ומלקוש בראשון	The early and the latter rain, as before.[375]
ומלאו הגרנות בר	Your threshing floors[376] will fill with grain
והשיקו היקבים תירוש ויצהר	And your winepresses flow with oil and wine.[377]

Step Four—"Accept Yhwh's compensation"

ושלמתי לכם את השנים	I will compensate you for the years[378]
אשר אכל הארב	Which the locust has devoured . . .
ואכלתם אכול ושבוע	You shall eat well and be satisfied,[379]
והללתם את שם יהוה אלהיכם	And praise the name of Yhwh your God
אשר עשה עמכם להפליא	Who deals wondrously with you.[380]

372. The oxymoron נאות מדבר ("pastures of the wilderness") occurs earlier in Joel (1:19) and elsewhere in Nevi'im (Jer 9:9; 23:10).

373. Contrast Jeremiah's negative focus on "unseminated" land which "produces no yield" (Jer 2:8). In Zechariah this agrarian prosperity is to be "inherited" (נחל) by שארית העם הזה, "the remnant of this people" (i.e., not the people as a whole; Zech 8:12; cf. Larkin, *Zechariah*, 196).

374. MT גשם is the term used in Kings to describe the "heavy rain" concluding the contest on Mt. Carmel (1 Kgs 18:45).

375. Deist (*Culture*, 125) recognizes that "the right kind of rain at the right time" (Deut 32:2) translates into "freedom from creditors" (11:14; 28:12).

376. Waters (*Threshing*, 40) observes that "though much of Joel focuses on lament, the threshing floor emerges as a symbol of survival, the place where Zion will be fed and nourished."

377. Joel 2:21–24. Crenshaw (*Joel*, 18) summarizes this section as "a rich résumé of assurances."

378. Barton (*Joel*, 47) wonders whether שנים might imply the possibility of "two separate locust plagues," but Allen (*Joel*, 95) suggests that "apparently the locusts' attacks are not confined to a single year," but perhaps "to several years in succession."

379. Joel 2:25a. The "consumption-restoration" polarity stands out clearly here.

380. Joel 2:26. Citing examples from Torah (Exod 21:37; Lev 24:18), Allen (*Joel*, 95) labels שלם ("to

Step Five—"Bear witness to Yhwh's compensation of the nations"[381]

וקבצתי את כל הגוים	I will gather all the nations
והורדתים אל עמק יהושפט	And bring them down to the Valley of Jehoshaphat[382]
ונשפטתי עמם שם על עמי	Where I will judge them on behalf of my people
ונחלתי ישׂראל אשר פזרו	And my inheritance,[383] Israel, whom they scattered,
בגוים וארצי חלקו	Parceling out my land among the Gentiles,
ואל עמי ידו גורל	Casting lots for my people,[384]
ויתנו הילד בזונה	Exchanging little boys for prostitutes,[385]
והילדה מכרו ביין וישתו	And little girls for flasks of wine.[386]
וגם מה אתם לי צר וצידון	What are you to me, O Tyre? O Sidon?
וכל גלילות פלשת	All you regions of Philistia?
הגמול אתם משלמים עלי	Would *you* compensate *me*?[387]
ואם גמלים אתם עלי	Should *you* try to repay *me* anything,[388]
קל מהרה אשיב גמלכם בראשכם	I will quickly turn it back upon your head.
אשר כספי וזהבי לכחתם	For you take my silver and my gold,[389]
ומחמדי הטבים הבאתם להיכליכם	And my precious treasures[390] to your palaces,

compensate") an "indemnifying term."

381. Crenshaw (*Joel*, 19) argues that since "Judah experiences an initial installment on the expected reward for faithful worship of Yhwh, Joel ponders an even fuller payment—complete revenge against foreigners for their cruelty toward Judeans."

382. Crenshaw (*Joel*, 19) believes that the "Valley of Jehoshaphat . . . is a nonexistent place created in the prophet's imagination by a verbal play on its meaning, 'Yhwh has judged.'"

383. N.B. the *Leitwort* נחלה ("inheritance"; cf. above).

384. Cf. Obad 11; Nah 3:10; Luke 23:34. Barton (*Joel*, 99) thinks that because of its use in divination, lot-casting is for many a "sign of contempt."

385. *Tg. Joel* 4.3 reads ויהבו עולימא באגר זניתא, "and they give the little boy over as wages for the prostitute." Like Ezekiel, Joel finds the business of human trafficking patently evil.

386. Lit. "the little girl for wine and they drink." Oppenheim ("Siege," 69–89) documents similar exchanges in wartime sieges, though peacetime child labor is legally permitted (cf., e.g., CH 114–18; Chirichigno, *Debt-Slavery*, 61–72). The practice today is vigilantly documented; cf. Genicot, "Child," 106–9; Fyfe, "Child," 82–85; Madrinan, "Child," 95–101; and Marriage, "Child," 102–5.

387. Cf. Gerleman, "Wurzel," 1–14. Inverted compensation arrangements occur in Ezek 16:33–34 and Hos 8:9. Cf. also Micah's use of שׁלם to denote "bribery" (Mic 7:3).

388. גמל // שׁלם is not unique to Joel; cf. קול יהוה משלם גמול לאיביו, "The voice of Yhwh delivers recompense to his enemies" (Isa 66:6).

389. Cf. גם כספם גם זהבם לא יוכל להצילם, "Neither their silver nor their gold will be able to save them" (Zeph 1:18).

390. MT מחמדי can refer to non-economic "treasures" (e.g., בטנם מחמדי, "treasures of their womb,"

ובני יהודה ובני ירשלם מכרתם	And sell the children of Judah and Jerusalem
לבני היונים	To the Greeks . . .[391]
ומכרתי את בניכם ואת בנותיכם לבני יהודה	But I will sell *your* children to the Jews
ומכרום לשבאים	And they will sell them to the Sabeans . . .[392]

Step Six—"Anticipate prosperity"[393]

והיה ביום ההוא יטפו ההרים עסיס	On that day[394] the mountains will drip wine
והגבעות תלכנה חלב	And the hills will flow with milk.[395]
וכל אפיקי יהודה ילכו מים	All of Judah's stream-beds will flow with water.
ומעין מבית יהוה יצא	A fountain will spring forth from Yhwh's house,
והשקה את נחל השטים	And irrigate the Wadi Shittim.[396]

Summary: John Barton insightfully observes that Joel begins with a "solemn lament assuring that it is still possible for Yhwh to relent," then follows it with the

Hos 9:16), but here probably refers to the temple furnishings stolen decades earlier by the Chaldeans (i.e., מחמד לכספם, "treasures of their silver," Hos 9:16; cf. Dan 5:2–3). As Crenshaw (*Joel*, 20) notes, "the later books of Daniel and 1 Esdras" tend to "insert the motif of stolen vessels from the Jerusalem temple into narrative plots."

391. Joel 4:2–6a. Challenging the belief that the laws laid down in Mishnah and Talmud always reflect actual practice, Martin ("Slavery," 113) insists that "slavery among Jews of the Graeco-Roman period" differs little "from the slave structures of those people among whom Jews are living" (*contra* Urbach, "Slavery," 1–94). Flesher (*Slaves*, xii) firmly insists that "no direct link necessarily exists between the behavior envisioned by a law and the behavior practiced by members of a community."

392. Joel 4:8. Herion ("Sabeans," 861) locates the home of the שׁבאים in Yemen and/or Ethiopia (the latter perhaps a colonial outpost). Nogalski (*Redactional*, 52) thinks "the Sabeans are mentioned because they are a distant nation, not because they are famous as slave traders," even though Joel emphasizes the latter over the former.

393. Toffelmire (*Joel*, 76) observes that many of the terms in the last chapter of Joel "fall within a semantic field associated with exchange and in some situations with trade or economic situations," but it cannot be overemphasized that prophetic notions of "prosperity" in Nevi'im have nothing to do with Western corporate notions of "prosperity," even though the latter "operates as a major force in American religion" (Bowler, *Prosperity*, 5).

394. Munch (*Expression*, 17–18) argues that (a) the phrase ביום ההוא has little to do with יום יהוה, but (b) operates as "an editorial connective formula." Rudolph (*Zephanja*, 264) and many others, however, disagree (e.g., Krinetzki, *Zefanjastudien*, 32–39; Irsigler, *Jahwetag*, 128, 168–69, 200–201).

395. Stern ("Land," 555) points out that Yhwh's ability to create a land flowing with "milk and honey" (Exod 3:8) closely parallels Ba'al's ability to provide "oil" and "honey" (*šmm // nbt*, *CAT* 1.6:3:6–7), thus finding it "difficult to imagine that 'a land flowing with milk and honey' does not have its origin in the rivalry with Ba'al."

396. Joel 4:18. Sweeney (*Twelve*, 184) points out that Shittim is the "site where the people of Israel turn to Ba'al" (Num 25:1–15), but Glenny (*Micah*, 155) suggests that the otherwise unknown GN "Wadi Shittim" is a "dry valley east of Jerusalem."

solemn assurance that "after this rite is carried out . . . disaster will be replaced with *prosperity*."[397]

Amos

Amos is less metaphorical than the first two scrolls of the Twelve, but in many ways its acerbic bluntness only deepens the significance of its socioeconomic impact.[398] The first oracle against Israel, for example, positioned at the end of a GN double-chiasm,[399] uses language which is *explicitly* economic:[400]

על שלשה פשעי ישראל ועל ארבעה	Because of Israel's many transgressions[401]
לא אשיבנו	I will not revoke it (i.e., her punishment).[402]
על מכרם בכסף צדיק	For they sell the righteous for silver[403]
ואביון בעבור נעלים	And the needy for[404] a pair of sandals,[405]
השאפים על עפר ארץ	Trampling[406] into the dust of the earth

397. Barton, *Joel*, 13.

398. Linville (*Amos*, 83) recognizes that "lying about at shrines and drinking confiscated wine (Amos 6:4–6) encapsulate both social and sacral offenses" and that Amos has to do with "an unjust political and economic system" (cf. Jaruzelska, *Amos*, 13–26).

399. The first four GNs (Damascus, Gaza, Tyre, Edom) make an "X" on the map with Israel at the center, the remaining four (Ammon, Moab, Judah, Israel) a westward "U" eventually landing upon Israel. As Barton (*Amos*, 49) recognizes, this opening literary structure makes it clear from the outset that "Israel's election does not indemnify her against punishment for sin."

400. Altmann (*Economics*, 66) recognizes that "the Prophets tend to be the first destination for investigations of economics in the preexilic period . . . and the Book of Amos puts economics on display in its denunciations." Schütte (*Schriftprophetie*, 4) believes that the first Israel-oracle (Amos 2:6–8) addresses Israelites "looking back at the destruction of their homeland and considering their new life as refugees in Judah."

401. Gesenius (*GKC* 158c) and Joüon (170h) explain the practical intentionality of the numerical idiom ועל ארבעה . . . על שלשה ("for three . . . and for four").

402. That the 3ms suffix refers to "punishment" becomes clear only a few verses later with the phrase אפקד עלכם את כל עונתיכם ("I will punish you for all your iniquities," Amos 3:2). Ceresko ("Amos," 485–90) discusses other possibilities.

403. MT מכר ("to sell"). Cf. Akk *makāru* in the command *ina alim Aššur ma-kà-ra-am ula taleʾe*, "you cannot sell (anything) in the land of Aššur" (TCL 4.5.11), and N.B. the repetitive use of מכר in Joel 4:6–8. Houston (*Amos*, 37) finds in this phrase an example where "the motivation for oppression is seen as financial."

404. MT בעבור ("for the sake of"). Cf. Akk *ebūru*, a cognate term sometimes denoting that portion of the "harvest yield to be paid as rent" (*CAD* E.19).

405. *Tg. Amos* 2.6 reads לא אשבוק להון על דזבינו בכספא זכאין וחשיביא בדיל דיחסנון, "I will not forget their selling of the innocent for silver and their confiscation of the poor's possessions." Pleins' understanding (*Visions*, 369) of the idiom in MT is doubtless correct: "the buying and selling of the אביון . . . refers to their falling into debt-servitude as a result of their failure or inability to pay off their debts."

406. Amos 2:7. Following OG πατέω ("to tread underfoot") and Syr ܕܝܫܝܢ (D form of ܕܘܫ, "to tread underfoot") with Wolff (*Amos*, 163), *HAL* (p. 1280) emends MT שאף ("to annoy") to שוף ("to trample"; cf. Gen 3:15).

The head of the poor,[407]	בראשׁ דלים
And obstructing the path of the afflicted.[408]	ודרך ענוים יטו
A man and his father go unto the same girl,[409]	ואישׁ ואבי וילכו אל הנערה
Thereby profaning my holy name.[410]	למען חלל את שׁם קדשׁי
Upon clothing taken in pledge[411]	ועל בגדים חבלים
They stretch out beside every altar,	אצל כל מצבח יטו
Drinking wine acquired via extortion[412]	ויין ענושׁים ישׁתו
In the house of their gods.[413]	בבית אלהיהם

Reacting to the term אלהים ("gods/God"),[414] and noting that אלהיהם in Amos ("their gods") never refers to the God of Moses, Jeremy Schipper and Mark Leuchter suggest that the first oracle against Israel condemns neither a northernly syncretized Yahwism nor the worship of Syro-Palestinian deities generally,[415] but the wealthy Isra-

407. Syr replaces this line with ܘܡܣܦܝܢ ܠܡܣܟܢܐ ("and they beat down the traders"), but *Tg. Amos* 2.7 reads דשׁיטין בעפרא דארעא רישׁ מסכיניא ודין חשׁיכיא, "trampling into the dust of the land the head of the poor and the cause of the 'desperate' (lit. 'darkened')."

408. Amos later condemns the "cows of Bashan" for עשׁקות דלים ("oppressing the poor") and רצצות אביונים ("crushing the needy," Amos 4:1). Elsewhere Yhwh's spirit does the exact opposite; i.e., "encourage the afflicted" (בשׂר ענוים, Isa 61:1).

409. Reading OG τὴν αὐτὴν παιδίσκην. Syr reads ܠܘܬ ("to join with"). Tracing this behavior into later texts, Fried ("Exploitation," 161) suggests that Neh 5:4–5 refers either to (a) the sale of children to raise money to pay rent on fields and vineyards, or (b) the payment of *ilku* (*CAD* I-J.73); i.e., that מדת המלך (5:4) refers to the "king's tax" required on land bequeathed to subjects by state officials. Thus, "for those who can afford it, the *ilku* will be paid off in silver," but for those who cannot, it must be paid off via military, domestic, or some other type of service, usually by a close relative. *Example:* Gedaliah, son of Raḫim-ili, works off the *ilku* owed by his father to Rimut-Ninurta son of Muršu (cited from Stolper, *Entrepreneurs*, 1–7; cf. van Driel, "Archive," 203–29).

410. MT חלל, "he profanes" (G ptc. sg.). Cf. OG βεβηλώσωσιν, "they might profane" (pf. subj. pl.); Vg *violarent*, "they might violate" (ipf. subj. pl.); Syr ܛܠܦܘܢ, "they have defiled" (ipf. pl.).

411. MT חבל, "to take as pledge of repayment, to borrow" (*HAL* 274; cf. Deut 24:12). In pre-Islamic Arabic اخبال "signifies the act of lending" (Lane 1.699); Cf. Akk *ḫabālu* ("to borrow"); e.g., *abua ma'da ḫabulli ša PN*, "my father borrowed much belonging to PN" (cited from *CAD* Ḫ.7). Ezekiel describes a צדיק ("righteous person") as someone who חבלתו חוב ישׁיב ("restores to the debtor his pledge") and חבל לא חבל ("never demands a pledge," Ezek 18:7, 16).

412. MT ענושׁים. OG οἶνον ἐκ συκοφαντιῶν, "wine from extortion." Cf. Ug *ġnṯ* in the epithet *il ġnṯ ʿgl il* ("the god who 'extorts' El's heifer," *CAT* 1.108.11); Akk *ḫ/kanāšu* ("to extort/levy a fine," *CAD* K.144–48); וענשׁו אתו מאה כסף, "and they will fine him one hundred shekels" (Deut 22:19).

413. Amos 2:6–8. *Tg. Amos* 2.8 reads בית טעותהון, "house of their idols" (cf. Thiel, "Amos," 285–97). Hadjiev (*Amos*, 109) sees the "theme of Israel's corrupt religion" as a major theme in Amos.

414. Cf. Draffkorn-Kilmer, "*Ilāni/Elohim*," 116–24; Moore, *Babbler*, 208; Gericke, *God*, 1–12.

415. Amos 2:6–8, *contra* Barstad, *Amos*, 37, 127–42; Mays, *Amos*, 47; and Hamborg, *Amos*, 116.

elite landowners attributing to their ancestors all their wealth.[416] Yet whether or not it engages the problem of ancestor-worship,[417] Amos maintains a clear focus:

בושסכם על דל יען	Because you trample upon the poor
ומשׂאת בר תקחו ממנו	And steal from him his grain allotment,[418]
בתי גזית בניתם	You will build stone-masoned houses[419]
ולא תשבו בם	But not inhabit them.[420]
כרמי חמד נטעתם	You will plant top-quality vineyards
ולא תשתו את יינם	But not drink their wine . . .[421]
צררי צדיק לקחי כפר	O attackers of the righteous, O bribe-takers[422]
ואביונים בשער הטו	Who push aside the needy at the gate . . .[423]
שמעו זות השאפים אביון	Listen to this, O tramplers of the needy,
ולשבית עניי ארץ	Who stifle the poor of the land,
לאמר מתי יעבר החדש	Muttering, "When will the new moon be over
ונשבירה שבר	So we can market grain?[424]
והשבת ונפתחה בר	And the sabbath, so we can sell wheat?"[425]

416. Schipper and Leuchter ("Amos," 441–48) read this into the phrase בתים רבים ("great houses") in Amos 3:15; Donner (*Botschaft*, 235) suggests that Amos condemns only "newly rich members of the civil service," but Schütte (*Schriftprophetie*, 520–42) contends that Amos lays the blame for Samaria's destruction squarely on the wealthy Israelites deported into Assyrian captivity.

417. Woo (*Marzēaḥ*, 174–95) argues that the *marzēaḥ* feast (cf. Amos 6:7) sometimes becomes a vehicle for venerating the dead.

418. Amos 5:11. Cf. MT משׂאת בר ("allotment of grain"); OG δῶρα ἐκλεκτὰ ("chosen gifts"); Vg *praedam electam* ("chosen loot"); Syr ܠܡܒܨܪܘ ܡܟܝܠܬܐ ܕܩܘܪܒܢܐ ܕܐܒܗܬܟܘܢ, "to reduce the *qorban*-measure of the parents" (on קרבן, see below; cf. McNamara, *Targum*, 229–31). Cf. the Aram phrases ממון שקר ("lying mammon," *Tg. Amos* 5.11) and ממון רשע ("evil mammon," *Tg. Hab*. 2.9 for MT בצע רע, "evil gain").

419. Jaruzelska (*Amos*, 150) cites textual and archaeological evidence suggesting (a) that בתי גזית ("hewn-stone houses") refers to construction technologies used in the building of "public structures," and (b) that this "corroborates the identification of those who despoil the needy . . . with royal officials living in the capital."

420. Why? Because Yhwh will הכה . . . רסיסים, "smash (them) to pieces" (Amos 6:11).

421. Amos 5:11 (repeated practically verbatim in Zeph 1:13).

422. MT כפר ("bribe," 1 Sam 12:3); OG ἀλλάγματα, (pl., "that which is taken in exchange," LSJ 149); Vg *munus* ("favor, obligation, tax"). Syr reads ܫܚܕ, "to bribe" (cf. Heb שׁחד, "to bribe," Ezek 16:33; Job 6:22).

423. Amos 5:12b. The שׁער ("gate"), of course, is where most village business is transacted (e.g., Ruth 4:2–11). *Tg. Amos* 5.12b reads לקבלא ממון דשקר ודין חשיכיא בבית כנישתכון מסטן, "to contract for deceitful mammon and darkened decision-making in the house of your satanic assembly."

424. Heb שׁבר has a wide semantic range (*HAL* 1303–10), but the basic meaning centers on that which "breaks away" (like grain from its husk).

425. Cf. 2 Kgs 4:23; Isa 1:13; Hos 2:13; Neh 10:32; Heschel, *Sabbath*, 86–93; Hasel, "Sabbath," 37–64.

You[426] deflate the bushel and inflate the shekel,	להקטין איפה ולהגדיל שקל
And rig the scales to commit fraud,	ולעות מאזני מרמה
Acquiring[427] the poor for silver	לקנות בכסף דלים
And the needy for a pair of sandals,	ואביון בעבור נעלים
Selling them chaff mixed in with the grain.[428]	ומפל בר נשביר

Like Jeremiah and other prophetic scrolls, Amos presumes that *the* factor responsible for the land's "mourning" (אבל) is fundamentally socioeconomic:

Shall not the land tremble over this,	העל זות לא תרגז הא
And every resident upon it mourn?[429]	ואבל כל יושב בה
Shall I turn your feasts into mourning . . . ?	והפכתי חגיכם לאבל
And make them like the mourning for an only child?[430]	ושמתיה כאבל יחיד

Even as Jeremiah "releases" (קרא דרור) Zedekiah to "pestilence, famine, and the sword" for pretending to "release" (קרא דרור) Jerusalem's slave population,[431] so Amos plays on the word רעב ("famine"):

I will send a famine on the land—	והשלחתי רעב בארץ
Not a famine from food,	לא רעב ללחם
Or a drought from water—	ולא צמה למים
But from the hearing of Yhwh's words.[432]	כי אם לשמע דברי יהוה

Like Isaiah, Amos dares to imagine a future in which

The one who plows overtakes the one who reaps,	ונגש חורש בקצר
And the treader of grapes the sower of seed.[433]	ודרך ענוים במשך הזרע

426. Amos 8:5, continuing 2 m pl. from בושסכם in 5:11.

427. OG κτᾶσθαι ("to purchase") maintains the inf. in MT, but Syr (ܢܙܒܢ, "we will buy off") and Vg (*possideamus*, "we will possess") change to 1st pl.

428. Amos 8:4–6. Simundson (*Amos*, 226–27) emphasizes that "Amos is particularly harsh in his accusations against those who use unfair business practices to cheat and oppress the poor" because they "cannot wait till the holy days are passed so they can make more money by fraudulent means."

429. Amos 8:8a (cf. Hayes, *Mourns*, 19–36).

430. Amos 8:10. Tobit cites this text centuries later to depict the world in which *he* lives (Tob 2:6; cf. below). For Hayes (*Mourns*, 34), the "mourning" metaphor "widens the scope of the social disorder . . . by connecting the human sphere with the natural sphere," thereby spawning "ramifications beyond any humanly conceived concept of punishment."

431. Jer 34:17 (cf. above).

432. Amos 8:11. Eidevall (*Amos*, 219) recognizes the depth of the socioeconomic problem in that "those who sell grain using immoral methods are, at the same time 'buying' the poor, as they bring them into indebtedness or outright enslavement."

433. Amos 9:13. Eidevall (*Amos*, 242) contends that "the hyperbolic image of activities that overlap, or overtake each other, is probably inspired by the blessing in Lev 26:5 . . . In other words, the epilogue of the book transforms the arid landscape envisioned in the prologue."

ונטעו כרמים ושתו את יינם	They shall plant vineyards and drink their wine
ועשׂו גנות ואכלו את פריהם	They shall establish gardens and eat their fruit.
ונטעתים על אדמתם	And I will plant them upon their land[434]
אשר נתתי להם	Which I give to them.[435]

Summary: Contemporary interpreters may identify the "poor" in Amos as settlers in the countryside[436] or urban residents in Samaria,[437] but regardless of their social location, Amos proves to be one of their fiercest champions.[438]

Micah

Micah champions the cause of every oppressed Hebrew forced to endure the systematic pilfering of his most important asset, his נחלה ("ancestral inheritance"):[439]

הוי חשבי און	Woe to those who plot malice[440]
ופעלי רע על משכבותם	While acting wickedly upon their beds.[441]
באור הבקר יעשׂוה	At morning light they execute it,[442]
כי יש לאל ידם	For it is in their power to do so.[443]

434. Jeremias (*Amos*, 169) recognizes in the symbolic agrarian language that "not only vineyards, but also the people of God can be 'planted.' The goal of the metaphor resides in the abiding and unthreatened quality of the change in fortune." Cf. the similar promise in Moses' "victory song": תבאמו ותטעמו בהר נחלתך, "you bring them in and plant them on the mountain of your inheritance" (Exod 15:17).

435. Amos 9:14–15. Few students of Amos any longer relegate this salvation-oracle to a (post-)exilic editor (*à la* Wellhausen, *Propheten*, 96; Westermann, *Heilsworte*, 76); yet cf. Rüterswörden, "Abschluss," 211–21.

436. Cf. Lang, "Poverty," 47–63.

437. Cf. Houston, *Contending*, 61.

438. Hamborg (*Amos*, 248) thinks it "unlikely that those poor enough to be selling themselves or family members as debt-slaves have any part at all in the literary processes that produce the Amos-text . . . However, if in the post-exilic period there are those who are not poor in socioeconomic terms, but who view themselves as the 'righteous poor' in religious terms, then there is the definite likelihood that some of these people take an interest in the preservation and development of the Amos-text."

439. Mic 2:2. Cf. Stade, "Mica"; Willis, "Micah"; Mays, *Micah*; Hillers, *Micah*; Allen, *Micah*; Ben Zvi, *Micah*; Jacobs, *Micah*; Wagenaar, *Micah*; Simundson, *Micah*; Smith-Christopher, *Micah*; Glenny, *Micah*; Cuffey, *Micah*. Schütte (*Schriftprophetie*, 4) thinks Micah "addresses a group of (refugee) Israelites living in Judah."

440. Mic 2:1. Mirroring those who חשבי און ("plot malice"), Yhwh חשב . . . רשע ("plots evil," 2:3).

441. This may refer to the musical behavior in Amos 6:4, activity also conducted on "couches/beds" (מטה/משכב)

442. The 3ms pronominal suffix appended to יעשׂו refers to the aforementioned און ("malice").

443. On Heb אל as "power" cf. Gen 31:9. *Tg. Mic.* 2.1 reads ארי אית חילא בידהון, "so that the strength of (their) existence (falls) into their hand."

וחמדו שׂדות וגזלו	They covet fields and seize them,[444]
ובתים ונשׂאו	And defraud people of their homes.[445]
ועשׁקו גבר וביתו	They oppress a man and his house,
ואישׁ ונחלתו	A man and his inheritance . . .[446]

The prophet believes, however, that the "shoe" (to use an old American idiom) will soon "wind up on the other foot"; i.e., that a righteous leader will some day arise courageous enough to challenge Judah's "robber barons":[447]

ביום ההוא ישׂא עליכם משׁל	On that day a taunt-song will drone overhead,[448]
ונהה נהי נהיה אמר	And (you will) wail bitterly,[449] saying,
שׁדוד נשׁדנו	"We are utterly ruined![450]
חלק עמי ימיר	He has redistributed[451] the parcel of my people,
איך ימישׁ לי	Plundering that which was once mine,[452]
לשׁובב שׂדינו יחלק	Parceling out our fields as a payoff."

444. Brueggemann (*Grace*, 164) sees here "the power class scheming about real estate even before they get out of bed in the morning. They lie awake at night thinking about how to buy up the land. And as soon as the sun comes up, they call their agents."

445. Mic 2:2 (lit. "and houses they lift away"). Soto (*Capitalism*, 207) contends that most people in the two-thirds world "view capitalism as a private club, a discriminatory system that benefits only the West and the elites who live inside the bell jars of poor countries."

446. Mic 2:1–2 (N.B., again, the *Leitwort* נחלה). *Tg. Mic.* 2.2 reads אחסנתיה ("his possessions"), but Syr ܩܢܝܢܗ ܘܝܪܬܘܬܗ ("his possessions and his inheritance") includes *everything* implied by נחלה. The crisis in Israel is twofold. *Externally*, the Assyrians are forcing Samaria to pay מנחה ("tribute," 2 Kgs 17:3; 18:14–16), money which the imperial government gathers through the imposition of exorbitantly high taxes. *Internally*, wealthy landowners take advantage of this as an "opportunity" to tack on all sorts of "handling fees." The result, as Hubbard observes ("Micah," 4), is that "these unrelenting taxes force peasants to mortgage their lands (and occasionally themselves) to moneylenders in order to pay them. Unable to keep up the mortgage payments, the poorest among them eventually lose their holdings to foreclosures."

447. Mic 5:2–4. Smith-Christopher (*Micah*, 168–69) asks, "What is to be done about unacceptable leadership among Israelites? Two solutions are often presented by the prophets. Either a new shepherd, an ideal one, will be appointed (or born, as in Isaiah's promises about the continued line of David), or God will change the terms of the agreement and take the job!" Cf. McNeese, *Barons*, 48–64.

448. Mic 2:4 (lit. "will lift up over you").

449. *GKC* 117r explains the semantic/syntactic significance of repetition.

450. Heb שׁדד. Cf. Ug *mlkn yšdd ḥwt ibh*, "the king will ravage the land of his enemies" (*CAT* 1.103+1.145.37). Citing the Akk cognate *šadādu* (*CAD* Š/1.27), Cathcart and Jeppeson ("Micah," 194–95) read "measure out for sale."

451. MT מור. Syr ܢܡܝܪ, "to trade" (ipf. of ܡܘܪ); OG μερὶς λαοῦ μου κατεμετρήθη ἐν σχοινίῳ, "part of my people is measured out with a cord" (cf. مير, "to provide," *DMWA* 933).

452. Heb מושׁ. (lit. "he touches," Gen 27:21; Judg 16:27; Ps 115:7); cf. Akk *mašā'u* (*CAD* M/1.361–62). Zechariah predicts a time when Judah והיו שׁלל לעבדיהם ("will become plunder for their own slaves," Zech 2:13).

לכן לא יהיה לך משליך חבל בגורל	Now no one champions your claim[453]
בקהל יהוה	In the assembly of Yhwh.[454]

Particularly deep are his feelings about *bribery*:

ראשיה בשחד ישפטו	Her rulers render verdicts for a bribe;[455]
וכהניה במחיר יורו	Her priests teach for a payoff;[456]
ונביאיה בכסף יקסמו	Her prophets divine[457] for silver . . .[458]

Nevertheless, in spite of all this Micah forecasts a prosperous future:

קומי ודושי בת ציון	Rise up and thresh, O daughter of Zion![459]
כי קרנך אשׂים ברזל	For I will turn your horn into iron,[460]
ופרסתיך אשׂים נחושה	And your hooves into bronze.[461]
והדקות עמים רבים	You shall pound many peoples to powder
והחרמתי ליהוה בצעם	And devote[462] their illicit estates to Yhwh;[463]

453. Lit. "casts your line by lot" (cf. Josh 18:10).

454. Mic 2:4–5. Presuming (a) that the genealogies in Chronicles are the product of "the cultic elite in Jerusalem in the Persian province of Yehud," and (b) that Boer's ("Economy," 29–48) Marxist model is a competent analytical tool, Jonker ("Agrarian," 97–98) reads the genealogies in Chronicles from a quasi-Marxist perspective, concluding that "the Chronicler's genealogies very clearly configure the relationship between Jerusalem and rural towns in the tribal areas in terms of donors and beneficiaries," the latter including "the Levite families who receive their land from all the tribal areas."

455. MT שחד (sg.). Cf. OG δώρων, "gifts" (pl.); Vg *muneribus*, "gifts, favors" (pl.). Where the English word "bribe" renders various Heb terms for "gift" (e.g., שלום, "compensation-gift," Mic 7:3), שחד always means "bribe" (*HAL* 1351). Cf. Syr ܫܘܚܕܐ, "bribe" (sg.); *Tg. Mic.* 3.11 שחד, "bribe" (sg.); and Old Aramaic שחד ("to bribe," *KAI* 224.28).

456. *Tg. Mic.* 3.11 reads כהנהא בממון מורן, "her priests teach for *mammon*."

457. This is the only place in Tanak where these roots converge: נביא-prophets "speak" (דבר) and "proclaim" (קרא), but in Tanak they do not "divine" (קסם), so the occurrence of the term here may well indicate some impropriety, socioeconomic or otherwise (cf. Ruppert, "קסם," 72–78; Moore, *Balaam*, 47–55). The targumist's lexicon includes Aram קסם ("to divine"), yet *Tg. Mic.* 3.11 still sanitizes this verse by reading נבייהא בכספא מלפין, "the prophets 'instruct' for money" (ילף).

458. Mic 3:11a; cf. כהן-נביא-חכם ("priest-prophet-sage") in Jer 18:18 and נביא-כהן-זקן ("prophet-priest-elder") in Ezek 7:26 (Moore, *Babbler*, 58–80). Premnath (*Prophets*, 173–76) sees the material in Mic 3:1–4, 9–12 directly critiquing the oppressive activities of wealthy landowners determined to seize ancestral land (e.g., 1 Kgs 21) in order to build large estates for themselves (a process he calls "latifundialization"), but Carroll (*Prophets*) finds this interpretation "forced" (cf. Moore, *Amos*, 760; Noonan, *Bribes*, 1–135).

459. Cf. Steck, "Zion," 261–81; and Maier, *Zion*, 91–93. The essays in Häusl (*Tochter*) examine the literary-historical afterlife of this epithet.

460. Amos condemns Damascus for similarly "threshing" (דוש) Gilead with sledges of "iron" (ברזל, Amos 1:3).

461. Oxen often do the work of threshing and winnowing at the גרן ("threshing floor," cf. Whittaker, "Threshing," 62–69).

462. "Devotion" (חרם) to Yhwh is not a peripheral notion in Nevi'im (cf. Lohfink, "חרם," 180–99).

463. Mic 4:13. MT בצע; OG πλῆθος ("great quantity/size"; cf. διὰ πλῆθος τῆς ζημίας, "because of the

וחילם לאדון כל הארץ	Their wealth[464] to the lord of all the land.[465]

Immediately following the justly famous oracle asking whether it is better to seek appeasement through sacrifice or to "walk humbly with your God,"[466] Micah denounces the cancerous corruption he sees devouring Judah:[467]

עוד האשׁ בית רשׁע	Am I to forget[468] the fraudulent[469] *bath*-measures[470]
אצרות רשׁע	In the compromised treasuries,[471]
ואיפה רזון זעומה	And the shrunken, tainted *ephah*-measures?[472]
האזכה במאזני רשׁע	Shall I justify[473] the rigged scales,
ובכיס אבני מרמה	And the canisters of false weights?[474]
אשׁר עשׁיריה מלאו חמס	For her rich men[475] are full of violence
וישׁביה דברו שׁקר	And her inhabitants manufacture lies,
ולשׁונם רמיה בפיהם	So deceitful is the language from their mouths . . .[476]

great size of the loss," *Thuc.* 3.70.5); Vg *rapinas* ("booty"); Syr ܢܟܣܬܗܘܢ ("their sacrifices"; from ܢܟܣ, "to slaughter, kill"). *Tg. Mic.* 4.13 reads נכסיהון, "their sacrifices."

464. MT חיל (meaning "strength" when paired with a synonym for "strength"; e.g. כח, Zech 4:6); "wealth" (when paired with a synonym for "wealth"; e.g., שׁלל, Isa 8:4; בצע, Mic 4:13). That its primary nuance here is perceived to be socioeconomic is confirmed by *Tg. Mic* 4.13, which reads ממון יקרהון, "their valuable *mammon*."

465. Mic 4:13. Is this a subtle reference to Ug *b`l arṣ* ("landlord," *CAT* 1.3.1.3–4)?

466. Mic 6:8. Following Seidel's (מיכה, 51–52) intertextual focus on the speeches of Samuel (1 Sam 12:3–17) and Micah (Mic 6:1–8), Joosten ("Micah," 455) concludes that "the most significant element these texts have in common is the protestation of innocence."

467. The oracle in Mic 6:9–15 specifically targets העיר ("the city," v. 9; cf. Chaney, "Micah," 149–60).

468. MT אשׁ. Since neither MT nor the versions make any sense (OG πῦρ; Vg *ignis*; Syr ܢܘܪܐ—all meaning "fire"), the majority of interpreters emend to האשׂא ("Shall I support?" from נשׂא) or האשׁה ("Shall I forget?" from נשׁה). Cf. McKane (*Micah*, 194–95) and Chaney ("Micah," 153).

469. At root Heb רשׁע means "evil" (*HAL* 1208–09), but the context here demands a wider semantic range.

470. Emending בית to בת, the בת referring to a liquid measure equal to the אפה (a dry measure).

471. Herzog ("Structures," 228–30) posits a distinction between מסכנות ("storehouses") and אוצרות ("treasuries"); where the former house grain, wine, oil and other agrarian items, the latter contain silver, gold, precious stones and weapons—products available only to the wealthy.

472. "The *ephah* and the *bath* are to be the same size" (Ezek 45:11). Cf. רזה את כל אלהי הארץ, Yhwh "will shrink down all the deities of the land" (Zeph 2:11). *Tg. Mic.* 6.10 reads מיתין לוט דשׁקר מכילן, "their accursed deceitful measure."

473. MT האזכה (lit. "make clean"); OG εἰ δικαιωθήσεται ("If he would justify"); Vg *numquid iustificabo* ("Am I expected to justify"); Syr ܐܙܟܐ ("Shall I acquit").

474. Lit. "fraudulent stones." *Tg. Mic.* 6.11 reads בכיס דביה מתקלין רברבין ודעקדין, "in the canister of reduced and significantly hollowed-out weights."

475. MT עשׁיר ("rich"). Cf. ואת עשׁיר במתיו ויתן את רשׁעים קברו, "He makes his grave with the wicked and a rich man in his death" (Isa 53:9). Cf. *Tg. Mic.* 6.11: דעתירהון מלן עוצריהון חטוף, "the warehouses of her rich men are filled with stolen items."

476. Mic 6:10–12.

You will eat, but not be satisfied,[477]	אתה תאכל ולא תשׂבע
For your stomach will remain empty.	וישחך בקרביך
You will put away,[478] but not save,[479] and	ותסג ולא תפליט
That which you do save I will "donate" to the sword.[480]	ואשר תפלט לחרב אתן
You will plant but not harvest;	אתה תזרע ולא תקצור
You will tread olives but find no use for the oil;	תדרך זית ולא תסוך שׁמן
You will tread grapes but not taste the wine.[481]	ותירוש ולא תשתה יין

Summary: Like other scrolls in the Twelve, opinions differ widely over how to read Micah. Some take the *external* view that the confiscation of Judahite property and possessions is an unavoidable response to excessive Assyrian demands for tribute.[482] Others take the *internal* view that the primary focus is the corrupt behavior of those Hebrew war profiteers willing to sacrifice others in the rush to line their own pockets.[483]

Habakkuk

The most socioeconomically pertinent passage in Habakkuk is also the most textually problematic:[484]

Surely wealth[485] corrupts[486] the arrogant man,	ואף כי היין בוגד גבר יהיר
And the one who opens wide his throat[487]	ולא ינוה אשר הרחיב

477. Cf. יאכלו ענוים וישׂבעו ("the poor will eat and be satisfied," Ps 22:27).

478. MT סוג (lit. "to remove"); cf. ס/שׂוג גבול, "remove the landmark" (Deut 19:14; Hos 5:10; Reiterer, "סוג," 165–70).

479. MT פלט (lit. "to escape"); cf. Prov 6:6–8; 21:5; 22:3; Hasel, "פלט," 551–67.

480. MT נתן ("to give"). Cf. the similar idiomatic expression in Jeremiah where Yhwh promises, in response to Zedekiah's duplicitous refusal to "declare a release" (דרור קרא) of Jerusalem's slaves, to "declare (his) release" (קרא דרור) to the "sword" (Jer 34:17).

481. Mic 6:14–15.

482. Wolff, *Micah*, 74–75 (Mic 2:1–2, 8–9).

483. Cf. McKane, *Micah*, 61–65; Hillers, *Micah*, 33; Houston, *Justice*, 66; and Kessler, *Micha*, 116–17.

484. "Problematic" is a relative term. Compared to the textual difficulties in, say, Mic 6:9–10 (cf. above), the "problems" in Hab 2:5–7 are minor.

485. MT יין ("wine") is followed by OG κατοινωμένος ("wine-addict"), Vg *vinum* ("wine"), and *Tg. Hab.* 2.5 (חמר, "wine"), but 1QpHab 8.3 reads הון ("wealth"). Whether 1QpHab 8.3–5 or MT Hab 2:5 is the "original text" (cf. Ramond, *Leçons*, 3–4) is not easily determined. Solid arguments support each option, yet Roberts' (*Habakkuk*, 113) seems least problematic: "One can do nothing with MT's 'wine is treacherous'; the many other emendations that are proposed lack textual support and involve more radical correction of the text."

486. MT בוגד ("corrupts," m. ptc.); 1QpHab 8.3 reads יבוגד ("corrupts," ipf. 3 m.).

487. Hab 2:5. Cf. *lyrt bnpš bn ilm mt*, "you must descend into the throat of divine Mot" (*CAT* 1.5.1.6–7). Since "throat" is the most likely translation for *npš* in this Ug text (*DULAT* 636–37), the same seems likely for נפשׁ in Hab 2:5.

Like Sheol will not succeed;[488]	כשאול נפשו
For like death, he is never satisfied.[489]	והוא כמות ולא ישׂבע
All the nations rally[490] against him, and	ויאספו אליו כל הגוים
All the peoples congregate against him.[491]	ויקבצו אליו כל העמים

The *Habakkuk Commentary* from Qumran Cave 1 is not the only witness to this ancient scroll,[492] but being the oldest it tends to command the most attention:

Will not all these (peoples) taunt him	הלא אלה כלם עליו משל ישׂאו
With sarcastic innuendos, saying,	ומליצה חדות לו ויאמר
"Woe to the man who amasses that which is not his.	הוי המרבה לא לו
How long will he burden himself[493] with debt?"[494]	עד מתי ומכביד עליו עבטיט
Will not your creditors[495] suddenly rise up	הלא פתע יקומו נשכיך
And those who scare you awaken . . .	ויקצו מזעזעיך
And make you *their* plunder?[496]	והיית למשסות למו

Although the prophet struggles with the deity's decisions in chapters 1–2, the mythopoeic hymn in chapter 3 reveals his determination to "wait quietly,"[497] even when

The fig-tree does not blossom	תאנה לא תפרח

488. *Tg. Hab.* 2.5 reads לא יתקיים, "he will not endure," but as Roberts points out (*Habakkuk*, 113), the Arabic cognate of MT נוה (نوى, Lane 3040) means "to aim for a goal, succeed."

489. Tromp (*Death*, 105) focuses on the obvious parallels with the behavior of the Canaanite deity Mot (cf. Hays, *Death*, 13–65).

490. Reading יאספו ("they gather, rally") with 1QpHab 8.5 instead of MT יאסף ("he gathers, rallies").

491. Hab 2:5. Reading יקבצו ("they congregate") with 1QpHab 8.5 instead of MT יקבץ ("he congregates"). Doubtless Roberts (*Habakkuk*, 117) is correct to identify the "arrogant man" as Nebuchadnezzar II.

492. Cf. Bernstein, "Habakkuk," 647–50.

493. Reading יכביד (lit. "he makes heavy") with 1QpHab 8.7 instead of MT מכביד (lit. "one causing heaviness").

494. Reading עבטט ("pledge-debt") with 1QpHab 8.8 (cf. MT עבטיט); cf. Heb עבט ("to lend"): העבט תעביטנו, "you shall indeed lend to him" (Deut 15:8; *HAL* 734–35; *DTTM* 1037). *Tg. Hab.* 2.6 reads חובין, "debts."

495. The primary meaning of נשך is "to bite" (Num 21:8); thus the one who "lends at interest" is the one who "takes a bite" out of the one owing him money (Deut 23:20). *Tg. Hab.* 2.7 reads אנס, a legal term denoting "one who is in possession of property bought from someone who obtains it by force or confiscation" (*DTTM* 86).

496. Hab 2:6–7, reading למו as emphatic. Cf. והיה חילם למשסה, "their wealth will become plunder" (Zeph 1:13).

497. Hab 3:16 (אנוח, lit. "I rest").

ואין יבול בגפנים	And there is no produce on the vines,
כחש מעשה זית	The work of the olive tree fails
ושדמות לא עשה אכל	And the fields produce nothing to eat,
גזר ממלכה צון	The flock is cut off from its fold
ואין בקר ברפתים	And there is no cattle in the corral.[498]

Summary: Portraying the "arrogant man" as a gluttonous shark devouring everything in his path, Habakkuk asks wounded readers to do something rather difficult for wounded readers to do: lay aside all doubt and despair. Empathizing with their struggle to survive the predations of a "stifled" economy,[499] Habakkuk promises that the southeastern peoples (the Chaldeans) so guilty of engaging in ruthless plunder will one day themselves be plundered:

כי אתה שלות גוים רבים	Because you (Babylon) plunder many nations
ישלוך כל יתר עמים	Everything "left over" will plunder you.[500]

Haggai

Whereas the pre-exilic prophets focus on the socioeconomic consequences of corrupt leadership, postexilic prophets like Haggai and Zechariah focus on the behavior of those Hebrew returnees more committed to rebuilding their own "houses" than Yhwh's "house."[501] Appalled by such priorities,[502] Haggai unleashes a stinging critique:

498. Hab 3:17.

499. Cf. Hit *wešuriyaš* in DT (Hoffner, *Hittite Myths*, 2a.2–3; cf. above). As is well known, the *Habakkuk Commentary* from Cave 1 applies this negative socioeconomic critique to a specific official—the הכוהן הרשע ("Wicked Priest," 1QpHab 8.8; 9.9; 11.4; 12.2, 8), a bureaucrat evidently adept at לוגיע רבים בעבודת שוו . . . להיות עמלם לריק גזל הון אביונים, "preoccupying many with useless busywork . . . , invalidating their labor . . . (and) robbing the poor of their wealth" (1QpHab 10.11–12; 12.10; cf. Lim, "Priest," 45–51).

500. Hab 2:6–8a. MT יתר is a *double entendre* because it addresses both economic (i.e., "profits") as well as human "leftovers" (i.e., "survivors"; cf. the יתר/שארית parallel in Zeph 2:9, "leftovers/remnant"). Addressing a much later context, the Qumran commentator identifies these antagonists as כוהני ירשלם האחרונים יקבוצו אשר הון ובצע משלל העמים ולאחרית הימים ינתן הונם עם שללם ביד חיל הכתיאים, "the last priests of Jerusalem who gather up riches and spoil from plundering the nations, but whose riches and plunder in the last days are given into the hand of the army of the Kittim" (1QpHab 9.4–7).

501. Stuhlmueller (*Haggai*, 20) contends that "Haggai can never be satisfied with a private religion of heart or home" because his "contact with the covenant is through the temple."

502. Haggai tends to get short shrift from (post)modern readers. Wolff (*Haggai*, 11), e.g., calls it "one of the most minor of the minor prophets, indeed one of the most despised," perhaps because some, like Taylor ("Haggai," 27) feel it to be "preoccupied with material things and devoid of the lofty concerns that characterize the writings of earlier biblical prophets." Cf. Kessler, *Haggai*, 103–53; Petersen, *Haggai*, 41–54; and Kippenberg, *Religion*, 23, 87.

העת לכם אתם לשבת בבתיכם ספונים	Is it time for you to settle into your paneled homes[503]
והבית הזה חרב	While *this* house lies desolate?[504]
שׂימו לבבכם על דרכיכם	Consider your situation.[505]
זרעתם הרבה והבא מעט	You sow much, but harvest little,
אכול ואין לשׂבעה	You eat, but never become satisfied,
שתו ואין לשכרה	You drink, but never to your fill,[506]
לבוש ואין לחם לו	You put on clothes, but never become warm,
והמשתכר משתכר אל צרור נקוב	You deposit your wages[507] in bags with holes.[508]

Then he challenges his audience to "connect the dots":

שׂימו לבבכם על דרכיכם	Consider your situation carefully:
עלו ההר הבאתם עץ ובנו הבית	Go up the hill, bring wood, and build the house,
וארצה בו ואכבד	So that I may be duly content.[509]
פנה אל הרבה והנה למעט	You search for much, but find little,
והבאתם הבית ונפחתי בו	And when you bring *that* home I take it away.[510]
יען מה	Why?
יען ביתי אשר הוא חרב	Because *my* house lies desolate
ואתם רצים איש לביתו	While each of you runs home to *his* house.[511]

503. *Tg. Hag.* 1.4 reads בתיא דמטללין בכיורי ארזיא, "cedar paneled booth/tent-houses."

504. *Tg. Hag.* 1.4 reads בית מקדשא הדין, "*this* holy house" (N.B. Aram demonstrative pronoun דין). Cf. the rhetorical question in Joel: בגמול אתם משלמים עלי, "Would *you* compensate *me*?" (Joel 4:4). Rhetorical questions are not uncommon in Nevi'im (cf. Held, "Rhetorical," 71–79; Brueggemann, "Rhetorical," 358–74; Regt, "Rhetorical," 51–78).

505. Lit. "Put it in your heart concerning your paths" (ipv. phrase in Hag 1:7b; 2:15, 18; interrogative in Job 1:8). *Tg. Hag.* 1.5 reads שוו לבכון על אורחתכון, "Let your heart consider your path." Kessler (*Haggai*, 105) translates "Ponder your conduct and its results." Petersen (*Haggai*, 41, 87) translates "Consider seriously your situation," referring to this Heb phrase as "the consider formula."

506. Reading with Kessler (*Haggai*, 105). Jacobs (*Haggai*, 56–57) posits a difference between the returnees and their neighbors in that the former "perceive drought to be a disaster" while the latter well understand "the tendencies of a nonarid climate" so that "drought and its resulting shortage of food and livestock would have been an unsurprising aspect of life for them."

507. MT והמשתכר משתכר (lit. "the one who hires himself out hires himself out"). N.B. the subtle wordplay between שכר ("to inebriate") and שׂכר ("to hire").

508. Hag 1:4b-6. *Tg. Hag.* 1.6 reads ולא שחין להון ודמיתגר מיתגר למאירתא, "do not lower yourselves to their level as traders making accursed trades."

509. Hag 1:7b-8.

510. *Tg. Hag.* 1.9 reads ואנא שלח ביה מאירתא, "but I send a curse against it."

511. Hag 1:9. N.B. the paronomastic use of חרב in Hag 1:4 ("ruins") and 1:11 ("famine").

This unresolved problem of "divine homelessness"[512] fuels all of Haggai's anxieties and concerns:

על כן עליכם כלאו שׂמים מטל	Thus the heavens withhold from you the dew,
והארץ כלאה יבולה	And the land its produce.[513]
ואקרא חרב על הארץ ועל ההרים	I call for a drought upon the land and the hills,
ועל הדגן ועל התירוש ועל היצהר	Upon the grain, the new wine, and the oil,
ועל אשׁר תוציא האדמה	Upon that which the ground brings forth,
ועל האדם ועל בהמה	Upon man and beast,
ועל כל יגיע כפים	Upon everything touched by human hands.[514]

Shifting gears, he then asks a priestly/cultic question:

הן ישׂא אישׁ בשׂר קדשׁ בכנף בגדו	If a man carries consecrated meat[515] in his pocket,
ונגע בכנפו אל הלחם	And his pocket touches bread,
ואל נזיד ואל היין ואל שׁמן ואל כל מאכל	Or porridge or wine or oil, or anything edible,
היקדשׁ	Does that make these things holy?[516]

When they answer "No,"[517] he inverts the question:

אם יגע טמא נפשׁ בכל אלה	If an unclean corpse touches any of these things,
היטמא	Does that make them defiled?[518]

512. Samuel highlights the positive aspects of this homelessness (2 Sam 7:5–7; cf. Acts 7:48–49), but Haggai stands more in line with the "house-erection" ideologies permeating the "great texts" of Israel's neighbors (cf. above).

513. Threats against the land's יבול ("produce") also appear in Torah (Lev 26:20; Deut 11:17), and the word pair טל/יבול ("dew"/"produce") recurs in the next book of the Twelve (Zech 8:12). *Tg. Hag.* 1.10 reads בדיל חוביכון פסקו שׁמיא מלאחתא מטרא וארעא פסקו מלמעבד פירין, "on account of your debts the heavens stop sending rain and the land stops making fruit." Cf. the mythopoeic parallels in DT, ID/DI, and the Eleusinian cults (Cosmopoulos, *Eleusis*, 12–24).

514. Hag 1:10–11. As Petersen (*Haggai*, 93) points out, in Haggai "the people are defined in terms of the work of their hands"; i.e., as "agricultural commodities."

515. Saul of Tarsus also deals with the question of what to do with "consecrated meat" (1 Cor 8:1–7).

516. Hag 2:12. The so-called *Halakic Letter* (4QMMT) focuses on this and other priestly questions (cf. Schiffman, "Miqtsat," 558–60). The anthropological analysis of Douglas (*Purity*, 42–58) structures and informs many contemporary discussions about the purity-defilement polarity.

517. Debate is lively on how exactly to define the character and parameters of the purity-defilement polarity. Cf. Schiffman, *Halakha*, 134–36; Harrington, *Impurity*, 69–110; Klawans, *Impurity*, 158–62; and Werrett, *Purity*, 288–306.

518. Hag 2:13. Petersen (*Haggai*, 81–85) argues that טמא ("defilement") refers not to the Samaritans (*pace* Rothstein, *Haggai*, 5–41), but to heterodox Yahwists whose sacrifices are defiled because of their impure, as-yet-unrestored altar.

When they answer "Yes," he deftly moves from priestly interrogation to prophetic application:

כן העם הזה וכן הגוי הזה לפני	So it is with this people and this nation before me,
וכן כל מעשׂה ידיהם	And all the work of their hands.[519]
ועתה שׂימו נא לבבכם מן היום הזה ומעלה	Now consider your possible future
מטרם שׂום אבן אל אבן בהיכל יהוה	Before a stone is (re-)set into Yhwh's temple.[520]
מהיותם	How would you feel[521]
בא אל ערמת עשׂרים	If you were to expect a stack of twenty units
והיתה עשׂרה	And find only ten?
בא אל היקב	Or if you were to come to the wine-vat
לחשׂף חמשׁים	To draw fifty units
והיתה עשׂרים פורה	And find only twenty?[522]
הכיתי אתכם בשׁדפון ובירקון	Or if I were to strike the work of your hands
ובברד את כל מעשׂה ידיכם	With blight and mildew and hail . . .,
ואין אתכם אלי	Would you still side with me?[523]

In short, should the purification of the still-defiled temple be *properly* conducted (i.e., according to the priestly procedure laid down in Torah),[524] then (a) Yhwh will gladly start accepting their sacrifices, (b) the economy will revive, and (c) more buoyant questions will begin to surface:

העוד הזרע במגורה ועד הגפן	Is there still seed left in the barn?
והתאנה והרמון ועץ הזית	Shall the vines, figs, pomegranates, and olives
לא נשׂא	Not yield (or)
מן היום הזה אברך	Shall I bless you from this day forward?[525]

519. Douglas (*Wilderness*, 22) insightfully points out that "it is a mistake in reading a religious text to keep curses and blessings (which we understand fairly easily) in a separate compartment from defilements and purifications (with which we have difficulty)."

520. Hag 2:15.

521. Following OG (τίνες ἦτε), Beuken (*Haggai*, 211–13) reads two words: מה היתם.

522. Wine production starts in the פורה ("press"), but ends up in the יקר ("vat"; cf. McGovern, *Wine*, 210–38).

523. Hag 2:14–17. *Tg. Hag.* 2.17 reads וליתיכון תיבין לפלחני, "would you return to work with me?"

524. The presumption, of course, is (a) that corpses have touched the altar during the bloody battle for Jerusalem in 586, and (b) that this altar has not yet been properly purified according to the instructions laid out in Torah (cf. Num 19:1–22, "the red heifer ritual"); cf. Petersen, *Haggai*, 70–85.

525. Hag 2:19 (presuming continuation into the third colon of the negative particle articulated in the first two cola). N.B. (a) the temple/fertility linkages in other ANE texts (cited above and in Hurowitz, *Temple*, 322–23); and (b) recent attempts to define "circumcision" as a "fertility rite"

Summary: Haggai addresses two concerns: (a) the embarrassing fact that so many returnees seem willing, like Elijah's audience on Mt. Carmel, to ignore the priestly instructions in Torah *vis-à-vis* how to segregate the *profane* from the *sacred*,[526] resulting in (b) the unsurprising result that sacrifices offered on the rebuilt but as yet unpurified altar remain completely unacceptable. Why? Because the defilement generated by the Chaldean holocaust decades earlier has yet to be removed.[527] Like Zechariah and Malachi, Haggai attends to these concerns from both a priestly and a prophetic perspective.[528]

Zechariah

Whatever the exact nature of the relationship between Haggai and Zechariah,[529] the socioeconomic motifs animating the former continue to resonate in the latter.[530] Beginning with the *inclusio* caveats framing the so-called "night-visions,"[531] Zechariah assures its audience that Yhwh's wrath remains more than capable of cleansing the land of defilement, particularly that resulting from the עשק ("exploitation") of widows, orphans, resident aliens, and the poor.[532] Like Haggai, Zechariah encourages readers (a) to understand that temple purification is in no way a peripheral concern, and (b)

(Eilberg-Schwarz, *Savage*, 141–48; Wyatt, *Whisper*, 41–45).

526. Eliade, *Sacred*, 8–19. N.B. that Elijah must "heal" Yhwh's altar before the heavenly fire can touch it (רפא, 1 Kgs 18:30). Janzen (*Boundaries*, 47) observes that "in any society dirt and pollution is what a society excludes from the socially acceptable (whether this involves morality or food or social relationships) because it does not fit into the categories established by the social purview."

527. Cf. Moore (*Balaam*, 20–65) on the various ways in which ANE priesthoods deal with the defilement-purification polarity.

528. Hanson (*Apocalyptic*, 240–62) overemphasizes the differences between "priest" and "prophet," but Meyers (*Haggai*, 717) justifiably posits that "priestly leadership expands in the postexilic era" at a time when an "enlarged priestly responsibility . . . belongs to the social, economic, and political—as well as religious—spheres."

529. Klostermann (*Geschichte*, 213) proposes a "single two-prophet book" thesis as early as 1896 which Wöhrle (*Zwölfprophetenbuch*, 384) declares to be "confirmed" (*bestätigt*), but Wolters (*Zechariah*, 525) strongly criticizes the "highly speculative form-critical and tradition-historical analysis which has characterized so much scholarly writing" about the Zechariah scroll. Hanson's (*Apocalyptic*, 410) sociological analysis tries to explain how "priest and prophet, while often engaged in controversy, are yet able to draw upon the traditions of the same cult."

530. For Boda (*Zechariah*, 323), two of the major factors contributing to the socioeconomic shape of Haggai-Zechariah include (a) the impact of the revolt of Gaumata/Bardiya against the regime of Darius I (cf. Briant, *Cyrus*, 105–6; Young, "Empire," 55–57); and (b) the evidence preserved in the scrolls themselves.

531. Zech 1:4 and 7:7 (cf. Boda, *Zechariah*, 17–23). Seybold (*Bilder*, 100) believes the night-visions to be about temple-renewal, but Petersen ("Visions," 196) sees them falling "somewhere between purely mundane concerns and a utopian vision of renewal."

532. Zech 7:10 (cf. Amos 4:1; Mic 2:2). Boda (*Zechariah*, 459) observes that "the most vulnerable to such abuse in ancient Israel are those who lay outside the basic social structure of the בית אב" ("house of the father"; cf. Schloen, *Father*, 51), and that this is "precisely the list of those oppressed in Zech 7:10."

that any decision to postpone it guarantees that ארץ שמה ("desolate land") will never become ארץ חמדה ("desirable land").[533]

One oracle in particular rather circuitously illustrates this:

כה אמר יהוה אלהי	Thus says Yhwh my God:
רעה את צון ההרגה	Shepherd the flock set aside for slaughter, (for)
אשר קניהן יהרגן ולא יאשמו	Those who buy it kill without compunction.[534]
ומכריהן יאמר	While those who sell it say,
ברוך יהוה ואעשר	"Blessed be Yhwh! I am rich!"[535]
ורעיהם לא יחמול עליהן	So, because their shepherds refuse to spare *them*,
כי לא אחמול עוד על ישבי הארץ	I will no longer spare the land's residents.[536]

Like several other prophetic texts, this one paronomasiacally plays on a common term, חמל ("to spare"). That is, just as Yhwh "proclaims freedom" (קרא דרור) in response to Zedekiah's bogus "emancipation proclamation,"[537] so here he refuses to "spare" (חמל) his "sheep" in spite of the promises of the "sheep-merchants" (כנעני הצון),[538] thereby provoking the "shepherd/prophet" to lay before these "sheep-merchants" an ultimatum:

אם טוב בעיניכם הבו שׂכרי	"Give me my wages,[539] if you will;
ואם לא חדלו	But if not, keep them."
וישקלו את שׂכרי	So they weighed out my wages—

533. Zech 7:14 (retreading phrases found in Jer 3:19; 4:7; 18:16; 19:8; 25:9; 51:29); cf. Petersen, *Haggai*, 295–96. Bedford (*Temple*, 259) argues that "like Haggai, Zechariah reworks the monarchical ideology to place temple rebuilding before the elevation of Zerubbabel to kingship."

534. Zech 11:4. MT ולא יאשמו (lit. "they are not guilty"); OG *μετεμέλοντο* ("and they are not remorseful/guilty"). *Tg. Zech.* 11.4 reads אתנבי על פרנסיא דאתמניאו לפרנסא עמא ואנון שליטו בהון כענא לנכסתא, "Prophesy against the appointed officials who officiate over the people and its rulers' estates, among whom they are like cattle for the slaughter."

535. *Tg. Zech.* 11.5 reads דקניהון קטלין להון ואמרין לית עלנא חובא ומזבניהון אמרין בריך יוי דעתרנא ורעיהון לא חיסין עליהון, "Those who acquire them kill them and (speaking to those under the yoke of debt) those who sell them say, 'Blessed be Yhwh! We are rich!'"

536. Zech 11:4–6a. Petersen (*Zechariah*, 93) argues that "the task of the shepherd, which has been conferred on the prophet, appears futile, given the plans that the owners have for their flock." Following Saebø (*Sacharja*, 234–52) and LaCocque (*Zacharie*, 174), Petersen (*Malachi*, 90) and Boda (*Zechariah*, 669) read this text as a "symbolic act report."

537. Jer 34:8, 17 (see above).

538. Zech 11:7, 11 (cf. 14:21). Reading כן עניי as one word, with OG (Χαναανῖτιν, "Canaanites/merchants") and Adams (*Economic*, 96). From Petersen's (*Zechariah*, 93) perspective, Yhwh here "abdicates his role as king and allows human rulers to exercise power over humanity, power that bears the promise of their annihilation (vv. 4–5). This view of the political order may reflect Judahite dismay at their lack of power in the Persian-period Levant."

539. *Tg. Zech.* 11.12 reads עבידו רעותי, "take care of my business" (lit. "do my wishes").

Thirty pieces of silver—[540]	שלשים כסף
And Yhwh said to me,	ויאמר יהוה אלי
"Throw it into the treasury"[541]	השליכהו אל היוצר
(so "precious" was my "value" to them).[542]	אדר היקר אשר יקרתי מעליהם
So I took the thirty shekels of silver,[543]	ואקחה שלשים הכסף
And cast it into the treasury of Yhwh's house.[544]	ואשליך אתו בית יהוה אל היוצר

Summary: "Thirty pieces of silver" is the sheep-merchants' way of insulting Zechariah because this paltry sum implies that the prophetic word affects them no more than an injured slave.[545] David Coldwell thus understands this parabolic socioeconomic exchange to "symbolize the broken relationship between the shepherd and the sheep."[546]

Malachi

The last scroll in the Twelve touches on many of the socioeconomic questions already discussed. Like Amos and Hosea, Malachi condemns the oppression of the poor, the widow, and the orphan.[547] Where Haggai chides Hebrew returnees for neglecting the task of temple restoration, Malachi focuses on what must be done to maintain the

540. Baldwin (*Zechariah*, 184) argues, in light of Neh 5:15 and other texts (Exod 21:32; 22:15–16; Lev 27:3–4), that 30 pieces of silver is a relatively large sum, but this flies in the face of evidence gathered by Reiner ("Thirty," 186–90), Sweeney (*Twelve*, 681), and Boda (*Zechariah*, 669). Rather than specify a number, *Tg. Zech.* 11.13 reads יקרת דחלתי, "the value of my *ḥallah*-portion" ("cake-portion," Lev 8:26).

541. MT יוצר ("potter"); OG χωνευτήριον ("smelting-furnace"); Vg *statuarium* ("sculpture-shop"); Syr ܒܝܬ ܓܙܐ ("treasury-house," trans. of בית אוצר). Petersen (*Malachi*, 87) reads with Syr; Boda (*Zechariah*, 669) reads with MT and OG ("house of the metalworker").

542. Boda (*Zechariah*, 671) reads this line as a sarcastic parenthesis.

543. Stuhlmueller (*Zechariah*, 140) notes that "thirty shekels of silver is sometimes interpreted as an impressive sum (the tax of forty shekels in Neh 5:15 is considered quite burdensome), or as ignominious (the price of a slave in Exod 21:32), or as a relatively small sum (all of two hundred shekels of silver is used in Judg 17:14 for making a statue)."

544. Zech 11:12–13. The targumic tradition is, again, more socioeconomically specific than MT or the versions. *Tg. Zech.* 11.13 reads ואמר יוי לי כתוב דוכרן עובדיהון בחילש כתבא ורמי יתיה לבית מקדשא לתחות יד אמרכלא חלף דיקרת דחלתי בעיניהון וכתבית ית דוכרן עובדיהון בחילש כתבא ורמית יתיה לבית מקדשא דיוי לתחות יד אמרכלא רבא, "Yhwh said to me, 'Write a receipt of their deeds with a writing instrument and take it to the holy house and submit it to the hand of the מרכל-official in lieu of the value of my *ḥallah* ("cake-portion," Lev 8:26),' so I wrote a receipt of their deeds in their presence with a writing instrument and I brought it to the holy house of Yhwh to submit it to the hand of the chief trustee" (N.B. the appearance of the מרכל-official in Tob 1:22 (4Q196 2.7; translated "treasurer" in *DSSSE* 1.385). The Nazarenes, of course, apply this text to Judas' economic exchange with the Sanhedrin (Matt 27:1–9; see below).

545. Exod 21:32.

546. Coldwell, *Zechariah*, 267.

547. Mal 3:5.

prosperity of a restored temple *economy*.[548] The usual first step toward achieving this goal is prophetic *analysis*:

היקבע אדם אלהים	Would a man rob God?[549]
כי אתם קבעים אתי	Yet you are robbing me![550]
ואמרתם במה קבענוך	You ask, "How are we robbing you?"
המעשׂר והתרומה	*Answer:* By your tithes and offerings![551]
במארה אתם נארים	You are deeply accursed,
ואתי אתם קבעים הגוי כלו	For the whole nation of you defraud me![552]

After this comes prophetic *admonition*:

הביאו את כל המעשׂר אל בית האוצר	Bring the full tithe[553] into the treasury[554]

548. Literature on the rebuilding of the Second Temple is vast. In addition to the primary sources (Ezek 40–48; Ezra-Nehemiah; 11Q19 [Temple Scroll]), cf. Hurowitz (*Temple*, 106–29), Edelman (*Temple*, 140–46), and Adams (*Economic*, 206–08).

549. N.B. the parallel rhetorical question in Joel 4:4: בגמול אתם משלמים עלי, "Would *you* compensate *me*?" (cf. Held, "Rhetorical," 71–79; Brueggemann "Rhetorical," 358–74; and Regt, "Questions," 51–78).

550. *HAL* (994) holds the meaning of קבע to be "disputed; either 'to walk behind one another' or 'to rob, steal,'" but the versions do not seriously conflict. Cf. OG πτερνίω ("to supplant"); Vg *adfiget* ("to annex, confine"); Syr ܠܡܢܐ ܢܛܠܡ ܒܪܢܫܐ ܠܐܠܗܐ ("Why would a son of man defraud God?"). *Tg. Mal.* 3.8 reads הירגיז גבר דיינא, "Will a man anger the judge?"

551. Elsewhere Malachi complains about the tendency of some not only to hold back their tithes, but offer substandard sacrifices as לחם מגאל ("defiled food," Mal 1:7; cf. Isa 59:3; Lam 4:14). Schiffmann (*Temple*, 541–56) documents from the Temple Scroll (11Q19) how some sectarians imagine the distribution of these offerings.

552. Mal 3:8–9. North ("עשׂר," 408) concludes, after a thorough survey of ANE sources (a) "that every human group sets aside a certain portion of private incomes for common concerns; (b) that the temple cult is dependant on such contributions; (c) that spontaneous (or honorific) contributions . . . suffice only until legal regulation becomes necessary; (d) that the number ten has no sacral character (unlike seven or forty), but is prominent when one counts on one's fingers (a tenth is roughly what an individual can afford, but is calculated only approximately and over the course of time comes to be considered a tax in the general sense); and (e) that as many social and economic concerns become secularized, tithes are reserved for cultic and priestly purposes and the term loses its association with a fixed percentage" (cf. Moore, "Tithes," 533–36; Downs, "Tithes," 156–68).

553. Köstenberger and Croteau ("Tithing," 70) suggest that כל־המעשׂר ("full tithe," Mal 3:10) refers to behavior free of duplicitousness and/or pretentiousness (i.e., the opposite of that displayed in Acts 5:1–4; cf. below).

554. MT בית האוצר (lit. "house of the storage"; from the root אצר, "to store up," 2 Kgs 20:17). Cf. אשלמ[נה] לך ירח בירח מן פרסי זי ינ[ת]נון לי מן אוצרא, "I shall recompense it to you each month from my salary which is given to me from the treasury" (*CAP* 11.5–6). Cf. اصار, "covenant, compact, contract, load" (*DMWA* 18); اوصر, "a written statement of a purchase of sale, transfer, bargain, or contract" (Lane 2945).

ויהי טרף בביתי	That there may be acceptable food[555] in my house.
ובחנוני נא בזות אמר יהוה צבאות	Test me on this, says Yhwh Ṣebaʾôth (and see)
אם לא אפתח לכם את ארבות השמים	If I do not open up for you the windows of heaven[556]
והריקתי לכם ברכה עד בלי די	And pour down upon you an incomparable blessing.[557]

Summary: Andreas Köstenberger and David Croteau identify four issues in Malachi: (a) the withholding of tithes signifies a deeper problem than money—viz., *disobedience*; (b) the "tithe" (מעשׂר) in question is the levitical tithe specified in Torah;[558] (c) the "offering" (תרומה) in question is not voluntary, but required;[559] and (d) the challenge to "test" the deity is not intended to be universally applicable.[560]

Summary

The socioeconomic motifs in Nevi'im cover a wide range of concerns, significant not least by the way in which they reformat those found in the "great texts" before them. Motifs focused on *socioeconomic identity*, for example, candidly engage a broad range of concerns, including *prosperity*, *(in)fertility*, *inheritance*, *slavery*, *profit*, *covenant loyalty*, *wealth*, and *poverty*, not to mention the always challenging problems associated with the question of *land*. As the versions and targums already show, early interpreters of these motifs read them though lenses which, if anything, focus on even more specific socioeconomic concerns.

How do the "great texts" of early Judaism engage the motifs on this prophetic trajectory?

555. MT טרף (cf. טרפה, "torn/prepared meat," Nah 3:12); OG διαρπαγή ("spoil, plunder"). *Tg. Mal.* 3.10 reads פרנוס לדמשמשין, "substantial provisions."

556. Cf. 2 Kgs 7:2, 19; Isa 24:18; *CAT* 1.4.5.62; 7.25–26 (LaBarbera, "Satire," 648; Moore, *Babbler*, 126–27).

557. Mal 3:10. *Tg. Mal.* 3.10 reads אחית לכון טובא, "I will graft good (things) into you."

558. Cf. Lev 27:30; Num 18:21; and below.

559. Cf. נדבה ("voluntary offering") in Lev 7:16; Amos 4:5; Ezek 46:12; Ezra 1:4.

560. Köstenberger and Croteau, "Tithing," 70.

4

Prophetic Socioeconomic Motifs in Early Jewish Texts

JEWISH TEXTS FROM THE Second Temple period manipulate a number of socioeconomic motifs similar to those identified above,[1] yet for reasons soon to become clear, three scrolls beg particular attention: Ezra-Nehemiah,[2] the Epistle of Jeremiah,[3] and Tobit.[4]

Ezra-Nehemiah

Early Christian readers split Ezra-Nehemiah into separate "books" even though no such division exists within Hebrew Bibles prior to the fifteenth century CE, nor does the *masora finalis* appear before the final words of Nehemiah.[5] The text begins with a

1. Definitions of Hebrew "prophecy" are many and varied, particularly in the post-exilic era (Stökl, *Prophecy*, 91–97; Nissinen, *Neo-Assyrian*, 4–9; "Perspective," 17–37; Moore, *Faith*, 237–41). Anthonioz (*Prophétisme*, 13–14) defines it as something "driven by a certain uniformity of presentation with regard to different types of personnel connected to divine revelation (diviners, seers, visionaries, men of God, prophets), resulting in a redefined prophetic ideal in which the social aspects, practices, techniques, and rituals of ancient prophecy become 'hidden' (*occulté*)."

2. Among others, Lortie ("Ezra," 169) recognizes that "Ezra 1–6 emphasizes the importance of the prophetic voice, with the actions of Haggai and Zechariah (Ezra 5:1; 6:14) being set out as the catalyst for the success of the temple rebuilding project."

3. Cf. Adams, *Epistle*, 147–64; Mendels, "Epistle," 721–22. Nickelsburg ("Rewritten," 146) recognizes that "satirical polemics against idols and idolatry are a developing mode of expression in exilic and postexilic literature."

4. Cf. Fitzmyer, *Tobit*, 3–90; Nowell, *Tobit*, 18–21; Moore, *Tobit*, 3–98. Of course, these three scrolls only exemplify, not exhaust this literature.

5. Klein ("Ezra-Nehemiah," 731–32) mentions Origen and Jerome by name. Whether Ezra-Nehemiah is part of a larger corpus produced by a "Chronicler" (i.e., Ezra-Nehemiah + 1–2 Chronicles)—a multifaceted question, to be sure—is marginally relevant to the present study (cf. Japhet, *Chronicles*, 3–7; Klein, "Chronicles," 993–94). The *masora finalis* is the scribal appendix/apparatus found at the end of every Tanak scroll indicating the midpoint of the exact number of letters.

Hebrew version of the Cyrus Edict,[6] a *mīšarum*-like decree[7] specifying how to care for Hebrew returnees:

וכל הנשאר מכל המכומות אשר הוא גר שם	Let all survivors wherever they travel
ינשאוהו אנשי מכמו	Be supported by the people of that place
בכסף ובזהב וברכוש ובבהמה	With silver and gold and property and animals,
עם הנדבה לבית האלהים	With freewill offerings[8] for the house of God
אשר בירושלם	Which is in Jerusalem.[9]

Of particular interest here is the Aramaic correspondence of government officials in Jerusalem and Persia: (a) Reḥum and Shimshi to King Artaxerxes (Ezra 4:8–16); (b) Artaxerxes' reply (Ezra 4:17–22); (c) Tattenai and Shethar-bozenai to King Darius (Ezra 5:6–17); (d) Darius' reply (Ezra 6:2–9); and (e) a general edict from Artaxerxes authorizing Ezra's mission to Jerusalem (Ezra 7:12–26).[10]

Letter of Reḥum and Shimshi to King Artaxerxes (Ezra 4:8–16)

רחום בעל טעם ושמשי ספרא	Reḥum the commissioner[11] and Shimshi the scribe
כתבו אגרה חדה על ירושלם	Wrote a letter about Jerusalem

6. Ezra 1:1–4 (cf. 2 Chr 36:22–23; Young, "Cyrus," 1231–32). An Aramaic version of this Edict appears in Ezra 6:2–5, a Greek version in 1 Esd 2:1–7. The decree itself is based on older building inscriptions (cf. Harmatta, "Modéles," 31–38).

7. In the seventeenth century BCE the Babylonian king Ammiṣaduqa issues a *mīšarum*-decree designed to release subjects from tax-induced debt (*CAD* M/2:116–17; *ANET* 526–28; *TDOT* 6:1–7). Hallo ("Edict," 205–16) illuminates the socioeconomic context of this decree, and Kraus (*Verfügungen*, 1–126) documents over one hundred examples of it in Babylonia, Mari, Assyria, Hana, Elam, Kanesh, and Eshnunna (cf. Otto, "Vertragsrecht," 125–60; Lemche, "Edicts," 11–22).

8. MT נדבה (cf. the PN נדביה, "Yhwh is generous," 1 Chr 3:18). A later account reads τοῖς ἄλλοις τοῖς κατ' εὐχὰς προστεθειμένοις, "with the other (gifts) prayerfully offered," 1 Esd 2:7). Torah lists several types of offering: עולה ("whole burnt offering"), זבח ("sacrifice"), מעשׂר ("tithe"), תרומה ("donation"), נדר ("votive offering"), and נדבה ("freewill offering," Deut 12:6). The last Aramaic epistle in Ezra-Nehemiah (Ezra 7:12–26) repeats נדבה several times to emphasize the advantages of maintaining a "volunteer spirit."

9. Ezra 1:4. Whatever the nature of the links between the Hebrew, Aramaic, and Greek versions of this edict, it is significant that each version focuses on Jerusalem's *socioeconomic* needs.

10. Some inevitably question the authenticity of (some or all of) these epistles (e.g. Gauger, "Artaxerxes," 196–225), but Steiner ("Archival," 676) argues persuasively that they most likely originate as "archival search reports" copied many times before their absorption into Tanak (cf. Folmer, *Aramaic*, 1–42). Altmann (*Economics*, 221) contends that "the narrative of Ezra 1–8" is "bound together by the overarching question, 'Who pays?'"

11. MT בעל טעם (lit. "lord of the order"; cf. Akk *bēl ṭēmi*, *AHw* 1387). This title occurs at Elephantine (בעל [טע]ם, *TADE* A6.2.23; *CAP* 26.23). N.B. that Artaxerxes' response is to "issue an order" (שׂים טעם, Ezra 4:19, 21).

לארתחששתא מלכא כנמא	To Artaxerxes[12] the king as follows . . .[13]
עלוהי על ארתחששתא מלכא	*To:* Artaxerxes the king
עבדיך אנש עבר נהרה	*From:* The servants of your people in `Eber-Nahara.[14]
וכענת ידיע להוה למלכא	Now let it be made known to the king
די יהודיא די סלקו מן לותך עלינא	That the Jews who came up to us from you[15]
אתו לירושלם	Have arrived in Jerusalem
קריתא מרדתא ובישתא בנין	To rebuild this shameful,[16] rebellious city,
ושוריא שכללו ואשיא יחיטו	Repairing the walls and reestablishing the foundations.
כעין ידיע להוה למלכא	But let the king be fully aware:
די הן קריתא דך תתבנא ושוריא ישתכללון	If this city repairs its walls and rebuilds
מנדה בלו והלך לא ינתנון	They will stop paying tribute,[17] produce-tax,[18] and property-tax,[19]

12. Suiter ("Artaxerxes," 463–64). Glatt (*Chronological*, 125–31) identifies this monarch according to what he calls the widely practiced tradition of "chronological displacement."

13. Ezra 4:8. In line with Steiner's analysis ("Archival," 641–85), the multiple introductions prefacing each of these epistles are here omitted.

14. עבר נהרה (lit. "beyond the river") is the GN for the Achaemenid territories west of the Euphrates.

15. Following Bordieu's ("Capital," 241–58) view that various types of *sociopolitical* "capital" always work alongside *economic* "capital," Laird (*Power*, 1–36) identifies four different groups contending for power in Ezra-Nehemiah: (a) official representatives of the Persian empire; (b) the group in and around Samaria construing itself as the rightful representatives of Persian power; (c) Jews in and around Jerusalem not exiled to Babylon; and (d) returning Jewish exiles (the group whose case Ezra-Nehemiah pleads).

16. MT באישתא; cf. Akk *bîšu* ("stinky"), from *ba'āšu* (A "to smell bad"; B "to come to shame," *CAD* B.270–71). Cf. *bēl qīptiya bāb ḫarrāniya ša qātātim la errišīma la a-ba-aš*, "lest I be 'ashamed' when my creditor asks me for guarantees at the outset of my journey" (*CCT* 3.8b.16).

17. MT מנדה; cf Akk *ma(n)dattu*: *eli bilti maḫrīti nadān šattišun man-da-at-tú uraddīma ukīn ṣēruššun*, "in addition to their former yearly tribute, I (Sennacherib) imposed upon them additional tribute"; *bilta u ma-da-at-ta eli ša panâ uttir ina muḫḫišu aškun*, "I (Tiglath-Pileser I) imposed upon him tax and tribute greater than before" (cf. *CAD* M/1.13). The Heb cognate appears in the phrase מדת המלך ("king's tax") in the lament laid before Nehemiah the governor: לוינו כסף למדת המלך שדתינו וכרמינו, "We must borrow silver for the 'king's tax' on our fields and our vineyards" (Neh 5:4; cf. Blenkinsopp, *Ezra-Nehemiah*, 253–60).

18. MT בלו. Cf. Akk *biltu*, "yield (of a field, garden, flock), produce (of a region)"; e.g., *ina bi-la-at kirîm šittīn ana bēl kirîm inaddin šaluštam šu ileqqi*, "he gives two-thirds of the 'yield' to the owner of the grove while he himself takes one third" (cf. *CAD* B.231).

19. Cf. *TADE* A7.4.13 and N.B. the tax categories listed in 1 Macc 10:29. Procopius (*Hist. arc.* 25.3)

ואפתם מלכים תהנזק	And the royal treasury[20] will suffer harm.[21]
כען כל קבל די מלח היכל מלחנה	Now, since we share the same palace salt[22]
וערות מלכא לא אריך לנא	And it is inappropriate for us
למחזא	To see the king 'dishonored,'[23]
על דנה שלחנא והודענא למלכא	We dispatch this invitation[24] to the king
די יבקר בספר דכרניא די אבהתך	To search in your historical annals,[25]
ותהשכח בספר דכרניא ותנדע די	Where you will discover that
קריתא דך קריא מרדא	This is a rebellious city with a
ומהנזקת מלכין ומדינן	History of offending kings and provinces,
ואשתדור עבדין בגוה מן יומת עלמא	Forever fomenting rebellion inside its walls
על דנה קריתא דך החרבת	(which is why it was destroyed).[26]
מהודעין אנחנה למלכא	So we urge the king to realize
די הן קריתא דך תתבנא ושוריה ישתכללון	That if this city is rebuilt and its walls refinished,
לקבל דנה חלק בעבר נהרה לא איתי לך	You will retain no assets in `Eber-Nahara.[27]

The rationale governing this correspondence is hardly atypical. Bureaucrats everywhere habitually dangle before their supervisors the specter of socioeconomic

documents the work of an ἄρχων ("ruler/magistrate") commissioned by the emperor to *πράττειν . . . τέλος* ("collect . . . a toll") from ships crossing the Hellespont, calling this toll *τινὰ μισθὸν ὁ ταύτην δὴ τὴν ἀρχὴν ἔχων τοῦ ἔργου τούτο λαμβάνειν ἠξίου*, "a wage of sorts claimed by the man holding this office as compensation for his labor."

20. Tadmor ("אפתם," 143–45) derives אפתם from Akk *iptu* ("tribute," *CAD* I-J.171), but Zadok ("Ezra," 261) posits an Old Persian root.

21. MT נזק ("damage"); cf. נזק//כפר in a contemporary Aramaic letter from Egypt: נזק ארשם וכפר צח]א, "the damage of PN and the indemnity of PN" (*TADE* A4.2.14; *CAP* 37.14). Explaining the fourth order of Mishnah (*Nezikin*), Talmud lists 24 types of נזיקין ("damages," *b. B. Qam.* 4b).

22. Evidently an idiomatic expression for "collegiality."

23. Lit. "to see the 'nakedness' of the king." Cf. OG *ἀσχημοσύνη* ("unseemliness, shamefulness"); Vg *laesiones* ("lesions, injuries"); Syr ܨܥܪܐ ("dishonor, wrong").

24. Lit. "to make known."

25. MT ספר דכרניא (lit. "scroll of the memories"); cf. the ספר הזכרנות examined by Esther's insomniac husband (Esth 6:1).

26. Kuhrt (*Ancient*, 660) suggests that "part of the effort to occupy and control the large territory that fell to the Persians as a consequence of the Babylonian defeat is the resettlement and strengthening of provincial centres. The reconstruction of Jerusalem could be part of such a policy."

27. Ezra 4:11–16. As noted above, Nevi'im often uses Heb חלק (sometimes in parallel with נחלה, "inheritance") to indicate "portion, assets, possession" (Isa 53:12; 57:6; Jer 10:16//51:19; Ezek 48:8, 21; Hos 5:7; Joel 4:2; Amos 7:4, 17; Mic 2:4; Hab 1:16; Zech 2:16).

injury as the surest way to protect their jobs.[28] These particular bureaucrats, having failed to accomplish this objective through "bribery" (סכר) and "terror" (בהל),[29] show no hesitation in slandering their new neighbors in order to manipulate the Achaemenid king into worrying whether these "invaders" somehow "threaten his prosperity."[30] This is a common groupthink strategy designed to exploit a familiar fear: (a) find a "problematic" area of "concern" (preferably one with a "checkered past");[31] (b) spotlight this "concern" before an authorized decision-maker;[32] and (c) ruthlessly exaggerate its "dangers."[33]

Response of King Artaxerxes (Ezra 4:17–22)

Compared, say, to the pharaohs,[34] the Achaemenid court responds relatively quickly to this type of correspondence:[35]

28. Cf. the statistics published by Transparency International (www.transparency.org, cited in Moore, *WealthWatch*, 225–28). With regard to Alatas' (*Corruption*, 1–62) three *types* of corruption—*extortative, manipulative, nepostic*—the situation in Ezra-Nehemiah best fits within category #2. Breaking "fear" down into *parochialism* ("control from within") and *territorialism* ("protection from outside"), Rieger (*Fear*, 33) might have a difficult time deciding which factor is more dominant here.

29. Ezra 4:4–5. Blenkinsopp (*Ezra-Nehemiah*, 252) contends that "while we can hardly speak of an imminent mutiny among the wall-builders . . . the Sanballat-Tobiah axis has sympathetic contacts within Jewish society."

30. Lysias (*Aristophanes* 5) passionately argues that πάντων δεινότατόν ἐστι διαβολή ("the most terrible of all things is slander"). Cf. the OB correspondence to King Zimri-Lim (excerpted above). Not all governmental correspondence is driven by paranoia, of course; bureaucratic motives can in some cases be quite mixed (e.g., the "Petition to the Governor of Yehud" in *TADE* A4.7; *CAP* 30). But it goes without saying that "immigration" and "invasion" tend to be synonymous terms in the nativistic mind (cf. Moore, "Monocultural," 39–53).

31. *Example:* Yedoniah of Egypt is careful to outline an historical context before submitting his request for help to the governor of Yehud (*TADE* A4.7; *CAP* 30).

32. In *EA* 9, for example, the Kassite king Burnaburiaš reminds Pharaoh that their ancestors have a history of making mutual declarations of *ṭabutu* (Akk "friendship," *EA* 9.8) by sending *šulmanū* ("peace-gifts," 9.9) to each other. This then sets up the context in which the Kassite king complains to his Egyptian "friend" about the latter's most recent "gift"—a "mere" 2 minas of gold. Obviously disappointed, he offers Pharaoh a face-saving way to "correct his mistake." Should gold no longer be as plentiful as it once was, he politely suggests, then perhaps he might send, say, one-half of what was originally "promised" (cf. Moore, *Babbler*, 140–55).

33. Michaels (*McCarthyism*, 118) documents how easily smear campaigns can become "a routine tool in the repertoire of political tactics."

34. Most of the vassal correspondence in the Amarna archive falls on deaf Egyptian ears, provoking in some cases whole *series* of increasingly desperate petitions (note, e.g., the extensive correspondence generated by the mayor of Byblos, Rib-Addi, in *EA* 68–95, 101–38). Na`aman ("Correspondence," 125) notes that "only six or seven pharaonic letters sent to . . . vassals are known . . . as against hundreds of letters sent by the vassals to Pharaoh."

35. Cf. Weninger (*Handbook*, 588–90) and N.B. the favorable response of Bagohi, governor of Yehud, to Yedoniah's request for help (*TADE* A4.9; *CAP* 32).

על רחום בעל טעם ושמשי ספרא	To Reḥum the commissioner and Shimshi the scribe
ושאר כנותהון די יתבין בשמרין	And the rest of their colleagues settled in Samaria[36]
ושאר עבר נהרה שלם	And `Eber-Nahara: Greetings.
וכעת נשתונא די שלחתון עלינא	Now the letter which you sent to us
מפרש קרי קדמי	Has been translated and read to me.
ומני שים טעם ובקרו והשכחו	So I gave the order to search,
די קריתא דך	And discovered that this city
מן יומת עלמא על מלכין מתנשאה	Does indeed have a history of offending kings,
ומרדו אשתדור מתעבד בה	Rebellion and revolt often recurring within it,
ומלכין תקיפין הוו על ירשלם	And that there have been great kings over Jerusalem
ושליטין בכל עבר נהרה	And rulers over all of `Eber-Nahara
ומדה בלו והלך	To whom tribute, produce-tax and property-tax[37]
מתיהב להון	Have been methodically paid.[38]
כען שימו טעם לבטלא גבריא אלך	Therefore I order these contractors to stop,
וקריתא דך לא תתבנא	And that this city be left unfinished
עד מני טעמא יתשם	Until further notice.
וזהירין הוו שלו למעבד על דנה	But take care not to be cavalier about the matter.
למה ישגא חבלא	Why should (the prospect of) debt[39] escalate
להנזקת מלכין	To the detriment of the crown?[40]

36. The Samaria connection is sensitive because Sanballat (one of Nehemiah's enemies, Neh 4:7–8), serves at one time as the פחת שמרין ("governor of Samaria," *TADE* A4.7.29; *CAP* 30.29). Whether the Persians ever consider Jerusalem to be under Samaria's "jurisdiction," however, is disputed (cf. Williamson, "Governors," 59–82).

37. These are the same three terms (in the same order) as those found in Ezra 4:13.

38. Syr adds ܠܐ ("not") into this line, yet apart from the historical question as to whether Jerusalem is a "good taxpayer," Williamson (*Ezra-Nehemiah*, 64) sees Reḥum and Shimsi arguing that since "many of Artaxerxes' predecessors . . . received tribute, even from the seditious Jerusalem . . . why, then, should not Artaxerxes take steps to ensure that he is no less powerful?"

39. That חבל (lit. "harm, damage") sometimes occurs in socioeconomic contexts is clear from the *Migdol Papyrus*, which refers to discrepancies surrounding the non-payment of a soldier's "salary" (lit. his "cut," Aram פרס, *SSI* 2.27.3–7).

40. Ezra 4:17–22. MT הנזקה (OG reads ἀφανισμός, "invisible, uncertain"). The fourth order of Mishnah is סדר נזקין, "Order of Damages"). In *CAP* 37.14 Grelot (*Documents*, 97) translates נזק as "to

Uninformed and uninvolved, the Achaemenid court defaults to the wishes of their branch managers. Jerusalem has a documented history of paying taxes,[41] yet in their minds the city is a ticking time-bomb because of its also-documented history of independent behavior. Thus the king decides to "nip the Jewish problem in the bud."[42] Otherwise the "crisis" for which these "invaders" are "responsible" may indeed generate a set of problems having the potential to drain the royal treasury.[43] This exchange shows (a) that the Achaemenid court is easily manipulated, and (b) that these Jerusalem envoys know exactly how to do it.[44]

Letter of Tattenai and Shethar-bozenai to King Darius (Ezra 5:6–17)

Another round of correspondence begins with another Jerusalem report:[45]

פרשגן אגרתא די שלח תתני	Copy of the letter sent by Tattenai,
פחת עבר נהרה	Governor of `Eber-Nahara,[46]
ושתר בוזני וכנותה	And Shethar-bozenai[47] and their[48] colleagues,
אפרסכיא די עבר נהרא	The investigators[49] in `Eber-Nahara,
על דריוש מלכא	Unto Darius the king:[50]
ידיע להוה למלכא די אזלנא	Let it be known to the king that we went
ליהוד מדינתא	To the province of Judah,
לבית אלהא רבא	To the house of the Great God
והוא מתבנא אבן גלל	Presently being constructed with hewn stone

suffer loss" in an epistle featuring Aram שחד ("bribe," 37.4) and פתפרס ("payment, ration," 37.3, 12).

41. That is, if ܠܐ ("not") is ignored in Syr Ezra 4:20.

42. Cuffari (*Judenfeindschaft*, 338–47) thinks that Tanak occasionally alludes to *Judenfeindschaft* ("hostility toward Jews"), but that it is not until c. 150 BCE that Jewish writers start intentionally educating future generations about the problem through documents like Esther and Maccabees.

43. In light of Syr ܠܐ ("not," Syr Ezra 4:20) it is not to be discounted that this letter cautions against overreaction; i.e., that no one wins if the Jerusalem treasury degenerates to the point of becoming unable to pay *any* taxes.

44. Cf. Altmann, *Economics*, 221.

45. Whether this report precedes or succeeds the one above is immaterial (cf. Steiner, "Aramaic," 642–85).

46. N.B. that *VSKMB* 4 (1907) #152 refers to an individual with the same name and title, ^{m}*Ta-at-[ta-ni] pāḫāt Ebir-nari* ("Tattenai, governor of `Eber-Nahara"; cf. Olmstead, "Tattenai," 46).

47. שתר בוזני, "Remnant of my plunder" (Ezra 5:6). The PN שתברזן from Elephantine (*CAP* 5.16) may well be a dyslexic echo (*pace* Cowley, *Papyri*, 15; cf. the PN שתר in Esth 1:4).

48. MT pronominal suffix here (Ezra 5:6) is 3ms (as in 4:7), but OG and Syr read 3mp (as in 5:3).

49. Ezra 5:6 MT אפרסכי; OG Αφαρσαχαῖοι; Vg *Apharsacei*; Ezra 4:9 MT reads אפרסתכי. Rudolph (*Esra*, 36) derives אפרסכי from Old Persian *fraštaka* ("envoy/ambassador, investigator"), but Lindenberger ("Vidranga," 134) reads "regional governor."

50. Ezra 5:6. Cf. Greenfield, "Darius," 434; and Young, "Darius," 37–38.

ועא מתשׂם בכתליא	And decorative wood paneling.
ועבידתא דך אספרנא מתעבדא	This project appears to be competently and
ומצלח בידה	Prudently managed.
אדין שׂאלנא לשׂביא אלך כנמא אמרנא להם	Speaking to the leaders, we asked,
מן שׂם לכם טעם ביתא דנה למבניה	"Who ordered you to rebuild this house
ואשרנא דנה לשכללה	And complete this edifice?". . .[51]
וכנמא פתגמא התיבונא לממר	And this is what they told us:
אנחנא המו עבדוהי די אלה שׂמיא וארעא	"We are servants of the God of heaven and earth
ובנין ביתא די הואבני מקדמת שׂנין שׂגיאן	Rebuilding the house built and completed
ומלך לישׂראל רב בנהי ושכללה	Many years ago by a great king of Israel.
להן מן די הרגזו אבהתנם	But because our ancestors
לאלא שׂמיא	Angered the God of heaven
יהב המו ביד נבוכדנצר	He gave them into the hand of Nebuchadnezzar,
מלך בבל כסדיא	The Chaldean king of Babylon
וביתא דנה סתרא	Who destroyed this house and
ועמה הגלי לבבל	Exiled its people to Babylon.[52]
ברם בשנת חדה לכורש מלכא דיבבל	But in the first year of Cyrus, king of Babylon,
כורש מלכא שׂם טעם	King Cyrus decreed that
בית אלהא דנה לבנא	This house of God was to be rebuilt.
ואף מאניא די בית אלהא	Further, the gold and silver vessels[53]
די דהבא וכספא	In the house of God
די נבוכדנצר הנפק	Which Nebuchadnezzar confiscated
מן היכלא די בירושלם	From the temple in Jerusalem
והיבל המו להיכלא די בבל	And carried with him to the temple of Babylon[54]

51. Ezra 5:6–9.

52. This, of course, is the Yahwistic prophetic explanation for the exile (2 Kgs 17:7–41; cf. Moore, *Faith*, 343–50).

53. Mention of these "gold and silver vessels" occurs in the Daniel scroll, where Belshazzar and his lieutenants drink from them until a mysterious hand starts writing on the palace wall (Dan 5:2).

54. Most presume this to be a reference to Esagila (the temple of Marduk), though a later account simply calls the place an εἰδωλίον ("idol chamber," 1 Esd 2:10).

הנפק המו כורש מלכא	King Cyrus removed
מן היכלא די בבל	From the temple of Babylon
ויהיבו לששבצר שמה	And gave them to a man named Sheshbazzar,[55]
די פחה שמה	Whom he appointed governor,
ואמר לה אל מאניא שא	Saying to him, 'Take these vessels (and)
אזל אחת המו בהיכלא די בירשלם	Go deposit[56] them in the Jerusalem temple,
ובית אלהא יתבנא על אתרה	That the house of God might be rebuilt on its site.'
אדין ששבצר דך אתא	Then this Sheshbazzar went (and)
יהב אשיא	Restored[57] the foundation
די בית אלהא די בירשלם	Of the house of God in Jerusalem
ומן אדין ועד כען מתבנא	And ever since construction has continued,
ולא שלם	However unfinished.
וכען הן על מלכא טב	So now, if the king approves,
יתבקר בבית גנזיא די מלכא	Let a search be conducted in the royal archive[58]
תמא די בבבל	There in Babylon
הן איתי די מן כורש מלכא	To ascertain whether King Cyrus indeed
שים טעם למבנא	Once filed a report regarding the rebuilding
בית אלהא דך בירשלם	Of this Jerusalem house of God.
ורעות מלכא	Then convey to us the king's wishes
על דנה ישלח עלינא	On this matter."[59]

Response from King Darius (Ezra 6:2–9)

Responding to *this* petition, the Achaemenid court issues a search warrant to find out (a) whether Cyrus in fact *does* issue a restoration decree for the Jerusalem temple, and

55. The etymology of this name is debated (cf. Eskenazi, "Sheshbazzar," 1207–09), but ששבצר looks to be a hebraicization of *Šamaš-bal-uṣur* ("May Šamaš protect the son"). In a later account the king entrusts these vessels to his γαζόφυλαξ ("treasurer"; lit. "wealth guard")—a man named Mithradates—who *then* entrusts them to Sheshbazzar (1 Esd 2:11).

56. MT אחת, "deposit" (causative ipv of נחת, "to descend").

57. Lit. "gave" (יהב).

58. MT בית גנזיא (lit. "house of treasure"); Vg *bibliotheca* ("library"); Syr ܒܟܬܒܐ ܕܐܝܬ ܒܒܝܬ ܓܙܐ ("records in the house of treasure").

59. Ezra 5:3–17.

(b) whether this decree in fact corroborates the claim of the Hebrew returnees. Failing to find a "copy" (דכרונה)[60] in Babylon, however, they keep on looking until one comes to light in the Median capital of Ecbatana:[61]

בשנת חדה לכורש מלכא	In the first year of Cyrus the king
כורש מלכא שׂם טעם	King Cyrus[62] issued an edict (concerning)
בית אלהא בירשלם	The house of God in Jerusalem:
ביתא יתבנא	"Let the house be restored (as)
אתר די דבחין דבחין	A place where sacrifices are slaughtered
ואשׁוהי מסובלין	And fire-offerings are submitted.
רומה אמין שׁתין פתיה אמין שׁתין	Make its height and width sixty cubits,
נדבכין די אבן גלל תלתא	(With) three rows of fine hewn stone
ונדבך די עא חדת	And one row of wood paneling,
ונפקתא מן בית מלכא תתיהב	The expense[63] deductible[64] from the 'royal budget.'[65]
ואף מאני בית אלהא	Also, let the gold and silver vessels
די דהבה וכספה	Of the house of God
די נבוכדנצר הנפק מן היכל	Which Nebuchadnezzar took from the temple
די בירשלם והיבל לבבל	In Jerusalem and transferred to Babylon[66]
יהתיבון ויהך להיכלא די בירשלם	Be taken back and given to the temple in Jerusalem,
לאתרה תחה בבית אלהא	Safely returned to their alcoves in the house of God."[67]
כען תתני פחת עבר נהרה	Now let Tattenai, governor of ʿEber-Nahara,

60. Ezra 6:2; OG ὑπόμνημα ("memorandum, notation"); Syr ܕܘܟܪܢܐ ("report"); cf. Heb זכר ("to remember").

61. MT אחמתה; cf. Ἐκβατανα (Tob 3:7). How "original" this document is, of course, is impossible to say (cf. Steiner, "Aramaic," 643–47). Media is an ancient Iranian kingdom which, after rising to power in the seventh century, allies with Babylon to overthrow the Neo-Assyrian empire in 612 BCE, after which it is eventually absorbed into the Achaemenid empire (Esth 1:3).

62. Twice the writer gives the king's name and title, but Bryce (*Letters*, 163) argues that it is "not the (usual) practice in (ancient) correspondence to address the recipients by their titles."

63. Aram נפקה appears repeatedly in expense-lists from Elephantine, once even distinguishing נפקת נפשה ("personal expenses") from נפקת מדינתא ("regional expenses," *CAP* 73.7, 14).

64. Aram תתיהב is reflexive of יהב ("to give"), implying "repeated giving."

65. Lit. "house of the king."

66. Constant mention of these "gold and silver vessels" indicates their importance to the author of Ezra-Nehemiah, whom Min (*Ezra-Nehemiah*, 4) views as more *levitical* than *priestly* in his thinking.

67. Ezra 6:2–5. Aramaic papyri from Egypt record the plundering of other "gold and silver" fixtures from a Jewish אגור in Egypt ("storehouse"/"temple"; *TADE* A4.7.12; *CAP* 30.12).

שתר בוזני וכנותהון	Shethar-bozenai and their colleagues, and
אפרסכיא די בעבר נהרה	The investigators in `Eber-Nahara,
רחיקין הוו מן תמה	All stay away from this construction site.
שבקו לעבידת בית אלהא דך	Leave the work on this house of God alone
פחת יהודיא ולשׂבי יהודיא	So that the governor and elders of the Jews[68]
בית אלהא דך יבנון על עתרא	May (re)construct it on its traditional site.
ומני שׂים טעם למא די תעבדון	In fact, I have decided that you are to do *this*
עם שׂבי יהודיא אלך	With the Jewish elders
למבניא בית אלהא דך	Presently rebuilding this house of God:
ומנכסי מלכא	From the royal funds[69]
די מדת עבר נהרה	Of the tribute collected in `Eber-nahara[70]
אספרנא נפקתא תהוא מתיהבא	You are to make sure that payment is duly given
די לא לבטלא לגבריא אלך	To these men without delay.
ומה חשחן ובני תורין ודכרין ואמרין	Whatever is needed—young bulls, rams, sheep—
לעלון לאלא שׂמיא	To sacrifice to the God of heaven—
חנטין מלח חמר ומשח	Wheat, salt, wine, oil—
כמאמר כהניא די בירשלם	At the direction of the Jerusalem priests
להוה מתיהב להום	Let it be readily given[71] to them
יום ביום די לא שׂלו	Daily without fail,
די להון מהקרבין ניחוחין	So that they may offer pleasing sacrifices
לאלא שׂמיא	To the God of heaven
ומצלין לחיי מלכא	And pray for the life of the king

68. Noth (*Israel*, 313) finds it "striking that in his report the satrap only passes on the information given by the elders in Jerusalem," and Min (*Levitical*, 126; following Gunneweg, "Esra-Nehemiah," 150) suggests a correspondence between the relaxation of "Persian vigilance" and what he perceives to be a power-shift from *priest*-leadership to *elder*-leadership in the Jerusalem rebuilding project, but he does not take into account the directive that no Persian aid is to be given to any of the Jews apart from the מאמר כהניא ("direction of the priests," Ezra 6:9). It is not clear whether שׂבי יהודיא ("elders of the Jews") refers to "city-elders" or "professional judges" (cf. Willis, *Elders*, 44).

69. Lit. "riches of the king." Aram נכס(י)ן appears repeatedly in the Aramaic papyri from Egypt. Cf., e.g., the Jewish reference to Vidranga, the Gentile commander responsible for plundering the temple of Yahu at Elephantine: וכל נכסין זי קנה אבדו, "all the riches he acquired (from this plunder) they destroyed" (*TADE* A4.7.16; *CAP* 30.16).

70. In other words, "you folks in Jerusalem pay for it yourselves out of *your* funds." In Pakkala's opinion (*Ezra*, 48), "the Achaemenids are less involved in local affairs than their Assyrian and Babylonian predecessors."

71. N.B. (again) the twice-repeated use of יהב in the reflexive ("to give," Ezra 6:8–9).

ובנוהי	And his children.[72]

Given its present context, it's not surprising to see this Aramaic version of the Cyrus Edict inflate the *degree* of economic support promised by the Achaemenids,[73] but it's also important to realize that this is not the only foreign temple Cyrus helps restore.[74] According to the so-called Cyrus Cylinder,[75] he helps rebuild *several* sanctuaries in the course of executing his "Marshall Plan" of post-war reconstruction,[76] judiciously returning "to these ruined sanctuaries the icons previously lodging in them."[77] According to Marty Stevens, the rationale for this strategy is essentially economic: (a) the more temples restored means (b) the more treasuries/depositories can be revived, which means (c) the more taxes can be collected.[78]

Letter of Artaxerxes to Ezra (Ezra 7:12–26)

The final Aramaic epistle in Ezra-Nehemiah is an edict from Artaxerxes designed to (a) authorize Ezra's mission to transport silver and gold to the Jerusalem temple, (b) temporarily exempt Jerusalem returnees from taxation, and (c) cap the overall amount of financial aid.[79] Opinions differ over how to read it. Erhard Gerstenberger believes "its language and perspectives (are) not of Persian, but of Jewish origin,"[80] but Lisbeth Fried sees several "archaic Persian period linguistic forms . . . and Persian loanwords" here, enough to suggest "that the biblical writer uses an existing royal authorization to a real historical Ezra":[81]

ארתחשסתא מלך מלכיא	Artaxerxes, king of kings
לעזרא כהנא ספר	To Ezra the priest, scribe of the
דתא די אלא שמיא	Law of the God of heaven:
גמיר	Greetings.

72. Ezra 6:2–9.

73. Herodotus, *Hist.* 1.209. Cf. Briant, *Empire*, 111.

74. Kuhrt ("Cyrus," 83–97) and Bedford (*Temple*, 87–156) question whether the Persian court extends *any* socioeconomic support to Jerusalem.

75. The منشور كوروش ("Charter of Cyrus/Cyrus Cylinder"), is a recovered sixth-century BCE foundation deposit detailing the reign of Babylon's new ruler, Cyrus II (cf. Finkel, "Cyrus," 129–35).

76. Bedford, *Restoration*, 85–179. The "Marshall Plan" (the brainchild of Gen. George C. Marshall enacted by the U.S. Congress on June 3, 1948), helps rebuild Europe after World War II rather than create another "Versailles Treaty" embarrassment like the one signed on June 28, 1919 (cf. Holm, *Marshall*, 51–82).

77. Akk *ma-ḫa-z[a e-be]r-ti* ÍD.IDIGNA *ša iš-tu pa-na-ma na-du-ú šu-bat-su-un* (cited from Finkel, "Cyrus," 132.31).

78. Stevens, *Temples*, 137.

79. Lim, *Canon*, 55.

80. Gerstenberger, *Persian*, 95.

81. Fried, *Ezra*, 21.

I issue a decree	וכענת מני שים טעם
That any of the people of Israel,	די כל מתנדב במלכותי מן עמא ישׂראל
Its priests or levites,	וכהנוהי ולויא
Who freely decide to go to Jerusalem with you,	למהך לירשׁלם עמך
May go.	יהך
For you are sent from the king and his 7 counselors[82]	כל קבל די מן קדם מלכא ושׁבעת יעטהי
To watch over[83] Judah and Jerusalem	שׁליח לבקרא על יהוד ולירשׁלם
With the law of your God which is in your hand,	בדת אלהך די בידך
To carry silver and gold	ולהיבלה כסף ודהב
Which the king and his counselors freely donate	די מלכא ויעטוהי התנדבו
To the God of Israel who dwells in Jerusalem,	לאלא ישׂראל די בירשׁלם משׁכנה
Along with all the silver and gold which you find[84]	וכל כסף ודהב די תהשׁכח
In every province of Babylon,	בכל מדינת בבל
With the freewill offerings of the people and the priests	עם התנדבות עמא וכהניא
Freely donated[85] to the house of their God in Jerusalem.	מתנדבין לבית אלההם די בירשׁלם
Accordingly, with all diligence	כל קבל דנה אספרנא
You shall acquire with this money	תקנא בכספא דנה
Bulls, rams, lambs, grain- and drink-offerings,	תורין דכרין אמרין ומנחתהון ונסכיהון
And you shall sacrifice them upon the altar	ותקרב המו על מדבחה
Of the house of your God in Jerusalem.	די בית אלהכם די בירשׁלם
And whatsoever seems good to you and your brothers	ומה די עלך ועל אחך

82. Since Briant (*Cyrus*, 130–37) contends that Persian monarchs do not share power, Fried (*Ezra*, 12) speculates that this "seven counselors" reference, as in Esth 1:14, is "added by the biblical writer to lend putative Persian coloring."

83. MT בקר ("to seek, investigate"); OG *ἐπισκέπτομαι* ("to watch over, care for"). Fried (*Ezra*, 19–21) speculates with Steiner ("Qumran," 623–46) that the meaning of לבקר likely resonates with מבקר in 1QS 6.11–12, 19–20, suggesting that since *ἐπισκέπτομαι* can mean "to act as an *ἐπίσκοπος*" (LSJ 657), לבקרא likely means "to act as the King's Ear."

84. Cf. the summary list of donations in Neh 7:70–72 (cf. below).

85. Repeated usage of נדב ("to donate freely") may well be intended to suggest that none of this wealth comes from "spoil" or "booty."

ייטב בשאר כספא ודהבה למעבד	To do with the rest of the silver and gold
כרעות אלהכם תעבדון	You may do according to the will of your God.
ומאניא די מתיהבין לך	The vessels[86] which have been given to you
לפלחן בית אלהך	For service in the house of your God
השלם קדם אלה ירשלם	You shall recompense[87] to the God of Jerusalem,
ושאר חשחות בית אלהך	And the rest of the needs of the house of your God
די יפל לך למנתן	Which falls to you to provide[88]
תנתן מן בית גנזי מלכא	You shall finance[89] from the king's treasury.
ומני אנה ארתחשסתא מלכא	Now I, King Artaxerxes,
שים טעם לכל גזבריא די בעבר נהרה	Issue a decree to all the treasurers of `Eber-Nahara
די כל די ישאלנכון עזרא כהנא	That everything asked of you by Ezra the priest,
ספר דתא די אלא שמיא	Scribe of the law of the God of Heaven,
אספרנא יתעבד	Be diligently done,
עד כסף ככרין מאה	Up to one hundred talents of silver
ועד חנטין כרין מאה	And one hundred cors of wheat
ועד חמר בתין מאה	And one hundred baths of wine
ועד בתין משח מאה	And one hundred baths of oil
ומלח די לא כתב	And unlimited salt . . .[90]
ולכם מהודעין די	And let it be known to you that against
כל כהניא ולויא זמריא תרעיא	Any priest, levite, singer, gatekeeper,
נתיניא ופלחי בית אלהא דנה	Temple slave, or laborer in the house of this God
מנדה בלו והלך	No tribute, produce-tax, or property-tax
לא שליט למרמא עליהם	Is to be levied.[91]

86. Williamson (*Ezra-Nehemiah*, 83) thinks that repeated mention of these vessels is significant because (a) they represent a "tangible point of contact" with pre-exilic temple worship; and (b) they possess "a symbolic value in the context of exile and restoration."

87. MT שלם (cf. Joel 2:25; 4:4; Gerleman, *Wurzel*, 1–2).

88. Lit. "give."

89. Lit. "give."

90. Ezra 7:12–22. In other words *this* Aramaic epistle, unlike the four previous, sets specific limits on the *amount* of Persian support to be distributed to the Hebrews (cf. Pakkala, *Ezra*, 28–30).

91. Ezra 7:24 (this is the same list of taxes—in the same order—as that found in Ezra 4:13 and 4:20). Exempting officials from taxation is one of a king's most important "weapons." According to the so-called Gadatas Inscription (Cousin and Deschamps, "Lettre," 529–42), Darius relieves Apollo's priests of *their* tax burden as well.

Authorized by this royal decree, Ezra conveys a small fortune to Jerusalem for the purpose of reviving its Second Temple economy.[92] In addition to the oft-mentioned "gold and silver vessels" recovered from the Chaldeans, he conveys 650 talents of silver, 100 silver vessels, 100 talents of gold, 20 golden bowls, and two vessels of polished bronze, entrusting the security of this treasure to a handpicked squadron of priestly guardians.[93] *Summary:* Regardless of the actual amounts spent or the motivation(s) for spending it, Ezra-Nehemiah understands Achaemenid support for Jerusalem to be only one small part of a much grander program of nation-building.[94] Nehemiah, however, casts a much darker shadow over the problems the returnees have to face in the course of trying to reclaim their ancestral landholdings.[95] Struggling to survive, several come to Nehemiah (now governor of `Eber-Nahara) to complain about the mistreatment they have to endure at the hands of their creditors, many of whom are fellow Jews.[96] The situation they describe is dire:

שדתינו וכרמינו ובתינו אנחנו ערבים	We have to mortgage[97] fields, vineyards, and houses
ונקחה דגן ברעב	To acquire grain during the famine . . .[98]
לוינו כסף למדת המלך	We have to borrow[99] money on our fields and vineyards.

92. Lipschitz ("Jerusalem," 26) observes that the Achaemenids try "to establish a strong military, political, and economic coalition *vis-à-vis* the Greeks," taking over the "maritime trade dominated by the Phoenicians," from whom they hire "many of the positions of authority on the local economic and political level." (Cf. Stern, "Province," 155).

93. Ezra 8:26–27. Williamson (*Ezra-Nehemiah*, 83) wonders whether the "vessels" mentioned in this final epistle might not be newly made (i.e., in addition to the "gold and silver vessels" originally plundered by the Chaldeans).

94. Cf. Wiesehöfer, "Empires," 199–234.

95. Janzen (*Witch-hunts*, 92–93) doubts whether this oppressed group consists of recent returnees, and Houston (*Justice*, 19) recognizes that "the circumstantial, though of course self-interested account of Nehemiah gives us a clear picture of a process of deprivation of the peasantry such as cannot be found in the rhetoric of the prophets."

96. Citrin ("Immigration," 859) contends that "those who experience job competition with immigrants, who bear a relatively heavy tax burden, or who have dimming financial prospects are more likely to favor restrictionist policies than people who are feeling more economically secure" (cf. the similar conclusion reported in Moore, "Monocultural," 53, n. 62).

97. MT ערב (cf. Ug `*rb*, "to stand surety for," *DULAT* 180–810); OG διεγγυάω ("to mortgage," but cf. ἀρραβὼν, "pledge, guarantee," Eph 1:14 // ערבן, "pledge, guarantee," *CAP* 10.9, 13, 17); Syr reads ܘܐܝܬ ܕܐܡܪܝܢ ܫܩܠܝܢ ܠ ܥܠܠܬܐ ܘܚܩܠܐ ܬܓܪܐ ܘܒܬܐ ܘܟܪܡܐ ܒܟܦܢܐ, "some say that 'merchants' (from ܙܒܢ, 'to buy') are seizing crops, fields, houses, and vineyards during the famine." Cf. the *irbū* ("gifts") and *katrū* ("bribes") brought to Marduk by the gods (*Ee* 7.111).

98. Neh 5:3. Whether this "famine" (רעב) is the result of natural or political factors is not clear (cf. Hag 1:6; 2:16).

99. MT לוה. OG δανείζω ("to lend"); Syr ܢܐܙܦ ܟܣܦܐ ܡܢ ܡܕܐܬܐ ܕܡܠܟܐ, "we borrow money *from* the king's tax"; cf. כמלוה כלוה ("like lender, like borrower," Isa 24:2).

שׂדתינו וכרמינו	To pay the king's tax.[100]

This situation is difficult to comprehend because

ועתה כבשׂר אחינו בשׂרנו	Our flesh is the same as that of our brothers,[101]
כבניהם בנינו	Our children are like their children.
והנה אנחנו כבשׁים	Yet we are being forced[102]
את בנינו ואת בנתינו לעבדים	To enslave our sons and our daughters.
ויש מבנתינו נכבשׁות	Our daughters are being assaulted[103]
ואין לאל ידנו	And we have to stand by powerless
ושׂדתינו וכרמינו לאחרים	As our fields and vineyards go to others.[104]

Shocked and appalled, Nehemiah responds to these complaints by convening a "town-hall meeting" to "sue" (ריב)[105] the "nobles" (חרים)[106] and "officials" (סגנים)[107] responsible for these egregious violations of Torah.[108] Using the strongest possible language, he charges that

100. Neh 5:4. Is the problem imperial taxation or usury from local officials (or both)? In addition to the persistent problems of drought, famine and disease (Hag 1:5–11), Hoglund (*Imperial*, 212–14) suggests that the Persian military desperately needs tax revenue to pay for the emperor's expanding army. Stern ("Palestine," 113) argues that "in contrast to the liberal approach of the Persian rulers towards the conquered people in matters of cult and administration, in questions of economy and taxation it is rather severe."

101. Noting the repeated use of אח ("brother") throughout this passage, Bautch ("Covenant," 15) contends that the "elite suffer none of the privation and familial dislocation that their brothers must undergo," even though Torah clearly states that לנכרי תשיך ולאחיך לא תשיך, "to the foreigner you may charge interest, but to your brother you may not" (Deut 23:20). Olyan ("Purity," 159–72) thinks Nehemiah is determined to classify אח as a "sacred boundary."

102. MT כבשׁ ("to subject"). This is the word Jeremiah uses to condemn Zedekiah for "subjecting" recently freed slaves (Jer 34:11). Explaining Kippenberg's (*Religion*, 56–58) model, Houston (*Justice*, 32) imagines here "successive phases of a process of degradation: first they pledge their children, then their land, then having lost their land their children are threatened with sale."

103. N.B. again the root כבשׁ ("to subject"), now in the N passive form, and cf. הגם לכבושׁ את המלכה, "Will he (Haman) 'assault' even the queen?" (Esth 7:8). Williamson (*Ezra-Nehemiah*, 238) sees sexual connotations in both of these texts.

104. Neh 5:5. Van Wijk-Bos (*Nehemiah*, 62) observes that "until this point the Jews are shown as a fragile, but united group bound together by . . . industrious eagerness to rebuild the city, beset only by troubles from outside. Now it is revealed that far more is amiss than can be accounted for by broken walls."

105. MT ריב ("to sue"; cf. the PN ירבעל, "Let Ba'al Sue," Judg 6:32; discussed above).

106. Cf. Isa 34:12; Jer 27:20; 39:6.

107. Cf. Ezra 9:2; Neh 2:16; 4:8.

108. Exod 22:24; Lev 25:36–37; Deut 23:20–21. The governor is careful to state in his suit that the behavior of *local* officials (not their Persian employers) makes up the bulk of what is לא טוב ("not good," Neh 5:9). Cf. Bautch, "Covenant," 14–18; Janzen, *Chronicles*, 214; Feldman, "Interest," 239–54.

משא איש באחיו אתם נשים	You are committing usury against your brothers . . .![109]
אנחנו קנינו את אחינו	We are (re)acquiring[110] as many of our brothers as possible
היהודים הנמכרים לגוים כדי בנו	(i.e., those Jews already sold to Gentiles),
וגם אתם תמכרו את אחיכם	But you are peddling your brothers,
ונמכרו לנו	Whom we must then reacquire,[111]
וגם אני אחי ונערי	As my brothers and I and my servants
נשים בהם כסף ודגן	Lend[112] them silver and grain.[113]

The mandate he issues to rein in this usury is thoroughly "prophetic":[114]

נעזבה נא את המשא הזה	Let us abandon this usury!
השיבו נא להם כהיום	Restore to them this day
שדתיהם כרמיהם זיתיהם ובתיהם	Their fields, vineyards, olive trees and houses,

109. Neh 5:7. MT נשא ("to lend"); cf. Vg *usurasne* ("you commit usury/charge interest"). Cf. نسا ("to defer, allow time"); نسيه ("credit"). Distinguishing between "interest" and "usury," Feldman ("Interest," 240) defines the latter as "predatory lending."

110. MT קנה ("to acquire"). Cf. the story of "the Acquirer" (i.e., קין, "Cain") in Gen 4:1–15 (Moore, *WealthWatch*, 105–17).

111. Neh 5:8. MT מכר appears in each line ("to buy/sell"; translated here as "peddling" and "reacquire"); N.B. that Elijah accuses Ahab of התמכרך לעשות הרע, "selling yourself to do evil" (1 Kgs 21:20). Smith (*Nehemiah*, 143) recognizes that "on the one hand, there is a group of generous Jewish brethren (including Nehemiah) who are graciously 'buying back' Jewish people forced to sell themselves as slaves to wealthy non-Jewish people because of large debts . . . But all this is for naught because a few months later these poor people are being forced back into slavery by wealthy Jewish nobles strictly enforcing their legal rights."

112. In LeFebvre's (*Collections*, 127) opinion, Nehemiah here "acknowledges the general propriety of secured loans," yet condemns the "distraint which leaves the debtor with no means to avoid subsequent bondage."

113. Neh 5:8. Cohen (*Jewishness*, 267–68) sees a parallel between Pericles' citizenship law in 450 BCE (Aristotle, *Ath. Pol.* 26.3) and the mass divorce in Ezra 10:1–44, attributing it to what he calls "the matrilineal principle" in Second Temple Judaism. Fried (*Ezra*, 24–27), however, cites the Periclean parallel to show (a) that the group complaining to Ezra about intermarriage is specifically called השׂרים (Ezra 9:1, lit. "the officials"), a group most likely to be identified as "officials of the Persian empire"; and (b) that the marriages between Judeans and the families of Sanballat and Tobiah are likely "seen by Persian officials as threatening to create a power base and source of wealth independent of the king." Thus, (c) Ezra-Nehemiah raises questions not simply with regard to "puritanical thinking about purity," but about the quotidian problems always generated by "insiders" seeking to maintain socioeconomic power over "outsiders."

114. N.B. that נבואה ("prophecy," Neh 6:12) is an active part of this "insider-vs.-outsider" discussion, what Brueggemann (*Imagination*, 39–58) calls "prophetic criticizing and the embrace of pathos." Grabbe (*Ezra-Nehemiah*, 50, 165–66) sees in contemporary prophetic circles both supporters and opponents of Nehemiah.

ומאת הכסף והדגן התירוש והיצהר	And the interest[115] on the money, grain, wine, and oil
אשר אתם נשים בהם	Which you are charging them.[116]

After the building of the Second Temple, the challenge to maintain the priestly economy outlined in Torah proves difficult,[117] especially when it comes to maintaining important "sacred boundaries" like (a) exclusion of work on the sabbath;[118] (b) exclusion of Ammonites and Moabites from קהל יהוה ("Yhwh's assembly);[119] and (c) fair financial compensation for the Levites:

ואדעה כי מניות הלוים	I discovered that the Levites' rations
לא נתנה	Were not being distributed,[120]
ויברחו איש לשדהו	And that each had retreated to his field.[121]

Careful policing of these boundaries, however, insures that the "storehouses/treasuries" (אוצרות) are better managed by supervisors more thoroughly committed to dispensing the correct amount mandated for "their brothers' portion" (לחלק אחיהם).[122]

Summary: Ezra-Nehemiah begins with great promise, but ends with great disappointment. Where oppression is "expected" one finds *external benevolence* (the Persian imperial policy of nation-building), yet where justice is "expected" (from Yhwh's covenant people) one finds *internal malevolence* (unfair usury practices). Struck by the depth of this irony,[123] Jeff McCrory holistically concludes that "the major task

115. Interest rates are outrageously high in this era. In Egypt a lady named Yehoḥen borrows four shekels at an interest rate of 60% APR, which, if not paid within two years, forces the forfeiture of her property (*TADE* 2.3.1.14–20; 2.4.2.1–5). In Mesopotamia two ladies named Nidintu and Adirtu borrow 940 and 950 shekels respectively from the Murašu family (major bankers in the fifth century BCE) at 40% APR (Cardascia, *Archives*, 30, 47–48; cf. Yoder, *Wisdom*, 69–70). Porten (*Archives*, 77–78) thinks the 20% difference suggests a tighter cash market in Egypt than in Mesopotamia.

116. Neh 5:10–11. Schoville (*Ezra-Nehemiah*, 181) lays the brunt of the blame on "the avarice of the elite of the society, wealthy enough to avoid the heart-wrenching circumstances of their Jewish brethren, but covetous enough to take advantage of their desperate situations."

117. Boer, "Economy," 29–48.

118. Exod 20:8. Many of the offenses listed in Neh 13:15–17 overlap those in Amos 4:5. *Contra* Philo (*Spec.* 2.60), Heschel (*Sabbath*, 13) views שׁבת not as a time to refresh for future work, but as something much deeper: "Six days a week we seek to dominate the world," but "on the seventh day we try to dominate the self."

119. Deut 23:4. While Nehemiah is away on business, Eliashib the priest empties a room in the temple used to store tithes and gifts earmarked for priests, levites and other temple staff, then helps Tobias the Ammonite—his "relative" (קרוב)—convert it into an office (Neh 13:4–5).

120. Num 7:1–6. Nehemiah's response is to "sue the officials" responsible (ריב הסגנים . . ., Neh 13:11; cf. Judg 6:25, 31; Jer 2:9; Hos 2:4; and discussion above).

121. Neh 13:10. N.B. that much like the first attacks against the Christian church (cf. below), the first attacks against the rebuilt temple community are profoundly *socioeconomic*.

122. Neh 13:12–13. N.B. the use of the root חלק ("portion") found repeatedly in Nevi'im (Josh 13:7; 14:4; 22:27; 2 Sam 20:1; Jer 10:16; Mic 2:4; cf. discussion above).

123. Goldingay's (*Esther*, 190) reflections on "irony" are *apropos* here: "Jewish readers . . . are no

of Nehemiah's reform is not just to build a wall, but to establish boundaries for an emerging postexilic community."[124]

Epistle of Jeremiah

Like the brief sent by the prophet Jeremiah to the exiles in Babylonia,[125] the Epistle of Jeremiah claims to come from the hand of Jeremiah of Anathoth.[126] Attending to it here would seem superfluous were it not for the fact that this document so pointedly, if hilariously, exposes the underbelly of a prominent socioeconomic institution—the *priesthood*.[127] Like Bel and the Dragon—the apocryphal text where a Hebrew vizier (Daniel) helps a Gentile king ascertain whether the food *offered* to Bel is *consumed* by Bel[128]—the Epistle of Jeremiah is a *farce*.[129] Derisively ridiculing Babylon's humanoid deities as lifeless objects unable to speak or move, much less eat,[130] it ruthlessly exposes the secret money-trail created by the corrupt priests responsible for maintaining the artificial machinery of the Babylonian cult:[131]

ἔστι δὲ καὶ ὅτε ὑφαιρούμενοι οἱ ἱερεῖς	Sometimes the priests pilfer[132]
ἀπὸ τῶν θεῶν αὐτῶν χρυσίον καὶ ἀργύριον	The gold and silver ornamenting their gods,[133]

more peace-loving and gentle than anyone else."

124. McCrory, "Nehemiah," 259.

125. Jer 29 (cf. Lied, "Trajectories," 288).

126. Cf. Jer 29:27. Mendels ("Epistle," 721–22) voices the majority opinion that this short document is a farce written in an artificial epistolary format long after the death of the prophet Jeremiah. Ball ("Epistle," 596–611) imagines a Hebrew original (cf. σκεῦος ἀνθρώπου, "vessel of a man," as a likely misreading of כלי אדמה, "earthen vessels," in EpJer 17), but the only surviving text is the OG.

127. Cf. Moore, *Babbler*, 25–41.

128. Bel 1–22 (cf. Wills, "Bel," 1051–53).

129. A "farce" is a "dramatic work (usually short) which has for its sole object to excite laughter" (*OED*, s.v. "farce," cited in Davis, *Farce*, 1).

130. EpJer 4–8. The author has difficulty understanding how humanoid wooden icons outfitted with gold and silver and fancy clothing can inspire so much "fear" in the heart of τοῖς ἔθνεσιν ("the nations," EpJer 4), but, as Walker and Dick point out (*Induction*, 6–7), the relationship between inanimate image and deity in Mesopotamian religion is similar to that between bread, wine and deity in Roman Christianity.

131. Specifying *which* priesthood in *which* particular temple is evidently immaterial to the author of EpJer (cf. Marttila, "Epistle," 225–46).

132. Gk ὑφαιρέω (ὑπο+αἱρέω, lit. "under + raise up"); Vg *subtrahent*, "they subtract"; Syr ܣܥܠܝܢ, "they conspire." Anxious to throw off the Athenian yoke, the Ionians urge the Spartans to take one of their towns καὶ τὴν πρόσοδον ταύτην μεγίστην οὖσαν Ἀθηναίων ὑφέλωσι, "and 'pilfer' from the Athenians that major revenue source" (Thucydides, *Hist.* 3.31).

133. EpJer 9. Syr ܚܠܠܬܐ ܘܟܠܝܠܝܢ ܒܪܫܐ ܕܐܠܗܝܗܘܢ, "the portions (of food) and crowns on the heads of their gods"; Vg *coronas . . . aureas*, "golden crowns." Beaulieu (*Pantheon*, 18–25) lists several types of *lubuštū* ("garments") worn on deified humanoid images.

εἰς ἑαυτοὺς καταναλώσουσιν δώσουσιν	Lavishly spending it upon themselves[134]
δὲ ἀπ᾽ αὐτῶν καὶ ταῖς ἐπὶ τοῦ τέγους πόρναις	As well as the prostitutes in the brothels.[135]

To hide these goings-on from "outsiders,"

ὀχυροῦσιν οἱ ἱερεῖς θυρώμασίν	The priests fortify the doors,
τε καὶ κλείθροις καὶ μοχλοῖς	The locks, and the barricades
ὅπως ὑπὸ τῶν λῃστῶν μὴ συληθῶσι	So that they cannot be robbed[136] by thieves.

In actuality, however, *they* are the thieves because

τὰς δὲ θυσίας αὐτῶν ἀποδόμενοι	The sacrifices they are supposed to give back
οἱ ἱερεῖς αὐτῶν καταχρῶνται	The priests redirect[137] to themselves;
ὡσαύτως δὲ καὶ αἱ γυναῖκες αὐτῶν	Likewise their wives
ἀπ᾽ αὐτῶν ταριχεύουσαι	Preserve their sacrifices (with salt?)[138]
οὔτε πτωχῷ οὔτε ἀδυνάτῳ μεταδιδόασιν	Never sharing with the poor or the powerless.[139]

All this takes place because

οὔτε πλοῦτον οὔτε χαλκὸν	Neither wealth[140] nor coin[141]
οὐ μὴ δύνωνται διδόναι	Are they able to manage.[142]

134. Gk καταναλίσκω ("to spend lavishly"). Wary of the Cypriot ruler Evagoras, the Persians declare war, εἰς τὴν στρατείαν ταυτήν πλέον ἢ τάλαντα πεντακισχίλια καὶ μύρια κατηνάλωσεν, "lavishing on that expedition more than fifteen thousand talents" (Isocrates, *Evagoras*, 60).

135. EpJer 9. Cf. Adams, *Epistle*, 178–79; Moore, *Additions*, 338.

136. EpJer 18. Gk συλάω ("to strip away"; pass. "to be stripped, robbed"). In a speech written in the voice of Archidamus III (king of Sparta, 360–338 BCE), Isocrates (*Archidamus* 19) refers to Herakles' tenth labor as a time when the demigod συληθεὶς γὰρ τὰς βοῦς τὰς ἐκ τῆς Ἐρυθείας, "was 'robbed' of the cattle from Eurytheia."

137. EpJer 27. Gk καταχράομαι, "to make full use of, apply, (re)direct." Describing the fundraising for a war effort, Lysias (*Aristophanes* 22) testifies that Aristophanes τοῦ ἀδελφοῦ τοῦ ὁμοπατρίου ἀποκειμένας παρ᾽ αυτῷ τεττεράκοντα μνᾶς λαβὼν κατεχρήσατο, "takes forty mina-units on deposit at his house for his brother on the father's side, and 'redirects' it."

138. That is, they hoard the meat for themselves and their families.

139. EpJer 27. Liverani (*Myth*, 21) emphasizes that "the food surplus the community reserves for the feeding of the gods should end up with the gods, not with the priests."

140. EpJer 34. That the Greeks deify Πλοῦτος ("wealth") as a DN inspires Cicero (*De natura deorum* 2.26.66) to hazard an explanation: *Terrena autem vis omnis atque natura Diti patri dedicata est, qui dives ut apud Graecos* Πλούτων, *quia et recedunt omnia in terras et oriuntur e teris*, "The entire bulk and substance of the land is dedicated to father Dis (i.e., Dives, 'the rich,' and so in Greek *Plouton*) because even as all things recede into the land they also arise from it."

141. Gk χαλκός (lit. "copper").

142. EpJer 35. Almsgiving, therefore, is apparently out of the question. N.B. the Epistle's repeated

Summary: Supplementing the prophetic tradition in Jeremiah,[143] the Epistle of Jeremiah focuses on the socioeconomic consequences generated by contrasting (a) dead humanoid images with a living, benevolent God, and (b) entrenched religious pretention with living, vibrant faith.[144]

Tobit

In contrast to the Epistle of Jeremiah, the namesake character of Tobit goes out of his way to avoid even the *hint* of corruption. Several socioeconomic motifs come together in this diaspora tale to construct a story which at one point cites a "prophecy from Amos":[145]

והפכתי חגיכם לאבל	I will turn your festivals into mourning
וכל שיריכם לקינה	And all your songs into lament.[146]

Tobit survives in several formats. Hebrew fragments from Qumran Cave 4 suggest it to have been originally semitic,[147] but the only complete witnesses known to have survived are preserved in Greek.[148] As with any ancient text, contemporary interpretations focus on matters of (a) historical context,[149] and (b) literary structure (i.e.,

use of the root δίδωμι ("to give"): ἀποδίδωμι ("to restore, give back," v. 27); μεταδίδωμι ("to share," v. 27); δίδωμι ("to give," v. 35).

143. Other contributors to this tradition include Lamentations and Baruch. N.B. that the reference to "the prophet Jeremiah" in 2 Macc 2:2 almost certainly alludes to EpJer, not the book of Jeremiah in Nevi'im.

144. Examining it alongside "idol parodies" in Tanak and elsewhere, Roth ("Parodies," 42) treats EpJer as a "homiletically expanded . . . collection of available idol parodying arguments."

145. Tob 2:6. BA τῆς προφητείας Αμος, "the prophecy of Amos"; S τοῦ ῥήματος τοῦ προφήτου ὅσα ἐλάλησεν Αμως, "the word of the prophet which Amos spoke"; Syr ܢܒܝܘܬܐ ܕܥܡܘܣ, "the prophecy of Amos"; Vg *sermonem quem dixit Dominus per Amos prophetam*, "the word which the Lord spoke to the prophet Amos." Cf. Humphreys, "Novella," 82–96; Deselaers, *Tobit*, 261–78; Nickelsburg, *Literature*, 29–35; Macatangay, *Tobit*, 116–18.

146. MT Amos 8:10 (cited in Tob 2:6). OG Tobit changes 1 sg act. μεταστρέψω ("I will turn") in OG Amos 8:10 to 3 pl. pass. στραφήσονται ("*they* [i.e., 'your festivals'] will be turned," Tob 2:6 S). One of the scroll's prominent characteristics, as Grabbe ("Tobit," 737) points out, is its "incorporation of didactic, hymnic, and prophetic elements . . . not usually found in a folktale."

147. Tobit is attested by four Aramaic fragments (4Q196–199) and one Hebrew (4Q200). Cf. *DSSSE* 382–99; Fitzmyer, *Tobit*, 18–28; Neubauer, *Tobit*.

148. OG Tobit survives in two formats: (a) S, underlying JB, NEB, and NAB; and (b) BA (1700 words shorter), underlying KJV and RSV. S is the preferred text because it most deeply resonates with the oldest witnesses from Qumran (4Q196–200). Moreover, S is "not only longer, but perhaps more sober" (Luciani, "Introduction," 8; cf. Tob 8:15). Cf. Weeks, *Tobit*; Hallermayer, *Tobit*, 15–19; Soll, "Tobit," 209–31; and Stuckenbruck, *Angels*, 126–27.

149. Cf. Zimmermann, *Tobit*; Fitzmyer, *Tobit*; Moore, *Tobit*; Otzen, *Tobit*, 1–66; Deselaers, *Tobit*; Nowell, *Tobit*; Schuller, "Tobit," 272–78; Grabbe, "Tobit," 736–47; Kiel, *Tobit*; Skemp, "Tobit," 43–70; Wills, *Novel*, 68–92.

micro-vs.-*macro*-literary).[150] Few, however, systematically attend to its socioeconomic motifs even though Tobit provides, in Micah Kiel's opinion, a "more extended picture of quotidian Jewish family life than any other book."[151]

The story begins with a focus on *tithing*.[152] Lamenting that his "brothers" in the "ancestral house of Naphtali" regularly offer sacrifice to the pagan calf-deity at Dan,[153] Tobit touts the frequency of his trips to Jerusalem to donate

τὰς ἀπαρχὰς καὶ τὰ πρωτογενήματα	The firstlings and the firstfruits and
καὶ τὰς δεκάτας τῶν κτηνῶν	The tithes of the cattle, and
καὶ τὰς πρωτοκουρίας τῶν προβάτων	The first shearings of the sheep.[154]

When registering his gifts with temple officials, he is careful to include

τὴν δεκάτην τοῦ σίτου καὶ τοῦ οἴνου	The tithe of the wheat and the wine,
καὶ ἐλαίου καὶ ῥοῶν καὶ τῶν σύκων	The oil, pomegranates, figs, and
καὶ τῶν λοιπῶν ἀκροδρύων	The rest of the fruits . . .[155]

In addition,

τὴν δεκάτην τὴν δευτέραν ἀπεδεκάτιζον	The second tithe I tithe[156]
ἀργυρίῳ τῶν ἓξ ἐτῶν	In silver every six years;
καὶ ἐπορευόμην καὶ ἐδαπάνων αὐτὰ	I go and distribute it
ἐν Ιερουσαλημ καὶ ἐδίδουν αὐτὰ	In Jerusalem; and give it[157]
τοῖς ὀρφανοῖς καὶ ταῖς χήραις	To the orphans and widows

150. Di Pede, "Enquête," 142–43. Explaining this design, McCracken ("Tobit," 401) argues that "Tobit is a comic narrator who, although pious, embodies the ludicrous through his limited perspective, a perspective that the third-person narrator and the reader transcend."

151. Kiel, "Tobit," 954. Machiela and Perrin ("Tobit," 132) argue from an intertextual analysis of Tobit and the *Genesis Apocryphon* that each scroll "shares a deep concern for Israelite identity and conduct in a world beset by the realities of widespread impiety and foreign domination."

152. Although they, too, emphasize "tithing," the medieval Hebrew/Aramaic manuscripts of Tobit only minimally parallel the fragments from Cave 4 (cf. Weeks, *Tobit*, 32).

153. Tob 1:5. Cf. 1 Kgs 12:26–29; Chung, *Calf*, 204–8.

154. Tob 1:6. The underlying Torah text is Deut 14:22–29.

155. Tob 1:7 (cf. Num 18:21–28). Baumgartner ("מעשׂר," 247) sees here an "ambiguity" which "results from the use of δεκάτη ('tenth') first in the extended sense of a priestly donation such as the תרומה ("wave-offering") and then literally for the levitical tithe."

156. Cf. the Mishnaic tractate *Ma'aser Sheni* ("second tithe"), discussed by Oppenheimer (*History*, 23–51).

157. B καὶ τὴν τρίτην ("the third"); Syr ܠܬܠܝܬܝܬܐ ("for the third"); Vg *in tertio anno* ("in the third year"). Does Tobit speak of a "third tithe" or a "third year?" N.B. that no OG version repeats δεκάτην ("tithe") a third time. Sanders' understanding (*Judaism*, 245) of the underlying Torah text (Deut 14:22–29) is that "there are two tithes every year (except the sabbatical year, when the land rests): one for the levites (who give ten per cent to the priests), and one to be spent in Jerusalem. In the third and sixth years there is still a third ten per cent for the poor." Dimant (*Tobit*, 203) basically agrees (cf. Jub 32:10–14; Josephus, *AJ* 4.68, 205, 240).

καὶ προσηλύτοις τοῖς προσκειμένοις	And proselytes[158] attached[159]
τοῖς υἱοῖς Ισραηλ	To the children of Israel.
εἰσέφερον καὶ ἐδίδουν αὐτοῖς	I bring and give (it) to them
ἐν τῷ τρίτῳ ἔτει	In the third year.[160]

Like the "forlorn scholar" Urad-gula,[161] Tobit is well aware of the challenges involved in working for the Assyrian government:

ἔδωκέν μοι ὁ ὕψιστος χάριν καὶ μορφὴν	The Most High[162] gave me favor and form[163]
ἐνώπιον Ενεμεσσαρου	Before Shalmaneser
καὶ ἠγόραζον αὐτῷ	And I made acquisitions for him,[164]
πάντα τὰ πρὸς τὴν χρῆσιν	Everything which he needed.
καὶ ἐπορευόμην εἰς Μηδίαν	I would go into Media[165]
καὶ ἠγόραζον αὐτῷ ἐκεῖθεν	And there purchase it for him
ἕως αὐτὸν ἀποθανεῖν	Until he died.
καὶ παρεθέμην Γαβαήλῳ βαλλάντια	Then I deposited with Gabael[166]
τῷ ἀδελφῷ τῷ Γαβρι	(the brother of Gabri
ἐν τῇ χώρᾳ τῆς Μηδίας	in the country of Media)
ἀργυρίου τάλαντα δέκα	Bags (containing) ten talents of silver.[167]

158. Tob 1:8. S reads "proselytes" alongside "widows" and "orphans," yet Vg omits the latter two groups, reading instead *proselytis et advenis* ("proselytes and arrivees"; cf. Deut 26:12).

159. That προσκεῖμαι can have overt religious connotations becomes clear from Epictetus' (*Diatr.* 4.7.20) complaint that too many too easily succumb to the temptation to say προσκείσομαι διάκονος καὶ ἀκόλουθος ἐκείνῳ, "I will attach myself as a servant and follower to that one" (i.e., that "deity").

160. Tob 1:8. Applying Becker's ("Theory," 493–517) household production model, Clain and Zech ("Household," 923–46) contend that of the two conventional presumptions—(a) that congregants' contributions of time and money are complementary; or (b) that congregations compete with other charitable organizations for money—only the first holds true.

161. Nissinen, *Prophets*, 108 (cf. above and van der Toorn, "Lions," 626–40).

162. Whether ὁ ὕψιστος refers to an (originally) independent deity or is simply an epithet for the God of Moses is an old debate (cf. Elnes and Miller, "Elyon," 294–96).

163. Fitzmyer (*Tobit*, 113) reads "favor and good standing."

164. Lit. "I purchased for him." The first part of Tobit resonates with the "court tale" genre; i.e., stories in which Jews serve Gentile kings (Joseph, Mordecai, Daniel, Tobit, Aḥiqar; Rosenthal, "Josephgeschichte" 278–84; Müller, "Lehrerzählung," 77–98). Macatangay (*Wisdom*, 218) thinks "the court is peripheral to the vision of the Tobit story despite the strong influence of a court story."

165. The capital of Media, Ecbatana, is where Achaemenid courtiers retrieve a copy of the Cyrus Edict (Ezra 6:2).

166. "Gabael" (גבאל, "El is lofty," cf. Tob 1:1) may be intentionally symbolic (McKenzie, *Dictionary*, 291), a PN used by the narrator "to reinforce yet another of the narrative's themes" (Schmidt, "Gabael," 861).

167. Tob 1:13–14. Tobit's government job, in other words, provides enough wealth to fund business

One of Tobit's pet peeves is the Assyrian monarch's nasty habit of killing Jews without burying the bodies, a practice he finds utterly reprehensible.[168] Like the government official Sinuhe, who flees for his life from political turmoil in Egypt,[169] Tobit comes to a point where he feels he has to flee for *his* life from political turmoil in Assyria. Here the Qumran Cave 4 fragments pick up the story:

כ]ל ד[י] הוה לי	Then all that was mine was seized.[170]
ולא שביק {פ} לי כל מנד]עם	And I was left with nothing
חנ]ה אנתתי וטוביה ברי	(except Han)nah my wife and Tobias my son.[171]

After Adrammelech and Sharezer assassinate their father Sennacherib and flee "to the mountains of Ararat,"[172] the throne transfers to the next-in-line, their brother Esarhaddon.[173] Responding to his new responsibilities, Esarhaddon then hires Aḥiqar—Tobit's kinsman—to help him manage the day-to-day activities of the sprawling Assyrian empire,[174] formalizing his appointment by assigning him several "titles": (a) על כל ש]זפנות מלכותא, "(the one) over all 'the kingdom's finances'" (lit. "lending-and-borrowing");[175] (b) ש]לטן על [כ]ל המרכלות מלכא, "the *sulṭan* over all the king's finances";[176] (c) רב שקה, "the chief cupbearer";[177] (d) רב עזקן, "the notary";[178] (e) המרכל, "the treasurer";[179] (f) שיזפן, "the administrator";[180] and (g) תנין לה, "the

partners miles away.

168. Cf. 2 Macc 5:10. Presuming that Sennacherib throws Jewish corpses over the wall because he wants to treat them as common criminals, Fitzmyer (*Tobit*, 119) believes that Tobit here portrays its main character engaging in *lèse majesté* ("insulting the monarch").

169. Lichtheim, *Literature* 1:222–35; Moore, *WealthWatch*, 121–24.

170. 4Q196.2.2 omits a verb, but cf. Syr ܘܐܬܚܛܦܘ ("then was seized/pillaged"); S καὶ ἡρπάγη ("then was seized/plundered").

171. Tob 1:20 (4Q196.2.2–3; reconstructed from OG).

172. 2 Kgs 19:37 // Isa 37:38; לטורי אררט, 4Q196.2.4 (Tob 1:21).

173. OG Σαχερδονος. Akk *Aššur-aḫ-iddin*, "Aššur has given a brother."

174. Aḥiqar does for Esarhaddon the same type of gritty "city-manager" work Tobit does for Sennacherib. Grabbe ("Tobit," 737) notes that "although he (Tobit) clearly does not rise as high as such other Jewish diaspora heroes as Daniel, Esther, and Joseph, for a short period of time he has a position of sufficient success to accumulate a large sum of money." Some of Aḥiqar's adventures appear in the Elephantine papyri (*TADE* C1.1; *CAP*, pp. 204–48; cf. Lindenberger, "Aḥiqar," 479–93).

175. 4Q196.2.5–6; cf. Tob 1:21 Syr ܥܠ ܟܠܗ ܚܘܫܒܢܐ ܕܡܠܟܘܬܐ ("over all the accounting of his kingdom"); S ἐπὶ πᾶσαν τὴν ἐκλογιστίαν τῆς βασιλείας αὐτοῦ ("over all the accounting of his kingdom").

176. 4Q196.2.6; cf. *šlyṭd šb`t rašm* ("seven-headed Sulṭan," *CAT* 1.3.3.39); Syr ܥܠ ܟܠܗ ܦܘܪܢܣܐ, "over all the supplies/revenues"; S ἐπὶ πᾶσαν τὴν διοίκησιν, "over all the housekeeping/administration."

177. 4Q196.2.7 (lit. "chief of the drink"). This is Nehemiah's title (משקה, Neh 1:11) before becoming "governor" (תרשתא, Neh 8:9).

178. 4Q196.2.7 (lit. "chief of the signet-ring").

179. 4Q196.2.7 (cf. המרכלות, "the finances," 4Q196.2.6).

180. 4Q196.2.8.

second-in-command."[181] Some of these titles reflect sociopolitical, others socioeconomic roles.[182]

Learning of Aḥiqar's appointment,[183] Tobit returns from exile to a celebratory meal hosted by his family.[184] Determined to share his good fortune,[185] he directs his son Tobias to

εὕρης πτωχὸν τῶν ἀδελφῶν ἡμῶν	Find a poor man[186] among our brothers[187]
ἐκ Νινευητῶν αἰχμαλώτων	Among the exiles in Nineveh,
ὃς μέμνηται ἐν ὅλῃ καρδίᾳ αὐτου	Who remembers the Lord[188] with all his heart
καὶ φάγεται κοινῶς μετ' ἐμου	That he might eat together with me.[189]

Obeying his father, Tobias leaves the feast to look for such a person, but instead finds another Hebrew corpse lying in the street.[190]

At this point the plotline takes what can only be described as a sudden, bizarre turn. Bird droppings "accidentally" fall onto Tobit's eyelids during an afternoon nap, and the medication used to treat the resultant problems produces total blindness.[191] How and why this occurs is never stated, only that the financial burden of caring for this angry blind man falls on the shoulders of Aḥiqar, who after two years passes it on to the man's wife:

181. 4Q196.2.8 (OG and Syr omit).

182. "Because politics and economics are always highly interdependent in advanced agrarian societies, the people who dominate the political system also dominate the economic system" (Nolan and Lenski, *Macrosociology*, 154).

183. Cf. Greenfield, "Aḥiqar," 195–202.

184. The Aramaic tradition adds a culinary detail not found elsewhere: וחזית נפתניא די קרבו עלוהי שגיאין, "I saw that the sweets they placed on it (i.e., the פתורא, 'table') were superb" (4Q296.2.11–12). S simply reads ὀψάρια πλείονα ("many tidbits," Tob 2.2).

185. Otzen (*Tobit*, 35–37) emphasizes that "almsgiving/charity" is one of the book's primary themes.

186. S πτωχὸν ("poor man"); Syr ܡܣܟܢܐ ("poor man"); B, Vg and 4Q196.2.12 omit.

187. 4Q196.2.12 reads [אזל דבר לכל מן [די ת]השכח בא]חינא, "Go fetch all [you] can find from among [our] bro[thers]"; cf. Vg *aliquos ex tribu nostra*, "someone from our tribe." Contrast the mistreatment doled out by the Hebrew "brothers" in Neh 5:1–5.

188. Syr reads ܡܪܝܐ ("the Lord"); B reads τοῦ κυρίου ("the Lord"); Vg reads *Deum* ("God"); S omits.

189. Tob 2:2. The root κοινῶς features prominently in early descriptions of the Christian church (e.g., κοινωνία, Acts 2:42; κοινά, 2:44; cf. below).

190. This incident is what triggers the aforementioned Amos citation in Tob 2:6.

191. "Granted that blindness itself is far from comic . . . there is something undeniably bizarre about this particular blindness" (McCracken, "Tobit," 402). Application of silver nitrate to diseased eyes still causes corneal ulceration in developing countries (Kong, "Blindness," 501–07). One ANE prescription reads: DIŠ NA IGI-*šú* LÙ.LÙ-*ḫa* LÀL Ì.NUN.NA Ì.SAG: *ḫal-ṣa* 1-*niš* . . . KÚM.KÚM-*am ta-šá-ḫal ana* IGI-*šú* ŠUB, "If a person's eyes are continually troubled, you heat honey, ghee (purified butter), (and) top-quality oil together, filter it, and let it fall into his eyes" (cited in Scurlock, *Medicine*, 363).

καὶ ἐν τῷ χρόνῳ ἐκείνῳ Αννα ἡ γυνή μου	At that time my wife Hanna
ἠριθεύετο ἐν τοῖς ἔργοις τοῖς γυναικείοις	Hired herself out[192] for women's work[193]
καὶ ἀπέστελλε τοῖς κυρίοις αὐτῶν	She delivered (a carpet?)[194] to her employers
καὶ ἀπεδίδουν αὐτῇ τὸν μισθόν	And they paid her a wage.[195]
καὶ ἐν τῇ ἑβδόμῃ τοῦ Δύστρου ἐξέτεμε τὸν ἱστὸν	On March 7 she cut down (a carpet?)[196]
καὶ ἀπέστειλεν αὐτὸν τοῖς κυρίοις	And sent it to her employers.
ἔδωκαν αὐτῇ τὸν μισθὸν πάντα	They paid her a full wage for it
καὶ ἔδωκαν αὐτῇ ἐφ' ἑστίᾳ ἔριφον ἐξ αἰγῶν	And gave her a goat to take home.[197]
καὶ ὅτε εἰσῆλθεν πρός με ὁ ἔριφος ἤρξατο κράζειν	When she came home the goat bleated
καὶἐκάλεσα αὐτὴν καὶ εἶπα	So I called out to her and said,
πόθεν τὸ ἐρίφιον τοῦτο	"Where did this goat come from?
μήποτε κλεψιμαῖόν ἐστιν	It's not stolen, is it?[198]
ἀπόδος αὐτὸ τοῖς κυρίοις αὐτου	Give it back to its owners,
οὐ γὰρ ἐξουσίαν ἔχομεν ἡμεῖς	For we have no right
φαγεῖν οὐδὲν κλεψιμαῖον	To eat something stolen."[199]

To this baseless accusation Hannah replies, *αὐτή δόσει δέδοταί μοι ἐπὶ τῷ μισθῷ*, "It's a gift given to me in addition to my wages."[200] Refusing to believe her, Tobit insists that she return the gift, a move which motivates her to ask two questions:

192. Gk ἐριθεύομαι. Aristotle (*Pol.* 1303a.16) observes that democracies where the wealthy become numerous often elect magistrates predisposed to "hiring themselves out" (ἐριθευόμενους).

193. Another woman forced to work because of an impaired husband is Job's wife Sitis (*T. Job* 21–25; cf. Moyo, "Workplaces," 261–62).

194. Later in the verse she ἐξέτεμε τὸν ἱστὸν, "cuts down a weaving/rug(?)" and "sends it to her employers." Macatangay ("Irony," 579) believes her to be a "textile weaver."

195. Macatangay, "Irony," 576–84.

196. Lit. "cut out from the warp/woof." "Dystrus" is "March" on the Roman calendar (Eusebius, *HE* 8.2.4).

197. Gk ἐφ' ἑστίᾳ (lit. "for the home/household/family/hearth"; cf. Herodotus 1.176).

198. Like her namesake in Nevi'im (1 Sam 3:8), Hannah lives with a man prone to groundless presumption.

199. Tob 2:11–13. Greenfield ("Tobit," 195–96) sees *marriage* and *death* as the two major themes of Tobit, but this analysis does not adequately address its socioeconomic concerns.

200. Tob 2:14. Macatangay ("Irony," 579) sees an ironic peculiarity distinguishing this husband-wife team. Where Hannah "works with diligence and skill and receives a bonus on top of her *μισθός* ('wage'), Tobit, a man known for his works of charity and righteousness, earns no reward other than

ποῦ εἰσιν αἱ ἐλεημοσύναι σου	Where are your "acts of charity". . .?[201]
ποῦ εἰσιν αἱ δικαιοσύναι σου	Where are your "acts of righteousness". . .?[202]

Rather than reflect on Tobit's anger/hypocrisy or Hannah's "right" to challenge it,[203] the narrator here (a) introduces the character of Sarah (Tob 3:7–15);[204] (b) relates how Tobit and Sarah, though separated by a great distance, simultaneously question whether death is preferable to life (3:6, 10);[205] and (c) affirms the "glory of God" (τῆς δόξης τοῦ θεοῦ, 3:16); i.e., that silent Partner behind the scenes presumably dictating his will through the angel Raphael (רפאל, "God heals").[206]

Introductions concluded, the plotline returns to the "treasure retrieval" theme:

ἐμνήσθη Τωβιθ τοῦ ἀργυρίου	Tobit remembered the silver
καὶ εἶπεν ἐν τῇ καρδίᾳ αὐτοῦ	And said to himself,
ἰδοὺ ἐγὼ ᾐτησάμην θάνατον	"Now since I have 'sought' death,
τί οὐχὶ καλῶ Τωβιαν τὸν υἱόν μου	Why don't I call for Tobias my son
καὶ ὑποδείξω αὐτῷ περὶ τοῦ ἀργυρίου τούτου	And explain to him about this silver
πρὶν ἀποθανεῖν με	Before I die?"[207]

Suspense builds, however, when the narrator inserts into Tobit's explanation a testamentary speech[208] directing Tobias to take care of three important matters: (a)

blindness and misery."

201. Macatangay (*Almsgiving*, 29) recognizes that "the book of Tobit is the only book in the Septuagint and the Christian Bible that makes 'acts of charity' (ἐλεημοσύναι) central to its narrative."

202. Tob 2:14, doubtless referring to (a) the verses above as well as (b) the חסד and צדקות Tobit later encourages his son to pursue (4Q200.2.6; Tob 4.7). Tob 2:22 Vg adds *atque his et aliis huiusmodi verbis exprobrabat ei*, "by these and other such words she reproached him," prompting Nowell (*Tobit*, 28) to comment sardonically that Hannah "does her husband a favor" because "her sharp words drive Tobit to prayer."

203. Both are wholly understandable, yet acutely (post)modern concerns (cf. Gross, *Tobit*, 21; Bow and Nickelsburg, "Patriarchy," 48–63).

204. Sarah is Raguel's daughter (Tob 3:7); Tobit is Raguel's first cousin (בר דדי, "my uncle's son," 4Q197.4.5; Tob 7:4 simply reads ἀδελφὸν ἡμῶν, "our brother"). *Conclusion:* Tobias and Sarah are probably second cousins. N.B. the numerous intertextual connections between "Sarah" (Gen 12, 21), "Sarah" (*Tobit*), "Sarah" (1QapGen), and "Sarah" (Gal 4), a trajectory on which McDonald (*Sarah*, 4) sees "a complex and sometimes contradictory figure whose individuality and agency often struggle to escape limitations placed upon her by other characters."

205. Miller (*Tobit*, 184–85) thinks that the primary difference between the two is that "whereas Tobit ends his prayer by stating that it is better to die than to hear insults (Tob 3:10), Sarah worries that her death will bring ignominy to her father and prays that God will do what he deems best" (3:15).

206. Cf. Barker, "Raphael," 118–28. Like the Book of Ruth, Tobit "stresses one particular aspect of God's providence, namely its hiddenness" (Hals, *Ruth*, 16).

207. Tob 4:1–2. *Contra* Nowell (*Tobit*, 33) the "treasure retrieval" theme is hardly an "afterthought." As with other "great texts" (see above), "death" and "wealth" inexorably go together.

208. Di Pede ("Tobie," 40–52) calls chapter 4 "*Le 'Testament' de Tobit.*"

how to treat his mother Hannah, (c) how to behave with regard to alcohol, sex, and ethno-tribal identity,[209] and (b) how to treat the corpses of his parents when they die. Here and there throughout the speech he alludes to *poverty*, *stewardship*, *work-ethic*, *land*, *inheritance*, *wages*, and *prosperity*, plus the scroll's most important socioeconomic motif—*almsgiving*.[210] Cloaking it under the generic term צדקות ("righteous deeds"),[211] he pleads,

כארך ידכה בני	According to the extent of your power,[212] my son,
[עושה בחסד] צדקות	[With kindness do] "righteous deeds."
ואל תס[תר פניכם	And do not with[hold your face
מן כל ע]נו	From any poor] person,[213]
אף ממכה לוא יס[תרו	So that from you will not be with[held
פני אלהי]ם	The face of Go]d.
אם יהיה לכה בנ[י רוב	If you have much, my [son, then
כרוב היה עוש]ה ממנו צד[קו]ת	Do righteous de]eds out of abundance.
אם יהיה לך מעט	If you have little, then
כמעט [היה עושה ממנו צדקות	[Do righteous deeds out of] scarcity.[214]

Linking "prosperity" to "moral merit,"[215] Tobit patiently lists what he believes to be the primary benefits of *almsgiving*: (a) it creates "good treasure" (שימה טובה) for the

209. Likely the latter part of this speech responds to exogamous programs like those promoted by Alexander of Macedon in which "it would be regarded as socially, politically, and economically advantageous by many Jews to seek a union with a well-placed Gentile family" (DeSilva, *Apocrypha*, 76). Kunin (*Incest*, 56–61) identifies some of the major factors responsible for historical shifts in the exogamy-endogamy polarity.

210. Motifs like these animate several Hebrew testaments; e.g., *T. Job* 9–12 (*OTP* 1.773–995; Greenfield, "Tobit," 196).

211. The usual OG equivalent is ἐλεημοσύναι (lit. "mercies"); Syr ܡܪܚܡܢܘܬܐ ("mercifulness," from ܪܚܡ, "to show mercy").

212. Lit. "the length of your hand" (Tob 4:8).

213. Sirach preserves a similar sentiment: *μὴ ἀποστρέψῃς τὸ πρόσωπόν σου ἀπὸπτωχοῦ*, "do not turn your face away from the poor" (Sir 4:4), a condition Tobit extends to *παντὸς* ("anyone," Tob 4:7).

214. Tob 4:7–8 (4Q200.2.6–9, reconstructed from OG). Cf. the incident of the poor widow giving away the final remnant of her estate (Luke 21:1–2), an act prompting the Nazarene prophet to comment: *πάντες γὰρ οὗτοι ἐκ τοῦ περισσεύοντος αὐτοῖς ἔβαλον εἰς τὰ δῶρα, αὕτη δὲ ἐκ τοῦ ὑστερήματος αὐτῆς πάντα τὸν βίον ὃν εἶχεν ἔβαλεν*, "for all these out of their abundance deposit gifts, but she out of her scarcity deposits her entire life" (21:4).

215. Jerome (cited from Skemp, *Vulgate*, 86–87) focuses on Tobit's struggle with the problem of suffering (his blindness), implying that his brittle "health-wealth" ideology is at least partially responsible: *Hanc autem temptationem ideo permisit Dominus evenire illi ut posteris daretur exemplum patientiae eius sicut et sancti Iob*, "The LORD thus allowed this trial to happen to him so that an example of his patience might be given to posterity, like that of holy Job."

"day of need" (ἡμέραν ἀνάγκης);[216] (b) it "delivers from death" (ἐκ θανάτου ῥύεται);[217] (c) it "refuses entry at the gate into darkness";[218] and (d) it propels a "good gift" (δῶρον . . . ἀγαθόν) into the "presence of the Most High" (ἐνώπιον τοῦ ὑψίστου).[219] Later the angel Raphael adds three more, arguing that almsgiving is (e) better than storing up gold;[220] (f) creates a "satisfying life" (χορτασθήσονται ζωῆς); and (g) purges away all sin.[221]

After this testamentary detour, Tobit again returns to topic:

καὶ νῦν παιδίον ὑποδεικνύω σοι	And now, child, let me explain to you
ὅτι δέκα τάλαντα ἀργυρίου παρεθέμην	That I have deposited ten talents of silver
Γαβαήλῳ τῷ τοῦ Γαβρι ἐν Ῥάγοις τῆς Μηδίας	With Gabael, son of Gabri, in Rages of Media.[222]
καὶ μὴ φοβοῦ παιδίον ὅτι ἐπτωχεύσαμεν	So do not be afraid because we are poor.[223]
ὑπάρχει σοι πολλὰ ἀγαθά	You possess great wealth
ἐὰν φοβηθῇς τὸν θεὸν	If you fear God . . .[224]

216. 4Q200.2.9. Elsewhere this translates into "heavenly investment" (*t. Pe'ah* 4.18; Matt 6:19–21; see below).

217. Tob 4:10 (OG). Cf. Syr ܡܢ ܡܘܬܐ ܡܦܨܝܐ, "delivers from death." Aḥikar escapes death-by-assassination because he is an almsgiver (Tob 14:10).

218. Tob 4:10 Syr (ܘܠܐ ܫܒܩܐ ܠܡܥܠ ܠܚܫܘܟܐ). OG reads only οὐκ ἐᾷ εἰσελθεῖν εἰς τὸ σκότος, "does not permit entering into darkness." The Syr reading concisely parallels the role of the gatekeeper Neti (ID 77), a role later enacted by the deity in Tobit's final prayer: ([מוריד עד שאול{ה} תחתיה והואה מעלה מתהו]ם, "He brings down to the deepest Sheol and brings up from the abyss," 4Q200.6.6; Tob 13:2).

219. Presuming ἐνώπιον to be a translation of לפני (lit. "before the face of").

220. One could argue that this benefit simply replicates the first benefit in Tobit's list ("creates good treasure").

221. Tob 12:8–9. Luke adds another "benefit" when he shows the almsgiving of Cornelius rising up to heaven as a μνημόσυνον ("memorial," Acts 10:4). Cf. also the admonition Paul makes to the Macedonians to engage in τὴν χάριν καὶ τὴν κοινωνίαν τῆς διακονίας τῆς εἰς τοὺς ἁγίους, "the grace and the fellowship of service to the saints" (2 Cor 8:4). Fitzmyer (*Tobit*, 169) argues that OG Tobit "seems to be advising Tobias to share his alms with those who practice righteousness" (cf. Tob 4:17), but Gregory (*Sirach*, 283) disagrees, arguing that "even when almsgiving is not explicitly limited to the righteous" in Tobit, "it is still limited to Jews" (1:3, 17; cf. Macatangay, *Almsgiving*, 31).

222. Rages is usually identified with the ruins of the city of Rai, approx. 5 miles SE of modern Teheran.

223. Like Urad-Gula (Nissinen, *Prophets*, 108), Tobit's finances plummet when he loses his Assyrian government job. Macatangay ("Irony," 576–77) observes that "Tobit persuades Tobias against fretting over any financial insecurity, telling his son not to fear poverty, for good things await those who fear God and do good deeds," but that "such advice is ironic given that Tobias is in fact on a journey to retrieve a considerable sum of money to secure the family from financial woes."

224. Tob 4:20–21. Di Pede ("Tobie," 51) thinks that Tobit's point is simple: Tobias should not "fear that poverty is his lot." Ignoring the socioeconomic context, Buechner (*Archangel*, 29) blithely suggests that Tobit here passes on to his son a "neurotic faith," but this contradicts Isaiah: "What will you do on the day of punishment, in the calamity that will come from far away? To whom will you flee for help, and 'where will you leave your wealth?'" (אנה תעזבו כבודכם, Isa 10:3).

To all these instructions Tobias finally responds:

πάντα ὅσα ἐντέταλσαί μοι ποιήσω πάτερ	Everything you command, father, I will do,
πῶς δὲ δυνήσομαι αὐτὸ λαβεῖν παρ᾽ αὐτου	But how will I be able to retrieve it from him?
καὶ αὐτὸς οὐ γινώσκει με	For he does not know me
καὶ ἐγὼ οὐ γινώσκω αὐτόν	And I do not know him.
τί σημεῖον δῶ αὐτῷ	What sign shall I give him
καὶ ἐπιγνῷ με καὶ πιστεύσῃ μοι	That he might recognize and trust me
καὶ δῷ μοι τὸ ἀργύριον	And give me the money . . .?[225]

At this Tobit instructs his son to look for a "sign":

χειρόγραφον αὐτοῦ ἔδωκέν μοι	His receipt[226] he gave to me
καὶ χειρόγραφον ἔδωκα αὐτῷ	And a receipt I gave to him.
καὶ διεῖλον εἰς δύο	I divided it in two:
καὶ ἐλάβομεν ἑκάτερος ἕν	We each took one
καὶ ἔθηκα μετὰ τοῦ ἀργυρίου	And I left one with the money.[227]
καὶ νῦν ἰδοὺ ἔτη εἴκοσι	Now it has been twenty years
ἀφ᾽ οὗ παρεθέμην τὸ ἀργύριον τοῦτο ἐγω	Since I left this silver in trust.
καὶ νῦν παιδίον	So now, child,
ζήτησον σεαυτῷ ἄνθρωπον πιστόν	Seek out for yourself a trustworthy man
ὃς πορεύσεται μετὰ σοῦ	Who will go with you,
καὶ δώσομεν αὐτῷ μισθόν ἕως ὅτου ἔλθῃς	And we will pay him a wage when you return.
καὶ λαβὲ παρ᾽ αὐτοῦ τὸ ἀργύριον τοῦτο	Go with him and retrieve this money.[228]

Taking his father's words to heart, Tobias seeks out a "trustworthy man," and much like Ruth's "random" encounter with Boaz, "happens" to bump into someone named

225. Tob 5:1–2.

226. Gk χειρόγραφον, lit. "handwritten note" (cf. כתב, "written," in 4Q197.5.10). To illustrate its usage, Perseus' allies deny complicity in his schemes even when "convicted to their face by their own receipts" (ἐλεγχόμενοι γὰρ κατὰ πρόσωπον ὑπὸ τῶν ἰδίων χειρογράφων, Polybius, *Hist.* 30.8.4); and "Job" describes how he tries to make funds available to individuals interested in helping the poor, cancelling their debt whenever it becomes too difficult for them to repay in spite of their signed "receipt" (χειρόγραφον, *T. Job* 11.11; cf. Col 2:14).

227. For Brown (*Buechner*, 326) "Tobias' charge is simple enough. Taking along his father's receipt for the treasure, he must find his way to Gabael and the silver and return the treasure for the sustenance of the family after Tobit's demise."

228. Tob 5:3.

"Azariah, son of Hananiah" (the angel Raphael wrapped in human disguise).[229] This pleases Tobit, who promises to pay this "man" a "wage" (μισθός) of "one drachma per day plus expenses."[230] Before they leave, however, Hannah asks two more questions:

τί ὅτι ἀπέστειλας τὸ παιδίον μου	Why are you sending my boy away?
οὐχὶ αὐτὸς ῥάβδος τῆς χειρὸς ἡμῶν ἐστιν	Is he not the staff of our hand[231]
καὶ αὐτὸς εἰσπορεύεται καὶ ἐκπορεύεται ἐνώπιον ἡμῶν	Who comes and goes before us?[232]

Then out comes her primary concern:[233]

אל ידבק [בכס]ף ברי	Let not my son cling [to silv]er![234]
ὡς δέδοται ζῆν ἡμῖν παρὰ τοῦ κυρίου	For the life given us by the Lord—
τοῦτο ἱκανὸν ἡμῖν	*This* is sufficient for us.[235]

Assuming the mantle of "maternal comptroller," Tobias' mother questions the wisdom of his "treasure-retrieval scheme" on three fronts: (a) she thinks it unnecessary because, in her opinion, the family's funds are already "sufficient" (ἱκανὸν); (b) she fears that the sight of so much money will tempt her son into something inappropriate; and (c) she fears that the trip itself might endanger his "life/soul" (Syr ܢܦܫܐ); i.e., that brigands might harm him, especially on the return trip home.[236] Dismissing these objections, Tobit glibly responds that she should

229. Tob 5:13. Cf Ruth 2:3: ויקר מקרה חלקת השדה לבעז, "and she just so happened upon the portion of the field belonging to Boaz."

230. Tob 5:14–15.

231. Vg reads *baculum senectutis nostrae* ("staff of our old age"; i.e., "caretaker").

232. Tob 5:18. Macatangay ("Metaphors," 79) contends that Hannah "obviously distances herself from her husband's decision regarding her son, accusing Tobit of prioritizing financial security over her son's well-being."

233. Tobit expressly tells his wife not to "fear" (דחל) or "worry" (יצף, 4Q197.4.1.3). Cf. the similar conversation between El and *his* wife, Lady Athirat, as she worries over the fate of her son Athtar (*CAT* 1.6.1.46–55).

234. 4Q197.4.1.1 (Tob 5:19). Syr reads ܢܗܘܐ ܐܠܐ ܬܬܚܠܦ ܢܦܫܐ ܕܒܪܢ ܕܗܠܟ ܟܣܦܐ ܠܟܣܦܐ ܠܐ ܢܚܠܦ, "Let us not entrap him with excessive silver! Let not the life of our only son be so lightly exchanged!" Cf. S ἀργύριον τῷ ἀργυρίῳ μὴ φθάσαι ἀλλὰ περίψημα τοῦ παιδίου ἡμῶν γένοιτο, "Do not heap silver upon silver, but let it be wiped away from our son."

235. Tob 5:20. Gk ζῆν might well be taken to refer to Tobias himself, except that Syr reads ܐܝܟ ܗܢ ܕܡܬܝܗܒܐ ܠܢ ܡܢ ܡܪܝܐ . . . ܗܘ ܗܢܐ ܕܣܦܩܐ ܠܢ ܐܬܘܬܗܝ, "But that which is given to us from the Lord . . . this suffices for us." Fitzmyer (*Tobit*, 198) sees little more here than Hannah "manifesting sound maternal instinct, for the boy is far more important than the money," but in actuality the primary contrast here is "moral-vs.-immoral use of wealth"—one of Tobit's most significant contributions to the prophetic socioeconomic trajectory arcing through Nevi'im.

236. 4Q197.4.1.2 (Tob 5:21; cf. Luke 10:30; Barker, "Raphael," 118–28). Where Raguel fears for his only daughter Sarah, Hannah "fears" for her only son Tobias (Tob 8:17, δύο μονογενεῖς, "two only-begottens"; cf. John 1:14). Fitzmyer (*Tobit*, 141) thinks that Hannah's character is one-dimensionally designed to exemplify "the human side of family life, and the continual possibility of misunderstandings," adding that she looks very much like "Job's wife" (Job 2:9; *T. Job* 21–26).

אל תדחלי בשלם יהך ברי	Have no fear; my son will be compensated.[237]

Fast-forwarding to the journey of the two travelers, Raphael notifies Tobias that a potential windfall awaits him at the estate of his kinsman Raguel (Sarah's father).[238] Apprising him that a great danger is threatening to destroy Raguel's family,[239] Raphael asks him to consider a few of the details:

υἱὸς ἄρσην οὐδὲ θυγάτηρ ὑπάρχει αὐτῷ	No male son follows him;
πλὴν Σαρρας μόνης	Only a daughter, Sarah.[240]

Tobias' visit would thus be prescient because

καὶ σὺ ἔγγιστα αὐτῆς εἶ	You are her closest relative
παρὰ πάντας ἀνθρώπους κληρονομῆσαι αὐτήν	Among all men to inherit her.[241]
καὶ τὰ ὄντα τῷ πατρὶ αὐτῆς	For the possessions belonging to her father[242]
σοὶ δικαιοῦται κληρονομῆσαι	You have the right to inherit.[243]

237. 4Q197.4.1.2 (Tob 5:21). This translation presumes (with Gerleman, "Wurzel," 1–14) that OG ὑγιαίνων πορεύσεται, "will go in good health," ignores the basic socioeconomic character of שלם.

238. McCracken ("*Tobit*," 412) sees the narrator using the character of Raguel to "heighten the comedy," and Miller (*Tobit*, 86) thinks that "although Sarah's inheritance may play a part in Tobias' decision to marry her, it is a minor part at best." Neither reading recognizes, much less reckons with Tobit*'s* socioeconomic trajectory.

239. The demon in Sarah's bridal chamber is not just removing potential sons-in-law, he is endangering Raguel's οἰκονομία ("household"). N. B. that the need to face economic crisis head-on is what motivates Inanna to descend into the Netherworld. Tobias does not descend to the Netherworld like Inanna and Orpheus, but he does "save" (שׁיזב, 4Q197.4.2.18) Sarah not simply from a ravaging demon, but from infertility, barrenness, childlessness, the absence of an heir, and all the other socioeconomic anxieties *symbolized* by the demon.

240. Tob 6:12. Otzen (*Tobit*, 38; *contra* Müller, *Tobit*, 5–9) insists that it is "untenable" to surmise from this that Sarah's seven husbands all die because they are not Jewish.

241. Syr reads a noun instead of a verb: ܡܛܠ ܕܠܟ ܡܛܠܟܐ ܝܪܬܘܬܐ ܕܝܠܗ ܘܐܬܝܐ ܠܡܣܘܪܢܝܢ, "For to you and you alone her own inheritance comes." Miller's (*Tobit*, 86) comment that "the notion of inheriting a bride is strange" betrays a profound ignorance of the economics of endogamous marriage. Levine ("Boundaries," 4, 5) thus contends (a) that readers of Tobit tend "to ignore the pivotal role played by boundary definition," and (b) that "in order to distinguish the Israelite from the Gentile" (an important theme in diaspora literature) "Tobit advances a program *centered* on endogamy." Wénin ("Tobias," 169) also recognizes that "all through the length of this narrative the idea of endogamous marriage . . . runs like a scarlet thread."

242. Tob 6:12. The narrator is careful to distinguish Raguel's "possessions" from his "daughter," whom he later calls Tobias' ἀδελφή ("sister," Tob 8:21).

243. Tob 6:12. 4Q197.4.1.19 reads דין ("right/claim/law"; cf. 2.2). Where Rab Eleazar (*b. Sanh.* 6b) depicts Aaron's leadership style as carefully examining all sides before making a decision, Moses' style is depicted as more direct: יקוב הדין את ההר ("he lets the law cut through the mountain"; i.e., he "trusts his gut"). Raphael imagines a similar דין at work here with regard to Tobias' "right" to inherit Sarah's family's estate.

Later, after Raphael "saves" (שיזב) Sarah from the danger threatening her family at the hands of Asmodeus,[244] Raguel affirms the socioeconomic "right" of his new son-in-law:

καὶ ὅσα μοι ὑπάρχει	Whatever is in my possession
λάμβανε αὐτόθεν τὸ ἥμισυ	Take half immediately,
καὶ ὕπαγε ὑγιαίνων πρὸς τὸν πατέρα σου	And depart for your father in good health.
καὶ τὸ ἄλλο ἥμισυ ὅταν ἀποθάνω	The other half is yours
ἐγώ τε καὶ ἡ γυνή μου ὑμέτερόν ἐστιν	When my wife and I die.
ἐγώ σου ὁ πατὴρ	I am your father,
καὶ Εδνα ἡ μήτηρ σου	And Edna is your mother.
καὶ παρὰ σοῦ ἐσμεν ἡμεῖς καὶ τῆς ἀδελφῆς σου	We belong to you and your sister
ἀπὸ τοῦ νῦν εἰς τὸν αἰῶνα	From now unto forever.[245]

Question: What role does Raphael play in this story—that is, what is the purpose of his "divine healing?" Is it to see his young travel-companion safe and happy? Is it to see the demon Asmodeus eliminated?[246] Or is it to ensure that Raguel's οἰκονομία ("household") fully "heals" (רפא) because of "the seed of humanity coming forth" via the endogamous marriage covenant between Sarah and Tobias?[247]

Contemporary interpreters often focus on the second of these three options. Chad Pierce, for example, observes that "Asmodeus is labeled a 'demon' in Tobit" even while admitting that he has no idea "what the author means by this term."[248] Like other contemporary readers he arbitrarily chooses to focus on the "demon angle," pondering (a) its resemblance to other "fallen angels" and their relationships with "human women,"[249] as well as (b) the way in which its "binding" resembles the "binding" of

244. 4Q197.4.2.18. 4Q197.4.2.9 reads simply שדא ("the demon"). Hutter ("Asmodeus," 106–07) posits a Persian origin for this creature, tracing it back to the Gathas.

245. Tob 8:21. *Question:* Is the Tobias-Sarah romance really a "romance?" Philonenko (*Joseph*, 43–44) excludes *Joseph and Aseneth* from the love-novel genre because its protagonists practice sexual abstinence, but Bloch (*Judentum*, 11–12) shows that the "intended-but-not-realized" chastity motif (suggested here in Tobit) is not foreign to Hellenistic love-novels.

246. Tob 8:3 (cf. Stuckenbruck, *Angels*, 126–27).

247. Tob 8:6 (ἐξ ἀμφοτέρων ἐγενήθη τὸ σπέρμα τῶν ἀνθρώπων). Pitt-Rivers (*Shechem*, 162) insists that Israelite families "keep their daughters as close to the nuclear family as the prohibition of incest permits," labeling this practice "Mediterranean endogamy." The story ends when Tobit and Tobias offer to pay Raphael the "wage" (μισθός) earlier promised (increasing it to half of their estate), at which point he reveals his true identity (Tob 12:1).

248. Pierce, *Spirits*, 155.

249. Gen 6:1–4 (cf. *1 En.* 1–36). The irony here, of course, is that Tobit never even implies sexual contact between Sarah and Asmodeus.

other demonic figures (like Shemiḥaza and Azazel).[250] Yet, as Pierce himself admits, the Tobit scroll "contains no reference to the 'watcher tradition.'"[251] So pursuit of this strategy contributes nothing to what this "demon" might *symbolize.*

Lawrence Wills, on the other hand, sees close parallels in Tobit to the folktales of "The Grateful Dead Man" and "The Blind Padishah," each featuring an "evil dragon."[252] In the first of these folktales a traveler ransoms a stranger's corpse by reimbursing the dead man's creditors in order to provide him a proper burial, a process which involves the slaying of a dragon to secure the betrothal of a wealthy princess. In the second folktale a wealthy blind man dreams that his eyes can be cured by contact with soil on which no horse has ever walked—soil which his youngest son finds defended by a dragon insisting that a *khoja* priestess be brought to him, whom the son then marries after successfully healing his father's eyes.

Obvious parallels with Tobit stand out in both tales, yet neither attempts to engage the deeper parallels rooted in the "great texts" surveyed above, especially those featuring the personification of fertility, maternity, and prosperity as divine figures "invading" the Netherworld,[253] "protecting" sacred boundaries,[254] and "conquering" Chaos.[255] Tobit stands firmly in this tradition, however, because Asmodeus, like Tiamat and Yam, is a dragon-like monster determined to kill anyone or anything "invading his territory,"[256] and Tobias (like Marduk and Ba'al) represents the victorious hero who succeeds in subduing it. These vignettes about Tobit and Sarah, in other words, address the problem of socioeconomic fragility from mythopoeic perspectives quite similar to those animating the "great literature" upon which they obviously draw. Where Sarah faces a "dragon" enslaving her to infertility and childlessness, Tobit faces a "dragon" intent on defining "creation" as "acquisition" *minus* "protection," a complete reversal of the Yahwistic imperative.[257]

Summary

These are not the only Second Temple texts engaging the prophetic socioeconomic motif trajectory, of course, but each text does represent a different literary genre—*epistle*,

250. *1 En.* 6–11. Cf. Hanson, "Azazel," 195–233; Nickelsberg, *Literature*, 47–50; Dimant, "Angels," 23–72; Pierce, *Spirits*, 33–36.

251. Pierce, *Spirits*, 154.

252. Wills, *Novel*, 73–76.

253. Cf. ID/DI and DT.

254. Cf. the "protector" role enacted by the monster Humbaba (GE 5.85–246).

255. Kiel (*Tobit*, 149) appears to understand this, at least partially: "Tobias fears that his death will leave his parents childless; his survival and promulgation are key plot elements. More pointedly, the threat to his virility is the very one provided by the demon Asmodeus to all who attempt to approach consummation of a marriage to Sarah."

256. Cf., e.g., its unwarranted claim on שׂרה ("Sarah"/"the princess"; cf. Yee, "Sarah," 982).

257. I.e., "creation = acquisition *plus* protection" (Moore, *WealthWatch*, 224).

narrative, and *farce*. The epistles in Ezra-Nehemiah expose the workings of a bureaucratic world populated by ruthless government officials driven by typical colonial prejudices about inheritance rights, taxes, temple/bank (re)construction, work-ethic, and land—all managed under the watchful eyes of employers preoccupied with the legendary "bottom line." The Tobit scroll shows many of these same socioeconomic concerns impacting the lives of "typical" Jewish families struggling to preserve their ancestral possessions on foreign soil, even as the Epistle of Jeremiah satirizes the corrupt behavior of religious officials defiling that soil.

How do the Nazarenes engage this motif trajectory?

5

Prophetic Socioeconomic Motifs in the Greek New Testament

THE GREEK NEW TESTAMENT chronicles the life of an individual widely regarded to be the greatest prophet who ever lived—Jesus of Nazareth.[1] This ancient library, a colloidal mixture of differing perspectives,[2] retreads the socioeconomic motifs found in earlier texts to express Nazarene notions about *wealth*, *poverty*, *investment*, *slavery*, *taxes*, *inheritance*, *theft*, *prosperity*, and other related concerns.[3] Where the previous volume in this series examines how the stewardship parables in the Gospel of Luke retread the socioeconomic motifs in Torah,[4] the following pages will examine the impact of these motifs on two other sections of GNT: (a) select episodes in the Gospel of Matthew depicting Yeshu'a of Nazareth as a נביא ("prophet");[5] and (b) select episodes in the Acts of the Apostles epitomizing his followers as בני הנביאים ("sons of the prophets").[6]

1. Aram ישוע דנזרת. Προφήτης ὡς εἷς τῶν προφητῶν, "He is a prophet like one of the prophets" (Mark 6:15); Οὗτός ἐστιν ἀληθῶς ὁ προφήτης ὁ ἐρχόμενος εἰς τὸν κόσμον, "This is truly the prophet who comes into the world" (John 6:14). Parrinder (*Jesus*, 16) contends that references to عيسى بن مريم ("Isa, son of Miriam") appear in Qur'an some 187 times—more than any other figure. Skiena and Ward's (*Historical*, 5) "top ten list" includes (in order) Jesus, Napoleon, Muhammad, Shakespeare, Lincoln, Washington, Hitler, Aristotle, Alexander the Great, and Jefferson.

2. Ezigbo and Williams ("Christology," 95) recognize that "in the New Testament we find different forms of Christianity professed by Syriac, Hebraic, Hellenistic, and Greco-Roman communities." Cf. Koester, *History*, 111–14; and Green and McDonald, "Introduction," 1–6.

3. Cf. Witherington, *Money*; Horsley, *Empire*; Wheeler, *Wealth*. Sandford (*Wealth*, 1–23) recognizes that one of the major motifs in the Gospels is "prophetic denouncement of the rich" (cf. Meeks, *Prophet-King*, 1–31).

4. Moore, *WealthWatch*, 202–22.

5. Nolland (*Matthew*, 33–36) recognizes that Matthew is the most consistently, openly, and intentionally prophetic of the four Gospels in GNT.

6. Cf. 2 Kgs 4:38–44. Horsley (*Covenant*, 115) recognizes that "like the prophet Elijah calling Elisha as his *protégé*, Jesus calls disciples to extend the work of his mission." Alongside Jeremias' ("Paulus," 88–94) view of Paul as a "rabbi" and Theis' (*Paulus*, 119–26) view of him as a "sage," Sandnes (*Paul*, 5–20) views the Tarsus native as a "prophet."

Gospel of Matthew

In light of the "great texts" surveyed above, it's no surprise that just as Tobit shows a beleaguered family fleeing the threats of an insecure king,[7] Matthew begins with a family caught in the throes of the same dilemma.[8] Just as Tobit features a "poor" man (Tobias) traveling a great distance to *retrieve* "treasure,"[9] so Matthew begins with a number of wealthy men (the Magi) traveling great distances to *dispense* "treasure."[10] Further, each text makes mention of a "sign" provided to help these travelers complete their journeys.[11] Motifs like these recur so often in this literature, critics like Leif Vaage wonder why "modern biblical scholarship . . . pays so little attention" to their "economic aspects."[12]

Matthew's portrayal of John the Baptist comes straight out of Nevi'im.[13] Depicting him as a prototypical prophet[14] in dress and diet,[15] Matthew marinates the words of this prophet in an agrarian gumbo pointing out how to "avoid the pruning knife,"[16] "winnow, separate, and gather"[17] from the "threshing floor,"[18] "produce fruit" (ποιήσατε καρπὸν),[19] and "deposit it in the storehouse" (εἰς τὴν ἀποθήκην).[20]

7. Tob 1:19. Cf. also the Egyptian *Tale of Sinuhe* (*AEL* 1.222–35; Parkinson, *Sinuhe*, 21–53).

8. Moreover, just as Tobit cites a prophet to explain Tobit's predicament (Amos 8:10), so Matthew cites a prophet to explain Yeshu`a's (Mic 5:2).

9. Tobit expressly says to his son Tobias, ἐπτωχεύσαμεν ("we are poor," Tob 4:21).

10. Cf. ἀνοίξαντες τοὺς θησαυροὺς αὐτῶν προσήνεγκαν αὐτῷ δῶρα, χρυσὸν καὶ λίβανον καὶ σμύρναν, "opening their treasuries they (i.e., μάγοι ἀπὸ ἀνατολῶν, 'Magi from the east,' Matt 2:1) offered him gifts—gold, frankincense, and myrrh" (2:11).

11. In Tob 5:2 Tobias asks what σημεῖον ("sign") he is to provide the man storing his father's silver; in Matt 2:2 the Magi observe a "sign" in the heavens leading them to the place where they are to deposit "treasure," and in 2:19 another sign appears to Joseph, telling him to take his family and go home to Nazareth. The twist in Tobit, of course, is that the angel Raphael is the major "sign."

12. Vaage, *Borderline*, 56; cf. Gen 16:6; 27:43; 31:21; Exod 2:15; 14:5; 1 Sam 19:12; 21:10; 23:6; 2 Sam 13:34; 15:14; 1 Kgs 11:17, 23; Dan 10:7; cf. Snell, *Flight*, 104–16.

13. Cf. Jer 2:2–7; 12:2; Ezek 17:3–10; Hos 2:24–25; Joel 1:7–12; 2:22; Amos 9:14. Pantoja (*Metaphor*, 116) thinks "these metaphors are drawn from the natural environment" because the lives of these writers "depend on an ecological balance between the necessary rainfall for a bountiful harvest versus drought or even inundation."

14. Dibelius (*Johannes*, 48) is one of the first modern critics to argue that regardless of what might be said about the Baptist, the Gospels portray him as "more than just a preacher of repentance," but "as a prophet."

15. Kelhoffer (*Diet*, 34) argues that "most prevalent interpretations maintain that "locusts and wild honey," however construed, distinguish John as a prophet, wilderness-dweller, and ascetic.

16. Cf. Isa 18:5 (or worse, the ax, 10:34).

17. Cf. Isa 17:5; 41:16; Jer 51:2.

18. Cf. Jer 51:33; Hos 9:2; 13:3; Mic 4:12; cf. Waters (*Threshing*, 1–28).

19. Lit. "make fruit." N.B. that καρπός can also mean "profit"—Xenophon (*Cyr.* 1.1.2), e.g., observes that unlike men, cattle follow their leaders without question, producing τοῖς καρποῖς τοίνυν τοῖς γιγνομένοῖς ἐξ αὐτῶν, "the profits generated by them" (cf. Ezek 17:23; Zech 8:12).

20. Matt 3:12 (τὸ πτύον ἐν τῇ χειρὶ αὐτοῦ καὶ διακαθαριεῖ τὴν ἅλωνα αὐτοῦ καὶ συνάξει τὸν σῖτον αὐτοῦ εἰς τὴν ἀποθήκην). Cf. Amos 8:6; Isa 10:33; Jer 22:7; Ezek 5:11; Mal 3:10. Davis (*Agriculture*, 22)

Galilean Encounters

The "beatitudes" are a collection of blessing-sayings formulaically structured, yet incontestably rooted in the mind of the Nazarene.[21] The collection in Luke's "Sermon on the Plain" engages the socioeconomic presumptions of a Hellenistic audience,[22] but the one in Matthew's "Sermon on the Mount" engages an Hebraic audience, depicting Yeshu`a as a נביא ("prophet") preparing בני הנביאים ("the sons of the prophets") for the future, and promising them that if they commit themselves to the Yahwistic imperative,[23]

ὁ μισθὸς ὑμῶν πολὺς ἐν τοῖς οὐρανοῖς	Your reward in heaven will be great,[24]
οὕτως γὰρ ἐδίωξαν τοὺς προφήτας	For thus they persecuted the prophets.[25]

Simultaneously he issues a directive designed to close the gap between external gesture and internal aspiration:[26]

Ἐὰν προσφέρῃς τὸ δῶρόν σου	If you offer your gift[27]
ἐπὶ τὸ θυσιαστήριον	Upon the altar[28]
κἀκεῖ μνησθῇς ὅτι	And there remember that

recognizes that "the essential understanding that informs the agrarian mind-set, in multiple cultures from ancient times to the present, is that agriculture has an ineluctably ethical dimension" because "food production entails at every stage judgments and practices that bear directly on . . . the emotional, economic, and physical well-being of families and communities, and ultimately on their survival."

21. Cf. the "blessing-lists" in Sir 14:20—15:10 and 4Q525.2.2.1–6 (Puech, "Sagesse," 297–329; "Matthieu," 80–106; Viviano, *Matthew*, 64–67; Fitzmyer, *Origins*, 116–18; Witherington, *Sage*, 239; Hartin, *James*, 144–45; Collins, "Beatitudes," 629–31).

22. Stanton ("Sermon," 735–37) and Betz ("Sermon," 1106–12) concisely lay out the major (dis) similarities between Matthew's Sermon on the Mount (Matt 5–7) and Luke's Sermon on the Plain (Luke 6:17–49). Autero (*Reading*, 117–68) applies the Sermon on the Plain to a Latin American context.

23. "Creation = acquisition *plus* protection" (Moore, *WealthWatch*, 110, 132, 160, 201, 224).

24. While it's possible to distinguish "wages" from "compensation," previous usage of שלם ("to compensate," 1 Sam 24:20; 2 Sam 3:39; 12:6; 2 Kgs 4:7; 9:26; Isa 57:18; 59:18; 65:6; Jer 18:20; 25:14; 51:6; Joel 2:25; 4:4; Tob 5:21) and μισθός ("wages," Tob 5:3, 7, 10, 15, 16) blurs this boundary. N.B. Jeremiah's description of Yhwh as אל גמלות שלם ישלם, "a requisitional deity who compensates completely" (Jer 51:56; cf. v. 6).

25. Matt 5:12. As Betz recognizes (*Sermon*, 152–53), the point is that "the persecuted disciples stand in parallel with the persecuted prophets" (cf. Gundry, *Better*, 139).

26. Jeremiah (22:9–32) condemns the prophets of Judah for severing this connection.

27. OG consistently uses δῶρον to translate Heb קרבן (Fabry, "קרבן," 153; see below).

28. With regard to נדבות ("freewill offerings"), the Qumran covenanters decree that אל ידור איש למזבח מאום אנוס, "no one is to place (lit. 'encircle') on the altar (anything obtained) from an 'oath of vengeance'" (CD 16.13). García Martínez and Tigchelaar (*DSSSE* 1.565) translate מאום אנוס as "unjust means."

ὁ ἀδελφός σου ἔχει τι κατὰ σου	Your brother has something against you,[29]
ἄφες ἐκεῖ τὸ δῶρόν σου	Leave your gift there
ἔμπροσθεν τοῦ θυσιαστηρίου	Before the altar.[30]
καὶ ὕπαγε πρῶτον διαλλάγηθι τῷ ἀδελφῷ σου	First be reconciled with your brother,[31]
καὶ τότε ἐλθὼν πρόσφερε τὸ δῶρόν σου	And then come offer your gift.[32]

Then he issues a prophetic mandate much like the one in Nehemiah:[33]

τῷ αἰτοῦντί σε δός	To the one who asks of you, give,
καὶ τὸν θέλοντα ἀπὸ σοῦ δανίσασθαι	And the one wishing to borrow from you
μὴ ἀποστραφῇς	Do not turn away.[34]

To help the בני הנביאים ("sons of the prophets") learn how to incarnate the Yahwistic imperative effectively he demands from them categorical submission to the principle of ἀγάπη-"love":[35]

29. Vaage (*Exegesis*, 64) insightfully suggests that the root of the donor's problem exists not "because you happen to discover that you are thinking bad thoughts about your brother, as though it is necessary for you to become inwardly pure before entering into contact with God. Rather, the problem exists when your piety, your offering (of yourself) to God, your payment of a divine debt, becomes a way of 'covering up' the obligation that the well-being of your brother ought to hold for you."

30. Matthew seems to have in mind the Torah "law of restitution" (Lev 6:4–6), but intertextually it's significant that where Haggai's view of altar defilement is *external* (bloodshed via the Chaldeans, Hag 2:14), Matthew's view is that altar defilement is *internal* (the decision to "give" without giving oneself in reconciliation).

31. At root, διαλλάσσω is a socioeconomic term meaning "to exchange." Herodotus (*Hist.* 1.22.2), e.g., describes the truce between Lydia and Miletus as a διαλλαγή ("exchange") of "enmity" for "friendship"; and Apollo informs Admetus of the Fates' promise to deliver him from death by ἄλλον διαλλάξαντα τοῖς κάτω νεκρόν, "exchanging (him) with the dead below for another" (Euripides, *Alc.* 14). N.B. that διαλλάσσω ("to exchange") and προσφέρω ("to offer") stand in parallel here, and that προσφοράς ("offerings/gifts") appears in an important speech in Acts of the Apostles (Acts 24:17; see below).

32. Matt 5:23–24. Cf. the parallel in Mishnah: עברות שבין אדם למקום יום כפרים מכפר עברות שבין אדם לחברו אין יום כפרים מכפר עד שירצה שבין את חברו, "Transgressions between a person and the Place (Deut 12:11) *yom kippur* covers over; transgressions between a person and his comrade *yom kippur* does not cover over until that person reconciles with his comrade" (*m. Yoma* 8.9; cf. Thelle, *Place*, 57–80; Pitkänen, *Sanctuary*, 1–24).

33. Neh 5:1–13 (cf. above).

34. Matt 5:42. Jones (*Usury*, 25) reminds us (a) that Torah condemns the charging of excessive interest on loans (Exod 22:24; Lev 25:36–37; Deut 23:20–21); (b) that GNT is "curiously silent" on the matter—with the incidental exception of τόκος ("interest") in Matt 25:27//Luke 19:23; but that (c) the Church Fathers and Councils universally condemn it.

35. As Nygren (*Agape*, 31) observes, "Eros and Agape belong . . . to two entirely separate spiritual worlds, between which no direct communication is possible" (cf. Lewis, "Charity," 116–46).

ἐὰν γὰρ ἀγαπήσητε τοὺς ἀγαπῶντας ὑμᾶς	If you love those who love you[36]
τίνα μισθὸν ἔχετε	What reward have you?
οὐχὶ καὶ οἱ τελῶναι τὸ αὐτὸ ποιοῦσιν	Do not the tax collectors do the same?[37]

Like Tobit, Yeshu`a champions the discipline of ἐλεημοσύνη ("almsgiving"):[38]

ὅταν οὖν ποιῇς ἐλεημοσύνην	Whenever you give alms[39]
μὴ σαλπίσῃς ἔμπροσθέν σου	Do not sound a trumpet before you
ὥσπερ οἱ ὑποκριταὶ ποιοῦσιν ἐν ταῖς συναγωγαῖς	Like the hypocrites do in the synagogues
καὶ ἐν ταῖς ῥύμαις	And the town squares
ὅπως δοξασθῶσιν ὑπὸ τῶν ἀνθρώπων	So that they may be glorified by men.
ἀμὴν λέγω ὑμῖν	Truly I tell you,
ἀπέχουσιν τὸν μισθὸν αὐτῶν	They have received their wages/reward.[40]
σοῦ δὲ ποιοῦντος ἐλεημοσύνην	But when *you* give alms
μὴ γνώτω ἡ ἀριστερά σου	Let not your left hand know
τί ποιεῖ ἡ δεξιά σου	What your right hand is doing[41]

36. The "first and greatest commandment" (Matt 22:38) is אהבת את יהוה אלהיך בכל לבבך ובכל נפשך ובכל מאדך, "You shall love Yhwh your God with all your heart, with all your soul and with all your strength" (Deut 6:5).

37. Matt 5:46. Demochares bluntly notifies Demetrius of Phalerum that "his conduct as a prince and the political presumptions in which he takes great pride are those championed by a 'petty tax collector' (τελώνης βάναυσος, Polybius, *Hist.* 12.13.9). Rejecting any association between Yeshu`a of Nazareth and the τελῶναι, Walker ("Jesus," 237) proposes an original Aram טלני transliterated here as τελῶναι, translating "playboys/demons/urchins." If טלני is a *nomen regens*, however, where is the *nomen rectum* (Rosenthal, *Grammar*, 47)? Schoberg (*Perspectives*, 36) and Adams (*Sinner*, 72) justifiably reject this proposal.

38. Tob 1:3–8 (cf. above). Luke sharply refocuses this motif in his second volume (Acts 6:1; cf. Hull, *Discipleship*, 62).

39. Matt 6:2—not ἐάν ("if"), but ὅταν ("whenever"). Some rabbis hold (a) that almsgiving "atones for sins" (ἐλεημοσύνη ἐξιλάσεται ἁμαρτίας, Sir 3:30; Clement compares it to "repentance from sin," μετάνοια ἁμαρτίας, 2 Clem 16.4); and (b) that withholding alms from the poor is "robbery" (*Num. Rab.* 5.2; *Ruth Rab.* 5.9). Tobit discusses several other benefits (cf. above).

40. Matt 6:5. Kloppenborg ("Alms," 327) argues that this line is "probably redactional," but repeated *Matthean* use of the term μισθός ("wages/reward") reflects a well-established prophetic worldview (cf. above on שׁלם and μισθός).

41. This appears to be an idiomatic expression for the notion of "healthy balance," a trait highly valued by the sages (cf. von Rad, *Wisdom*, 297). Marcus Aurelius (*Meditations* 8.9) relates a similar axiom: μηκέτι σου μηδεὶς ἀκούσῃ καταμεμφομένου τὸν ἐν αὐλῇ βίον μηδὲ σὺ σεαυτοῦ, "Let no one hear you finding fault in the courtyard, not even yourself."

ὅπως ᾖσου ἡ ἐλεημοσύνη ἐν τῷ κρυπτῷ	So that your almsgiving may be in secret,[42]
καὶ ὁ πατήρ σου ὁ βλέπων ἐν τῷ κρυπτῷ	And your father who sees in secret
ἀποδώσει σοι	May reward you.[43]

A significant *Leitwort* appears in the "Lord's Prayer":[44]

ἄφες ἡμῖν τὰ ὀφειλήματα ἡμῶν	Cancel for us our "debts"[45]
ὡς καὶ ἡμεῖς ἀφήκαμεν τοῖς ὀφειλέταις ἡμῶν	As we cancel those of our "debtors."[46]

The fact that Matthew reads ὀφείλημα ("debt") and Luke reads ἁμαρτία ("sin") is a problem for some readers. To "solve" it the suggestion is often made that Matthew represents an older version of the prayer and that the discrepancy with Luke must therefore be the result of later editorial activity.[47] Raymond Brown, however, rejects this "solution," pointing out (a) that ὀφείλημα ("debt") lacks religious nuance in secular Greek, and (b) that "Aramaic חוב is a financial and commercial term."[48] The difference between the two accounts, in other words, is probably due to the fact that the same Aramaic word (חוב) underlies each Greek text.[49] Where Luke gravitates to the nuance

42. Betz (*Sermon*, 358) interprets this to mean that "almsgiving should be done in such a way that the donor is not aware of the act; rather the donor's knowledge of the gift should not be used to let others know of it, but to keep it secret." Wierzbicka (*Sermon*, 142), however, thinks that "the question is not what the doer of a good deed *knows*, but what he or she *thinks*." Intertextual analysis suggests that where Tob 4:7 expresses the (nominal) *what*, Matt 6:4 addresses the (dative) *how*—i.e., ἐν τῷ κρυπτῷ ("in secret"). Bonhoeffer (*Discipleship*, 143) argues that "if the left hand knows what the right hand is doing, if we become conscious of our hidden virtue, we are forging our own reward."

43. Matt 6:2–4. Vaage (*Exegesis*, 73) fails to recognize that the father never pays "wages" (μισθός) to his children, only "donates/gives back" (ἀποδίδωμι) to them.

44. Cf. Oakman, "Prayer," 137–86.

45. The word for "indebtedness" here (ὀφείλω) occurs elsewhere in Matthew; e.g., ὁ κύριος αὐτοῦ παρέδωκεν αὐτὸν τοῖς βασανισταῖς ἕως οὗ ἀποδῷ πᾶν τὸ ὀφειλόμενον, "the master will hand him over to the jailors until he pays off (lit. 'donates back') the entire 'debt'" (Matt 18:34).

46. Matt 6:12. Eubank (*Wages*, 54) rejects the translation "forgive," arguing that it "obscures the fact that the petition uses the language of commerce," and that "cancel" is the most appropriate translation of ἀφίημι. Nel ("Debt," 87), however, insists that "the cancellation of monetary debt" is not "a condition for receiving forgiveness from God."

47. Bazzana ("Debt," 514) thinks (a) that ἁμαρτίας ("sins") is a "substituted word" in the Lucan version, and (b) that it "clearly aims at spiritualizing this demand." This conclusion, however, takes no account of the prayer's original semitic form (cf. below). Noting the presence of ὀφείλοντι in Luke 11:4b, Davies and Allison (*Matthew*, 1.611) suggest that Luke works with, or is at least aware of, an Aramaic (oral) tradition.

48. Brown, "Prayer," 200 (cf. Casey, *Aramaic*, 55). N.B. the שטר חוב, "writ of indebtedness" which can be מוחל, "cancelled" (*b. Ketub.* 85b; *DTTM* 428–29). Howard's (*Matthew*, 24) attempt to reconstruct an "original Hebrew text" in Matt 6:12 with the reading ומחול לנו חטאתינו ("and forgive us our sins") simply ignores the synoptic problem.

49. Eubank (*Wages*, 53–54) observes that "ἀφίημι and ὀφείλημα are not ordinarily used in contemporary Greek to refer to the forgiveness of sins, but if retrojected into a Semitic idiom the prayer

in the receptor language (Greek) most resonant with his theological agenda,[50] Matthew preserves the socioeconomic nuance in the original source language (Aramaic).[51]

Like other Second Temple rabbis, Yeshu`a's views on *investment* are clear:[52]

Μὴ θησαυρίζετε ὑμῖν θησαυροὺς ἐπὶ τῆς γῆς	Do not invest your treasures on earth[53]
ὅπου σὴς καὶ βρῶσις ἀφανίζει	Where moth and rust corrupt
καὶ ὅπου κλέπται διορύσσουσιν καὶ κλέπτουσιν	And thieves break in and steal.[54]
θησαυρίζετε δὲ ὑμῖν θησαυροὺς ἐν οὐρανῷ	Rather, invest your treasures in heaven[55]
ὅπου οὔτε σὴς οὔτε βρῶσις ἀφανίζει	Where neither moth nor rust corrupt
καὶ ὅπου κλέπται οὐ διορύσσουσιν οὐδὲ κλέπτουσιν	Nor thieves break in and steal.
ὅπου γάρ ἐστιν ὁ θησαυρός σου	For where your treasure is,[56]
ἐκεῖ ἔσται καὶ ἡ καρδία σου	There your heart is also.[57]

is not unusual at all."

50. Cf. Juel, "Prayer," 56–70. Conzelmann (*Luke*, 96) thinks that Luke recasts its sources to eliminate all expectation of an imminent return. Green (*Luke*, 79) responds that "lest we fail to appreciate the far-reaching importance of the release effected in Jesus' ministry, we should note that Luke portrays both forgiveness and healing in social terms."

51. Cf. Gerhardsson, "Prayer," 207–20; and Finkel, "Prayer," 131–69. Not to be forgotten is Ezekiel's definition of a צדיק ("righteous man," Ezek 18:9) as someone who חבלתו חוב ישיב, "restores to a debtor his pledge" (18:7), and לא יתן ותרבית לא יקח בנשך, "does not practice usury or demand high interest" (18:8). Brown's suggestion does not imply that redaction criticism is useless, only that it is sometimes too readily (and simplistically) applied (cf. Knierim, "Criticism," 123–66).

52. Cf. ὁ ἀγαθὸς ἄνθρωπος ἐκ τοῦ ἀγαθοῦ θησαυροῦ ἐκβάλλει ἀγαθά, καὶ ὁ πονηρὸς ἄνθρωπος ἐκ τοῦ πονηροῦ θησαυροῦ ἐκβάλλει πονηρά, "The good man out of a good treasure brings forth good things, but an evil man out of an evil treasure brings forth evil things" (Matt 12:35).

53. Lit. "Do not treasure your treasures." Kennedy (*Rhetorical*, 60) thinks the doubling of root-words in the Sermon on the Mount (cf. κρίνω in Matt 7:1) is designed to create a "gnomic effect," but semitists simply recognize it as the projection of emphasis in the original source language (*GKC* 113w).

54. First-century Palestinians tend to keep their valuables in strongboxes hidden inside their homes (Stambaugh and Balch, *Environment*, 73), and "thieves" (κλέπται) tend to be associated with "secrecy" (cf. Tob 1:18) and "violence" (John 10:10).

55. One way to do this—not the only way—is to ὕπαγε πώλησόν σου τὰ ὑπάρχοντα καὶ δὸς [τοῖς] πτωχοῖς, καὶ ἕξεις θησαυρὸν ἐν οὐρανοῖς, "go sell your possessions and give to the poor, and you will have treasure in heaven" (Matt 19:21).

56. Yeshu`a is not the only rabbi to link earthly obedience with heavenly "treasure" (cf. 4 Esd. 7:77; 2 Bar. 14.12; 24.1; 44.14; Tob 12:8; Gen. Rab. 9.9; Exod. Rab. 45.6). Torah describes "the heavens" (השמים) as Yhwh's "good treasury" (אוצרו הטוב) from which he "blesses" (ברך) the keepers of his covenant (Deut 28:12), and Talmud (*b. Taan.* 9a) alludes to this text when encouraging readers to understand the rationale behind the deity's desire to make the land prosper.

57. Matt 6:19–21. Recognizing that "such a polarization (between heaven and earth) is dangerous—or daring—to draw," Vaage (*Exegesis*, 74) warns against "facile misreading" of this text by those

Tosefta illustrates this mentality with a story about King Munbaz,[58] an Assyrian convert to Judaism famous for "distributing all his treasures in years of scarcity."[59] Asked to explain this behavior, he replies in language similar to that of the Nazarene:

אבותי גנזו אוצרות למטה	My fathers stored up treasures for below
ואני גנזתי למעלה	But I store up for above.[60]

Reflecting further, Munbaz lays out a thoughtful critique of "earthly treasure," arguing that it is (a) vulnerable to "human hands";[61] (b) unable to produce real "benefits";[62] (c) more about "mammon" than "souls";[63] and (d) only benefits "others" (i.e., "you can't take it with you").[64]

Likely aware of this usage,[65] Matthew shows Yeshu`a similarly utilizing the term ממון ("*mammon*/wealth"):

Οὐδεὶς δύναται δυσὶ κυρίοις δουλεύειν	No one can serve two masters.
ἢ γὰρ τὸν ἕνα μισήσει καὶ τὸν ἕτερον ἀγαπήσει	One either hates the one and loves the other,
ἢ ἑνὸς ἀνθέξεται καὶ τοῦ ἑτέρου καταφρονήσει	Or clings to the one and disdains the other.
οὐ δύνασθε θεῷ δουλεύειν καὶ μαμωνᾷ	You cannot serve both God and *mammon*.[66]

Other rabbis express similar sentiments, of course, but without the same degree of prophetic "bite." In Mishnah, for example, Rab Yose says,

יהי ממון חברך	Let the *mammon* of your comrade

determined to "turn the economy of the Kingdom of Heaven into a transcendental opiate for the poor and socially oppressed." Such a "false economy," he warns, "must be avoided at all costs because its consequence can only be a broken heart."

58. *b. B. Batr.* 11a. Josephus (*A.J.* 20.17) identifies him as Μονόβαζος ὁ τῶν Ἀδιαβηνῶν βασιλεύς (Monobazos, king of Adiabene). Adiabene (Syr ܚܕܝܐܒ) is a territory in Assyria surrounding the city of Arbela in northern Mesopotamia (historically a major center of Ištar worship).

59. בזבז את כל אוצרותיו בשני תבצור (*t. Pe'ah* 4.18).

60. *t. Pe'ah* 4.18.

61. *t. Pe'ah* 4.18, במקום שהיד שולטת בו (lit. "in the place where the hand reaches it").

62. *t. Pe'ah* 4.18, אין עושין פירות (lit. "they do not make fruit").

63. *t. Pe'ah* 4.18, ממון vs. נפשות ("*mammon*" vs. "souls"). This is one of Hannah's chief concerns in Tobit (4Q197.4.1.2//Tob 5:21; cf. above).

64. *t. Pe'ah* 4.18, לאחרים vs. לעצמי ("for others" vs. "for myself"). Cf. Tobit's list of almsgiving's benefits (Tob 4:7–11; 12:8–9).

65. Cf. *Tg. Amos* 5.11, 12; *Tg. Mic* 3.11, 4.13; and *Tg. Hab.* 2.9 (all discussed above). Cf. McNamara (*Targum*, 310–15).

66. Matt 6:24. McNamara (*Targum*, 228) thinks ממון here is "evidently a loanword," but more likely Matthew simply chooses to *transliterate* instead of *translate* a well-known term from the original source language (Aramaic).

חביב עליך כשלך	Be as dear to you as your own.[67]

Ben Zoma asks,

איזהו עשיר	Who is rich?
השמח בחלקו	The one who rejoices in his "portion."[68]

Medieval rabbi Yeḥiel ben Yekutiel counsels students to "honor the wealthy if they are benevolent and modest, but remember that contentment is the true riches."[69] Trying to explain Yeshu`a's words to contemporary Westerners, Leif Vaage argues that this "critique of the perils of envy and greed—the salient features of an economy exclusively devoted to constant gain"—is a prophetic warning . . . against "storing up treasure on earth."[70]

Like the prophets Jeremiah and John the Baptist, Yeshu`a gravitates to an agrarian vernacular heavily influenced by the lingo of *fruitful productivity*:[71]

Προσέχετε ἀπὸ τῶν ψευδοπροφητῶν	Beware of false prophets
οἵτινες ἔρχονται πρὸς ὑμᾶς ἐν ἐνδύμασιν προβάτων	Who come to you in sheep's clothing,
ἔσωθεν δέ εἰσιν λύκοι ἅρπαγες	But inwardly are ravenous wolves.[72]
ἀπὸ τῶν καρπῶν αὐτῶν ἐπιγνώσεσθε αὐτούς	By their fruits you shall know them.[73]
μήτι συλλέγουσιν ἀπὸ ἀκανθῶν σταφυλὰς	Are grapes gathered from thorns?
ἢ ἀπὸ τριβόλων σῦκα	Or figs from thistles?[74]

67. *m. Avot* 2.12.

68. *m. Abot* 4.1 (cf. Eccl 9:7–10; 11:9). Cf. the repeated use of חלק ("portion") in Isa 53:12; 57:6; Jer 10:16//51:19; Deut 32:9.

69. Yekutiel, *Bet Middot* (Constantinople, 1511, cited in Joseph, *Judaism*, 388). Sandoval (*Money*, 63) comments: "the sages hint that the pursuit and possession of wealth is fundamentally risky, precisely because it is so valuable and desirable and so often appears to hold the key to contentment," esp. for those who "cannot find a way to align themselves with a moral vision strong enough to counter this tendency."

70. Vaage (*Exegesis*, 75–76) goes on to argue that "having unthreatened treasure in heaven and an enlightened body is . . . equivalent to service in God's household, whereas the contrasting effort to store up treasure on earth and the body suffused with darkness are . . . characteristics of the minions of Mammon."

71. Kunene (*Holiness*, 1–16) discusses the significance of the "vine metaphor" and Summey ("Fruit," 73–108) reflects on whether *κάρπος* ("fruit") refers to "deeds" or "behavior."

72. The "wolf in sheep's clothing" motif goes back at least as far as *Aesop's Fables* (c. sixth century BCE).

73. Stack-Nelson ("Matthew," 230, 32) thinks the "switch from animal to botanical metaphors" helps emphasize that "sin is the natural result of pervasive internal corruption of character."

74. Job 31:40 preserves a jussive form of this line: תחת חטה יצא חוח ותחת שערה באשה, "Let thorns grow instead of wheat, and foul weeds instead of barley." France ("Fruits," 50) illustrates: "When I lived

οὕτως πᾶν δένδρον ἀγαθὸν καρποὺς καλοὺς ποιει	Even so every good tree makes good fruit,
τὸ δὲ σαπρὸν δένδρον καρποὺς πονηροὺς ποιει	And the rotten tree bad fruit . . .[75]
πᾶν δένδρον μὴ ποιοῦν καρπὸν καλὸν	Every tree which does not bear good fruit
ἐκκόπτεται καὶ εἰς πῦρ βάλλεται	Is cut down and thrown into the fire.
ἄρα γε ἀπὸ τῶν καρπῶν αὐτῶν	Thus by their fruits
ἐπιγνώσεσθε αὐτούς	You shall know them.[76]

In the so-called "Limited Commission,"[77] Matthew shows the נביא ("prophet") from Nazareth sending out the בני הנביאים ("sons of the prophets") on a training mission[78] designed to focus them on the principle

δωρεὰν ἐλάβετε δωρεὰν δότε	Freely have you received, freely give.[79]

At first glance the Nazarene's application of this principle seems severe:

Μὴ κτήσησθε χρυσὸν μηδὲ ἄργυρον	Take no gold, no silver,
μηδὲ χαλκὸν εἰς τὰς ζώνας ὑμῶν	No copper in your belts;
μὴ πήραν εἰς ὁδὸν	No pack for the journey,
μηδὲ δύο χιτῶνας	No extra shirt,
μηδὲ ὑποδήματα	Nor shoes,

in Nigeria, I wanted to plant a banana tree in our garden. There were saplings that looked like bananas in the bush nearby, but I had been there long enough to know that a plantain tree looks very much like a banana tree. So I asked my friend, a professor of botany, how I could tell the difference. 'You cannot,' he said, 'until the fruit comes: if it produces bananas, it's a banana tree; if it produces plantains, it's a plantain.'"

75. Matt 7:15–17 (cf. 12:33). As Manson (*Sayings*, 32) observes, the adjectives σαπρός and πονηρός refer primarily to that which is "worthless." Later the prophet expresses that among those who do "bear fruit" the "harvest" is not uniform, but variegated, both in *volume* (13:23) and *condition* (13:30).

76. Matt 7:19–20. For Crosby (*Economics*, 196–97) "bearing fruit for the Baptizer . . . must be expressed 'in fruit that befits repentance'" (Matt 3:8; see 3:10), yet "'bearing fruit'" for Yeshu`a (7:16–20; 12:3; 13:8, 24; 21:18–20, 33–43) "involves performing works that help reorder social life, esp. through the practice of justice." Repeated use of this proverb testifies to the depth of its significance.

77. I.e., limited to the "lost sheep of the house of Israel" (Matt 10:6) in contrast to the "Great Commission" ("Go into all the world," Matt 28:18). Without denying the significance of Matthew's *temporal axis*, Levine (*Social*, 191) calls for more attention to the *social axis* determined by the polarity between the egalitarian Kingdom community and the entrenched power-grids of the Mediterranean economy.

78. N.B. how Elisha similarly tutors *his* students, focusing them in one assignment on how to gauge the "purification"-"multiplication" polarity (2 Kgs 4:38–44; Moore, *Faith*, 143–46).

79. Matt 10:8b. Seneca (*Ben.* 1.1.1) states the axiom negatively: *nihil propemodum indignius . . . quam quod beneficia nec dare scimus nec accipere*, "there is nothing more unsettling . . . than the fact that we neither know how to bestow nor how to receive benefits." Thistleton ("Atkinson," 33) remembers a beloved colleague who was "envied" for "his unpharisaic capacity never to measure how much he gave."

μηδὲ ῥάβδον	Nor staff.[80]
ἄξιος γὰρ ὁ ἐργάτης τῆς τροφῆς αὐτου	For the laborer is worthy of his hire.[81]

Yet the severity of this application stands in direct correlation to what the בני הנביאים can reasonably expect to receive for their labor:

ὁ δεχόμενος προφήτην	Whoever receives a prophet
εἰς ὄνομα προφήτου	In a prophet's name
μισθὸν προφήτου λήμψεται	Will receive a prophet's wages/reward.[82]

Accused of abandoning the "ancestral traditions,"[83] the Nazarene shows little patience for those who hide behind such traditions to justify their mistreatment of the poor. Anchoring his critique in Torah, he quotes from the Decalogue:

τίμα τὸν πατέρα καὶ τὴν μητέρα καὶ	"Honor your father and mother" and
ὁ κακολογῶν πατέρα ἢ μητέρα	"Whoever speaks ill of father or mother,
θανάτῳ τελευτάτω	Let him be sentenced to death."[84]

Then he contrasts Torah with one of their "ancestral traditions":

ὑμεῖς δὲ λέγετε	But you say,
ὃς ἂν εἴπῃ τῷ πατρὶ ἢ τῇ μητρί	"Whoever says to father or mother,
δῶρον ὃ ἐὰν ἐξ ἐμοῦ	'The gift which should be from me
ὠφεληθῇς	Is now owed to you.'"[85]
οὐ μὴ τιμήσει τὸν πατέρα αὐτου	In this he fails to "honor/value"[86] his father,

80. Marcus (*Mark*, 389) argues that this "limited commission" follows the "model" laid out in Exod 12:11. Carson (*Matthew*, 245) thinks the prophet's restrictions apply only to the acquisition of *new* clothes, shoes, and/or walking sticks. As Thompson (*Francis*, 91–109) notes, the monk from Assisi is one of the very few readers to take this passage literally.

81. Matt 10:9–10 (cf. Mark 6:7–9; 1 Tim 5:18). Gk τροφή (lit. "food, sustenance"; cf. John the Baptist's τροφή in 3:4). The synoptic parallel in Luke reads μισθός ("wage," Luke 10:7).

82. Matt 10:41 (cf. Smith, *Gospels*, 163–84). N.B. that in Isaiah the Servant's חלק/שלל ("portion/spoil") for his "labor" is רב ("great," Isa 53:12).

83. Cf. Goodman, *Judaism*, 117–22.

84. Matt 15:4 (citing Exod 20:12; 21:17).

85. The Marcan parallel reads: ἐὰν εἴπῃ ἄνθρωπος τῷ πατρὶ ἢ τῇ μητρί κορβᾶν, ὅ ἐστιν δῶρον, ὃ ἐὰν ἐξ ἐμοῦ ὠφεληθῇς, "If a man says to father or mother, the קרבן ('gift/offering') which should be from me you are (now) owed" (Mark 7:11). Yeshu'a returns to this verb (ὠφελέω) in Matt 16:26, τί γὰρ ὠφεληθήσεται ἄνθρωπος ἐὰν τὸν κόσμον ὅλον κερδήσῃ τὴν δὲ ψυχὴν αὐτοῦ ζημιωθῇ, "What does it 'profit' a man to gain the whole world, but lose his soul?"

86. Exod 20:12 כבד ("to honor, glorify"); Syr ܝܩܪ ("to give honor, make valuable"); OG τιμάω ("to honor, assess value, set a price"). Plato (*Laws* 917c) describes the "ideal marketplace" as a place where a salesman "names only one price, and if he fails to get it, then he is entitled to take the article away," but "not increase its price" (μὴ τιμήσῃ πλέονος).

καὶ ἠκυρώσατε τὸν λόγον τοῦ θεοῦ	And you nullify[87] the word of God
διὰ τὴν παράδοσιν ὑμῶν	By means of your tradition.[88]

Instead of the Matthean term ὠφεληθῇς the Gospel of Mark in its parallel account uses the word κορβᾶν (a Greek transliteration of קרבן).[89] This well-known Hebrew word appears in Torah some eighty times, often in combination with its verbal root קרב, as in the priestly protasis כי תקריב קרבן, "if you bring near a 'brought-near thing' (i.e., 'gift')."[90] As early as the third century BCE the Greeks imagine it connoting any type of "gift" (δῶρον),[91] but the Athenian philosopher Theophrastus questions this custom when he learns that the Tyrians outlaw the קרבן along with several other "foreign vows."[92]

To the obvious question—"Why is קרבן a problem?"—Talmud offers a bit of insight.[93] In tractate *Ta'anith*, e.g., Abram and God have a conversation like the one in Genesis where the patriarch seeks to find out *how* his descendants will "inherit" the promised land.[94] In Torah the conversation concludes with Abram preparing a covenant sacrifice, but in *Ta'anith* it continues as Abram asks God whether "sacrifice" is even possible without a "temple."[95] To this the "deity" replies,

כבר תקנתי להם סדר קרבנות	I have already provided for them an "order of *qorbans*"[96]

87. Gk ἀκυρόω ("to nullify"). Cf. καὶ προσέταξεν ἵνα ὅσοι ἐὰν παραβῶσίν τι τῶν προειρημένων καὶ τῶν προσγεγραμμένων ἢ καὶ ἀκυρώσωσιν λημφθῆναι ξύλον ἐκ τῶν ἰδίων αὐτοῦ καὶ ἐπὶ τούτου κρεμασθῆναι καὶ τὰ ὑπάρχοντα αὐτοῦ εἶναι βασιλικά, "And he (Darius) commanded that if anyone transgressed or 'nullified' any of the things written or said, that a beam would be taken out of his house to impale him upon it, and his possessions confiscated by the crown" (1 Esd 6:31).

88. Matt 15:5–6 (παράδοσις, "tradition," lit. "that which is given over"). Plato (*Men.* 93b) doubts whether "good men" are able "to give over/transmit" (παραδοῦναι) virtue to others.

89. Mark 7:11. Vg transliterates as *corban*, the term often found in English Bibles (cf. McNamara, *Targum*, 229–31; Fabry, "קרבן," 152–58).

90. Lev 2:4. Vaux (*Sacrifices*, 31) sees קרבן as a "creation of the Priestly Code."

91. OG Lev 1:2 and *passim* (Eberhart, "Sacrifice," 23). Cf. חרם ("devoted thing") in the priestly refrain, כל חרם קדש קדשים הוא ליהוה, "every 'devoted thing' is a holy of holies to Yhwh" (Lev 27:28).

92. ξένικοι ὅρκοι. Cf. Theophrastus (d. 287 BCE, cited in Josephus, *C. Ap.* 1.167). Szegedy-Maszak (*Nomoi*, 74) thinks the Tyrians outlaw the קרבן not so much because it is an "oath" (ὅρκος), but because it is sworn over a sacrifice to a foreign deity.

93. The Aramaic inscription on a first-century ossuary reads כל די אנש מתהנה בחלתה דה קרבן אלה מן דבגוה, "All that one may find to his profit in this ossuary is a קרבן to God from him who is within" (Milik, "Tombeaux," 409), but whether this represents a "dedicatory formula in common use among the Jews," or the possibility that this "formula" is "a vestigial survival of much older mortuary offerings" (Fitzmyer, "Qorbān," 63) is not yet ascertainable.

94. Gen 15:1–9. N.B. that the issue driving this conversation is "inheritance" (ירש occurs five times in the biblical conversation).

95. בית המקדש (lit. "house of holiness," *b. Ta'an.* 27b).

96. Construct phrases beginning with סדר refer to major categories; cf., e.g., the six סדרים ("orders") of Mishna and the weekly סדרים-synagogue-readings.

בזמן שקוראין בהן לפני	So that whenever they are read out before me
מעלה אני עליהם כאילו הקריבום לפני	I lift up those who offer them
כאילו הקריבום לפני	As its[97] pillar "draws near" before me,[98]
ואני מוחל להם על כל עונתיה	And I "pardon" all their sins.[99]

The context of this talmudic conversation is a much larger discussion over how to gauge the importance of the מעמדות (lit. "standing places"); i.e., those primitive congregations most likely to have been the institutional forerunners of the συναγωγή ("synagogue").[100] The didactic goal of *Ta'anith* is to convince participants in these מעמדות that sacrificial giving can and should continue, even apart from a בית המקדש ("holy house/temple").[101]

One of the unintended results of this "divine solution," however, is that this "order of *qorbans*" (סדר קרבנות) becomes in less scrupulous minds an "authorized substitute" for *actual* sacrifice, and this in turn opens the door to the possibility that קרבן might include not only heavenly "pillars" connecting worshipers to God, but the "legal right" to substitute *imaginary* sacrifice for *actual* sacrifice. Alan Verhey explains: "To make a vow that something is קרבן is to declare that it is dedicated to God. It does not require that the thing actually be offered up in the temple, only that it be withdrawn from normal use," thereby making it possible for anyone to "vow something to God not so that it may be given to God, but so that some other person may not receive it."[102] This then evolves into a "bait-and-switch" policy authorizing neglect by default, even the neglect of one's elderly parents. What makes it so infuriating to the prophets is that even *Gentiles* like the Tyrians can see through it for what it is—a pretentious legal fiction.[103]

97. The 3ms suffix of אילו likely refers to the previously mentioned בית המקדש.

98. Repetition of the root קרב makes the visual image even more compelling: anyone who offers up a קרבן–"gift" is like a construction worker dutifully "bringing near" (קרב) one of the temple's "pillars" (איל).

99. *b. Ta'an.* 27b. The word חול means "to make smooth, lax, quiet, forgive" (*DTTM* 432–33) and parallels מעלה ("to lift up") in the preceding line (causative of עלה, "to go up").

100. Bowker (*Targums*, 9) observes that "the מעמדות are divisions of people throughout Judea which are intended to correspond to the twenty-four courses of the priests in the Temple. In this way all the people are involved in the duties and sacrifices of the Temple, even though they cannot be present in Jerusalem. Each מעמד assembles, when its turn comes, to read passages of Scripture according to the sacrifices taking place in Jerusalem. It is from these 'assemblies' that 'synagogues' in Palestine seem to have developed."

101. Levine (*Synagogue*, 39) believes that the Chronicler is already aware of the מעמדות (1 Chr 24:1–18; cf. Acts 7:48).

102. Verhey, *Jesus*, 409. This behavior presumes the prevalence of the "deprivation myth" (heartily condemned by Brueggemann, *Memory*, 69–76).

103. Josephus, *C. Ap.* 1.167.

Something similar occurs in the episode about the tax bill submitted to Yeshu`a through his disciple כיפא (Peter).[104] To understand its significance it is again helpful to examine the literary-historical context.[105] According to Torah, each Hebrew male over twenty years old must "give"[106] a half-shekel to "ransom his soul for Yhwh,"[107] a tradition which, like קרבן, eventually falls prey to priestly gerrymandering, in spite of Talmud's attempts to prevent it:

הילך מנה	(If someone says) "Take this *mina*[108]
על מנת שתחזירהו לי	On the condition that you restore it back to me,"
במכר לא קנה	For a purchase it cancels the sale;
באשה אינה מקודשת	For a wife it blocks the betrothal;
בפדיון הבן	For a son's redemption—
אין בנו פדוי	It invalidates the son's redemption.[109]

That such delimitations need to be stated at all becomes immediately clear from Rav Ashi's rejoinder:[110]

בכולהו קני לבר מאשה	All are valid except "betrothal" because
לפי שאין אשה נקנית בחליפין	No woman can be acquired[111] via barter/ exchange.[112]

In other words, the fact that "redemption of the firstborn" is to some extent "negotiable"[113] in early Jewish tradition helps explain the rationale behind the question,

104. Matt 17:24. Like "Yerubba'al" for "Gideon" (Judg 6:32), שמעון ("Simon") receives the nickname כיפא ("the Rock," John 1:42), which of course becomes πέτρος in GNT ("rock").

105. Trebilco (*Communities*, 16) observes that "some Jewish communities in Asia Minor (and elsewhere) feel sufficiently committed to the temple tax to take active measures to ensure they can pay for it." Why? Because it offers diaspora Jews a way to feel like they are "a tangible part of the worship offered in Jerusalem."

106. Exod 30:12 (נתן).

107. Exod 30:12 (ליהוה כפר נפשו; cf. Steiner, *Souls*, 124–27). Kaiser ("Bindung," 199–224) reconciles the tension between child-sacrifice and firstborn-redemption (Exod 13:13; 22:28; 34:20; Num 3:46–47) by suggesting that God foregoes this legal tradition in response to Abraham (Gen 22).

108. A mina is approx. 50–60 shekels.

109. *b. Qidd.* 6b.

110. Zobel, "Ashi," 565–66.

111. N.B. the homonymous wordplay on קנה ("to validate") and קנה ("to acquire").

112. *b. Qidd.* 6b. Cf., however, the תמורה ("exchange") engineered by Boaz for Ruth (Ruth 4:7). Hubbard (*Ruth*, vi) demarcates גאולה ("redemption") from תמורה ("exchange") by deriving the former "from Israelite family law" and the latter "from the realm of Israel's commercial life."

113. Some sources claim that all Jewish males are obligated to pay this tax annually (Josephus, *A.J.* 14.110; 18.312; *B.J.* 7.218; Philo, *Spec.* 1.77), but for the covenanters at Qumran רק פ[עם] אחת יתננו כול ימיו, "only on[ce] will he give it all his days" (4Q159.7).

ὁ διδάσκαλος ὑμῶν οὐ τελεῖ [τὰ] δίδραχμα	"Does your teacher not pay temple-taxes?"[114]

Peter's answer, of course, is a politically correct "Yes,"[115] but Yeshu`ạ seizes on this exchange as an optimal teaching moment. Whereas Peter's interrogators want to know whether his rabbi plans to support the business of the Jerusalem temple complex,[116] Peter's rabbi wants to know whether his student is ready to ponder a much deeper question:

οἱ βασιλεῖς τῆς γῆς	"The kings of the earth—
ἀπὸ τίνων λαμβάνουσιν τέλη ἢ κῆνσον	From whom do they take taxes or tribute?[117]
ἀπὸ τῶν υἱῶν αὐτῶν ἢ ἀπὸ τῶν ἀλλοτρίων	From their sons or from others?"[118]
εἰπόντος δέ ἀπὸ τῶν ἀλλοτρίων	When he answers, "From others,"[119]
ἔφη αὐτῷ ὁ Ἰησοῦς	Jesus says to him,
ἄρα γε ἐλεύθεροί εἰσιν οἱ υἱοί	"Then the sons are free.[120]

114. Matt 17:24. OG translates Exod 30:13 מחצית השקל בשקל הקדש ("the half-shekel according to the shekel of the sanctuary") as τὸ ἥμισυ τοῦ διδράχμου ὅ ἐστιν κατὰ τὸ δίδραχμον τὸ ἅγιον, "the half δίδραχμον according to the δίδραχμον of the sanctuary" (the same monetary term found here).

115. Cohen ("Antiquity," 35) thinks that payment of the temple tax "is perhaps the best statement of Jewishness for a Diaspora Jew in the pre-70 CE period."

116. Opinions are mixed on what exactly goes on in the Jerusalem temple. Schaper ("Temple," 200–206) thinks the Jerusalem temple operates much like any other ANE temple; i.e., as a depository for the imperial superpower under which the Jews, as vassals, must serve. Bedford, however ("Economic," 15–16), argues (a) that differences in scale, range of activities, and relative economic importance are too great to justify such comparisons, and (b) that temple taxes, unlike most taxes, are largely "self-imposed" (an opinion with which the Nazarene obviously disagrees). Further, Bickermann (*Maccabees*, 84–86) argues that Jason's establishment of a γυμνάσιον (2 Macc 4:9) in Jerusalem fundamentally changes everything, not least economically, and Bringmann (*Reform*, 66–96) builds on this to suggest that Jason never tries to replace the temple with a γυμνάσιον because such a move would destabilize the revenue-stream generated by the temple. Cf. Honigman, *Taxes*, 362–68; Ameling, "Gymnasion," 129–62.

117. Cf. the refrain מדה בלו והלך, "tribute, produce-tax, and property-tax" in the Aramaic letters of Ezra (4:13, 20; 7:24) as well as the numerous Hellenistic taxes listed in Maccabees: οἱ φόροι τῆς χώρας ("district taxes"); τιμῆς τοῦ ἁλός ("salt tax"); τιμῆς τῶν στεφάνων ("crown tax"); τοὺς φόρους καὶ τῶν κτηνῶν ("livestock taxes"); δαπάνην τοῖς ἁγίοις ("sanctuary expenses"; 1 Macc 3:29; 10:29, 33, 39; cf. Roth and Elon, "Taxation," 532–58).

118. "Sons" vs. "others," a common rabbinic polarity (e.g., *b. Bat.* 10a), demarcates a *very* "sacred boundary."

119. The tax mentioned in Torah (Num 3:46), however, is מבכור בני ישראל, "from the firstborn of the sons of Israel"—not "others."

120. Paul crafts a similar argument in the Sarah-Hagar allegory (Gal 4:22–31), an argument which Tamez ("Freedom," 265) thinks shows how "the free sons and daughters of Abraham are children of the promise and do not submit blindly to the law" (cf. Gorman, *Apostle*, 258–62).

ἵνα δὲ μὴ σκανδαλίσωμεν αὐτούς	Yet so that we do not offend them,[121]
πορευθεὶς εἰς θάλασσαν	Go to the sea,
βάλε ἄγκιστρον	Cast a hook,
καὶ τὸν ἀναβάντα πρῶτον ἰχθὺν ἆρον	And take out the first fish you catch.
καὶ ἀνοίξας τὸ στόμα αὐτοῦ	Opening its mouth
εὑρήσεις στατῆρα	You will find a coin.[122]
ἐκεῖνον λαβὼν	Take it out
δὸς αὐτοῖς ἀντὶ ἐμοῦ καὶ σου	And give it to them for me and for you."[123]

This deeper question, of course, is the one driving the actions of *every* prophet; viz., Who is the *just* "tax collector," and what are the mandates of *his* "tax policy?"[124]

Judean Encounters

Leaving Galilee for points south, the Nazarene encounters a wealthy young man[125] who asks what he must do to "inherit" eternal life.[126] In response to this question the prophet raises two more: (a) whether the selling of this young man's possessions to help the poor "completes" him; and (b) whether the acquisition of wealth *in se* prohibits the development of a kingdom ethic.[127] To the first question the young man

121. Derrett (*Law*, 256–57) thinks that σκανδαλίζω here means "cause the tax collectors to sin" by forcing the Son of God to pay taxes. Keener (*Matthew*, 445), however, thinks it "more likely that Jesus seeks simply to avoid turning people away from his gospel unnecessarily."

122. Regardless how one may feel about miracles generally or this miracle-story particularly (Richardson, *Miracle-Stories*, 31, 127), Keener (*Miracles*, 1) contends that "supernatural explanations should be welcome on the scholarly table along with other explanations." The fact that English translations of στατήρ differ (NRSV "coin"; NIV "four-drachma coin"; ESV "shekel") bothers Wenkel (*Coins*, 32) to the point that he feels compelled to warn readers that anyone "limited to research in English translations will likely experience confusion."

123. Matt 17:25–27. Josephus (*AJ* 14.110) remarks that no one should be "amazed that there is such 'wealth' (πλοῦτος) in our Temple, since all those in the 'Jewish economy' (οἰκουμένην Ἰουδαίων) and all those who worship God, even those of Asia and Europe, 'contribute' (συμφερόντων) to it, and this from very ancient times."

124. Similar questions hover over the epicenter of the messianic hope (Frankfort, *Kingship*, 341–44; Mowinckel, *Concept*, 49; Eaton, *Kingship*, 135–201; Childs, *Isaiah*, 106; Whitelam, *King*, 17–37). Staunchly critical of postmodernist definitions of "apocalyptic," Horsley (*Empire*, 81) calls for an approach in which the Nazarene's "pronouncement of judgment against rulers draws on a broader pattern" rooted not in "ancestral traditions," but "in ancient Israelite tradition."

125. According to Luke 18:18, he is πλούσιος σφόδρα ("very rich").

126. Matt 19:16 reads σχῶ ("I might have"); Luke 18:18 reads κληρονομήσω ("I might inherit").

127. Wogaman, *Economics*, 4–12. For Gushee and Stassen (*Kingdom*, 376) the "fundamental mandate" of a "Kingdom ethic" is "just distribution . . . of the good gifts of God."

cites from the Decalogue,[128] then asks what he still "lacks" (ὑστερέω).[129] This leads to the following response:

εἰ θέλεις τέλειος εἶναι	If you wish to be "complete,"[130]
ὕπαγε πώλησόν σου τὰ ὑπάρχοντα	Go, sell your possessions[131]
καὶ δὸς [τοῖς] πτωχοῖς	And give to the poor,
καὶ ἕξεις θησαυρὸν ἐν οὐρανοῖς	And you will have treasure in heaven.
καὶ δεῦρο ἀκολούθει μοι	Then come, follow me.[132]

The young man's response[133] to this invitation is to "grieve" (λυπούμενος) over his "many possessions" (κτήματα πολλά),[134] but turning to the בני הנביאים ("sons of the "prophets") the נביא ("prophet") pushes the question onto another plane by challenging them to ponder the addictive power of "wealth":

ἀμὴν λέγω ὑμῖν ὅτι πλούσιος δυσκόλως	Truly I tell you, it's hard[135] for a wealthy man[136]
εἰσελεύσεται εἰς τὴν βασιλείαν τῶν οὐρανῶν	To enter into the kingdom of heaven.
εὐκοπώτερόν ἐστιν κάμηλον	It's easier for a camel

128. I.e., the "ten commandments" (Exod 20:2–17).

129. In Matt 19:20 the young man asks τί ἔτι ὑστερῶ ("What do I yet lack?"); in Luke 18:22 Jesus says ἔτι ἕν σοι λείπει ("there is yet one thing left to you").

130. As is well known, τέλος means "complete, mature, perfect" (MacIntyre, *Virtue*, 61–64.) What is less known is that οἱ ἐν τέλει can mean "those in charge" (lit. "those with maturity," Sophocles, *Ajax* 1352).

131. Vermes (*Religion*, 148) conceptualizes Yeshu`a's teaching in three broad strokes: "detachment from possessions, unquestioning trust in God, and absolute submission."

132. Matt 19:17–22. Talmud (*b. Sot.* 49a) promises that any ת"ח ("student of the sages") who עוסק בתורה ("engages with Torah") מתוך הדחק ("in the midst of poverty") will (a) תפלתו נשמעת ("have his prayer heard"), and (b) משביעין אותו מזיו שכינה ("be glutted by the glory of the *šekinah*").

133. Whether this invitation is offered to only one particular person at only one particular moment is for many readers ambiguous—but not Bonhoeffer (*Discipleship*, 85): "The shocked question of the disciples, 'Who, then, can be saved?' (Matt 19:25), seems to indicate that they regard the case of the rich young man as not in any way exceptional, but as typical. For they do not ask, 'Which rich man?' but quite generally, '*Who* then can be saved?'"

134. Matt 19:22 (cf. ὑπάρχοντα in v. 21). Describing the behavior of Penelope's suitors, the swineherd Eumaios complains to Odysseus (in disguise as a beggar) that κτήματα δαρδάπτουσιν ὑπέρβιον οὐδ' ἔπι φειδώ, "they greedily devour (my master's) possessions, leaving nothing to spare" (Homer, *Od.* 14.92).

135. Gk δυσκόλως = δυς ("hard," opposite of εὖ, "good") + κόλον ("colon," LSJ 452, 458). Excessive pursuit of riches, in other words, causes "constipation."

136. Hesiod (*Op.* 20–24) dualistically describes two goddesses named Ἔρις ("Strife"): one a cruel deity responsible for conflict and war, the other an enterprising force responsible for "stirring up even the shiftless to toil; for a man grows eager to work when he considers his neighbor, a 'rich man' (πλούσιος) who hastens to plough and plant and put his house in good order, neighbor vying with neighbor in the pursuit of 'wealth' (ἄφενος; lit. α + φεναξ, 'cheating')."

διὰ τρυπήματος ῥαφίδος διελθεῖν	To go through the eye of a needle[137]
ἢ πλούσιον εἰσελθεῖν	Than for a wealthy man to enter
εἰς τὴν βασιλείαν τοῦ θεοῦ	Into the kingdom of God.[138]

The ancients view the "poverty-wealth" polarity from a number of perspectives,[139] and were this the only mention of it in GNT, it would be appropriate to argue (as some do) that "God is always on the side of the poor."[140] Reading this text in its literary-historical context, however,[141] precludes such one-sidedness.[142] As David Williams recognizes, it is too simplistic "to identify God with the poor or even to put God on the side of the poor" because "in the Old Testament God chooses the Jews, not the poor . . . and in the New Testament Jesus is seen as favoring not only the poor, but even those who collaborate with the oppressors" (e.g., the tax collector Levi).[143]

Finally arriving in Jerusalem, Yeshu`a and his students walk headlong into the parameters of another debate. Someone asks, "Who is this?" and a crowd answers,

οὗτός ἐστιν ὁ προφήτης Ἰησοῦς	This is the prophet Jesus
ὁ ἀπὸ Ναζαρὲθ τῆς Γαλιλαίας	From Nazareth in Galilee.

Then something rather remarkable happens:

εἰσῆλθεν Ἰησοῦς εἰς τὸ ἱερὸν	Yeshu`a entered into the temple

137. *Contra* Witherington, (*Sage*, 166) this saying may be an earlier version of "elephant through the eye of a needle," a phrase used to satirize scholarly conceit at Pumbeditha, the site of a rabbinic academy presided over by Rav Nachmani, the editor of what eventually becomes the Babylonian Talmud (cf. Eisenberg, *Talmud*, 198). Not coincidentally, the "elephant" phrase in *b. B. Meṣ.* 38b occurs within a discussion about the intricacies of inheritance law.

138. Matt 19:23–24. Marshall (*Luke*, 686) thinks these comments are "directed to non-disciples . . . to stir them up to realize the danger of riches."

139. Some acknowledge wealth's positive influence (Plato, *Leg.* 9.870ab; *Sib. Or.* 3.783); others warn of its dangers (Lucian, *Nigr.* 1.4; *1 En.* 97.8–10). A Qumranian legislator vows that להון חמס לוא תאוה נפשי, "My soul shall not crave wealth-through-violence" (1QS 10.19). A few recognize the difference between "money" and the "love of money" (Isocrates, *Demon.* 9.27–28; *Test. Jud.* 17.1; 18.2; 1 Tim 6:10).

140. Wierzbicka (*Sermon*, 385), e.g., notes that "Jesus' teaching on poverty and wealth . . . shares with the Psalms and the Prophets the key idea that God is somehow on the side of the poor."

141. Hegelian polarization is not only alien to prophetic Yahwism, but to *any* philosophy championing free will in the face of rigid determinism (Taylor, *Selfhood*, 100–103). Debunking Brandon's (*Zealots*, 284) attempt to disregard the Pella tradition (Eusebius, *HE* 3.5.3), Wink ("Revolution," 44) contends that "those Christians who find their way to Pella would be landless in an essentially agrarian society. Already for some time the Jerusalem church has a reputation for its destitution (2 Cor 8–9; Rom 15:25–27); and, if the Epistle of James in any way reflects Jerusalemite Christianity, its polemic against the rich (Jas 2:1–7) would be significant."

142. In this vein Deferrari (*Politics*, 149) justifiably criticizes Yoder (*Politics*) for presuming that his "political theories, (so) removed from the world, still apply to it." Not to be overlooked is the "health-wealth" extremism condemned by Barron (*Gospel*), Jones and Woodbridge (*Prosperity*), and Fee (*Wealth*).

143. Williams, *Poverty*, 267 (cf. de Villiers, *Liberation*, 67, *contra* Chopp, *Praxis*, 48).

καὶ ἐξέβαλεν πάντας τοὺς πωλοῦντας	And cast out all those buying
καὶ ἀγοράζοντας ἐν τῷ ἱερῷ	And selling in it,[144]
καὶ τὰς τραπέζας τῶν κολλυβιστῶν κατέστρεψεν	Overturning the money-changers' tables[145]
καὶ τὰς καθέδρας τῶν πωλούντων τὰς περιστεράς	And the seats of the dove merchants.[146]

Anticipating that some will react negatively to this behavior, he quotes from Nevi'im:

γέγραπται	"It is written,
ὁ οἶκός μου οἶκος προσευχῆς κληθήσεται	'My house shall be called a house of prayer,'
ὑμεῖς δὲ αὐτὸν ποιεῖτε σπήλαιον λῃστῶν	But you have made it a 'den of thieves.'"[147]

Several motifs occur here,[148] but Ron Witherup reasonably argues that the passage's primary intention is to spotlight the "image of a powerful and justifiably angry prophet . . . entering the temple . . . to exert his authority over it by expelling those who have corrupted it."[149]

Another lively exchange focuses (again) on the question of "taxation":

εἰπὲ οὖν ἡμῖν τί σοι δοκεῖ	Tell us what you think:
ἔξεστιν δοῦναι κῆνσον Καίσαρι ἢ οὔ	Is it "lawful"[150] to pay taxes to Caesar or not?[151]

144. N.B. that one of Aḥiqar's official titles is על כל ש]זפנות מלכותא, "(the one) over all the kingdom's lending-and-borrowing" (4Q196.2.5–6; cf. Tob 1:21 Syr ܥܠ ܟܠܗ ܚܘܫܒܢܐ, "over all the accounting").

145. As Harrington (*Matthew*, 294) points out, the κολλύβισται ("moneychangers") "give out Jewish or Tyrian coins in exchange for Greek or Roman money." Phrynicus (*Ecloga* 404, cited in Rutherford, *Phrynicus*, 497) perceives them to be οὐκ ὀρθῶς ("not straight"; i.e., "crooked").

146. Matt 21:11–12. Citing rabbinic tradition, Keener (*Jesus*, 292) cautions (a) that not all moneychangers are corrupt, and (b) that the problem depicted here is not economic activity in the temple *per se*, but its abuse.

147. Matt 21:13 (citing Isa 56:7 and Jer 7:11).

148. Blomberg (*Gospels*, 216–19) dutifully discusses several.

149. Witherup, *Matthew*, 145.

150. "Lawful" may well be too "legal" a translation for ἔξεστι, a term which simply means "appropriate," "possible," even "*kosher*" (cf. LSJ 591).

151. Matt 22:17.

Having earlier been quizzed about the "baptism of John,"[152] his detractors try to turn the tables on him.[153] Whatever their motives for bringing up this problem,[154] the Nazarene response remains to this day a timeless aphorism:[155]

ἐπιδείξατέ μοι τὸ νόμισμα τοῦ κήνσου	"Show me the coin for the tax."[156]
οἱ δὲ προσήνεγκαν αὐτῷ δηνάριον	And they brought him a denarius.[157]
καὶ λέγει αὐτοῖς	Then he said to them,
τίνος ἡ εἰκὼν αὕτη καὶ ἡ ἐπιγραφή	"Whose image and epigraph is this?"[158]
λέγουσιν αὐτῷ Καίσαρος	They said to him, "Caesar."
τότε λέγει αὐτοῖς	Then he said to them,
ἀπόδοτε οὖν τὰ Καίσαρος Καίσαρι	"Give to Caesar the things which are Caesar's
καὶ τὰ τοῦ θεοῦ τῷ θεῷ	And to God the things which are God's."[159]

Some try to stretch this aphorism into a theoretical rationale for the "separation of church and state,"[160] or (even more simplistically) an "anti-imperialist" manifesto,[161] but Joel Willitts rejects both options, arguing that "Matthew's problem with empire,

152. Matt 21:25: "The baptism of John, from God or man?" Hooker ("Baptism," 23) thinks that "whatever the background to John's baptism, it would have been understood as a 'prophetic sign'—a dramatic action which, like prophetic words, proclaims the divine will."

153. Wiker (*Religion*, 29) emphasizes how much "the Jews living in the Roman Empire are not keen on worshipping a pagan emperor (Tiberius) or paying oppressive taxes to the imperial government."

154. Perkins ("Taxes," 188) cautions that "common treatments of this story as an anti-zealot pronouncement, something which would be common enough from a Galilean . . ., or as a general principle about Christian obedience to the state do not attend either to its internal dynamics or to its setting."

155. Newspaper columnist Max Lerner (b. 1902), e.g., presumes a knowledge of this aphorism when he depicts Klaus Fuchs, the man convicted of selling American nuclear secrets to the Russians (thereby triggering the Big Red Scare of the 1950s) as "rendering to the British Caesar the things that are Caesar's, but to the Russian God the things that are God's" (cited in Bryant, "Lore," 140).

156. Vg. transliterates Gk κήνσος ("tax") as "*census*."

157. A denarius is a day's wage (Matt 20:2).

158. Rav Pappa (*b. B. Meṣ.* 45b) argues that a מטבע ("metal coin") cannot be used in חליפין ("exchanges") because of the צורתה ("image") stamped upon it, and how most images render the coin's עבידא ("value/adaptivity") בטלא ("void"). How much this "coin discussion" might influence/reflect the discussion here is impossible to say.

159. Matt 22:19–21. Should the epigraph on the denarius-coin read *Ti[berius] Caesar Divi Aug[usti] F[ilius] Augustus* ("Caesar Augustus Tiberius, son of Divine Augustus"), this considerably deepens the impact of this aphorism (cf. Wiker, *Religion*, 29).

160. DeBrabander ("Religion," 26), e.g., argues that "Jesus' new covenant is distinctive because it focuses on the prospect of a heavenly reward. The very condition of his new covenant is a separation of political and heavenly expectations: 'Give to Caesar what is Caesar's, and to God what is God's.'" Lenski (*Matthew*, 867) argues that this is "the only legitimate conclusion to be drawn."

161. Carter, *Margins*, 1–25.

if one can even put it that way, is not empire *per se*, but *which* empire."[162] In fact, "far from an empireless 'alternative' society, as Warren Carter labels it,[163] Matthew envisions the renewed and perfected kingdom of Israel (as) the coming of a society which finally expresses the fullness of Israel's potential shaped by Torah."[164]

Near the end of Matthew a socioeconomically revealing conversation takes place in the house of "Simon the leper":[165]

προσῆλθεν αὐτῷ γυνὴ ἔχουσα	A woman came to him holding
ἀλάβαστρον μύρου βαρυτίμου	An alabaster box of expensive ointment[166]
καὶ κατέχεεν ἐπὶ τῆς κεφαλῆς αὐτοῦ	And poured it upon his head
ἀνακειμένου	While he sat.
ἰδόντες δὲ οἱ μαθηταὶ	But when the disciples saw it
ἠγανάκτησαν λέγοντες	They were indignant,[167] saying,
εἰς τί ἡ ἀπώλεια αὕτη	"Why this waste?[168]
ἐδύνατο γὰρ τοῦτο πραθῆναι πολλοῦ	This might have been sold for a large sum[169]
καὶ δοθῆναι πτωχοῖς	And given to the poor."[170]
γνοὺς δὲ ὁ Ἰησοῦς εἶπεν αὐτοῖς	Aware of this, Yeshu`a said to them,
τί κόπους παρέχετε τῇ γυναικι	"Why do you trouble this lady?
ἔργον γὰρ καλὸν ἠργάσατο εἰς ἐμε	She has done something good for me.[171]

162. Willitts, *Matthew*, 85.

163. Carter, *Margins*, 43–50.

164. Willitts, "Matthew," 85. Longenecker ("Economic," 264) contends that with regard to Syro-Palestinians in Yeshu`a's day, 3% are wealthy, 17% form a "middle group" (though not what today would be called a "middle class"), 25% live barely above the subsistence level, 30% live right at it, and 25% live below it.

165. Matt 26:6 (// Mark 14:3–9).

166. Gk βαρυτιμός ("expensive, precious"). Strabo (*Geogr.* 17.1.13) describes the trade going in and out of Alexandria as activity where τῶν δὲ βαρυτιμῶν βαρέα καὶ τὰ τέλη, "the most expensive items produce the heaviest (tariffs)."

167. Josephus uses this term (ἀγανακτέω, *B.J.* 2.175) to describe Jewish "indignation" at Pilate's decision to pay for new city aqueducts from funds in the κορβωνᾶς (*korban*-vaults; see below), a curious response given the fact that these funds are designated for this purpose (*m. Šeqal.* 4.2 specifically mentions אמת המים, "water channels").

168. Gk ἀπώλεια ("destroyed, wasted"). Aristotle (*Eth. nic.* 1120a) defines the "prodigal" (ἄσωτος, lit. "unsaved") as δοκεῖ δ' ἀπώλειά τις αὑτοῦ εἶναι καὶ ἡ τῆς οὐσίας φθορά, "one who thinks he can wastefully destroy his possessions."

169. Other Gospels specify "300 denarii," roughly a year's salary (Mark 14:5; John 12:5).

170. The Fourth Gospel puts this response in the mouth of Judas Iscariot, "not because he cared about the poor, but because he was a thief who kept the common purse and used to steal what was put into it" (John 12:6).

171. Lit. "worked a good work" (another example of the cognate accusative; *GKC* 117p-r).

πάντοτε γὰρ τοὺς πτωχοὺς ἔχετε μεθ' ἑαυτῶν	The poor you have with you always,
ἐμὲ δὲ οὐ πάντοτε ἔχετε	But you do not always have me."[172]

Liz Theoharis complains that this passage too often is cited "to discredit antipoverty organizing, justify the foreordination of poverty, and support the idea that charity is the best response."[173] Against this tendency, however, she suggests that this text in fact provides "one of the strongest statements of the biblical mandate to *end* poverty." The rationale contrived to support this "mandate," however, comes from an "exegesis informed by a methodology and hermeneutic" based on a "conversation with contemporary issues"—issues like "taxation, debt, infrastructure and development, charity and patronage, poverty, wealth, and political power."[174] So nebulous a replacement for competent exegetical analysis, however, clearly undermines the substance of her thesis.[175]

The final episode of socioeconomic significance in Matthew focuses on a financial exchange between one of the בני הנביאים ("sons of the prophets") and the Sanhedrin.[176] Where Peter betrays his rabbi through a verbal denial,[177] Judas Iscariot sells him out to his enemies for a bribe.[178] Eventually he tries to return the money, but of central interest here is the rationale offered by the chief priests for taking it back:

οὐκ ἔξεστιν βαλεῖν αὐτὰ	"It is not lawful[179] to deposit it
εἰς τὸν κορβανᾶν	Into the *qorban*-vault,[180]
ἐπεὶ τιμὴ αἵματός ἐστιν	Since it is payment for blood."[181]

172. Matt 26:7–11. For Aristotle (*Nic. eth.* 1120a), the man who is ἐλευθέριος ("liberated/liberal") understands that ὁ πλοῦτος ("wealth") is simply χρήσιμος ("a useful thing") which can be χρῆσθαι καὶ εὖ καὶ κακῶς ("used for good or evil").

173. Theoharis, *Always*, 14.

174. Ibid., 147.

175. By contrast, cf. Wallis, *Politics*, xxvii-xxviii.

176. Gk συνέδριον, "council" (Matt 25:59; cf. Saldarini, "Sanhedrin," 975–80).

177. Matt 26:69–75 (cf. Aus, *Denial*, 95–178).

178. Matt 26:15. Peter calls Judas τοῦ γενομένου ὁδηγοῦ τοῖς συλλαβοῦσιν Ἰησοῦν, "the one who became a 'guide/pilot' to those who arrested Jesus" (Acts 1:16). As Noonan notes (*Bribes*, 58), the fact "that the betrayal is a sale is emphasized by Matthew's focus, in pursuit of his scriptural pedagogy, on the amount paid and its character of blood price." Both Peter and Judas suffer remorse for their actions, but only that felt by Peter leads to renewal (Matt 27:3–5).

179. Cf. ἔξεστι in Matt 22:17 (discussed above). Osborne (*Matthew*, 1012) thinks these Sanhedrin leaders may have a specific Torah prohibition in mind (e.g., Deut 23:18), while Nolland (*Matthew*, 1154) thinks the text has less to do with "guilt" than "ritual purity" (cf. 1 Chr 22:8–9).

180. Josephus (*B.J.* 2.175) calls the ἱερόν θαυσαρόν ("temple treasury") a κορβωνᾶς. Opinions differ over whether a קרבן inscription discovered near Jerusalem refers to a prison or stable or other type of room (cf. Power, "Criticism," 275–303; "Authenticity," 405; Evans, *Jesus*, 106–09; Longenecker, *Exegesis*, 133).

181. Matt 27:6. On τιμή ("price, value, payment") Aristotle (*Rhet.* 1391a) describes πλοῦτος ("wealth") as οἷον τιμή τις τῆς ἀξίας τῶν ἄλλων, ("something of a standard of value for other things"), condescendingly labeling a πλοῦτος ("wealthy man") as an ἀνοήτου εὐδαίμονος ἦθος ("fool favored by

συμβούλιον δὲ λαβόντες	So, after taking counsel together,
ἠγόρασαν ἐξ αὐτῶν τὸν ἀγρὸν τοῦ κεραμέως	They used it to buy a "potter's field"[182]
εἰς ταφὴν τοῖς ξένοις	(that is, a cemetery for foreigners).[183]
διὸ ἐκλήθη ὁ ἀγρὸς ἐκεῖνος	Thus that field today is called
ἀγρὸς αἵματος ἕως τῆς σήμερον	"Field of Blood."[184]

Not surprisingly, Matthew refracts this episode through a lens colored by an understanding of Nevi'im conditioned by his first-century environment:[185]

τότε ἐπληρώθη τὸ ῥηθὲν	Thus was fulfilled that which was spoken
διὰ Ἰερεμίου τοῦ προφήτου λέγοντος	By Jeremiah the prophet, saying,
καὶ ἔλαβον τὰ τριάκοντα ἀργύρια	"And they took thirty pieces of silver,
τὴν τιμὴν τοῦ τετιμημένου	The price which had been set,
ὃν ἐτιμήσαντο ἀπὸ υἱῶν Ἰσραήλ	Which had been set by the children of Israel,
καὶ ἔδωκαν αὐτὰ	And they put it
εἰς τὸν ἀγρὸν τοῦ κεραμέως	Into the potter's field[186]
καθὰ συνέταξέν μοι κύριος	Just as the Lord commanded me."[187]

Craig Keener focuses on one dimension of this incident; viz., "the hypocrisy of the chief priests—willing to pay out blood money for Jesus' capture, willing to allow Judas' suicide, but too pious to accept their own blood money into the temple treasury."[188] But it's more than a little ironic that the *type* of "temple treasury" accomodating this

fortune").

182. Lit. "a field of ceramics." Long (*Matthew*, 309) observes how "the picture of the religious leaders suddenly becoming ethically conscientious, not wanting to pollute the pure temple offerings . . . throws their own shameful involvement into high relief."

183. Osborne (*Matthew*, 1012) sardonically labels it "an unclean cemetery for unclean pagans purchased with unclean money."

184. Matt 27:6–8. Luke transliterates the name of the cemetery in Acts 1:19 (Ἀκελδαμάχ; i.e., חקל-דמא). Cf. above on the recurrent use of חקל ("portion") in Nevi'im.

185. Moss (*Zechariah*, 209–16) and Longenecker (*Exegesis*, 132–34) outline the contours and character of this environment. Paffenroth (*Judas*, 12) thinks that "the chief priests and elders render themselves guilty by returning the 'blood money,' not by the purchase of the field."

186. Jer 32:14 OG reads θήσεις αὐτὸ εἰς ἀγγεῖον ὀστράκινον, "put it (the deed of purchase) into a clay pot"; MT reads בכלי חרש, "in earthen vessels."

187. Matt 27:9–10. Searching for a way to depict the gravity of the situation, Matthew makes allusion to Jeremiah's purchase of his cousin's field (Jer 32:6–14—for 17 shekels, not 30; cf. above), but the clearer allusion is Zech 11:12–13, where "thirty pieces of silver is the wages of the faithful shepherd . . . who seeks to rescue Israel from worthless shepherds" (Keener, *Matthew*, 621; cf. above).

188. Keener, *Matthew*, 660; cf. Paffenroth, *Judas*, 12.

"blood money" is the very same type of *qorban* vault used to house the very same type of *qorban* gifts earlier censured by this very same prophet.[189]

Acts of the Apostles

Near the beginning of Acts of the Apostles one of the בני הנביאים ("sons of the prophets") addresses an assembly of Jews visiting Jerusalem from various parts of the Mediterranean world. The result, of course, is the birth of a fledgling movement resolutely pledged to the *ἀγάπη* ethic championed by the prophet from Nazareth:[190]

πάντες δὲ οἱ πιστεύοντες ἦσαν ἐπὶ τὸ αὐτὸ	All the believers were "together"[191]
καὶ εἶχον ἅπαντα κοινὰ	And had all things common,[192]
καὶ τὰ κτήματα καὶ τὰς ὑπάρξεις ἐπίπρασκον	Selling their goods and possessions[193]
καὶ διεμέριζον αὐτὰ πᾶσιν	And redistributing them to all
καθότι ἄν τις χρείαν εἶχεν	As any had need . . .[194]
οὐδὲ γὰρ ἐνδεής τις ἦν ἐν αὐτοῖς	No one was needy among them
ὅσοι γὰρ κτήτορες χωρίων ἢ οἰκιῶν ὑπῆρχον	For as many as owned fields or houses
πωλοῦντες	Sold them,
ἔφερον τὰς τιμὰς τῶν πιπρασκομένων	And brought the proceeds of what was sold
καὶ ἐτίθουν παρὰ τοὺς πόδας τῶν ἀποστόλων	And laid it at the apostles' feet
διεδίδετο δὲ ἑκάστῳ	Distributing it to each other

189. Matt 15:5–6 (cf. above).

190. Hays (*Wealth*, 1) recognizes that "Luke's teachings on wealth and possessions have been a bone of contention in the past half-century. Outside of the theses, articles, and monographs dedicated to Lukan ethics *in se*, historical studies on the life of Jesus examine the moral paradigm Luke transmits, biblical theology has entered the fray, theological ethicists discuss the question, and liberation theology demands that an account be given for the neglect and oppression of the poor."

191. Lit. "upon the same" (perhaps an abbreviation for "upon the same idea").

192. Gk (ἅ)*παντα κοινὰ* ("all things common") is a widely used phrase, and not just in utopian texts (cf. Davis, "*Utopia*," 37–38). Plato (*Phaed.* 110c-d), e.g., has Critias describe the Athenian military as a community in which *ἴδιον μὲν αὐτῶν οὐδεὶς οὐδὲν κεκτημένος ἅπαντα δὲ πάντων κοινὰ νομίζοντες αὐτῶν*, "no one acquires anything for themselves, but regard all that they have as common to all."

193. In the Letter to the Hebrews a Hellenized writer uses the term *ὕπαρξις* ("possession") to commend his audience for *τὴν ἁρπαγὴν τῶν ὑπαρχόντων ὑμῶν μετὰ χαρᾶς προσεδέξασθε γινώσκοντες ἔχειν ἑαυτοὺς κρείττονα ὕπαρξιν καὶ μένουσαν*, "cheerfully enduring the seizure of your 'possessions,' knowing that you have a greater and more abiding one" (Heb 10:34).

194. Acts 2:44–45. N.B. the verbatim repetition of this line in 4:32 (cf. below).

καθότι ἄν τις χρείαν εἶχεν	As any had need.[195]

The community depicted in this text is not the only "community-of-goods" in the ancient Mediterranean world.[196] Whether or not it embodies a "communist" worldview is an anachronistic question often raised by (post)modern readers.[197] Accommodating such terminology for the sake of argument, it's not insignificant that only a few chapters later Acts contrasts two *types* of would-be "communists."[198] One, a believer named Joseph (renamed Barnabas),[199] wholly epitomizes the Nazarene ἀγάπη ethic:

ὑπάρχοντος αὐτῷ ἀγροῦ πωλήσας	He sold a field he possessed,
ἤνεγκεν τὸ χρῆμα	He brought the money,
καὶ ἔθηκεν πρὸς τοὺς πόδας τῶν ἀποστόλων	And laid it at the apostles' feet.[200]

The other, however, epitomizes something else entirely:

ἀνὴρ δέ τις Ἁνανίας ὀνόματι	Now a man named Ananias,[201]
σὺν Σαπφίρῃ τῇ γυναικὶ αὐτου	With Sapphira his wife,

195. Acts 4:34–35. N.B. the verbatim repetition of this line in 2:45 (just cited above). Gushee and Stassen (*Kingdom*, 376) argue that the "fundamental mandate" of Christian ethics is "just distribution."

196. Cf. McCabe, *Words*, 57, 91–97. Capper ("Community," 323–56) recognizes similar "communities-of-goods" in the Pythagorean (cf. Euripides, *Orest.* 735; Aristotle, *Eth. nic.* 1159b20; cf. Zhmud, *Pythagoras*, 149–50) and Qumranian communities (1QS 6.21–25; CD 14.20–21).

197. Sandle (*Communism*, 7) argues that the "most significant thing to note" in Acts 2–6 "is that the elements which approximate most closely to communism in its 'modern' form—collective property, egalitarianism, social justice, co-operation, absence of hierarchy—are pursued . . . not as ends in themselves, but because they are seen as a means to a higher goal. Whereas the communist movements of the nineteenth century CE seek to abolish the existing capitalist system and replace it *in toto* with something morally, economically, politically and socially superior, these 'early' movements seek instead to escape from the existing society. They dream of creating 'colonies of heaven' on earth." Cf. Dawson, *Communist*, 258–63; Mönning, "Kommunismus," 175–81; and Schottroff and Stegemann, "Sozialutopie," 149–53.

198. Contemporary interpreters tend to avoid the term "communist" when describing the early Christian community, pointing out (a) that the selling of property is voluntary (not mandatory), and (b) that it ultimately fails when the Hellenistic widows are discriminated against, thereby leading to (c) Paul's collection for poor believers. On the first of these points Murphy (*Wealth*, 8–9) suggests that distinctions between Acts and 1QS/CD regarding the specifics of this mandatory-vs.-voluntary polarity "may in the end have more to do with the genres of our documents than with a difference in practice" (cf. Marshall, *Acts*, 84; Bruce, *Acts*, 131; Williams, *Acts*, 71; Klauck, "Antiken," 47–79; Finger, "Economic," 12–47).

199. "Barnabas" (בר־נביא) is an Aramaic PN meaning "son of the prophet." He is associated with "encouragement" because both Acts 4:36 and 1 Cor 14:3 associate "encouragement" with "prophecy."

200. Acts 4:37. Capper ("Community," 325), contends that "Luke presents the early Christians in Jerusalem in the dress of Greek thinking about ideal political organization, or a state of detachment from possessions realized by the ideally pious."

201. Gk Ἁνανίας (Heb חנניה, "Ḥananiah") is (a) the name of the prophet who attacks Jeremiah (Jer 28:1); (b) one of the pseudonyms of the angel Raphael (Tob 5:13); and (c) the name of the Damascus resident chosen to shelter the blinded Saul of Tarsus.

ἐπώλησεν κτῆμα	Sold a possession,[202]
καὶ ἐνοσφίσατο ἀπὸ τῆς τιμῆς	And held back some of the money
συνειδυίης καὶ τῆς γυναικός	(his wife being aware of it),[203]
καὶ ἐνέγκας μέρος τι	And brought a portion of it,
παρὰ τοὺς πόδας τῶν ἀποστόλων ἔθηκεν	And laid it at the apostles' feet.[204]

Cognizant of this duplicity,[205] Peter puts to Ananias a penetrating question:

διὰ τί ἐπλήρωσεν ὁ σατανᾶς τὴν καρδίαν σου	"Why has Satan filled your heart
ψεύσασθαί σε τὸ πνεῦμα τὸ ἅγιον	To lie to the Holy Spirit[206]
καὶ νοσφίσασθαι ἀπὸ τῆς τιμῆς τοῦ χωρίου	And hold back[207] from the proceeds of the field?
οὐχὶ μένον σοὶ ἔμενεν	While unsold, did it not remain yours, and
καὶ πραθὲν ἐν τῇ σῇ ἐξουσίᾳ ὑπῆρχεν	After the sale, were the profits not yours?"[208]

The fact that the apostolic response to Ananias' duplicity is swift and lethal troubles postmodern readers,[209] yet this is not an atypical response because, as historian David

202. Acts 5:1. According to 5:3, this κτῆμα is a χωρίον ("field").

203. Cf. Hannah's fear that the sight of money might tempt her son into doing something inappropriate (Tob 5:18–20). Ascertaining whether a spouse "collaborates" or is simply "aware" in cases involving corruption is notoriously difficult to ascertain (cf. the infamous Jeff Gillooly/Tonya Harding case discussed by Foote, "Tonya," 3–17).

204. Acts 5:1–2. Johnson (*Possessions*, 170–71, 233) believes (a) that "although Luke consistently talks about possessions, he does not talk about possessions consistently," and (b) that the Ananias and Sapphira incident demonstrates how an individual's use of wealth corresponds directly to that individual's attitude toward the ἀγάπη-ethic.

205. Baker (*Identity*, 98) reasons that "the audience knows about the deception, (but) they are not told how Peter acquires this knowledge. They must fill in this gap by remembering that Jesus is able to know the inner thoughts of others, and conclude that Peter is also granted this prophetic ability."

206. Reading this scene against other "stock scenes of divine judgment for the crime of perjury in Luke's Graeco-Roman culture," Harrill ("Ananias," 369) contends that Luke includes this episode to "encourage the audience to have confidence that 'the church' (ἡ ἐκκλησία) is blameless of 'impiety' (ἀσέβεια) and that promises about its deity are true."

207. Gk νοσφίζω can mean "to steal" (2 Macc 4:32; Josephus, *AJ* 4.274), but in a revealing parallel Polybius (*Hist.* 10.16.6) shows Roman legionnaires distributing the spoils of war so that everyone (active soldiers, reservists, and the wounded) receives an equal share; i.e., so that τοῦ μηδένα νοςφίζεσθαι ("no one is excluded") . . . κατὰ τὸν ὅρκον ὃν ὀμνοῦσι πάντες ὅταν ἀθροισθῶσι πρῶτον εἰς τὴν παρεμβολήν ("according to the oath which all swear when first mustered into camp"). Ananias and Sapphira, in other words, engage in corruption unacceptable even to Roman legionnaires.

208. Acts 5:3–4a (lit. "in your power"). In sociological terms, "Did you not still have the 'right to disconnect?'" (Bruhn, *Community*, 23).

209. E.g., Marguerat, *Historian*, 155; Taylor, "Community," 156; Strelan, *Acts*, 199. Lüdemann (*Acts*, 81) doubts "whether in the actual case the malefactor died," but admits that "according to sacred law he should have."

McCabe points out, "the *topos* of a representation of a community-of-goods would condition a Mediterranean auditor of Acts to expect . . . severe disciplinary action."[210] The Nazarenes, in other words, are not the only "community-of-goods" who discipline "miscreants who transgress the communal ethos of trust."[211] If the ANE "great texts" affirm anything, it is that *genuine* community is impossible to achieve apart from rigorously enforced boundaries.[212]

Soon afterwards this fledgling community faces yet another socioeconomic crisis,[213] this one generated by deep prejudices:[214]

Ἐν δὲ ταῖς ἡμέραις ταύταις	Now in those days,
πληθυνόντων τῶν μαθητῶν	As the disciples were multiplying,
ἐγένετο γογγυσμὸς τῶν Ἑλληνιστῶν	The Hellenists began murmuring[215]
πρὸς τοὺς Ἑβραίους	Against the Hebrews[216]
ὅτι παρεθεωροῦντο ἐν τῇ διακονίᾳ	Because their widows[217] were being ignored[218]
τῇ καθημερινῇ αἱ χῆραι αὐτῶν	In the daily distribution.[219]

210. McCabe, *Words*, 56.

211. McCabe, *Words*, 57, 91–97; cf. Moore, "Civic," 152–54. Harrill ("Ananias," 352–53) is quick to emphasize the multidimensional character of this text.

212. N.B. the boundary-guardians Humbaba (GE 2.221–29) and Neti (ID 77). Sociologist John Bruhn (*Community*, 56) insists that "social cohesion" is impossible to maintain outside "the boundaries of the group."

213. Tyson ("Christianity," 148) observes that "Acts consists of a series of threats; over and over the peace of the church is threatened."

214. According to ethnolinguistic identity theory (Gudykunst *et al.*, *Culture*, 20–25), divergence in communication occurs when (a) individuals view language as important to group membership; (b) individuals view boundaries between groups as hard and closed; and (c) individuals focus predominantly on group vitality.

215. Gk γογγύζω is the preferred OG translation of לון ("to grumble, murmur, complain") in the Torah wilderness tradition (Exod 16:7; Num 14:27, 36; Josh 9:18).

216. Baur's (*Christenthum*, 1–7, 42–46) attempt to polarize Christianity into Petrine (Hebraic) vs. Pauline (Hellenistic) factions no longer holds sway, but as Barrett (*Acts*, 308–9) points out, the term Ἑλληνιστής ("Hellenist") still denotes a specific *linguistic* category, and *does* document within the Church a deep cultural divide (cf. Lucian, *Philops.* 16; Dio Cassius, *Hist.* 55.3.5; Holladay, *Acts*, 151–53).

217. Thurston (*Widows*, 14–15) recognizes that "Jesus of Nazareth has an unprecedented attitude toward women and the plight of widows" and that "the legal status of women improves dramatically as the Roman Empire carries forward the liberating trends of Hellenistic Greece."

218. Gk παρεθεωρέω basically means "to examine, compare" and in some cases "to compare negatively" (i.e., "to ignore/overlook/neglect"). Dionysius of Halicarnassus (*Is.* 18), in a comparison of the orators Lysias and Isaeus, cautions students not to "ignore" (παραθεωροίη) stylistic differences.

219. Acts 6:1 (lit. "daily service"). The Nazarenes are not the only community-of-goods committed to helping the poor. Cf. the קופה ("community chest") and תמחוי ("soup kitchen") at Qumran (1QS 6.1–6) and elsewhere (*m. Pe'ah* 8.7; *t. Pe'ah* 4.9; cf. Hays, *Wealth*, 42).

Bonnie Thurston thinks that widows are (a) one of the most visible, active groups in the early church,[220] and (b) an "order" alongside other "orders" (bishops, presbyters, deacons, evangelists, pastors, teachers, missionaries).[221] The text often cited to prove the existence of this "order" is 1 Tim 5:3–6,[222] but as Rea McDonnell observes, many interpreters tend too quickly to read into it "Tertullian's use of *ordo*."[223] That being said, it is not insignificant that one of the earliest memories of Christian widows focuses on (a) the misappropriation of resources set aside to meet their socioeconomic needs,[224] followed by (b) the establishment of a program designed to prevent its recurrence.[225]

The longest speech in Acts comes from a young man named Stephen, one of "the Seven" appointed to resolve the aforementioned "widows problem."[226] In it he spotlights two important milestones of Hebrew history: (a) God's promise to give land to Abraham's "seed" as a κατάσχεσις ("possession");[227] and (b) the impact of "slavery" (δουλεία) on those Hebrews forced to live in Egypt as "resident aliens" (πάροικοι).[228] Elaborating the first milestone, Stephen illuminates the socioeconomic implications of God's promise to Abraham:

οὐκ ἔδωκεν αὐτῷ κληρονομίαν ἐν αὐτῇ	He did not give him an inheritance on it;[229]
οὐδὲ βῆμα ποδὸς	Not one square foot.
καὶ ἐπηγγείλατο δοῦναι αὐτῷ	But he promised[230] to give it to him
εἰς κατάσχεσιν αὐτὴν	For a possession,[231]

220. Thurston, *Widows*, 113–16.

221. Thurston, *Widows*, 7–8. Cf. Ignatius, *Smyrn.* 18.1; *Pol.* 4.1; Polycarp, *Phil.* 4.3.

222. Winter ("Widows," 83) attempts to read this text in light of "the legal stipulations and social conventions surrounding widows and their support in the Graeco-Roman world."

223. McDonnell, *Widows*, 328. Cf. Tertullian, *Virg.* 9; *Monog.* 11; *Mod.* 13. Bassler ("Widows," 41) doubts the existence of any "widows order."

224. N.B. the striking socioeconomic parallels between Acts 6:1–4 and Neh 5:1–5.

225. Thurston (*Widows*, 116) argues that the visibility of widows over time decreases in direct proportion to the embarrassment they bring to the male church hierarchy. Of the seven men chosen to deal with the socioeconomic problem in Jerusalem, however, it's important to note that all have Greek names (Acts 6:5; cf. Holladay, *Acts*, 154–55).

226. Acts 21:8 (cf. Parsons, "Seven," 108).

227. Acts 7:5. Sirach parallels κατάσχεσις ("possession") with κληρονομία ("inheritance," Sir 4:16).

228. Acts 7:6 (cf. Soards, *Speeches*, 59–70). Kilgallen (*Stephen*, 24–26) sees previous scholarship on Stephen's speech focusing on the theme of "God's Gifts, Israel's Ingratitude."

229. OG κληρονομία is the term most often used to translate נחלה ("inheritance"; cf. Lipiński, "נחל," 319–35). Gk ἐν αὐτῇ ("on it," 7:5) refers to τὴν γῆν ταύτην εἰς ἣν ὑμεῖς νῦν κατοικεῖτε, "the land upon which you now live" (7:4; cf. Heb 11:8).

230. Westermann (*Promises*, 162–63) observes that the promises in Genesis "attest to the oldest association we can discover between what a deity says (*promise*) and what he does (*fulfillment*)."

231. Gk κατάσχεσις (cf. Acts 7:45) is the most prominent OG translation of אחזה (Gen 17:8; Lev 25:25; Num 27:4), a term defined by Levine (*Numbers*, 346) as "land acquired through grant or purchase" which when "incorporated with the territory of the clan" becomes "an inheritance."

καὶ τῷ σπέρματι αὐτοῦ μετ᾽ αὐτόν	And to his seed[232] after him,
οὐκ ὄντος αὐτῷ τέκνου	Even though he was childless.[233]

Explaining the import of this second milestone he argues that

ἐλάλησεν δὲ οὕτως ὁ θεὸς	God likewise said that
ἔσται τὸ σπέρμα αὐτοῦ πάροικον	His seed would become a resident alien[234]
ἐν γῇ ἀλλοτρίᾳ	In another land, and
καὶ δουλώσουσιν αὐτὸ καὶ κακώσουσιν	Would be enslaved and mistreated
ἔτη τετρακόσια	Four hundred years.[235]

Reflecting on these promises, he then appears to misquote Torah:

καὶ τὸ ἔθνος ᾧ ἐὰν δουλεύσουσιν	"But the nation which they serve
κρινῶ ἐγώ, ὁ θεὸς εἶπεν	I will judge," says God,
καὶ μετὰ ταῦτα ἐξελεύσονται	"And after these things they will go out and
καὶ λατρεύσουσίν μοι ἐν τῷ τόπῳ τούτῳ	Worship me in this place."[236]

The text of Acts 7:7 appears to cite Gen 15:14b, but MT reads יצאו ברכש גדול ("they will go out with many possessions"), a reading supported by the major versions (OG, Syr, and Vg).[237] So, why does the text of Acts differ? Richard Coggins suggests that the discrepancy arises because Stephen cites not from MT or OG, but from the Samaritan Pentateuch, even though Sam *agrees* with MT and the versions *against* GNT.[238] Tracing the appearance of λατρεύω ("to worship") to OG Exod 3:15, F. F. Bruce suggests that Acts 7:7 might be the product of a narrative strategy designed to "telescope

232. Stephen uses an agrarian term, σπέρμα ("seed"; the usual OG translation of זרע), as a traditional metaphor for "descendants" because, as Preuss ("זרע," 161) emphasizes, "the patriarch lives on in his descendants."

233. Acts 7:5. In another Acts speech Peter posits that God καθελὼν ἔθνη ἑπτὰ ἐν γῇ Χανάαν κατεκληρονόμησεν τὴν γῆν αὐτῶν, "took down seven nations in Canaan and gave over their land as an inheritance" (Acts 13:19).

234. Later in the speech Stephen remembers Moses as a πάροικος ("resident alien") in the "land of Midian" (Acts 7:29). The closest equivalents to this Gk word are Heb גר (Exod 12:48; Ezek 22:7); Eg *retenu* (*ANET* 20–21); Akk *ḫupšu* (*EA* 117:90; 118:23; 125:27); and Gk λῃστής (Xenophon, *Cyr.* 2:4:23; Luke 10:30; cf. Moore, *WealthWatch*, 124). In Gen 46:34 the Egyptians assign the task of shepherding to the Hebrews because they find it a "detestable" profession (תועבה, *HAL* 1568–70).

235. Acts 7:6. GNT changes the m. pl. nouns in Gen 15:13 OG into n. sg. nouns (to match the n. sg. τὸ σπέρμα, "seed, offspring").

236. Acts 7:7.

237. OG ἐξελεύσονται ὧδε μετὰ ἀποσκευῆς πολλῆς ("thus they shall go out with much spoil"); Vg *egredientur cum magna substanti* ("they shall go out with great substance"); and Syr ܢܦܩܘܢ ܒܩܢܝܢܐ ܪܒܐ ("they shall go out with many possessions").

238. Coggins ("Samaritans," 423–34; cf. von Gall, *Pentateuch*, *ad loc*).

distinct quotations."[239] John Kilgallen curiously suggests that the discrepancy has to do with Stephen's obvious "desire to explain why the people are going free."[240] Against these proposals, however, it seems more likely that Luke's intention, like that of Josephus and Philo, is to avoid any historicizing which portrays the Hebrews as socially, politically, and/or economically independent.[241] Thus he simply changes the subject of Gen 15:14b to avoid offending readers accustomed to thinking of Hebrews as vulnerable dependants unable to take care of themselves.[242]

At any rate, Stephen's execution triggers an exodus of Nazarenes out of Jerusalem,[243] and those winding up in Samaria encounter a *μαγεύων* ("magician") named Simon who, like other magicians of this period,[244] makes a career out of *ἐξιστάνων τὸ ἔθνος* ("amazing the nation").[245] What makes this episode socioeconomically significant, however, is the not-so-subtle way Luke uses it to expose, like Ezekiel in his blistering critique of Tyre,[246] the self-indulgent spirit often associated with intemperate mercantilists:[247]

Ἰδὼν δὲ ὁ Σίμων ὅτι	Now when Simon saw that
διὰ τῆς ἐπιθέσεως τῶν χειρῶν τῶν ἀποστόλων	Through the laying on of the apostles' hands
δίδοται τὸ πνεῦμα	The Spirit was given,

239. Bruce (*Acts*, 194). In support of this theory, N.B. that Acts 7:16 telescopes information from Gen 23:2–20; 33:19; 49:29–30; 50:7–13; and Josh 24:32.

240. Kilgallen (*Stephen*, 38).

241. Philo (*Praem.* 24), e.g., paints the patriarchs as religious puritans altogether uninterested in "glory, wealth, and pleasure" (cf. Seland, *Philo*, 136–60), and Josephus (*A.J.* 4.280) interprets Exod 22:17 from a Roman legal perspective (*lex talionis*; cf. Jackson, "Law," 354).

242. Billings (*Acts*, 14) recognizes that Acts is "written in concert with broader representational trends and standards found in provincial representations and imperial monuments dating to the first two decades of the second century, and in a way reflects the dynamic exchange that produces an innovative narrative that hybridizes local and imperial forms."

243. Acts 8:1. Sterling (*Historiography*, 348) thinks that Acts from this point on seeks "to show how the church moves away from a strictly Jewish setting towards a universal stance."

244. Claiming that Empedocles, Democritus and even Pythagoras *ὁμιλήσαντες μάγοις* ("consort with magicians"), Philostratus of Athens (*Vit. Apoll.* 1.2) writes a treatise designed to "rehabilitate the reputation of Apollonius, and defend him from the charge of being a wizard addicted to evil magical practices" (Conybeare, *Apollonius*, viii).

245. Acts 8:9. Ancient documents refer constantly to magic and magicians, and Acts is no exception: Simon in Samaria (Acts 8:9); Elymas in Cyprus (13:8); and *Ἰουδαίων ἐξορκιστῶν* ("Jewish exorcists") in Ephesus (19:13–14). Whether such activity is "real" or not is disputed (cf. Klauck, *Magic*, 13–30), but Tuzlak ("Magician," 425; following Aune, "Sorcery," 17–45), defines "magic" in sociological terms; i.e., "an action is not 'magical' unless it is placed outside of the realm of the acceptable in the minds of the dominant religious group."

246. Cf. Joyce, *Ezekiel*, 176–77; Pohlmann, *Ezechiel*, 381–91; Saur, *Tyroszyklus*, 197–237; and Sedlmeier, *Ezechiel*, 34.

247. Cf. Aubet, "Polanyi," 17–39; Downs, "Economics," 156–62.

προσήνεγκεν αὐτοῖς χρήματα λέγων	He offered them money,[248] saying,
δότε κἀμοὶ τὴν ἐξουσίαν ταύτην	"Give me this power
ἵνα ᾧ ἐὰν ἐπιθῶ τὰς χεῖρας	So that anyone upon whom I lay *my* hands
λαμβάνῃ πνεῦμα ἅγιον	May receive the Holy Spirit."[249]

Whatever his motives, Peter's response, like that extended to Ananias and Sapphira, is quintessenitally "prophetic":

τὸ ἀργύριόν σου σὺν σοὶ εἴη εἰς ἀπώλειαν	"Let your money plunge with you into perdition[250]
ὅτι τὴν δωρεὰν τοῦ θεοῦ	Because the gift of God
ἐνόμισας διὰ χρημάτων κτᾶσθαι	You think you can acquire through money![251]
οὐκ ἔστιν σοι μερὶς οὐδὲ κλῆρος	You have no part or share[252]
ἐν τῷ λόγῳ τούτω	In this matter,[253]
ἡ γὰρ καρδία σου οὐκ ἔστιν εὐθεῖα	For your heart is not right
ἔναντι τοῦ θεοῦ	Before God."[254]

In short, Acts portrays Simon Magus as a "Balaam 2.0,"[255] a charlatan/celebrity who,[256] in the words of Stephen Haar, "imagines that the apostles will dispense some benefit" to him, but only after receiving an "appropriate donation."[257]

248. Derrett ("Simon," 55) finds it "gratuitous to impute to him the intention to use such a gift for his own exclusive profit," but Klauck (*Magic*, 22) contends that Simon refuses to recognize that "the Spirit is God's free gift and . . . not . . . an object of commercial transaction."

249. Acts 8:18–19. Klauck (*Magic*, 20–21) contends that "a shrill disharmony is introduced with this offer of cash," so that "if one bears in mind Luke's well-known sensitivity in matters of money and possessions, one perceives that this step on Simon's part will end badly."

250. For ἀπώλεια as "perdition," cf. 2 Thes 2:3. O'Toole ("Lie," 202) views the punishment meted out here as procedurally (if not essentially) parallel to that meted out against Ananias and Sapphira.

251. Cf. the much different response of the Ethiopian δυνάστης ("court official") in charge of Queen Candace's γάζα ("treasury," Acts 8:27).

252. Simon loses his κλῆρος ("allotment/share," Aristotle, *Ath. pol.* 9.2) just as quickly as Matthias gains his (Acts 1:26).

253. The elderly Plato (*Laws* 10.909b) proposes harsh punishments for those charlatan magicians who "'for the sake of money' (χρημάτων χάριν), make every effort to ruin individuals, whole families, and cities."

254. Acts 8:20–21. Satirizing the outrageous claims of magicians, Lucian (*Asin.* 11) tells the story of a man who (a) watches a magician rub "magic oil" on her body and turn into an owl, then (b) copies her behavior by rubbing oil on his body . . . and turning into a donkey (cf. Haar, *Simon*, 132–227).

255. Cf. Moore, *Balaam*, 110–22.

256. Derrett ("Simon," 53) views Simon as "a peripatetic practitioner in the occult, not necessarily a charlatan."

257. Haar, *Simon*, 186. Park (*Ḥerem*, 141) points out several connections between this text and

Traveling through southern Anatolia, Paul and Barnabas heal a congenitally lame man in Lycaonia,[258] thereby triggering a violent reaction from a populace shaped by the religious presumptions endemic to this part of the world.[259] Imagining Barnabas and Paul as avatars of Zeus and Hermes,[260] one Lycaonian priest even starts offering sacrifice to them,[261] provoking Paul to exclaim,

ἄνδρες, τί ταῦτα ποιεῖτε	"Men, why are you doing these things?
καὶ ἡμεῖς ὁμοιοπαθεῖς ἐσμεν ὑμῖν ἄνθρωποι	We are human beings like you,
εὐαγγελιζόμενοι ὑμᾶς	Evangelizing you[262]
ἀπὸ τούτων τῶν ματαίων ἐπιστρέφειν	To turn away from these futile things[263]
ἐπὶ θεὸν ζῶντα	To a living God[264]
ὃς ἐποίησεν τὸν οὐρανὸν καὶ τὴν γῆν	Who made the heaven and the earth
καὶ τὴν θάλασσαν καὶ πάντα τὰ ἐν αὐτοῖς	And the sea and everything in them . . .[265]
οὐρανόθεν ὑμῖν ὑετοὺς διδοὺς	Giving you rain from the heavens[266]
καὶ καιροὺς καρποφόρους	And seasons of fruit-bearing,[267]

several Nevi'im texts, and Ferreiro (*Simon*, 56) shows how some post-apostolic believers view Simon as "the chief Gnostic and founder of many such sects."

258. Bruce, "Lycaonia," 420–22.

259. Cf. Cumont, *Religions*, 46–72.

260. Like Paul, Lucian (*Astr.* 27) finds it "futile" (ματαίος) to imagine τὸν Ἄρεα ἢ τὸν Δία ἐν τῷ ἡμέων ἕνεκα κινέεσθαι, "Ares or Zeus moving around in heaven for our sake."

261. Ovid (*Metam.* 8.611–725) tells a tale of the deities Jupiter and Mercury disguising themselves as human beings to visit the home of a mortal couple named Baucis and Philemon in Phrygia. Swoboda (*Denkmäler*, 146) publishes epigraphic evidence establishing these deities as a team operating in southern Anatolia. Cf. Moore ("Sacrifice," 533).

262. Transliterating this Gk participle seems appropriate in light of its twenty-first-century semantic dynamics.

263. OG uses ματαίος ("futile, vain, worthless") to translate a variety of Heb terms; e.g., שׂעירים ("goat-demons," Lev 17:7); חטאות ("sins," 1 Kgs 16:2); הבלים ("puffs of vapor/smoke," 16:13). Barrett (*Acts*, 680) contends that "in non-biblical Greek ματαίος does not have the sense of 'false god,' but is used of empty talk and of vain and foolish persons."

264. Opposition to belief in a θεός ζῶν ("living God") comes not just from μάταιος ("futile thinking"), but also from καρδία πονηρὰ ἀπιστία, ("an evil, unbelieving heart," Heb 3:12; Moore, "Heart," 428–29).

265. Acts 14:15. Greenwood (*Cosmology*, 131–32) reminds readers that cosmological thinking before 1543 CE—the year Nicolaus Copernicus publishes *De Revolutionibus*—champions a "three-tiered model of heaven, earth, and sea."

266. Margalit (*Aqht*, 259) shows that reverence for "the Rainmaker" is deeply rooted (Ug *hrnmy*, *CAT* 1.17.1.19).

267. Paul often uses καρποφόρος ("fruit-bearing") metaphorically (e.g., Rom 7:4; Col 1:6), but his intention here is not so much to champion "natural revelation" (*pace* Gärtner, *Revelation*, 250) as to challenge Lycaonian notions of *fertility* and *prosperity*.

ἐμπιπλῶν τροφῆς	Filling you with food[268]
καὶ εὐφροσύνης τὰς καρδίας ὑμῶν	And gladness in your hearts.[269]

In Philippi Paul and his entourage come across a young woman exploited by mercantilistic entrepreneurs posing as her "masters" (κύριοι):

πορευομένων ἡμῶν εἰς τὴν προσευχὴν	While we were walking to a prayer meeting
παιδίσκην τινὰ ἔχουσαν πνεῦμα πύθωνα	A young woman with a python-spirit[270]
ὑπαντῆσαι ἡμῖν	Accosted us.[271]
ἥτις ἐργασίαν πολλὴν παρεῖχεν	She supplied much business[272]
τοῖς κυρίοις αὐτῆς μαντευομένη	To her masters as a diviner . . .[273]
ἔκραζεν λέγουσα	She cried out, saying,
οὗτοι οἱ ἄνθρωποι δοῦλοι	"These men, servants
τοῦ θεοῦ τοῦ ὑψίστου εἰσίν	Of the Most High God,
οἵτινες καταγγέλλουσιν ὑμῖν ὁδὸν σωτηρίας	Are proclaiming to you the way of salvation."[274]

Lucian of Samosota describes a similar scene in a village east of Philippi where a γόης ("sorcerer") named Alexander[275] (a) hides a small snake in a hollowed-out goose egg,

268. Yesh`ua redirects the thinking of his audience about food (Matt 6:25), esp. when emphasizing that workers deserve their food (10:10), arguing that ἡ γὰρ ψυχὴ πλεῖόν ἐστιν τῆς τροφῆς, "the soul is more than food" (Luke 12:23).

269. Acts 14:17.

270. The myth of Apollo's triumph over the πύθων ("serpent, snake"; Euripides, *Iph. Taur.* 1245, and Lucian, *Astr.* 23, read δράκων, "dragon") at Delphi, Didymus and elsewhere (van Henten, "Python," 670) echoes Marduk's triumph over Tiamat (*Ee* 4.93–106), Raphael's victory over Asmodeus (Tob 3:17), Michael's defeat of the great red dragon (Rev 12:7–9) and subsequent "dragon-tales" (cf. Ogden, *Drakōn*, 1–25).

271. Like פקד ("to visit," Judg 15:1; "to judge," Isa 26:14), ὑπαντάω can have positive or negative connotations.

272. Demosthenes (*Phor.* 36.6) uses this word in the idiomatic expression ἐργασία τῆς τραπέζης, "business of the bank" (lit. "work of the table").

273. Acts 16:16. Dillon (*Omens*, 89–90) recognizes that "apart from a few famous diviners who play an important role in significant political and military events, financial reward of a substantive nature would be an outcome for only a handful of μάντεις ("diviners"), usually in times of military crisis . . . As such, they do not therefore constitute an economic or 'upper-class' elite, though some high-profile μάντεις are doubtless well-rewarded." That the Philippian authorities so quickly respond to the complaints of these particular κύριοι ("masters") doubtless indicates their relative degree of influence.

274. Acts 16:17 (σωτηρία). Acts uses this term to foreshadow the question of the Philippian jailor who asks what he must do to be "saved" (σῴζω, 16:30). Whether these characters fully understand what the word means is neither clear nor relevant.

275. Lucian, *Alex.* 1. The town is Abonotichos, a Paphlagonian village on the southern shore of the Black Sea.

(b) buries it in a ditch beneath the temple of Apollo/Asclepius,[276] (c) "congratulates" a marketplace crowd "on receiving the god soon to appear among them,"[277] (d) "miraculously" unearths the previously buried goose egg, (e) takes out the snake inside, and (f) proclaims it as an epiphany of the god Asclepius.[278] Such is the fearful, gullible, predatory world of the first century CE, so that when Paul and Silas eliminate the revenue stream of these Philippians,[279] the response is predictable:

Ἰδόντες δὲ οἱ κύριοι αὐτῆς	When her masters saw
ὅτι ἐξῆλθεν ἡ ἐλπὶς τῆς ἐργασίας αὐτῶν	That the hope of their business was gone[280]
ἐπιλαβόμενοι τὸν Παῦλον καὶ τὸν Σιλᾶν	They seized Paul and Silas
εἵλκυσαν εἰς τὴν ἀγορὰν	And dragged them into the marketplace
ἐπὶ τοὺς ἄρχοντας	Before the authorities.[281]

This is not the only challenge to the Mediterranean "divination business,"[282] of course, but the reaction documented in Philippi practically pales in comparison to the one in Ephesus. That is, where the Philippian κύριοι ("masters") lose the services of a single diviner, the Ephesians experience a much greater loss:

ἱκανοὶ δὲ τῶν τὰ περίεργα πραξάντων	Several of those who practiced magic[283]
συνενέγκαντες τὰς βίβλους	Gathered up their books[284]

276. Lucian (*Alex.* 12–14) associates both deities with the same temple complex.

277. ἐμακάριζεν αὐτίκα μάλα δεξομένην ἐναργῆ τὸν θεόν (Lucian, *Alex.* 13). N.B. that this root (μακάριος, "blessed"), appears nine times in Matt 5 (the Beatitudes).

278. Lucian, *Alex.* 13–14. Asclepius, like Apollo, is often symbolized by a snake (Robinson, "Asclepius," 475–76), and Alexander the γόης claims to be descended from this "god of healing" (Lucian, *Alex.* 11, 14, 18, 35, 39–40).

279. Barrett (*Acts*, 788) believes "the incident is clearly regarded by Luke as an exorcism (cf. Luke 4:35)."

280. Lucian (*Astr.* 23) observes that μάντεις ("diviners") stand in great demand because the ancients "found no cities, invest themselves with no ramparts, slay no men, and wed no women until they are advised in all particulars by diviners."

281. Acts 16:17–19. Plutarch (*Def. orac.* 441e) complains about the Delphic oracle's general decline, which Klauck (*Magic*, 66–67) believes to be "due to the cheap offers available everywhere, with scaled-down Pythia and organizers who are . . . not much more than itinerant mountebanks."

282. Lucian's (*Alex.* 1–14) attacks are particularly relentless.

283. Acts 19:19. N.B. that the word here is περίεργός (not μαγκή or μαντεία), denoting "superstitious things," a category considerably larger than "magic" *per se*. Plutarch (*Alex.* 2) uses the term to describe Alexander the Great's mother Olympias, who (according to tradition) regularly engages in what he condescendingly calls περιεργοῖς ἱερουργίαις ("superstitious rites"; cf. below on Acts 19:25).

284. The exact nature of these βίβλοι ("scrolls, books") is difficult to identify, but Faraone ("Agonistic," 3–4) notes that "nearly six hundred Greek *defixiones* have been published to date and more than four hundred others have been unearthed and are awaiting study"—defining *defixiones* (Gk κατάδεσμοι) as "binding spells . . . usually inscribed on small sheets of lead, which are folded up, pierced with a bronze or iron nail, and then buried with the corpse of one of the 'untimely dead' (ἄωρον) or placed in a chthonic sanctuary."

κατέκαιον ἐνώπιον πάντων	And burned them publicly.[285]
καὶ συνεψήφισαν τὰς τιμὰς αὐτῶν	Calculating their value,[286]
καὶ εὗρον ἀργυρίου μυριάδας πέντε	It came to 50,000 pieces of silver.[287]

The Ephesians, moreover, mount a more organized defense:

Δημήτριος γάρ τις ὀνόματι	Now a man named Demetrius,
ἀργυροκόπος	A silversmith
ποιῶν ναοὺς ἀργυροῦς Ἀρτέμιδος	Who made silver shrines of Artemis,[288]
παρείχετο τοῖς τεχνίταις	Brought to the artisan-technicians[289]
οὐκ ὀλίγην ἐργασίαν	No little business.[290]
οὓς συναθροίσας καὶ	Gathering them together
τοὺς περὶ τὰ τοιαῦτα ἐργάτας εἶπεν	With other business associates,[291] he said,
ἄνδρες, ἐπίστασθε ὅτι ἐκ ταύτης τῆς ἐργασίας	"Men, you know that from this business
ἡ εὐπορία ἡμῖν ἐστιν	Comes our livelihood."[292]

Astute enough to recognize the practical advantages of including the "religious argument" in his "chamber of commerce" report, Demetrius continues:

οὐ μόνον δὲ τοῦτο κινδυνεύει ἡμῖν τὸ μέρος	"Not only is there danger that our entitlement[293]

285. That this burning occurs ἐνώπιον πάντων (lit. "before all") is not insignificant because "black magic" by definition occurs in secret, away from public view (cf. Versnel, "Cursing," 69).

286. The root of συνεψηφίζω is ψῆφος ("a small round worn stone," like that found on an abacus). That Luke feels a need to "calculate their value" is itself socioeconomically significant.

287. Acts 19:19. Christian missionaries are not the only group critical of Mediterranean diviners and magicians. Pliny (*Nat.* 28.4.19) complains that "there is no one who does not fear to be bound by curse-tablets," while Seneca (*Ben.* 6.35.4) condemns anyone who "calls down terrible curses upon those who ought instead to be held sacred."

288. Mussies ("Artemis," 91) recognizes this deity to be "the Greek virgin goddess originally of hunting and fertility."

289. English "technician" is a transliteration of this Gk word, τεχνίτης.

290. Of its six occurrences in GNT, ἐργασία occurs five times in Luke-Acts (Luke 12:58; Acts 16:16, 19; 19:24, 25).

291. Gk ἐργάτης ("worker") and ἐργασία ("business") come from the same root (ἔργον) which, according to Bertram ("ἔργον," 635), "denotes action or active zeal in contrast to 'idleness' (ἀεργία), or useful activity in contrast to useless busy-ness" (περίεργός; cf. Acts 19:19 above).

292. Acts 19:24–25. Failing to pay the Greek soldiers in his employ, Heracleides blames Xenophon, who defends himself by observing, as a fellow soldier, how they all stand on the cusp of great εὐπορία ("abundance," *Anab.* 7.2.36).

293. Gk μέρος (lit. "portion, share"). Like so many in power, Demetrius worries about losing his "piece of the pie" (cf. Sen, *Entitlement*, 1–8).

εἰς ἀπελεγμὸν ἐλθεῖν	Will be discredited,[294]
ἀλλὰ καὶ τὸ τῆς μεγάλης θεᾶς Ἀρτέμιδος	But the temple[295] of the great goddess
ἱερὸν εἰς οὐθὲν λογισθῆναι	Artemis may even be held accountable."[296]

Like the prophets Moses and Samuel, Paul recites his *résumé* in a "farewell address" to Ephesian Christians:[297]

ἀργυρίου ἢ χρυσίου ἢ ἱματισμοῦ	Silver or gold or clothing
οὐδενὸς ἐπεθύμησα	I coveted from no one.
αὐτοὶ γινώσκετε ὅτι ταῖς χρείαις μου	You yourselves know that for my needs
καὶ τοῖς οὖσιν μετ' ἐμου	And those with me
ὑπηρέτησαν αἱ χεῖρες αὗται	These hands have served.[298]
πάντα ὑπέδειξα ὑμῖν	I have provided for you an example[299]
ὅτι οὕτως κοπιῶντας δει	That by so laboring[300] it is necessary
ἀντιλαμβάνεσθαι τῶν ἀσθενούντων	To assist the weak,[301]

294. Lit. "come into disrepute." This is not the only time Ephesian silversmiths band together to promote their interests. According to a third-century CE inscription (published in Knibbe and Iplikçioglu, "Inschriften," 87–150), they come together to honor Valerius Festus for "making the harbor larger than that built by King Croesus."

295. The town clerk maintains the same order of priorities when he warns the crowd that the men they want to lynch are neither ἱερόσυλοι ("temple robbers") nor βλάσφημοι ("blasphemers," Acts 19:37). According to Plato (*Resp.* 1.344b), "temple-robbing" (ἱεροσύλησις) is as much a crime as kidnapping, burglary, and theft (see 2 Macc 4:24; Rom 3:22; Philo, *Jos.* 84; Josephus, *A.J.* 16:164–68).

296. Acts 19:27. Gk λογίζομαι ("to (ac)count for, reckon with") resonates with several other accounting terms in Acts 19:19–27: συνεψηφίζω, "to calculate"; τὰς τιμὰς, "value"; εὐπορία, "abundance"; τὸ μέρος, "share/entitlement"; ἀπελεγμός, "discredit"; and οἰκουμένη, "economy."

297. Cf. the similar apologies of Moses (Deut 1:1—11:32) and Samuel (1 Sam 12:1–6). Cf. Dupont, "Discours," 424–45; Schürmann, "Testament," 310–40; Aejmelaeus, *Rezeption*, 1–11; Lambrecht, "Farewell," 307–37.

298. Doubtless this is a reference to σκηνοποιία, "tent-making" (Acts 18:3), a marketable skill involving the handcrafting of leather and goat's hair (cf. Michaelis, "σκηνοποιός," 393–94).

299. Aristotle (*Oec.* 1345a) insists that in matters of stewardship οὐ γὰρ οἷόντε μὴ καλῶς ὑποδεικνύντος καλῶς μιμεῖσθαι, "there can be no good imitation without good example." Hock ("Workshop," 438–50) argues that vocational ministry is not only the province of Jewish sages, but Greek sages as well.

300. Whereas ὑπηρετέω signifies "subordinate service," the parallel κοπιάω denotes "wearisome labor." Aristotle (*Met.* 982b5) illustrates the first when he argues that ἐπιστημῶν . . . μᾶλλον ἀρχικὴ τῆς ὑπηρετούσης, "science . . . is superior to that which is 'subservient.'" The Gospel of John illustrates the second when it describes Yeshu`a as κεκοπιακὼς ἐκ τῆς ὁδοιπορίας, "weary from the journey" (John 4:6). Using a word easily twisted, some Corinthians accuse Paul of being τάπεινος ("humble," 2 Cor 10:1; Paul calls himself "ταπεινοφροσύνη," in Acts 20:19), but the apostle sardonically responds by asking them whether manual labor is ἁμαρτία ("sinful," 2 Cor 11:7; cf. Thompson, *Ethics*, 106–7).

301. Paul "pays" (δαπανάω) for the ritual head-shaving of four men (Acts 21:24), a type of "giving" partially overlapping ἐλεημοσύνη ("almsgiving").

μνημονεύειν τε τῶν λόγων τοῦ κυρίου Ἰησου	Remembering the words of Lord Yeshu`a,
ὅτι αὐτὸς εἶπεν	When he said,
μακάριόν ἐστιν μᾶλλον διδόναι	"It is more blessed to give
ἢ λαμβάνειν	Than to receive."[302]

Whether this *μακάριος* ("blessing/beatitude") comes from an established collection or not, the sentiment itself is hardly unique.[303] Yeshu`a ben Sirach, for example, admonishes his students: *μὴ ἔστω ἡ χείρ σου ἐκτεταμένη εἰς τὸ λαβεῖν καὶ ἐν τῷ ἀποδιδόναι συνεσταλμένη*, "Let not your hand be stretched out to receive, but closed when it is time to give."[304] The philosopher Epicurus teaches that *εὖ πάσχειν τὸ εὖ ποιεῖν οὐ μόνον κάλλιον ἀλλὰ καὶ ἥδιον εἶναί φησι*, "It is not only nobler, but more pleasant to give than receive benefits."[305]

Arriving in Jerusalem, Paul encounters detractors determined to incarcerate him for "defiling the temple"—a common priestly accusation.[306] Upon learning that he is a Roman citizen, however,[307] they turn him over to the tribune Claudius Lysias,[308] who asks,

σὺ Ῥωμαῖος εἶ	"Are you a Roman?"
ὁ δὲ ἔφη ναί	And he said, "Yes."
ἀπεκρίθη δὲ ὁ χιλίαρχος	The tribune replied,
ἐγὼ πολλοῦ κεφαλαίου	"For a large sum[309]
τὴν πολιτείαν ταύτην ἐκτησάμην	I acquired this 'citizenship.'"[310]

302. Acts 20:33–35.

303. Cf. discussion in Robinson and Koester, *Trajectories*, 97.

304. Sir 4:31.

305. Cited in Plutarch, *Mor.* 778c. Dio Chrysostom (*Or.* 3.14–15) and Lucian (*Nigr.* 25–26), e.g., emphasize that true philosophers refuse to accept money for their teaching (cf. Num 22:18; 1 Kgs 13:8–9; *T. Iss.* 4.2). The statement in 1 Clem 2:1 quotes the "Jesus-saying" here in Acts 20:35, but what makes the blessing in Acts so distinctive is its conspicuous lack of "preconditions" (Gregory, *Sirach*, 288).

306. From Luke's perspective this is a trumped-up charge, but the maintenance of temple boundaries is a priestly obsession (cf. Stokholm, "Tempelräubern," 1–28). The *Temple Scroll* from Qumran (11Q19 51.12–15), e.g., posits that acceptance of a "bribe" (שוחד) not only "perverts justice" (מטה משפט), but causes "great guilt" (אשמה גדולה) and "defiles the 'house' with sin" (מטמא הבית בעוון; cf. *ἁμαρτία* in 2 Cor 11:7).

307. That is, according to the *Lex Julia* (cf. Rapske, *Acts*, 52).

308. Act 23:26; 24:22.

309. Gk *κεφάλαιος* comes from a root meaning "head" (cf. *κεφαλή*, Eph 5:23), but in socioeconomic contexts can mean "sum total." Lysias (*Arist.* 19.40), e.g., itemizes several types and amounts of assets before posting a *κεφάλαιος* ("sum total").

310. Judge (*Groups*, 9) understands the social institutions of the Mediterranean world to include the "city-state" (*πολιτεία*), the "household" (*οἰκονομία*), and the "voluntary association" (*κοινωνία*; cf. Moore, "Associations," 149–55).

ὁ δὲ Παῦλος ἔφη ἐγὼ δὲ καὶ γεγέννημαι	But Paul said, "I was born a citizen."[311]

Whether the πολιτεία ("citizenship") allusions in this exchange come from Paul or Luke (or both),[312] Peter van Minnen views their appearance as a "decisive turn in the narrative" of Acts.[313]

Forced to defend himself before the procurator Marcus Antonius Felix,[314] Paul seizes this occasion as an opportunity to relate to Graeco-Roman leaders how he becomes a Christian, offhandedly mentioning in his testimony that while traveling through Anatolia he decides,

δι' ἐτῶν δὲ πλειόνων ἐλεημοσύνας ποιήσων	After several years, to bring alms
εἰς τὸ ἔθνος μου	To my nation,
παρεγενόμην καὶ προσφοράς	And gifts.[315]

The mention of "alms" and "gifts," however, triggers the procurator's attention, a politician widely reported to be utterly corrupt,[316] because from Paul's testimony he infers the existence of a sizeable treasure hidden away somewhere.[317] For two years he thus meets with his prisoner in the hope of securing a bribe in exchange for his release:[318]

ἐλπίζων ὅτι χρήματα	Hoping that money
δοθήσεται αὐτῷ ὑπὸ τοῦ Παύλου	Might be given to him by Paul;[319]

311. Acts 22:27–28. Most agree with Gardner (*Citizen*, 179–91) that there are five ways to become a Roman citizen: (a) be born to a Roman family; (b) be born in a city to which Roman citizenship has been granted; (c) be an honorably discharged Roman soldier; (d) be a slave freed by a citizen master; and/or (e) be a financial benefactor of Rome (or one of its agents). Purchasing citizenship is a quasi-legitimate activity. Plutarch (*Sulla* 8.1), e.g., condemns Publius Sulpicius Rufus (d. 88 BCE) for τὴν ρομαίων πολιτείαν ἐξελευθερικοῖς καὶ μετοίκοις πωλῶν ἀναφανδὸν, "publicly selling Roman citizenship to freedmen and aliens." Utterly groundless, however, is Maccoby's (*Mythmaker*, 162) contention that Paul purchases his citizenship with funds already earmarked for the poor.

312. *Paul:* Hengel, "Paulus," 177–291; *Luke:* Stegemann, "Bürger," 200–229. Cf. Bell, *Irrevocable*, 366.

313. Van Minnen, "Citizen," 45; cf. Sterling, *Historiography*, 348. The very first mention of Roman citizenship in Acts is in 16:37 (Tajra, *Trial*, 24–29).

314. Acts 23:26. According to Tacitus (*Hist.* 5.9), Felix is the grandson-in-law of the Roman emperor Claudius (d. 54 CE).

315. Acts 24:17. Gk προσφορά is a translation of מנחה ("gift") in OG Ps 39:7.

316. Tacitus (*Hist.* 5.9) describes him as someone known *per omnem saevitiam ac libidinem*, "for every kind of lustful barbarity."

317. Peters (*Humor*, 364) reads this text as an example of "biblical humor."

318. Josephus (*A.J.* 20.205) describes Ananias, the high priest who hires the Roman attorney Tertullus to prosecute Paul before Felix, as a χρημάτων ποριστικός ("money-hoarder") who bribes allies (213) and hires thugs to muscle in on poorer priests and steal their tithes (206–07).

319. Tacitus (*Hist.* 12.54) contends that Felix *cuncta malefacta sibi impune ratus*, "believed he could do anything evil with impunity," even to the point of competing with a rival (Cumanus) *raptare inter se immittere laltronum globos componere insidias . . . spoliaque et praedas ad procuratores referre*, "to plunder one another, release packs of thugs to ambush travelers . . . and refer to the procurators the

διὸ καὶ πυκνότερον αὐτὸν	He frequently
μεταπεμπόμενος ὡμίλει αὐτῷ	Sent for him to talk with him.[320]

Summary

From this brief survey several points stand out. *First*, the socioeconomic trajectory animating Nevi'im and subsequent texts continues to impact the "great literature" of the Nazarenes. *Second*, like the Ezra-Nehemiah scroll, the Gospel of Matthew focuses a good deal of attention on the problem of socioeconomic corruption within the Jerusalem temple-complex.[321] *Third*, the Acts of the Apostles continues to focus on the problems of *corruption* and *bribery* affecting not only Jews and Christians, but others as well, documenting these problems via prophetically shaped vignettes designed to emphasize the importance of safeguarding from defilement the Nazarene "community-of-goods."[322] *Fourth*, the avenue through which the first attacks come against this "community-of-goods" is unquestionably *socioeconomic* in nature. *Fifth*, the various sleight-of-hand activities used to camouflage these attacks (disguised as "magic" or "civic responsibility" or "creative exegesis") consistently fail to prohibit this fledgling community from carrying out its mission.

spoil and plunder." Not coincidentally, a later rabbi comments (*Qoh. Rab.* 11.1) that הדה מלכותא עבדא מידי על מגן, "this government does nothing without getting paid."

320. Acts 24:26. Bribing one's way out of jail is not an uncommon practice, in Paul's time or any other. Bunck and Fowler (*Bribes*, 262), e.g., note how commonplace it is for contemporary drug dealers to "employ bribery, violence, and threats as levers to gain cooperation and defeat law enforcement."

321. Matthew is not alone in this critique. The sectarian texts from Qumraṇ are just as critical, if not more so (cf. Murphy, *Wealth*, 447–55).

322. "The parallel deepens when we read of those who, contrary to God's express word, attempt to keep a secret store of manna for themselves. Moses' anger against them reminds us of Peter's wrath against Ananias and Sapphira" (Saxby, *Pilgrims*, 32).

6

Summary and Conclusions

As THE FOREGOING SURVEY tries to show, some socioeconomic motifs enjoy longer shelf lives than others, doubtless because of the way they "scratch" a deeper "itch."[1] Foremost among the most frequent are those motifs which engage the concentrated cultural concerns associated with *fertility/procreation*, *inheritance/possession*, *house/temple*, *tithing/taxation*, and *land*.

Fertility/Procreation

Two questions drive this motif trajectory: (a) "What causes infertility?" and (b) "How can it be reversed?" The first focuses on *diagnosis*, the second on *prognosis*. Bereft of the critical options available to postmoderns, ANE writers looking to voice their socioeconomic concerns manifestly gravitate to one type of writing in their literary arsenal: *mythopoeic epic*.[2] Since the ancients "imagine their gods in their own image,"[3] and since no other literary genre "provides a template or blueprint for the organization of social and psychological processes,"[4] *myth* is by far the safest place to go to register "statements critical of kings (and) royal policies."[5] Thus, where the Anatolians deal with the problem of infertility by imagining it as the god Telipinu "abandoning his post," the Sumerians imagine it as the goddess Inanna "suffering defeat in the Netherworld" at the hands of her sister Ereškigal.[6] Where Ištar removes an item of clothing at each gate before entering Ereškigal's presence, the exorcist Kamrušepaš strips Telipinu bare of all the negative

1. Van der Toorn (*Culture*, 217) cautions against overemphasizing this point, arguing that "if one has an eye for it, almost every period contains evidence to the effect that society is going through extensive changes."

2. Lemche ("Sovereign," 109) recognizes that myth reflects "economic processes in human society . . . transferred to the realm of divine beings."

3. *BWL* 7.

4. Buchan, *Frozen*, 84.

5. Launderville, *Piety*, 40.

6. Hoffner, *Hittite Myths*, 2a; ID 171.

traits tempting him to abandon his post repeatedly.[7] Where Ereškigal sends squadrons of demons to imprison Ištar, the demon Asmodeus kills a squadron of husbands before any of them can impregnate Sarah Bat-Raguel.[8]

The Hebrew prophets deal with the problems afflicting *their* economies as well, often by challenging audiences to present *their* explanations for crop failure, famine, drought, pestilence, locust plague, and death. Dismissing the polytheistic "solutions" offered by their neighbors, the Hebrew prophets dial up a wholly different set of solutions, baptizing each one in the cold, clear waters of Yahwism. Thus, where Ninšubur chants an Inanna lament comparing things precious to things mundane, Hosea and Jeremiah preach oracles contrasting the claims of Yhwh against those of Ba'al and the Queen of Heaven.[9] Where El argues with his wife Athirat over who is qualified to sit on Ba'al's throne, Jeremiah commends Yhwh's "bride" for loyally following him through the desert, even while Hosea rebukes her for nakedly exposing herself to "lovers" patently unable to sire children.[10] Where Enki sends servants to negotiate with Ereškigal on Inanna's behalf, Yhwh sends an unnamed servant to model "success" and "prosperity" before a broken people not by *avoiding* suffering, but by vicariously *engaging* it, thereby laying the foundation for an *ἀγάπη* ethic later championed by the Nazarenes.[11]

Inheritance/Possession

Ancestral inheritance is a socioeconomic prize over which siblings constantly quarrel, a harsh reality underlying a socioeconomic motif which, again, finds its deepest roots in the soil of ANE myth.[12] Where Yam attempts to seize Ba'al's inheritance, Naboth stubbornly refuses to surrender his inheritance to Yam-like bullies, even those pretending to be a "royal couple."[13] To Ba'al's seizure of Yam's estate (and Anat's attempt to muscle in on it), Micah condemns those wealthy landowners who regularly muscle in on the ancestral possessions of their Hebrew neighbors.[14] To Ba'al's claim that Mt. Zaphon is the "rock of my inheritance," Ḥanamel urges his cousin Jeremiah to take possession of *his* ancestral inheritance, even as Raphael and Raguel urge Tobias to do

7. DI 42–62; Hoffner, *Hittite Myths*, 2a.22.

8. DI 69; Tob 3:7–9.

9. ID 43–47; Hos 2:16–17; Jer 44:25.

10. *CAT* 1.6.1.43–48; Jer 2:6; Hos 2:9.

11. ID 224–25; Isa 52:13–53:12; Acts 4:34–35.

12. Liverani (*Myth*, 45) observes that in the later sections of DT "it is forbidden for killers to take the victims' goods, and the victim's sons, who have to inherit their father's goods," so that, "in this way economic incentives for political crimes are removed."

13. *CAT* 1.2.1.18–19; 1 Kgs 21:3.

14. *CAT* 1.2.4.26–28; 1.3.3.35–44; Mic 2:1–2.

the same.[15] To Ištar's reassurance to Esarhaddon that he is her legitimate "son" and "heir," Jeremiah reassures his audience that *Israel* is the "tribe of Yhwh's inheritance."[16] Where El challenges the generational tension plaguing Kirta's family, the prophet Nathan similarly challenges the dysfunctional family of David.[17] Where Yaṣṣib demands an inheritance from his father Kirta, Absalom demands the inheritance of *his* father David, even as Yeshu`a challenges his followers to *reimagine* "inheritance" in different categories altogether.[18] To Adad's attempt to dispossess Zimri-Lim of *his* inheritance, Raphael urges Tobias to take possession of *his* "rightful inheritance."[19] Where Marduk removes from Enlil the title "legitimate heir," Yhwh dispossesses Ba'al of the titles "Cloudrider," "Rainmaker," and "Landlord."[20] Where Marduk decides what can and cannot be inherited, Yhwh directs his support to those willing to include in their definition of "inheritance" a commitment to the dispossessed.[21]

"House"/Temple

As is well known, the semantic field enfolding various terms for "temple" also includes the generic term "house," a word which in the right context denotes "sanctuary" or "temple."[22] Victor Hurowitz form-critically suggests that mythopoeic accounts like the one in *Ee* depicting the construction of Marduk's "house" tend to "resemble in their structure the building stories regularly appearing in royal inscriptions."[23] Yet however perceptive this insight may be, it does not (a) identify the socioeconomic character of the "house/temple" motif in its intertextual context (e.g., the Ba'al epic), nor does it (b) assess the value of its contribution to the broader literary trajectory of "house/temple" motifs.[24]

Thus, where Marduk's "house" is a "wealth depository," Yhwh's "house" is a stockpile from which grain and drink offerings can be "cut off."[25] Where Marduk's house is a "tollbooth," Yhwh's "house" is a revenue source for the Achaemenid war machine.[26] Where El avenges Yam's dignity by advocating for him a "house," Haggai chides those

15. *CAT* 1.3.3.26–27; Jer 32:7; Tob 6:13.

16. Nissinen, *Prophets*, 73.5, 20; Jer 10:16//51:19.

17. *CAT* 1.16.4.11–5.49; 2 Sam 12:7; 1 Kgs 1:11, 24.

18. *CAT* 1.16.6.43–50; 2 Sam 16:21–22; Luke 12:13–23 (cf. Moore, *WealthWatch*, 209–12).

19. Nissinen, *Prophets*, 1.4, 20, 32; Tob 6:13.

20. *BWL* 212; *CAT* 1.17.1.19; 1 Kgs 18:21.

21. *Ee* 4.145–46; 5.8; Isa 58:6–7.

22. Hoffner, "בית," 111–13.

23. Hurowitz, *Temple*, 95–96 (cf. *Ee* 4.144–45 and above).

24. Limet ("Inanna," 27), e.g., identifies several parallels between the Ba'al epic and the Sum myth of Inanna and Ebiḫ (go to http://etcsl.orinst.ox.ac.uk/cgi-bin/etcsl.cgi?text=c.1.3.2&display=Crit&charenc=&lineid=c132.171#c132.171).

25. *Ee* 5.122; Joel 1:9.

26. *Ee* 5.123; Ezra 4:13, 20; Finkel (*Cyrus*, 129–35).

who trample on Yhwh's dignity by snubbing *his* "house."[27] To Athtar's realization that he cannot have his own "house," Haggai warns that Yhwh will not be content until *his* "house" is purified *properly*.[28] Where Cyrus helps finance the rebuilding of the "house of God" in Jerusalem, Stephen challenges those standing in the shadow of this same "house" to reimagine its original purpose.[29] Where the priests in the Epistle of Jeremiah contemptuously dismiss any connection between economics and religion, Demetrius the silversmith works hard to keep the two fused together, even as Yeshu`a simply recognizes their coexistence.[30] Where Talmud has Abram wondering whether worship is possible without a temple, Stephen (like Jeremiah) criticizes those who trust blindly in the power of the temple, even as Simon Magus foolishly tries to "acquire" the Holy Spirit for *his* "house."[31] Where Athtar fears that undertakers will one day prepare his corpse for burial in the "house" of Yam, Ezekiel predicts the explosion of a life-giving fountain from the northern court of Yhwh's "house" designed to bring the desert back to life.[32] Where the gods praise Marduk for provisioning their "houses," Malachi dares his audience to provision Yhwh's house sufficiently so that the "windows of heaven" might open up and pour down a divine blessing.[33]

Tithing/Taxation

Where the gods celebrate Marduk's conquest with "*erbu*-gifts,"[34] the language used to describe the transactions between Canaanite deities sometimes employs terms used in administrative texts to denote "tribute" (e.g., Ug *argmn*).[35] Where the gods gratefully bring "tribute" to Marduk at his coronation, Persian investigators warn Artaxerxes of the "danger" of losing Jerusalem's tax-and-tribute revenue.[36] Where Malachi urges his readers not to dismiss the connection between "tithing" and "blessing," Tobit contrasts the gifts donated by his brothers to the Dan calf-deity with the tithes he gives to the priests in the Jerusalem "house of God," the same "house" Yeshu`a later feels compelled to cleanse.[37] Where Persian envoys in Jerusalem warn their supervisors that taxes and tribute may soon become difficult to collect, Yeshu`a urges his disciples

27. *CAT* 1.2.3.16; Hag 1:4.
28. *CAT* 1.2.3.19–20; Hag 2:14–17.
29. Ezra 1:1–4; 6:2–5; 1 Esd 2:1–7; Acts 7:48.
30. EpJer 9; Acts 19:27; Matt 22:19–21.
31. *b. Ta`an* 27b; Acts 7:48: Jer 7:4; Acts 8:18–19.
32. *CAT* 1.2.3.19–20; Ezek 47:1–12.
33. *Ee* 4.11–14; Mal 3:10.
34. *Ee* 7.111 (using an administrative term often associated with taxation).
35. *CAT* 1.2.1.37–38 (cf. *CAT* 4.43.3; 181.1; cf. *DULAT* 100).
36. *Ee* 4.133–34; Ezra 4:20.
37. Mal 3:10; Tob 1:5; Matt 21:11–12.

to question the motives of tax collectors.[38] Where Micah condemns the "robber barons" who "rig the scales" against the poor, Peter asks Ananias, Sapphira and Simon Magus why they think they can go on doing the same thing.[39]

Land

In agrarian societies land is by far the most valuable economic resource, the precious commodity in which life-giving food is grown and over which violent conflict constantly recurs.[40] Like contemporary sociologists,[41] ancient scribes affirm this importance, primarily through the vehicle of mythopoeic epic. Thus, where the great god Enlil "decrees the fate of the land for Marduk," Marduk replaces Enlil because he has the ability to produce for his devotees a "surplus of land."[42] Where El awards the throne to Ba'al because he is "lord of the land," Elijah declares Yhwh to be the only *legitimate* "landlord."[43] Where famine "stifles" the land in Anatolia and Amos warns of Yhwh's power to send famine on the land, Isaiah promises those who take refuge in Yhwh that someday they will "inherit the land."[44] Where Canaanite scribes describe Ba'al's rain as a "delight to the land," Hosea insists that Yhwh is the only "husband" qualified to inseminate *his* "bride" on *his* land.[45] Where Anat's mutilation of Aqhat reflects the shriveling of the land, Amos contends that what actually causes the land to "mourn" is the unchecked prevalence of socioeconomic corruption.[46] Where Jeremiah reminds Judah that Yhwh brings them out of a land of slavery into a land of orchards, Zechariah warns that until or unless the temple is rebuilt the ארץ שמה ("desolate land") cannot become the ארץ חמדה ("desirable land"), and Isaiah warns that Yhwh will strip the land of those debasing the ברית עולם ("eternal covenant").[47] Where the Anatolians argue that Telipinu's return is the catalyst responsible for "replenishing the land," Amos declares Yhwh to be the deity responsible for "planting *his* people upon *their* land."[48] Where Joel informs Israel that Yhwh will judge the nations for "parceling

38. Ezra 4:13; Matt 17:25–27.

39. Mic 6:10–15; Acts 5:3–4; 8:20–21.

40. Nolan and Lenski, *Macrosociology*, 154.

41. Fager (*Land*, 1–37), e.g., wants to know why different societies address social issues the way they distinctively do, particularly how differing social forces affect the formulations of differing ideologies (like Jubilee, Lev 25:10–54).

42. CH 1.6–8; *Ee* 7.8.

43. *CAT* 1.3.5.43–44; 1 Kgs 18:37.

44. Hoffner, *Hittite Myths*, 2a.2–3; Amos 8:11; Isa 57:13.

45. *CAT* 1.16.3.7; Hos 2:24 (ET 2:22).

46. *CAT* 1.19.1.18–19; Amos 8:8.

47. Jer 2:7; Zech 7:14; Isa 24:1–6.

48. Hoffner, *Hittite Myths*, 2a.28; Amos 9:15.

out my land," Yeshu`a insists (with Isaiah) that the only people eligible to inherit/possess the land are the "meek."[49]

Conclusion

Much more may be said, of course, but space restrictions prohibit. Suffice it to say here in conclusion that the goal of this study was to identify and explain from a comparative intertextual perspective the primary prophetic socioeconomic motifs animating Nevi'im in the ancient library of texts called "the Bible." Whether this has been accomplished is a question for the reader to decide. Much is at stake in this decision, however, because, as the previous book in this series tries to show,[50] the Bible is *the* source most responsible for creating, maintaining, and potentially restoring the socioeconomic values of Western civilization.

49. Joel 4:2 (ET 3:2); Isa 11:4; Matt 5:5.

50. Cf. Moore, *WealthWatch*, 223–31.

Bibliography

Abernethy, Andrew A. *Eating in Isaiah: Approaching the Role of Food and Drink in Isaiah's Structure and Message*. BibIntSer 131. Leiden: Brill, 2014.

Abusch, I. Tzvi. "Ghost and God: Some Observations on a Babylonian Understanding of Human Nature." In *Self, Soul, and Body in Religious Experience*, edited by A. Baumgarten et al., 363–83. SHR 78. Leiden: Brill, 1998.

———. "Ishtar." In *DDD* 452–56.

———. "Marduk." In *DDD* 543–49.

———. *The Witchcraft Series* Maqlû. SBLWAW 37. Atlanta: SBL, 2015.

Ackerman, Jane. *Elijah, Prophet of Carmel*. Washington, DC: Institute of Carmelite Studies, 2002.

Ackerman, Susan. "'And the Women Knead Dough': The Worship of the Queen of Heaven in Sixth Century Judah." In *Gender and Difference in Ancient Israel*, edited by Peggy L. Day, 109–24. Minneapolis: Fortress, 1989.

———. "The Queen Mother and the Cult in Ancient Israel." 1993. Reprinted in *Women in the Hebrew Bible: A Reader*, edited by Alice Bach, 179–94. New York: Routledge, 1999.

———. *Under Every Green Tree: Popular Religion in Sixth-Century Judah*. HSM 46. Atlanta: Scholars, 1992.

———. *When Heroes Love: The Ambiguity of Eros in the Stories of Gilgamesh and David*. GTR. New York: Columbia University Press, 2005.

Ackroyd, Peter R. *Exile and Restoration*. OTL. London: SCM, 1968.

Adams, Dwayne H. *The Sinner in Luke*. ETSMS. Eugene, OR: Pickwick, 2008.

Adams, Samuel L. *Social and Economic Life in Second Temple Judea*. Louisville: Westminster John Knox, 2014.

Adams, Sean A. *Baruch and the Epistle of Jeremiah: A Commentary Based on the Texts in Codex Vaticanus*. SCS. Leiden: Brill, 2014.

Adkins, Arthur W. H. *Moral Values and Political Behavior in Ancient Greece from Homer to the End of the Fifth Century*. London: Chatto & Windus, 1972.

Aejmelaeus, Lars. *Die Rezeption des Paulusbriefe in der Miletrede (Apg 20, 18–35)*. AASF 232. Helsinki: Suomalainen Tiedeakatemia, 1987.

Ahlström, Gösta W. *Joel and the Temple Cult of Jerusalem*. VTSup 21. Leiden: Brill, 1971.

Alatas, Syed Hussein. *The Problem of Corruption*. Kuala Lumpur: The Other Press, 2015.

Albertz, Rainer. *A History of Israelite Religion in the Old Testament Period*, Vol. 1: *From the Beginnings to the End of the Monarchy*. Translated by John Bowden. OTL. Louisville: Westminster John Knox, 1994.

Albright, William F. "From the Patriarchs to Moses I: From Abraham to Joseph." In *The Biblical Archaeologist Reader IV*, edited by Edward F. Campbell and David Noel Freedman, 5–33. Sheffield: Almond, 1983.

———. *From the Stone Age to Christianity: Monotheism and the Historical Process*. New York: Doubleday, 1957.

Alexander, Joseph Addison. *Commentary on Isaiah*. 1867. Reprint, Grand Rapids: Kregel, 1992.

———. *The Gospel According to Matthew*. New York: Scribner, 1864.

Allen, James P. *Middle Egyptian: An Introduction to the Language and Culture of Hieroglyphs*. Cambridge: Cambridge University Press, 2014.

Allen, Leslie C. *The Books of Joel, Obadiah, Jonah, and Micah*. NICOT. Grand Rapids: Eerdmans, 1976.

———. *Ezekiel 20–48*. WBC 29. Dallas: Word, 1990.

———. "Jeremiah, Book of." In *DOTPr* 423–41.

———. *Jeremiah: A Commentary*. OTL. Louisville: Westminster John Knox, 2008.

Alster, Bendt. "NAM-EN, NAM-LAGAR." *JCS* 23 (1971) 116–17.

———. "Tammuz." In *DDD* 828–34.

———. "Tiamat." In *DDD* 867–69.

Alt, Albrecht. "The God of the Fathers." 1929. Translated by R. A. Wilson. In *Essays on Old Testament History and Religion*, 1–77. Oxford: Blackwell, 1966.

Alter, Robert. *The Art of Biblical Narrative*. New York: Basic Books, 2011

Altmann, Peter. "Ancient Comparisons, Modern Models, and Ezra-Nehemiah: Triangulating the Sources for Insights on the Economy of Persian Period Yehud." In *The Economy of Ancient Judah in Its Historical Context*, edited by M. Miller et al., 103–20. Winona Lake, IN: Eisenbrauns, 2015.

———. *Economics in Persian-Period Biblical Texts*. FAT 109. Tübingen: Mohr/Siebeck, 2016.

Ameling, Walter. "Wöhltater im hellenistischen Gymnasion." In *Das hellenistische Gymnasion*, edited by D. Kah and P. Scholz, 129–62. WGW 8. Berlin: Akademie, 2007.

Anbar, Moshé. "La libération des esclaves en temps de guerre: Jer 34 et ARM XXVI.363." *ZAW* 111 (1999) 253–55.

Anderson, Bernhard W. *Creation versus Chaos: The Reinterpretation of Mythical Symbolism in the Bible*. Minneapolis: Augsburg Fortress, 1987.

Anderson, Gary A., and Saul M. Olyan, eds. *Priesthood and Cult in Ancient Israel*. JSOTSup 125. Sheffield: Sheffield Academic, 1991.

Anderson, James S. *Monotheism and Yahweh's Appropriation of Ba'al*. LHBOTS 617. London: Bloomsbury, 2015.

Annus, Amar, and Alan Lenzi. *Ludlul bēl nēmeqi: The Standard Babylonian Poem of the Righteous Sufferer*. SAACT 7. Helsinki: Neo-Assyrian Text Corpus Project, 2010.

Antari, Amine. "When Bribery Becomes a Way of Doing Business." In *Bribery and Corruption Casebook: The View from Under the Table*, edited by J. T. Wells and L. Hymes, 43–52. Hoboken, NJ: Wiley, 2012.

Anthonioz, Stéphanie. *Le prophétisme biblique: De l'idéal à la réalité*. LD 261. Paris: Cerf, 2013.

Ap-Thomas, D. R. "Elijah on Mt. Carmel." *PEQ* 92 (1960) 146–55.

Arnold, Bill T., and Hugh G. M. Williamson, eds. *Dictionary of the Old Testament Historical Books*. Downers Grove, IL: InterVarsity, 2005.

Assis, Elie. *The Book of Joel: A Prophet Between Calamity and Hope*. LHBOTS 581. New York: Bloomsbury, 2013.

Assmann, Jan. *Moses the Egyptian: The Memory of Egypt in Western Monotheism*. Cambridge, MA: Harvard University Press, 1997.

Aubet, Maria Eugenia. "Karl Polanyi and His View of Ancient Economy." In *Commerce and Colonialization in the Ancient Near East*, 17–39. Cambridge: Cambridge University Press, 2013.

Aune, David E. "Sorcery, Demons, and the Rise of Christianity from Late Antiquity into the Middle Ages." In *Witchcraft Confessions and Accusations*, edited by Mary Douglas, 17–45. AE 2. New York: Tavistock, 1970.

Aus, Roger David. *Simon Peter's Denial and Jesus' Commissioning Him as His Successor in John 21:15–19: Studies in Their Judaic Background*. SJud. Lanham, MD: University Press of America, 2013.

Autero, Esa J. *Reading the Bible Across Contexts: Luke's Gospel, Socioeconomic Marginality, and Latin American Biblical Hermeneutics*. BI 145. Leiden: Brill, 2016.

Avigad, Naḥman. "Baruch the Scribe and Jeraḥmeel the King's Son." *IEJ* 28 (1978) 52–56.

Bachvarova, Mary. "Hurro-Hittite Stories and Hittite Pregnancy and Birth Rituals." In *Women in the Ancient Near East: A Sourcebook*, edited by M. Chavalas, 272–306. London: Routledge, 2014.

Baines, John, and Norman Yoffee. "Order, Legitimacy, and Wealth: Setting the Terms." In *Order, Legitimacy, and Wealth in Ancient States*, edited by J. Richards and M. van Buren, 13–17. NDA. Cambridge: Cambridge University Press, 2000.

Baker, Coleman A. *Identity, Memory, and Narrative in Early Christianity: Peter, Paul, and Recategorization in the Book of Acts*. Eugene, OR: Pickwick, 2011.

Baldwin, Joyce G. *Haggai, Zechariah, Malachi: An Introduction and Commentary*. TOTC. Downers Grove, IL: InterVarsity, 1981.

Balentine, Samuel E. *Prayer in the Hebrew Bible: the Drama of Divine-Human Dialogue*. OBT. Minneapolis: Augsburg Fortress, 1993.

Ball, C. J. "Epistle of Jeremy." In *The Apocrypha and Pseudepigrapha of the Old Testament*, edited by R. H. Charles, 1.596–611. Oxford, Clarendon, 1913.

Ballentine, Debra Scroggins. *The Conflict Myth and the Biblical Tradition*. New York: Oxford University Press, 2015.

Baltzer, Klaus. *Deutero-Isaiah: A Commentary on Isaiah 40–55*. Hermeneia. Minneapolis: Fortress, 1999.

Barker, Margaret. "The Archangel Raphael in the *Book of Tobit*." In *Studies in the Book of Tobit: A Multidisciplinary Approach*, edited by M. Bredin, 118–28. LSTS. New York: T. & T. Clark, 2006.

Barnouw, Jeffrey. *Odysseus, Hero of Practical Intelligence: Deliberation and Signs in Homer's Odyssey*. Lanham, MD: University Press of America, 2004.

Barr, James. *History and Ideology in the Old Testament: Biblical Studies at the End of a Millenium*. Oxford: Oxford University Press, 2000.

Barré, Michael L. "A Note on the Sin-Šumu-Lišir Treaty." *JCS* 39 (1987) 81–83.

Barrera, Albino. *Biblical Economic Ethics: Sacred Scripture's Teaching on Economic Life*. New York: Lexington, 2013.

Barrett, Charles K. *Acts 1–14*. ICC. London: T. & T. Clark, 1994.

Barrick, W. Boyd. "Funerary Character of High Places in Ancient Palestine: A Reassessment." *VT* 25 (1975) 565–95.

Barron, Bruce. *The Health and Wealth Gospel: What's Going On Today in a Movement that Has Shaped the Faith of Millions.* Downers Grove, IL: InterVarsity, 1987.

Barstad, Hans M. *The Religious Polemics of Amos: Studies in the Preaching of Amos 2:7b–8; 4:1–13; 5:1–27; 6:4–7; 8:14.* VTSup 34. Leiden: Brill, 1984.

Barth, John. *The End of the Road.* Garden City, NY: Doubleday, 1967.

Barton, John. *Amos's Oracles Against the Nations: A Study of Amos 1.3—2.5.* SOTSMS 6. Cambridge: Cambridge University Press, 1980.

———. *Joel and Obadiah: A Commentary.* OTL. Louisville: Westminster John Knox, 2001.

Bassler, Jouette M. "The Widows' Tale: A Fresh Look at 1 Timothy 5:3–16." *JBL* 104 (1984) 23–41.

Batto, Bernard F. "Behemoth." In *DDD* 165–69.

———. *Slaying the Dragon: Mythmaking in the Biblical Tradition.* Louisville: Westminster John Knox, 1992.

Baukal, Charles E. "Hydrotechnics on Mt. Carmel." *SJOT* 29 (2015) 63–79.

Baumann, Gerlinde. *Love and Violence: Marriage as Metaphor for the Relationship between Yhwh and Israel in the Prophetic Books.* 2000. Translated by L. M. Maloney. Collegeville, MN: Liturgical, 2003.

———. "Die prophetische Ehemetaphorik und die Bewertung der Prophetie im Zwölfprophetenbuch." In *Thematic Threads in the Book of the Twelve*, edited by P. L. Redditt and A. Schart, 214–31. BZAW 325. New York: de Gruyter, 2003.

Baumgartner, Joseph M. "On the Non-Literal Use of מעשׂר/δεκάτη." *JBL* 103 (1984) 245–51.

Baur, Ferdinand Christian. *Das Christenthum und die christliche Kirche in den ersten Jahrhunderten.* Tübingen: L. Fr. Fues, 1861.

Bautch, Richard J. "The Function of Covenant across Ezra-Nehemiah." In *Unity and Disunity in Ezra-Nehemiah: Redaction, Rhetoric, and Reader*, edited by M. Boda and P. Redditt, 8–24. HBM 17. Sheffield: Phoenix, 2008.

Bazzana, Giovanni Batista. "*Basileia* and Debt Relief: The Forgiveness of Debts in the Lord's Prayer in the Light of Documentary Papyri." *CBQ* 73 (2011) 511–25.

Beaulieu, Paul-Alain. *The Pantheon of Uruk during the Neo-Babylonian Period.* CM 23. Leiden: Brill, 2003.

Bechard, Raymond. *Unspeakable: The Hidden Truth Behind the World's Fastest-Growing Crime.* New York: Compel, 2006.

Beck, Martin. *Elia und die Monolatrie: Ein Beitrag zur religionsgeschichtlichen Rückfrage nach dem vorschriftprophetischen Jahwe-Glauben.* BZAW 281. Berlin: de Gruyter, 1999.

———. *Der "Tag YHWHs" im Dodekapropheton.* BZAW 356. Berlin: de Gruyter, 2005.

Becker, Gary. "A Theory of Allocation of Time." *Economic Journal* 75 (1965) 493–517.

Beckman, Gary. *Hittite Birth Rituals.* StBT 29. Wiesbaden: Harrassowitz, 1983.

———. "Royal Ideology and State Administration in Hittite Anatolia." In *CANE* 529–43.

———. "The Wrath of Telipinu." In *COS* 1.151–55.

Bederman, David J. *International Law in Antiquity.* CSICL. Cambridge: Cambridge University Press, 2001.

Bedford, Peter Ross. "The Economic Role of the Jerusalem Temple in Achaemenid Judah: Comparative Perspectives." In *Shai Le-Sara Japhet: Studies in the Bible, Its Exegesis, and Its Language*, edited by M. Bar-Asher et al., 3–20. Jerusalem: Bialik Institute, 2007.

———. *Temple Restoration in Early Achaemenid Judah.* JSJSup 65. Leiden: Brill, 2001.

Bell, Catherine. *Ritual: Perspectives and Dimensions.* Oxford: Oxford University Press, 2009.

Bell, Richard H. *The Irrevocable Call of God: An Inquiry into Paul's Theology of Israel*. WUNT 184. Tübingen: Mohr/Siebeck, 2005.

Ben Yekutiel, Yechiel. ספר מעלות המדות. Cremona, 1556.

Ben Zvi, Ehud. *Micah*. FOTL 21B. Grand Rapids: Eerdmans, 2000.

———. "Studying Prophetic Texts against Their Original Backgrounds: Preordained Scripts and Alternative Horizons of Research." In *Prophets and Paradigms: Essays in Honor of Gene M. Tucker*, edited by Stephen Breck Reid, 125–35. JSOTSup229. Sheffield: Academic, 1996.

———. "The Successful, Wise, Worthy Wife of Prov 31:10–31 as a Source for Reconstructing Aspects of Thought and Economy in the Late Persian/Early Hellenistic Period." In *The Economy of Ancient Judah in Its Historical Context*, edited by M. L. Miller et al., 27–51. Winona Lake, IN: Eisenbrauns, 2015.

———. "Twelve Prophetic Books or 'The Twelve?': A Few Preliminary Considerations." In *Forming Prophetic Literature: Essays on Isaiah and the Twelve in Honor of John D. W. Watts*, edited by James W. Watts and P. R. House, 131–38. JSOTSup 235. Sheffield: Academic, 1996.

Ben Zvi, Ehud, and James D. Nogalski. *Two Sides of a Coin: Juxtaposing Views on Interpreting the Book of the Twelve/the Twelve Prophetic Books*. AG 201. Piscataway, NJ: Gorgias, 2009.

Bergman, Claudia. *Childbirth as a Metaphor for Crisis: Evidence from the Ancient Near East, the Hebrew Bible, and 1QH XI, 1–18*. BZAW 382. Berlin: de Gruyter, 2008.

Bernstein, Moshe. "Pesher Habakkuk." In *EDSS* 2:647–50.

Berquist, Jon L. "Approaching Yehud." In *Approaching Yehud: New Approaches to the Study of the Persian Period*, edited by J. Berquist, 1–6. SemeiaSt 50. Atlanta: SBL, 2007.

Bertman, Stephen. *Handbook to Life in Ancient Mesopotamia*. New York: Facts on File, 2003.

Bertram, Georg. "ἔργον." In *TDNT* 2.635–55.

Betz, Hans Dieter. *A Commentary on the Sermon on the Mount, including the Sermon on the Plain (Matt 5:3—7:27 and Luke 6:20–49)*. Hermeneia. Minneapolis: Augsburg Fortress, 1995.

———. "Sermon on the Mount/Plain." In *ABD* 5.1106–12.

Beuken, Willem A. M. *Haggai-Sacharja 1–8: Studien zur Überlieferungsgeschichte der frühnachexilischen Prophetie*. SSN 10. Assen: Van Gorcum, 1967.

Beyerlin, Walter. "Gattung und Herkunft des Rahmens im Richterbuch." In *Tradition und Situation. Studien zur alttestamentlichen Prophetie: Artur Weiser zum 70 Geburtstag*, edited by Ernst Würthwein and Otto Kaiser, 1–29. Göttingen: Vandenhoeck & Ruprecht, 1963.

Bickerman, Elias. *The God of the Maccabees: Studies on the Meaning and Origin of the Maccabean Revolt*. 1937. Translated by H. R. Moehring. Leiden: Brill, 1979.

Bidmead, Julye. "The *Akītu* Festival: Religious Continuity and Royal Legitimation in Mesopotamia." PhD diss., Vanderbilt University, 2002.

Bienkowski, Piotr, and Alan Millard, eds. *Dictionary of the Ancient Near East*. Philadelphia: University of Pennsylvania Press, 2000.

Billings, Drew W. *Acts of the Apostles and the Rhetoric of Roman Imperialism*. Cambridge: Cambridge University Press, 2017.

Binger, Tilde. *Asherah: Goddesses in Ugarit, Israel, and the Old Testament*. JSOTSup 232. Sheffield: Sheffield Academic, 1997.

Black, Jeremy A. "Mother Goddesses." In *DANE* 202.

Black, Jeremy A., et al., eds. *A Concise Dictionary of Akkadian*. Wiesbaden: Harrassowitz, 2000.

———. *The Literature of Ancient Sumer*. New York: Oxford University Press, 2004.

Blackman, Aylward. "Some Remarks on an Emblem upon the Head of an Ancient Egyptian Birth-Goddess." *JEA* 3 (1916) 199–206.

Blenkinsopp, Joseph. *Abraham: The Story of a Life*. Grand Rapids: Eerdmans, 2015.

———. *Creation, Un-Creation, Re-Creation: A Discursive Commentary on Genesis 1–11*. New York: T. & T. Clark, 2011.

———. *Ezra-Nehemiah: A Commentary*. OTL. Philadelphia: Westminster, 1988.

Bloch, René. *Jüdische Drehbühnen: Biblische Variationen im antiken Judentum*. Tübingen: Mohr/Siebeck, 2013.

Block, Daniel I. *Ezekiel 25–48*. NICOT. Grand Rapids: Eerdmans, 1998.

Blomberg, Craig L. *The Historical Reliability of the Gospels*. Downers Grove, IL: InterVarsity, 2007.

Bluedorn, Wolfgang. *Yahweh versus Ba'alism: A Theological Reading of the Gideon- Abimelech Narrative*. JSOTSup 329. Sheffield: Sheffield Academic, 2001.

Boadt, Lawrence. *The Hebrew Prophets: Visionaries of the Ancient World*. CBS. New York: St. Martin's Griffin, 1997.

Böck, Barbara. "Überlegungen zu einem Kultfest der altmesopotamischen Göttin Inanna." *Numen* 51 (2004) 20–46.

Boda, Mark J. *The Book of Zechariah*. NICOT. Grand Rapids: Eerdmans, 2016.

———. "From Fasts to Feasts: The Literary Function of Zechariah 7–8." *CBQ* 65 (2003) 390–407.

———. *Praying the Tradition: The Origin and Use of Tradition in Nehemiah 9*. BZAW 277. Berlin: de Gruyter, 1999.

Bodi, Daniel. *The Book of Ezekiel and the Poem of Erra*. OBO 104. Göttingen: Vandenhoeck & Ruprecht, 1991.

Boer, Roland E. "The Sacred Economy of Ancient Israel." *SJOT* 21 (2007) 29–48.

———. *The Sacred Economy of Ancient Israel*. LAI. Louisville: Westminster John Knox, 2015.

Bonhoeffer, Dietrich. *The Cost of Discipleship*. 1937. Translated by R. H. Fuller. London: SCM, 1959.

Bons, Eberhard. *Das Buch Hosea*. NSKAT 23/1. Stuttgart: Katholisches Bibelwerk, 1996.

Bordieu, Pierre. "The Forms of Capital." In *Handbook of Theory and Research for the Sociology of Education*, edited by J. G. Richardson, 241–58. New York: Greenwood, 1986.

Bottero, Jean. *La plus vieille religion. En Mésopotamie*. FH 82. Paris: Gallimard, 1998.

Boulay, R. A. *Flying Serpents and Dragons: The Story of Mankind's Reptilian Past*. Escondido, CA: Book Tree, 1999.

Bow, Beverly, and George E. Nickelsburg. "Patriarchy with a Twist: Men and Women in Tobit." In *Tobit and Judith*, edited by A. Brenner-Idan and H. Efthimiadis-Keith, 48–63. FCB 537. London: Bloomsbury, 2015.

Bowker, John. *The Targums and Rabbinic Literature: An Introduction to Jewish Interpretations of Scripture*. Cambridge: Cambridge University Press, 1969.

Bowler, Kate. *Blessed: A History of the American Prosperity Gospel*. New York: Oxford University Press, 2013.

Braaten, Laurie J. "Earth Community in Hosea 2." In *The Earth Bible: Earth Story in the Prophets*, vol. 4, edited by Norman Habel, 190–95. Sheffield: Sheffield Academic, 2001.

———. "God Sows: Hosea's Land Theme in the Book of the Twelve." In *Thematic Threads in the Book of the Twelve*, edited by P. Redditt and A. Schart, 104–32. BZAW 325. New York: de Gruyter, 2003.

———. "Parent-Child Imagery in Hosea." PhD diss., Boston University, 1987.

Brandon, Samuel George Frederick. *Jesus and the Zealots: A Study of the Political Factor in Primitive Christianity*. Manchester: University of Manchester Press, 1967.

Brenner-Idan, Athalya. "Pornoprophetics Revisited: Some Additional Reflections." *JSOT* 70 (1996) 63–86.

Briant, Pierre. *From Cyrus to Alexander: A History of the Persian Empire*, 1996. Translated by P. T. Daniels. Winona Lake, IN: Eisenbrauns, 2002.

Bringmann, Klaus. *Hellenistische Reform und Religionsverfolgung in Judäa: Eine Untersuchung zur jüdische-hellenistischen Geschichte (175–163 v. Chr.)*. AAWG.PH 3/132. Göttingen: Vandenhoeck & Ruprecht, 1983.

Brodie, Thomas L. "Luke 7:36–50 as an Internalization of 2 Kings 4:1–37: A Study of Luke's Use of Rhetorical Imitation." *Bib* 64 (1983) 457–85.

Bronner, Leah. *The Stories of Elijah and Elisha as Polemics against Ba'al Worship*. POS 6. Leiden: Brill, 1968.

Brown, Dale. *The Book of Buechner: A Journey through His Writings*. Louisville: Westminster John Knox, 2006.

Brown, Raymond. "The Pater Noster as an Eschatological Prayer." *TS* 22 (1961) 175–208.

Bruce, Frederick Fyvie. *The Acts of the Apostles: Greek Text with Introduction and Commentary*. Grand Rapids: Eerdmans, 1990.

———. "Lycaonia." In *ABD* 4.420–22.

Brueggemann, Walter. *Deep Memory, Exuberant Hope: Contested Truth in a Post-Christian World*. Minneapolis: Augsburg Fortress, 2000.

———. *Disruptive Grace: Reflections on God, Scripture, and the Church*. Minneapolis: Fortress, 2011.

———. *Isaiah 40–66*. Westminster Bible Companion. Louisville: Westminster John Knox, 1998.

———. "Jeremiah's Use of Rhetorical Questions." *JBL* 92 (1973) 358–74.

———. *The Land: Place as Gift, Promise and Challenge in Biblical Faith*. 2nd ed. OBT. Minneapolis: Fortress, 2002.

———. *The Prophetic Imagination*. 2nd ed. Minneapolis: Augsburg Fortress, 2001.

Bruhn, John G. *The Sociology of Community Connections*. New York: Springer, 2011.

Bryant, Margaret M. "Proverbial Lore in American Life and Speech." *WF* 10 (1951) 134–42.

Bryce, Trevor. *The Kingdom of the Hittites*. New York: Oxford University Press, 1998.

———. *Life and Society in the Hittite World*. New York: Oxford University Press, 2002.

———. *Letters of the Great Kings of the Ancient Near East: The Royal Correspondence of the Late Bronze Age*. London: Routledge, 2003.

Buccellati, Giorgio. *"Quando in alto i cieli . . .": La spiritualità mesopotamica a confronto con quella biblica*. Milan: Jaca Book, 2012.

———. "The Descent of Inanna as a Ritual Journey to Kutha?" *SMS* 4/3 (1982) 3–7.

Buchan, James. *Frozen Desire: An Inquiry into the Meaning of Money*. New York: Farrar, Straus and Giroux, 1997.

Buechner, Frederick. *On the Road with the Archangel*. San Francisco: Harper & Row, 1997.

Bunck, Julie M., and Michael R. Fowler. *Bribes, Bullets, and Intimidation: Drug Trafficking and the Law in Central America*. State College: Pennsylvania State University Press, 2012.

Campbell, Joseph. *The Hero with a Thousand Faces*. 1949. Reprint, Novato, CA: New World Library, 2008.

Campbell, Michael. *Popular Music in America: The Beat Goes On*. Boston: Schirmer Cengage Learning, 2013.

Capper, Brian J. "The Palestinian Cultural Context of Earliest Christian Community of Goods." In *The Book of Acts in Its First Century Setting*, vol. 4: *Palestinian Setting*, edited by Richard Bauckham, 323–56. Grand Rapids: Eerdmans, 1995.

Caquot, André. "Le dieu ʿAthtar et les textes de Ras Shamra." *Syria* 35 (1958) 45–60.

———. "Une nouvelle interpretation de *CAT* 1.19.1.1–19." *SEL* 2 (1985) 93–114.

Cardascia, Guillaume. *Les archives des Murašû, une famille d'hommes d'affaires babyloniens à l'époque Perse (455–403 av. J.-C.)*. Paris: Imprimerie nationale, 1951.

Carlisle, Rodney P., ed. *Encyclopedia of Intelligence and Counterintelligence*. London: Routledge, 2015.

Carlson Robert A. *Preaching Like the Prophets: The Hebrew Prophets as Examples for the Practice of Pastoral Preaching*. Eugene, OR: Wipf & Stock, 2017.

Carroll, Michael P. *The Penitente Brotherhood: Patriarchy and Hispano-Catholicism in New Mexico*. Baltimore: Johns Hopkins University Press, 2002.

Carroll, Robert P. "Is Humour Also among the Prophets?" In *On Humour and the Comic in the Hebrew Bible*, edited by Y. T. Radday and A. Brenner-Idan, 169–90. BLS 23. Louisville: Westminster John Knox, 1992.

———. *Jeremiah*. London: SCM, 1986.

———. "Textual Strategies and Ideology in the Second Temple Period." In *Second Temple Studies*, vol. 1: *Persian Period*, edited by Philip R. Davies, 108–24. JSOTSup 117. Sheffield: Sheffield Academic, 1991.

Carroll R., M. Daniel. Review of *Eighth Century Prophets: A Social Analysis*, by D. N. Premnath. http://www.denverseminary.edu/article/eighth-century-prophets-a-social-analysis/.

Carson, David A. *Matthew*. EBC. Grand Rapids: Zondervan, 1984.

Carter, Charles E. *The Emergence of Yehud in the Persian Period: A Social and Demographic Study*. JSOTSup 294. Sheffield: Sheffield Academic, 1999.

Carter, Nancy Corson. Woman as Healer: Destruction and Renewal—Re-Membering Inanna." *Anima* 11 (1984) 3–10.

Carter, Warren. *Matthew and the Margins: A Sociopolitical and Religious Reading*, 2000. JSNTSup 204. London: T. & T. Clark, 2004.

Cartledge, Tony W. *Vows in the Hebrew Bible and the Ancient Near East*. JSOTSup 147. Sheffield: JSOT Press, 1992.

Casey, Maurice. *An Aramaic Approach to Q: Sources for the Gospels of Matthew and Luke*. SNTSMS 122. Cambridge: Cambridge University Press, 2002.

Cathcart, Kevin, and K. Jeppeson. "Micah 2:4 and Nahum 3:16–17 in the Light of Akkadian." In *Fucus: A Semitic/Afrasian Gathering in Remembrance of Albert Ahrman*, edited by Yoel L. Arbeitman, 191–200. Amsterdam: Benjamins, 1988.

Ceccarelli, Manuel. *Enki und Ninmaḫ: Eine mythische Erzählung in sumerischer Sprache*. ORA 16. Tübingen: Mohr/Siebeck, 2016.

Ceresko, Anthony R. "Janus Parallelism in Amos' Oracles against the Nations (Amos 1:3—2:16)." *JBL* 113 (1994) 485–90.

Chaney, Marvin L. "Accusing Whom of What? Hosea's Rhetoric of Promiscuity." In *Peasants, Prophets, and Political Economy*, 175-90. Eugene, OR: Cascade Books, 2017.

———. "Bitter Bounty: The Dynamics of Political Economy Critiqued by the Eighth-Century Prophets." In *Peasants, Prophets, and Political Economy*, 147–59. Eugene, OR: Cascade Books, 2017.

———. "Coveting Your Neighbor's House in Social Context." In *Peasants, Prophets, and Political Economy*, 67–82. Eugene, OR: Cascade Books, 2017.

———. "Debt Easement in Israelite History and Tradition." In *Peasants, Prophets, and Political Economy*, 106–20. Eugene, OR: Cascade Books, 2017.

———. "Micah—Models Matter: Political Economy and Micah 6:9–15." In *Ancient Israel: The Old Testament in Its Social Context*, edited by Philip F. Esler, 145–60. Minneapolis: Fortress, 2006. Reprinted in *Peasants, Prophets, and Political Economy*, 205–19. Eugene, OR: Cascade Books, 2017.

———. *Peasants, Prophets, and Political Economy: The Hebrew Bible and Social Analysis.* Eugene, OR: Cascade Books, 2017.

———. "The Political Economy of Peasant Poverty." In *Peasants, Prophets, and Political Economy*, 121–46. Eugene, OR: Cascade Books, 2017.

———. "Producing Peasant Poverty: Debt Instruments in Amos 2:6b-8, 13-16." In Peasants, Prophets, and Political Economy, 191–204. Eugene, OR: Cascade Books, 2017.

———. "Some Choreographic Notes on the Dance of Theory with Data: A Response to Roland Boer, *The Sacred Economy*." In *Peasants, Prophets, and Political Economy*, 243–49. Eugene, OR: Cascade Books, 2017.

———. "Whose Sour Grapes? The Addressees of Isaiah 5:1–7." In *Peasants, Prophets, and Political Economy*, 160–74. Eugene, OR: Cascade Books, 2017.

Charlesworth, James H., ed. *The Old Testament Pseudepigrapha.* 2 vols. Garden City, NY: Doubleday, 1983–85.

Charpin, Dominique. "L'*andurârum* à Mari." *MARI* 6 (1990) 253–70.

Chavel, Simeon. "'Let My People Go': Emancipation, Revelation, and Scribal Activity in Jeremiah 38:8–14." *JSOT* 76 (1997) 71–95.

Chelst, Kenneth. *Exodus and Emancipation: Biblical and African-American Slavery.* Jerusalem: Urim, 2009.

Childs, Brevard S. *Isaiah.* OTL. Louisville: Westminster John Knox, 2001.

———. *Isaiah and the Assyrian Crisis.* London: SCM, 1967.

Chirichigno, Gregory C. *Debt-Slavery in Israel and the Ancient Near East.* JSOTSup 141. Sheffield: Sheffield Academic, 1993.

Chopp, Rebecca S. *The Praxis of Suffering: An Interpretation of Liberation and Political Theologies.* Maryknoll, NY: Orbis, 1986.

Chung, Youn Ho. *The Sin of the Calf: The Rise of the Bible's Negative Attitude toward the Golden Calf.* LHBOT 523. New York: T. & T. Clark, 2010.

Cimok, Fatih. *The Hittites and Ḫattuša.* Istanbul: Yayinlari, 2008.

Citrin, Jack, et al. "Public Opinion Toward Immigration Reform: The Role of Economic Motivations." *JP* 59 (1997) 858–81.

Claassens, L. Juliana M. "'Give Us a Portion among Our Father's Brothers': The Daughters of Zelophehad, Land, and the Quest for Human Dignity." *JSOT* 37 (2013) 319–37.

Clain, Suzanne Heller, and Charles E. Zech. "A Household Production Analysis of Religious and Charitable Activity." *AJES* 58 (1999) 923–46.

Clark, Gordon R. *The Word Hesed in the Hebrew Bible.* JSOTSup 157. Sheffield: Sheffield Academic, 1993.

Clements, Ronald E. "Jeremiah: Prophet of Hope." *RevExp* 78 (1981) 345–63.

Clifford, Richard J. *Creation Accounts in the Ancient Near East and in the Bible*. CBQMS 26. Washington, DC: Catholic Biblical Association, 1994.

Cline, Eric H. *Biblical Archaeology: A Very Short Introduction*. New York: Oxford University Press, 2009.

Clines, David J. M. *The Theme of the Pentateuch*. JSOTSup 10. Sheffield: Sheffield Academic, 1997.

Clines, David J. M., and David M. Gunn. "'You Tried to Persuade Me' and 'Violence! Outrage!' in Jeremiah 20:7–8." *VT* 28 (1978) 20–27.

Cody, Aelred. "An Excursus on Priesthood in Israel." In *Ezekiel: With an Excursus on Old Testament Priesthood*, 256–63. OTM. Wilmington, DE: Glazier, 1984.

Cody, Diablo. *Juno: A Screenplay*. Santa Monica, CA: Mandate Pictures, 2007.

Cogan, Mordechai. *Imperialism and Religion: Assyria, Judah and Israel in the Eighth and Seventh Centuries BCE*. SBLMS 19. Missoula, MT: SBL, 1974.

Coggins, Richard J. "The Minor Prophets—One Book or Twelve?" In *Crossing the Boundaries: Essays in Biblical Interpretation in Honour of Michael D. Goulder*, edited by Stanley E. Porter et al., 57–68. BibIntSer 8. Leiden: Brill, 1994.

———. "The Problem of Isaiah 24–27." *ExpTim* 90 (1979) 328–33.

———. "The Samaritans and Acts." *NTS* 28 (1982) 423–34.

Cohen, Mark E. *Sumerian Hymnology: The Eršemma*. Cincinnati: Hebrew Union College, 1981.

Cohen, Shaye J. D. *The Beginnings of Jewishness: Boundaries, Varieties, Uncertainties*. Berkeley: University of California Press, 1999.

———. "Those Who Say They Are Jews and Are Not: How Do You Know a Jew in Antiquity When You See One?" In *Diasporas in Antiquity*, edited by Shaye J. D. Cohen and Ernest S. Frerichs, 1–46. BJS 288. Atlanta: Scholars, 1993.

Cohn, Seock-Tae. *Yhwh, the Husband of Israel: The Metaphor of Marriage between Yhwh and Israel*. Eugene, OR: Wipf & Stock, 2002.

Coldwell, David C. *Zechariah's Hope*. Dublin: Interact, 2018.

Collins, John J. "Marriage, Divorce, and Family in Second Temple Judaism." In *Families in Ancient Israel*, edited by Leo G. Perdue et al., 104–62. FRC. Louisville: Westminster John Knox, 1997.

Collins, Raymond F. "Beatitudes." In *ABD* 1.629–31.

Collins, Terence. *The Mantle of Elijah: The Redaction Criticism of the Prophetical Books*. New York: Continuum, 1993.

Coltman, Leycester. *The Real Fidel Castro*. New Haven, CT: Yale University Press, 2003.

Comte, Auguste. *Introduction to Positive Philosophy*. 1842. Translated by F. Ferré. Indianapolis: Hackett, 1988.

Conybeare, Frederick Cornwallis. *Philostratus: The Life of Apollonius of Tyana*. New York: MacMillan, 1912.

Conzelmann, Hans. *The Theology of St. Luke*. 1954. Translated by G. Buswell. New York: Harper, 1961.

Coogan, Michael D. *Stories from Ancient Canaan*. Louisville: Westminster, 1978.

Coogan, Michael D., and Mark Smith. *Stories from Ancient Canaan*. Louisville: Westminster John Knox, 2012.

Cook, Joan E. "The Song of Hannah: Texts and Contexts." PhD diss., Vanderbilt University, 1989.

Cook, Stephen L. *The Social Roots of Biblical Yahwism*. SBLStBL 8. Atlanta: SBL Press, 2004.

Cooper, Alan. "Two Exegetical Notes on *Aqht*." *UF* 20 (1988) 19–26.

Cooper, Jerrold. "Assyrian Prophecies, the Assyrian Tree, and the Mesopotamian Origins of Jewish Monotheism, Greek Philosophy, Christian Theology, Gnosticism, and Much More." *JAOS* 120 (2000) 430–44.

Coote, Robert A. (ed.). *Elijah and Elisha in Socioliterary Perspective*. Atlanta: Scholars, 1992.

Cornelius, Izak. *The Many Faces of the Goddess: The Iconography of the Syro-Palestinian Goddesses Anat, Astarte, Qedeshet, and Asherah*. OBO 204. Göttingen: Vandenhoeck & Ruprecht, 2004.

Corral, Martin Alonso. *Ezekiel's Oracles against Tyre: Historical Reality and Motivations*. BibOr 46. Rome: Editrice Pontificio Istituto Biblico, 2002.

Cosmopoulos, Michael B. *Bronze Age Eleusis and the Origins of the Eleusinian Mysteries*. Cambridge: Cambridge University Press, 2015.

Cousin, Georges, and Gaston Deschamps. "Lettre de Darius fils d'Hystapes." *BCH* 13 (1889) 529–42.

Cowley, A. E. *Aramaic Papyri of the Fifth Century B.C.* Oxford: Clarendon, 1923.

Craigie, Peter C. *Ezekiel*. DSB. Louisville: Westminster John Knox, 1983.

———. "Helel, Athtar and Phaeton, Jes 14:12–15." *ZAW* 85 (1973) 223–25.

———. "Ugarit and the Bible: Progress and Regress in Fifty Years of Literary Study." In *Ugarit in Retrospect: Fifty Years of Ugarit and Ugaritic*, edited by Gordon D. Young, 99–111. Winona Lake, IN: Eisenbrauns, 1981.

Creach, Jerome F. D. *Yahweh as Refuge and the Editing of the Hebrew Psalter*. JSOTSup 217. Sheffield: Sheffield Academic, 1996.

Crenshaw, James L. *Hymnic Affirmation of Divine Justice: The Doxologies of Amos and Related Texts in the Old Testament*. SBLDS 24. Missoula: Scholars, 1975.

———. *Joel: A New Translation with Introduction and Commentary*. AB 24C. New York: Doubleday, 1995.

———. *Old Testament Wisdom: An Introduction*. Louisville: Westminster John Knox, 2010.

———. "Why Knows What Yhwh Will Do?: The Character of God in the Book of Joel." In *Fortunate the Eyes That See: Essays in Honor of David Noel Freedman in Celebration of His Seventieth Birthday*, edited by A. B. Beek et al., 185–96. Grand Rapids: Eerdmans, 1995.

Crepeau, Richard C. *NFL Football: A History of America's New National Pastime*. Chicago: University of Illinois Press, 2014.

Crosby, Michael H. *House of Disciples: Church, Economics, and Justice in Matthew*. Maryknoll, NY: Orbis, 1988.

Cross, Frank Moore. *Canaanite Myth and Hebrew Epic*. Cambridge: Harvard University Press, 1973.

———. *From Epic to Canon: History and Literature in Ancient Israel*. Baltimore: Johns Hopkins University Press, 1998.

Crouch, Carly L. "Ištar and the Motif of the Cosmological Warrior: Assurbanipal's Adaptation of *Enuma Elish*." In *"Thus Says Ishtar of Arbela": Prophecy in Israel, Assyria, and Egypt in the Neo-Assyrian Period*, edited by R. P. Gordon and Hans M. Barstad, 129–42. Winona Lake, IN: Eisenbrauns, 2013.

Cuffari, Anton. *Judenfeindschaft in Antike und Altem Testament: Terminologische, historische und theologische Untersuchungen*. Hamburg: Philo, 2007.

Cuffey, Kenneth H. *The Literary Coherence of the Book of Micah: Remnant, Restoration, and Promise*. New York: Bloomsbury T. & T. Clark, 2015.

Cumont, Franz. *The Oriental Religions in Roman Paganism*. 1929. Reprint, New York: Dover, 1956.

Dalglish, Edward R. *Psalm Fifty-One in the Light of Ancient Near Eastern Patternism*. Leiden: Brill, 1962.

Dalley, Stephanie. *Myths from Mesopotamia*. New York: Oxford University Press, 2000.

———. "Near Eastern Myths and Legends." In *The Biblical World*, edited by John Barton, 1.41–64. London: Routledge, 2002.

Dandamaev, Muhammad A. "Neo-Babylonian Society and Economy." In *CAH* 3/2.252–75.

———. "Slavery." In *ABD* 6.56–85.

———. *Slavery in Babylonia from Nabopolassar to Alexander the Great*. DeKalb: Northern Illinois University Press, 1984.

Daniels. Dwight R. *Hosea and Salvation History: The Early Traditions of Israel in the Prophecy of Hosea*. BZAW 191. Berlin: de Gruyter, 1990.

Daube, David. "Absalom and the Ideal King." *VT* 48 (1998) 315–25.

Davenport, Tracy. "An Anti-Imperialist Twist to the 'Gilgamesh Epic.'" In *Gilgamesh and the World of Assyria*, edited by J. Azize and N. Weeks, 1–23. ANESSup 21. Leuven: Peeters, 2006.

David, Ellen. *Scripture, Culture, and Agriculture: An Agrarian Reading of the Bible*. New York: Cambridge University Press, 2009.

David, M. "The Manumission of Slaves Under Zedekiah." *OtSt* 5 (1948) 63–79.

Davidson, Steed Vernyl. *Empire and Exile: Postcolonial Readings of the Book of Jeremiah*. LHBOTS 542. London: T. & T. Clark, 2011.

Davies, Andrew. *Double Standards in Isaiah: Re-Evaluating Prophetic Ethics and Social Justice*. BibIntSer 46. Leiden: Brill, 2000.

Davies, William D., and Dale C. Allison Jr. *A Critical and Exegetical Commentary on the Gospel According to St. Matthew*. 3 vols. ICC. Edinburgh: T. & T. Clark, 1988–97.

Davis, Ellen F. *Scripture, Culture and Agriculture: An Agrarian Reading of the Bible*. Cambridge: Cambridge University Press, 2008.

Davis, James Colin. "Thomas More's *Utopia*: Sources, Legacy and Interpretation." In *The Cambridge Companion to Utopian Literature*, edited by G. Claeys, 28–50. Cambridge: Cambridge University Press, 2010.

Davis, Jessica Milner. *Farce*. 1978. Reprint, London: Routledge, 2017.

Dawson, Doyne. *Cities of the Gods: Communist Utopias in Greek Thought*. New York: Oxford University Press, 1992.

Day, John. "Asherah in the Hebrew Bible and Northwest Semitic Literature." *JBL* 105 (1986) 385–408.

———. "The Canaanite Inheritance of the Israelite Monarchy." In *King and Messiah in Israel and the Ancient Near East*, edited by John Day, 72–90. JSOTSup 220. Sheffield: Academic Press, 1998.

———. *From Creation to Babel: Studies in Genesis 1–11*. London: Bloomsbury, 2013.

———. *God's Conflict with the Dragon and the Sea: Echoes of a Canaanite Myth in the Old Testament*. Cambridge: Cambridge University, 1985.

———. "Why Does God 'Establish' Rather than 'Cut' Covenants in the Priestly Source?" In *Covenant as Context: Essays in Honour of E. W. Nicholson*, edited by A. D. H. Mayes and R. B. Salters, 91–110. Oxford: Oxford University Press, 2003.

———. *Yahweh and the Gods and Goddesses of Canaan*. JSOTSup 265. Sheffield: Sheffield Academic, 2000.

Day, Peggy L. "Anat." In *DDD* 36–43.

———. "Anat: Ugarit's 'Mistress of Animals.'" *JNES* 51 (1992) 181–90.

De Villiers, Pieter, ed. *Liberation Theology and the Bible*. Pretoria: University of South Africa Press, 1987.

Dearman, J. Andrew. *The Book of Hosea*. NICOT. Grand Rapids: Eerdmans, 2010.

———. *Jeremiah, Lamentations*. NIVAC. Grand Rapids: Zondervan, 2002.

DeBrabander, Firmin. "The Highest Form of Devotion: Spinoza on Piety, Patriotism, and the Therapy of Religion." *HPQ* 24 (2007) 19–37.

DeFerrari, Teresa M. Review of *The Politics of Jesus*, by John Howard Yoder. *CBQ* 36 (1974) 149–50.

Deist, Ferdinand E. *The Material Culture of the Bible: An Introduction*. BibSem 70. Sheffield: Sheffield Academic, 2000.

Derrett, J. Duncan M. *Law in the New Testament*. London: Dartman, Longman, and Todd, 1970.

———. "Simon Magus (Acts 8:9–24)." *ZNW* 73 (1982) 52–68.

Deselaers, Paul. *Das Buch Tobit*. Ostfildern: Patmos, 1990.

DeSilva, David A. *Introducing the Apocrypha: Message, Context, and Significance*. Grand Rapids: Baker Academic, 2002.

Dever, William G. *Did God Have a Wife? Archaeology and Folk Religion in Ancient Israel*. Grand Rapids: Eerdmans, 2005.

Diamond, A. R. Pete, and Kathleen O'Connor. "Unfaithful Passions: Coding Women Coding Men in Jer 2–3 (4.2)." In *Troubling Jeremiah*, edited by A. R. Pete Diamond et al., 123–45. JSOTSup 260. Sheffield: Sheffield Academic, 1999.

Dibelius, Martin. *Die urchristliche Überlieferung von Johannes dem Täufer*. Göttingen: Vandenhoeck & Ruprecht, 1911.

Dietrich, Manfred, Oswald Loretz, and Joaquín Sanmartín, eds. *The Cuneiform Alphabetic Texts from Ugarit, Ras Ibn Hani and Other Places*. ALASP 8. Münster: Ugarit, 1995.

Dietrich, Walter. "Der heilige Ort im Leben und Glauben Altisraels." In *The Land of Israel in Bible, History, and Theology: Studies in Honour of Ed Noort*, edited by J. van Ruiten and J. Cornelis de Vos, 219–36. VTSup 124. Leiden: Brill, 2009.

Diewert, David A. "Job 7:12: *Yam, Tannin*, and the Surveillance of Job." *JBL* 106 (1987) 203–15.

Dijkstra, Meindert. "The Law of Moses: The Memory of Mosaic Religion in and after the Exile." In *Yahwism After the Exile: Perspectives on Israelite Religion in the Persian Era*, edited by Rainer Albertz and Bob Becking, 70–98. Assen: Van Gorcum, 2003.

Dijkstra, Meindert, and Johannes C. de Moor. "Problematic Passages in the Legend of *Aqhatu*." *UF* 7 (1975) 171–215.

Dillon, Matthew. *Omens and Oracles: Divination in Ancient Greece*. London: Routledge, 2017.

Dimant, Devorah. "The Fallen Angels in the Dead Sea Scrolls and in Apocryphal and Pseudepigraphical Books Related to Them." PhD diss., Hebrew University, 1974.

———. *From Enoch to Tobit: Collected Studies in Ancient Jewish Literature*. FAT 114. Tübingen: Mohr/Siebeck, 2017.

Dinter, Paul E. *The Changing Priesthood: From the Bible to the 21st Century*. Chicago: Thomas More Association, 1996.

Di Pede, Elena. "Enquête sur l'identité du narrateur du livre de Tobit." In *Révéler les oeuvres de Dieu: Lecture narrative du livre de Tobie*, by E. Di Pede et al., 141–55. Paris: Lessius, 2014.

———. "Tobie au fil de recit." In *Révéler les oeuvres de Dieu: Lecture narrative du livre de Tobie*, by E. Di Pede et al., 15–137. Paris: Lessius, 2014.

Di Vito, Robert A. *Studies in Third Millenium Sumerian and Akkadian Personal Names: The Designation and Conception of the Personal God.* StPohl 16. Roma: Editrice Pontificio Istituto Biblica, 1993.

Donner, Herbert. "Die soziale Botschaft der Propheten im Lichte der Geschellschaftordnung in Israel." *OrAnt* 2 (1963) 329–45.

Donner, Herbert, and Wolfgang Röllig, eds. *Kanaanäische und aramäische Inschriften.* Wiesbaden: Harrassowitz, 1979.

Dossin, Georges. "Sur le prophétisme à Mari." In *La divination en Mésopotamie ancienne et dans les régions voisines*, 77–86. Paris: Presses universitaires de France, 1966.

Douglas, Mary. *In the Wilderness: The Doctrine of Defilement in the Book of Numbers.* Sheffield: Sheffield Academic, 1993.

———. *Purity and Danger: Analysis of Concepts of Pollution and Taboo.* 1966. Reprint, London: Routledge, 2003.

Downs, David J. "Economics, Taxes, and Tithes." In *The World of the New Testament*, edited by Joel Green and Lee McDonald, 156–68. Grand Rapids: Baker Academic, 2013.

Doyle, Brian. *The Apocalypse of Isaiah Metaphorically Speaking.* BETL 151. Leuven: Peeters, 2001.

Drabble, Margaret. *A Summer Bird-Cage.* New York: Morrow, 1969.

Draffkorn-Kilmer, Anne E. "How Was Queen Ereshkigal Tricked?: A New Interpretation of the *Descent of Ishtar.*" *UF* 3 (1971) 299–309.

———. "*Ilāni/Elohim.*" *JBL* 76 (1957) 216–24.

Driel, G. van. "The *Murašū* in Context." *JESHO* 32 (1989) 203–29.

Duguid, Iain. *Ezekiel.* NIVAC. Grand Rapids: Zondervan, 1999.

Duhigg, Charles. *Smarter, Faster, Better: The Transformative Power of Real Productivity.* New York: Random House, 2016.

Duhm, Bernhard. *Das Buch Jeremia.* KHC 11. Tübingen: Mohr, 1901.

———. *Israels Propheten.* Lebensfragen 26. Tübingen: Mohr/Siebeck, 1916.

Dupont, Jacques. "La construction du discours de Milet (Ac 20, 18–35)." In *Nouvelles études sur les Actes de Apôtres*, 424–45. Paris: Cerf, 1984.

Durand, Jean-Marie. *Les documents épistolaires du palais de Mari.* Paris: Cerf, 2000.

Eaton, John H. *Kingship and the Psalms.* London: SCM, 1976.

Ebeling, Erich. *Die akkadische Gebetsserie "Handerhebung."* Berlin: Akademie, 1953.

Eberhart, Christian. "Sacrifice? Holy Smokes!: Reflections on Cult Terminology for Understanding Sacrifice in the Hebrew Bible." In *Ritual and Metaphor: Sacrifice in the Bible*, edited by C. Eberhart, 17–32. Atlanta: SBL, 2011.

Edelman, Diana V. *King Saul in the Historiography of Judah.* JSOTSup 121. Sheffield: Sheffield Academic, 1991.

———. *The Origins of the "Second" Temple: Persian Imperial Policy and the Rebuilding of Jerusalem.* London: Routledge, 2014.

Eichrodt, Walther. *Ezekiel: A Commentary.* 1966. Translated by C. Quin. Philadelphia: Westminster, 1970.

———. *Theology of the Old Testament.* 2 vols. Philadelphia: Westminster, 1961, 1967.

Eidevall, Göran. *Amos: A New Translation with Introduction and Commentary.* AYB. New Haven, CT: Yale University Press, 2017.

Eilberg-Schwarz, Howard. *The Savage in Judaism*. Bloomington: Indiana University Press, 1990.

Eisenbeis, Walther. *Die Wurzel* שלם *im Alten Testament*. BZAW 113. Berlin: de Gruyter, 1969.

Eisenberg, Ronald L. *Essential Figures in the Talmud*. New York: Jason Aronson, 2013.

Eissfeldt, Otto. *El im ugaritischen Pantheon*. Berlin: Akademie, 1951.

Eliade, Mircea. *The Sacred and the Profane: The Nature of Religion*. 1956. Translated by W. R. Trask. New York: Harcourt, Brace and World, 1959.

———, ed. *The Encyclopedia of Religion*. New York: Macmillan, 1987.

Eliade, Mircea, and Ioan Peter Couliano, eds. *Dictionnaire des religions*. Paris: Presses Universitaires, 1983.

Elliott, James K. *New Testament Textual Criticism: The Application of Thoroughgoing Principles: Essays on Manuscripts and Textual Variation*. NovTSup 137. Leiden: Brill, 2010.

Elnes, Eric E., and Patrick D. Miller. "Elyon." In *DDD* 293–99.

Emerton, John. "Ugaritic Notes." *JTS* 16 (1965) 438–43.

Eskenazi, Tamara C. "Sheshbazzar." In *ABD* 5.1207–9.

Espak, Peeter. *The God Enki in Sumerian Royal Ideology and Mythology*. CSAWC 87. Wiesbaden: Harrassowitz, 2015.

Eubank, Nathan. *Wages of Cross-Bearing and Debt of Sin: The Economy of Heaven in Matthew's Gospel*. BZNW 196. New York: de Gruyter, 2013.

Evans, Craig A. *Jesus and His World: The Archaeological Evidence*. Louisville: Westminster John Knox, 2012.

Evans, Donald, ed. *Creating the Child: The Ethics, Law, and Practice of Assisted Procreation*. London: Nijhoff, 1996.

Exum, J. Cheryl. "Prophetic Pornography." In *Plotted, Shot, and Painted: Cultural Representations of Biblical Women*, 101–28. JSOTSup 215. Sheffield: Sheffield Academic, 1996.

Ezigbo, Victor Ifeanyi, and Reggie L. Williams. "Converting a Colonialist Christ: Toward an African Postcolonial Christology." In *Evangelical Postcolonial Conversations: Global Awakenings in Theology and Praxis*, edited by Kay Higuera Smith et al., 88–101. Downers Grove, IL: InterVarsity, 2014.

Fabry, Heinz-Josef. "קרבן." In *TDOT* 13.152–58.

Fafchamps, Marcel, and Agnes R. Quisumbing. "Household Formation and Marriage Markets in Rural Areas." In *Handbook of Development Economics*, vol. 4, edited by T. P. Schultz and J. Strauss, 3187–3248. Radarweg: North-Holland, 2008.

Fager, Jeffrey. *Land Tenure and the Biblical Jubilee: Discovering a Moral World-View through the Sociology of Knowledge*. JSOTSup 155. Sheffield: JSOT Press, 1993.

Falkenstein, Adam. "Zu 'Inannas Gang zur Unterwelt.'" *AfO* 14 (1941–44) 113–38.

Faraone, Christopher A. "The Agonistic Context of Early Greek Binding Spells." In *Magika Hiera: Ancient Greek Magic and Religion*, edited by C. Faraone and D. Obbink, 3–32. New York: Oxford University Press, 1991.

Farber, Walter. *Lamaštu: An Edition of the Canonical Series of the* lamaštu *Incantations and Rituals and Related Texts from the Second and First Millenia B.C.* Winona Lake, IN: Eisenbrauns, 2014.

Farber-Flügge, Gertrude. *Der Mythos "Inanna und Enki" unter besonderer Berücksichtigung der Liste der* me. StPohl 10. Rome: Biblical Institute Press, 1973.

Faust, Avraham. *Judah in the Neo-Babylonian Period: The Archaeology of Desolation*. ABS 18. Atlanta: SBL, 2012.

Favazza, Armando R. *Bodies under Siege: Self-Mutilation, Nonsuicidal Self-Injury and Body Modification in Culture and Psychiatry*. Baltimore: Johns Hopkins University Press, 2011.

Fee, Gordon D. *The Disease of the Health and Wealth Gospels.* Vancouver: Regent College, 1985.

Feinman, Gary M. "Mesoamerican Temples." In *Temple in Society*, edited by Michael V. Fox, 67–82. Winona Lake, IN: Eisenbrauns, 1988.

Feldman, Daniel Z. "The Jewish Prohibition of Interest: Themes, Scopes, and Contemporary Application." In *The Oxford Handbook of Judaism and Economics*, edited by A. Levine, 239–54. New York: Oxford University Press, 2010.

Feldman, Marian H. *Diplomacy by Design: Luxury Arts and an "International Style" in the Ancient Near East, 1400–1200 BCE*. Chicago: University of Chicago Press, 2006.

Ferch, Arthur J. "Daniel 7 and Ugarit: A Reconsideration." *JBL* 99 (1980) 75–86.

Ferguson, Everett. *Backgrounds of Early Christianity*. Grand Rapids: Eerdmans, 2003.

———. *The Church of Christ: A Biblical Ecclesiology for Today*. Grand Rapids: Eerdmans, 1996.

Ferrara, Anthony J. Review of *Der Mythos "Inanna und Enki" unter besonderer Berücksichtigung der Liste der* me, by G. Farber-Flügge. *JNES* 37 (1978) 350–54.

Ferreiro, Alberto. *Simon Magus in Patristic, Medieval, and Early Modern Traditions*. SHCT 125. Leiden: Brill, 2005.

Feuerbach, Ludwig. *The Essence of Christianity*. 1881. Translated by G. Eliot. Minneola, NY: Dover, 2008.

Finger, Reta Halteman. "Economic Sharing in Acts? A History of (Mis)Interpretation." In *Of Widows and Meals: Communal Meals in the Book of Acts*, 12–47. Grand Rapids: Eerdmans, 2007.

Finkel, Asher. "The Prayer of Jesus in Matthew." In *Standing before God: Studies on Prayer in Scriptures and in Tradition: Essays in Honour of John Oesterreicher*, edited by A. Finkel and L. Frizzell, 131–69. New York: KTAV, 1981.

Finkel, Irving. "Transliteration of the Cyrus Cylinder Text." In *The Cyrus Cylinder: The King of Persia's Proclamation from Ancient Babylon*, edited by I. Finkel, 129–35. London: Tauris, 2013.

Finley, Moses I. *The Ancient Economy*. SCL 43. Berkeley: University of California Press, 1973.

Finley, Thomas J. *Joel, Amos, Obadiah: An Exegetical Commentary*. Richardson, TX: Biblical Studies Press, 2003.

Fischlin, Daniel, and Mark Fortier. *James I: The True Law of Free Democracies and* Basilikon Doron. Toronto: Center for Reformation and Renaissance Studies, 1996.

Fishbane, Michael. *Biblical Interpretation in Ancient Israel*. New York: Oxford University Press, 1985.

Fisher, Loren R. "Creation at Ugarit and in the Old Testament." *VT* 15 (1965) 313–24.

Fitzenreiter, Martin. "Grabdekoration und die Interpretation funerarer Rituale im Alten Reich." In *Social Aspects of Funerary Culture in the Egyptian Old and Middle Kingdoms*, edited by H. Willems, 67–140. OLA 103. Leuven: Peeters, 2001.

Fitzmyer, Joseph A. "The Aramaic Qorbān Inscription from Jebel Ḫalle eṭ-Ṭûri and Mark 7:11 / Matt 15:5." *JBL* 78 (1959) 60–65.

———. *The Dead Sea Scrolls and Christian Origins*. SDSS. Grand Rapids: Eerdmans, 2000.

———. *The One Who Is to Come*. Grand Rapids: Eerdmans, 2007.

———. *Tobit*. CEJL. Berlin: de Gruyter, 2003.

Fleming, Daniel E. *The Installation of Ba'al's High Priestess at Emar: A Window on Ancient Syrian Religion*. HSM 42. Atlanta: Scholars, 1992.

———. *Time at Emar: The Cultic Calendar and the Rituals from the Diviner's House*. Winona Lake, IN: Eisenbrauns, 2000.

Flesher, Paul Virgil McCracken. *Oxen, Women, or Citizens? Slaves in the System of the Mishnah*. BJS 143. Atlanta: Scholars, 1988.

Fletcher, Joann. *Exploring the Life, Myth, and Art of Ancient Egypt*. New York: Rosen, 2010.

Floyd, Michael H. "The משא as a Type of Prophetic Book." *JBL* 121 (2002) 401–22.

———. "New Form Criticism and Beyond: The Historicity of Prophetic Literature Revisited." In *The Book of the Twelve and the New Form Criticism*, edited by M. J. Boda et al., 17–36. ANEM 10. Atlanta: SBL Press, 2015.

Flückiger-Hawker, Esther. *Urnamma of Ur in Sumerian Literary Tradition*. OBO 166. Göttingen: Vandenhoeck & Ruprecht, 1999.

Flusser, David. *Judaism of the Second Temple Period*, vol. 2: *The Jewish Sages and Their Literature*. 2002. Translated by A. Yadin. Grand Rapids: Eerdmans, 2009.

Fohrer, Georg. *Das Buch Jesaja*. 3 vols. ZBK. Zurich: Zwingli, 1964.

———. "Krankheit im Lichte des alten Testaments." In *Studien zu alttestamentlichen Texte und Themen*, 172–87. BZAW 155. Berlin: de Gruyter, 1981.

Folmer, Margaretha Louise. *The Aramaic Language in the Achaemenid Period: A Study in Linguistic Variation*. OLA 68. Leuven: Peeters, 1995.

Fontaine, Carole R. "The Deceptive Goddess in Ancient Near Eastern Myth: Inanna and Inaraš." *Sem* 42 (1988) 84–102.

Fontenrose, Joseph Eddy. *Python: A Study of Delphic Myth and Its Origins*. Berkeley: University of California Press, 1959.

Foote, Stephanie. "Making Sport of Tonya." *JSSI* 27 (Feb 2003) 3–17.

Foster, Benjamin. *Before the Muses: An Anthology of Akkadian Literature*. Bethesda, MD: CDL, 2005.

France, Richard T. "By Their Fruits: Thoughts on the Metaphor of Fruit in the Bible." *RT* 11 (2013) 50–56.

Franco, Zeno E., and Philip G. Zimbardo. "The Psychology of Heroism: Extraordinary Champions of Humanity in an Unforgiving World." In *The Social Psychology of Good and Evil*, edited by A. G. Miller, 494–523. New York: Guilford, 2016.

Frankena, Rintje. "Untersuchungen zum Irra-Epos." *BiOr* 14 (1957) 2–10.

Frankfort, Henri. *Kingship and the Gods: A Study of Ancient Near Eastern Religion as the Integration of Society and Nature*. Chicago: University of Chicago Press, 1962.

Frazer, James G. *The Golden Bough: A Study in Magic and Religion*. London: MacMillan, 1890.

Frechette, Christopher. "The Ritual-Prayer *Nisaba 1* and Its Function." *JANER* 11 (2011) 70–93.

Freedman, William. "The Literary Motif: A Definition and Evaluation." *Novel: A Forum on Fiction* 4 (Winter 1971) 123–31.

Frick, Frank S. "The Political and Ideological Interests of Female Sexual Imagery in Hosea 1–3." In *To Break Every Yoke: Essays in Honor of Marvin L Chaney*, edited by Robert B. Coote and Norman K. Gottwald, 200–208. Sheffield: Sheffield Phoenix, 2007.

Fried, Lisbeth S. "Exploitation of Depopulated Land in Achaemenid Judah." In *The Economy of Ancient Judah in Its Historical Context*, edited by M. Miller et al., 151–64. Winona Lake, IN: Eisenbrauns, 2015.

———. *Ezra and the Law in History and Tradition*. SPOT. Columbia: University of South Carolina Press, 2014.

Friedrich, Johannes. *Hethitisches Elementarbuch*. Heidelberg: Carl Winter, 1967.

Friedrich, Johannes, and A. Kammenhuber, eds. *Hethitische Wörterbuch*. Heidelberg: Carl Winter, 1975.

Frymer-Kensky, Tikva. *In the Wake of the Goddesses: Women, Culture and the Biblical Transformation of Pagan Myth*. New York: Free Press, 1992.

———. "Virginity in the Bible." 1998. Reprinted in *Gender and Law in the Hebrew Bible and the Ancient Near East*, edited by Victor H. Matthews et al., 79–96. New York: T. & T. Clark, 2004.

Fuchs, Esther. Review of *Sexual and Marital Metaphors in Hosea, Jeremiah, Isaiah and Ezekiel*, by Sharon Moughtin-Mumby. *ThTo* 66 (2009) 376, 379–80.

Fyfe, Alec. "Worst Forms of Child Labor: Agriculture." In *The World of Child Labor: An Historical and Regional Survey*, edited by H. Hindman, 82–85. London: M. E. Sharp, 2009.

Gabbay, Uri. *The Eršema Prayers of the First Millennium BCE*. Wiesbaden: Harrassowitz, 2015.

Gabriel, Gösta. Enūma eliš—*Weg zu einer globalen Weltordnung: Pragmatik, Struktur und Semantik des babylonischen "Lieds auf Marduk."* ORA 12. Tübingen: Mohr/Siebeck, 2014.

Gadotti, Alhena. "The Feminine in Myths and Epic." In *Women in the Ancient Near East: A Sourcebook*, edited by M. Chavalas, 28–58. London: Routledge, 2014.

———. *"Gilgamesh, Enkidu and the Netherworld" and the Sumerian Gilgamesh Cycle*. Berlin: de Gruyter, 2014.

Galil, Gershon. *The Lower Stratum Families in the Neo-Assyrian Period*. CHANE 27. Leiden: Brill, 2007.

Gall, August Freiherr von. *Der Hebräische Pentateuch der Samaritaner*. 1918. Reprint, Giessen: Töpelmann, 1966.

Galter, Hannes D. "Der Gott Ea/Enki in der akkadischen Überlieferung. Eine Bestandsaufnahme des vorhandenen Materials." PhD diss., Karl-Franzens-Universitat, 1983.

García Martínez, Florentino, and J. C. Tigchelaar. *The Dead Sea Scrolls: Study Edition*. Leiden: Brill, 1997–98.

Gardner, Barbara. "Earth Mother." In *Gods, Goddesses, and Mythology*, edited by C. Scott Littleton, 4.452–57. Tarrytown, NY: Marshall Cavendish, 2005.

Gardner, Jane F. *Being a Roman Citizen*. London, Routledge, 1993.

Gardner, John, and John Maier. *Gilgamesh*. New York: Knopf, 1984.

Garelli, Paul, and Dominique Collon, eds. *Cuneiform Texts from Cappadocian Tablets in the British Museum*. 1921. Reprint, London: Trustees of the British Museum, 1975.

Gärtner, Bertil. *The Areopagus Speech and Natural Revelation*. ASNU 21. Uppsala: Almqvist & Wiksell, 1955.

Gauger, Jörg-Dieter. "Antiochos III und Artaxerxes: Der Fremdherrscher als Wohltäter." *JSJ* 38 (2007) 196–225.

Gelb, Ignace. "From Freedom to Slavery." In *Gesellschaftsklassen im alten Zweistromland und in den abgrenzenden Gebieten*, edited by D. O. Edzard, 81–92. Munich: Bayerischen Akademie der Wissenschaften, 1972.

———. *Nuzi Personal Names*. Chicago: University of Chicago Press, 1943.

———. "Quantitative Evaluation of Slavery and Serfdom." In *Kramer Anniversary Volume: Cuneiform Studies in Honor of Samuel Noah Kramer*, edited by B. Eichler, 195–207. AOAT 25. Neukirchen-Vluyn: Neukirchener, 1976.

Geller, Markham J. *Ancient Babylonian Medicine: Theory and Practice*. Malden, MA: Wiley-Blackwell, 2010.

Genicot, Garance. "Worst Forms of Child Labor: Child Bonded Labor." In *The World of Child Labor: An Historical and Regional Survey*, edited by H. Hindman, 106–9. London: M. E. Sharp, 2009.

George, Andrew R. *The Babylonian Gilgamesh Epic: Introduction, Critical Edition, and Cuneiform Texts*. New York: Oxford University Press, 2003.

———. "Observations on a Passage of *Inanna's Descent*." *JCS* 37 (1985) 109–13.

Gerhardsson, Birger. "The Matthean Version of the Lord's Prayer." In *The New Testament Age*, edited by W. C. Weinrich, 1.207–20. Macon, GA: Mercer University Press, 1984.

Gericke, Jaco. *What Is a God?: Philosophical Perspectives on Divine Essence in the Hebrew Bible*. T. & T. Clark Biblical Studies. London: Bloomsbury T. & T. Clark, 2017.

Gerleman, Gillis. "Die Wurzel שלם." *ZAW* 85 (1973) 1–14.

———. "Was heisst פסח?" *ZAW* 88 (1976) 409–13.

Gerstenberger, Erhard S. *Israel in the Persian Period: The Fifth and Fourth Centuries BCE*. BibEnc 8. Atlanta: SBL, 2011.

———. *Theologies in the Old Testament*. Translated by John Bowden. Minneapolis: Fortress, 2002.

Gessel, B. H. L. van. *Onomasticon of the Hittite Pantheon*. HO 33. Leiden: Brill, 1998–2001.

Ginsberg, H. L. "Poems about Baʿal and Anath." In *ANET* 129–42.

Girard, Marc. *The Psalms: Mirror of the Poor*. Montréal: Médiaspaul, 1996.

Girgus, Sam B. *The Law of the Heart: Individualism and the Modern Self in American Literature*. Austin: University of Texas Press, 1979.

Glatt, David A. *Chronological Displacement in Biblical and Related Literatures*. SBLDS 139. Atlanta: Scholars, 1993.

Glenny, W. Edward. *Micah: A Commentary Based on Micah in Codex Vaticanus*. Septuagint Commentary Series. Leiden: Brill, 2015.

Glueck, Nelson. *Hesed in the Bible*. 1927. Translated by Alfred Gottschalk. Cincinnati: Hebrew Union College Press, 1967.

Gnuse, Robert. *You Shall Not Steal: Community and Property in the Biblical Tradition*. Maryknoll, NY: Orbis, 1985.

Godelier, Maurice. *The Enigma of the Gift*. Translated by Nora Scott. Chicago: University of Chicago Press, 1999.

Goetze, Albrecht. *Kulturgeschichte Kleinasiens*. HA 3/1/3. Munich: Beck, 1957.

Goldingay, John. *Ezra, Nehemiah and Esther for Everyone*. Louisville: Westminster John Knox, 2012.

Goldingay, John, and David Payne. *Isaiah 40–55*. Vol. 2. ICC. London: T. & T. Clark, 2006.

Goodchild, Philip. "The Market, God, and the Ascetic Life." In *Religion, Economy, and Cooperation*, edited by Ilkka Pyysiäinen, 219–36. Religion and Reason 49. Berlin: de Gruyter, 2010.

Goode, William J. "Magic and Religion: A Continuum." *Ethnos* 14 (1949) 172–82.

Goodman, Martin. *Judaism in the Roman World: Collected Essays*. AJEC 67. Leiden: Brill, 2007.

Gonnet, Hatice. "Un Rhyton en forme de *kurša* Hittite." In *Anatolia Antica: Studi in memoria di Fiorella Imparati*, edited by Stefano De Martino and Franca Pecchioli Daddi, 1.321–27. Florence: LoGisma, 2002.

Goody, Jack, and S. J. Tambiah. *Bridewealth and Dowry*. Cambridge Papers in Social Anthropology 7. Cambridge: Cambridge University Press, 1973.

Gordon, Cyrus H. Review of *In the World of Sumer*, by S. N. Kramer. *JCS* 39 (1987) 247–50.

———. *Ugaritic Textbook*. AnOr 38. Rome: Pontificium Institutum Biblicum, 1965.

Gordon, Barry J. "Scepticism and Apocalyptic." In *The Economic Problem in Biblical and Patristic Thought*, 33–42. SVC 9. Leiden: Brill, 1989.

Gordon, Kathryn, and Maiko Miyake. "Business Approaches to Combating Bribery: A Study of Codes of Conduct." *JBE* 34 (2001) 161–73.

Gordon, Robert P. "Prophecy in the Mari and Nineveh Archives." In *"Thus Says Ishtar of Arbela": Prophecy in Israel, Assyria, and Egypt in the Neo-Assyrian Period*, edited by R. P. Gordon and Hans M. Barstad, 37–58. Winona Lake, IN: Eisenbrauns, 2013.

Goren, Yuval, and Eran Arie. "The Authenticity of the Bullae of Berekhyahu son of Neriyahu the Scribe." *BASOR* 372 (2014) 147–58.

Gorman, Frank H. *The Ideology of Ritual: Space, Time, and Status in the Priestly Theology*. JSOTSup 91. Sheffield: Sheffield Academic, 1990.

Gorman, Michael. *Abortion and the Early Church: Christian, Jewish and Pagan Attitudes in the Graeco-Roman World*. 1982. Reprint, Eugene, OR: Wipf & Stock, 1998.

———. *Apostle of the Crucified Lord: A Theological Introduction to Paul and His Letters*. Grand Rapids: Eerdmans, 2017.

Gort, Jerald D., et al., eds. *Religion, Conflict and Reconciliation: Multifaith Ideals and Realities*. Amsterdam: Rodopi, 2002.

Gottwald, Norman K. "The Bible and Economic Ethics." In *Social Justice and the Hebrew Bible*, 1.14–20. Eugene, OR: Cascade Books, 2016.

———. "The Expropriated and the Expropriators in Nehemiah 5." In *Social Justice and the Hebrew Bible*, 3.35–53. Eugene, OR: Cascade Books, 2018.

———. *The Hebrew Bible: A Brief Socio-Literary Introduction*. Minneapolis: Fortress, 2009.

———. "Social Class as an Analytic and Hermeneutical Category in Biblical Studies." *JBL* 112 (1993) 3–22. Reprinted in *Social Justice and the Hebrew Bible*, 1.21–43. Eugene, OR: Cascade Books, 2016.

Grabbe, Lester L. *Ancient Israel: What Do We Know and How Do We Know It?* New York: Bloomsbury, 2017.

———. *Ezra-Nehemiah*. London: Taylor & Francis, 1998.

———. "Tobit." In *The Eerdmans Commentary on the Bible*, edited by James D. G. Dunn and John Rogerson, 736–47. Grand Rapids: Eerdmans, 2003.

Gray, John. *The* Krt *Text in the Literature of Ras Shamra*. Leiden: Brill, 1964.

Gray, Mark. *Rhetoric and Social Justice in Isaiah*. New York: T. & T. Clark, 2006.

Grayson, Albert Kirk. "Assyria: 668–635 B.C.: The Reign of Ashurbanipal." *CAH* 3/2 (1991) 142–161.

———. "Assyria: Sennacherib and Esarhaddon (704–669 B.C.)." *CAH* 3/2 (1991) 103–41.

———. "Assyria: Tiglath-pileser III to Sargon II (744–705 B.C.)." *CAH* 3/2 (1991) 71–102.

———. "Esarhaddon." In *ABD* 2.574.

———. "Nineveh." In *ABD* 4.1118–19.

Green, Alberto R. W. *The Storm-God in the Ancient Near East*. Winona Lake, IN: Eisenbrauns, 2003.

Green, Joel B. *The Theology of the Gospel of Luke*. Cambridge: Cambridge University Press, 1995.
———, ed. *Dictionary of Jesus and the Gospels*. Downers Grove, IL: InterVarsity, 1992.
Green, Joel B., and Lee M. McDonald. "Introduction." In *The World of the New Testament: Cultural, Social, and Historical Contexts*, edited by Joel B. Green and Lee M. McDonald, 1–6. Grand Rapids: Baker, 2013.
Green, Margaret W. Review of *Der Mythos* Inanna und Enki *unter besonderer Berucksichtigung der Liste der* me, by Gertrude Farber-Flügge. *JAOS* 96 (1976) 283–86.
Greene, John. *The Role of the Messenger and the Message in the Ancient Near East*. BJS 169. Atlanta: Scholars, 1989.
Greenfield, Jonas C. "Aḥiqar in Tobit." In *`Al Kanfei Yonah: Collected Studies of Jonas C. Greenfield on Semitic Philology*, 1.195–202. Leiden: Brill, 2001.
———. "Darius." In *EJ* 434.
Greenspahn, Frederick E. *When Brothers Dwell Together: The Preeminence of Younger Siblings in the Hebrew Bible*. New York: Oxford University Press, 1994.
Greenstein, Edward L. "Kirta." In *UNP* 9–48.
Greenwood, Kyle. *Scripture and Cosmology: Reading the Bible between the Ancient World and Modern Science*. Downers Grove, IL: InterVarsity, 2015.
Gregory, Bradley C. *Like an Everlasting Signet Ring: Generosity in the Book of Sirach*. DCLS 2. New York: de Gruyter, 2010.
Grelot, Pierre. *Documents araméens d'Égypte*. Paris: Cerf, 1972.
Grenz, Stanley J. *A Primer on Postmodernism*. Grand Rapids: Eerdmans, 1996.
Griffiths, John Gwyn. *The Origins of Osiris and His Cult*. SHR 40. Leiden: Brill, 1980.
Grøndahl, Frauke. *Die Personnamen der Texte aus Ugarit*. StPohl 1. Roma: Päpstliche Bibelinstitut, 1967.
Groneberg, Brigitte. "Ein Ritual an Ištar." *MARI* 8 (1996) 291–303.
———. "Towards a Definition of Literature as Applied to Akkadian Literature." In *Mesopotamian Poetic Language: Sumerian and Akkadian*, edited by M. E. Vogelzang and H. L. J. Vanstiphout, 59–84. CM 6. Gröningen: Styx, 1996.
Gross, Heinrich. *Tobit, Judit*. NEchtB 19. Würzburg: Echter, 1987.
Gruenwald, Ithamar. *Rituals and Ritual Theory in Ancient Israel*. BRLA 10. Leiden: Brill, 2003.
Gudykunst, William B., et al. *Culture and Interpersonal Communication*. Thousand Oaks, CA: Sage, 1988.
Guillaume, Philippe. "פרו ורבו and the Seventh Year: Complementary Strategies for the Economic Recovery of Depopulated Yehud." In *The Economy of Ancient Judah in Its Historical Context*, edited by M. L. Miller et al., 123–50. Winona Lake, IN: Eisenbrauns, 2015.
———. *Land and Calendar: The Priestly Document from Genesis 1 to Joshua 18*. New York: T. & T. Clark, 2009.
———. *Land, Credit and Crisis: Agrarian Finance in the Hebrew Bible*. London: Routledge, 2014.
Gundry, Robert H. *The Old Is Better: New Testament Essays in Support of Traditional Interpretations*. WUNT 178. Tübingen: Mohr/Siebeck, 2005.
Gunkel, Hermann. *Creation and Chaos in the Primeval Era and the Eschaton*. 1895. Translated by K. Whitney. Grand Rapids: Eerdmans, 2006.

———. *Elijah, Yahweh and Ba'al*. 1906. Translated by K. C. Hanson. Eugene, OR: Cascade, 2014.

———. *Schöpfung und Chaos in Urzeit und Endzeit*. Göttingen: Vandenhoeck & Ruprecht, 1895.

Gunneweg, Antonius H. J. "Zur Interpretation der Bücher Esra-Nehemiah: Zugleich ein Beitrag zur Methode der Exegese." In *Congress Volume: Vienna 1980*, edited by J. A. Emerton, 146–61. VTSup 32 Leiden: Brill, 1981.

Gurney, Oliver R. *The Hittites*. Baltimore. Penguin, 1954.

Gushee, David P., and Glen H. Stassen. *Kingdom Ethics: Following Jesus in Contemporary Context*. Grand Rapids: Eerdmans, 2016.

Güterbock, Hans Gustav. "Hittite *kurša* 'Hunting Bag.'" In *Essays in Ancient Civilisation Presented to Helene J. Kantor*, edited by A. Leonard and B. Williams, 113–19. Chicago: Oriental Institute, 1989.

———. "The Hittite Version of the Hurrian Kumarbi Myths: Oriental Forerunners of Hesiod." *AJA* 52 (1948) 123–34.

Gzella, Holger. "New Light on Linguistic Diversity in Pre-Achaemenid Aramaic: Wandering Arameans or Language Spread?" In *Wandering Arameans: Arameans Outside Syria*, edited by A. Berlejung et al., 19–37. LAS 5. Wiesbaden: Harrassowitz, 2017.

Haar, Stephen. *Simon Magus: The First Gnostic?* BZNW 119. Berlin: de Gruyter, 2003.

Haas, Volkert. "Death and the Afterlife in Hittite Thought." In *CANE* 2021–30.

———. *Hethitische Orakel, Vorzeichen und Abwehrstrategien*. Berlin: de Gruyter, 2008.

———. *Die Hethitisches Literatur*. Berlin: de Gruyter, 2006.

Habel, Norman C., ed. *The Earth Bible*, vol. 1: *Readings from the Perspective of Earth*. Sheffield: Sheffield Academic, 2000.

———. *Finding Wisdom in Nature: An Eco-Wisdom Reading of the Book of Job*. Sheffield: Sheffield Phoenix, 2014.

Hackett Jo Ann. *The Balaam Text from Deir 'Allā*. HSM 31. Chico, CA: Scholars, 1984.

———. "Can a Sexist Model Liberate Us?: Ancient Near Eastern 'Fertility' Goddesses." *JFSR* 5 (1989) 65–76.

Hadas, Moses. *A History of Greek Literature*. New York: Columbia University Press, 1950.

Haddox, Susan E. "Metaphor and Masculinity in Hosea." PhD diss., Emory University, 2005.

Hadjiev, Tchavdar S. *The Composition and Redaction of the Book of Amos*. BZAW 393. Berlin: de Gruyter, 2009.

Hadley, Judith M. *The Cult of Asherah in Ancient Israel and Judah: Evidence for a Hebrew Goddess*. University of Cambridge Oriental Publications 57. Cambridge: Cambridge Uni-versity Press, 2000.

Hägglund, Fredrick. *Isaiah 53 in the Light of Homecoming after Exile*. FAT 2/31. Tübingen: Mohr/ Siebeck, 2008.

Hall, Mark G. "A Study of Sumerian Moon God Nanna-Suen." PhD diss., University of Pennsylvania, 1985.

Hallermayer, Michaela. *Text und Überlieferung des Buches Tobit*. DCLS 3. Berlin: de Gruyter, 2008.

Hallo, William W. "New Viewpoints on Cuneiform Literature." *IEJ* 12 (1962) 13–26.

———. "The Road to Emar." *JCS* 18 (1964) 57–88.

———. "Sharecropping in the Edict of Ammi-ṣaduqa." In *Ḥesed ve-Emet: Studies in Honor of Ernest S. Frerichs*, edited by Jodi Magness and Seymour Gitin, 205–16. BJS 320. Atlanta: Scholars, 1998.

Hallo, William W. , and K. Lawson Younger, eds. *The Context of Scripture*. Leiden: Brill, 2003.

Halpern, Baruch. *The First Historians: The Hebrew Bible and History*. San Francisco: Harper and Row, 1988.

Hals, Ronald M. *The Theology of the Book of Ruth*. FBBS 23. Philadelphia: Fortress, 1969.

Hamborg, Graham R. *Still Selling the Righteous: A Redaction-Critical Investigation of Reasons for Judgment in Amos 2:6–16*. LHBOTS 555. London: T. & T. Clark, 2012.

Hamilton, Malcolm. *The Sociology of Religion: Theoretical and Comparative Perspectives*. London: Routledge, 2001.

Handy, Lowell. *Among the Host of Heaven: The Syro-Palestinian Pantheon as Bureaucracy*. Winona Lake, IN: Eisenbrauns, 1994.

———. "Dagon." In *ABD* 2.1–3.

Hanson, K. C. "When the King Crosses the Line: Royal Deviance and Restitution in Levantine Ideologies." *BTB* 26 (1996) 11–25.

Hanson, Paul D. *The Dawn of Apocalyptic: The Historical and Sociological Roots of Jewish Apocalyptic Eschatology*. Philadelphia: Fortress, 1979.

———. "Rebellion in Heaven, Azazel, and Euhemeristic Heroes in 1 Enoch 6–11." *JBL* 96 (1977) 195–233.

Hardmeier, Christof. "Wirtschaftliche Prosperität und Gottvergessenheit. Die theologische Dimension wirtschaftlicher Leistungskraft nach Dtn 8." *Leqach* 4 (2004) 15–24.

Harmatta, János. "Modéles littéraires de l'edit babylonien de Cyrus." In *Commemoration Cyrus: Hommage Universel 1*, 29–44. Tehran/Liege: Peeters, 1974.

Harrell, James E., et al. "Hebrew Gemstones in the Old Testament: A Lexical, Geological, and Archaeological Analysis." *BBR* 27 (2017) 1–52.

Harrill, J. Albert. "Divine Judgment against Ananias and Sapphira (Acts 5:1–11): A Stock Scene of Perjury and Death." *JBL* 130 (2011) 351–69.

Harrington, Daniel J. *The Gospel According to Matthew*. Collegeville Bible Commentary 1. Collegeville, MN: Liturgical, 1991.

Harrington, Hannah K. *The Impurity Systems of Qumran and the Rabbis: Biblical Foundations*. SBLDS 143. Atlanta: Scholars, 1993.

Harris, Rivkah. *Gender and Aging in Mesopotamia: The Gilgamesh Epic and Other Ancient Literature*. Norman: University of Oklahoma Press, 2000.

———. "Images of Women in the Gilgamesh Epic." In *Lingering Over Words: Studies in Ancient Near Eastern Literature in Honor of William L. Moran*, edited by Tzvi Abusch et al., 219–30. HSS 37. Atlanta: Scholars, 1990.

Hartin, Patrick J. *James and the Q Sayings of Jesus*. JSNTSup 47. Sheffield: Sheffield Academic, 1991.

Hasel, Gerhard F. "פלט." In *TDOT* 11.551–67.

———. "'New Moon and Sabbath' in 8th Century Israelite Prophetic Writings (Isa 1:13; Hos 2:13; Amos 8:5)." In *Wünschet Jerusalem Frieden: Collected Communications to the XIIth Congress of the International Organization for Study of the Old Testament*, 37–64. Frankfurt: Lang, 1988.

Hauser, Alan J., and Russell Gregory. *From Carmel to Horeb: Elijah in Crisis*. BLS 19. Sheffield: Sheffield Academic, 1990.

Häusl, Maria, ed. *Tochter Zion auf dem Weg zum himmlischen Jerusalem: Rezeptionslinien der "Stadtfrau Jerusalem" von den späten alttestamentlichen Texten bis zu den Werken der Kirchenväter*. DBGGKL 2. Berlin: Leipziger Universitätsverlag, 2011.

Hayes, John H. "The History of the Study of Israelite and Judean History." In *Israel's Past in Present Research: Essays on Ancient Israelite Historiography*, edited by V. P. Long, 7–42. Winona Lake, IN: Eisenbrauns, 1999.

Hayes, Katherine Murphey. *The Earth Mourns: Prophetic Metaphor and Oral Aesthetic*. SBLAB 8. Leiden: Brill, 2002.

Haymes, Brian. *The Concept of the Knowledge of God*. London: MacMillan, 1988.

Hays, Christopher B. *A Covenant with Death: Death in the Iron Age II and Its Rhetorical Uses in Proto-Isaiah*. 2011. Reprint, Grand Rapids: Eerdmans, 2015.

Hays, Christopher M. *Luke's Wealth Ethics*. WUNT 275. Tübingen: Mohr/Siebeck, 2010.

Hazell, Clive. *Alterity: The Experience of the Other*. Bloomington, IN: AuthorHouse, 2009.

Healey, John F. "Dagon." In *DDD* 216–19.

———. Review of *Goods, Prices and the Organization of Trade in Ugarit: Marketing and Transportation in the Eastern Mediterranean in the Second Half of the Second Millennium BCE*, by Michael Heltzer. *BSOAS* 43 (1980) 589.

Heidel, Alexander. *The Babylonian Genesis: The Story of Creation*. Chicago: University of Chicago Press, 1951.

Heider, George C. "Tannin." In *DDD* 835–36.

Heimpel, Wolfgang. *Letters to the King of Mari*. Winona Lake, IN: Eisenbrauns, 2003.

Held, Moshe. "Rhetorical Questions in Ugaritic and Biblical Hebrew." *ErIsr* 9 (1969) 71–79.

Heltzer, Michael. "The Economy of Ugarit." In *Handbook of Ugaritic Studies*, edited by W. G. E. Watson and N. Wyatt, 423–54. HO 39. Leiden: Brill, 1999.

Hendel, Ronald S. *The Epic of the Patriarch: The Jacob Cycle and the Narrative Traditions of Canaan and Israel*. HSM 42. Atlanta: Scholars, 1987.

Hengel, Martin. "Der vorchristliche Paulus." In *Paulus und die antike Judentum*, edited by Martin Hengel and U. Henkel, 177–291. WUNT 58. Tübingen: Mohr/Siebeck, 1991.

Herion, Gary A. "Sabeans." In *ABD* 5.861.

Hermisson, Hans J. "Voreiliger Abschied von den Gottesknechtslieder." *TRu* 49 (1984) 209–22.

Herms, Ronald. *An Apocalypse for the Church and for the World*. BZNW 143. Berlin: de Gruyter, 2006.

Herrmann, Wolfgang. "Ba`al." In *DDD* 132–39.

———. "El." In *DDD* 274–80.

———. *Yariḫ und Nikkal und der Preis de Kuṯarat-Göttinnen*. BZAW 106. Berlin: de Gruyter, 1968.

Herzog, Ze'ev. "Administrative Structures in the Iron Age." In *The Architecture of Ancient Israel: From the Prehistoric to the Persian Periods*, edited by A. Kempinski et al., 223–30. Jerusalem: Israel Exploration Society, 1992.

Heschel, Abraham Joshua. *The Sabbath: Its Meaning for Modern Man*. New York: Farrar, Straus and Giroux, 1951.

Hess, Richard S. *Amarna Personal Names*. Winona Lake, IN: Eisenbrauns, 1993.

Hibbard, J. Todd. *Intertextuality in Isaiah 24–27*. FAT 16. Tübingen: Mohr/Siebeck, 2006.

Hiebert, Theodore. Review of *Scripture, Culture, and Agriculture: An Agrarian Reading of the Bible*, by Ellen Davis. *BI* 18 (2010) 437–39.

Hillers, Delbert R. *Micah: A Commentary on the Book of the Prophet Micah*. Hermeneia. Minneapolis: Fortress, 1983.

Hobson, George. *The Episcopal Church, Homosexuality, and the Context of Technology*. Eugene, OR: Pickwick, 2013.

Hobson, John A. *God and Mammon: The Relations of Religion and Economics*. 1931. Reprint, London: Routledge, 2011.

Hock, Ronald F. "The Workshop as a Social Setting for Paul's Missionary Preaching." *CBQ* 41 (1979) 438–50.

Hoffman, Yair. "The Fasts in the Book of Zechariah and the Fashioning of National Remembrance." In *Judah and the Judeans in the Neo-Babylonian Period*, edited by O. Lipschitz and Joseph Blenkinsopp, 169–218. Winona Lake, IN: Eisenbrauns, 2003.

———. "The Status of the Decalogue in the Hebrew Bible." In *The Decalogue in Jewish and Christian Tradition*, edited by Hennig Graf Reventlow and Yair Hoffman, 32–49. New York: T. & T. Clark, 2011.

Hoffner, Harry A. "בית." In *TDOT* 2.107–16.

———. *Hittite Myths*. SBLWAW 2. Atlanta: Scholars, 1990.

———. *Letters from the Hittite Kingdom*. SBLWAW 15. Atlanta: Scholars, 2009.

Hoglund, Kenneth G. *Achaemenid Imperial Administration in Syria-Palestine and the Missions of Ezra and Nehemiah*. SBLDS 125. Atlanta: Scholars, 1992.

Holladay, Carl R. *Acts: A Commentary*. NTL. Louisville: Westminster John Knox, 2016.

Holm, Michael. *The Marshall Plan: A New Deal for Europe*. New York: Routledge, 2017.

Holt, Else K. "דעת אלהים and חסד im Buche Hosea." *SJOT* 1 (1987) 87–103.

———. . . . Urged On by His Wife Jezebel: A Literary Reading of 1 Kings 18 in Context." *SJOT* 9 (1995) 96.

Honigman, Sylvie. *High Priests and Taxes: The Books of the Maccabees and the Judean Rebellion against Antiochus IV*. Berkeley: University of California Press, 2014.

Hooker, Morna D. "John's Baptism: A Prophetic Sign." In *The Holy Spirit and Christian Origins: Essays in Honor of James D. G. Dunn*, edited by G. Stanton et al., 22–40. Grand Rapids: Eerdmans, 2004.

Hopkins, David L. *The Highlands of Canaan: Agricultural Life in the Early Iron Age*. SWBA 3. Sheffield: Almond, 1985.

Hoppe, Leslie J. *There Shall Be No Poor Among You: Poverty in the Bible*. Nashville: Abingdon, 2004.

Horsley, Richard A. *Covenant Economics: A Biblical Vision of Justice for All*. Louisville: Westminster John Knox, 2009.

———. *Jesus and Empire: The Kingdom of God and the New World Disorder*. Minneapolis: Augsburg Fortress, 2003.

House, Paul R. "Endings as New Beginnings: Returning to the Lord, the Day of the Lord, and Renewal in the Book of the Twelve." In *Thematic Threads in the Book of the Twelve*, edited by P. Redditt and A. Schart, 313–38. BZAW 325. New York: de Gruyter, 2003.

Houston, Walter J. *Amos: Justice and Violence*. London: Bloomsbury, 2017.

———. *Contending for Justice: Ideologies and Theologies of Social Justice in the Old Testament*. London: T. & T. Clark, 2008.

Houston Smith, Robert. "Lebanon." In *ABD* 4.269–70.

Howard, George. *Hebrew Gospel of Matthew*. Macon, GA: Mercer University Press, 1995.

Howgego, Christopher. *Ancient History from Coins*. London: Routledge, 1995.

Hubbard, Robert L. *The Book of Ruth*. NICOT. Grand Rapids: Eerdmans, 1988.

———. "Micah, Moresheth, and Martin: Keep Up the Beat (Micah 6:8)." *CovQ* 65 (2007) 3–10.

Huffmon, Herbert B. *Amorite Personal Names in the Mari Texts: A Structural and Lexical Study*. Baltimore: Johns Hopkins University Press, 1965.

———. "The Covenant Lawsuit in the Prophets." *JBL* 78 (1959) 285–95.

———. "Jezebel: The 'Corrosive' Queen." In *From Babel to Babylon: Essays on Biblical History and Literature in Honour of Brian Peckham*, edited by J. Wood et al., 273–84. London: T. & T. Clark, 2006.

———. "Prophecy in the Ancient Near East." In *ABD* 5.477–82.

———. "The Treaty Background of Hebrew ידע." *BASOR* 181 (Feb 1966) 31–37.

Hull, Bill. *Choose the Life: Exploring a Faith that Embraces Discipleship*. Grand Rapids: Baker Books, 2004.

Hulster, Izaak J. de, et al., eds. *Iconographic Exegesis of the Hebrew Bible/Old Testament: An Introduction to Its Method and Practice*. Göttingen: Vandenhoeck & Ruprecht, 2015.

Humphreys, Walter Lee. "A Lifestyle for Diaspora: A Study of the Tales of Esther and Daniel." *JBL* 92 (1973) 211–23.

———. "The Motif of the Wise Courtier in the Old Testament." ThD diss. Union Theological Seminary in Richmond, 1970.

———. "Novella." In *Saga, Legend, Tale, Novella, Fable: Narrative Forms in Old Testament Literature*, edited by G. W. Coats, 82–96. JSOTSup 35. Sheffield: Sheffield Academic, 1985.

Hunt, Alice M. W. *Palace Ware Across the Neo-Assyrian Imperial Landscape: Social Value and Semiotic Meaning*. CHANE 78. Leiden: Brill, 2015.

Hurowitz, Victor. *I Have Built You an Exalted House: Temple Building in the Bible in Light of Mesopotamian and Northwest Semitic Writings*. JSOTSup 115. Sheffield: JSOT Press, 1992.

———. "Joel's Locust Plague in Light of Sargon II's *Hymn to Nanāya*." *JBL* 112 (1993) 597–603.

———. "The Mesopotamian God Image: From Womb to Tomb." *JAOS* 123 (2003) 147–57.

———. "Name Midrashim and Word Plays on Names in Akkadian Historical Writings." In *A Woman of Valor: Jerusalem Ancient Near Eastern Studies in Honor of Joan Goodnick Westenholz*, edited by W. Horowitz et al., 87–104. Madrid: Consejo Superior de Investigaciones Científicas, 2010.

Hutter, Manfred. *Altorientalische Vorstellungen von der Unterwelt: Literar-und religions-geschichtliche Überlegungen zu* "Nergal und Ereškigal". OBO 63. Göttingen: Vandenhoeck & Ruprecht, 1985.

———. "Asmodeus." In *DDD* 106–08.

———. *Behexung, Entsuhnung und Heilung: Das Ritual der Tunnawiya for ein Konigspaar aus mittelhethitischer Zeit (KBo XXI 1 - KUB IX 34 - KBo XXI 6)*. OBO 82. Göttingen: Vandenhoeck & Ruprecht, 1988.

———. "Shaushka." In *DDD* 758–59.

Hutton, Jeremy M., and Aaron D. Rubin, eds. *Epigraphy, Philology, and the Hebrew Bible: Methodological Perspectives on Philological and Comparative Study of the Hebrew Bible in Honor of Jo Ann Hackett*. Atlanta: SBL Press, 2015.

Hyatt, James Philip. *Jeremiah: Prophet of Courage and Hope*. Nashville: Abingdon, 1958.

Inhorn, Marcia C. *Quest for Conception: Gender, Infertility, and Egyptian Medical Traditions*. Philadelphia; University of Pennsylvania Press, 1994.

Irsigler, Hubert. *Gottesgericht und Jahwetag: Die Komposition Zef 1,1—2,3 untersucht auf der Grundlage der Literarkritik des Zefanjabuches*. St. Ottilien: EOS, 1977.

Irving, John. *The Cider House Rules*. New York: William Morrow, 1985.

Isaac, Munther. *From Land to Lands, from Eden to the Renewed Earth: A Christ-Centered Biblical Theology of the Promised Land*. Cumbria, Canada: Langham Monographs, 2015.

Iser, Wolfgang. "Staging as an Anthropological Category." *NLH* 23 (1992) 877–88.

Izre'el, Shlomo. "The Amarna Letters from Canaan." In *CANE* 2411–19.

Jackson, Bernard S. "The Divorces of the Herodian Princesses: Jewish Law, Roman Law, or Palace Law?" In *Josephus and Jewish History in Flavian Rome and Beyond*, edited by J. Sievers and G. Lembi, 343–70. JSJSup 104. Leiden: Brill, 2005.

Jacobs, Mignon R. *The Conceptual Coherence of the Book of Micah*. JSOTSup 322. Sheffield: Sheffield Academic, 2001.

———. *The Books of Haggai and Malachi*. NICOT. Grand Rapids: Eerdmans, 2017.

Jacobsen, Thorkild. *"The Harps That Once"*. . . *Sumerian Poetry in Translation*. New Haven, CT: Yale University Press, 1987.

———. "Primitive Democracy in Ancient Mesopotamia." *JNES* 2 (1943) 159–72.

———. "Toward the Image of Tammuz." In *Toward the Image of Tammuz and Other Essays on Mesopotamian History and Culture*, edited by W. L. Moran, 73–103. 1970. Reprint, Eugene, OR: Wipf & Stock, 2008.

———. *The Treasures of Darkness: A History of Mesopotamian Religion*. New Haven, CT: Yale University Press, 1976.

Jacobson, Howard. "Elijah's Sleeping Ba`al." *Bib* 79 (1998) 413.

Jacques, Margaret. *Le vocabulaire des sentiments dans les textes sumériens. Recherche sur le lexique sumérien et akkadien*. AOAT 332. Münster: Ugarit, 2006.

Jagersma, Henk. "ישן in 1 Könige XVIII 27." *VT* 25 (1975) 674–76.

James, Phyllis Dorothy. *The Children of Men*. London: Faber and Faber, 1992.

Janowski, Bernd. "He Bore Our Sins: Isaiah 53 and the Drama of Taking Another's Place." 1993. Translated by D. P. Bailey. In *Suffering Servant: Isaiah 53 in Jewish and Christian Sources*, edited by B. Janowski and P. Stuhlmacher, 48–74. Grand Rapids: Eerdmans, 2004.

Janzen, David. *Chronicles and the Politics of Davidic Restoration: A Quiet Revolution*. London: Bloomsbury, 2017.

———. *Witch-Hunts, Purity, and Social Boundaries: The Expulsion of the Foreign Women in Ezra 9–10*. JSOTSup 350. Sheffield: Sheffield Academic, 2002.

Japhet, Sara. *1 and 2 Chronicles: A Commentary*. OTL. Louisville: Westminster John Knox, 1993.

Jaruzelska, Izabela. *Amos and the Officialdom in the Kingdom of Israel. The Socio-Economic Position of the Officials in the Light of the Biblical, the Epigraphic and Archaeological Evidence*. Poznan: Wydawnictwo Naukowe Uniwersytetu im. Adama Mickiewicza, 1998.

Jassen, Alex P. "Violent Imaginaries and Practical Violence in the *War Scroll*." In *The War Scroll, Violence, War and Peace in the Dead Sea Scrolls and Related Literature*, edited by K. Davis et al., 175–203. STDJ 115. Leiden: Brill, 2015.

Jauss, Hannelore. *Der liebebedürftige Gott und die gottbedürftige Liebe des Menschen: Ursprung und Funktion der Rede von der Liebe des Menschen zu Gott als alttestamtentlicher Beitrag zur Gotteslehre*. BVB 25. Münster: LIT, 2014.

Jemielity, Thomas. *Satire and the Hebrew Prophets*. LCBI. Louisville: Westminster John Knox, 1992.

Jeremias, Joachim. "Paulus als Hillelit." In *Neotestamentica et Semitica: Studies in Honour of Matthew Black*, edited by E. Ellis and M. Wilcox, 88–94. Edinburgh: T. & T. Clark, 1969.

Jeremias, Jörg. *The Book of Amos: A Commentary*. 1995. Translated by D. W. Stott. OTL. Louisville: Westminster John Knox, 1998.

———. *Der Prophet Hosea*. Göttingen: Vandenhoeck & Ruprecht, 1983.

Jindo, Job Y. "The Divine Courtroom Motif in the Hebrew Bible: A Holistic Perspective." In *The Divine Courtroom in Comparative Perspective*, edited by A. Mermelstein and S. E. Holtz, 76–93. Leiden: Brill, 2014.

Johnson, Dan G. *From Chaos to Restoration: An Integrative Reading of Isaiah 24–27*. JSOTSup 61. Sheffield: JSOT Press, 1988.

Johnson, Luke Timothy. *The Literary Function of Possessions in Luke-Acts*. SBLDS 39. Missoula, MT: Scholars, 1977.

Jones, David W. *Reforming the Morality of Usury: A Study of Differences that Separated the Protestant Reformers*. New York: University Press of America, 2004.

Jones, David W., and Russell S. Woodbridge. *Health, Wealth, and Happiness: Has the Prosperity Gospel Overshadowed the Gospel of Christ?* Grand Rapids: Kregel, 2011.

Jong, Jonathan, and Jamin Halberstadt. *Death Anxiety and Religious Belief: An Existential Psychology of Religion*. London: Bloomsbury, 2016.

Jonker, Louis. "Agrarian Economy through City-Elites' Eyes: Reflections of Late Persian Period Yehud Economy in the Genealogies of Chronicles." In *The Economy of Ancient Judah in its Historical Context*, edited by M. L. Miller et al., 77–101. Winona Lake, IN: Eisenbrauns, 2015.

Joosten, Jan. "Yhwh's Farewell to Northern Israel (Micah 6:1–8)." *ZAW* 125 (2013) 448–62.

Jordan, Hillary. *When She Woke*. San Francisco: HarperCollins, 2011.

Joseph, Morris. *Judaism as Creed and Life*. London: MacMillan, 1903.

Joyce, Paul M. *Ezekiel: A Commentary*. LHBOT 482. New York: T. & T. Clark, 2009.

Judge, Edwin A. *The Social Pattern of Christian Groups in the First Century: Some Prolegomena to the Study of New Testament Ideas of Social Obligation*. London: Tyndale, 1960.

Juel, Donald. "The Lord's Prayer in the Gospels of Matthew and Luke." In *The Lord's Prayer: Principles for Reclaiming Christian Prayer*, edited by D. Migliore, 56–70. Grand Rapids: Eerdmans, 1993.

Kaiser, Otto. "Die Bindung Isaaks: Untersuchungen zur Eigenart und Bedeutung von Genesis 22." In *Zwischen Athen und Jerusalem*, 199–224. BZAW 320. Berlin: de Gruyter, 2003.

———. *Die mythische Bedeutung des Meeres im Ägypten, Ugarit, und Israel*. BZAW 78. Berlin: Töpelmann, 1962.

———. *Isaiah 1–12: A Commentary*. OTL. Philadelphia: Westminster, 1983.

———. *Isaiah 13–39: A Commentary*. OTL. Philadelphia: Westminster, 1974.

Kammenhuber, Annelies. *Orakelpraxis, Traume, und Vorzeichenschau bei den Hethitern*. Heidelberg: Winter, 1976.

Karenga, Maulana. *Ma'at, The Moral Ideal in Ancient Egypt: A Study in Classical African Ethics*. London: Routledge, 2004.

Katz, Dina. *The Image of the Netherworld in the Sumerian Sources*. Bethesda, MD: CDL Press, 2003.

———. "Reconstructing Babylon: Recycling Mythological Traditions toward a New Theology." In *Babylon: Wissenskultur in Orient und Okzident*, by E. Cancik-Kirschbaum et al., 123–34. TBSAW 1. Berlin: de Gruyter, 2011.

Kawashima, Robert S. "Biblical Narrative and the Birth of Prose Literature." In *The Oxford Handbook of Biblical Narrative*, edited by D. N. Fewell, 51–60. New York: Oxford University Press, 2015.

Keefe, Alice A. "The Female Body, the Body Politic and the Land: A Sociopolitical Reading of Hosea 1–2." In *A Feminist Companion to the Latter Prophets*, edited by A. Brenner-Idan, 70–101. FCB 8. Sheffield: Sheffield Academic, 1995.

———. "Hosea." In *Fortress Commentary on the Bible: The Old Testament and the Apocrypha*, edited by G. Yee et al., 823–35. Minneapolis: Fortress, 2014.

———. *Woman's Body and the Social Body in Hosea*. JSOTSup 338. Sheffield: Sheffield Academic, 2001.

Keener, Craig S. *A Commentary on the Gospel of Matthew*. Grand Rapids: Eerdmans, 1999.

———. *The Historical Jesus of the Gospels*. Grand Rapids: Eerdmans, 2009.

———. *Miracles: The Credibility of the New Testament Accounts*. Grand Rapids: Baker, 2011.

Kelhoffer, James A. *The Diet of John the Baptist: "Locusts and Wild Honey" in Synoptic and Patristic Interpretation*. WUNT 176. Tübingen: Mohr/Siebeck, 2005.

Kelle, Brad E. *Hosea 2: Metaphor and Rhetoric in Historical Perspective*. AcBib 20. Atlanta: SBL Press, 2005.

Kennedy, Charles A. "Isaiah 57:5–6: Tombs in the Rocks." *BASOR* 275 (1989) 47–52.

Kennedy, George A. *New Testament Criticism through Rhetorical Criticism*. Chapel Hill: University of North Carolina Press, 1984.

Kessler, John. *The Book of Haggai: Prophecy and Society in Early Persian Yehud*. VTSup 91. Leiden: Brill, 2002.

———. "Building the Second Temple: Questions of Time, Text, and History in Haggai 1:1–15." *JSOT* 27 (2002) 243–56.

Kessler, Martin. "The Law of Manumission in Jer 34." *BZ* 15 (1971) 105–08.

Kessler, Rainer. *Micha. Übersetzt und Auslegt*. HTKAT. Freiburg im Brasgau: Herder, 1999.

———. *The Social History of Ancient Israel: An Introduction*. 2006. Translated by L. M. Maloney. Minneapolis: Fortress, 2008.

———. *Staat und Gesellschaft im vorexilischen Juda: Vom 8. Jahrhundert bis zum Exil*. VTSup 47. Leiden: Brill, 1992.

Kiel, Micah D. "Tobit." In *Fortress Commentary on the Bible: The Old Testament and Apocrypha*, edited by G. Yee et al., 953–62. Minneapolis: Fortress, 2014.

———. *The "Whole Truth": Rethinking Retribution in the Book of Tobit*. London: T. & T. Clark, 2012.

Kienast, Burkhart. *Die altassyrische Eherecht: Eine Urkundenlehre*. Unter Mitarbeit von S. Franke and K. Hecker. SANTAG 10. Wiesbaden: Harrassowitz, 2015.

Kilgallen, John J. *The Stephen Speech*. AnBib 67. Rome: Biblical Institute Press, 1976.

Kim, Brittany. "Yhwh as Jealous Husband: Abusive Authoritarian or Passionate Protector? A Reexamination of a Prophetic Image." In *Daughter Zion: Her Portrait, Her Response*, edited by M. Boda et al., 127–48. AIL 13. Atlanta: SBL, 2012.

Kim, Koowon. *Incubation as a Type-Scene in the 'Aqhatu, Kirta, and Hannah Stories: A Form-Critical and Narratological Study of CAT 1.14.1—1.15.3, 1.17.1–2, and 1 Samuel 1:1—2:11*. VTSup 145. Leiden: Brill, 2011.

Kimball, Sara, and Jonathan Slocum. *Hittite Online*. https://lrc.la.utexas.edu/eieol/hitol/20.

King, Leonard W. *The Seven Tablets of Creation, or the Babylonian and Assyrian Legends Concerning the Creation of the World and of Mankind*. London: Luzac, 1902.

King, Philip J. *Jeremiah: An Archaeological Companion*. Louisville: Westminster John Knox, 1993.

Kinsella, William Patrick. *Shoeless Joe*. New York: Houghton Mifflin, 1982.

Kinsley, David R. *Hindu Goddesses: Visions of the Divine Feminine in the Hindu Religious Tradition*. Berkeley: University of California Press, 1986.

Kippenberg, Hans G. *Religion und Klassenbildung in antiken Judäa: Eine religionssoziologische Studie zum Verhältnis von Tradition und gesellschaftlicher Entwicklung*. SUNT 14. Göttingen: Vandenhoeck & Ruprecht, 1978.

———. "Der Typik antiker Entwicklung." In *Seminar: Die Entstehung der antiken Klassengeschellschaft*, edited by H. Kippenberg, 9–61. STW 130. Frankfurt: Suhrkamp, 1977.

Kirk, Geoffrey Stephen. *Myth: Its Meaning and Functions in Ancient and Other Cultures*. Cambridge: Cambridge University Press, 1970.

Kitz, Anne Marie. "To Be or Not to Be, That Is the Question: Yhwh and Ea." *CBQ* 80 (2018) 191–214.

Klauck, Hans-Josef. "Gütergemeinschaft in der klassische Antiken, in Qumran, und in Neuen Testament." *RevQ* 11 (1982) 47–79.

———. *Magic and Paganism in Early Christianity: The World of the Acts of the Apostles*. 1996. Translated by B. McNeil. Edinburgh: T. & T. Clark, 2000.

Klawans, Jonathan. *Impurity and Sin in Ancient Judaism*. New York: Oxford University Press, 2000.

Klein, Ralph W. "Chronicles, Book of 1–2." In *ABD* 1.992–1002.

———. "Ezra-Nehemiah, Books of." In *ABD* 2.731–42.

Klengel, Horst. "Prolegomena zu einer hethitischen Wirtschaftgeschichte." In *Anatolia Antica: Studi in memoria di Fiorella Imparati*, edited by S. de Martino and F. Peccholi Daddi, 1.425–36. Trieste: LoGisma, 2002.

Kletter, Raz. "Land Tenure, Ideology, and the Emergence of Ancient Israel: A Conversation with Philippe Guillaume." In *The Land of Canaan in the Late Bronze Age*, edited by L. Grabbe, 112–24. New York: Bloomsbury, 2016.

Kline, Jonathan G. *Allusive Soundplay in the Hebrew Bible*. AIL 28. Atlanta: SBL Press, 2016.

Kloos, Carola. *Yahweh's Combat with the Sea: A Canaanite Tradition in the Religion of Ancient Israel*. Leiden: Brill, 1986.

Kloppenborg, John S. "Alms, Debt and Divorce: Jesus' Ethics in their Mediterranean Context." In *The Historical Jesus: Critical Concepts in Religious Studies*, vol. 2: *The Teaching of Jesus*, edited by C. A. Evans, 320–38. London: Routledge, 2004.

Klostermann, August. *Geschichte des Volkes Israel: Bis zur Restauration unter Esra und Nehemia*. Munich: C. H. Beck, 1896.

Knibbe, Dieter, and B. Iplikçioglu. "Neuen Inschriften aus Ephesos VIII." *JÖAI* 3 (1981/82) 87–150.

Knierim, Rolf. "Criticism of Literary Features, Form, Tradition and Redaction." In *The Hebrew Bible and Its Modern Interpreters*, edited by D. Knight and G. Tucker, 123–66. Chico, CA: Scholars, 1985.

Knoppers, Gary N. "Dissonance and Disaster in the Legend of Kirta." *JAOS* 114 (1994) 572–82.

———. "More than Friends?: The Economic Relationship between Huram and Solomon Reconsidered." In *The Economy of Ancient Judah in its Historical Context*, edited by M. L. Miller et al., 51–76. Winona Lake, IN: Eisenbrauns, 2015.

Knudtzon, Johannes A. *Die El Amarna Tafeln*. 1915. Reprint, Aalen: Zeller, 1964.

Koch, Klaus. "Die hebräische Gott und die Gotteserfahrungen der Nachbarvölker: Inklusiver und exklusiver Monotheismus im Alten Testament." In *Der Gott Israels und die Götter des Orients: Religionsgeschichtliche Studien II zum 80 Geburtstag von Klaus Koch*, edited by F. Hartenstein and M. Rösel, 9–41. Göttingen: Vandenhoeck und Ruprecht, 2007.

Koepf-Taylor, Laurel W. *Give Me Children or I Shall Die: Children and Communal Survival in Biblical Literature*. Minneapolis: Fortress, 2013.

Koester, Helmut. *Introduction to the New Testament*, vol. 1: *History, Culture, and Religion of the Hellenistic Age*. New York: de Gruyter, 1995.

Koller, Aaron. "Pornography or Theology?: The Legal Background, Psychological Realism, and Theological Import of Ezekiel 16." *CBQ* 79 (2017) 402–21.

Kong, I., M. Fry, M. Al-Samarraie, et al. "An Update on Progress and the Changing Epidemiology of Causes of Childhood Blindness Worldwide." *JAAPOS* 16 (2012) 501–7.

Konstan, D., and M. Dillon. "The Ideology of Aristophanes' Wealth." *AJP* 102 (1981) 371–94.

Korpel, Marjo C. A. "Exegesis in the Work of Ilimilku of Ugarit." In *Intertextuality in Ugarit and Israel*, edited by J. C. de Moor, 86–111. OtSt 40. Leiden: Brill, 1998.

Korpel, Marjo C. A., and Johannes C. de Moor. *Adam, Eve, and the Devil: A New Beginning*. HBM 65. Sheffield: Sheffield Phoenix, 2014.

———. "Fundamentals of Ugaritic and Hebrew Poetry." *UF* 18 (1986) 173–212.

Kossmann, Ruth. "Volk *ohne* Land: Überlegungen zur religiösen Neuorientierung des jüdischen Volkes in der persischen Diaspora." In *The Land of Israel in Bible, History, and Theology: Studies in Honour of Ed Noort*, edited by J. van Ruiten and J. Cornelis de Vos, 237–58. VTSup 124. Leiden: Brill, 2009.

Köstenberger, Andreas J., and David A. Croteau. "'Will a Man Rob God (Malachi 3:8)?': A Study of Tithing in the Old and New Testaments." *BBR* 16 (2006) 53–77.

Kramer, Samuel Noah. *History Begins at Sumer*. Garden City, NY: Doubleday, 1959.

———. "Inanna's Descent to the Netherworld." In *ANET* 52–57.

———, and John Maier. *Myths of Enki, the Crafty God*. New York: Oxford University Press, 1989.

Kratz, Reinhard G. *Die Komposition der erzählenden Bücher des alten Testaments*. UTB 2157. Göttingen: Vandenhoeck & Ruprecht, 2000.

Kraus, Fritz Rudolph. *Königliche Verfügungen in Altbabylonischer Zeit*. SDIOAP 11. Leiden: Brill, 1984.

Krinetzki, Günter. *Zefanjastudien: Motiv-und Traditionskritik + Kompositions-und Redaktionskritik*. RST 7. Frankfurt: Lang, 1977.

Kugel, James L. "Qohelet and Money." *CBQ* 51 (1989) 374–99.

Kühne, Cord. *Die Chronologie der internationalen Korrespondenz von El-Amarna*. Neikirchen-Vluyn: Neukirchener, 1973.

Kunene, Musa Victor Mdabuleni. *Communal Holiness in the Gospel of John: The Vine Metaphor as a Test Case with Lessons from African Hospitality and Trinitarian Theology*. Carlisle: Langham Monographs, 2012.

Kuhrt, Amélie. *The Ancient Near East*. New York: Routledge, 1995.

———. "The Cyrus Cylinder and Achaemenid Imperial Policy." *JSOT* 25 (1983) 83–97.

Kunin, Seth D. *The Logic of Incest: A Structuralist Analysis of Hebrew Mythology*. JSOTSup 185. Sheffield: Sheffield Academic, 1995.

Laato, Antti. *The Servant of YHWH and Cyrus: A Reinterpretation of the Exilic Messianic Programme in Isaiah 40–55*. ConBOT 35. Stockholm: Almqvist & Wiksell, 1992.

LaBarbera, Robert. "The Man of War and the Man of God: Social Satire in 2 Kings 6:8—7:20." *CBQ* 46 (1984) 637–51.

LaCocque, André. *Zacharie 9–14*. Commentaire de l'ancien testament 11c. Neuchâtel: Delachaux and Niestlé, 1981.

Lafont, Bertrand. "La roi de Mari et les prophètes du dieu Adad." *RA* 78 (1984) 7–18.

Laird, Donna. *Negotiating Power in Ezra-Nehemiah*. AIL 26. Atlanta: SBL Press, 2016.

Lalleman-de Winkel, Hattie. *Jeremiah in Prophetic Tradition: An Examination of the Book of Jeremiah in the Light of Israel's Prophetic Traditions*. CBET 26. Leuven: Peeters, 2000.

Lambdin, Thomas O. *Egyptian Loanwords and Transcriptions in the Ancient Semitic Languages*. Baltimore: Johns Hopkins University Press, 1952.

Lambert, Wilfrid G. *Babylonian Creation Myths*. Winona Lake, IN: Eisenbrauns, 2013.

———. *Babylonian Wisdom Literature*. Oxford: Clarendon, 1960.

———. "Studies in Marduk." *BSOAS* 47 (1984) 1–9.

Lambert, Wilfrid G., and Alan R. Millard. *Atra-Ḫasīs: The Babylonian Story of the Flood*. Oxford: Clarendon, 1969.

Lambrecht, Jan. "Paul's Farewell Address at Miletus (Acts 20,17–38)." In *Les Actes des Apôtres: Traditions, rédaction, théologie*, edited by J. Kremer, 307–37. BETL 48. Gembloux: Ducolot, 1979.

Lang, Bernhard. "Sklaven und Unfreie im Buch Amos (2:6; 8:6)." *VT* 31 (1981) 482–88.

———. "The Social Organization of Peasant Poverty in Biblical Israel." *JSOT* 24 (1982) 47–63.

———. *Wisdom and the Book of Proverbs: A Hebrew Goddess Redefined*. New York: Pilgrim, 1986.

Lanner, Laurel. *Who Will Lament Her?: The Feminine and the Fantastic in the Book of Nahum*. New York: T. & T. Clark, 2006.

Larkin, Katrina J. A. *The Eschatology of Second Zechariah: A Study of the Formation of a Mantological Wisdom Anthology*. CBET 6. Kampen: Kok Pharos, 1994.

Laroche, Emmanuel. "Koubaba, déesse anatolienne, et le problème des origins de Cybèle." In *Elements orientaux dans la religion grecque ancienne*, 113–28. Paris: Presses Universitaires de France, 1960.

Lasine, Stuart. *Knowing Kings: Knowledge, Power and Narcissism in the Hebrew Bible*. SemeiaSt 40. Atlanta: SBL, 2001.

Launderville, Dale. *Celibacy in the Ancient World: Its Ideal and Practice in Pre-Hellenistic Israel, Mesopotamia, and Greece*. Collegeville, MN: Liturgical, 2010.

———. *Piety and Politics: The Dynamics of Royal Authority in Homeric Greece, Biblical Israel, and Old Babylonian Mesopotamia*. Grand Rapids: Eerdmans, 2003.

Lee, Andrew Y. "The Canonical Unity of the Scroll of the Minor Prophets." PhD. diss., Baylor University, 1985.

Lee, Robert Greene. *Payday Someday and Other Sermons*. Nashville: Broadman & Holman, 1995.

LeFebvre, Michael. *Collections, Codes, and Torah: The Re-Characterization of Israel's Written Law*. LHBOTS 451. New York: T. & T. Clark, 2006.

Leichty, Erle. "Esarhaddon, King of Assyria." In *CANE* 949–58.

Lemche, Niels Peter. "*Andurārum* and *Mīšarum*: Comments on the Problem of Social Edicts and Their Application in the Ancient Near East." *JNES* 38 (1979) 11–22.

———. *Biblical Studies and the Failure of History*. London: Routledge, 2014.

———. "The Manumission of Slaves—The Fallow Year—The Sabbatical Year—The Jobel Year." *VT* 26 (1976) 38–59.

———. "Our Most Gracious Sovereign: On the Relationship between Royal Mythology and Economic Oppression in the Ancient Near East." In *Ancient Economy in Mythology: East and West*, edited by M. Silver, 109–34. Savage, MD: Rowan & Littlefield, 1991.

Lemos, Tracy Maria. *Marriage Gifts and Social Change in Ancient Palestine 1200 BCE—200 CE*. Cambridge: Cambridge University Press, 2010.

Lenski, Gerhard E. *Power and Privilege: A Theory of Social Stratification*. New York: McGraw-Hill, 1966.

Lenski, Richard C. H. *The Interpretation of St. Matthew's Gospel 15–28*. 1943. Reprint, Minneapolis: Augsburg Fortress, 2008.

Leota, Peniamina. "'For the Right of Possession and Redemption Is Yours; Buy It for Yourself: Who Is the Implied Reader of Jeremiah 32:8?" *PJT* 22 (1999) 59–65.

Lesko, Barbara S. *The Great Goddesses of Egypt*. Norman: University of Oklahoma Press, 1999.

Leslau, Wolf. *Comparative Dictionary of Ge`ez (Classical Ethiopic)*. Wiesbaden: Harrassowitz, 2006.

Leuchter, Mark. *The Levites and the Boundaries of Israelite Identity*. New York: Oxford University Press, 2017.

Levenson, Jon D. *The Hebrew Bible, The Old Testament, and Historical Criticism: Jews and Christians in Biblical Studies*. Louisville: Westminster John Knox, 1993.

———. Review of *In the Wake of the Goddesses: Women, Culture, and the Biblical Transformation of Pagan Myth*, by T. Frymer-Kensky. *First Things* 27 (1992) 50–53.

Levi della Vida, Giorgio, and Maria Giula Amadasi Guzzo. *Iscrizioni puniche della Tripolitania (1927-67)*. Rome: "L'Erma" di Bretschneider, 1987.

Levin, Yigal. "Ba`al Worship in Early Israel: An Onomastic View in Light of the 'Eshba`al' Inscription from Khirbet Qeiyafa." *Maarav* 21 (2014) 203–22.

Levine, Amy-Jill. "Redrawing the Boundaries: A New Look at 'Diaspora as Metaphor: Bodies and Boundaries in the Book of Tobit.'" In *A Feminist Companion to Tobit and Judith*, edited by A. Brenner-Idan and H. Efthimiadis-Keith, 3–22. FCB 537. New York: Bloomsbury, 2015.

———. *The Social and Ethnic Dimensions of Matthean Salvation History: "Go Nowhere among the Gentiles . . ." (Matt 10:5b)*. Lewiston: Edwin Mellen, 1988.

Levine, Baruch A. "The Descriptive Ritual Texts from Ugarit: Some Form and Functional Features of the Genre." In *The Word of the Lord Shall Go Forth: Essays in Honor of David Noel Freedman in Celebration of his Sixtieth Birthday*. Philadelphia: ASOR, 1983.

———. *In the Presence of the Lord: A Study of Cult and Some Cultic Terms in Ancient Israel*. SJLA 5. Leiden: Brill, 1974.

———. *Numbers 21–36: A New Translation with Introduction and Commentary*. AB 4A. New York: Doubleday, 2000.

Levine, Lee I. *The Ancient Synagogue: The First Thousand Years*. New Haven, CT: Yale University Press, 2005.

Levine, Phillip B. *Sex and Consequences: Abortion, Public Policy, and the Economics of Fertility*. Princeton, NJ: Princeton University Press, 2004.

Lévi-Strauss, Claude. *Structural Anthropology*. 1958. Translated by C. Jacobson and B. G. Schoepf. New York: Basic Books, 1963.

Lewis, Clive Staples. "Charity." In *The Four Loves*, 116–46. New York: Harcourt, Brace, 1960.

———. "On Myth." In *An Experiment in Criticism*, 40–49. Cambridge: Cambridge University Press, 1961.

Lewis, Theodore J. *Cults of the Dead in Ancient Israel and Ugarit*. HSM 39. Atlanta: Scholars, 1989.

———. "Dead." In *DDD* 223–31.

———. "Death Cult Imagery in Isaiah 57." *HAR* 11 (1987) 267–84.

———. "First-Born of Death." In *DDD* 332–35.

Lied, Liv Ingeborg. "Between 'Text Witness' and 'Text on the Page': Trajectories in the History of Editing the Epistle of Baruch." In *Snapshots of Evolving Traditions: Jewish and Christian Manuscript Culture, Textual Fluidity and New Philology*, edited by L. I. Lied and H. Lundhaug, 277–96. TUGAL 175. Berlin: de Gruyter, 2017.

Lim, Timothy H. *The Formation of the Jewish Canon*. AYBRL. New Haven, CT: Yale University Press, 2013.

———. "The Wicked Priest or the Liar?" In *The Dead Sea Scrolls in Their Historical Context*, edited by T. Lim et al., 45–51. Edinburgh: T. & T. Clark, 2000.

Limet, Henri. "Le poème épique 'Inanna et Ebiḫ': Une version des lignes 123 à 182." *Or* 40 (1971) 11–28.

Linafelt, Tod. *The Hebrew Bible as Literature: A Very Short Introduction*. Oxford: Oxford University Press, 2016.

Lindenberger, James M. "Ahiqar." In *OTP* 2.479–507.

———. "What Ever Happened to Vidranga?: A Jewish Liturgy of Cursing from Elephantine." In *The World of the Aramaeans III: Studies in Language and Literature in Honour of Paul-Eugène Dion*, edited by P. M. Michèle-Daviau et al., 134–57. JSOTSup 325. Sheffield: Sheffield Academic, 2001.

Linville, James R. *Amos and the Cosmic Imagination*. Burlington, VT: Ashgate, 2008.

Lipiński, Eduard. "Adad." In *ER* 1:27–29.

———. "מהר." In *TDOT* 8.142–49.

———. "נחל." In *TDOT* 9.319–35.

———. "תרשיש." In *TDOT* 15.790–93.

Lipschitz, Oded. "Achaemenid Imperial Policy, Settlement Processes in Palestine, and the Status of Jerusalem in the Fifth Century BCE." In *Judah and the Judeans in the Persian Period*, edited by O. Lipschitz and M. Oeming, 19–53. Winona Lake, IN: Eisenbrauns, 2006.

Litke, Richard L. *A Reconstruction of The Assyro-Babylonian God-Lists, An: ^{d}A-nu-um and An: Anu ša amēli*. New Haven, CT: Yale Babylonian Collection, 1998.

Liverani, Mario. "The Great Powers' Club." In *Amarna Diplomacy: The Beginnings of International Relations*, edited by R. Cohen and R. Westbrook, 15–27. Baltimore: Johns Hopkins University Press, 2000.

———. *Myth and Politics in Ancient Near Eastern Historiography*. Ithaca, NY: Cornell University Press, 2004.

———. *Prestige and Interest: International Relations in the Near East*. Padova: Sargon, 1990.

———. "The Trade Network of Tyre According to Ezekiel 27." In *Ah, Assyria . . . !: Studies in Assyrian History and Ancient Near Eastern Historiography Presented to Hayim Tadmor*, edited by M. Cogan and I. Eph`al, 65–79. Jerusalem: Hebrew University Press, 1991.

Lohfink, Norbert. "חרם." In *TDOT* 5.180–99.

———. "ירש." In *TDOT* 6.368–96.

Long, Thomas G. *Matthew*. Louisville: Westminster John Knox, 1997.

Longenecker, Bruce W. "Exposing the Economic Middle: A Revised Economy Scale for the Study of Early Urban Christianity." *JSNT* 31 (2009) 243–78.

Longenecker, Richard N. *Biblical Exegesis in the Apostolic Period.* Grand Rapids: Eerdmans, 1999.

Lortie, Christopher R. "These Are the Days of the Prophets: A Literary Analysis of Ezra 1–6." *TynBul* 64 (2013) 161–69.

Loucas, Ioannis. "La déesse de la prospérité dans les mythes mésopotamien et égéen de la descente aus enfers." *RHR* 205 (1988) 227–44.

Luciani, Didier. "Introduction." In *Révéler les oeuvres de Dieu: Lecture narrative du livre de Tobie,* by E. di Pede et al., 5–11. Paris: Lessius, 2014.

Lüdemann, Gerd. *The Acts of the Apostles: What Really Happened in the Earliest Days of the Church.* Amherst, NY: Prometheus, 2005.

Lundbom, Jack R. *Jeremiah 1–20.* AB 21A. New York: Doubleday, 1999.

———. *Jeremiah: A Study in Ancient Hebrew Rhetoric.* Winona Lake, IN: Eisenbrauns, 1997.

———. *Jeremiah: Prophet Like Moses.* Eugene, OR: Cascade, 2015.

———. *Jeremiah Among the Prophets.* Eugene, OR: Cascade, 2012.

Macatangay, Francis M. "Metaphors and the Character Constitution of Tobias in the Book of Tobit." In *The Metaphorical Use of Language in Deuterocanonical and Cognate Literature,* edited by M. Witte and S. Behnke, 75–86. Berlin: de Gruyter, 2015.

———. "Μισθός and Irony in the Book of Tobit." *Bib* 94 (2013) 576–84.

———. *The Wisdom Instructions in the Book of Tobit.* DCLS 12. Berlin: de Gruyter, 2011.

———. *When I Die, Bury Me Well: Death, Burial, Almsgiving and Restoration in the Book of Tobit.* Eugene, OR: Pickwick, 2016.

Maccoby, Hyam. *The Mythmaker: Paul and the Invention of Christianity.* New York: Barnes & Noble, 1998.

MacDowell, Douglas M. "Athenian Laws about Bribery." *RIDA* 30 (1983) 57–78.

Machiela, Daniel A. and Andrew B. Perrin. "*Tobit* and the *Genesis Apocryphon*: Toward a Family Portrait." *JBL* 133 (2014) 111–32.

Machinist, Peter. "The Question of Distinctiveness in Ancient Israel." In *Essential Papers on Israel and the Ancient Near East,* edited by F. Greenspahn, 420–42. New York: NYU Press, 1991.

MacIntosh, Andrew A. *A Critical Commentary on Hosea.* ICC. Edinburgh: T. & T. Clark, 1997.

MacIntyre, Alasdair C. *After Virtue: A Study in Moral Theory.* 1981. Reprint, New York: Bloomsbury, 2007.

Madrinan, Carmen. "Worst Forms of Child Labor: Commercial Sexual Exploitation of Children." In *The World of Child Labor: An Historical and Regional Survey,* edited by H. Hindman, 95–101. London: M. E. Sharp, 2009.

Magdalene, F. Rachel. "Ancient Near Eastern Treaty-Curses and the Ultimate Texts of Terror: A Study of the Language of Divine Sexual Abuse in the Prophetic Corpus." In *A Feminist Companion to the Latter Prophets,* edited by A. Brenner-Idan, 326–52. FCB 8. Sheffield: Sheffield Academic, 1995.

Maier, Christl. *Daughter Zion, Mother Zion: Gender, Space, and the Sacred in Ancient Israel.* Minneapolis: Fortress, 2008.

Maier, John R., ed. *Gilgamesh: A Reader.* Wauconda, IL: Bolchazy-Carducci, 1997.

Maier, Walter A. "Anath." In *ABD* 1.225–27.

Malamat, Abraham. *Mari and the Bible.* SHANE 12. Leiden: Brill, 1998.

———. "Mari and the Bible: Some Patterns of Tribal Organization and Institutions." *JAOS* 82 (1962) 143–50.

Mandolfo, Carleen. *Daughter Zion Talks Back to the Prophets: A Dialogic Theory of the Book of Lamentations*. SemeiaSt 58. Atlanta: SBL, 2007.

Mann, Thomas. *The Book of the Former Prophets*. Cambridge: James Clark, 2012.

Manning, Gary T. "Shepherd, Vine, and Bones: The Use of *Ezekiel* in the *Gospel of John*." In *After Ezekiel: Essays on the Reception of a Difficult Prophet*, edited by A. Mein and P. Joyce, 25–44. LHBOTS 535. London: T. & T. Clark, 2011.

Manson, Thomas W. *The Sayings of Jesus*. 1957. Reprint, Grand Rapids: Eerdmans, 1979.

Marcus, David. "The Betrothal of Yarikh and Nikkal-Ib." In *UNP* 215–18.

Marcus, Joel. *Mark 1–8: A New Translation with Introduction and Commentary*. AYB 27. New York: Doubleday, 2000.

Margalit, Baruch. *A Matter of "Life" and "Death": A Study of the Ba'al-Mot Epic*. AOAT 206. Kevelaer: Butzon & Bercker, 1980.

———. *The Ugaritic Poem of Aqht*. BZAW 182. Berlin: de Gruyter, 1989.

Marguerat, Daniel. *The First Christian Historian: Writing the "Acts of the Apostles"*. Translated by K. McKinney et al. Cambridge: Cambridge University Press, 2004.

Margueron, Jean-Claude. "Mari: A Portrait of a Mesopotamian City-State." In *CANE* 885–99.

Mark, Joshua A. "Inanna's Descent: A Sumerian Tale of Injustice." In *Ancient History Encyclopedia*. http://www.ancient.eu/article/215/.

Marriage, Zoë. Worst Forms of Child Labor: Children and War." In *The World of Child Labor: An Historical and Regional Survey*, edited by H. Hindman, 102–5. London: Sharp, 2009.

Marshall, I. Howard. *The Acts of the Apostles: An Introduction and Commentary*. TNTC. Grand Rapids: Eerdmans, 1980.

———. *The Gospel of Luke: A Commentary on the Greek Text*. NIGTC. Grand Rapids: Eerdmans, 1978.

Marsman, Hennie J. *Women in Ugarit and Israel: Their Social and Religious Position in the Context of the Ancient Near East*. Leiden: Brill, 2003.

Martin, Dale B. "Slavery and the Ancient Jewish Family." In *The Jewish Family in Antiquity*, edited by S. J. D. Cohen, 113–29. Atlanta: Scholars, 1993.

Marttila, Marko. "Babylonian Priests in the Description of the Epistle of Jeremiah." In *Various Aspects of Worship in Deuterocanonical and Cognate Literature*, edited by G. Xeravits et al., 225–46. Berlin: de Gruyter, 2017.

Mason, Steven D. "Another Flood? Genesis 9 and Isaiah's Broken Eternal Covenant." *JSOT* 32 (2007) 177–98.

Massie, Robert K. *The Romanovs: The Final Chapter*. New York: Ballantine, 1995.

Mastnjak, Nathan. *Deuteronomy and the Emergence of Textual Authority in Jeremiah*. FAT 87. Tübingen: Mohr/Siebeck, 2016.

Maul, Stefan M. "Die altorientalische Hauptstadt—Abbild und Nabel der Welt." In *Die Orientalische Stadt: Kontinuität, Wandel, Bruch*, edited by G. Wilhelm, 109–24. CDOG 7. Wiesbaden: Harrassowitz, 2013.

Mauss, Marcel. *The Gift: Forms and Functions of Exchange in Archaic Societies*. Translated by Ian Cunnison. 1925. Republished, New York: Norton, 1967.

May, Elaine Tyler. *Barren in the Promised Land: Childless Americans and the Pursuit of Happiness*. Cambridge: Harvard University Press, 1995.

May, Herbert G. "Some Cosmic Connotations of מים רבים, 'Mighty Waters.'" *JBL* 74 (1955) 9–21.

Mayer, Wendy, and Bronwen Neil, eds. *Religious Conflict from Early Christianity to the Rise of Islam*. AKG 121. Berlin: de Gruyter, 2013.

Mays, James L. *Amos: A Commentary*. OTL. Philadelphia: Westminster, 1969.
———. *Hosea*. OTL. Philadelphia: Westminster, 1969.
———. *Micah: A Commentary*. OTL. Philadelphia: Westminster, 1976.
Mazoyer, Michel. *Télipinu, le dieu au marécage: Essai sur les mythes fondateurs du royaume hittite*. Paris: Kubaba, 2003.
McCabe, David R. *How to Kill Things with Words: Ananias and Sapphira under the Prophetic Speech-Act of Judgment (Acts 4:32—5:11)*. New York: T. & T. Clark, 2011.
McCracken, David. "Narration and Comedy in the Book of Tobit." *JBL* 114 (1995) 401–18.
McCrory, Jeff. "Nehemiah." In *The IVP Women's Bible Commentary*, edited by C. Kroeger and M. Evans, 256–63. Downers Grove, IL: InterVarsity, 2002.
McDonald, Joseph Loren. *Searching for Sarah in the Second Temple Era: Portraits in the Hebrew Bible and Second Temple Narratives*. Fort Worth: TCU Press, 2015.
McDonnell, Rea. Review of *The Widows*, by Bonnie Thurston. *Horizons* 17 (1990) 328–29.
McGeough, Kevin M. *Exchange Relationships at Ugarit*. ANESSup 26. Leuven: Peeters, 2007.
McGovern, Patrick. *Ancient Wine: The Search for the Origins of Viniculture*. Princeton, NJ: Princeton University Press, 2003.
McKane, William L. *A Critical and Exegetical Commentary on Jeremiah*. ICC. Edinburgh: T. & T. Clark, 1996.
———. *Micah: A Critical and Exegetical Commentary*. ICC. Edinburgh: T. & T. Clark, 1998.
McKenzie, John L. *Dictionary of the Bible*. New York: MacMillan, 1965.
———. "Knowledge of God in Hosea." *JBL* 74 (1955) 22–27.
McLaren, Brian D. *Finding Faith: A Self-Discovery Guide for Your Spiritual Quest*. Grand Rapids: Zondervan, 1999.
McLaughlin, John L. *The* marzēaḥ *in the Prophetic Literature: References and Allusions in Light of the Extra-Biblical Evidence*. VTSup 86. Leiden: Brill, 2001.
McMahon, Gregory. "Theology, Priests, and Worship in Hittite Anatolia." In *CANE* 1981–95.
McNamara, Martin. *Targum and Testament Revisited: Aramaic Paraphrases of the Hebrew Bible*. Grand Rapids: Eerdmans, 2010.
McNeese, Tim. *The Robber Barons and the Sherman Antitrust Act: Reshaping American Business*. New York: Chelsea House, 2009.
Mead, James K. "Elijah." In *DOTHB* 249–54.
Meeks, Wayne A. *The Prophet-King: Moses Traditions and the Johannine Christology*. NovTSup 14. Leiden: Brill, 1967.
Melchert, H. Craig. "Marginalia to the Myth of Telipinu." In *Audias Fabulas Veteres: Anatolian Studies in Honor of Jana Součková-Siegelová*, edited by S. Velhartická, 210–20. CHANE 79. Leiden: Brill, 2016.
Melugin, Roy. "Prophetic Books and the Problem of Historical Reconstruction." In *Prophets and Paradigms: Essays in Honor of Gene M. Tucker*, edited by S. Reid, 63–78. JSOTSup 229. Sheffield: Sheffield Academic, 1996.
Mendels, Doron. "Jeremiah, Epistle of." In *ABD* 3.721–22.
Mendenhall, George E. "The Hebrew Conquest of Palestine." *BA* 25 (1962) 66–87.
Mendenhall, George E., and Gary A. Herion. "Covenant." In *ABD* 1.1179–1202.
Merkur, Dan. "Biblical Terrorism." In *A Cry Instead of Justice: The Bible and Cultures of Violence in Psychological Perspective*, edited by D. Daschke and A. Kille, 55–79. New York: T. & T. Clark, 2010.

Métral, Francoise. "Managing Risk: Sheep-Shearing and Agriculture." In *The Transformation of Nomadic Society in the Syrian Steppe*, edited by M. Mundy and B. Musallam, 123–44. Cambridge: Cambridge University Press, 2000.

Mettinger, Tryggve N. D. *A Farewell to the Servant Songs: A Critical Examination of an Exegetical Axiom*. Lund: Gleerup, 1983.

———. *The Riddle of Resurrection: "Dying and Rising Gods" in the Ancient Near East*. ConBOT 50. Stockholm: Almqvist & Wiksell, 2001.

Meyers, Carol L. Review of *Haggai and Zechariah 1–8: A Commentary*, by David L. Petersen. *JBL* 105 (1986) 716–17.

———. "'Women of the Neighborhood' (Ruth 4:17): Informal Female Networks in Ancient Israel." In *Ruth and Esther: A Feminist Companion to the Bible*, edited by Athalya Brenner-Idan, 110–28. FCB 3. Sheffield: Sheffield Academic, 1999.

Meyers, Carol L., and Eric Meyers. *Zechariah 9–14*. AB 25C. New Haven, CT: Yale University Press, 1998.

Michaelis, Wilhelm. "σκηνοποιός." In *TDNT* 7.393–94.

Michaels, Jonathan. *McCarthyism: The Realities, Delusions, and Politics behind the 1950s Big Red Scare*. London: Routledge, 2017.

Milgram, Jonathan S. "Gifting and Inheriting in Tannaitic Law and in the Ancient World." In *From Mesopotamia to the Mishnah: Tannaitic Inheritance Law in Its Legal and Social Contexts*, 39–65. TSAJ 64. Tübingen: Mohr/Siebeck, 2016.

Milgrom, Jacob. *Cult and Conscience: The* אשם *and the Priestly Doctrine of Repentance*. SJLA 18. Leiden: Brill, 1976.

Milik, Jozef T. "Trois tombeaux juifs récemment découverts au Sud-Est de Jerusalem." *RB* 65 (1958) 409.

Millar, William R. *Isaiah 24–27 and the Origin of Apocalyptic*. HSM 11. Missoula, MT: Scholars, 1976.

Miller, Geoffrey David. *Marriage in the Book of Tobit*. DCLS 10. New York: de Gruyter, 2011.

Miller, James Maxwell, and John H. Hayes. *A History of Israel and Judah*. Louisville: Westminster John Knox, 1986.

Miller, Patrick D. *Israelite Religion and Biblical Theology: Collected Essays*. JSOTSup 267. Sheffield: Sheffield Academic, 2000.

———. "Vocative *lamed* in the Psalter." *UF* 11 (1979) 617–38.

Miller, Patrick D., and J. J. M. Roberts. *The Hand of the Lord: A Reassessment of the "Ark Narrative" in 1 Samuel*. Baltimore: Johns Hopkins University Press, 1977.

Millgram, Hillel I. *The Elijah Enigma: The Prophet, King Ahab, and the Rebirth of Monotheism in the Book of Kings*. Jefferson, NC: McFarland, 2014.

Min, Kjung-Jin. *The Levitical Authorship of Ezra-Nehemiah*. JSOTSup 409. New York: T. & T. Clark, 2004.

Minnen, P. van. "Paul the Roman Citizen." *JNTS* 56 (1994) 43–52.

Miranda, José Porfirio. *Marx and the Bible: A Critique of the Philosophy of Oppression*. 1974. Reprint, Eugene, OR: Wipf & Stock, 2004.

Moberly, R. Walter L. "'In God We Trust?' The Challenge of the Prophets." *Ex Auditu* 24 (2008) 18–33.

———. *The Old Testament of the Old Testament: Patriarchal Narratives and Mosaic Yahwism*. Minneapolis: Augsburg Fortress, 1992.

Momigliano, Arnaldo Dante. *Essays on Ancient and Modern Judaism*. Chicago: University of Chicago Press, 1994.

Mönning, B. H. "Die Darstellung des urchristlichen Kommunismus nach der Apostelgeschichte des Lukas." PhD diss., Georg August Universität, 1978.
Monroe, Christopher M. *Scales of Fate: Trade, Tradition, and Transformation in the Eastern Mediterranean ca. 1350–1175 BCE.* Münster: Ugarit, 2009.
Moor, Johannes C. de. *An Anthology of Religious Texts from Ugarit.* Leiden: Brill, 1987.
———. *The Seasonal Pattern in the Ugaritic Myth of Ba'alu.* AOAT 16. Kevelaer: Butzon and Bercker, 1971.
Moore, Carey A. *Daniel, Esther, and Jeremiah: The Additions.* AB 44. New Haven, CT: Yale University Press, 1977.
———. *Tobit: A New Translation with Introduction and Commentary.* AB 40A. New York: Doubleday, 1996.
Moore, Michael S. "הגאל—The Cultural Gyroscope of Ancient Hebrew Society." *ResQ* 23 (1980) 27–35.
———. "America's Monocultural Heritage." *Fides et Historia* 15 (1982) 39–53.
———. "Are Our Wounds Incurable? (Micah 1:9)." In *Today Hear His Voice: The Minor Prophets Speak*, edited by D. Shackelford, 313–24. Searcy, AR: Harding University Press, 1993.
———. *The Balaam Traditions: Their Character and Development.* SBLDS 113. Atlanta: Scholars, 1990.
———. "Bathsheba's Silence." In *Inspired Speech: Prophecy in the Ancient Near East: Essays Presented to Herbert B. Huffmon*, edited by J. Kaltner and L. Stulman, 336–46. JSOTSup 378. New York: Continuum, 2004.
———. "Civic and Voluntary Associations in the Graeco-Roman World." In *The World of the New Testament: Cultural, Social, and Historical Contexts*, edited by J. Green and L. McDonald, 149–55. Grand Rapids: Baker Academic, 2013.
———. "David and His Teenagers." In *Reconciliation: A Study of Biblical Families in Conflict*, 49–60. Joplin, MO: College Press, 1994.
———. "Divine Presence." In *DOTPr* 166–70.
———. *Faith Under Pressure: A Study of Biblical Leaders in Conflict.* Abilene, TX: Abilene Christian University Press, 2003.
———. "Jehu's Coronation and Purge of Israel." *VT* 53 (2003) 97–114.
———. "Jeremiah's Progressive Paradox." *RB* 93 (1986) 386–414.
———. "Job's Texts of Terror." *CBQ* 55 (1993) 662–75.
———. "Numbers." In *The Transforming Word*, edited by M. Hamilton, 185–202. Abilene, TX: Abilene Christian University Press, 2009.
———. "Obduracy, Hardness of Heart." In *EHJ* 428–29.
———. *Reconciliation: A Study of Biblical Families in Conflict.* Joplin, MO: College Press, 1994.
———. Review of *Amos and the Officialdom in the Kingdom of Israel: The Socio-Economic Position of the Officials in the Light of the Biblical, Epigraphic and Archaeological Evidence*, by Izabela Jaruzelska. *JBL* 119 (2000) 758–60.
———. Review of *Assyrian Prophecies*, by Simo Parpola. *CBQ* 61 (1999) 551–53.
———. Review of *The Standard Babylonian Creation Myth* Enūma Eliš, by P. Talon. *CBQ* 69 (2007) 800–802.
———. Review of *Finding Wisdom in Nature: An Eco-Wisdom Reading of the Book of Job*, by Norman C. Habel. *RBL*, 2016. http://www.bookreviews.org/pdf/10227_11347.pdf.

———. Review of *Flight and Freedom in the Ancient Near East*, by Daniel C. Snell. *JBL* 121 (2002) 337–39.
———. Review of *Goddesses in Religions and Modern Debate*, edited by Larry Hurtado, and *In the Wake of the Goddesses*, by Tikva Frymer-Kensky. *Int* 47 (1993) 178–81.
———. Review of *The Riddle of Resurrection: "Dying and Rising Gods" in the Ancient Near East*, by T. N. D. Mettinger. *RBL*, 2003. http://www.bookreviews.org/pdf/2958_3037.pdf.
———. "Role Preemption in the Israelite Priesthood." *VT* 46 (1996) 316–29.
———. "Ruth." In *Joshua, Judges, Ruth*, 293–383. UBCS. Grand Rapids: Baker Academic, 2000.
———. "Sacrifice, Tithes, Offerings." In *EHJ* 533–36.
———. "Two Textual Anomalies in Ruth." *CBQ* 59 (1997) 324–43.
———. *WealthWatch: A Study of Socioeconomic Conflict in the Bible*. Eugene, OR: Pickwick, 2011.
———. *What Is This Babbler Trying to Say? Essays on Biblical Interpretation*. Eugene, OR: Pickwick, 2016.
———. "'Wise Women' in the Bible: Identifying a Trajectory." In *Essays on Women in Earliest Christianity*, edited by C. D. Osburn, 2.87–103. Joplin, MO: College Press, 1995.
Moran, William L. *The Amarna Letters*. Baltimore: Johns Hopkins University Press, 1992.
———. "Ancient Near Eastern Background of the Love of God in Deuteronomy." *CBQ* 25 (1963) 77–87.
Morgenstern, Julian. "The Elohist Narrative in Exodus 3:1–15." *AJSL* 37 (1920–21) 242–62.
Morley, Neville. *Theories, Models, and Concepts in Ancient History: Approaching the Ancient World*. London: Routledge, 2004.
Morse, Merrill. *Isaiah Speaks: A Voice from the Past for the Present*. Eugene, OR: Resource, 2012.
Moss, Candida R., and Joel S. Baden. *Reconceiving Infertility: Biblical Perspectives on Procreation and Childlessness*. Princeton, NJ: Princeton University Press, 2015.
Moss, Charlene McAfee. *The Zechariah Tradition and the Gospel of Matthew*. BZNW 156. New York: de Gruyter, 2008.
Moughtin-Mumby, Sharon. *Sexual and Marital Metaphors in Hosea, Jeremiah, Isaiah, and Ezekiel*. New York: Oxford University Press, 2008.
Mouton, Alice. *Rêves Hittites: Contribution à une histoire et une anthropologie du rêve en Anatolie ancienne*. CHANE 28. Leiden: Brill, 2007.
Mowat, Barbara A. "Shakespeare and the Geneva Bible." In *Shakespeare, the Bible, and the Form of the Book: Contested Scriptures*, edited by T. DeCook and A. Galey, 25–39. New York: Routledge, 2012.
Mowinckel, Sigmund. *Die Erkenntnis Gottes bei den Propheten*. Oslo: Grøndahl, 1941.
———. *He That Cometh: The Messianic Concept in the Old Testament and Later Judaism*. 1951. Translated by G. W. Anderson. Nashville: Abingdon, 1956.
———. *The Psalms in Israel's Worship*. Nashville: Abingdon, 1962.
Moyo, Fulata Lusungu. "We Demand Bread and Roses When We Are Hired: Gender Justice in Workplaces—A Feminist Ethical Perspective." *Ecumenical Review* 64 (2012) 254–66.
Muellner, Leonard. *The Anger of Achilles: μῆνις in Greek Myth*. Ithaca, NY: Cornell University Press, 1996.
Mugerauer, Robert. "Literature as Reconciliation: The Art of Hypothetical Vision." *Soundings* 58 (1975) 407–15.

Muhs, Brian. *The Ancient Egyptian Economy, 3000–30 BCE*. Cambridge: Cambridge University Press, 2016.

Muilenberg, James. "A Study in Hebrew Rhetoric: Repetition and Style." In *Congress Volume: Copenhagen 1953*, 97–111. VTSup 1. Leiden: Brill, 1953.

Mulder, Martin J. "Ba`al Berith." In *DDD* 141–44.

———. *Ba`al in het Oude Testament*. Kampen: Gravenhage, 1962.

Mullen, E. Theodore. *The Divine Council in Canaanite and Early Hebrew Literature*. HSM 24. Atlanta: Scholars, 1980.

Müller, Gerfrid G. W. *Quaestio Thesauri*. http://www.hethport.uni-wuerzburg.de/txhet_myth/q2.php/.

Müller, Hans-Peter. "Die weisheitliche Lehrerzahlung im Alten Testament und seiner Umwelt." *WO* 9 (1977) 77–98.

Müller, Johannes. *Beiträge zur Erklärung und Kritik des Buches Tobit*. BZAW 13. Giessen: Töpelmann, 1908.

Munch, Peter A. *The Expression* ביום ההוא*: Is It an Eschatological Terminus Technicus?* Oslo: Dybwad, 1936.

Munn, Mark. *The Mother of the Gods, Athens, and the Tyranny of Asia: A Study of Sovereignty in Ancient Religion*. Berkeley: University of California Press, 2006.

Murphy, Aaron G. *Foreign Corrupt Practices Act: A Practical Resource for Managers and Executives*. Hoboken, NJ: Wiley, 2011.

Murphy, Catherine. *Wealth in the Dead Sea Scrolls and in the Qumran Community*. STDJ 40. Leiden: Brill, 2002.

Mussies, Gerard. "Artemis." In *DDD* 91–97.

Na`aman, Nadav. "The Egyptian-Canaanite Correspondence." In *Amarna Diplomacy: The Beginnings of International Relations*, edited by R. Cohen and R. Westbrook, 125–38. Baltimore: Johns Hopkins University Press, 2000.

Nakash, Yitzhaq. "The *Muharram* Rituals and the Cult of the Saints among Iraqi Shiites." In *The Other Shiites: From the Mediterranean to Central Asia*, edited by A. Monsutti et al., 115–36. WI 2. New York: Peter Lang, 2007.

Nel, Marius J. "The Forgiveness of Debt in Matthew 6:12, 14–215." *Neot* 47 (2013) 87–106.

Neubauer, Adolf. *The Book of Tobit: A Chaldee Manuscript from a Unique Manuscript in the Bodleian Library*. Oxford: Clarendon, 1878.

Neusner, Jacob. *The Economics of the Mishnah*. Chicago: University of Chicago, 1990.

Nicholson, Ernest W. *Preaching to the Exiles: A Study of the Prose Tradition in the Book of Jeremiah*. Oxford: Blackwell, 1970.

Nickelsburg, George W. E. "The Bible Rewritten and Expanded." In *Jewish Writings of the Second Temple Period: Apocrypha, Pseudepigrapha, Qumran Sectarian Writings, Philo, Josephus*, edited by M. E. Stone, 89–156. CRINT. Philadelphia: Fortress, 1984.

———. *Jewish Literature Between the Bible and Mishnah: An Historical and Literary Introduction*. Minneapolis: Fortress, 2005.

Niebuhr, H. Richard. *Theology, History and Culture: Major Unpublished Writings*. Edited by W. S. Johnson. New Haven, CT: Yale University Press, 1996.

Nissinen, Martti. *Ancient Prophecy: Near Eastern, Biblical, and Greek Perspectives*. New York: Oxford University Press, 2018.

———. *Prophets and Prophecy in the Ancient Near East*. SBLWAW 12. Atlanta: SBL, 2003.

———. *References to Prophecy in Neo-Assyrian Sources*. SAAS 7. Helsinki: Neo-Assyrian Text Corpus Project, 1998.

———. "What Is Prophecy?: An Ancient Near Eastern Perspective." In *Inspired Speech: Prophecy in the Ancient Near East: Essays in Honor of Herbert B. Huffmon*, edited by John Kaltner and Louis Stulman, 17–37. JSOTSup 378. New York: T. & T. Clark, 2004.

Noegel, Scott B. "God of Heaven and Sheol and the 'Unearthing' of Creation." *HS* 58 (2017) 119–44.

———. *Puns and Pundits: Word Play in the Hebrew Bible and Ancient Near Eastern Literature.* Bethesda, MD: CDL Press, 2000.

Nogalski, James D. "The Day(s) of Yhwh in the Book of the Twelve." In *Thematic Threads in the Book of the Twelve*, edited by P. Redditt and A. Schart, 192–213. BZAW 325. New York: de Gruyter, 2003.

———. "Intertextuality and the Twelve." In *Forming Prophetic Literature: Essays on Isaiah and the Twelve in Honor of John D. W. Watts*, edited by J. W. Watts and P. R. House, 102–24. JSOTSup 235. Sheffield: Sheffield Academic, 1996.

———. *Redactional Processes in the Book of the Twelve*. BZAW 218. New York: de Gruyter, 1993.

Nolan, Patrick, and Gerhard Lenski. *Human Societies: An Introduction to Macrosociology.* London: Paradigm, 2011.

Nolland, John. *The Gospel of Matthew: A Commentary on the Greek Text.* NIGTC. Grand Rapids: Eerdmans, 2005.

Noonan, John T. *Bribes: The Intellectual History of a Moral Idea.* Berkeley: University of California Press, 1984.

Noonan, John T. , and Dan M. Kahan. "Bribery." In *Encyclopedia of Crime and Justice*, edited by J. Dressler, 105–11. New York: MacMillan, 2002.

North, Robert. "עשׁר." In *TDOT* 11.404–8.

———. *Sociology of the Biblical Jubilee.* AnBib 4. Roma: Pontificio Istituto Biblico, 1954.

Noth, Martin. *The Deuteronomistic History*, 1943. Translated by J. Doull. Sheffield: JSOT Press,

———. *The History of Israel.* 1958. Translated by P. R. Ackroyd. New York: Harper & Row, 1960.

———. *Die israelitischen Personnamen im Rahmen der gemeinsemitischen Namengebung.* Hildesheim: Georg Olms, 1928.

Nougayrol, Jean. *Textes accadiens des archivs sud. PRU* 4. Paris: Imprimerie Nationale, 1956.

Nowell, Irene. "The Book of Tobit: Narrative Technique and Theology." PhD diss., Catholic University of America, 1983.

———. *Jonah, Tobit, Judith.* Collegeville, MN: Liturgical, 2015.

Nutkowicz, Hélène, and Michel Mazoyer. *La disparition du dieu dans la Bible et les mythes hittites: Essai anthropologique.* Paris: L'Harmattan, 2014.

Nygren, Anders. *Agape and Eros: The Christian Idea of Love.* 1936. Translated by P. S. Watson. Chicago: University of Chicago Press, 1982.

Oakman, Douglas E. "The Lord's Prayer in Social Perspective." In *Authenticating the Words of Jesus*, edited by Bruce Chilton and Craig Evans, 137–86. Leiden: Brill, 2002.

Ober, Josiah. "Civic Ideology and Counterhegemonic Discourse: Thucydides on the Sicilian Debate." In *Athenian Identity and Civic Ideology*, edited by A. Boegehold and A. Scafuro, 102–26. Baltimore: Johns Hopkins, 1994.

O'Brien, Mark A. *The Deuteronomistic History Hypothesis: A Reassessment.* OBO 92. Göttingen: Vandenhoeck & Ruprecht, 1989.

Oded, Bustanay. "Ahab." In *EJ* 1.522–25.

Ogden, Daniel. *Drakōn: Dragon Myth and Serpent Cult in the Greek and Roman Worlds.* Oxford: Oxford University Press, 2013.

Ohrenstein, Roman A., and Barry Gordon. *Economic Analysis in Talmudic Literature: Rabbinic Thought in the Light of Modern Economics.* Leiden: Brill, 1992.

Oldenburg, Ulf. *The Conflict between El and Ba'al in Canaanite Religion.* Leiden: Brill, 1969.

Olmo Lete, Gregorio del. "The Offering Lists and the God Lists." In *Handbook of Ugaritic Studies*, edited by W. G. E. Watson and N. Wyatt, 305–52. Leiden: Brill, 1999.

Olmo Lete, Gregorio del, and Joaquín Sanmartín. *A Dictionary of the Ugaritic Language in the Alphabetic Tradition.* Leiden: Brill, 2003.

Olmstead, A. T. "Tattenai, Governor of 'Across the River.'" *JNES* 3 (1944) 46.

Olson, Charles. "The Gate and the Center." In *Human Universe and Other Essays*, edited by D. Allen, 17–23. New York: Grove, 1967.

Olyan, Saul. "Honor, Shame, and Covenant Relations in Ancient Israel." *JBL* 115 (1996) 201–18.

———. "Purity Ideology in Ezra-Nehemiah as a Tool to Reconstitute the Community." In *Social Inequality in the World of the Text: The Significance of Ritual and Social Distinctions in the Hebrew Bible*, 159–72. Göttingen: Vandenhoeck & Ruprecht, 2011.

———. "Some Observations concerning the Identity of the Queen of Heaven." *UF* 19 (1987) 161–74.

Oort, Henricus. "Jezaja 24–27." *ThT* 20 (1886) 166–94.

Oppenheim, A. Leo. "Mesopotamian Mythology III." *Or* 19 (1950) 139–52.

———. "Siege Documents from Nippur." *Iraq* 17 (1955) 69–89.

Oppenheimer, Aharon. *The 'Am Ha-aretz: A Study in the Social History of the Jewish People in the Hellenistic-Roman Period.* ALGHJ 8. Leiden: Brill, 1977.

Osborne, Grant R. *Matthew.* Grand Rapids: Zondervan, 2010.

Oshima, Takayoshi. *Babylonian Poems of Pious Sufferers.* ORA 14. Tübingen: Mohr/Siebeck, 2014.

———. *Babylonian Prayers to Marduk.* ORA 7. Tübingen: Mohr/Siebeck, 2011.

Oswalt, John N. *The Book of Isaiah: Chapters 40–66.* NICOT. Grand Rapids: Eerdmans, 1998.

O'Toole, Robert F. "You Did Not Lie to Us (Human Beings), but to God (Acts 5:4c)." *Bib* 76 (1995) 182–209.

Otto, Eckhart. *Deuteronomium: Politische Theologie und Rechtsreform in Juda und Assyrien.* BZAW 284. Berlin: de Gruyter, 1999.

———. *Krieg und Frieden in der Hebräischen Bibel und im Alten Orient: Aspekte für eine Friedensordnung in der Moderne.* ThF 18. Stuttgart: Kohlhammer, 1999.

———. "Soziale Restitution und Vertragsrecht: *mīšarum, (an)-durāru(m), kirenzi, parā tarnumar, šemiṭṭa* und *derôr* in Mesopotamien, Syrien, in der hebraischen Bibel und die Frage des Rechtstransfers im alten Orient." *RA* 92 (1998) 125–60.

Otzen, Benedikt. *Tobit and Judith.* GAP 11. London: Sheffield Academic, 2002.

Overholt, Thomas W. "Jer 2 and the Problem of Audience Reaction." *CBQ* 41 (1979) 262–73.

Paffenroth, Kim. *Judas: Images of the Lost Disciple.* Louisville: Westminster John Knox, 2001.

Pakkala, Juha. *Ezra the Scribe: The Development of Ezra 7–10 and Nehemiah 8.* BZAW 347. Berlin: de Gruyter, 2004.

Pallis, Svend Aage. *The Babylonian* Akītu *Festival.* Copenhagen: Andr. Fred Host and Son, 1926.

Pantoja, Jennifer Metten. *The Metaphor of the Divine as Planter of the People: Stinking Grapes or Pleasant Planting?* BibIntSer 155. Leiden: Brill, 2017.

Pardee, Dennis. *Ritual and Cult at Ugarit*. SBLWAW 10. Leiden: Brill, 2002.

———. "Ugaritic Proper Nouns." *AfO* 36–37 (1989–90) 390–513.

———. "West Semitic Canonical Compositions." In *COS* 1.239–75.

Park, Hyung Dae. *Finding Ḥerem?: A Study of Luke-Acts in the Light of Ḥerem*. LNTS 357. New York: T. & T. Clark, 2007.

Parker, Simon B. "Aqhat." In *UNP* 49–80.

———. "Some Methodological Principles in Ugaritic Philology." *Maarav* 2 (1979–80) 7–41.

———, ed. *Ugaritic Narrative Poetry*. SBLWAW 9. Atlanta: SBL, 1997.

———. "The Vow in Ugaritic and Israelite Literature." *UF* 11 (1979) 693–700.

Parkinson, Richard B. *The Tale of Sinuhe and Other Ancient Egyptian Poems*. Oxford: Oxford University Press, 1997.

Parpola, Simo. *Assyrian Prophecies*. SAA 9. Helsinki: Helsinki University Press, 1997.

———. *Letters from Assyrian Scholars to the Kings Esarhaddon and Assurbanipal*. Vol. 2: *Commentary and Appendices*. 1983. Reprint, Winona Lake, IN: Eisenbrauns, 2007.

Parrinder, Geoffrey. *Jesus in the Qur'ān*. Oxford: OneWorld, 1995.

Parsons, Mikeal C. "Stephen and the Seven." In *Acts*, 81–108. Paideia. Grand Rapids: Baker Academic, 2008.

Patai, Raphael. "The Control of Rain in Ancient Palestine." *HUCA* 14 (1939) 251–86.

———. *The Hebrew Goddess*. Detroit: Wayne State University Press, 1990.

Patterson, Orlando. *Slavery and Social Death: A Comparative Study*. Cambridge, MA: Harvard University Press, 1982.

Paul, Shalom M. *Isaiah 40–66: Translation and Commentary*. ECC. Grand Rapids: Eerdmans, 2012.

Pecchioli-Daddi, Franca, and Anna Maria Polvani. *La mitologia ittita*. Brescia: Paideia, 1990.

Peckham, Brian J. "Phoenicia and the Religion of Israel: The Epigraphic Evidence." In *Ancient Israelite Religion: Essays in Honor of Frank Moore Cross*, edited by P. D. Miller et al., 79–99. Philadelphia: Fortress, 1987.

———. *Phoenicia: Episodes and Anecdotes from the Ancient Mediterranean*. Winona Lake, IN: Eisenbrauns, 2014.

Penglase, Charles. *Greek Myths and Mesopotamia: Parallels and Influence in the Homeric Hymns and Hesiod*. London: Routledge, 1994.

Peponi, Anastasia-Erasmia. "Theorizing the Chorus in Greece." In *Choruses, Ancient and Modern*, edited by J. Billings et al., 15–34. New York: Oxford University Press, 2013.

Perdue, Leo G. *Wisdom Literature: A Theological History*. Louisville: Westminster John Knox, 2007.

Perera, Sylvia Brinton. *Descent to the Goddess: A Way of Initiation for Women*. Toronto: Inner City Books, 1981.

Perkins, Phoebe. "Taxes in the New Testament." *JRE* 12 (1984) 182–200.

Peters, David A. *The Many Faces of Biblical Humor*. New York: Hamilton Books, 2008.

Petersen, David L. "A Book of the Twelve?" In *Reading and Hearing the Book of the Twelve*, edited by J. Nogalski and M. Sweeney, 3–10. SymS 15. Atlanta: SBL, 2000.

———. *Haggai and Zechariah 1–8: A Commentary*. OTL. Philadelphia: Westminster, 1984.

———. "Zechariah's Visions: A Theological Perspective." *VT* 34 (1984) 195–206.

Peterson, Brian Neil. *The Authors of the Deuteronomistic History: Locating a Tradition in Ancient Israel*. Minneapolis: Fortress, 2014.

Peterson, Eugene. "Ba'alism and Yahwism Updated." *ThTo* 29 (1972) 138–43.

———. *A Long Obedience in the Same Direction*. Downers Grove, IL: InterVarsity, 2000.

Philips, Anthony. *Ancient Israel's Criminal Law: A New Approach to the Decalogue*. Oxford: Blackwell, 1970.

Philonenko, Marc. *Joseph et Aséneth: Introduction, texte critique, traduction et notes*. Leiden: Brill, 1968.

Pierce, Chad T. *Spirits and the Proclamation of Christ: 1 Peter 3:18–22 in Light of Sin and Punishment Traditions in Early Jewish and Christian Literature*. WUNT 305. Tübingen: Mohr/Siebeck, 2011.

Pikor, Wojciech. *The Land of Israel in the Book of Ezekiel*. New York: T. & T. Clark, 2018.

Pitard, Wayne T. "Just How Many Monsters Did Anat Fight?" In *Ugarit at Seventy-Five*, edited by K. Lawson Younger Jr., 75–88. Winona Lake, IN: Eisenbrauns, 2007.

Pitkänen, Pekka. *Central Sanctuary and Centralization of Worship in Ancient Israel: From the Settlement to the Building of Solomon's Temple*. Piscataway, NJ: Gorgias, 2004.

Pitt-Rivers, Julian. *The Fate of Shechem: Essays in the Anthropology of the Mediterranean*. Cambridge: Cambridge University Press, 1977.

Pleins, J. David. In *The Social Visions of the Hebrew Bible: A Theological Introduction*. Louisville: Westminster John Knox, 2001.

Podella, Thomas. צום*-Fasten: Kollektive Trauer um den verborgenen Gott im Alten Testament*. AOAT 224. Neukirchen-Vluyn: Neukirchener, 1989.

Pohlmann, Karl-Friedrich. *Der Prophet Hesekiel Kapitel 20–48*. ATD 22/2. Göttingen: Vandenhoeck & Ruprecht, 2001.

Polanyi, Karl. *The Livelihood of Man*. New York: Academic, 1977.

Polaski, Donald C. *Authorizing an End: The Isaiah Apocalypse and Intertextuality*. BibIntSer 50. Leiden: Brill, 2001.

Pongratz-Leisten, Beate. Ina šulmi īrub*: Die kulttopographische und ideologische Programmatik der* akītu*-Prozession in Babylonien und Assyrien im I. Jahrtausend v. Chr.* Mainz an Rhein: Philipp von Zabern, 1994.

Pope, Marvin H. *El in the Ugaritic Texts*. Leiden: Brill, 1955.

———. *Job: A New Translation with Introduction and Commentary*. AB 15. Garden City, NY: Doubleday, 1965.

Porten, Bezalel. *Archives from Elephantine: The Life of an Ancient Jewish Military Colony*. Berkeley: University of California Press, 1968.

Porten, Bezalel, and Ada Yardeni, eds. *Textbook of Aramaic Documents from Ancient Egypt*. Winona Lake, IN: Eisenbrauns, 1986–99.

Porter, Barbara Nevling. *Trees, Kings and Politics: Studies in Assyrian Iconography*. OBO 197. Göttingen: Vandenhoeck & Ruprecht, 2003.

Postgate, Nicholas. *Bronze Age Bureaucracy: Writing and the Practice of Government in Assyria*. Cambridge: Cambridge University Press, 2013.

———. *Early Mesopotamia: Society and Economy at the Dawn of History*. London: Routledge, 1994.

Power, Edmond. "The House of Caiaphas and the Church of St. Peter: Criticism of an Erroneous Interpretation of the Texts." *Bib* 10 (1929) 275–303.

———. "The House of Caiaphas and the Church of St. Peter II: Archaeological Proof of the Authenticity of the Site." *Bib* 10 (1929) 394–416.

Premnath, D. N. "Amos and Hosea: Sociohistorical Background and Prophetic Critique." *WW* 28 (2008) 125–32.

———. *Eighth Century Prophets: A Social Analysis*. St. Louis: Chalice, 2003.

Preuss, Horst Dietrich. "זרע." In *TDOT* 4.143–62.

Prinsloo, Willem S. *The Theology of the Book of Joel*. BZAW 163. Berlin: de Gruyter, 1985.

Provan, Iain W. "Ideologies, Literary and Critical: Reflections on Recent Writing on the History of Israel." *JBL* 114 (1995) 585–606.

Puech, Émile. "4Q525 et les péricopes des béatitudes en Ben Sira et Matthieu." *RB* 98 (1991) 80–106.

———. "La sagesse dans les beátitudes de Ben Sira: Étude du texte de Sir 51:13–30 et de 14:20–15:10." In *The Texts and Versions of the Book of Ben Sira: Transmission and Interpretation*, edited by J.-S. Rey et al., 297–329. Leiden: Brill, 2011.

Rabe, David. *Hurlyburly: A Stageplay*. Los Angeles: Landmark Entertainment, 1988.

Raczka, Witt. *Unholy Land: In Search of Hope in Israel/Palestine*. Lanham, MD: Hamilton Books, 2016.

Rad, Gerhard von. *Old Testament Theology*. 1957. Translated by D. M. G. Stalker. New York: Harper & Row, 1962.

———. *Wisdom in Israel*. 1970. Translated by J. D. Martin. Nashville: Abingdon, 1972.

Radine, Jason. *The Book of Amos in Emergent Judah*. FAT 45. Tübingen: Mohr/Siebeck, 2010.

Rahmouni, Aicha. *Divine Epithets in the Ugaritic Alphabetic Texts*. HO 1/93. Leiden: Brill, 2008.

Rainey, Anson F., and William Schniedewind. *The El-Amarna Correspondence*. Leiden: Brill, 2015.

Ramond, Sophie. *Les leçons et les énigmes du passé: Une exégèse intrabiblique des psaumes historiques*. Berlin: de Gruyter, 2014.

Rand, Herbert. "David and Ahab: A Study of Crime and Punishment." *JBQ* 24 (1996) 90–97.

Rappaport, Helen. *The Last Days of the Romanovs: Tragedy at Ekaterinburg*. New York: St. Martin's, 2008.

Rapske, Brian. *The Book of Acts and Paul in Roman Custody*. Grand Rapids: Eerdmans, 1994.

Raschke, Carl. *GloboChrist: The Great Commission Takes a Postmodern Turn*. Grand Rapids: Baker Academic, 2008.

Regt, Lénart J. de. "Discourse Implications of Rhetorical Questions in Job, Deuteronomy, and the Minor Prophets." In *Literary Structure and Rhetorical Strategies in the Hebrew Bible*, edited by L. J. de Regt et al., 51–78. Assen: Van Gorcum, 1996.

Reimer, David J. "The 'Foe' and the 'North' in Jeremiah." *ZAW* 101 (1989) 223–32.

Reiner, Erica. "Die akkadische Literatur." In *Neues Handbuch der Literatur-Wissenschaft: Altorientalische Literature*, edited by W. Röllig, 1.15–210. Wiesbaden: Athenaion, 1978.

———. "Thirty Pieces of Silver." *JAOS* 88 (1968) 186–90.

Reiterer, Friedrich V. "סוג." In *TDOT* 10.165–70.

Rendsburg, Gary A. "The Mock of Ba`al in 1 Kings 18:27." *CBQ* 50 (1988) 414–17.

Rendtorff, Rolf. "How to Read the Book of the Twelve as a Theological Unity." *SBLSP* 36 (1997) 420–32.

Renger, Johannes. "Untersuchungen zum Priestertum in der altbabylonischen Zeit." *ZA* 58 (1967) 110–88; 59 (1969) 104–230.

Renz, Thomas. *The Rhetorical Function of the Book of Ezekiel*. VTSup 76. Leiden: Brill, 2002.

Reventlow, Henning Graf. *Liturgie und prophetisches Ich bei Jeremia*. Gütersloh: Mohn, 1963.

Richardson, Alan. *The Miracle-Stories of the Gospels*. London: SCM, 1941.

Richardson, Mervyn E. J. *Hammurabi's Laws: Text, Translation, and Glossary*. London: T. & T. Clark, 2004.

Richter, Sandra L. *The Deuteronomistic History and the Name Theology*. BZAW 318. Berlin: de Gruyter, 2002.

Richter, Wolfgang. *Traditionsgeschichtliche Untersuchungen zum Richterbuch*. BBB 18. Bonn: Hanstein, 1966.

Rieger, Tom. *Breaking the Fear Barrier: How Fear Destroys Companies from the Inside Out and What to Do About It*. New York: Gallup, 2011.

Rieken, Elisabeth, et al. "CTH 324.1: Erste Version des Telipinu-Mythos. Translatio." In *Mythen der Hethiter*, edited by Elisabeth Rieken et al. June 6, 2012. http://www.hethport.uni-wuerzburg.de/txhet_myth/.

Ringgren, Helmer. "ריב." In *TDOT* 13.473–79.

Ro, Johannes Unsok. *Poverty, Law, and Divine Justice in Persian and Hellenistic Judah*. AIL 32. Atlanta: SBL, 2018.

Roaf, Michael. "Mesopotamian Kings and the Built Environment." In *Experiencing Power, Generating Authority*, edited by J. A. Hill, et al., 331–60. Philadelphia: University of Pennsylvania Press, 2013.

Roberts, J. J. M. "The Ancient Near Eastern Environment." In *The Hebrew Bible and Its Modern Interpreters*, edited by D. Knight and G. Tucker, 75–121. Chico, CA: Scholars, 1985.

———. "A Christian Perspective on Prophetic Prediction." *Int* 33 (1979) 240–53.

———. *The Earliest Semitic Pantheon: A Study of the Semitic Deities Attested in Mesopotamia before Ur III*. Baltimore: Johns Hopkins University Press, 1972.

———. "The Mari Prophetic Texts in Transliteration and English Translation." In *The Bible and the Ancient Near East: Collected Essays*, 157–253. Winona Lake, IN: Eisenbrauns, 2002.

———. *Nahum, Habakkuk, and Zephaniah*. OTL. Louisville: Westminster John Knox, 1991.

Roberts, Kathleen G. *Alterity and Narrative: Stories and the Negotiation of Western Identities*. Albany: SUNY Press, 2007.

Roberts, Kathryn L. "God, Prophet, and King: Eating and Drinking on the Mountain in 1 Kings 18:41." *CBQ* 18 (2000) 632–44.

Robinson, Thomas L. "Asclepius, Cult of." In *ABD* 1.475–76.

Robinson, James M., and Helmut Koester. *Trajectories through Early Christianity*. Philadelphia: Fortress, 1971.

Rodin, Therese. *The World of the Sumerian Mother Goddess: An Interpretation of Her Myths*. HRel 35. Uppsala: Uppsala Universitet, 2014.

Rofé, Alexander. *The Prophetical Stories: The Narratives about the Prophets in the Hebrew Bible, Their Literary Types and History*. Jerusalem: Magnes, 1988.

Roller, Lynn E. *In Search of God the Mother: The Cult of Anatolian Cybele*. Berkeley: University of California Press, 1999.

Rollston, Christopher A. *Writing and Literacy in the World of Ancient Israel: Epigraphic Evidence from the Iron Age*. ABS 11. Atlanta: SBL, 2010.

Ronczkowski, Michael. *Terrorism and Organized Hate Crime: Intelligence Gathering, Analysis, and Investigations*. Boca Raton: CRC, 2012.

Rose, Martin. "Names of God in the Old Testament." In *ABD* 4.1001–11.

Rosenthal, Franz. *A Grammar of Biblical Aramaic*. Wiesbaden, Harrassowitz, 1974.

Rosenthal, Ludwig A. "Die Josephgeschichte mit den Büchern Ester und Daniel verglichten." *ZAW* 15 (1895) 278–84.

Roth, Cecil, and Menahem Elon. "Taxation." In *EJ* 19:532–58.

Roth, Wolfgang. "For Life, He Appeals to Death (Wis 13:18): A Study of Old Testament Idol Parodies." *CBQ* 37 (1975) 21–47.

Rothstein, Johann Wilhelm. *Juden und Samaritaner: Die grundlegende Scheidung von Judentum und Heidentum. Eine kritische Studie zum Buche Haggai und zur judischen Geschichte im ersten nachexilischen Jahrhundert*. BWAT 3. Leipzig: Hinrichs, 1908.

Rouland, Robert. "Sociological Norms and the Heroic Epic." *Journal of Comparative Literature and Aesthetics* 12–13 (1989–90) 90–99.

Rudolph, Wilhelm. *Esra und Nehemia*. HAT 20. Tübingen: Mohr/Siebeck, 1949.

———. *Jeremia*. HAT 12. Tübingen: Mohr, 1968.

———. *Micha, Nahum, Habakuk, Zephanja*. KAT 13/3. Gütersloh: Gerd Mohn, 1975.

Rüger, Hans-Peter. "Das Tyrusorakel Ezechiel 27." PhD diss., University of Tübingen, 1961.

Ruiz, Eleuterio R. *Das Land ist für die Armen da: Psalm 37 und seine immer aktuelle Bedeutung*. SBS 232. Stuttgart: Bibelwerk, 2015.

Ruppert, Lothar. "קסם." In *TDOT* 13.72–78.

Rusak, Tal. "The Clash of Cults on Mt. Carmel: Do Archaeological Records and Historical Documents Support the Biblical Episode of Elijah and the Ba`al Prophets?" *SJOT* 22 (2008) 29–46.

Rüterswörden, Udo. "'Rosen und Lavendel statt Blut und Eisen': Zum Abschluss des Amosbuches." In *Geschichte Israels und deuteronomisches Geschichtsdenken*, edited by P. Mommer and A. Scherer, 211–21. AOAT 380. Münster: Ugarit, 2010.

Rutherford, W. Gunion. *The New Phrynicus: A Revised Text of the* Ecloga *of the Grammarian Phrynicus*. London: MacMillan, 1881.

Saebø, Magne. *Sacharja 9–14: Untersuchungen von Text und Form*. WMANT 34. Neukirchen-Vluyn: Neukirchener, 1969.

Saggs, H. W. F. *The Encounter with the Divine in Mesopotamia and Israel*. London: Athlone, 1978.

Sakenfeld, Katherine Doob. "In the Wilderness, Awaiting the Land: The Daughters of Zelophehad and Feminist Interpretation." *PSB* 9 (1988) 179–96.

———. *The Meaning of Hesed in the Hebrew Bible: A New Inquiry*. 1978. Reprint, Eugene, OR: Wipf & Stock, 2002.

Saldarini, Anthony J. "Sanhedrin." In *ABD* 5.975–80.

Sallaberger, Walther. "Ur III Zeit." In *Mesopotamien: Akkade-Zeit und Ur III-Zeit*, by W. Sallberger and A. Westenholz, 121–335. OBO 160/3. Göttingen: Vandenhoeck & Ruprecht, 1999.

Salvini, Mirjo. *Les textes hourrites de Meskéné/Emar*. AnOr 57. Rome: Gregorian and Biblical, 2015.

Sancisi-Weerdenberg, Heleen. "Gifts in the Persian Empire." In *Le tribut dans L'Empire perse: Actes de la table ronde de Paris, 12–13 Décembre 1986*, edited by P. Briant and C. Herrenschmidt, 129–45. Travaux de l'Institut d'Etudes Iraniennes de l'Université de la Sorbonne Nouvelle 13. Paris: Peeters, 1989.

Sandars, Nancy K. *The Sea Peoples: Warriors of the Ancient Mediterranean, 1250–1150 B.C.* London: Thames & Hudson, 1978.

Sanders, Ed Parish. *Judaism: Practice and Belief, 63 BCE—63 CE*. 1992. Reprint. Minneapolis: Fortress, 2016.

Sanders, Paul. *The Provenance of Deuteronomy 32*. OtSt 37. Leiden: Brill, 1996.

Sandford, Michael J. *Poverty, Wealth, and Empire: Jesus and Postcolonial Criticism*. Sheffield: Phoenix, 2014.

Sandle, Mark. *Communism*. London: Routledge, 2012.

Sandnes, Karl Olav. *Paul—One of the Prophets?: A Contribution to the Apostle's Self-Understanding*. WUNT 2/43. Tübingen: Mohr/Siebeck, 1991.
Sandoval, Timothy. *The Discourse of Wealth and Poverty in the Book of Proverbs*. BibIntSer 77. Leiden: Brill, 2007.
———. *Money and the Way of Wisdom: Insights from the Book of Proverbs*. Woodstock, VT: Skylight Paths, 2008.
Sasson, Jack. "Literary Criticism, Folklore Scholarship, and Ugaritic Literature." In *Ugarit in Retrospect: Fifty Years of Ugarit and Ugaritic*, edited by G. D. Young, 81–98. Winona Lake, IN: Eisenbrauns, 1982.
Sassoon, John. *From Sumer to Jerusalem: The Forbidden Hypothesis*. Oxford: Intellect Books, 1993.
Saur, Markus. *Der Tyroszyklus des Ezechielbuches*. BZAW 386. Berlin: de Gruyter, 2008.
Saxby, Trevor J. *Pilgrims of a Common Life: Christian Community of Goods through the Centuries*. Scottdale, PA: Herald, 1987.
Schaper, Joachim. "The Temple Treasury Committee in the Times of Nehemiah and Ezra." *VT* 47 (1997) 200–206.
Schein, Seth L. *The Mortal Hero: An Introduction to Homer's Iliad*. Berkeley: University of California Press, 1984.
Schiffman, Lawrence H. *The Courtyards of the House of the Lord: Studies on the Temple Scroll*. STDJ 75. Leiden: Brill, 2008.
———. *The Halakhah at Qumran*. SJLA 16. Leiden: Brill, 1975.
———. "Miqtsat Ma`asei Ha-Torah." In *EDSS* 1:558–60.
Schipper, Jeremy, and Mark Leuchter. "A Proposed Reading of בית אלהיהם in Amos 2:8." *CBQ* 77 (2015) 441–48.
Schloen, J. David. *The House of the Father as Fact and Symbol: Patrimonialism in Ugarit and the Ancient Near East*. Winona Lake, IN: Eisenbrauns, 2001.
Schmidt, Frederick W. "Gabael." In *ABD* 2.861–62.
Schmutzer, Andrew J. *Be Fruitful and Multiply: A Crux of Thematic Repetition in Genesis 1–11*. Eugene, OR: Wipf & Stock, 2009.
Schneider, Dale. "The Unity of the Book of the Twelve." PhD diss., Yale University, 1979.
Schneider, Tammi J. *An Introduction to Ancient Mesopotamian Religion*. Grand Rapids: Eerdmans, 2011.
Schniedewind, William M. *How the Bible Became a Book: The Textualization of Ancient Israel*. Cambridge: Cambridge University Press, 2004.
———. *A Social History of Hebrew: Its Origins through the Rabbinic Period*. AYBRL. New Haven, CT: Yale University Press, 2013.
Schoberg, Gerry. *Perspectives of Jesus in the Writings of Paul*. Cambridge: James Clarke, 2014.
Schottroff, Luise, and Wolfgang Stegemann. "Die konkrete Socialutopie des Lukas." In *Jesus von Nazareth: Hoffnung der Armen*, 149–53. Stuttgart: Kohlhammer, 1978.
———. "Luke's Concrete Social Utopia." In *Jesus and the Hope of the Poor*, 116–20. Translated by Matthew J. O'Connell. 1986. Reprint, Eugene, OR: Wipf & Stock, 2009.
Schottroff, Willy. "'Unrechtmässige Fesseln auftun, Jochstricke lösen' Jesaja 58, 1–2. Ein Textbespiel zum Thema 'Bibel und Ökonomie.'" *BI* 5 (1997) 263–78.
Schoville, Keith N. *Ezra-Nehemiah*. CPNIV. Joplin, MO: College Press, 2001.
Schroer, Silvia, and Othmar Keel. *Die Ikonographie Palästinas/Israels und der Alte Orient: Eine Religionsgeschichte in Bildern*, Vol. 1: *Vom ausgehenden Mesolithikum bis zur Frühbronzezeit*. Fribourg: Academic Press, 2005.

Schuller, Eileen M. "Tobit." In *Women's Bible Commentary*, edited by C. Newsom and S. H. Ringe, 272–78. Louisville: Westminster John Knox, 1998.

Schürmann, Heinz. "Das Testament des Paulus für die Kirche." In *Traditionsgeschichtliche Untersuchungen zu den synoptischen Evangelien: Beiträge*, 310–40. KBANT. Düsseldorf: Patmos, 1967.

Schütte, Wolfgang. *Israels Exil in Juda: Untersuchungen zur Entstehung der Schriftprophetie*. OBO 279. Göttingen: Vandenhoeck & Ruprecht, 2016.

Schwartz, Joshua. Review of *Tales of High Priests and Taxes: The Books of the Maccabees and the Judean Rebellion against Antiochos IV*, by Sylvie Honigman. *RBL*, 2017. https://www.bookreviews.org/pdf/11059_12293.pdf.

Schwesig, Paul-Gerhard. *Die Rolle der Tag-JHWHs-Dichtungen im Dodekapropheton*. BZAW 366. Berlin: de Gruyter, 2006.

Scurlock, Jo Ann. *Sourcebook for Ancient Mesopotamian Medicine*. SBLWAW 36. Atlanta: SBL, 2014.

Sedlmeier, Franz. *Das Buch Ezechiel: Kapitel 25–48*. NSKAT 21/2. Stuttgart: Katholisches Bibelwerk, 2013.

Seidel, Moshe. ספר מיכה. Jerusalem: מוסד הרב קוק, 1990.

Seitz, Christopher R. *Joel*. ITC. New York: Bloomsbury, 2016.

Segal, Charles. *The Theme of the Mutilation of the Corpse in the Iliad*. MBCBSup 17. Leiden: Brill, 1971.

Seitz, Christopher R. "Isaiah." In *ABD* 3.472–88.

Seland, Torrey. *Establishment Violence in Philo and Luke: A Study of Non-Conformity to the Torah and Jewish Vigilante Reactions*. BibIntSer 15. Leiden: Brill, 1995.

Selms, A. van. *Marriage and Family Life in Ugaritic Literature*. London: Luzac, 1954.

Selz, Gebhard J. "Babilismus und die Gottheit ^{d}Nindagar." In *Ex Mesopotamia et Syria Lux: Festschrift für Manfred Dietrich zu seinem 65. Geburtstag*, edited by O. Loretz et al., 647–84. AOAT 281. Münster: Ugarit, 2002.

Sen, Amartya. *Poverty and Famines: An Essay on Entitlement and Deprivation*. Oxford: Oxford University Press, 1981.

Seri, Andrea. "The Fifty Names of Marduk in *Enūma eliš*." *JAOS* 126 (2006) 507–19.

———. "The Role of Creation in *Enūma eliš*." *JANER* 12 (2012) 4–29.

Setel, T. Drorah. "Prophetics and Pornography: Female Sexual Imagery in Hosea." In *Feminist Interpretations of the Bible*, edited by L. M. Russell, 86–94. Oxford: Blackwell, 1985.

Seybold, Klaus. *Bilder zum Tempelbau: Die Visionen des Propheten Sacharja*. SBS 70. Stuttgart: Katholisches Bildungswerk, 1974.

Sharp. Carolyn J. *Irony and Meaning in the Hebrew Bible*. Bloomington: Indiana University Press, 2009.

Sheldon, Rose Mary. "Ancient Intelligence." In *EIC* 29–34.

Sherwood, Yvonne. *The Prostitute and the Prophet: Reading Hosea in the Late Twentieth Century*. JSOTSup 212. Sheffield: Sheffield Academic, 1996.

Simian-Yofre, Horace. "Ezek 17:1–10 como enigma y parábola." *Bib* 65 (1984) 27–43.

Simkins, Ronald A. "Care for the Poor and Needy." In *Religion and Politics*, edited by Ronald A. Simkins and Zachery B. Smith, 4–13. Journal of Religion & Society Supplement Series 14. Omaha, NE: Creighton University, 2017.

———. "Family in the Political Economy of Monarchic Judah." *The Bible and Critical Theory* 1 (2004) 1–17.

———. "Patronage and the Political Economy of Monarchic Israel." *Semeia* 87 (1999) 123–44.

———. "The Widow and Orphan in the Political Economy of Ancient Israel." In *The Bible, the Economy, and the Poor*, edited by Ronald M. Simkins and Thomas M. Kelly, 20–33. Journal of Religion & Society Supplement Series 10. Omaha, NE: Creighton University, 2014.

———. *Yhwh's Activity in History and Nature in the Book of Joel*. Lewiston, NY: Mellen, 1991.

Simmons, Bill. *The Book of Basketball*. New York: Ballentine, 2009.

Simundson, Daniel J. *Hosea, Joel, Amos, Obadiah, Jonah, Micah*. AOTC. Nashville: Abingdon, 2005.

Singer, Ithamar. "A Political History of Ugarit." In *Handbook of Ugaritic Studies*, edited by W. G. E. Watson and N. Wyatt, 603–733. HO 39. Leiden: Brill, 1999.

Sivan, Daniel. *A Grammar of the Ugaritic Language*. HO 28. Leiden: Brill, 1997.

Sjöberg, Åke. *Der Mondgott Nanna-Suen in der sumerischen Überlieferung. I Teil: Texte*. Uppsala: Almqvist & Wiksell, 1969.

Ska, Jean-Louis. *Introduction to Reading the Pentateuch*. 1998. Translated by P. Dominique. Winona Lake, IN: Eisenbrauns, 2006.

Skehan, Patrick W. "A Fragment of the 'Song of Moses' (Deut 32) from Qumran." *BASOR* 136 (1954) 12–15.

Skemp, Vincent T. M. "Avenues of Intertextuality between Tobit and the New Testament." In *Intertextual Studies in Ben Sira and Tobit*, edited by J. Corley and V. Skemp, 43–70. CBQMS 38. Washington, DC: Catholic Biblical Association of America, 2005.

———. *The Vulgate of Tobit Compared with Other Ancient Witnesses*. SBLDS 180. Atlanta: SBL 2000.

Skiena, Steven, and Charles B. Ward. *Who's Bigger?: Where Historical Figures Really Rank*. Cambridge: Cambridge University Press, 2014.

Sladek, William R. "Inanna's Descent to the Netherworld." PhD. diss., Johns Hopkins University, 1974.

Smend, Rudolf. "Anmerkungen zu Jes. 24–27." *ZAW* 4 (1884) 161–224.

Smith, Gary V. *Ezra, Nehemiah, Esther*. Carol Stream, IL: Tyndale House, 2010.

Smith, Jonathan Z. "Dying and Rising Gods." In *ER* 4.521–27.

———. *Imagining Religion: From Babylon to Jonestown*. Chicago: University of Chicago Press, 1982.

Smith, Mark S. "ברית עם / ברית עולם: A New Proposal for the Crux of Isa 42:6." *JBL* 100 (1981) 241–48.

———. "The Ba`al Cycle." In *UNP* 81–180.

———. *The Early History of God: Yahweh and the Other Deities in Ancient Israel*. Grand Rapids: Eerdmans, 2002.

———. *The Origins of Biblical Monotheism*. New York: Oxford University Press, 2001.

———. *Poetic Heroes: Literary Commemorations of Warriors and Warrior Culture in the Early Biblical World*. Grand Rapids: Eerdmans, 2014.

———. *The Ugaritic Ba`al Cycle*. Vol. 1: *Introduction with Text, Translation, and Commentary of CAT 1.1—1.2*. VTSup 55. Leiden: Brill, 1994.

———. "Ugaritic Studies and the Hebrew Bible, 1968–1998 (with an Excursus on Judean Monotheism and the Ugaritic Texts)." In *Congress Volume: Oslo 1998*, edited by A. Lemaire and M. Saebø, 327–52. VTSup 80. Leiden: Brill, 2000.

Smith, Mark S., and Wayne T. Pitard. *The Ugaritic Ba`al Cycle*. Vol. 2: *Introduction with Text, Translation, and Commentary of CAT 1.3—1.4*. VTSup 114. Leiden: Brill, 2009.

Smith, Morton. *Tannaitic Parallels to the Gospels*. JBLMS 6. Philadelphia: SBL, 1951.

Smith-Christopher, Daniel L. *Micah: A Commentary*. OTL. Louisville: Westminster John Knox, 2015.

Sneed, Mark R. "הבל as 'Worthless' in Qohelet: A Critique of Michael V. Fox's 'Absurd' Thesis." *JBL* 136 (2017) 879–94.

———. "Theodicy Strategies in the Hebrew Bible." In *The Politics of Pessimism in Ecclesiastes: A Social-Science Perspective*, 180–83. AIL 12. Atlanta: SBL, 2012.

Snell, Daniel C. *Flight and Freedom in the Ancient Near East*. CHANE 8. Leiden: Brill, 2001.

———. *Religions of the Ancient Near East*. Cambridge: Cambridge University Press, 2011.

———. "Slavery in the Ancient Near East." In *The Cambridge World History of Slavery*, vol. 1, *The Ancient Mediterranean World*, edited by K. Bradley and P. Cartledge, 4–21. Cambridge: Cambridge University Press, 2011.

Soards, Marion L. *The Speeches in Acts: Their Content, Context, and Concerns*. Louisville: Westminster John Knox, 1994.

Sohn, Seock-Tae. *YHWH, the Husband of Israel: The Metaphor of Marriage between YHWH and Israel*. Eugene, OR: Wipf & Stock, 2002.

Soll, Will. "Misfortune and Exile in Tobit: The Juncture of a Fairy Tale Source and Deuteronomic Theology." *CBQ* 51 (1989) 209–31.

Sollberger, E. *The Business and Administrative Correspondence under the Kings of Ur*. Locust Valley, NY: Augustin, 1966.

Sommerfeld, Walter. *Der Aufstieg Marduks: Die Stellung Marduks in der babylonischen Religion des zweiten Jahrtausends v. Chr.* AOAT 213. Kevelaer, Germany: Butzon and Bercker, 1982.

Soto, Hernando de. *The Mystery of Capital: Why Capitalism Triumphs in the West and Fails Everywhere Else*. New York: Basic Books, 2000.

Soulen, R. Kendall. *The God of Israel and Christian Theology*. Minneapolis: Fortress, 1996.

Sowada, Karin N. *Egypt in the Eastern Mediterranean during the Old Kingdom: An Archaeological Perspective*. OBO 237. Göttingen: Vandenhoeck & Ruprecht, 2009.

Speiser, Ephraim A. "The Creation Epic." In *ANET* 60–72.

———. "The Descent of Ishtar to the Netherworld." In *ANET* 106–9.

Spencer, Neal. "Priests and Temples, Pharaonic." In *A Companion to Ancient Egypt*, edited by A. B. Lloyd, 255–73. Oxford: Wiley-Blackwell, 2010.

Sperber, Alexander. *The Bible in Aramaic*. Leiden: Brill, 1959–73.

Spieckermann, Hermann. "The Conception and Prehistory of the Idea of Vicarious Suffering in the Old Testament." 1997. Translated by D. P. Bailey. In *The Suffering Servant: Isaiah 53 in Jewish and Christian Sources*, edited by B. Janowski and P. Stuhlmacher, 1–15. Grand Rapids: Eerdmans, 2004.

Spretnak, Charlene. *Missing Mary: The Queen of Heaven and Her Re-Emergence in the Modern Church*. New York: Palgrave MacMillan, 2004.

Spronk, Klaas. *Beatific Afterlife in Ancient Israel and in the Ancient Near East*. AOAT 219. Neukirchen-Vluyn: Neukirchener, 1986.

Stack-Nelson, Judith. "The Metaphorical Portrayals of the Causes of Sin and Evil in the Gospel of Matthew." PhD diss., Princeton Theological Seminary, 2013.

Stade, Bernard. "Bemerkungen über das Buch Mica." *ZAW* 1 (1881) 161–72.

Stambaugh, John E., and David L. Balch. *The New Testament in Its Social Environment.* LEC 2. Philadelphia: Westminster, 1986.

Stanley, Christopher D. *The Hebrew Bible: A Comparative Approach.* Minneapolis: Fortress, 2010.

Stansell, Gary. "How Abraham Became Rich." In *Ancient Israel: The Old Testament in Its Social Context*, edited by P. Esler, 92–110. Minneapolis: Fortress, 2006.

Stanton, Graham N. "Sermon on the Mount/Plain." In *DJG* 735–44.

Starr, Charlie W. "So How *Should* We Teach English?" In *Contemporary Perspectives on C. S. Lewis'* The Abolition of Man*: History, Philosophy, Education, and Science*, edited by T. M. Mosteller and G. J. Anacker, 63–82. New York: Bloomsbury Academic, 2017.

Starr, Chester G. "An Overdose of Slavery." *Journal of Economic History* 18 (1958) 17–32

Steck, Odil Hannes. "Zion als Gelände und Gestalt: Überlegungen zur Wahrnehmung Jerusalems als Stadt und Frau im Alten Testament." *ZTK* 86 (1989) 261–81.

Stegemann, Wolfgang. "Was der Apostel Paulus ein römische Bürger?" *ZNW* 78 (1987) 200–229.

Steinberg, Naomi. Review *of Marriage Gifts and Social Change in Ancient Palestine: 1200 BCE to 200 CE*, by Tracy M. Lemos. *BI* 19 (2011) 525–27.

Steiner, Richard C. "Bishlam's Archival Search Report in Nehemiah's Archive: Multiple Introductions and Reverse Chronological Order as Clues to the Origin of the Aramaic Letters in Ezra 4–6." *JBL* 125 (2006) 641–85.

———. *Disembodied Souls: The Nefesh in Israel and Kindred Spirits in the Ancient Near East, with an Appendix on the Katumuwa Inscription.* Atlanta: SBL, 2015.

———. "The מבקר at Qumran, the ἐπίσκοπος in the Athenian Empire, and the Meaning of לבקרא in Ezra 7:14: On the Relation of Ezra's Mission to the Persian Legal Project." *JBL* 120 (2001) 623–46.

Steinmetz, Devorah. *From Father to Son: Kinship, Conflict and Continuity in Genesis.* LCBI. Louisville: Westminster John Knox, 1991.

Sterling, Gregory A. *Historiography and Self-Definition: Josephos, Luke-Acts, and Apologetic Historiography.* NovTSup 64. Leiden: Brill, 1992.

Stern, Ephraim. "The Archaeology of Persian Palestine." In *The Cambridge History of Judaism*, vol. 1: *The Persian Period*, edited by W. D. Davies et al., 88–114. Cambridge: Cambridge University Press, 1984.

———. "The Dor Province in the Persian Period in Light of Recent Excavations at Dor." *Transeu* 2 (1990) 147–55.

Stern, Philip D. "The Origin and Significance of 'The Land Flowing with Milk and Honey.'" *VT* 42 (1992) 554–57.

Stevens, Marty E. *Temples, Tithes and Taxes: The Temple and the Economic Life of Ancient Israel.* Grand Rapids: Baker Academic, 2006.

Stiebert, Johanna. *The Construction of Shame in the Hebrew Bible: The Prophetic Contribution.* JSOTSup 346. Sheffield: Sheffield Academic, 2002.

Stieglitz, Robert R. "The Ideology of Divine Kingship at Ugarit." In *Visions of Life in Biblical Times: Essays in Honor of Meir Lubetski*, edited by C. Gottlieb et al., 225–34. Sheffield: Sheffield Phoenix, 2015.

Stienstra, Nelly. *YHWH Is the Husband of His People: Analysis of a Biblical Metaphor with Special Reference to Translation.* Kampen: Kok Pharos, 1994.

Stokholm, Niels. "Zur Überlieferung von Heliodor, Kuturnahhunte and anderen missglückten Tempelräubern." *ST* 22 (1968) 1–28.

Stökl, Jonathan. "Female Prophets in the Ancient Near East." In *Prophecy and Prophets in Ancient Israel*, edited by J. Day, 47–61. New York: T. & T. Clark, 2010.

———. *Prophecy in the Ancient Near East: A Philological and Sociological Comparison*. CHANE 56. Leiden: Brill, 2012.

Stol, Marten. *Women in the Ancient Near East*. Berlin: de Gruyter, 2016.

Stolper, Matthew W. *Entrepreneurs and Empire: The Murašû Archive, the Murašû Firm, and Persian Rule in Babylonia*. Leiden: Nederlands Historische-Archaeologische Instituut te Istanbul, 1985.

Stolz, Fritz. "Sea." In *DDD* 737–42.

Stovell, Beth M. "'I Will Make Her Like a Desert': Intertextual Allusion and Feminine and Agricultural Metaphors in the Book of the Twelve." In *The Book of the Twelve and the New Form Criticism*, edited by M. Boda et al., 37–61. ANEM 10. Atlanta: SBL, 2015.

Streck, Michael P., and Nathan Wasserman. "More Light on Nanāya." *ZA* 102 (2012) 183–201.

Strelan, Rick. *Strange Acts: Studies in the Cultural World of the Acts of the Apostles*. BZNW 126. New York: de Gruyter, 2004.

Stuart, Douglas. "Exegesis." In *ABD* 2.682–88.

Stuckenbruck, Loren T. *The Myth of Rebellious Angels: Studies in Second Temple Judaism and New Testament Texts*. Grand Rapids: Eerdmans, 2017.

Stuhlman, Louis. *Order Amid Chaos: Jeremiah as Symbolic Tapestry*. BibSem 57. Sheffield: Sheffield Academic, 1998.

Stuhlmueller, Carroll. *Rebuilding with Hope: A Commentary on the Books of Haggai and Zechariah*. ITC. Grand Rapids: Eerdmans, 1988.

Sturtevant, Edgar H. "A Hittite Text on the Duties of Priests and Temple Servants." *JAOS* 54 (1934) 363–406.

Suiter, David E. "Artaxerxes." In *ABD* 1.463–64.

Summey, David C. "The Meaning of 'Bearing Fruit' in Gospel Illustrations." PhD diss., Southeastern Baptist Theological Seminary, 2015.

Suter, Kevin. "Christians and Personal Wealth." *AJT* 3 (1989) 643–50.

Sweeney, Marvin A. *1 and 2 Kings: A Commentary*. OTL. Louisville: Westminster John Knox, 2007.

———. "The Place and Function of Joel in the Book of the Twelve." In *Thematic Threads in the Book of the Twelve*, edited by P. Redditt and A. Schart, 133–54. BZAW 325. New York: de Gruyter, 2003.

———. *The Twelve Prophets*. 2 vols. Berit Olam. Collegeville, MN: Liturgical, 2000.

Swoboda, Heinrich, et al., eds. *Denkmäler aus Lykaonien, Pamphylien, und Isauren*. Leipzig: Brünn, 1935.

Szegedy-Maszak, Andrew. *The Nomoi of Theophrastus*. New York: Arno, 1981.

Tadmor, Ḥayim. "אפתם בעזרא ד, יג." In *Michael: Historical, Epigraphical, and Biblical Studies in Honor of Michael Heltzer*, edited by Y. Avishur and R. Deutsch, 143–45. Tel Aviv-Jaffa: Archaeological Center, 1999.

Tajra, Harry W. *The Trial of St Paul: A Juridical Exegesis of the Second Half of the Acts of the Apostles*. 1989. Reprint, Eugene, OR: Wipf & Stock, 2010.

Talmon, Shemaryahu. "The 'Comparative Method' in Biblical Interpretation—Principles and Problems." In *Essential Papers on Israel and the Ancient Near East*, edited by F. Greenspahn, 320–56. New York: New York University Press, 1991.

Talon, Philippe. *The Standard Babylon Creation Myth* Enūma Eliš. SAACT 4. Helsinki: Neo-Assyrian Text Corpus Project, 2005.

Tamez, Elsa. "Hagar and Sarah in Galatians: A Case Study in Freedom." *WW* 20 (2000) 265–71.

Tandy, David W. *Warriors into Traders: The Power of the Market in Early Greece*. Berkeley: University of California Press, 1997.

Tarun, Robert W. *The Foreign Corrupt Practices Handbook: A Practical Guide for Multinational General Counsel, Transactional Lawyers, and White Collar Criminal Practitioners*. Chicago: American Bar Association, 2010.

Taylor, Justin. "The Community of Goods among the First Christians and among the Essenes." In *Historical Perspectives from the Hasmoneans to Bar Kokhba in Light of the Dead Sea Scrolls: Proceedings of the Fourth International Symposium of the Orion Center for the Study of the Dead Sea Scrolls and Associated Literature*, edited by D. Goodblatt et al., 147–64. STDJ 37. Leiden: Brill, 2001.

Taylor, Mark C. *Journeys to Selfhood: Hegel and Kierkegaard*. New York: Fordham University Press, 2000.

Taylor, Richard A. "Haggai." In *Haggai, Malachi*, by Richard A. Taylor and E. Tay Clendenen, 23–202. NAC 21A. Nashville: Broadman & Holman, 2004.

———. *Interpreting Apocalyptic Literature: An Exegetical Handbook*. Grand Rapids: Kregel, 2016.

Thamm, Robert A. "The Classification of Emotions." In *Handbook of the Sociology of Emotions*, edited by J. Stets and J. Turner, 11–37. New York: Springer, 2007.

Theis, Joachim. *Paulus als Weisheitslehrer: Die Gekreuzigte und die Weisheit Gottes in 1 Kor 1–4*. Regensburg: Pustet, 1991.

Thelle, Rannfrid Irene. *Approaches to the "Chosen Place": Accessing a Biblical Concept*. New York: T. & T. Clark, 2012.

Theoharis, Liz. *Always with Us?: What Jesus Really Said about the Poor*. Grand Rapids: Eerdmans, 2017.

Thiel, Winfried. "Ahab." In *ABD* 1.100–104.

———. "Amos 2,6–8 und der Einfluss Hoseas auf die Amos-Traditionen." In *Verbindungslinien: Festschrift fur Werner H. Schmidt zum 65 Geburtstag*, edited by A. Graupner et al., 385–97. Neukirchen-Vluyn: Neukirchener, 2000.

Thistleton, Anthony C. "James Atkinson: Theologian, Professor, and Churchman." In *The Bible, the Reformation, and the Church: Essays in Honour of James Atkinson*, edited by W. P. Stevens, 11–35. JSNTSup 105. Sheffield: Sheffield Academic, 1995.

Thompson, Augustine. *Francis of Assisi: A New Biography*. Ithaca, NY: Cornell University Press, 2012.

Thompson, James W. *Moral Formation According to Paul: The Context and Coherence of Pauline Ethics*. Grand Rapids: Baker Academic, 2011.

Thompson, John Arthur. *The Book of Jeremiah*. NICOT. Grand Rapids: Eerdmans, 1980.

———. "The Debt of Jeremiah to Hosea." In *The Book of Jeremiah*, 81–85. NICOT. Grand Rapids: Eerdmans, 1980.

———. "Joel's Locusts in the Light of Near Eastern Parallels." *JNES* 14 (1955) 52–55.

Thurston, Bonnie Bowman. *The Widows: A Women's Ministry in the Early Church*. Minneapolis: Fortress, 1989.

Tillich, Paul. *Theology of Culture*. Oxford: Oxford University Press, 1959.

Timmer, Daniel C. *The Non-Israelite Nations in the Book of the Twelve: Thematic Coherence and the Diachronic-Synchronic Relationship in the Minor Prophets*. BibIntSer 135. Leiden: Brill, 2015.

Toffelmire, Colin M. *A Discourse and Register Analysis of the Prophetic Book of Joel*. SSN 66. Leiden: Brill, 2016.

Toombs, Lawrence E. "Ba`al, Lord of the Earth: The Ugaritic Ba`al Epic." In *The Word of the Lord Shall Go Forth: Essays in Honor of David Noel Freedman in Celebration of his Sixtieth Birthday*, edited by C. Meyers and M. O'Connor, 613–23. Winona Lake, IN: ASOR, Eisenbrauns, 1983.

Toorn, Karel van der. "Anat-Yahu, Some Other Deities, and the Jews of Elephantine." Numen 39 (1992) 80–101.

———. *Family Religion in Babylonia, Syria and Israel: Continuity and Change in the Forms of Religious Life*. SHANE 7. Leiden: Brill, 1996.

———. "In the Lions' Den: the Babylonian Background of a Biblical Motif." *CBQ* 60 (1998) 626–40.

———. *Scribal Culture and the Making of the Hebrew Bible*. Cambridge, MA: Harvard University Press, 2007.

Törnqvist, Rut. *The Use and Abuse of Female Sexual Imagery in Osea: A Feminist Critical Approach to Hosea 1–3*. Uppsala Women's Studies A; Women in Religion 7. Uppsala: Uppsala University Library, 1998.

Tov, Emanuel. *Textual Criticism of the Hebrew Bible*. Minneapolis: Fortress, 1992.

Townsend, Joan. "Fact, Fallacy, and Revitalization Movement." In *Goddesses in Religions and Modern Debate*, edited by Larry Hurtado, 179–203. Atlanta: Scholars, 1990.

Trebilco, Paul. *Jewish Communities in Asia Minor*. Cambridge: Cambridge University Press, 1991.

Trible, Phyllis. "Exegesis for Storytellers and Other Strangers." *JBL* 114 (1995) 3–19.

Tromp, Nicholas J. *Primitive Conceptions of Death and the Nether World in the Old Testament*. BibOr 21. Rome: Pontifical Biblical Institute, 1969.

Tropper, Josef. *Ugaritische Grammatik*. AOAT 273. Münster: Ugarit, 2000.

Trotter, James M. "Reading the 'Prophetic Lawsuit' Genre in the Persian Period." In *The Book of the Twelve and the New Form Criticism*, edited by M. J. Boda et al., 63–74. ANEM 10. Atlanta: SBL, 2015.

Tsumura, David. *Creation and Destruction: A Reappraisal of the Chaoskampf Theory in the Old Testament*. Winona Lake, IN: Eisenbrauns, 2005.

Tuckett, Christopher M. "The Parable of the Mustard Seed and the Book of Ezekiel." In *The Book of Ezekiel and Its Influence*, edited by H. J. de Jonge and J. Tromp, 87–102. Burlington, VT: Ashgate, 2007.

Turcan, Robert. *Les cultes orientaux dans le monde romain*. Paris: Les Belles Lettres, 1989.

Tuzlak, Ayse. "The Magician and the Heretic: The Case of Simon Magus." In *Magic and Ritual in the Ancient World*, edited by P. Mirecki and M. Meyer, 416–26. RGRW 141. Leiden: Brill, 2002.

Tyson, Joseph B. "Acts 6:1–7 and Dietary Regulations in Early Christianity." *PRSt* 10 (1983) 145–61.

Urbach, Efraim E. "The Laws Regarding Slavery as a Source for Social History of the Period of the Second Temple, the Mishnah, and Talmud." In *Papers of the Institute of Jewish Studies, London*, edited by J. G. Weiss, 1–94. Lanham, MD: University Press of America, 1964.

Urbin-Chofray, T. "Déesse-mère." In *DR* 380–81.

Vaage, Leif E. *Borderline Exegesis*. University Park: Pennsylvania State University Press, 2014.

Vancil, Jack W. "The Symbolism of the Shepherd in Biblical, Intertestamental, and New Testament Material." PhD diss., Dropsie College, 1975.

Van den Hout, Theo P. J. "Another View of Hittite Literature." In *Anatolia Antica: Studi in memoria di Fiorella Imparati*, edited by S. de Martino and F. Peccholi Daddi, 1.857–78. Trieste: LoGisma, 2002.

Van Dijk, J. J. A. "L'hymne à Marduk avec intercession pour le roi Abī'ešuḫ." *MIO* 12 (1966) 57–74.

Van Henten, Jan Willem. "Python." In *DDD* 669–71.

Van Ruiten, J. T. "The Use of Deuteronomy 32:39 in Monotheistic Controversies in Rabbinic Literature." In *Studies in Deuteronomy in Honour of C. J. Lambuschagne on the Occasion of his 65th Birthday*, edited by F. G. Martínez et al., 223–42. VTSup 53. Leiden: Brill, 1994.

Van Seters, John. *Abraham in History and Tradition*. New Haven, CT: Yale University Press, 1975.

Vanstiphout, Herman L. J. "Ambiguity as a Generative Force in Standard Sumerian Literature, or Empson in Nippur." In *Mesopotamian Poetic Language: Sumerian and Akkadian*, edited by M. Vogelzang and H. Vanstiphout, 155–66. Groningen: Styx, 1996.

Van Wijk-Bos, Johanna W. H. *Ezra, Nehemiah, and Esther*. Louisville: Westminster John Knox, 1998.

Vaughn, Andrew G., and Christopher A. Rollston. "The Antiquities Market, Sensationalized Textual Data, and Modern Forgeries: Introduction to the Problem and Synopsis of the 2004 Israel Indictment." *SBL Forum*, March 2005. http://sbl-site.org/Article.aspx?ArticleID=373/.

Vaux, Roland de. "Sur quelques rapports entre Adonis et Osiris" *RB* 42 (1933) 31–56.

———. *Les Sacrifices de l'Ancien Testament*. Paris: Gabalda, 1964.

Veerkamp, T. *Die Vernichtung des Baal*. Stuttgart: Alektor, 1981.

Veldhuis, Niek. *History of the Cuneiform Lexical Tradition*. GMTR 6. Münster: Ugarit, 2014.

Verbrugge, Verlyn D., and Keith R. Krell. *Paul and Money: A Biblical and Theological Analysis of the Apostle's Teachings and Practices*. Grand Rapids: Zondervan, 2015.

Verhey, Alan. *Remembering Jesus: Christian Community, Scripture, and the Moral Life*. Grand Rapids: Eerdmans, 2002.

Vermes, Geza. *The Religion of Jesus the Jew*. Minneapolis: Fortress, 1993.

Versnel, Hendrick S. "Beyond Cursing: The Appeal to Justice in Judicial Prayers." In *Magika Hiera: Ancient Greek Magic and Religion*, edited by C. Faraone and D. Obbink, 33–59. New York: Oxford University Press, 1991.

Viviano, Benedict. *Matthew and His World: The Gospel of the Open Jewish Christians*. NTOA 61. Göttingen: Vandenhoeck & Ruprecht, 2007.

Wagenaar, Jan A. *Judgement and Salvation: The Composition and Redaction of Micah 2–5*. VTSup 85. Leiden: Brill, 2001.

Wakeman, Mary K. *God's Battle with the Monster: A Study in Biblical Imagery*. Leiden: Brill, 1973.

Walker, Christopher, and Michael Dick. *The Induction of the Cult-Image in Ancient Mesopotamia: The Mesopotamian* mīs pī *Ritual*. SAALT 1. Helsinki: Neo-Assyrian Corpus Project, 2001.

Walker, William O. "Jesus and the Tax Collectors." *JBL* 97 (1978) 221–38.

Wallis, Jim. *God's Politics: Why the Right Gets It Wrong and the Left Doesn't Get It*. San Francisco: HarperCollins, 2005.

Walls, Neal H. *The Goddess Anat in Ugaritic Myth*. SBLDS 135. Atlanta: Scholars, 1992.
Walsh, Jerome T. *Ahab: The Construction of a King*. Collegeville, MN: Liturgical, 2006.
———. *1 Kings*. Collegeville, MN: Liturgical, 1996.
———. "Elijah." In *ABD* 2.463–66.
Walton, John H. *Ancient Near Eastern Thought and the Old Testament: Introducing the Conceptual World of the Hebrew Bible*. Grand Rapids: Baker Academic, 2018.
———. "The Imagery of the Substitute King Ritual in Isaiah's Fourth Servant Song." *JBL* 122 (2003) 734–43.
Wang, Martin Chen-Chang. "Jeremiah's Message of Hope in Prophetic Symbolic Action: The 'Deed of Purchase' in Jer 32." *SEAJT* 14 (1973) 13–20.
Wanke, Gunther. "Jeremias Ackerkauf: Heil im Gericht?" In *Prophet und Prophetenbuch: Festschrift für Otto Kaiser zum 65. Geburtstag*, edited by V. Fritz et al., 265–76. BZAW 185. Berlin: de Gruyter, 1989.
Washington, Harold C. *Wealth and Poverty in the Instruction of Amenemope and the Hebrew Proverbs*. SBLDS 142. Atlanta: Scholars, 1996.
Waters, Jaime L. *Threshing Floors in Ancient Israel: Their Ritual and Symbolic Significance*. Minneapolis: Fortress, 2015.
Waters, Matt. *Ancient Persia: A Concise History of the Achaemenid Empire, 550–330 BCE*. Cambridge: Cambridge University Press, 2014.
Watson, Paul L. "Mot, the God of Death, at Ugarit and in the Old Testament." PhD diss., Yale University, 1970.
Watson, Wilfred G. E. "Comments on Some Ugaritic Lexical Items." *JNSL* 22 (1996) 73–84.
———. "Ugaritic Poetry." In *Handbook of Ugaritic Studies*, edited by W. G. E. Watson and N. Wyatt, 165–92. HO 39. Leiden: Brill, 1999.
Watson, Wilfred G. E., and Nicolas Wyatt, eds. *Handbook of Ugaritic Studies*. HO 39. Leiden: Brill, 1999.
Watters, William R. *Formula Criticism and the Poetry of the Old Testament*. BZAW 138. Berlin: de Gruyter, 1976.
Watts, John D. W. "Babylonian Idolatry in the Prophets as a False Socio-Economic System." In *Israel's Apostasy and Restoration: Essays in Honor of Roland K. Harrison*, edited by A. Gileadi, 115–22. Grand Rapids: Baker, 1988.
———. "A Frame for the Book of the Twelve: Hosea 1–3 and Malachi." In *Reading and Hearing the Book of the Twelve*, edited by J. Nogalski and M. Sweeney, 209–17. SBLSymS 15. Atlanta: SBL, 2000.
———. *Isaiah 1–33*. WBC 24. Waco, TX: Word, 1985.
Weber, Max. *The Sociology of Religion*. Translated by E. Fischoff, 1956. Reprint, Boston: Beacon, 1963.
Weeks, Noel. *Admonition and Curse: The Ancient Near Eastern Treaty/Covenant Form as a Problem in Inter-Cultural Relationships*. JSOTSup 407. New York: T. & T. Clark, 2004.
Weeks, Stuart, et al. *The Book of Tobit: Texts from the Principal Ancient and Medieval Traditions*. FoSub 3. New York: de Gruyter, 2004.
Wehr, Hans, and J. M. Cowan. *A Dictionary of Modern Written Arabic*. Ithaca, NY: Cornell University Press, 1966.
Weider, Andreas. *Ehemetaphorik in prophetischer Verkündigung: Hos 1–3 und seine Wirkungsgeschichte im Jeremiabuch. Ein Beitrag zum alttestamentlichen Gottes-Bild*. FB 71. Würzburg: Echter, 1993.
Weidner, Ernst F. "Hochverrat gegen Nebukadnezar II." *AfO* 17 (1954–5) 1–9.
Weinfeld, Moshe. *Deuteronomy 1–11*. AB 5. New York: Doubleday, 1991.

Weippert, Manfred. "Assyrische Prophetien der Zeit Asarhaddons und Assurbanipals." In *Assyrian Royal Inscriptions*, edited by F. M. Fales, 71–113. Rome: Istituto per l'Oriente, Centro per le antichità e la storia dell'arte del vicino Oriente, 1981.

———. *Götterwort in Menschenmund: Studien zur Prophetie in Assyrien, Israel, und Juda.* FRLANT 252. Göttingen: Vandenhoeck & Ruprecht, 2014.

Wellhausen, Julius. *Die Kleinen Propheten.* Berlin: Reimer, 1898.

Weigle, Marta. *Creation and Procreation: Feminist Reflections on Mythologies of Cosmology and Parturition.* Philadelphia: University of Pennsylvania Press, 1989.

Weiss, H. "Excavations at Tell Leilan and the Origins of North Mesopotamian Cities in the Third Millenium BC." *Pal* 9 (1983) 39–52.

Wénin, André. "Le mariage de Tobias et ceux d'Isaac et de Jacob en Genèse." In *Révéler les oeuvres de Dieu: Lecture narrative du livre de Tobie*, by E. Di Pede et al., 168–81. Paris: Lessius, 2014.

Weninger, Stefan. *The Semitic Languages: An International Handbook.* HSK 36. Berlin: de Gruyter, 2011.

Wenkel, David H. *Coins as Cultural Texts in the World of the New Testament.* New York: Bloomsbury, 2017.

Werrett, Ian C. *Ritual Purity and the Dead Sea Scrolls.* Leiden: Brill, 2007.

Westbrook, Raymond L. "International Law in the Amarna Age." In *Amarna Diplomacy: The Beginnings of International Relations*, edited by R. Cohen and R. Westbrook, 28–41. Baltimore: Johns Hopkins University Press, 2000.

———. *Old Babylonian Marriage Law.* Horn, Austria: Berger, 1988.

Westenholz, Joan G. "Symbolic Language in Akkadian Narrative Poetry: The Metaphorical Relationship Between Poetical Images and the Real World." In *Mesopotamian Poetic Language: Sumerian and Akkadian*, edited by M. Vogelzang and H. Vanstiphout, 183–206. Groningen: Styx, 1996.

Westermann, Claus. *Isaiah 40–66.* 1966. Translated by D. Stalker. OTL. Philadelphia: Westminster, 1969.

———. *The Promises to the Fathers: Studies on the Patriarchal Narratives.* 1976. Translated by D. E. Green. Philadelphia: Fortress, 1980.

———. *Prophetic Oracles of Salvation in the Old Testament.* Louisville: Westminster John Knox, 1991.

———. *Prophetische Heilsworte im Alten Testament.* FRLANT 145. Göttingen: Vandenhoeck & Ruprecht, 1987.

Wheeler, Sondra Ely. *Wealth as Peril and Obligation: The New Testament on Possessions.* Grand Rapids: Eerdmans, 1995.

Whitelam, Keith W. *The Just King: Monarchical Judicial Authority in Ancient Israel.* JSOTSup 12. Sheffield: Department of Biblical Studies, University of Sheffield, 1979.

Whittaker, John C. "The Ethnoarchaeology of Threshing in Cyprus." *NEA* 63 (2000) 62–69.

Whybray, Roger N. *Thanksgiving for a Liberated Prophet: An Interpretation of Isaiah 53.* JSOTSup 4. Sheffield: JSOT Press, 1978.

———. *Wealth and Poverty in the Book of Proverbs.* JSOTSup 99. Sheffield: Sheffield Academic, 1990.

Wierzbicka, Anna. *What Did Jesus Mean?: Explaining the Sermon on the Mount and the Parables in Simple and Universal Concepts.* Oxford: Oxford University Press, 2001.

Wiesehöfer, Josef. "Iranian Empires." In *The Oxford Handbook of the State in the Ancient Near East and Mediterranean*, edited by P. F. Bang and W. Scheidel, 199–234. New York: Oxford University Press, 2013.

Wiggermann, Franciscus Antonio Maria. *Mesopotamian Protective Spirits: The Ritual Texts*. CM 1. Groningen: Styx, 1992.

Wiker, Benjamin. *Worshiping the State: How Liberalism Became Our State Religion*. Washington, DC: Regnery, 2013.

Wilder, Amos N. *The Bible and the Literary Critic*. 1991. Reprint, Eugene, OR: Wipf & Stock, 2014.

Wilhelm, Gernot. *The Hurrians*. 1982. Translated by J. Barnes. Warminster: Aris & Phillips, 1989.

Williams, Charles S. Conway. *The Acts of the Apostles*. New York: Harper & Row, 1957.

Williams, David T. *Christian Approaches to Poverty*. New York: Authors Choice, 2001.

Williamson, Hugh G. M. *Ezra-Nehemiah*. WBC 16. Nashville: Thomas Nelson, 1985.

———. "The Governors of Judea under the Persians." *TynBul* 39 (1988) 59–82.

Willis, John T. Review of *Haggai and Zechariah 1–8: A Commentary*, by David L. Petersen. *ResQ* 31 (1989) 115–16.

———. "The Structure of the Book of Micah." *SEÅ* 34 (1969) 5–42.

Willis, Timothy M. *The Elders of the City: A Study of the Elders-Laws in Deuteronomy*. SBLMS 55. Atlanta: SBL, 2001.

Wills, Lawrence M. "Bel and the Dragon." In *Fortress Commentary on the Bible: The Old Testament and Apocrypha*, edited by G. Yee et al., 1051–53. Minneapolis: Fortress, 2014.

———. *The Jewish Novel in the Ancient World*. Ithaca, NY: Cornell University Press, 1995.

Wildberger, Hans. *Isaiah 1–12: A Commentary*. CC. Minneapolis: Fortress, 1991.

Willitts, Joel. "Matthew." In *Jesus Is Lord, Caesar Is Not: Evaluating Empire in New Testament Studies*, edited by S. McKnight and J. B. Modica, 82–100. Downers Grove, IL: InterVarsity, 2013.

Wilt, Judith. *Abortion, Choice, and Contemporary Fiction: The Armageddon of the Maternal Instinct*. Chicago: University of Chicago Press, 1990.

Wink, Walter. "Jesus and Revolution: Reflections on S. G. F. Brandon's *Jesus and the Zealots*." *USQR* 25 (1969) 37–59.

Winter, Bruce W. "Providentia for the Widows in 1 Timothy 5:3–16." *TynBul* 39 (1988) 83–99.

Wiseman, Donald J. "The Vassal-Treaties of Esarhaddon." *Iraq* 20 (1958) 1–99.

Witherington, Ben, III. *Jesus and Money: A Guide for Times of Financial Crisis*. Grand Rapids: Brazos, 2010.

———. *Jesus the Sage: The Pilgrimage of Wisdom*. Minneapolis: Fortress, 2000.

Witherup, Ronald D. *Matthew: God With Us*. Hyde Park, NY: New City, 2000.

Wogaman, J. Philip. *Economics and Ethics: A Christian Enquiry*. London: SCM, 1986.

Wöhrle, Jakob. *Die frühen Sammlungen des Zwölfprophetenbuches: Entstehung und Komposition*. BZAW 360. Berlin: de Gruyter, 2006.

Wolff, Hans Walter. *Haggai: A Commentary*. 1986. Translated by M. Kohl. CC. Minneapolis: Augsburg, 1988.

———. *Hosea: A Commentary on the Book of the Prophet Hosea*. 1965. Translated by G. Stansell. Hermeneia. Philadelphia: Fortress, 1974.

———. *Joel and Amos: A Commentary on the Books of the Prophets Joel and Amos*. 1969. Translated by W. Janzen et al. Hermeneia. Philadelphia: Fortress, 1977.

———. *Micah: A Commentary*. 1982. Translated by G. Stansell. CC. Minneapolis: Augsburg, 1990.

Wolff, Hope Nash. "Gilgamesh, Enkidu, and the Heroic Life." *JAOS* 89 (1969) 392–98.

Wolters, Al. Review of *Zechariah 9–14 and Malachi: A Commentary*, by D. L. Petersen. *CBQ* 58 (1996) 525–27.

Woo, Taek Joo. "The *Marzēaḥ* Institution and Rites for the Dead: A Comparative and Systemic Study with Special Attention to the Eighth Century Prophets." PhD diss., Graduate Theological Union, 1998.

Wright, David P. *Inventing God's Law: How the Covenant Code of the Bible Used and Revised the Laws of Hammurabi*. New York: Oxford, 2009.

———. *Ritual in Narrative: The Dynamics of Feasting, Mourning, and Retaliation Rites in the Ugaritic Tale of Aqhat*. Winona Lake, IN: Eisenbrauns, 2001.

Wyatt, Nicolas. "Asherah." In *DDD* 99–105.

———. "Astarte." In *DDD* 109–14.

———. "The Concept and Purpose of Hell: Its Nature and Development in West Semitic Thought." *Numen* 56 (2009) 161–84.

———. *The Mythic Mind: Essays on Cosmology and Religion in Ugaritic and Old Testament Literature*. New York: Routledge, 2014.

———. *Myths of Power: A Study of Royal Myth and Ideology in Ugaritic and Biblical Tradition*. Münster: Ugarit, 1996.

———. *Religious Texts from Ugarit*. BibSem 53. Sheffield: Sheffield Academic, 2002.

———. *Word of Tree and Whisper of Stone, and Other Papers on Ugaritian Thought*. Piscataway, NJ: Gorgias, 2007.

Yee, Gale A. "Jezebel." In *ABD* 3.848–49.

———. "Sarah." In *ABD* 5.981–82.

Yoder, Christine Roy. *Wisdom as a Woman of Substance: A Socioeconomic Reading of Proverbs 1–9 and 31:10–31*. BZAW 304. Berlin: de Gruyter, 2001.

Yoder, John Howard. *The Politics of Jesus: Vicit Agnus Noster*. Grand Rapids: Eerdmans, 1972.

Yon, Marguerite. *The City of Ugarit at Tell Ras Shamra*. Winona Lake, IN: Eisenbrauns, 2006.

Young, T. Cuyler. "The Consolidation of the Empire and Its Limits of Growth under Darius and Xerxes." In *CAH*, vol. 4, *Persia, Greece and the Western Mediterranean c. 525 to 479 B.C.*, edited by J. Boardman et al., 93–99. Cambridege: Cambridge University Press, 1988.

———. "Cyrus." In *ABD* 1.1231–32.

———. "Darius." In *ABD* 2.37–38.

Zadok, Ran. "Two Terms in Ezra." *AS* 5 (2007) 255–61.

Zelizer, Viviana. *Pricing the Priceless Child*. New York: Basic Books, 1985.

Zhmud, Leonid. *Pythagoras and the Early Pythagoreans*. 1994. Translated by K. Wendle and R. Ireland. New York: Oxford University Press, 2012.

Zimmerli, Walther. *Ezekiel: A Commentary on the Book of the Prophet Ezekiel*. Hermeneia. Philadelphia: Fortress, 1983.

Zimmermann, Frank. *The Book of Tobit*. New York: Harper, 1958.

Zobel, Hans Jürgen. "כנען." In *TDOT* 7.211–28.

Zobel, Moshe Nahum. "Ashi." *EJ* 2.565–66.

Zsolnay, Ilona. "The Misconstrued Role of the *Assinnu* in Ancient Near Eastern Prophecy." In *Prophets, Male and Female: Gender and Prophecy in the Hebrew Bible, the Eastern Mediterranean, and the Ancient Near East*, edited by J. Stökl and C. Carvalho, 81–99. AIL 15. Atlanta: SBL, 2013.

Subject Index

Aaron, 153n243
Abigail, 14n92, 34n295
abortion, 5, 5n11
Abra(ha)m, 49, 49n458, 72n140, 168, 170n107, 171n120, 184, 199
Absalom, 53n496, 54, 59n499, 54n503, 54n504, 198
abundance, 23n176, 25, 32n274, 83n222, 149, 191n292, 192n296
Abzu, 8n44
Achaemenid, 124n14, 126, 128, 130, 131n61, 132n70, 133, 136, 136n92, 144n165, 198
Achan, 61n46
Achilles, 33n284, 33n289, 49n460
acquisition, 11n65, 80n202
Acts of the Apostles, 2, 41n375, 157, 160n31, 180, 181n198, 183, 183n213, 184, 185, 185n233, 186n242, 186n243, 186n245, 189n274, 193n305, 194, 195
Adad, 30, 33, 37n331, 38n338, 49n454, 198
Adapa, 26n211
Adiabene, 164n58
Adirtu, 139n115
Admetus, 160n31
adoption, 5n8
Adrammeleḫ, 27n218, 145
adultery, 75n165, 91n300, 92n313, 97n350
Aesop, 165n72
Agade, 9n48, 44n404
Agamemnon, 33n289
agrarian, 2n20, 16n108, 24n184, 25, 32, 57n13, 66, 66n91, 71, 74, 74n151, 75n163, 78n191, 81n208, 90, 92, 93n318, 93n324, 94n326, 95n337, 96, 100n373, 107n434, 109n454, 110n471, 146n182, 158, 159n20, 165, 174n141, 185n232, 200
Ahab, 33n287, 59n29, 59n30, 59n33, 60, 61, 61n47, 61n48, 61n51, 82, 138n111
Aḫiqar, 144n164, 145, 145n174, 146, 146n183, 150n217, 175n144
Aitukima, 90n294
akītu, 17, 18n124, 55n510
Akizzi, 90n294
Akkadian, 12, 13, 16, 17n116, 34n294, 49n454, 98n360
Aleppo, 30
Alexander of Macedon, 149n209, 190n283
Alexandria, 177n166
alien, 74n153, 117, 184, 185, 185n234, 194n311
almsgiving, 67n101, 141n142, 145n185, 148n210, 149, 150, 150n217, 150n221, 161, 161n39, 161n40, 162, 162n42, 164n64, 192n301, 194
altar, 31, 31n268, 60, 62, 62n58, 62n61, 63, 65, 65n81, 83, 99, 104, 115n518, 116n524, 117, 117n526, 134, 159, 159n28, 160, 160n30, 115n518, 116n524, 117, 117n526, 134, 159, 159n28, 160, 160n30
Amarna, 20n147, 21n160, 25n204, 30, 81n211, 126n34
Amenhotep III, 90n294
Ammiṣaduqa, 82n214, 123n7
Ammon(ite), 103n399, 139, 139n119
Amnon, 54n503
Amos, 4n5, 32n279, 54, 78n187, 80n201, 103, 103n397, 103n399, 103n400, 103n406, 104n408, 104n413, 105, 105n416, 106, 106n428, 107, 107n435, 107n438, 109n460, 119, 142, 142n145, 146n190, 200
Amun, 41n375
Ananias, 181, 182, 182n204, 182n207, 187, 187n250, 194n317, 195n322, 200
Anat, 6, 6n16, 6n18, 6n27, 27, 33n284, 33n289, 33n290, 39, 39n350, 39n353, 39n354, 39n356, 40, 43, 44n402, 45, 46, 47, 48, 48n441, 50, 197, 200

Anathoth(ian), 6n18, 57n15, 79, 140
Anatolia(n), 1, 4, 9n50, 31, 32, 34n295, 34n301, 35n306, 35n307, 51n476, 54, 95n333, 188, 188n261, 194, 196, 200
Anat-Yahu, 6n18
Annunaki, 13, 13n85, 16, 16n109, 16n111
Anšar, 17n120, 18, 18n125, 19
anthropological, 1, 51, 51n476, 56, 56n6, 63n64, 68n105, 75n164, 89, 115n516
Anu, 19n140, 20, 23, 25n200, 47n439, 98n360
Anzu, 8n44, 19n140
apocalyptic, 1, 25n204, 71, 71n133, 72n139, 73n146, 96n343, 172n124
Apollo, 135n91, 160n31, 189n270, 190, 190n278
Apollonius, 186n244
Aqhat, 1, 39, 39n353, 45, 46n426, 54n502, 58n22, 200
Arabia, 85n245
Arabic, 104n411, 112n488
Aramaic, 70n124, 71n127, 109n455, 123, 123n6, 123n8, 123n9, 125n11, 128n45, 131n67, 132n68, 133, 135n90, 142n147, 143n152, 146n184, 162, 162n47, 163, 164n66, 168n93, 71n117, 181n199
Ararat, 145
Arbela, 164n58
Archidamus, 141n136
Ares, 188n260
Aristophanes, 126n30, 141n137
Aristotle, 80n202, 138n113, 147n192, 177n168, 178n172, 178n181, 181n196, 187n252, 192n299, 192n300
Artaxerxes, 123, 123n10, 123n11, 124, 126, 127n38, 133, 135, 199
Artemis, 191, 191n288, 192
Asclepius, 190, 190n278
Aseneth, 154n245
A/asherah, 43n393, 57n14, 60, 60n41, 61, 77n180
Asia (Minor), 170n105, 172n123
Asmodeus, 154, 154n244, 154n249, 155, 155n255, 189n270, 197
Aššur, 26n212, 27n218, 28n233, 103n403, 145n173
Assurbanipal 4, 27, 28, 28n234
Assyria(n), 6n17, 18n124, 18n132, 25n203, 26, 26n208, 27n218, 51n476, 61n48, 78, 82n214, 90n294, 105n416, 108n446, 111, 122, 123n7, 131n61, 132n70, 144, 145, 150n223, 164, 164n58
Aštabi, 34n297, 41n372
Astarte, 6, 6n16, 6n25, 43
Aṣušunamir, 15n102, 16
Athens, 140n132, 168, 180n192, 186n244
Athirat, 6, 43, 47n437, 47n438, 47n440, 48, 49, 50, 52, 53, 53n494, 152n233, 197
Athtar, 34, 34n297, 41, 41n372, 42, 42n379, 42n386, 43, 50, 53, 53n487, 53n494, 53n495, 152n233, 199
Atraḫasis, 4, 14, 15n101, 17n120, 20n146, 20n151, 48, 48n441, 49n451, 49n454, 52n480, 81n208
Attis, 91n300
Augustine, 91n300
Augustus, 176n159
Azariah, 152
Azazel, 155, 155n250

betrothal, 1, 49, 50, 51, 51n472, 96, 96n344, 96n346, 155, 170
Ba'al, 1, 9n50, 18, 18n133, 22, 27, 32n269, 33n284, 33n289, 37, 37n331, 38, 38n336, 38n338, 38n348, 39, 39n350, 39n351, 39n352, 39n354, 41, 41n371, 42, 42n380, 43, 43n391, 44, 44n397, 45, 45n417, 46, 47, 48, 48n441, 48n444, 48n445, 49n459, 50, 52, 53, 53n487, 53n489, 53n490, 53n491, 53n494, 53n495, 57, 57n10, 57n14, 58, 58n18, 58n19, 58n21, 58n22, 58n23, 58n25, 59, 59n27, 59n29, 60, 60n38, 60n44, 61, 62, 62n58, 62n61, 63, 63n62, 63n65, 64, 64n73, 64n74, 65n81, 65n83, 68n111, 69n118, 75n165, 76, 76n170, 76n172, 77n180, 89n290, 91, 91n299, 102n395, 102n396, 137n105, 155, 197, 198, 200
Babylon(ian), 5n12, 17, 17n123, 18n124, 18n129, 18n132, 19n139, 24, 25n203, 30, 31, 41n375, 42n386, 45n413, 56n2, 78n183, 80n206, 81n208, 82n214, 82n216, 82n219, 87, 113, 123n7, 125n26, 129, 130, 131, 131n61, 132n70, 133n75, 134, 140
Bagohi, 126n35
Balaam, 187, 187n255
Bardiya, 117n530
Barnabas, 181, 181n199, 188
Baruch ben Neriah, 80, 80n203, 142n143
Batista, Fulgencio, 19
beatitudes, 159
Behemoth, 40n360
Bel, 140, 140n128
Belial, 54n498, 75n165
Belshazzar, 129n53
benefactor, 194n311
Benjamin, 79
Beowulf, 44n407

Bible/biblical, 1, 2n20, 3, 40n364, 55n509, 58n15, 60n36, 73n145, 76n167, 85, 90, 91n301, 93n320, 113n502, 122, 133, 134n82, 148n201, 158, 168n94, 178, 180n190, 188n263, 194n317, 180n190, 188n263, 201
birthright, 40n368
bless(ing), 5, 23n176, 40n370, 45, 75n163, 106n433, 116, 118n535, 121, 159, 159n21, 163n56, 190n277, 193, 199
Blind Padishah, 155
Boaz, 29n45, 151, 152n229, 170n112
borrow, 29n243, 73, 104n411, 124n17, 136, 136n99, 139n115, 145, 160, 175n144, 136n99, 139n115, 145, 160, 175n144
bribe(ry), 21n161, 25n201, 47, 48, 48n441, 48n449, 49, 61n45, 101n387, 105, 105n422, 109, 109n455, 126, 128n40, 136n97, 178, 193n306, 194, 195, 195n320
bridewealth, 47, 47n432, 49, 51, 51n472, 155
Burnaburiaš, 126n32
business, 50m469, 58n17, 68n105, 70, 70n123, 84n239, 85n248, 87, 105n423, 106n428, 118n539, 144n167, 189, 189n272, 190, 191, 191n291
Byblos, 126n34

Caesar, 14n92, 175, 176, 176n159
Cain, 138n110
capital(ism), 2, 2n20, 124n15, 181n197
Canaan(ite), 4, 6, 6n16, 6n18, 9n50, 32, 33n284, 33n289, 33n290, 34, 34n297, 36, 36n327, 37, 37n327, 37n330, 39, 39n352, 40, 41n371, 41n372, 44, 44n397, 45, 45n413, 48, 50, 53n495, 54, 58, 58n19, 61, 62n54, 62n56, 64n73, 65n83, 83n231, 86n252, 95n333, 98n356, 112n489, 185n233, 199, 200
Carmel, 60, 62n61, 65, 65n83, 75n161, 79, 83n224, 100n374, 117
Carthage, 68n111
Castro, Fidel, 19
Cedar Forest, 8
Chaldea(n), 78n183, 79, 82, 82n216, 86, 102n390, 113, 117, 129, 136, 136n93, 160n30
charity, 146n185, 147n200, 148, 148n201, 178
child(ren), 5n8, 5n9, 5n11, 5n13, 10, 15n99, 36, 36n325, 66, 66n90, 66n91, 68, 68n111, 76, 81n113, 85n248, 88n268, 92n310, 92n311, 94n328, 97n350, 100, 101n386, 102, 104n409, 106, 133, 137, 137n102, 144, 150, 170n107, 179, 185, 197
Christian(ity), 15n100, 60n33, 67n100, 69n119, 122, 139n121, 140n130, 146n189, 148n201, 157n2, 174n141, 176n154, 181n195, 181n198, 181n200, 183n216, 184, 191n287, 192, 194, 195
Chronicles, 1n6, 58n16, 72n140, 109n454, 122n5, 169n101
church, 139n121, 146n189, 160n34, 174n141, 176, 182n206, 183n213, 183n216, 185n225
Cicero, 141n140
circumcision, 116n525
civilization, 2n20
Claudius, 194n314
Clement, 161n39
coin, 172, 172n122, 175n145, 176, 176n158
commerce, 38n342, 52n478, 88n269, 162n46
communism, 181, 181n197, 181n198
compensation/wages, 22, 24n190, 29n240, 28n224, 67n100, 71, 83n222, 95, 95n335, 98, 98n355, 100, 101, 101n380, 101n385, 101n387, 101n388, 109n455, 114, 114n504, 118, 120n549, 120n554, 125n19, 135, 139, 147, 149, 152, 153, 154n247, 155, 159n24, 161, 161n40, 162n43, 167, 167n81
consumer, 2n20
Copernicus, 188n265
Cornelius, 150n221
corrupt(ion), 2, 110, 111, 111n486, 126n28, 140, 142, 156, 165n73, 175, 175n146, 182n203, 182n207, 194, 195, 200
cosmogony, 19, 39n352, 45n417
covenant, 57, 57n10, 57n12, 59, 59n28, 59n32, 61, 67n96, 68n108, 71, 72n134, 76, 80, 81n208, 81n209, 82, 82n217, 86, 86n255, 88, 88n268, 90, 90n297, 91, 94, 95, 96, 96n343, 96n344, 97, 113n501, 120n544, 121, 137n101, 137n108, 139, 154, 159n28, 163n56, 168, 170n113, 176n160, 200
credit(or), 28n230, 73, 100n375, 112, 124n16, 136, 138n109, 155, 192, 192n296
Critias, 180n192
Croesus, 192n294
curse(d), 30n254, 45, 72, 97n352, 114n510, 116n519, 120, 191n285
Cybele, 6, 91n300
Cyprus, 21n161, 84n240, 141n134, 186n245
Cyrus, 117n530, 123, 129, 130, 131, 133, 133n74, 133n75, 144n165, 199

Dagan, 30, 38, 38n339, 52, 53, 98n362
Damascus, 103n399, 109n460, 181n201

Dan(ite), 78n185, 143
Dan'el, 46n426, 54n502
Daniel, 56n2, 65n86, 69n113, 102n390, 129n53, 140, 144n164, 145n174
Darius, 117n530, 123, 128, 130, 135n91, 168n87
David(ic), 14n92, 34n295, 40n370, 41n376, 43n394, 44n405, 52n485, 53n496, 54n503, 54n504, 60n36, 72n134, 83n231, 86, 108n447, 198
death, 6, 7, 7n37, 8, 9, 11n64, 13n87, 16n112, 43, 56, 56n1, 62n58, 64n71, 67, 67n96, 69, 69n114, 74n156, 82n216, 93n320, 105n417, 112, 112n489, 147n199, 148, 148n207, 150, 150n217, 155n256, 160n31, 167, 197
debt(or), 2n19, 29, 31n262, 70, 70n124, 71n127, 73, 76, 82n214, 88n268, 103n405, 104n411, 106n432, 112, 112n494, 115n513, 118n535, 123n7, 127, 138n111, 138n112, 151n226, 160n29, 162, 162n45, 163n51, 178
debt-slavery, 31, 52n478, 52n479, 52n480, 71n127, 76n168, 82n214, 101n386, 103n405, 107n438
decalogue, 57n12, 62, 167, 173
defile(ment), 35, 74n149, 75, 75n164, 75n165, 89n290, 97n350, 104n410, 115, 115n516, 115n517, 115n518, 116, 116n519, 117, 117n527, 120n551, 160n30, 193n306, 195, 120n551, 160n30, 193, 193n306, 195
Delphi, 189n270, 190n281
Demetrius, 41n375, 161n37, 191, 191n293, 199
Demochares, 161n37
Democritus, 186n244
Demosthenes, 189n272
destiny, 11n66, 13n78, 19n140, 20, 20n154, 22, 22n173
Deuteronomy, 1n2, 72n140, 77n182, 84n233, 84n235, 84n237, 88n268
diaspora, 45n418, 142, 145n174, 153n241, 170n105, 171n115
Dinah, 51
Dio Cassius, 183n216
Dio Chrysostom, 193n305
Diodorus Siculus, 80n207
Dionysius of Halicarnassus, 183n218
disciples, 157n6, 159n25, 174n138, 177, 183, 199
divin(ation), 68n105, 101n384, 109, 109n457, 122n1, 189, 189n273, 190, 190n280, 191n287
divorce, 90, 92n310, 94n327, 97, 138n113
dowry, 47n432, 50n470, 51, 51n472, 94, 96, 96n344
dragon, 35n306, 39n354, 45n413, 64n78, 140, 155, 189n270
drought, 33n287, 49n452, 54n504, 58n18, 58n22, 59, 60, 74, 106, 114n506, 137n100, 158n13, 197
Druze, 43n396
Dumuzi, 9n48, 16, 16n108, 16n111, 17
Dunnu, 17n120

Eanna, 7n34
Ebabbara, 30, 30n254, 30n255
'Eber-Nahara, 124, 125, 127, 128, 128n46, 131, 132, 135, 136
Ebiḫ, 22n164, 198n24
Eblaite, 400n403
Ecbatana, 131, 144n165
Ecclesiastes, 1n6
economic(s), 2n21, 3, 5n6, 5n11, 8, 8n45, 16n106, 17, 19n144, 23n174, 23n178, 24n185, 26n211, 31, 31n266, 32, 32n274, 35, 36, 36n319, 36n327, 37n330, 41n376, 48n448, 50, 50n461, 50n464, 51n472, 57n13, 59, 62n56, 62n58, 62n61, 67n100, 69n119, 70n121, 70n124, 72, 72n140, 75n159, 75n165, 76n171, 76n175, 78n191, 79n198, 81n208, 81n212, 81n213, 82, 84, 86n253, 86n255, 88n269, 89n289, 90n296, 91n307, 92, 92n312, 93n318, 94n326, 94n327, 96n344, 97n350, 99, 100, 102n393, 103, 103n397, 103n400, 109n454, 113, 113n500, 116, 117n528, 120, 120n548, 120n552, 124n15, 133, 136, 136n92, 136n96, 137n100, 139, 146n182, 149n209, 153n239, 153n241, 158, 159n20, 164n57, 165, 166n77, 171n116, 172n123, 175n146, 177n164, 181n197, 186, 189n273, 192n296, 196n2, 197, 197n12, 199, 200
Edna, 154
Edom, 103n399
Egypt(ian), 5n9, 6, 6n20, 6n24, 28n229, 30, 31, 41n375, 42n384, 42n385, 48n441, 55, 56n2, 59, 74, 78, 78n104, 83n222, 83n227, 87, 87n262, 87n266, 88, 90n294, 94n332, 125n21, 126n31, 126n32, 126n34, 131n67, 132n69, 139n115, 145, 158n7, 184, 185n234
El, 9n50, 18, 37, 37n334, 38, 38n343, 38n348, 40, 41, 42, 43, 43n391, 45, 46, 47, 47n437, 47n438, 47n440, 48, 48n441, 49, 52, 53, 53n487, 57n10, 104n412, 144n166, 152n233, 197, 198, 200
Elam(ite), 11n65, 82n214, 123n7

elegy, 2n17
Elephantine, 123n10, 128n47, 131n63, 132n69, 145n174
Eliashib, 139n119
Elijah, 34n301, 57, 57n14, 58, 58n16, 58n21, 58n22, 58n23, 59, 59n25, 59n26, 59n29, 60, 60n44, 61, 61n49, 62, 62n57, 62n58, 63, 64, 64n69, 64n70, 64n73, 65, 65n80, 65n83, 79, 82, 89n285, 117, 117n526, 138n111, 157n6, 200
Elisha, 64n69, 157n6, 166n78
Elymas, 186n245
'Elyon, 84, 144n162
Empedocles, 186n244
Emar, 37n331, 64n71
endogam(ous), 149n209, 153n241, 154, 154n247
Enki, 8, 8n44, 9n54, 10, 10n54, 10n58, 14, 14n91, 14n94, 15, 15n101, 16, 17n120, 22, 22n173, 23, 23n173, 34n303, 38, 38n343, 47n436, 47n439, 49, 197
Enkidu, 30n254, 45, 91n303
Enlil, 10, 10n58, 14, 18, 18n129, 18n132, 19, 23, 24n184, 24n193, 27, 27n214, 30n254, 41n375, 42n386, 47n436, 47n439, 48n441, 49, 49n452, 56n1, 64n73, 78n183, 198, 200
Enmešarra, 17n120
Enuma Eliš, 1, 8n46, 17, 21n158, 21n159, 22n170, 23n176, 45n413, 198
Ephesus, 186n245, 190, 191, 192, 192n294
epic, 2n17, 4, 17, 37, 39n353, 49, 78n183, 196, 198, 200
Ephraim, 90n294, 90n297
Epictetus, 144n159
Epicurus, 193
Epistle of Jeremiah, 122, 122n3, 140, 141, 142, 156, 199
Ereškigal, 7, 7n36, 9n49, 9n50, 11, 11n62, 13, 13n79, 13n83, 13n85, 14, 14n94, 15, 15n98, 15n99, 64, 196, 197
Erišti-Aya, 30, 30n256
Erra, 4, 78n183, 78n190
Eršema, 11, 11n60, 11n61
Ešmunazar, 6n25
Ešnunna, 82n214, 123n7
Esagila, 18, 18n132, 129n54
Esarhaddon, 26, 26n207, 26n209, 27, 27n214, 27n218, 28, 145, 145n174, 198
Esdras, 102n390
estate, 20n148, 22n172, 30n253, 80, 81n213, 108n444, 109, 109n458, 118n534, 149n214, 153, 153n243, 154n247, 197
Esther, 1n6, 47n436, 56n2, 125n25, 128n42, 139n123, 145n174
Ethiopia, 102n392187n251
Euphrates, 22, 22n172, 37n331, 124n14
Euripides, 92n312, 160n31, 181n196, 189n270
Eurytheia, 141n136
Eusebius, 174n141
Evagoras, 141n134
exchange, 2n21, 16, 16n110, 18n127, 37n330, 41n371, 48n450, 50n465, 51n476, 61, 63, 72n140, 76, 76n174, 77, 95n335, 101n386, 102n393, 105n422, 119, 119n544, 128, 152n234, 160n31, 170, 170n112, 171, 175, 175n145, 176n158, 178, 186n242, 194
exile, 6, 71n128, 78n184, 87n266, 92n315, 124n15, 129, 129n52, 135n86, 140, 146
Exodus, 1n2, 56n2
Ezekiel, 1n16, 16n112, 65n84, 66n91, 84, 84n238, 84n239, 85n241, 85n245, 85n248, 85n249, 86n251, 87, 87n260, 87n265, 87n266, 88, 88n268, 88n269, 88n270, 88n271, 88n272, 89n290, 92n315101n385, 104n411, 163n51, 186, 186n246, 199
Ezra, 1n6, 2, 58n16, 120n548, 122, 122n2, 122n5, 123, 123n8, 124n15, 126n28, 131n66, 133, 135, 136, 136n93, 138n113, 139, 156, 171n117, 195

family, 5, 9n54, 27, 29n244, 47n432, 51, 51n477, 55n507, 70n121, 79n195, 79n198, 91n298, 107n438, 109n454, 137n101, 141n138, 146, 150n223, 151, 151n227, 152, 152n236, 153n243, 154n247, 158, 158n11, 159n20, 170n112
famine, 6, 7, 32, 32n279, 49n452, 56, 69, 82, 106, 114n511, 136, 136n97, 136n98, 137n100, 197, 100
farce, 140, 140n126, 140n129, 156
fast(ing), 70, 70n122, 70n125, 71
Felix, 194, 194n314, 194n318, 194n319
feminist, 5n7
fertility, 4, 5, 5n6, 5n9, 5n13, 6, 6n21, 6n28, 7, 8n43, 9, 13n87, 24n186, 26, 32n271, 36n323, 56, 59n27, 69, 91, 97, 116n525, 121, 153n239, 155, 188n267, 196
financ(ial), 79n198, 90, 103n403, 133, 135, 136n96, 139, 245, 145n179, 150n223, 152n232, 162, 178, 189n273, 194n311, 199
firstborn, 40, 40n368, 40n370, 49n454, 53n487, 54n503, 170, 170n107, 171n119
folktale, 3n25, 142n146, 155
fortune, 23n176, 26n210, 28n223, 47, 47n438, 77n181, 107n434, 136, 146

Francis of Assisi, 167n80
frankincense, 158n10
fraud(ulent), 29n238, 106, 106n428, 108, 110, 110n474, 120, 120n550
fund(raising), 141n137, 151n226, 152, 177n167, 194n311

Gabael, 144, 144n166, 150, 151, 151n227
Gadatas, 135n91
Galile(an), 159, 172, 174, 176n154
Gathas, 154n244
Gaza, 103n399
Gedaliah, 104n409
Gehazai, 64n69
Gaumata, 117n530
gender, 5n7, 6n28, 16n108
Genesis, 1n2, 5n13, 43n392, 45n413, 49, 51, 168, 184n230
Genesis Apocryphon, 143n151
Geštinanna, 9n48, 16, 16n108, 16n111, 17
Gideon, 60, 62, 62n61, 69, 77n177, 92n310, 170n104
gift/giving, 7n34, 21, 21n161, 23, 23n174, 24n185, 25n201, 27, 27n219, 27n222, 36n327, 37n330, 38, 38n347, 41n371, 47, 47n439, 48, 48n441, 48n442, 48n443, 48n447, 48n448, 48n450, 49, 50, 50n465, 50n470, 51, 93n320, 94, 94n332, 95n335, 96, 96n345, 97n350, 98n355, 98n360, 105n418, 109n455, 111n480, 123n8, 126n32, 131n64, 136n97, 139n119, 142n142, 143, 147, 149n214, 150, 158n10, 159, 160, 160n29, 160n31, 162n42, 167, 167n85, 168, 169, 169n98, 172n127, 173, 180, 184n228, 187, 187n248, 194, 194n315, 199
Gilead, 57n14, 109n460
Gilgamesh, 4, 7, 8, 12n69, 20n146, 30n254, 40n360, 43n394, 44n407, 45, 86n250, 91n302, 91n303, 91n304
goddess, 4, 5, 6n15, 6n16, 6n17, 6n18, 6n19, 6n20, 6n22, 6n23, 6n28, 7, 7n29, 7n32, 8n44, 11n64, 12, 33n289, 36n322, 39n353, 47, 57n10, 98n360
gold, 9n48, 38n342, 40, 44, 48, 49n460, 50, 50n461, 51, 84n239, 85, 88, 94, 96n346, 101, 101n389, 123, 126n32, 129, 129n53, 131, 131n66, 131n67, 133, 134, 135, 136, 136n93, 140, 140n130, 150, 158n10, 166, 192
Gomer, 90n296, 90n297, 92n311
goods, 2n20, 21n162, 36n327, 48n450, 92n312, 180, 181, 181n196, 183, 183n219, 195, 197n12
G/gospel, 157n3, 157n5, 158, 158n14, 168, 172n121, 177n169, 177n170, 195
Grateful Dead, 155
Greek, 2n19, 12, 12n77, 15n100, 16n109, 33n284, 33n289, 37n328, 37n332, 48, 55n509, 88n270, 91n300, 102, 102n391, 123n6, 123n9, 136n92, 141n140, 142, 157, 157n2, 162, 162n49, 163, 168, 175n145, 181n200, 182n206, 183n217, 184n222, 184n225, 190n284, 191n288, 192n299
greed(y), 2, 55n508, 68n107, 81n212, 165
Gudea, 44n404

Habakkuk, 111, 111n485, 112, 112n488, 113, 113n499
Hades, 12, 12n77
Hagar, 171n120
Haggai, 113, 113n501, 113n502, 114n505, 115, 115n452, 115n514, 115n518, 116n521, 116n524, 117, 117n528, 118n533, 119, 122n2, 160n30, 198, 199
Halakic Letter, 115n516
Hana, 82n214, 123n7
Hannah, 145, 147, 147n198, 147n200, 148, 148n202, 149, 152, 152n232, 152n235, 152n236, 164n63, 182n203
Hathor, 6, 6n16, 6n21
Haman, 137n103
Hammurabi, 24n184, 30, 31, 31n261, 80n207
Ḥanamel, 79, 79n197, 79n199, 80, 197
Ḥananiah, 152, 181n201
Ḫanḫana, 35n307
Harmal, 22n168
harvest, 75n158, 75n163, 77n177, 85n248, 103n404, 111, 114, 158n13, 166n75, 77n177, 103n404, 158n13, 166n75
Hasmonean, 48n447
Ḫattuša, 33n286
Ḫauran, 43, 43n396, 44n399
Hebrew, 6, 6n19, 7n29, 16n112, 34n301, 36, 37n335, 38n338, 43n390, 46, 49n460, 54n501, 56, 56n2, 57n12, 59, 62n56, 64n70, 74n150, 77n180, 80n201, 81, 81n208, 82, 82n218, 82n221, 84n235, 88n268, 107, 111, 113, 119, 122, 123, 123n9, 131, 135n90, 140, 140n126, 142, 142n147, 143n152, 146, 146n187, 149n210, 157n2, 159, 162n48, 168, 170, 180n193, 183, 183n216, 184, 185n234, 186, 197
Hector, 49n460
Hellenistic, 54n503, 81n213, 154n245, 157n2, 159, 171n117, 181n198, 183n216,

183n217, 157n2, 159, 171n117, 180n193, 181n198, 183, 183n216, 183n217
Hellespont, 125n19
Heracleides, 191n292
Herakles, 141n136
Hermes, 188
hero(ism), 8n41, 9n54, 19n140, 33n289, 42, 42n387, 44n407, 145n174
Herodotus, 133n73, 147n197, 160n31
Hesiod, 19n135, 99n370, 173n136
Ḫirḫib, 50
histor(ical), 3n25, 27, 53n491, 55, 55n509, 57n15, 58n16, 58n24, 65n79, 73n145, 78n183, 81n208, 81n212, 91n300, 109n459, 125, 126n32, 127, 133, 142, 157n1, 157n2, 170, 174, 180n190, 182, 184, 186
Hittite, 9n50, 13n87, 24n192, 31, 31n263, 31n265, 31n267, 32, 32n275, 33n284, 33n286, 33n289, 34, 34n294, 34n295, 34n297, 34n298, 34n299, 34n301, 34n302, 34n304, 35n305, 35n306, 35n308, 35n315, 35n316, 35n317, 35n318, 36n319, 36n320, 37n328, 37n331, 37n333, 38n339, 43n390, 49n460, 57n9, 64n73, 74n151, 90n294, 98n362, 113n499, 196n6, 197n7, 200n44, 200n48
hokum, 91n302
Homer(ic), 44n403, 49n460, 55n509, 99n370, 173n134
honeybee, 34, 34n298, 35
Horeb, 64n69
Hosea, 58n17, 59n27, 68, 73, 73n148, 76n169, 76n172, 76n173, 80n201, 89, 89n285, 89n290, 90, 90n295, 90n297, 90n298, 91, 91n307, 92, 93, 94n326, 94n330, 94n340, 96, 97, 97n347, 97n348, 97n349, 119, 197, 200
Hoshea, 90n294
house(hold), 2n20, 11, 20n148, 22, 23, 23n178, 24n192, 25n200, 26, 26n210, 27n214, 31n260, 41n376, 42, 43, 43n394, 44, 44n404, 45, 47, 48, 49, 61n45, 62n61, 63, 67n100, 75, 75n158, 80, 80n205, 85n241, 86n252, 90n292, 90n294, 104, 104n413, 105, 105n416, 105n419, 105n423, 108, 108n445, 113, 114, 114n503, 115n512, 117n532, 119, 119n541, 119n544, 120n554, 121, 123, 128, 129, 130, 130n58, 131, 131n65, 132, 134, 135, 136n97, 138, 141n137, 143, 144n160, 145n176, 147n197, 153n239, 154, 165n70, 168n95, 169, 173n136, 175, 193n310, 196, 198, 199
hospitality, 14, 15, 15n100
Humbaba, 12n69, 155n254, 183n212
hunger, 32, 33n287, 71
Ḫuraya, 40n367, 49, 50, 53
Hurrian, 19n134, 24n192, 33n288, 34n295, 34n297, 35n309, 41n372, 43n395, 55
hymn, 2n17

Ignatius, 184n221
Ilimilku, 48, 48n445, 49n459
immigrant, 75n164, 136n96
Inanna, 1, 4, 7, 7n30, 7n35, 8, 8n44, 9, 9n48, 9n49, 9n50, 9n52, 9n54, 10, 10n54, 10n56, 10n57, 10n59, 11, 11n62, 11n63, 11n64, 11n65, 12n67, 12n68, 12n73, 12n76, 13, 13n82, 13n84, 14n90, 15, 15n98, 15n99, 15n104, 16, 16n111, 17, 17n118, 21n155, 22n164, 23n173, 32, 35n318, 45, 59n31, 64, 92n314, 95n333, 153n239, 196, 197, 198n24
Inara, 34n304
income/revenue, 24n190, 25n201, 75n158, 76n175, 120n552, 137n100, 140n132, 145n176, 171n116, 198, 199
inherit(ance), 22n169, 24, 24n190, 26, 27, 27n214, 27n218, 27n219, 27n221, 30, 30n253, 37, 38n340, 40, 40n364, 41, 41n371, 44n405, 55, 61n47, 67n103, 68, 68n112, 69n112, 69n117, 69n118, 70n121, 71, 73, 75, 75n165, 76n175, 79, 79n196, 79n197, 79n198, 79n199, 83, 83n230, 83n231, 84, 84n232, 86, 90, 92n311, 97n350, 98n357, 99, 99n368, 100n373, 101, 101n383, 107, 107n434, 108, 108n446, 121, 125n27, 149, 153, 153n238, 153n239, 153n241, 153n243, 156, 157, 168, 168n94, 172, 172n126, 174n137, 184, 184n227, 184n229, 184n231, 185n233, 196, 197, 197n12, 198, 200
insurance, 5n11
interest, 48n441, 112n495, 137n101, 137n108, 138n109, 139, 139n115, 160n34, 163n51
invest(ment), 45, 70, 70n124, 79, 87, 150n216, 157, 163, 190n280, 157, 163
Ionia, 140n132
Iran, 131n61
Isaeus, 183n218
Isaiah, 1n16, 65, 65n84, 65n85, 65n86, 67n96, 68, 68n104, 69, 69n118, 70, 70n122, 70n123, 70n124, 70n125, 71. 71n128, 71n132, 72n136, 72n139, 72n141, 73n144, 73n146, 76n171, 76n173, 78n192, 81n210, 84n236, 87n263, 99n371, 106, 108n447, 150n224, 167n82, 172n124, 200, 201

Ištar, 6n17, 7n29, 8n43, 9n50, 11n66, 13, 13n84, 16, 18n132, 26, 26n208, 26n209, 26n212, 28n223, 43n394, 57, 91n302, 91n303, 164n58, 196, 197, 198
Isis, 6, 6n23
Islam(ic), 104n411
Isocrates, 141n134, 141n136, 174n139
Israel(ite), 2n19, 3n35, 5n7, 6n19, 21n160, 36n327, 37n328, 38n336, 38n345, 51, 56n2, 58, 58n16, 59, 59n26, 60, 61, 61n46, 61n47, 62, 63, 63n62, 65n79, 65n83, 67n100, 72n134, 74, 75n158, 75n162, 76n169, 77n177, 83, 83n231, 84, 84n233, 84n235, 85n241, 86n252, 89, 89n287, 89n289, 89n290, 90, 90n294, 90n296, 90n297, 90n298, 92n310, 92n314, 93, 94n328, 94n329, 94n330, 95n335, 95n336, 97, 97n349, 101, 102n396, 103, 103n399, 103n400, 104, 104n413, 105n416, 107n439, 108n446, 108n447, 115n512, 117n532, 129, 134, 143n151, 144, 153n241, 154n247, 166n77, 170n112, 171n119, 172n124, 177, 179, 179n187, 184n227
Italy, 2n19, 55n509

Jacob, 67n102, 70n121, 71n131, 83, 83n230, 84
James, 159n21, 174n141
James I, 44n403
Jason, 171n116
Jehoshaphat, 61n49, 101, 101n382
Jehu, 61n48
Jeremiah, 1n16, 2, 6, 6n18, 56n2, 63n62, 69n112, 73, 73n148, 74n148, 74n149, 74n151, 76, 76n169, 76n170, 76n172, 76n173, 76n175, 77, 77n180, 77n182, 78n184, 79, 79n193, 79n195, 79n197, 79n199, 80, 80n204, 80n205, 80n206, 80n207, 80n208, 81, 81n212, 82, 81n216, 82n219, 83n227, 84, 84n233, 89n289, 89n290, 92n310, 93, 100n373, 106, 111n480, 137n102, 140, 140n126, 142, 142n143, 159n24, 159n26, 165, 179, 179n187, 181n201, 197, 198, 199, 200
Jerome, 122n5, 149n215
Jerubba`al, 60, 76n172, 77n177, 170n104
Jerusalem, 16n112, 68n111, 70n125, 75n165, 79, 80, 81, 81n208, 82, 86n253, 88n268, 89, 102, 102n390, 102n396, 106, 109n454, 111n480, 113n500, 116n524, 123, 123n9, 124, 124n15, 125n26, 127, 127n36, 127n38, 128, 128n43, 129, 130, 131, 132, 132n68, 132n70, 133, 133n74, 134, 135, 136, 136n92, 143, 143n157, 169n100, 170n105, 171, 171n116, 174, 174n141, 178n180, 180, 181n200, 184n225, 186, 193, 195, 199
Jesse, 83n231
Jethro, 59n26
Jew(ish), 1, 56n2, 71n127, 73n145, 102, 102n391, 122, 124, 124n15, 126n29, 128, 128n42, 131n67, 132, 132n68, 133, 136, 137n104, 138, 138n111, 139n116, 139n123, 143, 144n164, 145, 145n174, 149n209, 150n221, 153n240, 156, 168n93, 170, 170n105, 170n113, 171n115, 171n116, 172n123, 174, 175n145, 176n153, 177n167, 180, 186n243, 192n299, 195
Jezebel, 58n22, 59, 59n31, 60n41
Jezreel, 97, 97n347
Job, 1n6, 40n360, 93n321, 147n193, 149n215, 151n226, 152n236
Joel, 75n162, 97, 97n351, 97n352, 97n353, 98n354, 98n356, 98n360, 99, 99n364, 99n369, 100n372, 199n376, 101n381, 101n385, 101n388, 102, 102n392, 102n393, 114n504, 200
John the Baptist, 78n191, 158, 158n14, 158n15, 165, 166n76, 167n81, 176
Jonathan, 47n436, 61
Joppa, 85
Joseph, 144n164, 154n245, 158n11, 181
Josephus, 54n503, 88n275, 143n157, 164n58, 168n92, 169n103, 170n113, 172n123, 177n167, 178n180, 182n207, 186, 186n241, 192n295, 194n318
Joshua, 1n16
Jubilee, 73, 73n145, 80n207, 81n213, 200n41
Judah(ite), 37n328, 51, 52n485, 67n102, 76, 76n172, 77, 79, 79n193, 80n205, 81, 82, 82n217, 84, 85n241, 86n255, 88, 89n289, 90n297, 98n359, 101n381, 102, 103n399, 103n400, 107n439, 108, 108n452, 110, 111, 118n538, 128, 134, 159n26, 200
Judaism, 75n165, 121, 138n113, 164, 165n69, 167n83
Judas Iscariot, 119n544, 177n170, 178, 178n178, 179
Judea(n), 48n447, 57n12, 81n208, 81n213, 101n381, 138n113, 169n100, 172
Judges, 1n16
Judith, 56n2
Jupiter, 188n261
just(ice), 2, 41, 53, 59n31, 69n119, 91n307, 95, 95n341, 96, 103n398, 110, 110n473, 111n483, 136n95, 137n102, 139, 159n28, 166n76, 167, 171n116, 172, 172n127,

174n142, 175, 178, 181n195, 181n197, 193n306

Kamrušepaš, 32n269, 35, 196
Kanesh, 82n214, 123n7
Karnak, 41n373
Kassite, 25n203, 126n32
Kataḫzipuri, 35n309
khoja, 155
Kings, 1n16, 57, 18, 58n16, 58n23, 59, 61, 62n57, 62n58, 64n74, 65n80, 82, 100n374
Kirta, 1, 40, 40n366, 40n367, 40n368, 40n370, 43n392, 49, 49n456, 49n459, 50n461, 51n472, 53, 53n496, 54, 54n498, 54n502, 54n504, 63n65, 198
Kišar, 19
Kittim, 113n500
Koṯar-wa-Ḫasis, 15n101
Koubaba, 34n294
Kubaba, 6
Kumarbi, 19

Labbu, 17n120
labor/work, 9n54, 57n13, 60n33, 67, 82n216, 85n248, 101n386, 113n499, 125n19, 147, 147n193, 139, 156, 167, 167n82, 173n136, 189n268, 192n300
Lagash, 44n404
Laḫamu, 19
Laḫmu, 19
lament, 2n17
Lamentations, 1n6, 19n142, 142n143
land, 2n20, 6n23, 24, 24n187, 24n191, 24n193, 31, 31n265, 31n266, 34n301, 36, 43n396, 45, 45n414, 45n418, 46, 50n461, 51n472, 59n27, 59n33, 60n34, 61, 61n47, 66, 66n95, 69, 69n117, 72, 72n136, 72n137, 73, 74, 74n152, 74n153, 74n155, 74n156, 75, 75n163, 76n168, 79, 81n208, 82, 83, 83n231, 87n260, 87n266, 89, 89n287, 89n289, 92n315, 93, 93n320, 95n340, 96, 97, 97n349, 97n350, 97n352, 98, 98n357, 98n359, 98n361, 99, 100n373, 101, 102n395, 103n400, 104n409, 106, 107, 108n444, 109n454, 109n458, 111n478, 115, 115n513, 117, 118, 121, 136, 137n102, 141n140, 143n157, 149, 156, 163n56, 168, 174n141, 184n231, 185, 185n233, 196
Landlord/owner, 44, 45, 46, 52, 81n213, 110n465, 198, 200, 81n213, 105, 108n446, 109n458, 110, 110n465, 124n18, 184n229, 197, 198, 200
lapis-lazuli, 10, 11, 44, 50, 51, 96n346
law(suit), 13, 60n38, 60n39, 60n42, 76, 76n172, 78, 78n187, 78n189, 92, 92n310, 137, 137n105, 137n108, 139n120, 153n243, 170n112, 171n120, 175, 175n150, 178, 182n209, 183n217, 184n222, 186n241, 193n307
Leah, 43n395
Lebanon, 43n396, 86, 86n250
lend(er), 73, 104n411, 108n446, 112n494, 112n495, 136n99, 138, 138n109, 145, 175n144, 136n99, 138, 138n109, 145, 175n144
Lenin, Vladimir I., 19
leviathan, 22, 39, 39n351, 39n354
Leviticus, 1n2, 98n355
levit(ical), 109n454, 131n66, 132n68, 134, 135, 139, 139n119, 143n155, 143n157
Liḫzina, 35, 35n307
literary, 1n17, 3, 3n35, 4n4, 5n11, 6, 6n15, 8, 8n46, 17, 19, 25, 27n221, 31n265, 41, 45n418, 55n507, 56, 58n15, 67, 73, 82, 91, 96n343, 103n399, 107n438, 109n459, 142, 143, 155, 170, 174, 196, 198
literature, 4n1, 13n81, 17, 31n263, 31n265, 32n273, 34n299, 36n323, 37, 37n328, 41, 41n374, 42n385, 54, 55, 56, 56n2, 82n221, 89n291, 120n548, 122n3, 122n4, 153n241, 155, 95
livestock, 13n87, 28, 29, 31, 31n268, 32, 36, 36n323, 59, 74n151, 74n152, 85, 94n326, 109n461, 113, 114n506, 118n534, 123, 132, 134, 141n136, 143, 147, 158n19, 165, 166n77, 171n117
loan, 71n127, 138n112, 160n34
locust, 86n253, 97, 97n352, 97n353, 98n356, 98n358, 98n360, 99n369, 100, 100n378, 158n15, 197
Lot, 15n100
Lotan, 39n354
loyalty, 2n21, 30, 57, 57n10, 74, 74n149, 74n153, 86n255, 88n268, 91, 91n301, 95, 96, 121, 74n153, 88n268, 91, 91n301, 95, 96, 121
Lucian, 15n100, 174n139, 183n216, 187n254, 188n260, 189, 189n270, 189n275, 190n276, 190n278, 190n280, 190n282, 193n305
Luke, 150n221, 157, 159, 161n38, 162, 162n47, 163n50, 167n81, 180n190, 181n200, 186, 187n249, 190n279, 193n306, 194
Lycaonia(n), 65n83, 188, 188n258, 188n267
Lydia, 160n31
lyric, 2n17
Lysias, 126n30, 141n137, 183n218, 193n309

Ma'at, 6, 6n24
Macedon(ian), 149n209, 150n221
Maccabees, 56n2, 67n103, 128n42, 171n116
Magi, 158, 158n10, 158n11
magic, 28n226, 30n252, 35n315, 36n319, 57n13, 63, 63n63, 63n64, 91n301
Malachi, 53n496, 117, 119, 120n551, 121
mammon, 73n147, 105n418, 195n423, 109n456, 110n464, 164, 164n63, 165n70
manage(ment), 67n100
manna, 195n322
manumission, 80n207, 81n212, 82n214
Marcus Aurelius, 161n41
Marduk, 9n51, 9n53, 11n65, 13n78, 17, 17n123, 18, 18n124, 18n125, 18n129, 18n132, 19n139, 19n140, 20, 20n154, 21, 22, 23n178, 24, 24n182, 24n184, 24n193, 25, 25n197, 25n203, 27, 27n214, 31n260, 39, 41n375, 45, 47n439, 64, 66n90, 78n183, 83n223, 83n227, 84n232, 93n323, 129n54, 136n97, 155, 189n270, 198, 199, 200
Mari, 4, 4n5, 24n195, 25, 30, 30n251, 30n252, 31n262, 82n214, 84n232, 123n7
Mark, 167n80, 167n85, 168
market(place), 2n20, 5n9, 61n47, 81n213, 85n243, 105, 167n86, 190
marriage, 16n112, 50n465, 50n470, 51, 51n472, 51n476, 56n5, 68, 89, 89n283, 90, 94n332, 95, 96n344, 97, 97n348, 138n113, 147n199, 153n238, 153n241, 154, 155, 155n256
Mary/Miriam, 157n1
marzeaḥ, 69n114, 105n417
Matthew, 2, 157, 157n5, 158, 158n8, 159, 159n22, 160n30, 161n40, 162, 162n45, 163, 164, 164n66, 165n73, 166, 166n77, 167n80, 168, 175n145, 176, 177, 178n178, 179, 195, 195n321
Matthias, 187n252
Media, 131, 131n61, 144, 144n165, 150, 179n187
Mediterranean, 85, 85n240, 154n247, 180, 181, 183, 190, 191n287, 193n310
Melqart, 64n74
merc(h)an(tile), 2n18, 36, 44n397, 80n201, 85, 86, 86n252, 136n97, 186, 189
Mercury, 188n261
Meskene, 37n331
Mesoamerican, 41n376
Mesopotamia, 1, 4, 6, 7, 8, 9n48, 11n65, 12n68, 13n81, 14n91, 16, 16n109, 17, 17n120, 18n129, 18n131, 19n139, 20n154, 25, 32, 34n303, 36n322, 37, 37n328, 37n331, 38n343, 43n390, 43n392, 44n404, 50n466, 52n478, 54, 139n115, 140n130, 164n58
metaphor(ical), 16n108, 25, 50n469, 51n471, 55n507, 66, 68, 72n137, 72n139, 73, 73n147, 74, 78n191, 87n260, 89n283, 89n288, 90, 91, 91n300, 91n308, 96, 97, 97n348, 98n353, 103, 107n434, 152n232, 158n13, 165n71, 165n73, 185n232, 188n267
Micah, 57n12, 60n33, 70n121, 76n168, 78n185, 101n387, 107, 107n439, 108n446, 109, 110n466, 110n467, 110n468, 111, 111n482, 111n483, 197, 200
Micaiah ben Imlah, 61n49
Michael, 189n270
Midian(ite), 59, 59n26, 185n234
Miletus, 160n31
Mishnah, 102n391, 125n21, 127n40, 160n32, 164, 125n21, 127n40, 143n156, 160n32
Mitanni, 20n147, 94n332
Mithradates, 130n55
Moab(ite), 68n111, 103n399, 139
Moloch, 68n111
money, 50n469, 76n174, 83n228, 84n239, 88, 104n409, 106n428, 108n446, 109n457, 112n495, 121, 134, 136, 139, 140, 144n160, 145n174, 150n223, 151, 152, 152n235, 157n3, 162n46, 171n114, 174n139, 175, 175n145, 175n146, 178, 179, 179n183, 179n185, 180, 181, 182, 182n203, 187, 187n249, 187n253, 193n305, 194, 194n318
moral(ity), 2, 5, 117n526, 152n235
Mordechai, 47n436, 144n164
mortgage, 108n446, 136, 136n97
Moses, 58, 58n21, 60n36, 61, 70n121, 72n140, 78n189, 81n208, 84, 84n233, 104, 107n434, 144n162, 153n243, 185n234, 192, 192n297, 195n322
Mot, 33n284, 39, 39n351, 39n353, 43, 43n388, 45, 46, 52, 53n489, 53n495, 64n74, 74n156, 111n487, 112n489
mother/maternity, 3n25, 4, 5n13, 6n2, 13n87, 16n108, 26n209, 34, 34n294, 34n295, 48, 48n444, 53, 77n180, 92n310, 92n311, 152, 155, 167, 167n85
motif, 1, 3, 4, 5n11, 25n204, 27, 31, 33n284, 36, 37, 47, 54, 55, 55n507, 67n100, 67n102, 68, 71, 72n135, 82, 84, 85, 87, 89, 117, 122, 143, 155, 156, 157, 157n3, 158, 161n38, 165n72, 175, 196, 197, 198
mourn(ing), 46, 72n137, 98, 98n361, 106, 106n429, 106n430, 142, 200
Muḥammad, 44n400

Munbaz, 164
Muraba`at, 88n276
Murašu, 139n115
Muršu, 104n409
Mut, 6, 6n22
myrrh, 158n10
myth(ological), 2n17, 9n49, 9n50, 11, 11n65, 13n87, 14n92, 15n102, 17n119, 18, 18n131, 26n211, 31, 31n267, 32, 32n275, 33n284, 33n289, 33n290, 34n297, 34n298, 34n299, 34n301, 34n302, 34n304, 35n305, 35n306, 35n308, 35n316, 36n321, 36n325, 37n328, 39n352, 42n379, 45n417, 50n466, 56, 57n9, 64n73, 64n78, 74n151, 95n333, 98n362, 113n499, 141n139, 160n102, 189n270, 196, 196n2, 197, 197n7, 200n44, 200n48
mythopoeic, 1, 4, 6n23, 13n81, 17, 18, 27, 37, 38n340, 38n342, 45n418, 73n141, 78n183, 86n258, 91, 112, 115n513, 155, 196, 198, 200

Nabal, 14n92, 34n295
Naboth, 59n33, 61n47, 84n232, 197
Naḥal Ḥever, 88n276
Nahar, 38, 39, 39n354, 41, 42, 52
Nahum, 86n253
Namtar, 13n85, 14, 49, 49n454
Nanāya, 98n360
Nanna, 10, 10n58, 14, 14n89, 50n466
Naomi, 50, 50n462
Naphtali, 143
Naram-Sin, 44n404
Nathan, 198
nations/Gentiles, 56n9, 60n33, 62n56, 72n134, 76n172, 76n175, 84, 85n285, 89, 89n284, 90n293, 93n318, 94n326, 99, 99n369, 101, 112, 113, 113n500, 132n69, 138, 140, 140n130, 144, 144n164, 149n209, 153n241, 169, 185n233, 200
Nazarene, 2, 119n544, 149n214, 156, 157, 159, 164, 167, 171n116, 172, 172n124, 176, 181, 183, 183n219, 186, 195, 197
Nazareth, 157, 158n11, 161n37, 166, 174, 180, 183n217, 166, 174, 180, 183n217
Nebuchadnezzar, 25n203, 82n217, 83n222, 86n255, 112n491, 129, 131
Nehemiah, 1n6, 2, 62n59, 81n213, 86n253, 120n548, 122, 122n5, 123n8, 124n15, 124n17, 126n28, 127n36, 131n66, 133, 136, 136n93, 136n95, 137, 137n101, 137n104, 138n111, 138n112, 138n114, 139, 139n119, 139n120, 140, 145n177, 156, 160, 195
Nergal, 7n36, 9n50, 11n62, 15n99, 30n259
Netherworld, 7, 7n36, 8, 8n44, 9, 9n48, 9n49, 9n50, 10, 10n56, 11n65, 12, 12n67, 12n69, 14, 14n90, 16, 16n108, 33n284, 35n318, 36n325, 49n452, 153n239, 155, 196
Neti, 12, 12n69, 15, 15n98, 35n318, 150n218, 183n212
Nevi'im, 1, 4, 6, 11n66, 13, 35n305, 53n496, 55, 56, 57n15, 62n61, 64n70, 65, 67, 73, 76, 78n185, 79n196, 82, 89, 89n290, 90n292, 100n372, 102n393, 109n462, 114n504, 121, 125n27, 139n122, 142n143, 147n198, 152n235, 158, 175, 179, 179n184, 188n257, 195, 201
Nidintu, 139n115
Nikkal, 1, 49, 50, 50n466, 51n472, 96n346
Nimmureya, 20n147
Nineveh, 4, 25, 26n208, 146
Ningal, 50, 50n466
Ninhursanĝa, 34n294
Ninmaḫ, 10n54, 17n120, 34n294
Nintur, 34n294
Ninurta, 8n44
Nippur, 18n129, 41n375, 44n404
Ninšubur, 8, 9n49, 10, 10n57, 11, 14, 16n111, 197
Nisaba, 36n322
Noah, 72n140
Numbers, 1n2
Nur-Sîn, 30, 75n165
Nut, 6, 6n20, 6n21

oath, 14n94, 15, 58n17
Obadiah, 62n58
Odysseus, 44n405, 173n134
Odyssey, 44n405, 44n407
offering, 24n185, 25n201, 49, 66, 66n88, 69, 75n158, 75n159, 83n225, 98, 98n360, 120, 120n541, 121, 121n559, 123, 123n8, 131, 134, 159n28, 160n29, 160n31, 167n85, 168n93, 179n182, 198
Omri, 61n48
oracle, 26, 26n205, 26n207, 27n219, 88n269, 90, 103, 103n400, 104, 107n435, 110, 110n467, 118, 190n281, 197
Origen, 122n5
orphan, 54, 54n502, 78n191, 117, 119, 143, 144
Orpheus, 153n239
Osiris, 6n23, 45, 45n413
Ovid, 188n261

Paĝit, 46n426

palace, 3n25, 12, 12n67, 18n132, 22n164, 33n286, 37, 41, 42, 43, 44, 59, 101, 125, 129n53
Palestin(ian), 1, 36, 67n96, 73n145, 99n366, 104, 163n54, 169n100, 177n164
parable, 14n95, 65n84, 66n91, 85, 86, 87, 87n261, 88n268, 96n342, 119, 157
patron-client, 2, 2n21, 72n140, 178
Paul(ine), 150n221, 157n6, 171n120, 181n198, 183n216, 188, 188n260, 188n267, 189, 190, 192, 192n301, 193, 194, 194n318, 195n320
payment, 16
peasant, 2n18
Pekah, 90n294
Pella, 174n141
Penelope, 173n134
Pericles, 138n113
Perseus, 151n226
Persia(n), 48, 55, 75n163, 81n213, 109n454, 118n538, 123, 124n15, 125n20, 125n26, 127n36, 128n49, 132n68, 133, 133n74, 135n90, 137n100, 137n108, 138n113, 139, 141n134, 154n244, 199
Peter, 170, 171, 178, 178n178, 182, 182n205, 183n216, 185n233, 187, 195n322, 200
Phalerum, 161n37
Pharaoh, 20n147, 21n161, 59, 60n36, 90n294, 99n371, 126, 126n32, 126n34
Philippi(an), 189, 189n273, 189n274, 190
Philistine, 95n333, 101
Philo, 77n181, 90n296, 139n118, 186, 186n241, 192n295
Philostratus, 186n244
Phoenicia(n), 62, 64n78, 136n92
Phrygia, 188n261
Phrynicus, 175n145
Pidray, 50, 50n468
Plato, 168n88, 174n139, 180n192, 187n253, 192n295
pledge, 104, 104n411, 112n494, 136n97, 137n102
Pliny, 191n287
Plouton/Dis, 141n140
plunder/booty/spoil, 9n54, 11n65, 24n190, 61n46, 67n103, 83n222, 86n255, 108, 108n452, 110n463, 112, 112n496, 113, 113n500, 121n555, 128n47, 132n69, 134n85, 136n93, 145n170, 182n207, 185n237, 194n319, 195n319
Plutarch, 91n301, 190n281, 190n283, 193n305, 194n311
poetry, 2n17, 37n335, 39n352, 53n493
Polybius, 151n226, 161n37, 182n207
Polycarp, 184n221
pornograph(ic), 85n248, 89, 89n290, 91, 91n303, 91n308
portion/share, 67, 67n102, 68, 68n112, 69n112, 71, 71n131, 83, 83n230, 83n231, 84, 84n236, 92n311, 119, 120n552, 125n27, 139, 139n122, 140n133, 152n229, 165, 165n68, 167n82, 179n184, 182, 187n252, 191n293, 192n296
possess(ions), 22n172, 26, 37, 40, 41, 45n414, 55,67n96, 69, 69n117, 70n121, 79n196, 79n197, 79n198, 79n199, 83n230, 90, 99n368, 106n427, 108n446, 111, 112n495, 125n27, 153, 154, 156, 163n55, 165n69, 168n87, 172, 173, 173n131, 173n134, 180, 180n190, 180n193, 181n200, 182, 182n204, 184, 184n227, 185, 185n237, 187n249, 196, 197
postmodern, 5, 5n11, 8, 46, 91, 91n301, 113n502, 153n242, 181, 182, 196, 198
poverty/poor/needy, 2, 3n25, 24n185, 27, 27n221, 28, 54, 55n508, 55n510, 63n62, 67n96, 69n117, 71, 71n128, 103, 103n405, 104, 104n407, 104n408, 105, 105n419, 106, 106n428, 106n432, 107, 107n435, 107n438, 108n445, 111n477, 113n499, 117, 119, 121, 138n111, 141, 146, 146n186, 149, 149n213, 149n214, 150, 150n223, 150n224, 151n226, 157, 158, 158n9, 161n39, 163n54, 164n57, 167, 172, 173, 173n132, 174, 174n140, 177, 177n170, 178, 180, 180n190, 181, 181n198, 183n219, 194n311, 194n318, 200
pregnancy, 6n14, 26, 26n210, 28n223, 32n276
priest(hood), 7n34, 9, 17, 18, 18n124, 18n132, 25, 26, 26n211, 27n219, 39n351, 41, 41n373, 41n374, 41n375, 41n376, 43, 43n390, 45, 55, 55n508, 55n510, 58n24, 59, 59n26, 66n90, 67n96, 71n127, 73, 73n143, 75n165, 76, 76n169, 80n205, 90, 98, 98n361, 99, 99n365, 99n366, 109, 109n456, 109n458, 113n499, 113n500, 115, 115n516, 116, 117, 117n527, 117n528, 120n552, 131n66, 132, 132n68, 134, 135, 136, 139, 139n119, 140, 140n131, 141, 141n139, 143n155, 143n157, 155, , 168n90, 168n91, 169, 169n100, 170, 178, 179, 179n185, 188, 193, 193n306, 194n318, 199
primogeniture, 50n463
Procopius, 124n19
procreation, 5, 5n7, 13, 15n98, 26, 66n90, 91, 92n315, 97n348, 196

produc(tion), 2n20, 75, 75n158, 75n163, 77n175, 77n178, 8131n213, 84n239, 88, 89n277, 93, 93n325, 94n326, 97n349, 98n362, 100n373, 113, 115, 115n513, 124n18, 127, 135, 144n160, 158, 159n20, 165, 171n117
profit(ability), 61n45, 73, 76, 76n171, 76n175, 77, 77n177, 83n228, 85n248, 99n371, 113n500, 121, 158n19, 167n85, 168n93, 182, 187n148
property/asset, 21n219, 30n253, 36n327, 70n121, 79n198, 80n202, 80n204, 90, 111, 112n495, 123, 124, 125, 127, 135, 139n115, 171n117, 181n197, 181n198, 193n309
prose, 2n17
prosper(ity), 5, 6, 7, 13, 17, 23, 24n184, 25, 35, 36, 53, 65, 65n86, 66, 66n87, 66n90, 67, 68, 71n127, 73, 73n146, 77, 77n181, 78, 78n185, 78n189, 78n191, 79, 79n196, 87, 88, 88n269, 97n347, 97n351, 100n373, 102, 102n393, 103, 109, 120, 121, 126, 149, 155, 157, 163n56, 174n142, 188n267, 197
prostitut(ion), 68, 69n112, 75n165, 85n248, 89n289, 91n300, 92, 92n312, 93, 97n348, 101, 101n385, 141
Proverbs, 1n6
provision, 14n94, 21, 21n157, 23, 24, 24n189, 28, 29n141
prophecy, 4n4, 4n5, 6n17, 8n43, 11n66, 20n146, 26n206, 26n209, 30n249, 54, 95n336, 122n1, 138n114, 142, 142n145, 181n199
prophet(ic), 3, 4, 4n4, 6, 6n18, 10, 11n66, 25, 25n204, 27n219, 30n252, 34n301, 54, 55, 56, 58, 58n15, 58n16, 60n33, 60n38, 61, 65n79, 67n96, 71, 71n133, 72, 77n182, 79, 87, 88n273, 89, 89n290, 91, 91n308, 96n342, 102n393, 117, 118, 119, 120, 121, 122, 122n2, 129n52, 138, 138n114, 142, 142n143, 142n146, 152n235, 155, 157, 157n3, 157n5, 160, 161n40, 164, 174n141, 176n152, 182n205, 187, 195, 201
prophet(s), 1, 36, 41n371, 46, 55n508, 57, 58, 58n15, 58n22, 59, 59n31, 60, 61n47, 62, 62n58, 63, 63n62, 64n71, 65, 65n80, 65n83, 65n84, 70n119, 70n122, 70n124, 71, 73n148, 75n162, 75n165, 76, 78n191, 79, 82, 84, 88, 88n275, 91n300, 97, 98n362, 101n382, 103n400, 107n435, 108, 108n447, 109, 109n457, 109n458, 112, 113, 113n502, 116, 117n528, 118n536, 122n1, 136n95, 140, 140n26, 142n145, 149n214, 157, 157n6, 158, 158n8, 158n14, 158n15, 159, 159n25, 159n26, 160, 161n40, 165, 166, 166n75, 167, 167n80, 169, 172, 173, 174, 174n140, 175, 178, 180, 181n199, 181n201, 197
Psalms, 1n6, 174n140
Pumbeditha, 174n137
Punic, 62
purchase, 79, 79n199, 80, 80n202, 80n206, 106n427, 120n554, 144, 144n164, 170, 179n183, 179n185, 179n186, 179n187, 184n231, 194n311
puritan, 1
Pythagoras, 181n196, 186n244

Qatna, 90n294
Qingu, 18, 21, 22
Qohelet, 83n228
qorban, 98n360, 105n418, 167n85, 168, 168n89, 168n93, 169, 169n98, 170, 177n167, 178, 178n180, 180
Qudšu, 6n16
Qumran, 72n140, 88n276, 92n315, 112, 113n500, 134n82, 142, 142n148, 145, 159n28, 170n113, 174n139, 181n196, 183n219, 193n306, 195n321
Qur'an, 60n44, 65n83, 157n1

Ra, 18n133
rabbinic, 1, 73n147, 88
Rages, 150, 150n222
Raguel, 148n204, 152n236, 153, 153n238, 153n242, 154, 197
Raḫim-ili, 104n409
rain, 58n18, 60n34, 64n73, 65n81, 65n83, 77n177, 83, 83n224, 95, 95n341, 100, 100n374, 100n375, 115n513, 158n13, 188, 200
Rainmaker, 58, 58n22, 60, 65, 188n266, 198
Raphael, 62n61, 79n196, 148, 150, 152, 152n236, 153, 153n243, 154, 154n247, 158n11, 181n201, 189n270, 197, 198
Ras Shamra, 37, 48n445, 51
receipt, 18n127, 31n265, 119n544, 151, 151n226, 151n227
redemption/redeemer, 52n482, 67, 67n100, 79, 79n197, 79n198, 170, 170n107, 170n112
Reḥum, 123, 127, 127n38
remnant, 84n236, 100n373, 113n500, 128n47, 149n24, 113n500, 128n47
rent, 2, 29n240, 103n404, 104n409
revitalization, 92n308

reward, 19n140, 101n381, 147n200, 159, 161, 161n40, 162, 162n42, 167, 176n160, 189n273, 167, 176n160, 189n273
Rib-Addi, 126n34
Rim-Sin, 14n91
Rimut-Ninurta, 104n409
ritual, 8n46, 14, 18n124, 34, 35, 35n316, 36n322, 38n339, 39, 39n352, 42n384, 46n419, 46n421, 46n428, 49n460, 55, 55n508, 58n24, 63, 63n67, 63n68, 64n71, 64n73, 69n114, 116n524, 116n525, 122n1, 178n179
Roman, 48n447, 91n3n50400, 102n391, 140n130, 147n196, 157n2, 175n145, 176n153, 182n206, 182n207, 183n217, 184n222, 186n241, 193, 194, 194n311, 194n313, 194n314, 194n318
Romanov, 19
Ruth, 1n6, 49, 148n206, 170n112

sabbath, 104, 105n425, 139, 139n118
Sabean, 102, 102n392
sacrific(ial), 7n34, 13n80, 63n65, 65, 68n111, 75n165, 90n297, 98n355, 110, 110n463, 111, 116, 117, 120n551, 123n8, 131, 132, 134, 141, 143, 168, 168n91, 168n92, 169, 169n100, 170n107, 188
sage, 109n458, 157n6, 159n21, 161n41, 165n69, 173n132, 174n137, 192n299, 157n6, 192n299
Šakkan, 36n323
Salvius, 80n207
Samaria, 63n62, 90, 90n292, 105n416, 107, 108n446, 124n15, 127, 127n36, 186, 186n245
Samaritan, 115n518, 185
Šamaš, 31n261, 33, 33n285, 130n55
Samuel, 1n16, 21n160, 77n177, 110n466, 115n512, 192, 192n297
Samson, 33n289
Sanballat, 126n29, 127n36, 138n113
Sanhedrin, 119n544, 178, 178n179
Sapphira, 181, 182n204, 182n207, 187, 187n250, 195n322, 200
Šapšu, 6n16, 42
Sarah, 148, 148n204, 148n205, 152n236, 153, 153n238, 153n239, 153n240, 153n243, 154, 154n245, 154n249, 155, 155n255, 155n256, 171n120, 197
satire/sarcasm/parody, 53, 60n38, 64n70, 64n73, 64n74, 112, 121n556, 122n3, 142n144, 148n202, 156, 174n137, 179n183, 187n254, 192n300
Saul, 42n379, 44n405, 47n436, 60n36, 61, 61n45
Šauška, 6, 6n28
security, 86n253, 88, 96n344
seminated, 74, 74n152, 86, 87, 93, 97, 97n347, 100n373, 200
Seneca, 166n79, 191n287
Sennacherib, 26, 27n214, 27n218, 84n240, 124n17, 145, 145n168, 145n174
Sermon on the Mount, 159, 159n22, 163n53
Sermon on the Plain, 159, 159n22
servant/worker, 2n21, 30, 37n333, 52n479, 65, 65n84, 65n85, 66n87, 67, 67n99, 67m101, 71, 72n134, 74n149, 75n165, 86n251, 87n263, 124, 129, 138, 144n159, 167n82, 189, 191n291, 197
Seth, 45
sex(ual), 6n28, 15n98, 15n99, 68, 68n106, 73, 85n248, 89, 89n290, 91, 91n298, 91n302, 92n308, 92n312, 95n336, 97n348, 137n103, 149, 154n245, 154n249
Sharezer, 27n218, 145
Shalmeneser, 61n48, 144
Shamḫat, 91n302, 91n303
shekel, 70n124, 104n412, 106, 119, 119n543, 139n115, 170, 170n108, 171n114, 172n122, 179n187
Shekinah, 63n62
Shemiḫaza, 155
shepherd, 9n54, 16, 16n111, 24, 24n184, 76, 108n447, 118, 118n536, 119, 179n187, 185n234
Sheol, 56n1, 68n108, 112, 150n218
Sheshbazzar, 130, 130n55
Shethar-bozenai, 123, 128, 132
Shimshi, 123, 127, 127n38
Shittim, 102, 102n396
Sicily, 80n207
Sidon, 6n25, 49, 62n58, 85, 101
Silas, 190
silver, 10, 11, 20n150, 22n169, 23n174, 28, 28n225, 29, 29n242, 29n243, 38n342, 40, 41n375, 44, 48, 49, 50n461, 51, 51n476, 75n159, 80, 84n239, 85, 88, 94, 96n346, 101, 101n389, 102n390, 103, 103n405, 104n409, 106, 109, 110n471, 119, 119n540, 119n543, 123, 124n17, 129, 129n53, 131, 131n66, 131n67, 133, 134, 135, 136, 136n93, 138, 140, 140n130, 143, 144, 146n191, 148, 150, 151, 151n227, 152, 152n234, 158n11, 166, 179, 179n187, 191, 192, 192n294, 199
Simon, 48n447, 170n104, 186, 186n245, 187, 187n249, 187n256, 188n257, 199, 200
Sinuhe, 28n229, 42n385, 145, 158n7
Sippar, 30, 30n256

Sirach, 97n350, 149n213, 150n221, 184n227, 193
Sitis, 147n193
slave(ry), 47, 50n461, 52, 52n478, 52n482, 73, 76n172, 80, 80n207, 81, 81n208, 81n212, 81n213, 82, 85n248, 86n255, 91n303, 102n391, 106, 106n432, 108n452, 119, 121, 135, 137n102, 138n111, 157, 171n116, 184, 185, 194n311, 200
socioeconomic, 2n19, 4, 5n9, 8, 13, 13n79, 15n100, 17, 18, 19, 21n159, 21n160, 22n169, 24n184, 24n191, 25, 25n197, 205n204, 26, 26n205, 27, 29n242, 31, 31n265, 36, 36n325, 37, 38n342, 40, 41, 45, 45n418, 47, 48, 49, 50n463, 51, 52, 52n478, 54, 54n503, 55, 56, 60n33, 62n58, 64n78, 65n85, 65n86, 67, 69n114, 69n118, 70n127, 71, 72n236, 72n139, 73, 73n147, 75n158, 76, 79, 81, 81n211, 81n213, 82, 82n214, 83n229, 83n230, 84, 84n232, 85, 89, 90, 91, 91n303, 93, 94n326, 99n370, 101n390, 103, 106, 106n432, 107n438, 109n457, 110n464, 111, 113n499, 117, 117n530, 119, 119n544, 121, 122, 123n7, 123n9, 125, 133n74, 138n113, 139n121, 140, 142, 143, 146, 150n224, 152n235, 153n237, 153n238, 153n239, 154, 155, 156, 157, 159, 160n31, 163, 177, 178, 183, 184, 184n224, 184n225, 186, 191n286, 193n309, 195, 196, 197, 198, 200, 201
Sodom, 15n100
Solomon, 14n92
Solon, 88n269
Song of Songs, 1n6
Sophia, 6n19
Sophocles, 173n130
Sparta, 140n132, 141n136
Stephen, 184, 184n228, 185, 185n232, 185n233, 185n234, 186, 199
stewardship, 149, 157
Strabo, 177n166
success(ful), 5, 13, 23, 25, 32, 66n87, 68, 70, 76n171, 78n185, 197
sufficiency, 12, 28n225, 29n241, 36n327, 65n85, 152, 152n235
Sumer(ian), 7, 7n37, 8n44, 8n45, 9n54, 10, 10n55, 10n56, 12, 16, 16n108, 16n111, 17n116, 18n127, 19n139, 23n173, 34n294, 38n343, 41n375, 49n452, 50, 50n466, 98n356, 196
surplus, 2n20, 24, 28
Sutean, 46n420
Syria(c), 1, 30, 36, 43n396, 90n294, 104, 157n2, 177n164
Tacitus, 194n314, 194n315, 194n319
Talmud(ic), 1n12, 58n18, 59n28, 60n38, 61, 63n62, 64n72, 80n202, 90n296, 96n344, 102n391, 125n21, 163n56, 168, 169, 170, 173n132, 174n137, 199
Tamar, 54n503
Tammuz, 16, 16n112, 17
Tanak, 5n13, 21n160, 27n218, 33n289, 38n339, 43n392, 43n394, 45n413, 60n36, 60n40, 61n45, 67n96, 67n102, 109n457, 122n5, 123n10, 128n42, 142n144
Tarshish, 84, 84n240, 85n240
Tarsus, 65n83, 157n6, 181n201
targum(ic), 13, 119n544, 121, 169n100
Tattenai, 123, 128, 128n46, 131
tax(ation)/tariff, 2n20, 21n162, 31n265, 41n375, 67n96, 75n163, 76n168, 81n213, 82n214, 90n296, 104n409, 105n422, 108n446, 120n552, 123n7, 124, 124n17, 124n19, 125n19, 127, 127n38, 128, 128n43, 133, 135n91, 136n96, 136n99, 137, 137n100, 156, 157, 161, 161n37, 170, 170n105, 170n113, 171, 171n115, 171n116, 171n117, 171n119, 172, 172n121, 174, 175, 176, 176n153, 176n156, 177n166, 178, 196, 199, 199n34, 200
technology, 2n20
Teheran, 150n222
Telipinu, 1, 9n50, 13n87, 31, 31n264, 31n266, 31n268, 32n268, 32n269, 33, 33n284, 33n289, 33n293, 35, 35n307, 35n309, 35n310, 35n313, 35n318, 36, 36n321, 36n323, 57n9, 64n73, 64n74. 71n131, 196, 200
Tertullian, 184, 184n223
Tertullus, 194n318
T/temple, 9, 11n65, 11n66, 16n112, 18n132, 23, 23n178, 25n201, 30n257, 36, 36n320, 41n376, 44n404, 75n165, 84n238, 99n365, 102n390, 113n501, 116, 116n525, 117, 117n531, 118n533, 120, 120n548, 120n551, 120n552 122, 122n2, 129, 130, 131n67, 133, 133n74, 135, 135n86, 136, 138n113, 139, 139n119, 139n121, 140n131, 143, 155, 156, 168, 169, 169n100, 170n105, 171, 171n115, 171n116, 172n123, 174, 175, 175n146, 178n180, 179, 179n182, 190n276, 192, 192n295, 193, 193n306, 195, 196, 198, 199, 200
Tešub, 18, 33n288, 37n331, 43n395

Thebes, 41n375
theft/confiscation/robbery, 8n44, 75n165, 83n227, 112n495, 113n499, 120, 120n550, 140n132, 141, 141n136, 145, 147, 157, 161n39, 163, 163n54, 168n87, 175, 177n170, 182n207, 192n295, 200
theogony, 17n120
Theophrastus, 168, 168n92
theory, 2, 3n25, 3n35
Thucycides, 140n132
Thutmosis, 41n375
Tiamat, 18, 18n125, 18n126, 21, 22, 22n165, 39, 64, 155, 189n270
Tiberius, 176n153, 176n159
Tiglath-Pileser, 84n239, 124n17
Tigris, 22, 28n233
Titans, 19, 19n135
tithe, 75n158, 83n225, 120, 120n551, 120n552, 121, 121n560, 123n8, 139n119, 143, 143n152, 143n155, 143n157, 194n318, 196, 199
Tobiah, 126n29, 138n113
Tobias, 79n196, 139n119, 144, 146, 148, 148n204, 150n221, 150n223, 150n224, 151, 151n227, 152, 152n236, 153, 153n238, 153n241, 153n242, 153n243, 154, 154n245, 154n247, 155, 155n256, 158, 158n9, 158n11, 197, 198
Tobit, 2, 62n61, 67n101, 106n430, 122, 122n4, 142, 142n145, 142n146, 142n147, 143, 143n150, 143n151, 143n157, 144, 144n163, 144n164, 144n167, 145, 145n168, 145n174, 146, 147n199, 148, 148n210, 148n202, 148n204, 148n205, 148n208, 149, 149n213, 149n215, 150, 150n218, 150n220, 150n221, 150n223, 150n224, 151, 151n227, 152, 152n232, 152n233, 152n235, 153n238, 153n241, 154, 154n245, 154n247, 154n249, 155, 156, 158, 158n8, 158n9, 158n11, 161, 161n39, 164n63, 164n64, 199
Torah, 1, 4, 11n66, 47n438, 52n482, 67n96, 72, 73, 75n158, 76, 77n182, 83n230, 84, 85n245, 93n320, 94n327, 97, 97n350, 100n380, 115n513, 116, 116n524, 117, 121, 123n8, 137, 137n101, 139, 143n154, 143n157, 157, 160n30, 160n34, 163n56, 167, 168, 170, 171n119, 173n132, 177, 178n179, 183n215, 185
Tosefta, 164
trade(r), 2n20, 36, 84n239, 85, 85n245, 86n253, 102n392, 102n393, 104n407, 114n508, 136n92
trafficking, 85, 85n248, 101n385
transaction, 16, 50n469, 80, 80n205, 187n248
treasur(y)/storehouse, 24n192, 25, 26, 83, 83n225, 85n241, 91n303, 101, 101n390, 102n390, 110, 110n471, 119, 119n541, 119n544, 120, 120n544, 125, 128, 128n43, 130n55, 130n58, 131n67, 133, 136, 139, 145, 148, 148n207, 149, 150n220, 151, 151n227, 152, 158, 158n10, 158n11, 163, 163n52, 163n53, 163n55, 163n56, 164, 165n70, 173, 178n180, 179, 187n251, 194
tribal, 2n19, 4n1, 5, 51, 79n195, 91n298, 109n454, 149
tribe, 5, 70n121, 83, 146n187, 198, 146n187
tribute, 19, 38, 38n347, 108n446, 111, 124, 124n17, 127, 127n38, 132, 135, 171, 171n117, 199
Tunnan, 39, 39n354, 40n357
Tušratta, 20n147
Twelve, 1n16, 72n135, 74n152, 88, 88n273, 88n275, 89, 89n280, 89n287, 93n320, 102n396, 103, 111, 115n512, 119
Typhoeus, 37n332
Typhon, 37n332
Tyr(ian), 49, 59n31, 84, 84n238, 84n239, 85, 85n241, 85n244, 85n245, 88n269, 101, 103n399, 168, 168n92, 169, 175n145, 186

Ugarit(ic), 34, 37, 37n328, 37n329, 37n330, 37n332, 38n340, 38n342, 38n347, 39n350, 39n352, 39n354, 40n360, 40n366, 40n370, 44n403, 50n468, 51, 53n489, 53n490, 53n494, 56n3, 57n13, 57n14, 58n24, 62, 62n54, 63, 64n74, 82n219, 96n346
Urad-Gula, 27, 28, 28n229, 144, 150n223
Uruk, 7n34, 9n48
usury, 137n100, 138, 138n109, 163n51
Utu, 18n123

value(s)/precious/expensive, 4n1, 5n7, 8n45, 26n213, 28n225, 37n327, 45, 59, 59n33, 61n47, 72, 96n345, 119, 135n86, 163n54, 165n69, 167n86, 176n158, 177n166, 178n181, 191, 192n296, 201
Vedic, 53n495
Vidranga, 132n69
vineyard, 51, 65, 76, 80, 96n346, 104n409, 105, 107, 107n434, 124n17, 136, 136n97, 137, 138

warfare, 2n20

wealth(y)/rich, 2, 2n20, 14n91, 19n144, 20n153, 20n154, 23, 23n176, 23n178, 24, 24n189, 24n194, 25, 30, 31n260, 40, 41, 41n373, 41n375, 53n494, 55n508, 63n62, 66, 67, 67n96, 68n105, 73n146, 73n147, 75n165, 76n168, 77, 77n176, 81n213, 83n222, 84, 84n238, 85, 88, 88n270, 90n296, 93n321, 104, 105, 105n416, 108n446, 109n458, 110, 110n464, 110n471, 110n475, 111, 111n485, 112n496, 113n499, 113n500, 118, 118n535, 121, 130n55, 132n69, 134n85, 138n111, 138n113, 139n116, 141, 141n140, 144n167, 147n192, 148n207, 149n215, 150, 150n224, 152n235, 155, 157, 157n3, 158, 164, 165, 165n69, 172, 172n123, 172n125, 173, 173n133, 173n135, 173n136, 174, 174n138, 174n139, 174n140, 174n141, 174n142, 177n164, 178, 178n172, 178n181, 180n190, 182n204, 186n241, 197, 198
welfare, 26
widow, 54, 54n502, 117, 119, 143, 144, 149n214, 181n198, 183, 183n217, 184, 184n222, 184n223
wine, 36n323, 85, 94, 95, 96, 96n345, 99, 99n366, 100, 101, 101n386, 102, 103n398, 104, 104n412, 105, 110n471, 111, 111n485, 116n522, 139, 140n130, 143
wisdom, 2n17, 9n54, 47, 47n437, 65n86, 67n96, 71n133, 76n171, 82, 82n221, 144n164m 152
wise woman, 34n295, 35n315
women, 5n6, 5n7, 170, 183n217, 190n280
worthless/futile, 58n23, 76n175, 77n179, 83, 83n228, 166n75, 173n136, 177, 177n168, 179n187, 188, 188n260, 188n263, 188n264
Writings, 1

Xenophon, 158n19, 185n234, 191n292

Yabrudemay, 50, 50n468
Yam, 22n165, 27, 37, 37n332, 38, 39, 39n349, 39n350, 39n351, 39n354, 41, 41n371, 42, 43, 43n393, 45, 46, 48, 49, 52, 53n487, 53n495, 64, 155, 197, 198, 199
Yariḫ, 50, 96n346
Yaṣṣib, 53, 53n496, 54n502, 54n504, 198
Yaṭpan, 33n290, 46, 46n420
Yazilikaya, 33n286
Yedoniah, 126n31, 126n35
Yehud, 126n30, 126n31, 126n35
Yekutiel, 165, 165n69
Yemen, 102n392
Yeshu`a/Jesus/Isa, 14n92, 157, 157n1, 157n6, 158n8, 159, 161, 161n37, 163, 163n50, 163n56, 164, 165, 166n76, 167n85, 170, 171, 172n121, 173n131, 174, 174n140, 176n160, 177, 177n164, 178n178, 179, 180n190, 182n205, 183n217, 189n268, 192n300, 193, 193n305, 198, 199, 201
Yhwh(ism), 6n19, 24n184, 33n287, 38n338, 38n344, 41n376, 43n394, 47n430, 57, 57n10, 57n12, 58, 58n17, 59, 59n25, 59n26, 59n27, 59n29, 59n31, 60, 61, 61n53, 62, 62n56, 63n64, 64, 64n69, 64n78, 65, 65n81, 65n83, 66, 66n90, 67, 67n99, 67n102, 69n118, 71, 72, 72n135, 74, 75n158, 75n162, 75n163, 75n165, 76, 76n169, 76n172, 78, 79, 79n199, 81, 82n216, 82n219, 83n224, 83n230, 84, 84n233, 86n251, 89, 89n280, 89n287, 90, 92, 92n310, 93, 93n321, 94n326, 94n328, 94n329, 95, 96, 97, 97n349, 97n350, 97n351, 98, 98n358, 99, 100, 101, 101n381, 101n382, 101n388, 102, 102n395, 104, 104n408, 106, 107n440, 109, 109n462, 110n472, 111n480, 113, 115n518, 116, 117, 118, 118n535, 118n538, 119, 119n544, 121, 123n8, 129n52, 132n69, 139, 155, 59, 159n24, 160, 161n36, 163n56, 168n91, 170, 174n141, 197, 198, 199, 200

Zechariah, 67n102, 70n125, 84n239, 86n255, 100n373, 108n452, 113, 117, 117n529, 117n532, 118n533, 118n536, 119, 119n540, 119n541, 119n542, 119n543, 119n546, 122n2, 179n185, 200
Zedekiah, 80, 81, 82, 82n217, 86, 86n255, 87n266, 106, 111n480, 118, 137n102
Zelophehad, 40n365
Zephaniah, 102n394
Zerubbabel, 118n533
Zeus, 19, 19n135, 188, 188n260
Zimri-Lim, 4, 30, 30n259, 31, 75n165, 126n30, 198
Zion, 49n460, 69n118, 89, 94n328, 100, 100n376, 109, 109n459, 100n376

Author Index

Abernethy, Andrew A., 70n125
Abusch, I. Tzvi, 7n30, 13n85, 25n203, 57n12
Ackerman, Susan, 6n16, 6n28, 60n41, 62n57, 68n106, 68n110
Adams, Dwayne H., 161n37
Adams, Samuel L., 51, 51n474, 118n538, 120n548
Adams, Sean A., 122n3, 141n135
Adkins, Arthur W. H., 88n270
Aejmelaeus, Lars, 192n297
Ahlström, Gösta W., 97n353
Alatas, Syed Hussein, 126n28
Albertz, Rainer, 2n23
Albright, William F., 15n101, 91n300
Alexander, Joseph Addison, 73n146
Allen, James P., 6n24
Allen, Leslie C., 82n216, 82n219, 85n245, 88n269, 99n366, 100n378, 100n380, 107n439
Allison, Dale C., 162n47
Alster, Bendt, 9n52, 9n53, 16n112, 18n126
Alter, Robert, 3n29, 12n68, 82n218
Altmann, Peter, 86n253, 103n400, 123n10, 128n44
Ameling, Walter, 171n116
Anbar, Moshé, 80n207, 80n208
Anderson, Bernhard W., 91n305
Anderson, Gary A., 43n390
Anderson, James S., 59n25
Anthonioz, Stéphanie, 122n1
Ap-Thomas, D. R., 65n83
Arie, Eran, 80n203
Assis, Elie, 97n353, 99n369
Assmann, Jan, 56n2
Aubet, Maria Eugenia, 8n45, 186n147
Aune, David E., 186n245
Aus, Roger David, 178n177
Autero, Esa J., 159n22
Avigad, Naḥman, 80n203
Bachvarova, Mary, 6n14
Baden, Joel S., 5n6, 5n13
Baines, John, 43n389
Baker, Coleman A., 182n205
Balch, David L., 163n54
Baldwin, Joyce G., 119n540
Balentine, Samuel E., 79n193
Ball, C. J., 140n126
Ballentine, Debra Scroggins, 52n479, 64n78
Baltzer, Klaus, 65n84
Barker, Margaret, 148n206, 152n236
Barnouw, Jeffrey, 44n405
Barr, James, 69n119
Barré, Michael L., 58n17
Barrett, Charles K., 183n216, 188n263, 190n279
Barrick, W. Boyd, 67n96
Barron, Bruce, 174n142
Barstad, Hans M., 104n415
Barth, John, 5n8
Barton, John, 97n351, 98n356, 100n378, 101n384, 102, 103n397, 103n399
Bassler, Jouette, 184n223
Batto, Bernard F., 18n131, 40n360, 64n78
Baukal, Charles E., 65n81
Baumann, Gerlinde, 89n283, 89n288, 91n308, 95n336
Baumgartner, Joseph M., 143n155
Baur, Ferdinand C., 183n216
Bautch, Richard J., 137n101, 137n108
Bazzana, Giovanni Batista, 162n47
Beaulieu, Paul-Alain, 140n133
Bechard, Raymond, 85n248
Beck, Martin, 57n12, 72n135
Becker, Gary, 144n160
Beckman, Gary, 5n13, 31n264, 31n265, 33n293, 35n313, 36n321, 36n323, 71n131
Bederman, David J., 39n350
Bedford, Peter Ross, 118n533, 133n74, 133n76, 171n116
Bell, Catherine, 18n124

Bell, Richard H., 194n312
Ben Zvi, Ehud, 57n14, 76n171, 88n273, 89, 89n278, 107n439
Bergman, Claudia, 5n11
Bernstein, Moshe, 112n492
Bertman, Stephen, 16n109, 38n343, 50n466
Bertram, Georg, 191n291
Betz, Hans Dieter, 159n22, 159n25, 162n42
Beuken, Willem A. M., 116n521
Beyerlin, Walter, 60n44
Bickerman, Elias, 171n116
Bidmead, Julye, 18n124
Billing, Drew W., 186n242
Black, Jeremy A., 6n14, 12, 12n74, 14n90, 15n99, 41n375, 49n452
Blackman, Aylward, 5n13
Blenkinsopp, Joseph, 49n458, 81n213, 93n320, 124n17, 126n29
Bloch, René, 154n245
Block, Daniel I., 85n245, 85n247
Blomberg, Craig L., 175n148
Bluedorn, Wolfgang, 58n21, 60n40
Boadt, Lawrence, 61n47
Böck, Barbara, 8n46
Boda, Mark J., 70n125, 78n187, 117n530, 117n531, 117n532, 118n536, 119n540, 119n541, 119n542
Bodi, Daniel, 78n183
Boer, Roland E., 109n454, 139n117
Bonhoeffer, Dietrich, 162n42, 173n133
Bons, Eberhard, 90n290
Bordieu, Pierre, 124n15
Bottero, Jean, 10n154
Boulay, R. A., 12n77
Bow, Beverly, 148n203
Bowker, John, 100
Bowler, Kate, 102n393
Braaten, Laurie J., 51n472, 74n152, 76n173, 89, 89n285, 89n287, 92n309, 92n310, 93n320
Brandon, Samuel G. F., 174n141
Brenner-Idan, Athalya, 89n290, 92n208
Briant, Pierre, 117n530, 133n73, 134n82
Bringmann, Klaus, 171n116
Bronner, Leah, 59n25
Brown, Raymond, 162, 162n48, 163n51
Brownson, Orestes, 5n10
Bruce, F. F., 181n198, 185, 186n239, 188n258
Brueggemann, Walter, 45n418, 108n444, 114n504, 120n549, 138n114, 169n102
Bruhn, John G., 182n208, 183n212
Bryant, Margaret M., 176n155
Bryce, Trevor, 31n265, 36n325, 52n483, 131n62
Buccelatti, Giorgio, 11n63, 11n64, 17n122
Buchan, James, 6n28, 50n469, 196n4
Buechner, Frederick, 150n224
Bunck, Julie M., 195n320

Campbell, Joseph, 17, 17n117
Campbell, Michael, 91n302
Capper, Brian J., 181n196, 181n200
Caquot, André, 41n372, 42n386, 46n421, 50n467
Cardascia, Guillaume, 139n115
Carlson, Robert A., 61n47
Carroll, Michael P., 64n72
Carroll, Robert P., 79n194, 80n205, 80n206, 109n458
Carson, David A., 167n80
Carter, Nancy Corson, 7n35
Carter, Warren, 176n161, 177, 177n163
Casey, Maurice, 162n48
Cathcart, Kevin, 108n450
Ceccarelli, Manuel, 10n54, 14n91, 34n294
Ceresko, Anthony R., 103n402
Chaney, Marvin L., 60n33, 76n168, 82n215, 110n4678, 110n
Charpin, Dominique, 31n262
Chavel, Simeon, 81n208, 81n212
Chelst, Kenneth, 1n5
Childs, Brevard, 67n96, 69n118, 172n124
Chirichigno, Gregory C., 52n478, 76n168, 101n386
Chopp, Rebecca S., 174n143
Chung, Youn Ho, 143n152
Cimok, Fatih, 33n286
Citrin, Jack, 136n96
Claasens, L. Juliana M., 40n365
Clain, Suzanne Heller, 144n160
Clark, Gordon R., 74n149
Clements, Ronald E., 80n205
Cline, Eric H., 55n509
Clines, David J. M., 79n193, 93n320
Cody, Aelred, 43n390
Cody, Diablo, 5n10
Cogan, Mordechai, 6n16
Coggins, Richard J., 71n132, 88n273, 185, 185n238
Cohen, Mark E., 11n60, 11n61
Cohen, Shaye J. D., 138n113, 71n115
Coldwell, David C., 119, 119n546
Collins, John J., 94n327
Collins, Raymond F., 159n21
Collins, Terence, 89n285
Coltmann, Leycester, 19n137
Comte, Auguste, 56n9
Conybeare, Frederick C., 186n244
Conzelmann, Hans, 163n50
Coogan, Michael D., 44n397

Cook, Stephen L., 61n53
Cooper, Jerrold, 26n213
Cornelius, Izak, 39n353
Cosmopoulos, Michael B., 115n513
Cousin, Georges, 135n91
Cowley, A. E., 128n47
Crabble, Margaret, 5n8
Craigie, Peter C., 34n297, 41n372, 53n494, 56n3, 87n266, 88, 88n272
Crenshaw, James L., 78n187, 97n352, 98n354, 98n358, 100n377, 101m381, 101n382, 102n390
Crepeau, Richard C., 45n409
Crosby, Michael H., 166n76
Cross, Frank Moore, 19n138, 39n351, 39n352, 41n375, 43n390, 43n391, 45n417
Croteau, David A., 120n553, 121, 121n560
Crouch, Carly L., 18n132
Cuffari, Anton, 56n2, 128n42
Cuffey, Kenneth H., 107n439
Cumont, Franz, 188n259

Dalglish, Edward R., 11n60
Dalley, Stephanie, 13n78, 13n84, 15n102, 17n115, 17n122, 21n159, 22n170, 23n176, 24n191, 50n466
Dandamaev, Muhammad A., 27n217, 52n478, 85n248
Daniels, Dwight R., 97n349
Daube, David, 54n503
Davenport, Tracy, 4n1
David, M., 81n212
Davidson, Steed Vernyl, 79n195, 79n198
Davies, Williwm D., 162n47
Davis, Ellen F., 93n320, 158n20
Davis, James Colin, 180n192
Davis, Jessica Milner, 140n129
Dawson, Doyne, 181n197
Day, John, 34n297, 39n354, 40n360, 41n372, 43n393, 45n413, 47n430, 48n444, 53n490, 59n32, 64n78, 81n209
Day, Peggy L., 6n27, 39n353
Dearman, J. Andrew, 80n204, 90n297, 97n247
DeBrabander, Firmin, 176n160
Deferrari, Teresa M., 174n142
De Hulster, Izaak J., 3n32
Deist, Ferdinand E., 100n375
De Moor, Johannes C., 39n352, 41n372, 42n380, 45n413, 46n419, 46n422, 49n456, 50n465, 53n490, 53n494
De Regt, Lénart J., 114n504, 120n549
Derrett, J. Duncan M., 172n121, 187n248, 187n256
Deschamps, Gaston, 135n91
Deselaers, Paul, 142n145, 142n149
DeSilva, David A., 149n209
De Soto, Hernando, 108n445
De Villiers, Peeter, 174n143
Dever, William G., 3n26
Diamond, A. R., 91n308
Dibelius, Martin, 158n14
Dick, Michael, 11n63, 140n130
Dietrich, Walter, 45n418
Diewert, David A., 39n357
Dijkstra, Meindert, 46n422, 61n53
Dillon, Matthew, 189n273
Dimant, Devorah, 143n157, 155n250
Dinter, Paul E., 80n205
Di Pede, Elena, 143n150, 148n208, 150n224
Di Vito, Robert A., 49n453
Donner, Herbert, 105n416
Dossin, Georges, 30n253
Douglas, Mary, 45n415, 75n164, 115n516, 116n519
Downs, David, 120n552, 186n247
Doyle, Brian, 71n132, 72n139
Draffkown-Kilmer, Anne E., 14n94, 33n287, 104n414
Duguid, Ian, 88, 88n269, 88n271
Duhm, Bernhard, 80n208, 97n352
Dupont, Jacques, 192n297
Durand, Jean-Marie, 30n256

Eaton, John H., 172n124
Eberhart, Christian, 168n91
Edelman, Diana V., 61n46, 120n548
Eichrodt, Walter, 61n53, 85n249
Eideval, Göran, 106n432, 106n433
Eilberg-Schwartz, 117n525
Eisenbeis, Walther, 98n355
Eisenberg, Ronald L., 174n137
Eissfeldt, Otto, 43n391
Eliade, Mircea, 8n41, 18n124, 117n526
Elliott, James K., 3n28
Elnes, Eric E., 84n234, 144n162
Elon, Menahem, 171n117
Emerson, Ralph Waldo, 5n10
Emerton, John, 53n490
Eskenazi, Tamar C., 130n55
Espak, Peeter, 14n91
Eubank, Nathan, 162n46, 162n49
Evans, Craig A., 178n180
Evans, Donald, 5n8
Exum, J. Cheryl, 89n290
Ezigbo, Victor I., 157n2

Fabry, Heinz Josef, 159n27, 168n89
Fafchamps, Marcel, 51n472

Fager, Jeffrey, 200n41
Falkenstein, Adam, 12n76
Faraone, Christopher A., 190n284
Farber, Walter, 5n13
Farber-Flügge, 10n54
Faust, Avraham, 3n26
Favazza, Armando R., 62n56, 64n72
Fee, Gordon D., 174n142
Feinman, Gary M., 41n376
Feldman, Daniel Z., 137n108, 138n109
Feldman, Marian H., 37n330
Ferch, Arthur, 57, 57n13
Ferrara, Anthony J., 12n68
Ferreiro, Alberto, 188n257
Feuerbach, Ludwig, 56n8
Finger, Reta Halteman, 181n198
Finkel, Asher, 163n51
Finkel, Irving, 133n75, 133n76, 198n26
Finley, Moses I., 45n418
Finley, Thomas J., 98n359
Fischlin, Daniel, 44n403
Fishbane, Michael, 60n40
Fisher, Loren R., 39n351
Fitzenreiter, Martin, 42n384
Fitzgerald, F. Scott, 5n10
Fitzmyer, Joseph A., 67n99, 122n4, 142n147, 142n149, 144n163, 145n168, 150n221, 152n235, 152n236, 159n21, 168n93
Fleming, Daniel E., 30n253, 37n331
Flesher, Paul V. M., 102n391
Fletcher, Joann, 41n375
Floyd, Michael H., 57n15, 88n273
Flückiger-Hawker, Esther, 7n36, 9n51, 12, 12n75
Flusser, David, 76n167
Fohrer, Georg, 6n19, 70n124
Folmer, Margaretha Louise, 123n10
Fontaine, Carole R., 14n92
Fontenrose, Joseph Eddy, 36n325, 39n349
Foote, Stephanie, 182n203
Fortier, Mark, 44n403
Foster, Benjamin, 2n17, 9n50, 11n62, 12n78, 13n84, 15n99, 17n122, 21n159, 22n170, 23n176, 24n190, 24n191, 41n375, 49n454
Fowler, Michael R., 195n320
France, Richard T., 165n74
Franco, Zeno E., 8n41
Frankena, Rintje, 78n183, 78n190
Frankfort, Henri, 172n124
Frazer, Fames, 47n430
Frechette, Christopher, 36n322
Freedman, William, 55n507
Frick, Frank S., 90n298, 91n298
Fried, Lisbeth, 104n409, 133, 133n81, 134n82, 138n113
Friedrich, Johannes, 32n272, 32n273, 32n274, 33n292, 34n294, 36n323
Frymer-Kensky, Tikva, 5n11, 6n15, 6n28, 7n30, 7n32, 8n44, 57n11
Fuchs, Esther, 91n300
Fuchs, Klaus, 176n155
Fyfe, Alec, 101n386

Gabbay, Uri, 11n60
Gabriel, Gösta, 17n121, 19n138, 19n141, 20n154, 45n417
Gadotti, Alhena, 6n14, 7n37
Galil, Gershon, 29n244
Gall, August Freherr von, 185n238
Galter, Hannes D., 14n91
García Martínez, Florentino, 159n28
Gardner, Barbara, 16n108
Gardner, Jane F., 194n311
Gardner, John, 91n304
Gärtner, Bertil, 188n267
Gauger, Jörg-Dieter, 123n10
Gelb, Ignace, 24n183, 52, 52n478, 52n481
Geller, Markham J., 6n19
Genicot, Garance, 101n386
George, Andrew R., 10n59, 11n62, 11n65, 85n250
Gerhardsson, Birger, 163n51
Gericke, Jaco, 104n414
Gerleman, Gillis, 63n63, 98n355, 101n387, 135n87, 153n237
Gerstenberger, Erhard S., 2n23, 133, 13n80
Gesenius, Wilhelm, 103n401
Gibson, J. C. L., 38n336, 40n359, 40n368, 42n380, 43n396, 46n419, 48n444, 49n456, 50n467, 53n494, 54n497
Ginsberg, H. L., 48n444
Girard, Marc, 1n7
Girgus, Sam B., 5n10
Glatt, David E., 124n12
Glenny, W. Edward, 102n396, 107n439
Glueck, Nelson, 74n149
Gnuse, Robert, 36n327
Godelier, Maurice, 41n371
Goetze, Albrecht, 6n28, 31n265, 31n266
Goldingay, John, 65n84, 139n123
Gonnet, Hatice, 36n321
Goodchild, Philip, 5n9
Goodman, Martin, 167n83
Goody, Jack, 47n432, 51n472, 63n64
Gordon, Barry J., 1n12, 1n14

Gordon, Cyrus H., 38n336, 38n343, 40n359, 42n380, 43n396, 44n399, 44n401, 48n443, 52n486
Gordon, Robert P., 4n5, 30n249
Goren, Yuval, 80n203
Gorman, Frank L., 58n24
Gorman, Michael, 5n11, 171n120
Gort, Jerald D., 60n36
Gottwald, Norman K., 2n20, 2n23, 58n16
Grabbe, Lester L., 138n114, 142n146, 142n149, 145n174
Gray, John, 40n368, 40n370. 71n128
Grayson, A. Kirk, 26n207, 26n208
Green, Alberto R. W., 39n351, 41n372
Green, Margaret W., 8n44, 14n90
Green, Joel B., 157n2, 163n50
Greene, John, 39n350
Greenfield, Jonas C., 128n50, 146n183, 147n199, 149n210
Greenspahn, Frederick E., 40n364, 50n463
Greenstein, Edward L., 40n368, 49n456, 49n459, 54n498
Greenwood, Kyle, 188n165
Gregory, Bradley C., 150n221, 193n305
Grelot, Pierre, 127n40
Grenz, Stanley J., 91n301
Gregory, Russell, 58n21
Griffiths, John Gwyn, 45n413
Grøndahl, Frauke, 24n183
Groneberg, Brigitte, 3n35, 8n46
Gross, Heinrich, 148n203
Gruenwald, Ithamar, 55n508
Gudykunst, William B., 183n214
Guillaume, Philippe, 2n24, 30n253, 45n414, 75n163
Gundry, Robert H., 159n25
Gunkel, Hermann, 18n125, 61, 61n49, 64n78
Gunn, David M., 79n193
Gunneweg, Antonius H. J., 132n68
Gurney, Oliver R., 31n264, 33n289, 35n306
Gushee, David P., 172n127, 181n195
Güterbock, Hans G., 19n134, 35n305, 36n320

Haar, Stephen, 187, 187n254
Haas, Volkert, 7n37, 31n263, 31n264, 31n266, 33n293, 34n299, 35n307, 35n315, 36n323
Habel, Norman C., 3n33, 89n287
Hackett, Jo Ann, 5n6
Hadas, Moses, 19n135
Haddox,, Susan E., 91n307, 94n328
Hadjiev, Tchavdar S., 104n413
Hadley, Judith M., 43n393
Hägglund, Frederick, 65n84, 65n86
Halberstadt, Jamin, 56n8
Hall, Mark G., 14n89, 50n466
Hallermeyer, Michaela, 142n148
Hallo, William W., 3n35, 82n214, 123n7
Halpern, Baruch, 3n30
Hals, Ronald M., 148n206
Hamborg, Graham R., 104n415, 107n438
Hamilton, Malcolm, 56m9
Handy, Lowell, 37n335, 38n343, 42n378, 95n333
Hanson, Paul D., 117n528, 117n529, 155n250
Harding, Tonya, 182n203
Harmatta, János, 123n6
Harrell, James L., 85n244
Harrill, J. Albert, 182n206, 183n211
Harrington, Daniel J., 175n145
Harrington, Hannah K., 115n517
Harris, Rivkah, 8n42, 43n392
Hartin, Patrick J., 159n21
Hasel, Gerhard F., 88n267, 105n425, 111n479
Häusl, Maria, 109n459
Hauser, Alan J., 58n21
Hays, Christopher B., 43n388, 52n483, 64n74, 67n96, 68n106, 68n108, 69n114, 112n489
Hays, Christopher M., 180n190, 183n219
Hayes, John H., 53n491
Hayes, Katherine Murphey, 46n423, 82n220, 98n361, 106n429, 106n430
Haymes, Brian, 94n330
Hazell, Clive, 56n2
Healey, John F., 38n339, 38n342, 95n333
Hegel, Georg Wilhelm Friedrich, 174n141
Heidel, Alexander, 17n122
Heider, George C., 40n357
Heimpel, Wolfgang, 30n248
Held, Moshe, 114n504, 120n549
Heltzer, Michael, 37n330
Hendel, Ronald S., 49n458, 91n304
Hengel, Martin, 194n312
Herion, Gary A., 57n10, 102n392
Hermisson, Hans J., 65n84
Herms, Ronald, 73n146
Herrmann, Wolfgang, 37n331, 37n334, 43n391, 50n466, 58n25
Herzog, Ze'ev, 110n471
Heschel, Abraham Joshua, 105n425, 139n118
Hess, Richard S., 24n183
Hibbard, J. Todd, 71n132
Hiebert, Theodore, 81n208
Hillers, Delbert R., 107n439, 111n483
Hobson, George, 60n33, 65n80
Hobson, John A., 7n34

Hock, Ronald F., 192n299
Hoffman, Yair, 62n55, 70n125
Hoffner, Harry A., 9n50, 13n87, 31n264, 31n267, 32n269, 32n271, 32n272, 32n273, 32n274, 32n275, 32n279, 32n280, 33n284, 33n293, 34n294, 34n297, 34n298, 34n299, 34n301, 34n302, 34n304, 35n305, 35n306, 35n308, 35n313, 35n314, 35n315, 35n316, 35n317, 35n318, 36n319, 36n320, 36n321, 36n323, 37n333, 57n9, 64n73, 74n151, 95n333, 98n362, 113n499, 196n6, 197n7, 198n22, 200n44, 200n48
Hoglund, Kenneth G., 137n100
Holladay, Carl R., 183n216, 184n225
Holm, Michael, 133n76
Holt, Else K., 58n22, 94n330
Honigman, Sylvie, 171n116
Hooker, Morna D., 176n152
Hopkins, David L., 55n510
Horsley, Richard A., 82n217, 157n3, 157n6, 172n124
House, Paul R., 88n273
Houston, Walter J., 2n22, 103n403, 107n437, 111n483, 136n95, 137n102
Houston Smith, Robert, 86n250
Howard, George, 162n48
Howells, William Dean, 5n10
Howgego, Christopher, 3n31
Hubbard, Robert L., 108n446, 170n112
Huffmon, Herbert B., 24n183, 25n204, 30n249, 30n252, 78n187, 94n330
Hull, Bill, 161n38
Humphreys, Walter Lee, 142n145
Hunt, Alice M., 26n213
Hurowitz, Victor, 11n64, 11n65, 18n123, 98n360, 116n525, 120n548, 198m 198n23
Hutter, Manfred, 6n28, 7n35, 36n319, 154n244
Hutton, Jeremy M., 3n27
Hyatt, James Philip, 81n212

Inhorn, Marcia C., 5n9
Iplikçioglu, I., 192n294
Irsigler, Hubert, 102n394
Irving, John, 5n10
Isaac, Munther, 45n418
Iser, Wolfgang, 37n328
Ives, Charles, 5n10
Izre'el, Shlomo, 30n247

Jackson, Bernard S., 186n241
Jacobs, Mignon R., 107n439, 114n506
Jacobsen, Thorkild, 6n28, 7n29, 7n31, 7n38, 8n43, 11n63, 12, 12n77, 13n81, 15n98, 15n99, 16n112
Jacobson, Howard, 64n73
Jacques, Margaret, 14n91
Jagersma, Henk, 64n73
James, Henry, 5n10
James, William, 5n10
Janowski, Bernd, 67, 67n98
Janzen, David, 117n526, 136n95, 137n108
Japhet, Sara, 122n5
Jaruzelska, Izabela, 103n398, 105n419
Jassen, Alex P., 96n343
Jastrow, Marcus, 68n105, 71n127
Jauss, Hannelore, 74n150
Jemielty, Thomas, 36n327, 64n70
Jeppeson, A., 108n450
Jeremias, Joachim, 157n6
Jeremias, Jörg, 95n340, 107n434
Jindo, Job Y., 38n343
Johnson, Dan G., 71n132
Johnson, Luke Timothy, 182n204
Jones, David W., 160n34, 174n142
Jong, Jonathan, 56n8
Jonker, Louis, 109n454
Jordan, Hillary, 5n10
Joseph, Morris, 165n69
Joosten, Jan, 110n466
Joüon, Paul, 103n401
Joyce, Paul M., 84n238, 85n241, 87n265, 186n246
Judge, Edwin A., 193n310
Juel, Donald, 163n50

Kaiser, Otto, 38n336, 72n141, 170n107
Kammenhuber, Annelies, 35n315, 36n323
Karenga, Maulana, 6n24
Katz, Dinah, 7n37, 10n56, 25n203
Keefe, Alice A., 5n6, 5n7, 90, 90n297, 90n298
Keel, Othmar, 3n32
Keener, Craig S., 172n121, 172n122, 175n146, 179, 179n187, 179n188
Kelhoffer, James A., 158n15
Kelle, Brad E., 60n40, 90, 90n294, 90n295, 90n299
Kennedy, Charles A., 69n114
Kennedy, George A., 163n53
Kessler, John, 113n503, 114n505, 114n506
Kessler, Martin, 81n212
Kessler, Rainer, 2n23, 73n147, 111n483
Kiel, Micah D., 142n149, 143, 143n151, 155n255
Kienast, Burkhart, 51n476
Kilgallen, John J., 184n228, 186, 186n240
Kim, Brittany, 94n328

Kim, Koowon, 49n460, 54n504
Kimball, Sara, 32n272, 32n273, 32n274
King, Leonard W., 17n122
King, Philip J., 80n204
Kinsley, David R., 6n19
Kinsella, W. P., 45n410
Kippenberg, Hans G., 2n19, 113n503, 137n102
Kitz, Ann Marie, 14n91
Klauck, Hans-Josef, 181n198, 186n245, 187n248, 187n249, 190n281
Klawans, Jonathan, 115n517
Klein, Ralph W., 122n5
Klengel, Horst, 31n265
Kletter, Raz, 45n414
Kline, Jonathan G., 82n217
Kloppenborg, John S., 161n40
Kloos, Carola, 37n335
Klostermann, August, 117n529
Knibbe, Dieter, 192n294
Knoppers, Gary N., 48n448, 54n504, 72n140
Knierim, Rolf, 163n51
Koch, Klaus, 61n53
Koepf-Taylor, Laurel W., 5n9
Koester, Helmut, 157n2, 193n303
Koller, Aaron, 88n268, 89n290
Kong, I. M., 146n191
Kossman, Ruth, 45n418
Köstenberger, Andrea J., 120n553, 121, 121n560
Korpel, Marjo C. A., 39n352, 40n366, 45n413, 48n445
Kramer, Samuel N., 4n2, 9n54, 10n55, 12, 12n73, 38n343
Kratz, Reinhard G., 58n16
Kraus, Fritz R., 31n262, 82n214, 123n7
Krinetzki, Günter, 102n394
Kugel, James L., 83n228
Kühne, Cord, 94n332
Kuhrt, Amélie, 125n26, 133n74
Kunene, Musa Victor Mdabuleni, 165n71
Kunin, Seth D., 149n209

Laato, Antti, 65n84
LaBarbera, Robert, 121n556
LaCocque, André, 118n536
Lafont, Bertrand, 30n253
Laird, Donna, 124n15
Lalleman-de Winkel, Hattie, 73n147
Lambdin, Thomas O., 54n501
Lambert, Wilfrid G., 4n2, 10n54, 13n79, 17n120, 17n122, 18, 18n123, 18n127, 18n128, 18n130, 19n139, 19n140, 21n159, 22n170, 24n182, 24n187, 24n190, 24n191, 25n202, 25n203, 39n352, 49n451
Lambrecht, Jan, 192n297
Lane, Edward W., 47n438, 50n468, 79n196, 104n411, 112n488, 120n544
Lang, Gerhard, 2n18, 6n19, 107n436
Lanner, Laurel, 95n334
Larkin, Katrina J. A., 100n373
Laroche, Emmanuel, 34n294
Lasine, Stuart, 30, 30n250
Launderville, Dale, 7n36, 96n344, 196n5
Lee, Andrew Y., 88n273
Lee, Robert G., 59n31
LeFebvre, Michael, 138n112
Leichty, Erle, 26n207, 27n218
Lemche, Niels Peter, 31n262, 73n145, 81n212, 82n214, 123n7, 196n2
Lemos, Tracy M., 36n327, 47n432, 51, 51n472, 51n476, 56n5
Lenski, Gerhard, 2n23, 3n25, 31n266, 41n375, 57n13, 73n143, 146n182, 200n40
Lenski, Richard C. H., 176n160
Leota, Peniamina, 79n198
Lerner, Max, 176n155
Lesko, Barbara S., 6n20, 6n21, 6n22, 6n23
Leslau, Wolf, 41n372, 42n384
Leuchter, Mark, 84n236, 104, 105n416
Levenson, Jon D., 3n30, 7n29
Levin, Yigal, 60n38
Levine, Amy-Jill, 153n241, 166n77
Levine, Baruch A., 63n68, 66n88, 75n159, 98n355, 184n231
Levine, Lee I., 169n101
Levine, Phillip B., 5n11
Lévi-Strauss, Claude, 14n92, 56n6
Lewis, C. S., 17n119, 160n35
Lewis, Theodore J., 42n378, 49n454, 69n112, 69n114
Lichtheim, Miriam, 28n229, 42n385, 145n169
Lied, Liv Ingeborg, 140n125
Lim, Timothy H., 133n79
Limet, Henri, 198n24
Lindenberger, James M., 128n49, 145n174
Linfelt, Tod, 76n167
Linville, James R., 103n398
Lipiński, Eduard, 49n454, 51n472, 85n240, 184n229
Lipschitz, Oded, 136n92
Litke, Richard L., 24n182
Liverani, Mario, 25n204, 26n211, 31n265, 33n287, 48n441, 85n245, 141n139, 197n12
Lohfink, Norbert, 27n219, 109n462
Long, Thomas, 179n182
Longenecker, Bruce N., 177n164
Longenecker, Richard N., 178n180, 179n185

Lortie, Christopher R., 122n2
Loucas, Ioannis, 13n88
Luciani, Didier, 142n148
Lüdemann, Gerd, 182n209
Lundbom, Jack R., 73n148, 77n180, 78n189, 82n218
Luther, Martin, 65n86

Macatangay, Francis M., 142n145, 144n164, 147n194, 147n195, 147n200, 148n201, 150n221, 150n223, 152n232
Maccoby, Hyam, 194n311
MacDowell, Douglas M., 48n449
Machiela, Daniel A., 143n151
Machinist, Peter, 56n9
MacIntosh, Andrew A., 290n292, 92n313
MacIntyre, Alasdair C., 173n130
Madrinan, Carmen, 101n386
Magdalene, F. Rachel, 95n334
Maier, Christl, 109n459
Maier, John R., 7n38, 38n343, 91n304
Maier, Walter A., 39n353
Malamat, Abraham, 30n253
Mandolfo, Carleen, 94n328
Mann, Thomas, 11n66, 65n80, 65n83
Manning, Gary T., 87n261
Manson, Thomas W., 166n75
Marcus, Joel, 167n80
Margalit, Baruch, 53n489, 58n22, 188n266
Marguerat, Daniel, 182n209
Margueron, Jean-Claude, 30n249
Mark, Joseph, 7, 17n118
Marriage, Zoë, 101n386
Marshall, George C., 133n76
Marshall, I. Howard, 174n138, 181n198
Marsman, Hennie J., 40n366, 40n369, 40n370, 50n465, 50n466, 53n489, 53n492
Martin, Dale B., 102n391
Marttila, Marko, 140n131
Mason, Steven D., 72n140
Massie, Robert K., 19n136
Mastnjak, Nathan, 77n182, 84n233, 84n237
Maul, Stefan M., 18n129
Mauss, Marcel, 41n371
May, Elaine Tyler, 5n8
May, Herbert G., 86n258
Mayer, Wendy, 60n36
Mays, James L., 90n292, 104n415, 107n439
Mazoyer, Michel, 31n267, 35n310
McCabe, David R., 181n196, 183, 183n210, 183n211
McCracken, David, 143n150, 146n191, 153n238
McCrory, Jeff, 139, 140n124
McDonald, Joseph Loren, 148n204
McDonald, Lee Martin, 157n2
McDonnell, Rea, 184, 184n223
McGeough, Kevin M., 37n330
McGovern, Patrick, 116n522
McKane, William L., 80n208, 110n468, 111n483
McKenzie, John L., 94n330, 144n166
McLaren, Brian D., 94n328
McLaughlin, John L., 69n114
McMahon, Gregory, 33n285
McNamara, Martin, 105n418, 164n65, 164n66, 168n89
McNeese, Tim, 108n447
Mead, James K., 58n16
Meeks, Wayne A., 157n3
Melchert, H. Craig, 31n268, 35n309
Melugin, Roy, 57n14
Mendels, Doron, 122n3, 140n126
Mendenhall, George E., 57n10, 62n56
Merkur, Dan, 63n63
Métral, Francoise, 75n163
Mettinger, Tryggve N. D., 15n105, 33n284, 47n430, 64n74
Meyers, Carol L., 1n8, 117n528
Michaelis, Wilhelm, 192n298
Michaels, Jonathan, 126n33
Milgram, Jonathan S., 27n219
Milgrom, Jacob, 66n88, 73n141, 75n159
Milik, Jozef T., 168n93
Millar, William R., 71n132
Millard, Alan R., 17n120, 49n451
Miller, Geoffrey David, 148n205, 153n238, 153n241
Miller, James Maxwell, 53n491
Miller, Patrick D., 11n66, 39n356, 63n65, 65n83, 84n234, 144n162
Millgram, Hillel I., 58n23
Min, Kjung-Jin, 131n66, 132n68
Moberly, R. Walter L., 61n53, 69n119
Mönning, B. H., 181n197
Monroe, Christopher M., 37n330
Moore, Carey A., 122n4, 141n135, 142n149
Moore, Michael S., 1n4, 1n15, 3n33, 3n36, 4n1, 6n19, 6n28, 7n37, 7n38, 8n40, 8n41, 8n46, 14n93, 15n100, 15n105, 19n142, 20n146, 20n151, 21n161, 25n204, 26n213, 28n229, 34n295, 35n315, 36n327, 38n343, 40n370, 42n381, 43n390, 45n417, 47n431, 47n433, 48n441, 49n458, 50n463, 52n480, 52n482, 52n485, 54n505, 57n14, 58n16, 60n33, 64n74, 67n96, 67n103, 69n113, 70n126, 71n133, 72n135, 74n157, 78n186, 79n193, 79n197, 81n208, 81n211, 83n229, 89n287, 90n294,

91n302, 104n414, 109n457, 109n458, 117n527, 120n552, 121n556, 122n1, 126n28, 126n30, 126n32, 129n52, 136n96, 138n110, 140n127, 145n169, 155n257, 157n4, 159n23, 166n78, 183n211, 185n234, 187n255, 188n261, 188n264, 193n310, 198n18, 201n50
Moran, William A., 21n160, 90n294
Morgenstern, Julian, 59n26
Morley, Neville, 3n25
Morse, Merrill, 73n144
Moss, Candida R., 5n6, 5n13
Moss, Charlene McAfee, 179n185
Moughtin-Mumby, Sharon, 68, 68n104, 73n148, 89n288, 97n348
Mowat, Barbara A., 40n364
Mowinckel, Sigmund, 39n351, 94n330, 172n124
Moyo, Fulata Lusungu, 147n193
Muellner, Leonard, 33n289
Mugerauer, Robert, 4n1, 17n119
Muhs, Brian, 55n506
Muilenberg, James, 82n218
Mulder, Martin J., 57n10, 83n224
Mullen, E. Theodore, 37n335, 38n343
Müller, Gerfrid G. W., 32n271, 32n272, 32n273, 32n274
Müller, Johannes, 144n164, 153n240
Munch, Peter A., 102n394
Munn, Mark, 92n312
Murphy, Catherine, 1n13, 181n198, 195n321
Mussies, Gerard, 191n288

Na'aman, Nadav, 126n34
Nakash, Yitzhaq, 64n72
Neil, Bronwen, 60n36
Nel, Marius J., 162n46
Neubauer, Adolf, 142n147
Neusner, Jacob, 1n12
Nicholson, Ernst W., 80n208
Nickelsburg, George E., 122n3, 142n145, 148n203, 155n250
Niebuhr, H. Richard, 59n26
Nissinen, Martti, 4n4, 4n5, 11n66, 24n190, 26n205, 26n206, 26n209, 26n210, 26n212, 27n214, 27n219, 27n220, 27n221, 27n222, 28n224, 28n225, 28n228, 28n230, 28n231, 28n232, 28n233, 28n234, 29n235, 29n236, 29n237, 29n238, 29n239, 29n241, 29n242, 29n243, 29n244, 29n245, 29n246, 30n253, 30n254, 30n256, 30n257, 30n258, 30n259, 31n260, 31n261, 31n262, 41n371, 75n165, 84n232, 122n1, 144n161, 150n223, 198n16, 198n19
Nogalski, James, 89, 89n279, 89n280, 102n392
Nolan, Patrick, 2n23, 3n25, 31n266, 57n13, 146n182, 200n40
Noegel, Scott B., 58n18, 82n217
Nolland, John, 157n5, 178n179
Noonan, John T., 109n458, 178n178
North, Robert C., 73n145, 120n552
Noth, Martin, 24n183, 58n16, 132n68
Nowell, Irene, 122n4, 142n149, 148n202, 148n207
Nutkowicz, Hélène, 31n267
Nygren, Anders, 160n35

Oakman, Douglas E., 162n44
Ober, Josiah, 39n350
O'Brien, Mark A., 58n16
O'Connor, Kathleen M., 91n308
Oded, Bustanay, 59n30
Ogden, Daniel, 189n270
Ohrenstein, Roman A., 1n12
Oldenburg, Ulf, 43n391
Olmo Lete, Gregorio del, 24n182, 52n479
Olmstead, A. T., 128n46
Olson, Charles, 8n45
Olyan, Saul, 6n25, 43n390, 90n294, 137n101
Oort, Henricus, 72n136
Oppenheim, A. Leo, 13n84, 101n386
Oppenheimer, Aharon, 143n156
Osborne, Grant R., 178n179, 179n183
Oshima, Takayoshi, 18n132, 57n12
Oswalt, John N., 65n85, 70n122, 70n123
O'Toole, Robert F., 187n250
Otto, Eckhart, 82n214, 88n268, 123n7
Otzen, Benedikt, 142n149, 145n185, 153n240

Paffenroth, Kim, 179n185, 179n188
Pakkala, Juha, 132n70
Pallis, Svend Aage, 18n124
Pantoja, Jennifer M., 158n13
Pardee, Dennis, 42n380, 43n395, 46n428, 48n441, 63n68
Park, Hyung Dae, 187n257
Parker, Simon B., 46n419
Parkinson, Richard B., 158n7
Parpola, Simo, 4n5, 6n17, 8n43, 26, 26n209, 26n210, 26n211, 26n212, 26n213, 28n234
Parrinder, Geoffrey, 157n1
Parsons, Mikeal C., 184n226
Patai, Raphael, 6n18, 83n224
Patterson, Orlando, 52n478
Paul, Shalom, 65n85

Payne, David, 65n84
Pecchiolo-Daddi, Franca, 33n293, 36n323
Peckham, Brian J., 57n14, 59n26, 62n54, 64n78, 84n239, 85n242
Penglase, Charles, 7n36, 9n49
Peponi, Anastasia-Erasmia, 12n68
Perdue, Leo G., 52n480
Perera, Sylvia Brinton, 13n8
Perkins, Phoebe, 176n154
Perrin, Andrew B., 143n151
Peters, David A., 194n317
Petersen, David L., 72n135, 88n273, 113n503, 114n505, 115n514, 115n518, 116n524, 117n531, 118n533, 118n536, 118n538, 119n541
Peterson, Brian Neil, 57n15
Peterson, Eugene, 62n58, 96n346
Philips, Anthony, 62n55
Philonenko, Marc, 154n245
Pierce, Chad T., 154, 154n248, 155, 155n250, 155n251
Pikor, Wojciech, 87n260
Pitard, Wayne T., 39n354, 48n441, 50n468
Pitkänen, Pekka, 160n32
Pitt-Rivers, Julian Alfred, 154n247
Pleins, J. David, 1n3, 103n405
Podella, Thomas, 70n125
Poe, Edgar Allen, 5n10
Pohlmann, Karl-Friedrich, 85n241, 186n246
Polanyi, Karl, 3n34, 8n45, 16n106, 25n203, 186n247
Polaski, Donald C., 71n132, 72n135, 72n140, 72n141, 84n232, 91n306
Polvani, Anna Maria, 33n293, 36n323
Pongratz-Leisten, Beate, 18n124, 55n510
Pope, Marvin H., 18n133, 37n334, 40n360, 43n391
Porten, Bezalel, 139n115
Porter, Barbara Nevling, 8n43
Postgate, Nicholas, 27n222, 31n262
Power, Edmond, 178n180
Premnath, D. N., 109n458
Preuss, Horst Dietrich, 185n232
Prinsloo, Willem S., 99n364
Provan, Iain W., 91n301
Puech, Émile, 159n21
Puhvel, Jaan, 33n293

Quisumbing, Agnes R., 51n472

Rabe, David, 5n10
Raczka, Witt, 43n396
Rad, Gerhard von, 58n16, 161n41
Radine, Jason, 4n5
Rahmouni, Aicha, 38n348, 48n444
Rainey, Anson F., 30n247
Ramond, Sophie, 111n485
Rappaport, Helen, 19n136
Rapske, Brian, 193n307
Reiner, Erica, 1n17, 3n35, 119n540
Reiterer, Friedrich V., 111n478
Rendsburg, Gary A., 64n74
Rendtorff, Rolf, 89n280
Renger, Johannes, 43n390
Renz, Thomas, 85n249
Reventlow, Henning Graf, 79n193
Richardson, Alan, 172n122
Richter, Sandra L., 58n16
Richter, Wolfgang, 99n364
Rieger, Tom, 126n28
Rieken, Elisabeth, 31n264, 32n270, 33n293, 35n305, 35n310
Ringgren, Helmer, 60n43
Ro, Johannes Unsok, 3n35, 55n510, 73n143
Roaf, Michael, 44n404
Roberts, J. J. M., 4n5, 11n66, 30n253, 56n7, 86n253, 111n485, 112n488, 112n491
Roberts, Kathleen J., 56n2
Roberts, Kathryn L., 60n36
Robinson, James M., 193n303
Robinson, Thomas L., 190n278
Rodin, Therese, 34n295
Rofé, Alexander, 65n79
Roller, Lynn E., 6n28
Rollston, Christopher A., 3n27
Ronczkowski, Michael, 30n251
Rose, Martin, 43n391, 84n234
Rosenthal, Franz, 161n37
Rosenthal, Ludwig A., 144n164
Roth, Cecil, 171n117
Roth, Wolfgang, 142n144
Rothstein, Johann Wilhelm, 115n518
Rouland, Robert, 44n407
Rubin, Aaron D., 3n27
Rudolph, Wilhelm, 80n205, 80n206, 80n208, 102n394, 128n49
Rüger, Hans-Peter, 85n245
Ruppert, Lothar, 109n457
Rusak, Tal, 57n14
Rüterswörden, Udo, 107n435
Rutherford, W. Gunion, 175n145

Saebø, Magne, 118n536
Saggs, H. W. F., 56n9
Sakenfeld, Katherine Doob, 40n365, 74n149
Saldarini, Anthony J., 178n176
Sallaberger, Walther, 10n57
Salvini, Mirjo, 43n395

Sancisi-Weerdenberg, 48n448
Sandford, Michael J., 157n3
Sandle, Mark, 181n197
Sanmartín, Joaquín, 52n479
Sandars, Nancy K., 31n265
Sanders, Ed Parish, 143n157
Sanders, Paul, 84n235, 84n237
Sandnes, Karl Olav, 157n6
Sandoval, Timothy, 1n10, 82n221, 165n69
Sasson, Jack, 82n219
Sassoon, John, 9n54
Saur, Markus, 85n241, 85n245, 186n246
Saxby, Trevor J., 195n322
Schaper, Joachim, 171n116
Schein, Seth L., 44n407
Schiffmann, Lawrence H., 115n516, 115n517, 120n551
Schipper, Jeremy, 104, 105n416
Schloen, J. David, 117n532
Schmidt, Frederick W., 144n166
Schmutzer, Andrew J., 5n13
Schneider, Dale, 88n273
Schneider, Tammi J., 7n36
Schniedewind, William M., 30n247, 54n501, 62n56
Schoberg, Gerry, 161n37
Schottroff, Luise, 181n197
Schottroff, Willy, 70n121, 70n127
Schoville, Keith N., 139n116
Schroer, Silvia, 3n32
Schuller, Eileen M., 142n149
Schürmann, Heinz, 192n297
Schütte, Wolfgang, 85n241, 103n400, 105n416, 107n439
Schwartz, Joshua, 90n296
Schwesig, Paul-Gerhard, 72n135
Scurlock, Jo Ann, 6n19, 13n85, 146n191
Sedlmeier, Franz, 84n239, 186n246
Segal, Charles, 39n353, 46n422
Seidel, Moshe, 110n466
Seitz, Christopher R., 97n352
Seland, Torrey, 186n241
Selz, Gebhard J., 14n91
Sen, Amartya, 191n293
Seri, Andrea, 17n123, 24n182
Setel, T. Drorah, 89n290
Seybold, Klaus, 117n531
Sharp, Calolyn J., 11n66
Sheldon, Rose Mary, 30n251
Sherwood, Yvonne, 91n300
Simian-Yofre, Horace, 85n254
Simkins, Ronald A., 2n21, 99n369
Simmons, Bill, 45n409
Simundson, Daniel J., 106n428, 107n439
Singer, Ithamar, 38n340
Sivan, Daniel, 39n356, 40n359, 52n486, 53n488
Sjöberg, Åke, 14n89, 50n466
Skehan, Patrick W., 84n235
Skemp, Vincent T. M., 142n149, 149n215
Skiena, Steven, 157n1
Sladek, William R., 7n38, 9n48, 9n52, 9n54, 10n56, 12, 12n67, 12n76, 13n84, 14n90, 15n98, 15n99, 21n155
Slocum, Jonathan, 32n272, 32n273, 32n274
Smend, Rudolf, 72n136
Smith, Gary V., 138n111
Smith, Jonathan Z., 15n105, 18n124, 47n430
Smith, Mark S., 33n284, 38n336, 38n347, 38n348, 39n351, 40n359, 41n372, 42n380, 42n386, 43n392, 43n396, 44n397, 45n410, 46n420, 47n430, 48n441, 48n444, 50n468, 52n479, 53n489, 53n492, 53n494, 57n12, 58n19, 64n73, 72n134
Smith, Morton, 167n82
Smith-Christopher, Daniel, 70n121, 107n439, 108n447
Sneed, Mark R., 78n186, 83n228
Snell, Daniel C., 12n77, 31n262, 52, 52n478, 52n480, 52n482, 56n8, 158n12
Soards, Marion L., 184n228
Soden, Wolfram von, 13n84, 24n187
Sohn, Seock-Tae, 97n349
Soll, Will, 142n148
Sollberger, E., 14n91
Sommerfeld, Walter, 18, 18n129, 18n131, 25n203, 41n375, 78n183
Soulen, R. Kendall, 67n100
Sowada, Karin N., 48n441
Speiser, Ephraim A., 13n78, 17n122
Spencer, Neal, 41n373
Spieckermann, Hermann, 67n97
Spretnak, Charlene, 6n19
Spronk, Klaas, 68n111
Stack-Nelson, Judith, 165n73
Stade, Bernard, 107n438
Stambaugh, John E., 163n54
Stanley, Christopher D., 57n12
Stanton, Graham N., 159n22
Starr, Charlie W., 89n291
Starr, Chester G., 52n478
Stassen, Glen H., 172n127, 181n195
Steck, Odil Hannes, 109n459
Stegemann, Wolfgang, 181n197, 194n312
Steinberg, Naomi, 51, 51n475
Steiner, Richard C., 32n269, 42n383, 66n88, 123n10, 124n13, 128n45, 131n61, 134n82, 170n107

Steinmetz, Devorah, 43n392
Sterling, Gregory A., 186n243, 194n313
Stern, Ephraim, 136n92, 137n100
Stern, Philip D., 47n430, 102n395
Stevens, Marty E., 133, 133n78
Stiebert, Johanna, 61n47
Stieglitz, Robert R., 44n403
Stienstra, Nelly, 60n35, 97n349
Stokholm, Niels, 193n306
Stökl, Jonathan, 4n5, 30n252, 64n71, 122n1
Stol, Marten, 5n6
Stolper, Matthew W., 104n409
Stolz, Fritz, 37n332
Stovell, Beth M., 89n286
Streck, Michael P., 98n360
Strelan, Rick, 182n209
Stuart, Douglas, 65n85
Stuckenbruck, Loren T., 142n148, 154n246
Stuhlmueller, Carroll, 113n501, 119n543
Sturtevant, Edgar H., 43n390
Suiter, David E., 124n12
Summey, David L., 165n71
Suter, Kevin, 60n33
Sweeney, Marvin A., 62n59, 88n273, 88n281, 102n396, 119n540
Swoboda, Heinrich, 188n261
Szegedy-Maszak, Andrew, 168n92

Tadmor, Ḥayim, 125n20
Tajra, Harry W., 194n313
Talmon, Shemaryahu, 56n4
Talon, Philippe, 17n122, 21n158, 21n159, 22n170, 23n176
Tambiah, S. J., 47n432, 51n472
Tamez, Elsa, 117n120
Tandy, David W., 448n450
Taylor, Justin, 182n209
Taylor, Mark C., 174n141
Taylor, Richard A., 71n133, 113n502
Thamm, Robert A., 44n407
Theis, Joachim, 157n6
Thelle, Rannfrid I., 160n32
Theoharis, Liz, 178, 178n173
Thiel, Winfried, 29n30, 104n413
Thistleton, Anthony C., 166n79
Thompson, Augustine, 167n80
Thompson, James W., 192n300
Thompson, John Arthur, 73n148, 81n212, 98n356
Thurston, Bonnie Bowman, 183n217, 184, 184n220, 184n221, 184n225
Tigchelaar, J. C., 159n28
Tillich, Paul, 56n2
Timmer, Daniel C., 89n284
Toffelmire, Colin N., 102n393
Toombs, Lawrence E., 45n417
Toorn, Karel van der, 6n15, 6n18, 27, 27n220, 44n406, 51, 51n477, 144n161, 196n1
Törnqvist, Rut, 89n288
Tov, Emanuel, 3n28, 84n235
Townsend, Joan, 6n28, 92n308
Trebilco, Paul, 170n105
Trible, Phyllis, 59n31
Tromp, Nicholas J., 112n489
Tropper, Josef, 53n490
Trotter, James M., 60n43
Tuckett, Christopher M., 87n261
Turcan, Robert, 91n300
Tuzlak, Ayse, 186n245
Tyson, Joseph B., 183n213

Urbach, Efraim E., 102n391
Urbin-Chofray, T., 6n14

Vaage, Leif E., 158, 158n12, 160n29, 162n43, 163n57, 165, 165n70
Vancil, Jack W., 24n184
Van den Hout, Theo P. J., 31n265
Van Dijk, J. J. A., 9n51, 9n53
Van Driel, G., 104n409
Van Gessel, B. H. L., 33n286
Van Henten, Jan Willem, 189n270
Van Minnen, Peter, 194, 194n313
Van Ruiten, J. T., 84n233
Van Selms, A., 40n370
Van Seters, John, 49n458
Vanstiphout, Herman L. J., 17n116
Van Wijk-Bos, Johanna W. H., 137n104
Vaux, Roland de, 47n430, 168n90
Veldhuis, Niek, 17n116
Verhey, Alan, 169, 169n102
Vermes, Geza, 173n131
Versnel, Hendrick S., 191n285
Viviano, Benedikt, 159n21

Wagenaar, Jan A., 63n65, 107n435
Walker, Christopher, 11n63, 140n130
Walker, William O., 161n37
Wallis, Jim, 178n175
Walls, Neal H., 33n289, 39n353, 47n434
Walsh, Jerome T., 58n16, 59n30
Walton, John, 42n387, 65n84, 66n95
Wang, Martin Chen-Chang, 80n205
Wanke, Gunther, 80n205
Ward, Charles B., 157n1
Washington, Harold C., 1n11
Wasserman, Nathan, 98n360
Waters, Jaime L., 46n425, 100n376, 158n18

Waters, Matt, 55n506
Watson, Paul L., 43n388, 52n484
Watson, Wilfred G. E., 42n380, 53n493
Watters, William R., 65n85, 69n118
Watts, John D. W., 72n136, 83n229, 89n282
Weber, Max, 41n374, 43, 43n390
Weeks, Noel, 58n17
Weeks, Stuart, 142n148, 143n152
Weider, Andreas, 73n147
Weidner, Ernst F., 58n17
Weigle, Marta, 91n305
Weippert, Manfred, 4n5, 26n213
Weiss, H., 30n251
Wellhausen, Julius, 77n182, 107n435
Wénin, André, 153n241
Weninger, Stefan, 126n35
Wenkel, David H., 172n122
Werrett, Ian C., 115n517
Westbrook, Raymond L., 47n432, 90n294
Westenholz, Joan G., 17n116
Westermann, Claus, 26n207, 65n86, 70n123, 107n435, 184n230
Wheeler, Sondra Ely, 157n3
Whitelam, Keith W., 172n124
Whitman, Walt, 5n10
Whybray, Roger N., 1n9, 65n84
Wierzbicka, Anna, 162n42, 174n140
Wiesehöfer, Josef, 136n94
Wiggerman, F. A. M., 18n128
Wiker, Benjamin, 176n153, 176n159
Wilder, Amos N., 3n29
Wilhelm, Gernot, 55n506
Williams Charles S., 181n198
Williams, David T., 174, 174n143
Williams, Reggie L., 157n2
Williamson, H. G. M., 127n36, 127n38, 135n86, 136n93, 137n103
Willis, John T., 107n439
Willis, Timothy M., 132n68
Willitts, Joel, 176, 177n162, 177n164
Wills, Lawrence W., 140n128, 142n149, 155, 155n252
Wilt, Judith, 5n8
Wink, Walter, 174n141
Winter, Bruce W., 184n222
Wiseman, Donald J., 97n352
Witherington, Ben, 157n3, 159n21, 174n137
Witherup, Ronald D., 175, 175n149
Wogaman, J. Philip, 172n127
Wöhrle, Jakob, 88, 89n277, 89n284, 117n529
Wolff, Hans Walter, 89n280, 90n292, 99n364, 103n405, 111n482, 113n502
Wolff, Hope Nash, 45n412
Wolters, Al, 117n529
Woo, Taek Joo, 105n417
Woodbridge, Russell S., 174n142
Wright, David P., 42n384, 46n419, 46n421, 46n428
Wyatt, Nicolas, 6n25, 6n26, 37n328, 37n332, 38n336, 38n338, 39n351, 39n355, 40n368, 40n370, 41n372, 42n379, 42n380, 43n396, 44n397, 44n401, 46n421, 46n422, 48n441, 48n444, 49n456, 50n461, 50n468, 53n487, 53n490, 53n494, 53n495, 57n14, 58n19, 59n26, 68n111, 117n525

Yee, Gale A., 59n31, 155n256
Yehoḥen, 139n115
Yoder, Christine Roy, 139n115
Yoder, John Howard, 174n142
Yoffee, Norman, 43n389
Yon, Marguerite, 37n329
Young, T. Cuyler, 517n530, 123n6, 128n50

Zadok, Ran, 125n20
Zech, Charles E., 144n160
Zelizer, Viviana, 5n8
Zhmud, Leonid, 181n196
Zimbardo, Philip G., 8n41
Zimmerli, Walther, 85n245
Zimmermann, Frank, 142n149
Zobel, Hans Jürgen, 36n325
Zobel, Moshe Nahum, 170n110
Zsolnay, Ilona, 15n98

www.ingramcontent.com/pod-product-compliance
Lightning Source LLC
Chambersburg PA
CBHW060508300426
44112CB00017B/2590
* 9 7 8 1 5 3 2 6 3 8 1 2 1 *